To Be a Minority Teacher in a Foreign Culture

Mary Gutman • Wurud Jayusi • Michael Beck
Zvi Bekerman
Editors

To Be a Minority Teacher in a Foreign Culture

Empirical Evidence from an International Perspective

Editors
Mary Gutman
Efrata College of Education
Jerusalem, Israel

Michael Beck
St. Gallen University of Teacher Education
St. Gallen, Switzerland

Wurud Jayusi
Beit Berl College
Arab Academic Institute
Beit Berl, Israel

Zvi Bekerman
The Seymour Fox School of Education
Hebrew University of Jerusalem
Jerusalem, Israel

The open access publication of this book has been published with the support of the Swiss National Science Foundation

ISBN 978-3-031-25583-0   ISBN 978-3-031-25584-7   (eBook)
https://doi.org/10.1007/978-3-031-25584-7

This work was supported by Schweizerischer Nationalfonds zur Förderung der Wissenschaftlichen Forschung (215000/1)

© The Editor(s) (if applicable) and The Author(s) 2023. This book is an open access publication.
Open Access This book is licensed under the terms of the Creative Commons Attribution 4.0 International License (http://creativecommons.org/licenses/by/4.0/), which permits use, sharing, adaptation, distribution and reproduction in any medium or format, as long as you give appropriate credit to the original author(s) and the source, provide a link to the Creative Commons license and indicate if changes were made.
The images or other third party material in this book are included in the book's Creative Commons license, unless indicated otherwise in a credit line to the material. If material is not included in the book's Creative Commons license and your intended use is not permitted by statutory regulation or exceeds the permitted use, you will need to obtain permission directly from the copyright holder.
The use of general descriptive names, registered names, trademarks, service marks, etc. in this publication does not imply, even in the absence of a specific statement, that such names are exempt from the relevant protective laws and regulations and therefore free for general use.
The publisher, the authors, and the editors are safe to assume that the advice and information in this book are believed to be true and accurate at the date of publication. Neither the publisher nor the authors or the editors give a warranty, expressed or implied, with respect to the material contained herein or for any errors or omissions that may have been made. The publisher remains neutral with regard to jurisdictional claims in published maps and institutional affiliations.

This Springer imprint is published by the registered company Springer Nature Switzerland AG
The registered company address is: Gewerbestrasse 11, 6330 Cham, Switzerland

Contents

1	**Introduction**... Mary Gutman, Wurud Jayusi, Michael Beck, and Zvi Bekerman	1
Part I	**Immigrant and Immigrant Origin Teachers as Unrepresented Groups** Mary Gutman, Wurud Jayusi, Michael Beck, and Zvi Bekerman	
2	**Ethiopian Origin Teachers in Israel: Prejudices, Pedagogical Expectations and the Pygmalion Effect in the Shadow of the COVID-19** .... Mary Gutman	15
3	**Belonging and Otherness: Teachers of Ethiopian and Russian Origins in Israeli Schools** .... Shahar Gindi and Rakefet Erlich Ron	27
4	**Switzerland: Diversity in the Classroom, Uniformity in the Faculty**................................ Michael Beck, Carola Mantel, and Sonja Bischoff	45
5	**Sweden and Germany: Top-Down and Bottom-Up Policy Making in the Re-professionalization of International Teachers** .... Galina Putjata, Catarina Economou, Elin Ennerberg, and Jana Arnold	61
6	**"After Building Relationships, Language Is No Longer a Barrier": Two Bilingual Mathematics Teachers' Growth Through Student Teaching Experiences** .... Ji Yeong I and EunJin (E. J.) Bahng	75

| 7 | "Crossing the River by Feeling the Stones": Understanding Chinese Minority Teachers' Transnational and Transitional Experiences | 91 |

Pei-Ying Wu

| 8 | Research on Minority Teachers in Germany: Developments, Focal Points and Current Trends from the Perspective of Intercultural Education | 107 |

Lisa Rosen and Drorit Lengyel

| 9 | Teachers with Migration Background in German Discourse: Insights into Research on Education, Professional Integration and Self-Perception | 125 |

Evghenia Goltsev, Galina Putjata, and Anastasia Knaus

| 10 | Germany: Professional Networks of Minority Teachers and Their Role in Developing Multicultural Schools | 139 |

Josef Strasser

Part II Migrant and Indigenous Teachers as Minorities in Bilingual and Multilingual Schools
Mary Gutman, Wurud Jayusi, Michael Beck, and Zvi Bekerman

| 11 | "Welcome to the Club": Palestinian-Israeli Teachers in Bilingual Integrated and in Hebrew Speaking Schools | 159 |

Wurud Jayusi and Zvi Bekerman

| 12 | Independent Schools in South Africa: Acculturation of Zimbabwean Immigrant Teachers | 183 |

Tshatiwa Makula

| 13 | Netherlands: Teachers' Perspectives and Practices in Chinese and Polish Language and Culture Teaching | 201 |

Sjaak Kroon, Jinling Li, and Agnieszka Dreef

| 14 | Convergences and Divergences in Career Paths: Recruiting Foreign Teachers in Binational Schools in Argentina | 217 |

Liliana Mayer and Verónica Gottau

| 15 | Argentina: Minority Indigenous Teachers of Bilingual Intercultural Education | 233 |

Ana Carolina Hecht

Part III	Journeys and Identities of International Minority Teacher Educators Mary Gutman, Wurud Jayusi, Michael Beck, and Zvi Bekerman	
16	The Growth of Minority Supervisors: Supervision of Pre-service Teachers' Field Experiences Bing Xiao	253
17	Foster Child of the Family: An Autoethnography of an International Minority Teacher Educator in a U.S. University Yiting Chu	269
18	Pedagogical Challenges of Immigrant Minority Teacher Educators: A Collaborative Autoethnography Study Xuexue Yang and Byungeun Pak	285
19	Linguicism in U.S. Higher Education: A Critical Autoethnography Hyesun Cho	301
20	Science Teacher Education in Canada: Addressing Diversity by Living and Teaching Intersectionality Lydia E. Carol-Ann Burke	317
21	White College Students' Cognitive Dissonance When Taught by Immigrant Professor of Color Amani Zaier and Faith Maina	333
Part IV	Ethnic Minority Teachers as a Cultural Mediators Mary Gutman, Wurud Jayusi, Michael Beck, and Zvi Bekerman	
22	Kurdish Teachers in Turkey Within the Context of History Education Fatih Yazıcı	351
23	"They Respect Me as a Person Who Can Help" Roma Teaching Assistants in the Czech Republic Zbyněk Němec	365
24	South Africa: Desegregated Teaching, Democratic Citizenship Education and Integrating of Ethnic Minority Teachers Nuraan Davids	381

25 "Why Are We Only Learning About White People?"
    The Role of Identity in the Curricular and Pedagogical
    Considerations of One Latino Educator 395
    Kelly R. Allen

26 China: Decolonization and Teaching: An American Professor's
    Experience at Yunnan University 409
    MaryJo Benton Lee

27 Finland and Sweden: Muslim Teachers as Cultural Brokers 425
    Inkeri Rissanen

28 Ethnic Identity as a Cultural Mediator in Teaching:
    An Autoethnography of a Latinx Teacher 439
    Jennifer M. Barreto

29 New Zealand: The Experiences of Māori Teachers
    as an Ethnic Minority in English-Medium Schools 453
    Hana Turner-Adams and Christine Rubie-Davies

30 Transformation or 'Training the Dog'? Approaches to Access
    Within an Historically White University in South Africa 471
    Dina Zoe Belluigi and Gladman Thondhlana

31 Minority Status, Majority Benefits: Stories of Minority
    Teachers in U.S and What They Bring to the Classroom 489
    Atifa Manzoor

Conclusions and Implications 503

Chapter 1
Introduction

Mary Gutman, **Wurud Jayusi**, **Michael Beck**, and **Zvi Bekerman**

Abstract The introductory chapter begins by clarifying the rationale that led the editors to delve into this project despite the many challenges in this field of study. First, we outline the rationale that preceded our journey, while explaining the gap in the academic literature in this field. Thereafter, we address each of the four parts of this book. The first part deals with immigrant and immigrant-origin teachers. It reviews the social and linguistic challenges they face in geopolitical contexts in Israel, Europe, and the USA. The second part reviews the experiences of indigenous teachers as minorities in multilingual and bilingual schools. The third focuses on international minority teacher educators, and examines the pedagogical and cultural challenges they face as educators, instructors, and supervisors of pre-service teachers. The fourth and final part showcases ethnic minority teachers integrated into educational frameworks around the globe, highlighting the challenges and benefits involved. We conclude this chapter by presenting the potential contributions of the empirical evidence contained in this open-access book to the growing theoretical and practical understanding of the potential benefits and risks involved in these processes.

M. Gutman (✉)
Efrata College of Education, Jerusalem, Israel
e-mail: maria_g@inter.net.il

W. Jayusi
Beit Berl College, Arab Academic Institute, Beit Berl, Israel
e-mail: wurud.jayusi@beitberl.ac.il

M. Beck
St. Gallen University of Teacher Education, St. Gallen, Switzerland
e-mail: michael.beck@phsg.ch

Z. Bekerman
The Seymour Fox School of Education, Hebrew University of Jerusalem, Jerusalem, Israel
e-mail: zvi.bekerman@mail.huji.ac.il

The thirty chapters included in the present volume were conducted in fourteen countries spread across five continents. Their main aim is to improve the understanding of the status and potential influence of teachers from 'different' cultural, ethnic, racial, and national minority groups working in mainstream schools. For a variety of reasons, increasing migration flows around the world has led many education systems to consider including minority teachers among the teaching staff in schools. It is assumed that these teachers' cultural knowledge will help them mediate cultural and linguistic boundaries in school contexts with empathy, and thus effectively contribute to the success of minority students, while at the same time supporting prejudice reduction.

The search for potential studies for this book was conducted over a year. It resulted from the identification of a shortage of research literature examining the subject in depth, as has already been argued in meta-research in this field (Rubenko, 2018). As part of this process we faced challenges, the first of which was the heterogeneity of frameworks that integrate minority teachers into school staff. Most of these frameworks contain mixed populations of students from diverse backgrounds studying together, as found in recent studies (Bonner et al., 2018; Hajisoteriou et al., 2018; Whitaker & Valtierra, 2018). In other words, minority teachers tend to be assigned to heterogeneous classrooms rather than homogeneous classes that are dominant in the cultural and linguistic culture. Few studies that examine minority teachers (e.g., Rocheleau, 2017) focus on the interactions between them and students from the same ethnic group, thus ignoring the potential contribution of these teachers to the classroom climate as a whole, and to the resilience-building processes that teachers themselves undergo. Moreover, the existing literature does not examine in depth issues of policy in the education system on this subject, or the data regarding under-representation of minority teachers in the various frameworks.

Nevertheless, there were a number of ideological frameworks that led us to embark on this challenging journey. First, the research experience of the book's editors (Gutman, 2019; Jayusi & Bekerman, 2019, 2020) shows that one of the challenges of the education system and teacher training lies in preparing graduates for life in a diverse, cosmopolitan, and multicultural society. This conclusion is consistent with the literature (Bartanen & Grissom, 2019; Smith Kondo, 2019) which holds that ensuring diversity among staff indicates overt support and contribution by the institution and the education system vis-à-vis such preparation. Since most societies in the world today are characterized by a diverse cultural mosaic, the chances of graduates of the education system meeting people with diverse identities are high. Moreover, defining cultural identity has become a complex, hybrid, and multidimensional craft. Recent changes in communication methods have contributed to the blurring of geopolitical boundaries, thereby creating the ability to make intercultural encounters accessible through technological-virtual environments. Moreover, multiple migrations and international mobility as part of career transitions that seek to improve the quality of life have created countless opportunities for such encounters.

In keeping with the discourse emerging in the academic literature, the book is divided into four parts. The first deals with the challenges faced by immigrant teachers integrating into schools in a 'foreign' culture, while emphasizing language issues and culture-dependent teaching skills. The second part focuses on the most topical issue in academic discourse, in light of the rise of the international mobility of the global middle classes, which, as part of their mobility patterns, are routinely engaged in seeking educational frameworks for their children, among other parenting issues. These families, as well as families of immigrants, often choose bilingual and international schools for their children (Maxwell et al., 2019). Accordingly, this part deals with the issues arising from international and bilingual schools in the context of the minority teachers' role. The third part deals with minority teacher educators, and is based on self-studies that present a variety of attempts by researchers, who also serve as minority teacher educators, to position themselves under the guidance of 'majority' pre-service teachers. The fourth and final part deals with ethnic minority teachers, and it raises an interpretation of under-representation of teachers from ethnic backgrounds who serve in mainstream education settings.

The purpose of this book is to provide a theoretical basis for the discourse surrounding the issues of diversity among teaching staff in a variety of education systems around the world, with an emphasis on integrating teachers of different identities. As a secondary goal, the book indirectly identifies a set of strengths among all of these teachers, drawn from empirical evidence.

Part I: Immigrant and Immigrant Origin Teachers as Unrepresented Groups

The part includes nine chapters which reveal the challenges of integration of immigrant teachers and their descendants in schools in a 'foreign' culture, while emphasizing language issues and culture-dependent teaching skills.

Chapter 2, written by Mary Gutman focuses on the unique positioning of Ethiopian origin teachers in Israeli schools, with the aim of examining COVID-19 as an extreme situation in which unique characteristics of minority- majority relations in the education system may be revealed and intensified. Interviews with seven teachers of Ethiopian origin in the early years of their work indicated two solid phenomena faced during the period of closure in the education system related to prejudices and low expectations towards their pedagogical abilities relevant to COVID-19. The study findings are discussed in the context of the Pygmalion effect.

In Chap. 3, Shahar Gindi and Rakefet Erlich Ron, present a qualitative study comparing the two largest migrations groups which have arrived in Israel in recent decades; teachers arriving from Ethiopia and teachers from the Former Soviet Union working in Israeli schools The findings offer insights into the differential sense of belonging and alterity experienced by teachers in these groups.

In Chap. 4, Michael Beck, Carola Mantel and Sonja Bischoff provide an overview of studies dealing with transitions of pre- and in- service immigrant teachers in Swiss Universities of Teacher Education (UTED) and Swiss schools. The chapter discusses the reason for the rather low representation of immigrant teachers in these settings even though the demand for teachers in Switzerland is high and jobs are secure and well paid. The discussion is supported by empirical data on practicing teachers with a so-called immigrant background who experience a lack of recognition and rather subtle forms of social exclusion, and exposes a range of strategies developed by these teachers in coping with these experiences.

Chapter 5 presented by Galina Putjata, Catarina Economou, Elin Ennerberg and Jana Arnold address training programmes for immigrant teachers in Sweden and in Germany, with a particular focus on multilingualism. The results highlight the importance of top-down- and bottom-up approaches to overcome the monolingual mind-set and the urgent need to include course leaders in the process of policy making, while raising their language awareness.

Chapter 6, written by Ji Yeong I and EunJin (E. J.) Bahng follows the journeys of two bilingual mathematics teachers, immigrants from Mexico and Korea. It describes the teachers' first experiences of anxiety when speaking English as a Second Language in their school contexts. Following their interaction with supportive and cooperative teachers and with culturally and linguistically diverse students, both teachers underwent a crucial shift in their thinking from deficit views to asset-rich views in terms of their own cultural and linguistic identities. The results of this case study suggest that teacher preparation programs should integrate ways of supporting bilingual teachers to promote their positive cultural identity and to bring enrichment through their linguistic capabilities.

Chapter 7 authored by Pei-Ying Wu focuses on six minority teachers from China as an analytical lens to elucidate what happened when they were teaching while simultaneously learning new ideas and practices in U.S. public elementary school contexts. The findings illustrate a number of personal and professional challenges encountered by newly-arrived minority teachers in their initial transitions to life and work in the U.S. The challenges include the unfamiliarity with U.S. public schools, inadequate teaching materials, a heavy teaching load, and other teaching-related issues.

In Chap. 8 Lisa Rosen and Drorit Lengyel present a meta-analysis of studies on ethnic minority (pre-service) teachers in Germany and in German-speaking countries. The meta-analysis identifies five main research areas focusing on intercultural education: intersectional perspectives on professional self-concepts of minority teachers; discrimination and anti-Muslim racism experienced by prospective minority teachers; language and multilingualism as relevant social categories of difference and inequality in the context of (prospective) minority teachers; and comparisons between (prospective) minority and majority teachers with a focus on the effects of representation of (prospective) minority teachers. They conclude, that in Germany and German speaking countries there is an urgent need to develop inclusive policies for minority teachers to overcome the ethnizized attributions of professional competence and to focus on the discriminatory structures of the German education system, including teacher education.

In Chap. 9, Evghenia Goltsev, Galina Putjata and Anastasia Knaus apply a narrative review method to present a meta-analysis of the issues typical of teachers with an immigrant background in Germany and their strategies for integration.

Among the prominent issues they raise: ascriptions and self-perception of immigrant origin teachers' role in education; immigrant origin teachers 'importance for students, students'own perspectives on immigrant teachers; and professional integration of immigrant teachers in schools.

With the aim to explore the conditions for successfully realizing the supposed positive impact in immigrant teachers, the tenth chapter by Josef Strasser focuses on the role of the school context, assuming that a supportive context offers better options for cooperation and cohesion. Based on two case studies, the author highlights how such an impact can come about and claims that the implementation of professional networks and learning communities of minority teachers may be a major step in developing multicultural schools. He concludes that schools with such communities seem to be open to professional impulses of minority teachers and give them space to develop a "diversity agenda", whereas other schools tend to marginalize them.

Part II: Indigenous Teachers as Minorities in Multilingual and Bilingual Schools

The part focuses on the most topical issue in academic discourse, in light of the rise of international mobility of the global middle class which, as part of their mobility patterns, are routinely engaged in seeking educational frameworks for their children (e.g. international schools) and other parenting practices.

The chapters in this part deal with the variety of obstacles encountered by these teachers and examine their perceptions as minority teachers in the local context. The five chapters included in this part are based on qualitative studies conducted in bilingual schools.

Chapter 11, written by Wurud Jayusi and Zvi Bekerman, deals with Arab-Palestinian teachers in Israeli schools and contributes to a better understanding of how minority teachers in majority schools experience their work and how their participation in such educational contexts helps shape their sense of ethno-cultural belonging and their sense of self-efficacy. Through comparative work, between teachers working at National Hebrew speaking schools and those working at bilingual (Hebrew, Arabic) integrated schools they gain insights into the context-specific conditions which might help support or undermine minority teachers' inclusion. Though differences are exposed in the analysis, both groups of teachers express satisfaction regarding their work at the schools. They are satisfied with their work and feel they belong to a very special 'club' a metaphor that affords them a strong and positive positioning within the school context.

Chapter 12, written by Tshatiwa Makula, aims at shedding light on Zimbabwean migrant teachers' experiences of acculturation in culturally diverse independent multilingual schools in Johannesburg, South Africa. It also seeks to identify educational leadership approaches that promote multiculturalism and acculturation in culturally diverse independent schools. The findings indicate absence of cultural assimilation; immigrant teachers are treated differently from their South African peers and they do not blend in easily. It is suggested that changing this situation implies developing school policies and practices that are sensitive to cultural differences as well as the need for all stakeholders to face head-on the specific needs of educational multiculturalism.

In Chap. 13, Sjaak Kroon, Jinling Li and Agnieszka Dreef present two high-quality case studies at a multilingual community supplementary school teaching both the Chinese and Polish languages in the Netherlands. The authors claim that the migrant teachers who teach at these schools are generally community members who are not necessarily qualified as language (or culture) teachers. The findings reveal that these teachers are more oriented toward highlighting and promoting their home country's national history, identity, ideology and values than to preparing their students for living in the Netherlands' super diverse society in which Dutch language and culture are dominant.

Chapter 14 authored by Liliana Mayer and Verónica Gottau seeks to analyze the reasons for hiring migrant teachers in bi-national multilingual schools, and the motives of foreign residents in Argentina to work in schools of their own country of origin. The author states that one of the main reasons for this is the school ethos which closely aligns with values of cultural diplomacy added to the working conditions offered at these institutions. The authors conclude that bi-national multilingual schools tend to legitimate their added value through the hiring of foreign teachers, and foreign teachers find solid ground for a successful career path, granted by their place of birth.

In Chap. 15, the last one in this part, Ana Carolina Hecht describes the co-teaching practices of a non-indigenous teacher and a minority indigenous teacher in a Toba/Qom neighborhood in Chaco, Argentina. The ethnographic data shows that the indigenous teacher played a key role as a translator/mediator between the school and monolingual children in their indigenous languages thus the goal of bilingualism has not been fully realized. Considering this complex sociolinguistic panorama, this chapter analyzes specific aspects of these new practices among the Toba/Qom teachers whose pedagogical tasks have shifted from teaching the indigenous language to reversing language shift. Additionally, it examines the experiences and knowledge of the native tongue among these minority teachers, who range from fluid bilingual speakers to less competent ones. As a consequence, from an anthropological perspective, the question of Bilingual Intercultural Education is raised.

Part III: Journeys and Identities of International Minority Teacher Educators

The experiences of skilled international teacher educators who have integrated into foreign institutions for teacher education for varying periods of time are described in this part. The chapters in this part present empirical evidence and auto-ethnographic studies based on authors' international career trajectories that emphasize multifaceted impacts of such integration on their personal and cultural identity as foreign staff members, as well as a broad discussion of their potential and actual contributions to the local teacher education curriculum and culture.

Bing Xiao, in Chap. 16, documents her journey as a China born minority teacher educator of American pre-service teachers. She describes her efforts to balance her two identities as an "insider" in the teacher education program, but an "outsider" to American school culture. The research used a video-cued multifocal ethnographic method as well as interviews with university supervisors and instructors and demonstrates her growth as both instructor and supervisor in a foreign culture.

In Chap. 17 Yiting Chu explores how his intersectional identities as a foreign-born of Chinese descent, non-White, non-native English speaking; pre-tenure teacher educator had influenced his experiences and journeys at a predominantly White university in the United States. He used tenets of critical race theory (CRT) and Asian critical theory (AsianCrit), as analytic lenses to frame his auto-ethnographic recollections and explorations of what it meant to be a minority educator in a foreign cultural and institutional context and the strategies he used to navigate the White dominant academic space. He concludes by calling for a more inclusive framework in order to broaden our understandings of international minority teacher educators' journeys and experiences.

Chapter 18 describes two journeys saturated with pedagogical and linguistic challenges from two novice international minority teacher educators, natives of China and South Korea, who teach in a transcultural context in the U.S. Using a collaborative auto-ethnography, the authors, Xuexue Yang and Byungeun Pak investigate language, cultural and socio-political dimensions of the first space (teaching practice at the home country), and the second space (teaching practice at the host-country) while trying to design the notion of a third possible space.

Chapter 19, an auto-ethnography by Hyesun Cho, a native of South Korea, describes the linguistic discrimination she experienced during her professional trajectory as an international minority teacher educator, employed at an institution of higher education in the United States. The researcher describes the processes of negotiating her professional identity as a researcher and teacher educator in a foreign culture. It delineates various events she encountered in her journey with an emphasis on linguistic challenges and a process of acquiring self-efficacy in a foreign culture.

Chapter 20 begins with Lydia E. Carol-Ann Burke's past reflections on the fact that she was never taught by a science teacher from a racial or ethnic minority group. Later in the chapter, she documents her journey as an immigrant science teacher educator of racial minority status at a Canadian university. She documents significant events in her academic career with an emphasis on her racial, ethnic and gender identity as a Black woman from England of Caribbean heritage. Through an inter-sectionality theoretical framework, she examines her role and impact on the perceptions of diversity among peers and student-teachers.

The third part ends with Chap. 21, written by Amani Zaier's and Faith Maina', who describe the cognitive dissonance of White college students when taught by immigrant professors of colour, and the way these professors restore harmony and balance in order to complete the course successfully. Using a qualitative method, the authors found that the students manifested dissonance by "othering" the professor through cultural and racial profiling, questioned his qualification, professionalism and credentials, and tend to express anger and anxiety towards the course. The authors claim that these processes have significant implications for the career trajectory of the immigrant professor of colour, while at the same time impacting the knowledge access for White college students.

Part IV: Ethnic Minority Teachers as Cultural Mediators

The fourth and final part deals with ethnic minority teachers who serve in mainstream educational settings. It contains diverse empirical evidence from various countries around the world that reveals the potential inherent in employing ethnic minority teachers in schools in terms of agency, mediation, "cultural brokering", and its inestimable value for students in majority educational settings.

Chapter 22, written by Fatih Yazıcı focuses on Kurdish teachers teaching history in Turkey, trapped in between the 'truths' of official history and their own understandings of 'truth' The chapter describes in detail the identity problems they face in the social and political spheres. The interviews conducted with Kurdish teachers of different religious/sectarian, political and sexual identities reveal the complex relationship existing between such teachers and their students, colleagues and the educational establishment while trying to uncover the meaning of being a history Kurdish teacher in Turkey.

Chapter 23 by Zbyněk Němec touches on the unique context of Roma teaching assistants in the Czech Republic, who traditionally provide an irreplaceable form of support for the education of socially disadvantaged Roma students. The study shows the potential benefits these assisting teachers can offer when serving as cultural mediators for students in the foreign culture and while supporting communication between the school and the Roma students' families. Moreover, Roma assistants also represent an important resource of information for local teachers which can help them overcome their own prejudices.

In Chap. 24, Nuraan Davids offers an in-depth narrative account of the experiences of a first-year 'black' teacher at a historically advantaged ('white') school. Her narrative sheds light on the intersectional complexities and discourses, which led to her eventual departure from the school. In concluding the author turns her attention to what the implications of her experiences are for democratic citizenship in South Africa. According to her view, these teachers (as well as the presence of a diverse student cohort) are of great importance as cultural mediators and as such contribute to the enactment and preservation of democratic values.

Kelly R. Allen, in Chap. 25, focuses on the experiences and perspectives of Ricardo, a Latino educator in US adopting a post positivist realist approach to identity. This chapter analyzes a collection of focus groups, individual interviews, and curriculum artifacts as a means of approaching and analyzing Ricardo's experiences as a cultural mediator. The analysis makes visible how language and hybrid classroom discourse practices were used to connect with students so as to create bridges to the official curriculum. The findings underscore the need for teacher education programs to better support ethnic minority educators in navigating the complex position they assume, as educators and as minoritized individuals, and the ways that these multiple identities intersect with their practice.

Chapter 26, an auto-ethnography written by MaryJo Benton Lee, describes her work, as an ethnic minority professor (a white American) teaching at a University in China. The author describes her own self- perception as a "cultural ambassador" in this context and describes how her learning about educators' work in China, brought her to a deeper understanding of her own USA culture. a process which reflected on her Chinese students' understanding of their own country.

Chapter 27 focuses on the experiences and perspectives of Muslim teachers, who serve informally as "cultural brokers and mediators" in Finnish and Swedish schools. The author, Inkeri Rissanen, presents qualitative data from semi-structured interviews conducted with fourteen such teachers. The results offer insights on who is perceived to be a good cultural broker and how this role should be encouraged and developed in educational settings. In the conclusions the simplistic view of cultural brokerage as a role for teachers is critically reviewed while questioning the practice of outsourcing "all things multicultural" in school settings.

Chapter 28, authored by Jennifer M. Barreto, examines her ethnic identity, through the inter-sectionality of language, culture, and teaching as a Latinx teacher in the United States. The auto-ethnographic effort acknowledges and validates her Latinx presence as well as draws attention to her marginal position inside dominant structures of education. The author investigates the importance of similarities and differences that permeate everyday life as a teacher in complex ways and discusses the everyday negotiations of being Latinx, culture and teaching in an elementary school.

In Chap. 29 Hana Turner-Adams and Christine Rubie-Davies discuss the experiences of Māori teachers who are currently or were previously employed in English-medium schools and centers in New Zealand. Their study clearly shows Māori teachers connecting and engaging more readily with Māori students due to their shared culture and background while, in contrast, many Pākehā/New Zealand European teachers show a limited understanding of Māori language, knowledge systems, values, and customs, which often brings them to hold low expectations for Māori student achievement.

In Chap. 30, Dina Zoe Belluigi and Gladman Thondhlana presents a critical theoretical discussion and analysis of sources reflecting the under-representation of black female teachers in institutions of higher education in South Africa. The analysis reveals multiple factors (structural, cultural, and political), which stand in the way of minority faculty members serving as cultural mediators in the diverse South African society.

The last chapter in this part, Chap. 31, authored by Atifa Manzoor, closely examines the life-stories of three minority female teachers, seeking to answer the question: How does their cultural identity influence their teaching in regards to classroom curriculum, environment and relationships with students? Major themes to emerge from the data referred to minority teachers as role models and culturally responsive teaching. They provided a unique perspective to which some students might relate. Manzoor claims that with an ever-changing demographic, it is advantageous to have diversity among educators that mirrors that of the student population.

All in all this volume wishes to contribute to the growing theoretical and practical understanding of the potential benefits and risks involved in the process of integrating minority teachers in mainstream educational systems. This goal was implemented by empirical and theoretical studies made by the authors from diverse academic worlds and contexts. Most of the chapters in this volume present studies using the qualitative approaches, with the exception of three chapters which were done using the systematic review approach and meta-analysis of studies in the field. Given present migratory trends, it is clear that the need to include 'minority' teachers in mainstream educational settings will only grow. Their proper inclusion can clearly benefit all – locals and new comers – but these benefits can only be realized if we are careful when developing policies and programs which honestly confront the many obstacles clearly described in the thirty chapters included in this volume. Doing so will take courage and personal transformation, from the part of all relevant stakeholders, and a profound understanding that contexts are always local and complex and do not allow for 'one fits all' solutions. Yet what we have learned while producing the volume has enriched us and hopefully will enrich its readers too by suggesting a few common directions which cannot be ignored.

References

Bartanen, B., & Grissom, J. A. (2019). *School principal race and the hiring and retention of racially diverse teachers* (EdWorkingPaper No. 19–59). Annenberg Institute at Brown University.

Bonner, P. J., Warren, S. R., & Jiang, Y. H. (2018). Voices from urban classrooms: Teachers' perceptions on instructing diverse students and using culturally responsive teaching. *Education and Urban Society, 50*(8), 697–726.

Gutman, M. (2019). International mobility and cultural perceptions among senior teacher educators in Israel: 'I have learned to suspend judgment'. *Journal of Education for Teaching, 45*(4), 461–475.

Hajisoteriou, C., Karousiou, C., & Angelides, P. (2018). Successful components of school improvement in culturally diverse schools. *School Effectiveness and School Improvement, 29*(1), 91–112.

Jayusi, W., & Bekerman, Z. (2019). Does teaching on the "other" side create a change. *Teaching and Teacher Education, 77*(1), 160–169.

Jayusi, W., & Bekerman, Z. (2020). Yes, we can! Palestinian-Israeli teachers in Jewish-Israeli schools. *Journal of Teacher Education, 71*(3), 319–331.

Maxwell, C., Yemini, M., Koh, A., & Agbaria, A. (2019). The plurality of the Global Middle Class (es) and their school choices – Moving the 'field' forward empirically and theoretically. *Discourse, 40*, 609.

Rocheleau, M. (2017). Mass. Students are increasingly diverse. But their teachers are not. *The Boston Globe*.

Rubenko, R. (2018). *The influence of teachers from a social minority group on students from the social majority group*. Merhavim Institute. (in Hebrew).

Smith Kondo, C. (2019). Front Streeting: A challenge in preparing culturally diverse teachers for diverse students. *Anthropology and Education Quarterly, 50*(2), 135.

Whitaker, M. C., & Valtierra, K. M. (2018). Enhancing preservice teachers' motivation to teach diverse learners. *Teaching and Teacher Education, 73*, 171–182.

Mary Gutman is researcher, teacher educator and a head of the research authority at Efrata College of Education in Jerusalem, Israel. She is a graduate of the excellent programs of Ph.D. studies (President's Scholarship Program, Bar Ilan University) and the Postdoctoral Program (Mofet Institute). Her main research interest refers to multiculturalism in teaching and teacher education, minority-majority relationships and immigration in educational contexts. In recent years she has published dozens of articles in leading international journals and received a number of competitive research scholarships and grants.

Wurud Jayusi is the Head of the Arab Academic Institute - Beit Berl College. She is the former head of the Center for the Advancement of Shared Society at the College. She teaches planning & evaluation for learning at the Education faculty. Her main interests are in the study of peace education, multicultural\multiethnic education, and minority-majority relations in the education system. Her recent work has examined cross-cultural teaching. Wurud has published multiple papers in a variety of academic journals and presented her research at multiple international conferences.

Michael Beck is a research fellow and lecturer at St. Gallen University of Teacher Education, Switzerland. He studied social sciences with a focus on sociology and research methodology in Manheim, Germany, and received his Ph.D. in Educational Sociology at the University of Bern, Switzerland. His fields of interest are social mobility, educational inequality, research in teacher education and assessment of student competencies.

Zvi Bekerman teaches anthropology of education at the School of Education, Hebrew University of Jerusalem (Israel), and is a faculty member at the Mandel Leadership Institute in Jerusalem. He is also an Associate Fellow at The Harry S. Truman Research Institute for The Advancement of Peace. His main interests are in the study of cultural, ethnic and national identity, including identity processes and negotiation during intercultural encounters and in formal/informal learning contexts. He is particularly interested in how concepts such as culture and identity intersect with issues of social justice, intercultural and peace education, and citizenship education. His recent work has examined the intersection between civic and religious epistemologies in educational contexts. In addition to publishing multiple papers in a variety of academic journals, Bekerman is the founding editor of the refereed journal Diaspora, Indigenous, and Minority Education: An International Journal. Among his most recent books: Bekerman, Z., & Zembylas, M. (2017). Psychologized language in education: Denaturalizing a regime of truth, Palgrave Macmillan – Springer; Bekerman, Zvi (2016), The Promise of Integrated and Multicultural Bilingual Education: Inclusive Palestinian-Arab and Jewish Schools in Israel, Oxford University Press; Bekerman, Z. & Michalinos, Z. (2012), Teaching Contested Narratives Identity, Memory and Reconciliation in Peace Education and Beyond. London, Cambridge University Press; C. McGlynn, M. Zembylas, & Z. Bekerman (Eds.) (2013) Integrated Education in Conflicted Societies, Palgrave, Mcmillan; and Bekerman, Z. & Geisen, T. (Eds. 2012) International Handbook of Migration, Minorities and Education Understanding Cultural and Social Differences in Processes of Learning. New York: Springer.

Open Access This chapter is licensed under the terms of the Creative Commons Attribution 4.0 International License (http://creativecommons.org/licenses/by/4.0/), which permits use, sharing, adaptation, distribution and reproduction in any medium or format, as long as you give appropriate credit to the original author(s) and the source, provide a link to the Creative Commons license and indicate if changes were made.

The images or other third party material in this chapter are included in the chapter's Creative Commons license, unless indicated otherwise in a credit line to the material. If material is not included in the chapter's Creative Commons license and your intended use is not permitted by statutory regulation or exceeds the permitted use, you will need to obtain permission directly from the copyright holder.

Part I
Immigrant and Immigrant Origin Teachers as Unrepresented Groups

Mary Gutman ⓘ, Wurud Jayusi ⓘ, Michael Beck ⓘ, and Zvi Bekerman ⓘ

Chapter 2
Ethiopian Origin Teachers in Israel: Prejudices, Pedagogical Expectations and the Pygmalion Effect in the Shadow of the COVID-19

Mary Gutman

Abstract The present study focuses on that unique positioning of Ethiopian origin teachers in Israeli schools, with the aim of examining COVID-19 as an extreme situation in which unique characteristics of minority-majority relations in the education system may be revealed and intensified. Interviews with seven teachers of Ethiopian origin during the early years of their careers indicated two specific phenomena that they faced during the period of closure in the education system. These phenomena related to prejudices and low expectations regarding their pedagogical abilities relevant to COVID-19. The findings raise two tensions encountered regularly by Ethiopian origin teachers during this period. The methodology employed the conceptual framework of 'agility' – a term that reflects the teacher's ability to exercise discretionary flexibility and demonstrate the required access to students in socially distanced conditions. The first tension relates to the relationship between the interviewees' culture and that of the students, with emphasis on the students' low expectations of the interviewees' abilities as distance teachers. The second tension discussed in the findings relates to the organizational culture and school management. Additionally in this context, the interviewees felt that low expectations prevailed regarding their ability to establish innovative technological conditions and develop professionally in accordance with the requirements of this challenging period within the education system. The evidence is discussed in the context of the Pygmalion effect.

M. Gutman (✉)
Efrata College of Education, Jerusalem, Israel
e-mail: maria_g@inter.net.il

© The Author(s) 2023
M. Gutman et al. (eds.), *To Be a Minority Teacher in a Foreign Culture*,
https://doi.org/10.1007/978-3-031-25584-7_2

Introduction

Reducing gaps in education systems has been defined as one of the key issues in global discourse, and even the most important challenge in the coming decade. This discourse intensified even more in the wake of the global crisis of the COVID-19 epidemic that erupted like a storm, reshaping an educational reality around the world. Beyond distance learning in conditions of emergency and social isolation, it has created a new benchmark for teachers in the context of a wide range of skills and required resources, such as access to innovative infrastructures, overnight change in teaching pathways and immediate pedagogical adaptation. All of these undoubtedly highlighted cultural, social and economic gaps between different sectors and classes in the education system and even created new ones, between both students and teachers from different backgrounds (Greenfeld-Jonah, 2013).

In Israel, as in many countries in the world, awareness of multicultural issues in the education system is increasing. According to Reichman (2009), at the beginning of the present century, about one-third of the Jewish population in Israel are natives of other countries who made a return to the historic homeland (immigrated to Israel; in local terms, made Aliya), and another third are second-generation immigrants. Following that, the central vision that stood out in the various education committees was to place increased emphasis and a deliberate effort to integrate the multicultural teaching force who will serve as social-cultural agents, and as mediators of language and educational values. All that in accordance with the spirit of the 'melting pot' ideology which aims to educate one Jewish-Israeli joint culture (Baratz & Kalnisky, 2017; Halper, 1987; Ran, 2017). However, Nevo (2016) claims that the attempt to apply such spirit in the education system has not been successful throughout history. Likewise, the deliberate effort to ignore (or minimize an effect of) cultural diversity in social and educational terms did not go well, and the education system perceived itself as unwilling to absorb immigrants from countries that hold a non-Western-progressive culture. An example of this can be seen in Ethiopian origin teachers, who although born in Israel or arrived at an early age, are sometimes considered "foreign" socialization agents and those who cannot represent the dominant Israeli white culture which combines identities of the Middle East and the West (Weininger, 2014).

Admittedly, the attempt to culturally correlate the teaching force with the students of the education system was inconsistent with these aspirations: while immigrants from the other countries have integrated into Israeli schools as teachers, the percentage of Ethiopian origin teachers is inconsistent with Ethiopian community representation in Israel (Brener & Avisher, 2017; Ran, 2017). Other sources (e.g. Ran, 2017) claim that this situation was caused as a result of low expectations in society towards this group of teachers, both at the stage of teacher education and their entering to teaching. In these two stages, they are integrated into dedicated support programs on behalf of the Ministry of Education, which aim to support Ethiopian origin teachers in a variety of aspects and thus ensure optimal integration into the education system. Although, paradoxically, it has been found that these programs often even perpetuate prejudices in society and low expectations for generations (Schatz-Oppenheimer, 2015, 2020). The present study focuses on that unique positioning of Ethiopian origin teachers in Israeli schools, with the aim of examining COVID-19 as an extreme situation in which unique characteristics of minority- majority relations in the education system may be revealed and intensified.

Ethiopian Origin Teachers in Israel

Ethiopian immigration in Israel, which took place by four main waves from 1980 to 1992, is one of the most controversial ones Israel has known (Cohen, 1998). This migration, more than the others, was faced with challenges of de- and re-socialization, which means a disengagement from the norms and cultural codes of the country of origin, and the adoption of the new and local ones (Berry et al., 2006). Thus, in the case of the Ethiopian community in Israel, most of them serve as an example of self-fulfilling prophecy: due to increased discrimination and exclusion in different life systems, they demonstrated an affinity for preserving old cultural patterns (Brenner & Avishar, 2017). Thus, although the last wave of the immigration occurred three decades ago, and most of Ethiopian origins are second-generation Israelis, the image and stereotype of the lower class has remained constant over time, and makes it difficult for social and professional integration. The sense of difference and strangeness of this minority group and their descendants is explained by variant cultural codes, skin color, external appearance and distinct customs (Amit, 2012; Cohen, 2016).

Researchers (Kalnisky & Brenner, 2016) claim that as a result of the gaps in the signs of culture and status, many Israelis of Ethiopian origin report a decline in their sense of self-cultural value and state that they find it difficult to find a way to contribute to Israeli society (Parfitt & Semi, 2013). Thus, in practice, the stereotype of their lowest status in the Israeli-Jewish society that failed to integrate them into professional, sociological and social aspects is preserved. This did not skip the teacher population, which as the largest and most cohesive professional group in Israel serves as the mirror, the 'microcosm' of socialization processes in this multicultural society. These processes have taken a sharp turn in light of the outbreak of the state of the COVID-19 epidemic, and have thrown a lot at the pedagogical and educational abilities of teachers from minority groups. In this article, I will review the implications of educational reforms that occurred due to the COVID-19 epidemic on pedagogical expectations among Ethiopian origin teachers, and the impact of these expectations on Ethiopian origin teachers' self-expectations. In other words, I will examine the Pygmalion effect in the shadow of COVID-19 in the context of Ethiopian origin teachers in Israeli schools, in an effort to contribute to the understanding of minority-majority relations that sometimes tend to intensify during a global educational crisis.

Challenges in Integrating Ethiopian Origin Teachers in Israeli Schools

Brenner and Avishar (2017) attribute a supreme importance to the integration of Ethiopian origin teachers into the Israeli education system. The main factor stems from the need for correcting an ongoing tradition of under-representation of the Ethiopian community in the education system as a teaching force and the breaking of the initial challenge of "flag bearers". Weiner-Levy (2006) defines this term as the lack of harnessing and commitment of a minority group to a particular process due to the lack of a role model. In the case of Ethiopian origin teachers, the challenge stems from the lack of pioneering and the visible justification to embark on teacher education acquisition processes, to integrate into key positions and to serve the education system. The main victims of the situation are children and adolescents of Ethiopian origin who are not exposed to role models and inspirations for building self-confidence and a better class future.

Apart from the initial challenge, researchers (Schatz-Oppenheimer & Kalnisky, 2014) noted that integration of Ethiopian origin teachers into the education system packs quite a few difficulties with regard to their starting point, which differs in the light of economic, social and cultural gaps. Others (Mehert et al., 2018; Schatz-Oppenheimer, 2015; Weininger, 2014) claim that during their professional encounter with peer teachers, school administrators, students and their parents, they often perceive themselves as having reduced value, due to a social expectation of educators to meet high standards of "educational language" in terms of oral and written ability, educational leadership, social engagement, and the ability to take initiatives. Another prominent area in this regard is difficulty in the field of technology skills which are requested in this era even more than in the past, due to the COVID-19 crisis that has disrupted schools and required teachers to create a sharp transition from traditional classroom teaching to online lessons (UNESCO, 2020). This reality has further sharpened the need for the implementation of the usual "educational language": flexibility in methods of teaching and education, entrepreneurship and creativity, mastery of online teaching in both technological and methodological aspects and implementing communication skills. Thus, according to educational experts (Dahan et al., 2020), the COVID-19 crisis has exposed class gaps in the ethnic, social and cultural aspects of Israel, even expanding it on a daily basis. Admittedly, while most of the discourse around the implications of socioeconomic disparities in the shadow of COVID-19 mostly focuses on students in schools and higher education, a relative minority of the material deals with the not-so-simple struggles of teachers during this period with an emphasis on cultural and professional diversity. This study attempts to help close this lacuna.

Methodology

Sample and Sampling

This qualitative study included seven early careers Ethiopian origin teachers teaching in three elementary religious schools throughout Jerusalem. The sample was selected according to cross-referencing among the main criteria: seniority in school (1–5 years) and the level of technological skills of online teaching (medium and above). Choosing these criteria is intended, firstly, to allow the interviewees to examine their position as teachers over a period of time, relative to COVID-19, and secondly, to rule out another interpretation of the findings, such as the variety in pedagogical-technological skills.

Research Process

The qualitative-narrative approach was conducted in Hebrew through semi-structured interviews, during which interviewees were asked about their feelings and emotions as it was in the past, before the outbreak of COVID19 viz. the lockdown of education system and the distance learning routine. The interview was constructed in five parts: (1) the biographical section and the demographic data; (2) questions about unique characteristics of their work routine before and during the COVID-19; (3) questions about feelings and emotions that accompanied Ethiopian origin teachers during these two periods, emphasizing interaction with school principals, colleagues and students. The interviews lasted an average of 30 min. Adhering to the ethical principles of educational research (AERA, 2004), interviewees were assured of complete privacy and anonymity. The interviewees signed for the interview recording knowing that their quotes would be used for writing and publishing future research papers.

The Data Analysis

The interview and analysis procedure was deductive: the aim was to glean information and examples in the context of Ethiopian origin teachers in the shadow of COVID-19 and to create a theoretical framework that interprets these experiences. This research approach, known in the literature as 'grounded theory', with the aim of coming up with an up-to-date and innovative theory following the collection of qualitative data in unique contexts. This is in contrast to more traditional research processes, which are based on inquiring into the use of existing models and theories in innovative contexts.

Accordingly, data analysis began by identifying issues that emerged from the narrative data as dominant and recurring in different interviews. In the second stage, a quote and example for each prominent theme was chosen. In this case, the themes touched on the interviewees' feelings and interpretation of school reality in the shadow of COVID-19 and their attitudes, expectations and prejudices towards them. In the final stage, a theory that reflects findings obtained was adapted to the specific context in which the study was conducted and was used for the purpose of discussing the findings of this chapter. In the current case, a theoretical framework that has been found to be appropriate for these findings was the "Pygmalion effect theory," which emphasized the impacts of pedagogical expectations and prejudices.

Findings and Discussion

The new reality created in the education system due to the onslaught of the COVID-19 epidemic required a shift from frontal to online learning from educators and their students. According to Burgess and Sievertsen (2020), reality has greatly influenced the widening of gaps and the creation of new ones, between those accustomed to traditional teaching and assessment methods and those open to innovation and entrepreneurship. According to Kidd (2020), among the factors influencing the gaps among teachers – a changing teaching culture, the ability (or inability) of flexibility-accessibility (that appears in the academic-educational literature in the field of COVID-19 by the innovative concept of "agility"), the uniqueness of the character of certain professions, characteristics of the students Additional sources (Dvir & Schatz-Oppenheimer, 2020) also pointed to possible gaps in teachers' ability to adapt to this crisis situation due to age, ethnic culture or organizational culture in the school where they teach.

Against these claims, the present study pointed to emotional challenges that outweigh the technological ones, among Ethiopian origin teachers. Interviewees argued that the difficulty was created due to a reduced sense of value, low self-esteem and a sense that the environment's expectations towards the mentioned abilities were significantly lower relative to their majority peers. Evidence also emerged that argued for the latent tensions between them as representatives of a minority group of teachers, the majority culture (the students) and organizational culture (i.e., peers and principals in the school). These cultures were reflected in the students' and principals' high expectations from the pedagogical staff to catch up with gaps in the field of professional development, teamwork, other soft skills and technologies within a limited time and at short notice. To the sense of the interviewed teachers, they felt excluded from these cultures and had to face low expectations directed towards them and the Pygmalion effect that created a self-fulfilling prophecy when the prevailing expectations affected performance.

Yuan (2019) brought up the positive influences of "Pygmalion effect theory" which conceived first at 1964, believing that the level of motivation of the individual depends directly on the expectation conveyed to him or her in overt and covert ways, both from the educational environment, and the work environment.

According to the study, a good application of the expectation effect has great inspiration for promoting an individual's development. Alongside this, White and Locke (2000) present the negative consequences of the Pygmalion effect, and present a number of limitations of its application in different settings. In the context of this study, the findings revealed aspects that produced the Pygmalion effect under the influence of prejudices of students, principals and pedagogical staff.

Tension Between Majority and Minority Cultures H. (an elementary school teacher and Bible teacher), talked about her role of combining professional teaching with classroom education:

As I am both a professional teacher and an educator accustomed to the simple and traditional teaching aids, I had the same difficulty as many other teachers switching to remote teaching and implementing these two roles using Zoom. For me, I have not taught a distance lesson so far and have seen a challenge despite the stress and frustration. Although I have seen that students do not expect me to be good at such teaching. I have seen that some take it in the absence of seriousness. Many of them "overlap", do not join to the zoom meetings or do not open cameras in the hope that I will not find out. Some of them did not take care of homework and assignments. From conversations with the other teachers, it seems that with them it is different and the participation and commitment of the students is high. I felt that the decrease in their motivation was related to lower expectations of me in the technological field because in the past these things did not happen, the students were attentive to me. For some reason their low motivation also affected my motivation to be interesting in zoom classes.

It can be seen in this testimony, which was typical of other testimonies that H. attributes to herself the disdainful behaviors of students in the Zoom learning and she interprets this as proof of their low pedagogical expectations toward her. This interpretation influences her expectations of herself and creates the perpetuation of the situation.

Tension Between Organizational and Minority Cultures According to the interviewees, the prejudices and low expectations were expressed by the colleagues and the school management regarding the ability of the teachers to assimilate innovative technological environments and develop professionally. D. (an elementary school teacher) talked about the organizational culture of the school where she worked in everything related to expectations and requirements towards the teaching staff, and they were different from the expectations towards her.

It was important for the school management to provide an assessment of the success of distance learning. They looked mainly at the ways to manage a Zoom lesson, the content of the lessons, and creativity and maintaining personal contact with the students. But I have not seen them refer to the lessons I teach and what I do. The feeling was that they were trying to skip me. I think it is important to see the investment as well, and some obstacles we went through to get to distance learning and it did not happen. To say it did not hurt me? It actually did.

T., an elementary school teacher, shared this testimony.

The school asked for a report on the amount of lessons, each teacher had to report what lessons s/he gave and also share the recordings of the lessons. I was not asked and did not understand the reason. When I asked, the coordinator replied: if you have and recorded, send. It felt strange and I felt that the expectations from me are actually low during Corona, which didn't help my motivation to strive and show involvement.

So far one can see the voices of distress and insult that indicate a tension between the organizational cultures of the school, the ways of assessment practiced in the COVID-19 period, and the Ethiopian origin teachers' low status in this situation. According to the interviewee, this even hurt her desire to persevere and show involvement, thus creating the aforementioned Pygmalion effect.

Conclusions and Implications

The evidence heard in the study indicated tensions between the interviewees as representing a minority group in the teaching staff, and the majority and organizational cultures of the school in which they teach. The interviewees testified that the pedagogical expectations were low compared to the other teachers, which is reflected in a variety of overt and covert situations. This study sheds light on three cornerstones that underlie Ethiopian origin teachers' coping, which are influenced by pedagogical expectations, prejudices and the skills of 'agility', that is the new term refering to the teachers' skills of flexibity and available adoption of new technological practices in a significant but pragmatic way (Kidd, 2020). In practice, the study reveals the concept of "teacher expectations" with the reference of skills of "agility" (Kidd, 2020). Theoretically the study contributes to the discourse about widening gaps in the lens of the Pygmalion effect and prejudices toward minorities in the education system. The study redefines the impact of pedagogical expectations and prejudices in the context of minority and majority relations and in the shadow of COVID-19 in the education system. A combination of these two terms is reflected in a variety of recent studies, and it appears to be a major factor in determining a teacher's professional success. For example, Turner et al. (2015) found a relationship between teachers' expectations of students and the ethnicity of both. Also, my previous study (Gutman, 2019) pointed to the "Pygmalion effect" formulated following principals 'expectations towards new teacher educators. The present study adds to these findings the voices of a group of minority teachers who testified to frustration following low pedagogical expectations placed on them by principals and students in the context of pedagogical abilities required in the COVID-19 period.

These findings are consistent with previous studies showing that the period of lockdown and the COVID-19 epidemic revolutionized the definition of the teacher role (Huber & Chem, 2020; Reimers & Schleicher, 2020; Schleicher, 2020), and the importance of agility as an ability to quickly adaptat to changing circumstances (Kidd & Murray, 2020; Nissim & Simon, 2020). According to them, the COVID-19 period that befell the education system is emerging in academic discourse as an extreme situation that puts to the test a wide range of professional, emotional, technological, adaptive, personal and interpersonal abilities of teachers and educators. The present study shows that this test does not miss the skills of multiculturalism and relationship between minority and majority among teachers. Interviewees in this study indicated, first, low expectations of the majority group in relation to their ability to effect a change in their role definition and daily functioning. Second, the interviewees testified to the Pygmalion effect that intensified during this period due to the special nature of daily routine in the education system.

This chapter presents a limited pilot study with the aim to explore the challenges of Ethiopian origin teachers during COVID-19, on the one hand, and expands the discourse on society's expectations of minority teachers in times of crisis in the education system. Cultural gaps, which widened during COVID-19, now occupy a prominent place in the academic and professional discourse surrounding teacher training and teacher work during COVID-19.

Despite the great specificity of the case and the context in which relationships between minority and majority groups were examined, it is difficult to ignore the applicability of the insights that emerge from these narratives. Recognizing the great difference between the educational and cultural circumstances and contexts in institutions where minority teachers integrate, it is extremely important to follow new phenomena that are created against the background of the systemic, security and social crises and to examine how each group interprets them. In the theoretical aspect, this study sets a precedent for future discourse on social expectations towards minority education teams, both in an overall view and in crisis situations in the education system. I hope that this paper makes a modest contribution to this discourse.

Acknowledgement This project was supported by the Applied Research Foundation in Teaching and Teacher Education, Mofet Institute.

References

AERA. (2004). *Ethical standards – III*. Guiding standards: Intellectual ownership. American Educational Research Association.

Amit, K. (2012). Social integration and identity of immigrants from western countries, the FSU and Ethiopia in Israel. *Ethnic and Racial Studies, 35*(7), 1287–1310.

Baratz, L., & Kalnisky, E. (2017). The identities of the Ethiopian community in Israel. *Journal for Multicultural Education, 11*, 37.

Berry, J. W., Phinney, J., Sam, D., & Vedder, P. (Eds.). (2006). *Immigrant youth in cultural transition: Acculturation, identity, and adaptation across national contexts*. Erlbaum.

Brener, R. A., & Avisher, N. J. (2017). Ethiopian teachers and teachers in the education system: The story of an ongoing under-representation. *Opinion, 12*, 92–63. (in Hebrew).

Burgess, S., & Sievertsen, H. H. (2020). *Schools, skills, and learning: The impact of COVID-19 on education*. CEPR Policy Portal. Retrieved from https://voxeu.org/article/impact-covid-19-education

Cohen, J. J. (1998). Time to shatter the glass ceiling for minority faculty. *The Journal of the American Medical Association, 280*(9), 821–822.

Cohen, J. B. (2016). Ethiopian-Israeli community. *Case Reports*, bcr2016216074.

Dahan, Y., Kwider, S., Yona, Y., Biton, A., Hasan, S., Gali, L., Masalha, M., Safrai, L., & Pinson, H. (2020). *The Corona crisis and its impact on the Israeli education system*. Position Paper by a team of crisis experts (in Hebrew).

Dvir, N., & Schatz-Oppenheimer, O. (2020). Novice teachers in a changing reality. *European Journal of Teacher Education, 43*(4), 639–656.

Greenfeld-Jonah, L. A. (2013). *What solutions do educational systems in selected countries offer to the challenges of student diversity?* Invited review as background material for discussions in the "Education system for everyone – and everyone". The Initiative for Applied Research in Education (in Hebrew).

Gutman, M. (2019). Retrospective view of the early career: Three landmarks in building resilience in academic administration among Israeli teacher training college principals. *Journal of Educational Administration and History, 52*(2), 165–177.

Halper, J. (1987). The absorption of Ethiopian immigrants: A return to the fifties. *Ethiopian Jews and Israel,* 112–139.

Huber, S. G., & Chem, C. (2020). COVID-19 and schooling: Evaluation, assessment and accountability in times of crises – Reacting quickly to explore key issues for policy, practice and research with the school barometer. *Educational Assessment, Evaluation and Accountability,* 1–34. https://doi.org/10.1007/s11092-020-09322

Kalnisky, E., & Brenner, R. (2016). The contribution and of personal and social resources towards the prediction of Ethiopian students' academic achievements. *Open Science Journal, 1*(3), 1–21.

Kidd, W. (2020). *Agility, return and recovery: Our new covid context for schooling and teacher education?* [Blog post]. https://www.bera.ac.uk/blog/agility-return-and-recovery-our-new-covid-context-for-schooling-and-teacher-education

Kidd, W., & Murray, J. (2020). The Covid-19 pandemic and its effects on teacher education in England: How teacher educators moved practicum learning online. *European Journal of Teacher Education, 43*(4), 542–558.

Mehert, D., Fulbramacher, J., & Davies, R. A. (2018). *Integrating Ethiopian Israeli teachers into the education system.* Position paper of an inter-college think tank. Kerem Institute – Oranim College. (in Hebrew).

Nevo, G. (2016). From melting pot to multiculturalism: Eshkol Nevo's Ashkenazi comedy. *Jewish Culture and History, 17*(3), 264–281.

Nissim, Y., & Simon, E. (2020). Agility in teacher training: Distance learning during the Covid-19 pandemic. *International Education Studies, 13*(12).

Parfitt, T., & Semi, E. T. (Eds.). (2013). *The Jews of Ethiopia: The birth of an élite.* Routledge.

Ran, A. (2017). *Educating Ethiopian origin teachers and integrating them into teaching subjects* (L. Josefsberg Ben-Yehoshua, Eds.). Mofet Institute.

Reichman, R. A. (2009). Immigration to Israel: Mapping trends and empirical studies 1990–2006. *Israeli Sociology, 10*(2), 339–379.

Reimers, F. M., & Schleicher, A. (2020). *A framework to guide an education response to the COVID19 pandemic of 2020.* OECD. https://www.hm.ee/sites/default/files/framework_guide_v1_002_harward.pdf2

Schatz-Oppenheimer, O. (2015). The Tesfa program: The unique program for teacher education of Ethiopian community members. *Digital Letter to Presidents/Heads of Teaching Colleges, 2,* 7–13.

Schatz-Oppenheimer, O. (2020). Program for Ethiopian community: Tesfa contents. In O. Schatz-Oppenheimer & Z. Mevarech (Eds.), *Opening a door: Social-responsibility initiatives in teacher education* (pp. 173–195). Mofet Institute.

Schatz-Oppenheimer, O., & Kalnisky, E. (2014). Travelling far—Drawing closer: Journeys that shape identity. *Diaspora, Indigenous, and Minority Education, 8*(3), 170–187.

Schleicher, A. (2020*). How can teachers and school systems respond to the COVID-19 pandemic? Some lessons from TALIS.* OECD Education and Skills Today. https://oecdedutoday.com/how-teachers-school-systems-respond-coronavirus-talis/

Turner, H., Rubie-Davies, C. M., & Webber, M. (2015). Teacher expectations, ethnicity and the achievement gap. *New Zealand Journal of Educational Studies, 50*(1), 55–69. https://doi.org/10.1007/s40841-015-0004-1

UNESCO (United Nations Educational, Scientific and Cultural Organization). (2020). *COVID-19 educational disruption and response.* UNESCO. https://en.unesco.org/covid19/educationresponse. Accessed 3 Apr 2020.

Weiner-Levy, N. (2006). The flag-bearers: Israeli Druze women challenge traditional gender roles. *Anthropology & Education Quarterly, 37*(3), 217–235.

Weininger, A. (2014). *The integration of Ethiopian teachers in the education system.* Submitted to the Education, Culture and Sports Committee. Research and Information Center (in Hebrew).

White, S. S., & Locke, E. A. (2000). Problems with the Pygmalion effect and some proposed solutions. *The Leadership Quarterly, 11*(3), 389–415.

Yuan L. (2019). *The application of Pygmalion effect in the work of university teachers.* In 9th international conference on education and social science, pp. 617–621.

Mary Gutman is researcher, teacher educator and a head of the research authority at Efrata College of Education in Jerusalem, Israel. She is a graduate of the excellent programs of Ph.D. studies (President's Scholarship Program, Bar Ilan University) and the Postdoctoral Program (Mofet Institute). Her main research interest refers to multiculturalism in teaching and teacher education, minority-majority relationships and immigration in educational contexts. In recent years she has published dozens of articles in leading international journals and received a number of competitive research scholarships and grants.

Open Access This chapter is licensed under the terms of the Creative Commons Attribution 4.0 International License (http://creativecommons.org/licenses/by/4.0/), which permits use, sharing, adaptation, distribution and reproduction in any medium or format, as long as you give appropriate credit to the original author(s) and the source, provide a link to the Creative Commons license and indicate if changes were made.

The images or other third party material in this chapter are included in the chapter's Creative Commons license, unless indicated otherwise in a credit line to the material. If material is not included in the chapter's Creative Commons license and your intended use is not permitted by statutory regulation or exceeds the permitted use, you will need to obtain permission directly from the copyright holder.

Chapter 3
Belonging and Otherness: Teachers of Ethiopian and Russian Origins in Israeli Schools

Shahar Gindi and Rakefet Erlich Ron

Abstract This chapter investigates minority teachers' experience in light of the power relations in society and their expression in schools. The study population included 20 teachers from an Ethiopian background and 34 Russian-speaking teachers in Israeli schools. The teachers responded to an online questionnaire about what made them work at their school, and about feelings of otherness and belonging toward it. The analysis revealed similarities in the issues that contributed to a sense of belonging in both groups, while the issues that contributed to a sense of otherness were different. Teachers described their sense of belonging on three levels: national belonging (e.g., holidays, war times), organizational belonging (professional merit, roles at school, care for students, and school events), and personal belonging (comradeship and team spirit). When it comes to otherness, Russian-speaking teachers noted cultural gaps, slight school involvement, and professional gaps, while teachers of Ethiopian origin emphasized prejudice and feeling patronized. It is noteworthy that all the sources of belonging and otherness are determined by the minority's resemblance to the majority demonstrating the power relations between minorities and the hegemony. The differences in the symbolic assets that each of the minority groups import, point to the "diversity of diversity" among Israeli minorities. We conclude that the hegemonic group use symbolic assets that minority groups have difficulty acquiring fully (language, Jewishness, skin color), and that construct teachers' experiences.

Introduction

This chapter focuses on two immigrant populations and their relationship with the majority group. We chose to examine this relationship within the educational field by studying minority teachers' experiences of belonging and otherness within schools in Israel. These groups provide a glimpse into minority-majority relations

S. Gindi (✉) · R. E. Ron
Beit-Berl College, Beit Berl, Israel
e-mail: shaharg@beitberl.ac.il

in general, which is examined through a sociological lens using the theories of social fields, exclusion, and symbolic capital. We outline the theoretical underpinning, followed by a sketch of the Israeli context, before presenting the empirical work that serves as the basis for this study.

Integration of Minorities into the Workplace

Observations on minority integration in the workplace suggest that some minority groups find it more difficult to integrate than others (Shdema, 2013). Moreover, differences are often explained by the extent of similarity between the minority group and the majority group, and especially by the way the minority group is perceived by the majority group. The more a majority group views a minority group as similar to it, the simpler the integration process will be and vice versa (Johnston et al., 2010; Khattab, 2003).

This study seeks to examine two immigrant groups through their workplace experience. The staffroom is a microcosm of social gatherings. With teachers' personal descriptions of their sense of belonging at school, and revealing the motives behind their choice and acceptance into the school, we can gain a better understanding of the degree of integration, inner experience and discourse that exists around their identity. Based on the premise that social fields shape everyday experiences, we seek the meeting point of the formal and informal that builds their everyday experience. The research examines the way individuals draw on external categorizations of otherness, and the characteristics of the organization they work in, to make sense of their experiences. We explore the meaning that these experiences acquire in different minority groups, the variations in individuals' experiences and understanding, and how they lead to different formulations of belonging and otherness between the two immigrant groups, thus constituting an opportunity for an original examination of a new discourse concerning skin color and religiosity in relation to the dominant group. The two immigrant groups have a broad common denominator: a common religion and nationality that gave them the legitimacy and possibility to immigrate to Israel. At the same time, Ethiopian immigrants are of different skin color, high religiosity, and originate from the African continent; whereas, former Soviet Union immigrants came from a European, Soviet culture, and were less closely related to religion.

Social Fields

Theory and research have shown how social fields are created around many different lines including class (Bourdieu, 1984), race (Wallace, 2017), ethnicity Brubaker et al., 2006)), national belonging (Halfman, 2019), citizenship (Wood, 2015), immigrant status (Guetzkow & Fast, 2016; Lamont, 2000), and religion (Edgell et al., 2006).

The research is rich with data and theory about the way people demarcate social fields that, in turn, form power relations and distinctions internalized by social actors. Less attention and insight, however, has been generated when it comes to the question of how social fields shape individuals' life experiences. Specifically, do people 'belong' and experience 'otherness' differently depending on the social fields that outline their exclusion?

Bourdieu (1990) argued that there are several forms of capital: cultural, social, economic, and symbolic capital that individuals can use to cope with exclusion and power relations. According to Bourdieu (1990), practices of 'taste' and 'distinction' serve as tools of control, exclusion and subordination in the symbolic social market of assets. He considered this control 'symbolic violence', since it is not the result of choice and consent, but is created by symbolic categories.

Israel as an Immigrant Society

Israel presents a thought-provoking case for understanding immigrants' experience of belonging/otherness. It was founded based on the Jewish *Yishuv* that comprised Zionist Jews who came mostly from European countries. Throughout its years of existence, Israel has encouraged the emigration of diaspora Jews on the basis of the Law of Return. Israel has been accepting Jewish immigrants that constitute (along with their descendants) most of the Israeli population (Raijman, 2009). The first decades following the establishment of the state were characterized by a policy of cultural unification and renunciation of cultures of origin. This tendency has been changing in recent decades to social and cultural pluralism, i.e., recognizing the existing differences between cultural groups and legitimizing them (Ben-Rafael & Peres, 2005). The national-religious basis that is common to all immigrant groups provides an entry ticket to Israeli society, but those who arrive, like immigrants everywhere in the world, face challenges. There is an expectation of the dominant majority group that immigrants acquire the local habitus comprised of language, local history, and behavior.

Immigration from the Former Soviet Union (FSU) and from Ethiopia

The Ethiopian and FSU immigration in the 1980s and 1990s is central for understanding the immigrant-host relationships in Israel. While the dialogue between the FSU immigration and Israeli society changed both the immigrant community and Israeli society, by and large, the Ethiopian immigration was not successful and stirs frustration to this day. The two waves of immigration are vastly different. To name just a few major differences, the immigration from the Soviet Union to Israel was massive – one million immigrants up to the year 2000, while the Ethiopian immigration was only around 35,000 people during the same period (Kaplan & Salamon, 2004). Secondly, one cannot ignore the skin color of the Ethiopian Jews, that is unfortunately connected to discrimination in many countries and cultures around the world including Israel (e.g., Hochschild & Weaver, 2007). Finally, the FSU immigration was characterized by professionals, people with academic degrees and specializations, primarily in the sciences, while the Ethiopian immigration was mostly from rural areas with limited education. This last point is also connected to these communities' respective incorporation as teachers in Israel.

The socioeconomic status of these two groups is significantly different to this day, with the Ethiopian population (hereafter EO) being one of the lowest in Israel in many indices. For example, a 2018 report showed that EO individuals experienced higher proportions of residential segregation and workplace discrimination (Hendels, 2013), and their household income was 55% of the rest of the population's average income. Only about 20% of high school graduates attended university (compared to about 40% of the general population), and 88% of the marriages were within the community (Central Bureau of Statistics, 2018). Finally, there was a higher rate of police arrests and cruelty toward EO citizens leading to a number of mass demonstrations (Abu et al., 2017). In comparison, a 2016 report indicated that the income of FSU households was 67% of veteran Israelis' average income, their attendance at universities was higher than the national average, and only 59% of their marriages were within their community, with lower unemployment rates than veteran Israelis (Central Bureau of Statistics, 2016).

FSU Teachers in Israel

Approximately 5% of the million immigrants who came in the late 1980s and 1990s were qualified teachers in their home countries (Michael et al., 2004). The teaching profession was one of the only ones allowed Jews under the anti-Semitic Soviet regime, and was therefore common (Remennick, 2002). The immigrants nonetheless encountered difficulties as Israeli institutions do not readily acknowledge foreign teaching qualifications.

FSU teachers have encountered various barriers over the years with language issues being paramount. Language is a teacher's main instruction tool, as well as a major vehicle to interact with students, parents and colleagues, and language barriers proved to be difficult for many FSU teachers to overcome. FSU teachers were often made to understand that they should abandon Russian at school and adhere to Hebrew (Putjata, 2019). The attitude to Hebrew and Russian is especially important because of many immigrants' pride in the Russian culture and language on one hand (Epstein & Kheimets, 2000), and their negative attitude to Hebrew on the other hand (Putjata, 2019).

The differences between the Israeli school system and the education systems that characterized the Soviet Union also proved challenging for FSU teachers

(Remennick, 2002). For example, there were considerable disparities between FSU teachers and their native-born colleagues with regards to educational perceptions in teaching sciences and mathematics (Amit, 2010). In the FSU, the study regime that they were used to was typically structured and rigid, with a uniform textbook that did not allow teachers any freedom. In Israel, various approaches and styles are used with a variety of textbooks. As a result, they were labeled by their colleagues and students stereotypically as authoritative and inflexible (Remennick, 2002).

Michael (2006) found that FSU teachers' enrolment in professional organizations, participation in decision-making forums at school and in professional courses were significantly lower than veteran Israeli teachers. The study concluded that despite the general perception that the FSU immigration was a national priority, the education system found it difficult to incorporate immigrant teachers, and did not make the most of their potential contribution.

Teachers of Ethiopian Origin (EO)

In the Jewish society in Israel, Ethiopian immigrants stand out as excluded from various social frameworks and low socio-economic status (Ben-Eliezer, 2008; Central Bureau of Statistics, 2018; Dayan, 2014). This situation is reflected in the lack of representation of Ethiopian immigrants in various institutions and frameworks. In addition, Ethiopian immigrants live in a predominantly white Jewish public space that lacks socio-cultural representations of their heritage and culture. These limitations are manifest also in the educational system and in various educational settings. Until recently, it was rare to find Ethiopian young people educated by Ethiopian teachers. This situation has implications for Ethiopian immigrants – the way they perceive themselves and their social status (Avishar & Bernner, 2017). Examining the condition of Ethiopian immigrants exposes the social power relations in Israel, which, among other things, are organized according to skin tone, and produce 'white privilege' (McIntosh, 1990). Various studies demonstrated the white hegemony's bearing on Ethiopian Jews' experiences, which emphasizes the significance and consequences of skin tone and the racial and discriminatory treatment that follows (Ringel et al., 2005; Walsh & Tuval-Mashiach, 2012).

In a retrospective study among EO teachers, they reported that their training had not adequately taken into consideration some of the barriers and academic gaps. Pre-service EO teachers perceived their starting point as different and often at a disadvantage socially, culturally, and academically. Many found it difficult to adjust to the academic environment, and many dropped out. Those who did not drop out were often overworked, and often felt lonely (Avishar & Bernner, 2017).

Avishar and Bernner (2017) further found that EO teachers who had succeeded in overcoming the cultural transition, and integrated into teaching positions, found great value for themselves, for their immediate environment, and for Israeli society as a whole. EO teachers indicated that they spoke 'two languages': they represented the educational system and at the same time represented the social margins, and thus became change agents and role models (Ran, 2017).

Ran (2017) noted that today, in the field of teacher training in Israel, six colleges of education offer unique training programs for Ethiopian Israeli students in addition to the standard curricula available at universities and colleges of education. Few EO teachers are graduates of university programs, and data on the number of substitute teachers among them are unclear.

For reasons that will be outlined below, some EO teachers teach part-time or are not considered official education workers, but NGO employees.

Discriminatory Practices Toward FSU and EO Israeli Citizens

The initial admission ticket to Israeli society is being Jewish. Because of Israel's unique status as a state that defines its nationalism in accordance with its religion, this has further significance (Gindi & Erlich Ron, 2020). Often, a complex debate develops regarding the Jewishness of the FSU immigrants, coming from a culture that was influenced by communist ideology for many years, which did not allow them to maintain their religion. Many Soviet Union Jews married non-Jews over the years, and many adopted Christian holidays (Raijman & Pinsky, 2013). Similarly, the question arises from time to time about the Jewishness of Ethiopian immigrants, some of whom came to Israel with cross tattoos from Christian missionaries, and testified to experiences of religious coercion (Kaplan & Salamon, 2004). The questions surrounding their Judaism undermine these two groups' legitimacy for emigrating to Israel, and cause great difficulty marrying outside their community.

Israeli society is largely a mosaic of immigrants who have arrived at different stages of local history, and there have always been cultural differences based on countries of origin. The first migrant groups to come from Europe became the dominant group that held symbolic capital and the desired local habitus. Within this symbolic pyramid, religion and nationality are followed by the Hebrew language. Language is a significant symbolic capital to which social exclusion is associated. Hebrew-speakers command much greater symbolic capital than speakers of other languages, and Russian or Amharic accents denote inferior status in most social fields (Ben-Rafael & Peres, 2005).

Sense of Belonging/Otherness

Belonging has far greater implications than its dictionary definition 'being a member or part of a group' implies. There is wide consensus that belonging is a basic human motivation, and teachers' sense of belonging to their school is no exception (Leary & Baumeister, 2000). For example, teacher-trainees' sense of belonging to their college or university was found to promote the development of their new professional identity (Williams et al., 2012).

There is a close link between belonging and identity. In one relevant study that examined Arab, EO, and FSU Israelis, Tannenbaum (2009) noted the importance of their native language to their self-identity. There are many interface points between language, identity and conflict, and they can be investigated in various contexts and with various tools. FSU immigrants view the Russian language as a way to maintain access to the cultural treasures that they came from, and as a tool of self-definition versus other parts of Israeli society, while immigrants from Ethiopia see their language as a means of communication and preservation of key values such as honor and family values.

The flip side of belonging – otherness – has been the focus of sociological research for many decades (e.g., Lee & Brown, 1994). It is important to note that feelings of otherness are significant beyond denoting a lack of sense of belonging. The concept of otherness has helped formulate how a perception of 'we' is structured, and how a concept of 'others' is built into it in different societies. In the field of psychology, as well, the concept of otherness has increasingly been used as one of the elements of the constitution of the self and of becoming singular subjects (Laplanche, 2005). Thus, feelings of otherness do not merely represent one's lack of belonging, but also processes of self- definition.

In the present study, we examine immigrant teachers' senses of belonging and otherness among FSU and EO teachers in Israel. These groups of teachers were chosen with the intent of highlighting two aspects of diversity: skin color and religiosity. Both groups have much in common with one another and with the majority, but their otherness from the majority is different. FSU immigrants' Judaism is questioned by the Jewish majority, while EO immigrants have a different skin color. We examined teachers' experience in the wider institutional context of the education system, and not in their day-to-day social and professional relationships.

Methodology

The present research is based on a larger study that included 1197 post-primary education teachers from all districts and educational streams in Israel (Gindi & Erlich Ron, 2019). From this sample, this study uses the answers to the optional qualitative questions in the survey completed by 20 teachers from an Ethiopian background and 34 FSU teachers. The three open-ended questions were: (1) Describe an event where you felt you belonged in the staffroom; (2) Describe an event where you felt different in the staffroom; and (3) What motivated you to choose to teach at your school?

The responses were uploaded to qualitative analysis software (Atlas.ti, version 7.5.6.), and the information was analyzed thematically in accordance with Braun and Clarke's guidelines (Braun et al., 2019). First, the writers each studied the information and read the material several times. Subsequently, initial codes were produced, and themes and subthemes were identified, reviewed and compared. The responses were reviewed one by one, and the results of the two analyses were compared to reach the final theme matrix. This triangulation method is designed to strengthen the validity of the findings (Leech & Onwuegbuzie, 2007).

Population

The sample characteristics, presented in Table 3.1, demonstrate the vast differences between the two groups studied. First, the FSU teachers seem to have actually been born in the FSU, while the EO teachers were mostly born in Israel. The questionnaire did not include questions about place of birth, but we can deduce it from the teachers' age and their first language. The mean age for EO teachers was 33.1 years with a standard deviation of 5.9 years. They had been working as teachers for 5.65 years on average (SD = 4.9). The mean age for the FSU teachers was 49.5 (SD = 11.2) and they had been working as teachers for 23.7 years on average (SD = 12.7). In addition, the proportion of first language Hebrew-speakers was 30% among EO teachers compared to only 9% among FSU teachers.

The two groups also differ in their academic background: FSU teachers have a higher proportion of Master's degree graduates. There is a much higher proportion of EO homeroom teachers than FSU homeroom teachers. Finally, FSU teachers in the sample were distributed among different districts, while most EO teachers were concentrated in the Jerusalem district. The groups were also similar on a few variables. The proportion of men to women, as well as the distribution among the different educational tracks, was similar in the two groups. The majority of teachers in both groups taught exact sciences.

Research Findings

Open-Ended Question Analysis: When Do You Feel That You Belong?

Before delving into the themes that emerged in the qualitative analysis, it should be noted that most of the responses received reflected a sense of belonging. For example, many teachers' response to the question "Describe an event where you felt different" was that they did not feel otherness at all: "I never felt this way"; "None"; "I do not feel different in the staffroom"; and so on. In the summary of the responses, 33 responses expressed belonging, while only 15 related to otherness. Moreover, both EO and FSU teachers exhibited similar themes regarding their feelings of belonging.

Table 3.1 Sample characteristics

Characteristic	FSU teachers (N = 35) Frequency (%)	EO teachers (N = 20) Frequency (%)
Gender		
Men	13 (23%)	6 (32%)
Women	44 (77%)	13 (68%)
Education		
BA	17 (30%)	13 (65%)
MA	39 (68%)	7 (35%)
Other	1 (2%)	0 (0%)
1st language		
Hebrew	3 (9%)	6 (30%)
Russian	32 (91%)	0 (0%)
Amharic	0 (0%)	12 (60%)
Tigrinya	0 (0%)	1 (5%)
Homeroom teacher		
Yes	11 (19%)	14 (70%)
No	46 (81%)	6 (30%)
Education track		
State	31 (55%)	12 (60%)
State-religious	8 (14%)	5 (25%)
Settlement admin.	15 (26%)	2 (10%)
Arab	0 (0%)	0 (0%)
Orthodox	1 (2%)	1 (5%)
Other	1 (2%)	0 (0%)
Heterogeneity of training college		
1 – Very homogenous	5 (9%)	3 (16%)
2	5 (9%)	2 (11%)
3	13 (23%)	3 (16%)
4	19 (35%)	6 (31%)
5 – Very heterogeneous	13 (23%)	5 (26%)
District		
North	12 (21%)	2 (10%)
Haifa	6 (11%)	3 (15%)
Center	14 (25%)	3 (15%)
Tel Aviv	7 (12%)	1 (5%)
Jerusalem	5 (9%)	10 (50%)
South	13 (23%)	1 (5%)
Teaching discipline[a]		
Exact sciences	30 (53%)	7 (39%)
Humanities	10 (18%)	3 (17%)
Social sciences	4 (7%)	1 (6%)
Languages	5 (9%)	4 (22%)
Technology	3 (5%)	1 (6%)
Arts	3 (5%)	1 (6%)
Physical education	3 (5%)	1 (6%)
Computer sciences	5 (9%)	0 (0%)

[a]Percentage adds up to more than 100%; some teachers reported more than one teaching discipline

The qualitative analysis of belonging revealed sub-themes on three levels: (1) national belonging; (2) organizational relationship; (3) personal relationship. In terms of national belonging, teachers cited holidays and wartime as unifying factors that contributed to their sense of belonging. For example, an FSU teacher noted a sense of belonging on "all holidays, celebrating the first day of the Jewish month". Interestingly, EO teachers not only mentioned their feelings of belonging on all Jewish holidays but also on the Ethiopian Jewish holiday (*Sigd*) marking the yearning for Jerusalem: "Truthfully, I feel I belong and am part of the teachers and the staffroom throughout the year, but the *Sigd* period can be mentioned as an event when I feel I particularly belong". Another EO teacher wrote about the feeling of belonging on "the Israeli Defense Forces' memorial days." The teachers' shared fate also reinforces their sense of belonging, as this FSU teacher said: "Identifying with the fighting spirit over the defense of the State of Israel."

At the organizational level, teachers' sense of belonging was expressed in various ways: in school roles, in concern for students, and in school events. Despite the low percentage of office holders among FSU teachers, some respondents reported key positions. In the following quote an EO teacher wrote how her leadership in preparing a school event made her feel that she belonged: "After my class performance for the Pentecost (*Shavuot*) holiday that I prepared - the teachers were in total shock how it (the performance) turned out perfect, and I proved that I'm like everyone else and can do anything." The teachers' struggle against feelings of inferiority (or perhaps the environment's manifest superiority) is almost palpable in this quote, and connected to the prejudice that EO teachers feel, which will be elaborated upon below.

One teacher from the FSU noted that she chaired the teachers' union at her school, and another FSU teacher wrote: "Each time I turn to teachers and ask for help with things that are not in their role definition, they decisively tell me: 'Whatever you need'." An EO teacher wrote: "This (belonging) is a feeling that accompanies me from the first instance I began working at the school. I have countless examples. Team meetings, pedagogical conferences, leading activities, etc. etc."

The teachers unite around helping students, as one FSU teacher said: "When we talk about students, the concern for them, the difficulties working with them." School events that acknowledged teachers' contribution were another factor that contributed to teachers' feeling of belonging.

The third sub-theme was that of personal friendship. The vast majority of teachers wrote about the sense of team spirit that exists in the school, beyond working relationships. For example, an EO teacher was excited about a surprise birthday party organized by the other teachers, and an FSU teacher wrote of a peak event on a trip to Poland: "The pinnacle for me was at the second time I accompanied a trip to Poland with problem students. On Friday night, I received a big package of surprises and letters from teachers I did not expect to receive." Many teachers noted the sociable and pleasant atmosphere in the staffroom: "The laughs at recess - laughter among us, for all kinds of situations." Contrary to the veteran teachers-young teachers tension that will be referred to below, there was an FSU teacher who found the age gap between veteran and new teachers to be an advantage: "End-of-year breaks and conversations, they accepted me as their son."

One unique example should be mentioned, in which a teacher cited her advantage as a teacher who immigrated from the FSU when working with immigrant students. This advantage increased her sense of belonging to the entire staff, as she felt she belonged "when teachers contact me and consult about new Russian-speaking students." Naturally, there were also teachers who noted their sense of belonging in several environments at the same time as one FSU teacher wrote: "The warm attitude in the staffroom, full support of the professional coordinator, attentive ear in management and a pleasant atmosphere in general."

Open-Ended Question Analysis: When Do You Feel Otherness?

The responses of EO teachers to the above question were all about prejudice, while teachers from the FSU wrote about four topics, prejudice being only one. The subthemes included: (1) prejudice; (2) cultural gaps; (3) little involvement in school; (4) professional gaps.

Prejudice against EO teachers was evident in five teachers writing about others feeling surprised when they found out their profession. Several teachers were thought to be janitors: "When I (first) arrived they thought I was a student's mother or a cleaning lady"; "Sometimes when parents get confused and think that I'm the janitor." Another teacher was dismissed as a teaching aide and felt disrespected: "When I was called an assistant the first time they met me, without asking or trying to get to know me, while I fought tooth and nail to become a teacher, equal among equals." Yet other EO teachers wrote about the implicit ways people exhibit their surprise. For example, when they are treated as unique: "When they talk about me as an exceptional case for Ethiopians: 'You don't represent, you're not like everyone'." Some teachers reported prejudice in the way others look at them: "People's looks of amazement. Racism comes up implicitly when they admire the way that you talk excellent Hebrew, and ask when you immigrated."

EO teachers felt otherness when they spoke to other teachers about the broader picture of racism and prejudice against Ethiopian Jews in Israel. This EO teacher felt that her colleagues were disconnected from the wider context: "When there is police violence against Israelis of EO. I often feel that the other teachers don't understand the kind of racism that exists in Israeli society." Police prejudice against black people led to several large "Black Lives Matter" demonstrations in Israel. These demonstrations are referred to in the following quotation: "In discussing the demonstrations, other teachers don't understand what it means to be Ethiopian. As a woman, I feel racism less, but young Ethiopian men, who walk in the street and get arrested, feel humiliated."

The prejudice against FSU teachers reflected the stereotype of veteran Israelis who perceive FSU immigrants as loosely connected to Judaism: "When you make a refreshment list for a meeting, and you're told to buy something, without even asking if my kitchen is *kosher*, and it is!" FSU teachers also noted being perceived as cold and having a high work ethic: "When I put in a lot of work and was told I was a 'Russian', and all that interests me is work."

In terms of cultural disparities, one FSU teacher noted her difficulty getting involved in the discussion due to a lack of knowledge about Israeli society, and noted that she felt different "when differences between groups in Israeli society were discussed". Two other FSU teachers referred to the cultural gaps arising from *Novi God* (the Russian New Year's Eve celebration), for example: "When there is no time off for the civic New Year, because I celebrate."

The following quotation includes a reference to the disparity that results from the low participation of FSU teachers in administrative roles and their consequent small impact on the school:

> *We have minimal impact on the school climate. We are less aware of our rights. In our city, there is no principal or vice principal who is from the Russian sector, and in our district, there is not one teacher from the Russian sector with a significant role, except for some profession coordinators.*

This quote coincides with other studies, showing FSU teachers' low involvement in education and management roles (Michael, 2006), which is also reflected in the low proportion of homeroom FSU teachers in this study. Despite the positive findings about FSU integration, the barrier to organizational influence has persisted for years. It should be noted that in Israel, being a homeroom teacher is a prerequisite for many promotional channels in the system.

The feeling of otherness of some of the FSU teachers had a prosaic and familiar background, disconnected from their origin. Teachers mentioned seniority, personal characteristics or teaching profession as making them feel otherness. The issue of seniority is reflected in the following quotation: "Veterans allow themselves to raise their voices at young women." Another teacher describes herself as a non-conformist and emphasizes that it has nothing to do with her origin: "I felt differently because I was a non-conformist person, not because I was Ukrainian." Another teacher complains about the sense of otherness that comes from teaching different subjects: "They don't like to talk about math, those who don't teach the subject." These descriptions are like teachers' descriptions all over the world, regardless of ethnicity.

Discussion

The present study focuses on minority-majority relations using teachers' reports about their senses of belonging and otherness. On the face of it, it would seem that the sources of otherness were different between the two groups, while the sources of belonging were similar. Nonetheless, if we look at it from a bird's eye view, we can see that all the sources of belonging and otherness are determined by the minority's resemblance to the majority (Johnston et al., 2010; Khattab, 2003). Similarities are used as markers of inclusion, while differences are used as markers of exclusion

(Bourdieu, 1984). We can see how, in many instances, the power relations are manifested in response to an external characteristic a priori to any interaction taking place, defining the hierarchy in minority-majority relations.

EO teachers differ from the majority group by their skin color (Kaplan & Salamon, 2004). While teachers did not report direct comments about their skin color, they did describe events in which their different appearance provoked reactions that they found upsetting. In addition, there was evidence of micro-aggression in response to their appearance. The discriminatory micro-aggressive practices are often subtle, and merely raising the issue of ethnicity ("When did you immigrate?") in response to the teachers' experience can be used to remind the teacher of the power hierarchy.

It is also noteworthy that despite the sociological research that indicates religion as another marker of exclusion for Israeli EO citizens (Kaplan & Salamon, 2004), the EO respondents never mentioned this issue, in contrast to FSU teachers. FSU teachers are different from the majority group in their lack of religious upbringing, which they are often upbraided for (Raijman & Pinsky, 2013). Other markers of exclusion included FSU teachers' stigmatization as rigid, cold, and too hard-working.

The themes that emerged concerning the belonging questions indicated that the sources for belonging are similar for both groups, and include their professionalism and their social and professional relations with other teachers. Professionalism – being teachers – is a currency of great value that both FSU and EO teachers noted as bridging the gaps between them and their colleagues. The symbolic capital that teachers bring with them includes their social proficiencies, and both FSU and EO teachers mentioned social relationships as an important source of belonging. It is noteworthy that the sources of belonging were similar despite exceeding differences between the groups. The FSU teachers were mostly born in the FSU, and were on average 16 years older than the EO teachers. The EO teachers were most likely born in Israel (second generation), were much younger and less experienced in the education system. Nonetheless, these two groups found that their sense of belonging stemmed from the same sources.

Conclusions and Implications

Minorities struggle with many discriminatory practices and use different inclusion strategies in order to restore equality. The findings indicated that they face different discriminatory practices, with ethnicity and language being salient in the experience of EO teachers. The mechanisms of exclusion that FSU teachers confront include devaluing their religious status, their language, teaching habits, and other stereotypes. The sources of symbolic capital, on the other hand, are quite similar and mostly related to the teaching profession. Given the power of the national narrative in Israel, EO and FSU teachers subjugate their ethnic identities to their professional identity. We propose that professional identity gives minorities an anchor, and can serve as an important source of symbolic capital for minority teachers worldwide.

A comprehensive look at the two research groups shows that each of the groups has a different starting point. Each group has come equipped with a different set of symbolic assets within the Israeli context. The question of FSU immigrants' Judaism is poised to linger as much as Ethiopian immigrants cannot change their skin color. FSU immigrants' academic education is an asset, while Ethiopian immigrants have the benefit of being a more religious community within an Israeli context that values that. Both groups suffer from stereotypes, and have a significant deficit in mastering the local language. The different starting points are an important aspect of understanding diversity within diversity. Parallel lines can be seen between commanding the macro-level symbolic assets and belonging at the micro-level. The dominant group serves as a gatekeeper that reminds immigrants that they did not acquire, and perhaps may never acquire, the full inventory of symbolic assets (language, Jewishness, skin color), and indirectly produces each teacher's private, individual sense of otherness (Bourdieu, 1984).

This study demonstrates that professional identity is a moderating tool that enables participation in a social arena of partnership. In addition to the research focus on the importance of minority teachers for students, we propose to explore the shared environment of role partners and the social forces at work within these fields. This study brings to the front a social arena that provokes a meeting and discourse between ethnic, lingual and religious identities, from which much can be learned about the experience of immigrants and minorities as a part of our project on boundary-crossing teachers. In this project, we have explored beyond the Ethiopian background and the Russian speaking teachers focused on in the chapter, also Arab teachers in Jewish schools, religious teachers in secular schools, and ethnic diversity in staffrooms. We suggest further study and research of sense of belonging and otherness of minority groups and the relationships with the majority group. On the practical side, the research paved the way for the formation of the cross-teach program in various institutions and research studies.

References

Abu, O., Yuval, F., & Ben-Porat, G. (2017). Race, racism, and policing: Responses of Ethiopian Jews in Israel to stigmatization by the police. *Ethnicities, 17*(5), 688–706. https://doi.org/10.1177/2F1468796816664750

Amit, M. (2010). Cultural conflicts in mathematics classrooms and resolution: The case of immigrants from the former Soviet Union and Israeli 'old-timers'. *Montana Mathematics Enthusiast, 7*(2), 263–274.

Avishar, N., & Bernner, R. (2017). 'Like living for millennia': Ethiopian women students become teachers. *Zman Hinuch, 3*(1), 35–66. (Hebrew).

Ben-Eliezer, U. (2008). Multicultural society and everyday cultural racism: Second generation of Ethiopian Jews in Israel's 'crisis of modernization'. *Ethnic and Racial Studies, 31*(5), 935–961. https://doi.org/10.1080/01419870701568866

Ben-Rafael, E., & Peres, Y. (2005). *Is Israel one? Religion, nationalism, and multiculturalism confounded*. Brill.

Bourdieu, P. (1984). *Distinction: A social critique of the judgement of taste*. Harvard University Press.
Bourdieu, P. (1990). Structures, habitus, practices. In P. Bourdieu (Ed.), *The logic of practice* (pp. 52–65). Stanford University Press.
Braun, V., Clarke, V., Hayfield, N., & Terry, G. (2019). Thematic analysis. In P. Liamputtong (Ed.), *Handbook of research methods in health social sciences*. Springer.
Brubaker, R., Feischmidt, M., Fox, J. E., & Grancea, L. (2006). *Nationalist politics and everyday ethnicity in a Transylvanian town*. Princeton University Press.
Central Bureau of Statistics (2016). *Immigrants from the FSU on the 25th anniversary of their immigration*. Author. Retrieved from https://www.cbs.gov.il/he/Statistical/immigration_ussr_h148.pdf (Hebrew).
Central Bureau of Statistics (2018). *The population of Ethiopian origin in Israel: Data collection on the occasion of the Sigd holiday*. Author. Retrieved from https://www.cbs.gov.il/he/mediarelease/DocLib/2018/326/11_18_326b.pdf (Hebrew).
Dayan, N. (2014). *The integration of Ethiopian immigrants in Israel: A snapshot*. Ruppin Academic Center/Institute for Immigration and Social Inclusion. (Hebrew).
Edgell, P., Gerteis, J., & Hartmann, D. (2006). Atheists as 'other': Moral boundaries and cultural membership in American society. *American Sociological Review, 71*, 211–234. https://doi.org/10.1177/2F000312240607100203
Epstein, A. D., & Kheimets, N. G. (2000). Cultural clash and educational diversity: Immigrant teachers' efforts to rescue the education of immigrant children in Israel. *International Studies in Sociology of Education, 10*(2), 191–210. https://doi.org/10.1080/09620210000200055
Gindi, S., & Erlich Ron, R. (2019). Bargaining with the system: A mixed-methods study of Arab teachers in Israel. *International Journal of Intercultural Relations, 69*, 44–53. https://doi.org/10.1016/j.ijintrel.2018.12.004
Gindi, S., & Erlich Ron, R. (2020). *Has religiosity become a key factor in Jewish Israelis' attitudes toward minorities? A call for research*. Equality, Diversity and Inclusion. https://doi.org/10.1108/EDI-03-2020-0064
Guetzkow, J., & Fast, I. (2016). How symbolic boundaries shape the experience of social exclusion: A case comparison of Arab Palestinian citizens and Ethiopian Jews in Israel. *American Behavioral Scientist, 60*(2), 150–171. https://doi.org/10.1177/2F0002764215607581
Halfman, J. (2019). An educated Sint Maartener? National belonging in a primary school on Sint Maarten. *Globalisation, Societies and Education, 1-13*. https://doi.org/10.1080/14767724.2019.1662280
Hendels, S. (2013). *The feelings of discrimination among workers and employment seekers, and what the public thinks about this*. Ministry of Industry, Commerce, and Employment. (Hebrew).
Hochschild, J. L., & Weaver, V. (2007). The skin color paradox and the American racial order. *Social Forces, 86*(2), 643–670. https://doi.org/10.1353/sof.2008.0005
Johnston, R., Sirkeci, I., Khattab, N., & Modood, T. (2010). Ethno-religious categories and measuring occupational attainment in relation to education in England and Wales: A multilevel analysis. *Environment and Planning A, 42*(3), 578–591. https://doi.org/10.1068/a42180
Kaplan, S., & Salamon, H. (2004). Ethiopian Jews in Israel: A part of the people or apart from the people? In U. Rebhun & C. Waxman (Eds.), *Jews in Israel: Contemporary social and cultural patterns* (pp. 118–148). Brandeis University Press.
Khattab, N. (2003). Segregation, ethnic labour market and the occupational expectations of Palestinian students in Israel. *British Journal of Sociology, 54*(2), 259–285. https://doi.org/10.1080/0007131032000080230
Lamont, M. (2000). *The dignity of working men: Morality and the boundaries of race, class, and immigration*. Harvard University Press/Russell Sage Foundation.
Laplanche, J. (2005). *Essays on otherness*. Routledge.
Leary, M. R., & Baumeister, R. F. (2000). The nature and function of self-esteem: Sociometer theory. In *Advances in experimental social psychology* (Vol. 32, pp. 1–62). Academic.
Lee, N., & Brown, S. (1994). Otherness and the actor network: The undiscovered continent. *American Behavioral Scientist, 37*(6), 772–790. https://doi.org/10.1177/2F0002764294037006005

Leech, N. L., & Onwuegbuzie, A. J. (2007). An array of qualitative data analysis tools: A call for data analysis triangulation. *School Psychology Quarterly, 22*(4), 557–584. https://doi.org/10.1037/1045-3830.22.4.557

McIntosh, P. (1990). White privilege: Unpacking the invisible knapsack. *Independent School, 50*(2), 31–36.

Michael, O. (2006). Multiculturalism in schools: The professional absorption of immigrant teachers from the former USSR into the education system in Israel. *Teaching and Teacher Education, 22*(2), 164–178. https://doi.org/10.1016/j.tate.2005.09.005

Michael, O., Sever, R., & Tamir, P. (2004). The professional positioning of FSU immigrant teachers in Israeli schools. *Dapim (Pages), 38*, 103–126. (Hebrew).

Putjata, G. (2019). Immigrant teachers' integration and transformation of the linguistic market in Israel. *Language and Education, 33*(1), 51–67. https://doi.org/10.1080/09500782.2018.1458860

Raijman, R. (2009). Immigration to Israel: Mapping trends and empiric studies: 1990–2006. *Israeli Sociology, 10*(2), 339–379. (Hebrew).

Raijman, R., & Pinsky, Y. (2013). Religion, ethnicity and identity: Former soviet Christian immigrants in Israel. *Ethnic and Racial Studies, 36*(11), 1687–1705. https://doi.org/10.1080/01419870.2012.669486

Ran, A. (2017). *Training and integration of Israeli Ethiopian teachers in the teaching professions.* Mofet Institute Press. http://library.macam.ac.il/study/pdf_files/d12592.pdf

Remennick, L. (2002). Survival of the fittest: Russian immigrant teachers speak about their professional adjustment in Israel. *International Migration, 40*(1), 99–121. https://doi.org/10.1111/1468-2435.00187

Ringel, S., Ronell, N., & Gatehune, S. (2005). Factors in the integration process of adolescent immigrants: The case of Ethiopian Jews in Israel. *International Social Work, 48*, 63–76. https://doi.org/10.1177/2F0020872805048709

Shdema, I. (2013). Social and spatial examination of Palestinian employment in Israel in single municipalities. In N. Khattab & S. Miaari (Eds.), *Palestinians in the Israeli labor market* (pp. 241–261). Palgrave Macmillan.

Tannenbaum, M. (2009). What's in a language? Language as a core value of minorities in Israel. *Journal of Ethnic and Migration Studies, 35*(6), 977–995. https://doi.org/10.1080/13691830902957742

Wallace, D. (2017). Reading 'race' in Bourdieu? Examining black cultural capital among black Caribbean youth in South London. *Sociology, 51*(5), 907–923. https://doi.org/10.1177/2F0038038516643478

Walsh, S. D., & Tuval-Mashiach, R. (2012). Ethiopian emerging adult immigrants in Israel: Coping with discrimination and racism. *Youth and Society, 44*, 49–75. https://doi.org/10.1177/0044118X10393484

Williams, J., Ritter, J., & Bullock, S. M. (2012). Understanding the complexity of becoming a teacher educator: Experience, belonging, and practice within a professional learning community. *Studying Teacher Education, 8*(3), 245–260.

Wood, B. E. (2015). Teacher interpretations of 'active' citizenship curricula: Shared identities and spatial orientations. In M. Y. Eryaman & B. Bruce (Eds.), *International handbook of progressive education* (pp. 339–354). Peter Lang.

Shahar Gindi is a Senior Lecturer at Beit Berl College in Israel and a clinical psychologist. His main research interests include psychology, education and controversial political issues in Israeli schools.

Rakefet Erlich Ron is a Lecturer at Beit Berl College in Israel. Her fields of research include the sociology of Israeli society, gender, cross-cultural interactions, and consumerism. She serves as a head of the Excellence Program and pedagogic instructor.

Open Access This chapter is licensed under the terms of the Creative Commons Attribution 4.0 International License (http://creativecommons.org/licenses/by/4.0/), which permits use, sharing, adaptation, distribution and reproduction in any medium or format, as long as you give appropriate credit to the original author(s) and the source, provide a link to the Creative Commons license and indicate if changes were made.

The images or other third party material in this chapter are included in the chapter's Creative Commons license, unless indicated otherwise in a credit line to the material. If material is not included in the chapter's Creative Commons license and your intended use is not permitted by statutory regulation or exceeds the permitted use, you will need to obtain permission directly from the copyright holder.

Chapter 4
Switzerland: Diversity in the Classroom, Uniformity in the Faculty

Michael Beck, Carola Mantel, and Sonja Bischoff

Abstract Switzerland is a country with a long immigration history. Today, 27% of all pupils in compulsory education are foreign nationals (Federal Statistical Office (FSO) Switzerland, Obligatorische Schule: Lernende nach Grossregion, Schulkanton, Bildungstyp und Staatsangehörigkeit (je-d-15.02.01.05). Retrieved from https://www.bfs.admin.ch/bfs/de/home/statistiken/bildung-wissenschaft/personen-ausbildung/obligatorische-schule.assetdetail.11787900.html, 2020). On the other hand, teachers of immigrant background constitute a small minority even though the demand for teachers is high, with secure jobs that pay well. Moreover, there is a debate on the question whether teachers with an immigrant background are especially qualified for teaching culturally diverse classes. Given that persons with an immigrant background tend to aspire to higher educational and occupational goals than non-immigrant individuals (Van De Werfhorst & Van Tubergen, Ethnicities 7(3):416–444, 2007), the question arises why individuals with an immigrant background do not choose to become teachers more often.

In light of this question, we provide an overview of studies from Switzerland and examine transitions of individuals into and out of Universities of Teacher Education in Switzerland as well as studies concerning active teachers.

We will discuss current research evidence, that suggests that social background as well as motivations for choosing the fields of study (which usually play a significant role in explaining differing educational decisions) do not provide an explanation for the low enrolment rate into teacher education among students with immigrant background. Evidence indicates that dichotomizing into immigrant and non-immigrant might conceal differences in attitudes which particularly those from stigmatized cultural backgrounds face. These findings are highlighted by empirical insights on practicing teachers who experience a lack of recognition and who develop a range of strategies in response to these experiences.

M. Beck (✉)
St. Gallen University of Teacher Education, St. Gallen, Switzerland
e-mail: michael.beck@phsg.ch

C. Mantel · S. Bischoff
University of Teacher Education, St. Gallen, Switzerland

Diversity and Uniformity – The Swiss Case

With regard to the concept of minorities teaching in a majority society, this article deals with the perception of otherness and othering in the context of transnational migration in Switzerland. Despite relatively strict immigration laws, Switzerland is an immigration country with a high percentage of inhabitants with an immigrant background which are very heterogenous in terms of ethnic or national origin, socioeconomic history or reasons for migration (Federal Statistical Office (FSO) Switzerland, 2017).

At the same time, Switzerland's educational system is considered to be relatively highly structured, with an early division of students into different achievement levels, which usually takes place at the age of 12. In the current literature, this transition is often cited as being responsible for a strong relationship between educational success and social as well as immigrant background. When it comes to naming migration-related diversity, words are (obviously) important. Surveys and operationalizations of the so-called "immigrant background" in the context of (official) statistics as well as (educational) scientific studies have three possible consequences: First, different data collection types and operationalizations often have very different implications for theory-based explanations of the studied 'faits sociaux', in Emile Durkheim's words, which in our view are not always made sufficiently explicit. Second, the nature of data collection and operationalization naturally affects the nature and strength of the effects and results as well as their interpretations. And third, the terms, definitions, and operationalizations used, in turn, naturally influence the 'faits sociaux', for example, by not only not reflecting but possibly also preserving stereotypes, minority status and thus power relations.

In contrast to the heterogeneity and abundance of different immigrant backgrounds and histories in Switzerland, there has been little research on teachers with an immigrant background. This article shows the current state of research, and at the same time, points out the gaps in the state of research, based on different theoretical backgrounds.

Throughout this article, we look at the construction of difference in the choice of studying to become a teacher. We assume that the choice of apprenticeship or study is a result of weighing the advantages and disadvantages one expects from the associated career options. These advantages and disadvantages can be, for example, more economic/material factors such as salary or job security. They can also be more psychological/non-material factors such as self-worth and a sense of belonging, but also anticipated interactions (for example, the risk of experiencing discrimination on the basis of origin in daily interactions) with superiors, colleagues and "customers" (in the case of teachers: students and parents).

This article is structured as follows: First, we will show examples of the problems involved in constructing the immigrant background on an operational and theoretical level. We then provide theoretical considerations with regard to explaining differing educational pathways, leading to differential outcomes concerning the choice of studying to become a teacher. Following this, the Swiss educational system is briefly explained, with a focus on the training of teachers for compulsory education.

Then, based on figures from official education statistics, we present distributions of the proportions of persons with an immigrant background in relation to the total population as well as various indicators of educational success. Furthermore, we show the results of studies to choose a course of study to become a teacher and the experiences of teachers with a migrant background when on the job or looking for a job. The article concludes with implications of the results for research and educational policy.

The findings presented here come from various data sources: First, we draw on previously published studies, official data and surveys to look more closely at educational aspirations and the choice of a course of study to become a teacher among individuals with an immigrant background. In addition, we use data that we have collected in the context of our own projects at universities of teacher education. On the one hand, these are data from the projects DIVAL and DIVAL_transition, which we collected from 2013 onwards at the St.Gallen University of Teacher Education. In the project DIVAL, additional to a standardized questionnaire survey of all students in 2013 (N = 891), 8 focus group discussions with 18 students and 4 focus group discussions with 17 lecturers[1] were conducted on the relevance they attribute to immigrant backgrounds during teacher education (Beck et al., 2014; Bischoff et al., 2016; Edelmann et al., 2015; Ha & Bischoff, 2020; Ha et al., 2019). In addition, in the project DIVAL_transition (Bischoff & Edelmann, 2017) we interviewed students with an immigrant background during their transition into the profession using problem-centred interviews (Witzel, 2000). Finally, we refer to another one of our own studies in which we generated data by biographical-narrative interviews with 19 teachers and analyzed the data with a hermeneutical approach (Mantel, 2017, 2020). We include findings from other research in Switzerland in our reflections, drawing largely on the work of Edelmann (2006, 2008), who examined interviews with 40 practicing teachers in the context of her studies.

Who? Otherness and Othering

To analyze differences in outcomes for different groups of a population, one must first define the different groups. In doing so, there is a danger of reproducing social categories and the inequalities they entail. Therefore, it should be pointed out that operational definitions are artificial and must always be interpreted with regard to the object of investigation. Starting from a (as far as possible) value-free approach, the distinctions presented here should therefore be understood as theory-based. Their construction should neither be understood as a justification of unequal

---

[1] Due to limited space and the focus of this paper, we only use data from the focus group discussions with students.

treatment nor as a negation of other relevant distinctions. In terms of content, the following descriptions largely follow the considerations in Beck and Edelmann (2016), which in turn are strongly oriented on Gresch and Kristen (2011) and Kemper (2010).

When analyzing group differences related to family migration biographies, terms such as "foreigner," "ethnic or cultural affiliation," or "migration/migratory background" are used in the (German-language) social sciences. Operationalizations of immigrant backgrounds in studies that draw on existing (often large) data sets are naturally made on the basis of information available on nationality, country of birth, but also first language. This implies different restrictions in the analytical depth of possible results, since the set of theoretical explanations is naturally limited. However, this does not automatically mean that "simple" operationalizations via nationality or residence status, for example, cannot be meaningful, since naturalization, at least in Germany and Switzerland, is associated with both increased educational success and increased integration (see for example Hainmueller & Hangartner, 2013; Söhn, 2014). Therefore, we propose a definition of a person having a migratory/immigrant background analogous to the statistical advice, given by the European commission as "a person who has: (a) migrated into their present country of residence; and/or (b) previously had a different nationality from their present country of residence; and/or (c) at least one of their parents previously entered their present country of residence as a migrant" (European Commission, 2020). While we should be aware that this demarcation is not sufficient to describe social categories, this definition nevertheless may highlight the common denominator, namely the aspect of movement/mobility.[2] Usual (statistical) categories available in pre-existing data are nationality, country of birth of the respondents and if born abroad, the year in which they immigrated. Especially when the data are related to education, the languages spoken by the respondents and/or their respective households are used to distinguish autochthonous and immigrant population. In a narrower sense, nationality is only a meaningful operationalization when it comes either to aspects related to citizenship or to the fact that it can be used as an "instrument" for discrimination (when it is stated in job applications, for example). The use of country of birth as a distinguishing criterion is based on the assumption that comparable regions of origin are associated with more or less comparable "ethnic" or "cultural" contexts of origin.[3] This is often combined with the indication of the so-called generational status of immigrants, usually distinguishing between "first" (born "abroad") and "second" (born "at country of residence", at least one parent born "abroad") generation.

Using statistical categorizations (or variables) that already exist in data comes with different problems: First, when analyzing such data, researchers rely on the variables collected to construct exhaustive categories. Second, these constructions

---

[2] This is an assumption on our part, to our knowledge there are currently no systematic studies on this.

[3] And with it, differences in socioeconomic background and in basic norms and values.

should also be able to represent categories that are valid and have theoretical content. One danger of such approaches, which is not emphasized enough by Beck and Edelmann (2016), is the following: An approach that is predominantly oriented towards statistical categories may overlook the fact that these categories are not "objectively given". Rather, the relevance of these categories in relation to outcomes (such as experiences of discrimination in the job search) may be rooted deeply in the social processes that both helped to create such categorizations, as well as working as a mechanism responsible for the phenomena of interest.

Especially studies with qualitative research approaches proceed in a different way by primarily recording or interpreting self-attributions or perceived attributions by others with reference to an immigrant background. The relevance of the categorization is either left to the actors themselves or revealed with the help of analytical (mostly hermeneutical) methods in combination with attributions from others. This has the advantage for different lines of difference to be drawn when analyzing different situations. Furthermore, the subjective view of the actors can be better documented. Of course, this approach also poses challenges that have to be addressed by the researcher with the help of adequate methodology: Potentially important processes that take place outside the perception of the actors can almost not be captured. Furthermore, there is a danger that certain situations and their consequences are over- or under-interpreted with regard to the underlying lines of difference. Relevant attributions of an immigrant background can also be discovered within the framework of a specific analysis by analyzing patterns. Ideally, this can also uncover patterns of action and interpretations hidden from the persons involved in the social processes under investigation.

The use of existing categories should therefore be theory-guided so that they do not only represent otherness, but also take the processes of categorizing in the sense of othering into account. Thus, existing differences should not be interpreted as objectively and permanently existing differences but should be understood as situational as well as addressed and interpreted as a consequence of social processes and resulting attributions.

From Diverse Schools to Universities: Choice or Restriction?

Compulsory education in Switzerland today starts at the age of four and comprises (simplified) 2 years of kindergarten, 6 years of primary education and 3 years of lower secondary education (Swiss Conference of Cantonal Ministers of Education (EDK), 2019). Subsequently, approximately two-thirds of a cohort enters dual vocational education, which lasts between 3 and 4 years, and one-third attends a tertiary educational institution (university, teacher-training college or university of applied sciences). As Switzerland is a federal state with a very high degree of autonomy of the cantons (federal states), there are great differences in the actual organization of compulsory education. As mentioned above, Switzerland is an immigration country despite rigid immigration policies. This is also reflected in the educational institutions. The public education statistics record any immigrant background in Switzerland only via nationality. According to this categorization, around 28% of students in kindergarten and elementary school and 26% of students in secondary schools were of foreign nationality in the 2018/2019 school year (Federal Statistical Office (FSO) Switzerland, 2020). In level-separated secondary schools, around 37% of foreign students were at basic levels, while at advanced levels the figure is only 17%. However, with the PISA survey (which includes secondary school students at the age of 15) and the so-called Assessment of the Achievement of Basic Educational Competences, large, representative data sets are available that allow for a more differentiated analysis with a more precise operationalization. According to data from the Swiss Assessment of the Achievement of Basic Educational Competences, in 2017, approximately 67% of students in 6th grade at the primary level did not have an immigrant background. The breakdown of students with an immigrant background (33% overall) is 21% for the second generation and around 12% for the first (Konsortium ÜGK (Ed.), 2019). Students with only one parent born abroad are not counted as having immigrant background. Using a similar operationalization, according to the 2018 PISA survey data, approximately 34% of 15-year-old students at the lower secondary level had an immigrant background, an almost identical proportion (Konsortium PISA.ch, 2019). However, as we will show below, the composition of the teaching force in Switzerland does not remotely reflect this migration-related diversity. In order to get closer to this problem of underrepresentation, we therefore first address what moves people to start a teacher-training program. Psychological as well as sociological and educational theories often assume educational decisions as realizations of educational aspirations in decision-making situations, which are associated with more or less uncertainty, depending on different factors such as socioeconomic and psychological resources and the expected benefits of the chosen educational pathway (Boudon, 1974; see Maaz et al., 2006 for an overview). However, although such models have a strong focus on the choice of individuals, one should not assume that this choice is completely free for all individuals. Rather, we must emphasize here that restrictions can massively limit the "freedom of choice". These restrictions can be of a material nature, for example in the form of excessively high opportunity costs for completing a course of study. But they can also be immaterial, for example in the sense that people expect not to be accepted by their fellow students and lecturers during their studies, or in the form of being exposed to discrimination when looking for a job or later in their career. Research shows that people with an immigrant background in particular often report higher educational aspirations (Van De Werfhorst & Van Tubergen, 2007). These high aspirations are described by some authors as immigrant optimism (Heath & Brinbaum, 2007; Kao & Tienad, 1995). According to this conception, persons with an immigrant background represent a particularly selective group and tend to regard their low socioeconomic status in the country of arrival as temporary and accordingly changeable. However, if this attitude is confronted with the reality of possible discrimination in the job search, this optimism would presumably be reversed in the case of minorities who were already born in the country under consideration. Whether or not this discrimination objectively takes place is irrelevant from an analytical viewpoint,[4] as the awareness of having to perform better than non-migrants in order to achieve comparable professional success might still lead to higher educational aspirations, however, it could also lead to educational aspirations being directed at areas where less discrimination is expected.

Suter (2016) found evidence of high parental educational aspirations among educationally successful students with a migrant background in Switzerland in the context of a guideline-based interview study. Beck (2015) however, finds no evidence for increased aspirations among parents of primary school students with an immigrant background from "typical" migration countries (former Yugoslavian states, Turkey and Portugal). Glauser (2015) finds no clear influence of migration status on the educational motivation of school leavers in Switzerland, while Tjaden and Scharenberg (2017), using a different data set, find more favorable transitions after lower secondary school for students with an immigrant background (controlling for social origin and school performance) in Switzerland, which they attribute predominantly to immigrant optimism. Similarly, Griga and Hadjar (2014) finds that second-generation immigrant women in Switzerland are more likely to enter university than natives, controlling for social background and school performance. However, it is not clear whether this is due to higher educational aspirations or expected discrimination in the search for apprenticeships.

Overall, one might consider the profession of a teacher in Switzerland as very secure nowadays due to a shortage of teachers (Dachverband Lehrerinnen und Lehrer Schweiz (LCH), 2020). It is also well paid compared to the level of demands of the training (Wolter et al., 2003) and since pay is based on established salary categories, there is actually little possibility of wage discrimination. So based on these considerations and assumptions, there are actually many reasons why people with a migrant background could choose to study to become a teacher more often, as long as they meet the entry requirements. But this consideration is also based on the restriction that no discrimination on the basis of origin is to be expected in the search for a job or in the job itself.

Few studies examine the reasons for choosing to study teaching in Switzerland (Denzler et al., 2005; Denzler & Wolter, 2009, 2010), even fewer with a focus on students with an immigrant background. Beck and Edelmann (2016) examine the choice using educational statistics with the application of different statistical operationalizations of immigrant background. They find that there are strong differences in the distribution of students across different types of higher education institutions (universities (Uni), universities of applied sciences (UAS), and universities of teacher education (UTED)), but not only in terms of immigrant background, but also depending on the type of operationalization (see Fig. 4.1).

Two findings stand out (Beck & Edelmann, 2016): First, students with an immigrant background are significantly underrepresented at Swiss universities of teacher education compared to universities and universities of applied sciences, and this can

---

[4]As the Thomas theorem states: "If men define situations as real, they are real in their consequences" (Thomas & Thomas, 1928, p. 572).

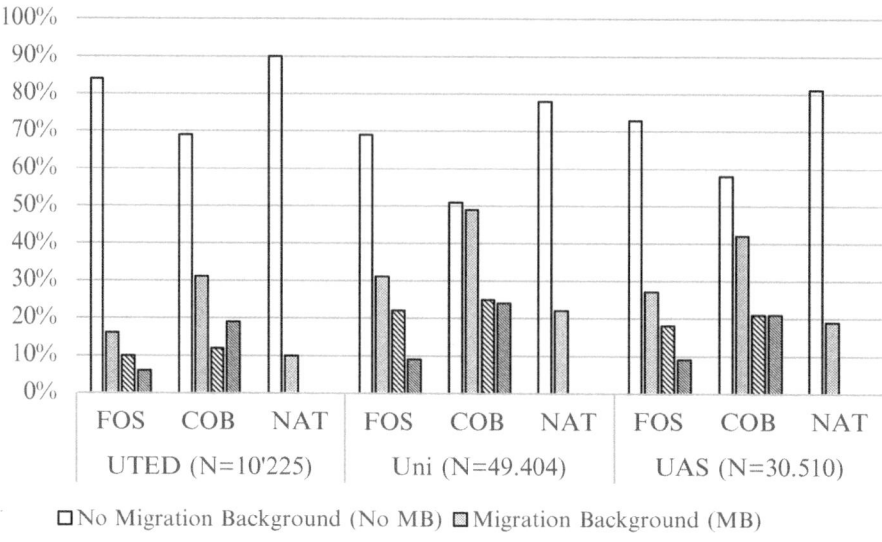

Fig. 4.1 Students by Immigrant background (No, 1st Generation, 2nd Generation), Operationalization (*FOS* According to Federal Office of Statistics Switzerland, *COB* Country of birth of respondent and their parents, *NAT* Nationality of Respondent) and Type of University (UTED: University of Teacher Education, Uni: University, UAS: University of Applied Sciences). (Data: Federal Office of Statistics (FOS) Switzerland, 2013)

probably not be explained by the career choice motives considered in the study (Beck & Edelmann, 2016, p. 185). Second, the extent of the underrepresentation depends strongly on what counts as an immigrant background. It is particularly interesting to note that the definition of an immigrant background as made by the official statistics of Switzerland, takes into account the nationality in addition to the countries of birth of the respondents and their parents (Federal Statistical Office (FSO) Switzerland, 2017). This has consequences, for example, when people have one parent born in Switzerland and one born abroad; in this case, nationality at birth determines whether a person is categorized as having an immigrant background or not.

At University: One of Us?

For prospective teachers, the path from educational decision to the profession normally leads through the University of Teacher Education. Among other things, fellow students and the interactions with the lecturers can have an influence on whether the training can be successfully completed. Literature on dropping out of higher education with a focus on students with an immigrant background is relatively scarce until now, especially when it comes to teacher education. One of the problems is the adequate operationalization of dropout and the associated problems in the study of such phenomena. However, there are indications that a low socioeconomic status as well as general conditions of study have an influence on the risk of dropping out from university in general (see, for example Wolter et al., 2014). One conceivable factor here for students with an immigrant background would be, how integrated they feel at university and the sense of belonging conveyed to them by fellow students and lecturers. Furthermore, research on the sense of belonging at universities in Switzerland is rare to non-existent (see Federal Statistical Office (FSO) Switzerland, 2018 for results related to overall wellbeing). Recent studies from the United States of America (Gopalan & Brady, 2020) show a significant difference depending on the racial-ethnic origin of students in the sense of belonging, even if the reported effect sizes are rather small. We use selected examples to show the extent to which integration and a sense of belonging at university might play a role for prospective teachers.

Results from the survey of 14 students with an immigrant background as part of the project DIVAL (cf. Paragraph 1) indicate that the question of representativeness and belonging is relevant to some of the students with an immigrant background and that they would welcome an increased proportion of students with an immigrant background at university. This is illustrated with the following selected statements from the interviews (cf. Edelmann et al., 2015, p. 217):

> When I started here, I was, I believe, the only dark-skinned student. And now at undergraduate level there are, I think, two or three more dark-skinned students that have recently started. And I think that's good.
>
> I have asked myself this question before I started teacher education: If I become a teacher as a person with an immigrant background, how many other such students are currently at this university? Will I be the only one? And if you already know, aha, yes, there are other students with an immigrant background at this university and it is seen as something positive, then you simply don't need to have this discussion with yourself and worries at the beginning.

Other students emphasized that they hardly perceive an immigrant background as a relevant distinguishing feature at St. Gallen University of Teacher Education. One reason mentioned is that all students have already completed a successful educational path in Switzerland and acquired the Certificate of Access to Higher Education (Edelmann et al., 2015, p. 217).

These results show several aspects: On the one hand, a perceived relevance of the sense of belonging, which, however, is rather defined by belonging to the minority (in this case there seems that "migration" and "skin color/race" are mixed together). The risk of not feeling a sense of belonging can be interpreted as a cost aspect, which can lead to an overall negative evaluation of the teacher education program, even among those who are inclined to study. On the other hand, a meritocratic attitude is reported, where only the entrance qualification counts.

Into and on the Job: What to Expect?

The decision as to whether students choose to enter the teaching profession may also depend on what they anticipate encountering as teachers. This anticipation may be based on what they experience during their practical courses as well as what they observe about and hear from practicing teachers.

There are indications from the DIVAL and DIVAL_transition projects that prospective teachers with a so-called immigrant background are indeed concerned about their future role, as they tend to think much more about certain aspects than their fellow students. For example, considerations are made regarding the extent to which languages shared with students or parents may or may not be used in a school context or to what extent a common national or ethnic origin with the pupils and their parents may lead to more closeness and when it is appropriate or necessary to make delimitations.

So, the question arises, what kind of stories may reach the students during their pre-service teacher education – or, in other words: What *are* the experiences of teachers for whom a so-called immigrant background has become relevant?

Edelmann (2006, 2008) has studied with a content analysis approach (Mayring, 2010), how teachers in the city of Zurich who consider themselves as someone 'with immigrant background' (and therefore using self-identification as an operationalization) deal with cultural diversity among their students. Surprisingly, she has found these teachers to feel fully recognized. They considered their 'background' as a resource for their teaching by – for instance – acting as role models for their students or by being particularly empathetic to those with similar migration experiences. Edelmann (2008) suggests to interpret these results against the background that the teachers in the city of Zurich at the time of research had a particularly high working satisfaction, as the working conditions were attractive and there was an overall teacher shortage so that they were usually able to choose the particular school neighborhood they most preferred (ibid., p. 200ff).

The question why teachers choose or avoid to work in particular neighborhoods has also been addressed in a study by Mantel (2017, 2020). She has investigated how teachers' ways of dealing with diversity are interconnected with their biographical experiences of being someone 'with immigrant background'. The study is framed by the social constructivist theory of boundary making by Wimmer (2013) referring to Weber (1921–1922), Barth (1969) and Bourdieu (1982). It focuses on the question of how teachers experience and deal with processes of boundary making in the pursuit of their life story as well as in their pedagogical orientations. The hermeneutical analysis of biographical-narrative interviews (Rosenthal, 1995; Schütze, 1983) reveals three[5] types that each show specific ways of dealing with social boundaries which are closely related to the teachers' ways of dealing with student diversity:

---

[5] The original study describes four ideal types. However, the fourth type does not have sufficient data saturation and is therefore not presented here (for details, see Mantel, 2017, 2020).

The first type has an overall orientation of *striving towards appreciation for all*. This type has biographically experienced only lightly effective processes of boundary making which he or she has been able to influence by constantly modifying boundaries in claiming both sides to be equally valuable in some way. As a teacher, this type avoids schools in the rural context and consciously prefers schools in urban-immigrant neighborhoods for a negative as well as a positive reason: The negative reason is the anticipation to be less exposed to stigmatization or denigration as would presumably be the case in the rural context, while the positive reason is to feel familiar with the milieu of the urban-immigrant environment. Nevertheless, this type experiences precarious lack of belonging and recognition as a teacher, is particularly cautious not to offend anyone and tends to think of those 'with immigrant background' – including his or her own students – as those who will always be limited in their career opportunities.

The second type orientates towards a *struggle against social exclusion* and has experienced social boundaries that have been almost impossible to overcome, including physical and/or psychological violence such as being strongly stigmatized based on one's national or ethnic family history, which in turn leads to a constant feeling of vulnerability. As a teacher, this type avoids the migration context altogether and seeks to find an environment in which migration is on the agenda as little as possible for fear of again being addressed as someone of foreign origin. Due to the feeling of vulnerability, this type seeks to keep and defend the relatively high social position as a teacher, while at the same time teaching the students not to exclude or denigrate anyone.

The third type is structured along *self-determined belonging through upward mobility*. In this case, there is a strong desire for change because of unsatisfying family conditions and limiting socioeconomic circumstances. Social upward mobility becomes a main biographical orientation. Having reached this social advancement by becoming a teacher, the social position feels strong and secure. Consequently, this type feels free to choose a school neighborhood independently of concerns of being recognized as a teacher, while sometimes urban-immigrant neighborhoods are chosen for reasons of familiarity. These teachers typically distance themselves from the 'new immigrants' who – in their eyes – have not yet 'earned' their belonging while showing strongly optimistic performance expectations towards all of their students combined with the idea that assimilation is needed in order to achieve full integration and educational success.

In all three types, the boundaries that are most strongly experienced and lead to strongly contoured type structures are those that refer to socioeconomic background as well as migration, typically having a parental labor migration history.

In sum, the overall picture of experienced teachers for whom a so-called immigrant background has become significant, shows various kinds of tensions between different resources in dealing with student diversity and limitations based on experienced boundary making processes. Those feeling vulnerable in their recognition as teachers tend to avoid rural environments and choose urban-immigrant neighborhoods instead, while nevertheless experiencing precarious conditions of belonging (Ha & Bischoff, 2020; Mantel, 2020).

Conclusions and Implication

In this article, we have tried to summarize the current state of research on teachers with a migration history in Switzerland. The focus was on the construction of the immigrant background as an object of investigation in scientific works, on the choice of a study program to become a teacher as well as on the experiences of prospective and practicing teachers with an immigrant background. Based on the results presented here, we would like to briefly discuss what we already know and, building on this, focus on the question of what we do not know.

Although we first discussed the question of operationalizing immigrant background, this discussion is by no means completed. Especially in a strongly heterogeneous immigration society like Switzerland, it is important that this heterogeneity is also anticipated in research. For this, studies with a focus on specific immigrant backgrounds would be promising in the first instance, since dichotomizing operationalizations (with/without an immigrant background) are mainly demarcations in relation to the autochthonous population, but they blur the boundaries within the immigrant population. At the same time, the examples of skin color/race and religion described here show once more that national origin in this context is not sufficient to examine relevant boundary demarcations and questions of representation and belonging. This raises the problem of which categories can be used in research and how. Categorizations like skin color or race are easily misused for biologizing explanations and therefore subject to data protection for good reasons.

We have seen that differences in operationalization, which seem trivial at first glance, already result in large quantitative differences in the categorization into "minority" and "majority". If, for example, nationality is taken into account in the construction of the "2nd generation", we could see that the proportion of students with an immigrant background is clearly underestimated according to the official statistical definition of Switzerland. This leads to the question: Does "opening up" the term "immigrant background" in the true sense of the word (here, for example, if at least one parent was born abroad, regardless of current nationality), which leads to a markedly higher proportion of students with an immigrant background, enable the normalization of diversity in the context of migration? Does the "assimilation" by definition of persons with an actual immigrant background as described above lead to a stronger delimitation of the then so-called "immigrants"?

A promising approach could be to use extended concepts of (self-identified) ancestry to measure specific group memberships in future (quantitative) studies. While measurements of origin via cultural and ethnic background as well as self-identified ancestry are already standard in surveys in countries such as Australia or the USA, such operationalizations have only recently been applied in the European context (cf. European Standard Classification of Cultural and Ethnic Groups (ESCEG) by Heath et al., 2016). It has been shown that these are also suitable for identifying distinctions based on sub-national and regional categories (Heath et al., 2016, p. 45) and are suitable for uncovering connections with, for example, experiences of discrimination that cannot be identified exclusively with operationalizations based on countries of birth and nationalities (Schneider & Heath, 2020, p. 549).

A central question remains to what extent one overlooks relevant lines of difference with too rigid categorizations based on simple observable facts (such as country of birth). At the same time, however, focusing on the complexity of heterogeneity, especially in the Swiss context, can obscure the bigger picture. This an make it difficult to distinguish structural realities and mechanisms from the assessment of individual preferences and choices. Another aspect of this is to return to the fit between operationalization and theoretical explanation: perhaps the question should not be who chooses to study to become a teacher, but who chooses not to. Further studies thereby address the question of the extent to which "objective" or self-assessed factors are relevant in determining who becomes a teacher, or whether there is also the question of who, why, and what categorizations of "otherness" are made and whether this may already be discouraging school leavers from becoming teachers. Certainly, studies that start much earlier in the career choice process could provide more clarity here. In the context of recognition and belonging, this is immediately followed by the question of who drops out of teacher training or leaves the teaching profession prematurely and why. This could provide valuable clues as to which aspects of categorization can help explain the low representation of minority teachers in Switzerland.

References

Barth, F. (1969). Introduction. In F. Barth (Ed.), *Ethnic groups and boundaries: The social organization of culture difference* (pp. 9–38). Allen & Unwin.

Beck, M. (2015). *Bildungserfolg von Migranten: der Beitrag von Rational-Choice-Theorien bei der Erklärung von migrationsbedingten Bildungsungleichheiten in Bern und Zürich*. Haupt Verlag.

Beck, M., & Edelmann, D. (2016). Migrationshintergrund und Gender: Eine Überprüfung der statistischen Konstruktion von Differenz am Beispiel der Lehrerinnen- und Lehrerbildung in der Schweiz. In I. Kriesi, B. Liebig, I. Horwarth, & B. Riegraf (Eds.), *Gender und Migration an Universitäten, Fachhochschulen und in der höheren Berufsbildung* (Forum Frauen- und Geschlechterforschung, Band 46). (pp. 168–192). Westfälisches Dampfboot.

Beck, M., Bischoff, S., & Edelmann, D. (2014). *Migrationsbedingte und soziale Diversität von Studierenden der Pädagogischen Hochschule St. Gallen*. Pädagogische Hochschule St. Gallen (PHSG).

Bischoff, S., & Edelmann, D. (2017). «Ich habe zwar den Schweizerpass, bin aber türkisch, und dann kommt halt diese Religionsfrage…» – Einblicke in das qualitative Forschungsprojekt «DIVAL_transition» zur beruflichen Einmündung von Lehramtsstudierenden in der Migrationsgesellschaft. In S. Barsch, N. Glutsch, & M. Massumi (Eds.), *Diversity in der LehrerInnenbildung. Internationale Dimensionen der Vielfalt in Forschung und Praxis* (pp. 175–188). Waxmann.

Bischoff, S., Edelmann, D., & Beck, M. (2016). Students with a migration background in teacher education: A potential or a challenge? In *Teacher education in the 21st century: A focus on convergence* (p. 66). Cambridge Scholars Publishing.

Boudon, R. (1974). *Education, opportunity, and social inequality: Changing prospects in Western society*. Wiley.

Bourdieu, P. (1982). *Die feinen Unterschiede. Kritik der gesellschaftlichen Urteilskraft*. Suhrkamp.

Dachverband Lehrerinnen und Lehrer Schweiz (LCH). (2020). *LCH sehr besorgt über Personalmangel an Schulen* [Press release]. Retrieved from https://www.lch.ch/fileadmin/user_upload_lch/Aktuell/Medienmitteilungen/200615_MedienmitteilungLCH_PersonalmangelAnSchulen2020.pdf

Denzler, S., & Wolter, S. C. (2009). Sorting into teacher education: How the institutional setting matters. *Cambridge Journal of Education, 39*(4), 423–441. https://doi.org/10.1080/03057640903352440

Denzler, S., & Wolter, S. C. (2010). Der Einfluss des lokalen Hochschulangebots auf die Studienwahl. *Zeitschrift für Erziehungswissenschaft, 13*(4), 683–706. https://doi.org/10.1007/s11618-010-0143-6

Denzler, S., Fiechter, U., & Wolter, S. C. (2005). Die Lehrkräfte von morgen. *Zeitschrift für Erziehungswissenschaft, 8*(4), 576–594.

Edelmann, D. (2006). Pädagogische Professionalität im transnationalen sozialen Raum. Eine Studie über Sichtweisen und Erfahrungen von Primarlehrpersonen in Bezug auf die kulturelle Heterogenität ihrer Schulklassen. In C. Allemann-Ghionda & E. Terhart (Eds.), *Kompetenzen und Kompetenzentwicklung von Lehrerinnen und Lehrern* (pp. 235–249). Beltz.

Edelmann, D. (2008). *Pädagogische Professionalität im transnationalen sozialen Raum. Eine qualitative Untersuchung über den Umgang von Lehrpersonen mit der migrationsbedingten Heterogenität ihrer Klassen*. Lit.

Edelmann, D., Bischoff, S., Beck, M., & Meier, A. (2015). More students with migration backgrounds at Universities of Teacher Education. Theoretical reflections and empirical insights on potential aspects and challenges from the perspectives of pre-service teachers and lecturers. *Tertium Comparationis, 21*(2), 205.

European Commission. (2020). *European Migration Network (EMN) Glossary: Person with a migratory background*. Retrieved from https://ec.europa.eu/home-affairs/what-we-do/networks/european_migration_network/glossary_search/person-migratory-background_en

Federal Office of Statistics (FOS) Switzerland. (2013). *Social and economic conditions of student life (SSEE)* (Vol. 2013). Federal Office of Statistics (FOS).

Federal Statistical Office (FSO) Switzerland. (2017). *Statistischer Bericht zur Integration der Bevölkerung mit Migrationshintergrund*. Federal Statistical Office (FSO).

Federal Statistical Office (FSO) Switzerland. (2018). *Gesundheit der Studierenden an den Schweizer Hochschulen. Themenbericht der Erhebung 2016 zur sozialen und wirtschaftlichen Lage der Studierenden*. Federal Statistical Office (FSO) Switzerland.

Federal Statistical Office (FSO) Switzerland. (2020). *Obligatorische Schule: Lernende nach Grossregion, Schulkanton, Bildungstyp und Staatsangehörigkeit* (je-d-15.02.01.05). Retrieved from https://www.bfs.admin.ch/bfs/de/home/statistiken/bildung-wissenschaft/personen-ausbildung/obligatorische-schule.assetdetail.11787900.html

Glauser, D. (2015). *Berufsausbildung oder Allgemeinbildung: Soziale Ungleichheiten beim Übergang in die Sekundarstufe II in der Schweiz*. Spinger VS.

Gopalan, M., & Brady, S. T. (2020). College students' sense of belonging: A national perspective. *Educational Researcher, 49*(2), 134–137. https://doi.org/10.3102/0013189x19897622

Gresch, C., & Kristen, C. (2011). Staatsbürgerschaft oder Migrationshintergrund? Ein Vergleich unterschiedlicher Operationalisierungsweisen am Beispiel der Bildungsbeteiligung. *Zeitschrift für Soziologie, 40*, 208–227.

Griga, D., & Hadjar, A. (2014). Migrant background and higher education participation in Europe: The effect of the educational systems. *European Sociological Review, 30*(3), 275–286. https://doi.org/10.1093/esr/jct031

Ha, J., & Bischoff, S. (2020). «[…] halt einfach viel Wert legen auf Gleichberechtigung». Zukunftsorientierte Perspektiven angehender Lehrpersonen mit Migrationshintergrund im Umgang mit Schüler*innen und deren Eltern. In R. Schneider-Reisinger & M. Oberlechner (Eds.), *Diversitätssensible PädagoInnenbildung in Forschung und Praxis. Utopien, Ansprüche und Herausforderungen* (pp. 241–250). Verlag Barbara Budrich GmbH.

Ha, J., Bischoff, S., & Beck, M. (2019). „Wir reden Deutsch, als wäre ich Schweizerin."Hinweise angehender Lehrpersonen zur migrationsbedingten Mehrsprachigkeit *Mehrsprachigkeit im Fokus: Sprachenprofile der Pädagogischen Hochschulen* (pp. 183–194). Studienverlag.

Hainmueller, J., & Hangartner, D. (2013). Who gets a Swiss passport? A natural experiment in immigrant discrimination. *The American Political Science Review, 107*(1), 159–187. https://doi.org/10.2307/23357762

Heath, A., & Brinbaum, Y. (2007). Explaining ethnic inequalities in educational attainment. *Ethnicities, 7*, 291–305.

Heath, A., Schneider, S. L., & Butt, S. (2016). Developing a measure of socio-cultural origins for the European Social Survey. *GESIS Papers, 2016/16*. GESIS – Leibniz-Institut für Sozialwissenschaften. https://doi.org/10.21241/ssoar.49503

Kao, G., & Tienad, M. (1995). Optimism and achievement: The educational performance of immigrant youth. *Social Science Quarterly, 76*, 1–19.

Kemper, T. (2010). Migrationshintergrund – Eine Frage der Definition! *Die Deutsche Schule, 102*, 315–326.

Konsortium ÜGK (Ed.). (2019). *Überprüfung der Grundkompetenzen. Nationaler Bericht der ÜGK 2017: Sprachen 8. Schuljahr*. Retrieved from Bern/Genf: https://doi.org/10.18747/PHSG-coll3/id/385

Konsortium PISA.ch. (2019). *PISA 2018: Schülerinnen und Schüler der Schweiz im internationalen Vergleich*. Bern und Genf: SBFI/EDK und Konsortium PISA.ch. https://www.sbfi.admin.ch/dam/sbfi/de/dokumente/2019/12/bericht-pisa-2018.pdf.download.pdf/pisa-2018-bericht_d.pdf

Maaz, K., Hausen, C., McElvany, N., & Baumert, J. (2006). Stichwort: Übergänge im Bildungssystem. *Zeitschrift für Erziehungswissenschaft, 9*(3), 299–327.

Mantel, C. (2017). *Lehrer_in, Migration und Differenz. Fragen der Zugehörigkeit bei Grundschullehrer_innen der zweiten Einwanderungsgeneration in der Schweiz*. transcript.

Mantel, C. (2020). Being a teacher with a so-called 'immigrant background': Challenges of dealing with social boundaries. *Intercultural Education, 31*(2), 173–189.

Mayring, P. (2010). *Qualitative Inhaltsanalyse*. Beltz.

Rosenthal, G. (1995). *Erlebte und erzählte Lebensgeschichte. Gestalt und Struktur biographischer Selbstbeschreibungen*. Campus.

Schneider, S. L., & Heath, A. F. (2020). Ethnic and cultural diversity in Europe: Validating measures of ethnic and cultural background. *Journal of Ethnic and Migration Studies, 46*(3), 533–552. https://doi.org/10.1080/1369183X.2018.1550150

Schütze, F. (1983). Biographieforschung und narratives Interview. *Neue Praxis, 13*(3), 283–293.

Söhn, J. (2014). How legal status contributes to differential integration opportunities. *Migration Studies, 2*(3), 369–391. https://doi.org/10.1093/migration/mnu022

Suter, R. (2016). *Bildungserfolg trotz Migrationshintergrund. Ressourcen von bildungserfolgreichen jungen Erwachsenen mit Migrationshintergrund in der Schweiz*. University of Bern.

Swiss Conference of Cantonal Ministers of Education (EDK). (2019). *The Swiss education system*. Retrieved from https://www.edk.ch/dyn/16833.php

Thomas, W. I., & Thomas, D. S. (1928). *The child in America behavior problems and programs*. Alfred A. Knopf.

Tjaden, J. D., & Scharenberg, K. (2017). Ethnic choice effects at the transition into upper-secondary education in Switzerland. *Acta Sociologica, 60*(4), 309–324.

Van De Werfhorst, H. G., & Van Tubergen, F. (2007). Ethnicity, schooling, and merit in the Netherlands. *Ethnicities, 7*(3), 416–444. https://doi.org/10.1177/1468796807080236

Weber, M. (1921–1922). *Wirtschaft und Gesellschaft*. J.C.B. Mohr (Paul Siebeck).

Wimmer, A. (2013). *Ethnic boundary making*. Oxford University Press.

Witzel, A. (2000). Das problemzentrierte Interview. *Forum Qualitative Sozialforschung, 1*(1), 8.

Wolter, S. C., Denzler, S., & Weber, B. a. (2003). Betrachtungen zum Arbeitsmarkt der Lehrer in der Schweiz. *Vierteljahrshefte zur Wirtschaftsforschung, 72*(2), 305–319. https://doi.org/10.3790/vjh.72.2.305

Wolter, S. C., Diem, A., & Messer, D. (2014). Drop-outs from Swiss universities: An empirical analysis of data on all students between 1975 and 2008. *European Journal of Education, 49*(4), 471–483. https://doi.org/10.1111/ejed.12096

Michael Beck is a research fellow and lecturer at St. Gallen University of Teacher Education, Switzerland. He studied social sciences with a focus on sociology and research methodology in Manheim, Germany, and received his Ph.D. in Educational Sociology at the University of Bern, Switzerland. His fields of interest are social mobility, educational inequality, research in teacher education and assessment of student competencies.

Carola Mantel is head of the Institute for International Cooperation in Education at the University of Teacher Education Zug, Switzerland. She studied Social Anthropology, International Law and Religious Studies at the University of Zurich. From the same University, she received her PhD on her research about minority teachers. Her research interests include social justice in and through education, recognition, social boundary making, migration-related diversity, professional development of teachers, learning through study abroad and South-North cooperation.

Sonja Bischoff is a researcher fellow and lecturer at the St. Gallen University of Teacher Education, Switzerland. She is a qualified primary school teacher and studied Social Anthropology and Sociology at the University of Zurich. Sonja Bischoff received her Ph.D. in Social Anthropology at the University of Bern, Switzerland. Her fields of interests are educational inequality, migration-related diversity and qualitative research methodology.

Open Access This chapter is licensed under the terms of the Creative Commons Attribution 4.0 International License (http://creativecommons.org/licenses/by/4.0/), which permits use, sharing, adaptation, distribution and reproduction in any medium or format, as long as you give appropriate credit to the original author(s) and the source, provide a link to the Creative Commons license and indicate if changes were made.

The images or other third party material in this chapter are included in the chapter's Creative Commons license, unless indicated otherwise in a credit line to the material. If material is not included in the chapter's Creative Commons license and your intended use is not permitted by statutory regulation or exceeds the permitted use, you will need to obtain permission directly from the copyright holder.

Chapter 5
Sweden and Germany: Top-Down and Bottom-Up Policy Making in the Re-professionalization of International Teachers

Galina Putjata, Catarina Economou, Elin Ennerberg, and Jana Arnold

Abstract Flight has developed into a new research focus worldwide, but, only a few projects are concerned with newly immigrated teachers. Meanwhile, increasing importance is politically assigned to them and their linguistic resources. Despite these expectations, there are hardly any studies that address language diversity in the professional training of immigrant teachers. As a reaction to this lacuna, we have conducted a qualitative study in two countries: Sweden and Germany. These cases are particularly interesting to compare as they approach the re-professionalization of immigrant teachers in very different ways. In Sweden the introductory programs are the result of a political measure (top-down-policy making) and hold no language requirement in Swedish, whereas in Germany these programs are the result of bottom-up initiatives on behalf of universities and academics, which consequently result in a varying dealing with linguistic diversity. The difference in approach is of extreme interest with regard to top-down- and bottom-up processes of language education policy making, as the chapter will explicate with a specific focus on research review thus far. It will then present a qualitative study that focuses on multilingual practices in teacher training. To access this level, interviews were conducted with the respective actors – programme coordinators and lecturers. The results allow deep insights into the process of language policy making and their implementation on the institutional level. Finally, we will discuss the potentials of top-down- and bottom-up approaches and formulate implications for international teacher education.

G. Putjata (✉)
University of Frankfurt, Frankfurt, Germany
e-mail: Putjata@em.uni-frankfurt.de

C. Economou · E. Ennerberg
Malmo University, Malmö, Sweden

J. Arnold
University of Munster, Münster, Germany

Introduction

While expectations towards immigrant teachers as "role models" and "bridge-builders" have been broadly researched, little is known about their professional integration (Bräu et al., 2013, see also Goltsev et al. in Chap. 9, this volume), specifically, how languages are dealt with in professional training (Terhart et al., 2018). As a reaction to this lacuna, we conducted a qualitative study in two countries: Sweden and Germany. These contexts are interesting to compare as they approach the programmes for immigrant teachers in different ways (Bonoli, 2012; Terhart et al., 2020).

The contextual framework constitutes "re-professionalisation" programmes in Sweden and Germany. These programmes are of particular interest because they differ in their educational policy structure: while the Swedish programme is the result of political decisions and top-down policy-making, the German programme was developed through bottom-up initiatives by university actors.

In Sweden, the professional integration of immigrants can look back on a long experience in education policy (Bonoli, 2012; Ennerberg, 2017). In addition to an already existing programme, the Swedish government introduced a fast track procedure in 2016: The measure lasts 26 weeks and is currently offered at six Swedish universities. No knowledge of Swedish is required for participation. Translanguaging seminars allow for quick access to the course content. Participants as well as teachers use their different language resources in order to understand and discuss the content. The concept of translanguaging also suggests a positive attitude towards multilingualism. The existing linguistic basics of the (mainly Arabic-speaking) participants are the prerequisite for learning, while teaching the educational language Swedish in parallel. On 2 days a week they take part in university lectures on the Swedish school system, on two further days they gain practical experience at school and on 1 day they attend the Swedish language course. The successful completion of the course gives them access to regular teacher training or employment as assistants.

In Germany, due to institutional and structural requirements, only a few teachers with foreign qualifications are integrated into the regular school system (Krüger-Potratz, 2013). In the course of new immigration, qualification projects in educational fields emerged in recent years. In contrast to Sweden, all programmes were initiated by university actors and are not politically binding (Putjata 2018; Terhart et al., 2020). Upon successful completion of the programmes, participants receive a certificate that qualifies them to work as replacement teachers, heritage language teachers, in all-day care at German schools or to pursue a regular teacher training. The second difference is the language requirements: Most of the courses require knowledge of German at least at level B1 of the Common European Framework of Reference for Languages. In addition to the language courses, the programme aims to prepare participants for the regular teacher training programme with methodological-didactic contents and information about the German education system.

Teachers with an Immigrant Background and Their Access to Educational Market

The professionalization programmes presented in the last section constitute a significant research context specifically with regard to language requirements. We will show this in the following, basing on the theoretical concepts of linguistic market and language policy making and including the literature review on the role of languages in teachers' access to labour and education markets.

Research on international teachers is extremely scarce, as teachers from other countries are rarely integrated into the national school system. Apart from speakers of prestigious languages like English from the UK, Canada and the United States (Collins & Reid, 2012), or French speakers from France (Liboy & Mulatris, 2016), teachers with an immigrant background often experience downward mobility, as shown in studies from Canada, Europe, the USA and Australia (Putjata, 2018; Remennick, 2002). Studies with refugee teachers analyse their access to the educational market and confirm numerous barriers on their way to professional integration (Putjata, 2018, 2019; Santoro, 2013) which results in 'brain waste'- a phenomenon widely criticized in migration studies (Bauder, 2003). A recent study on newly immigrated teachers in Germany analysis the mechanisms of this restriction. Framed by Bourdieu's capital theory, the results show the role of language as symbolic capital in this process: in migration, all three forms of capital (embodied in skills, objectified as in books and institutionalized in diplomas) undergo repositioning, since individuals lack the most relevant capital – the state language. The books are not in the legitimate language, the embodied skills cannot be presented, the diplomas are often not accepted, and access to formal education in order to adopt these diplomas is only possible when there is knowledge of the majority language (Putjata, 2018). Exceptions were shown in studies from Israel, where languages were included in the courses and thus positioned as an embodied and institutionalized capital (Putjata, 2018).

Following Bourdieu's model (Bourdieu, 1990), individuals are assigned a certain social position according to the value of their languages, whereby this value corresponds to the prevailing power relations. In everyday interaction, this positioning results in view of the role of certain languages. At the individual level of the speakers, these views are reflected in the so-called language beliefs. They include, for example, ideas about what role language skills play, how languages are learned and how useful they are. These language hierarchies are reproduced and circulated in educational institutions. Knowledge of certain linguistic forms (e.g. the state language, Swedish, or the family language[1] of the course participants, Arabic) is certified and institutionalised as capital. Documented in certificates, the linguistic capital

---

[1] The terms "heritage language" or "mother tongue" are subject to controversial discussion in German pedagogical discourse as they bear an idea of a (foreign) heritage or one specific language with no actual relevance for the child's life. Hence, the present paper adopts the term "family languages" or "language practices" (for further discussion, see Fürstenau & Gomolla, 2011).

is a decisive criterion for educational success and access to work. What functions as relevant knowledge, whether English or Arabic, is defined by the groups with the largest volume of capital – policy makers, who are themselves mostly speakers of prestigious languages and act as ideology brokers (Blommaert, 1999). Hence, following this sociolinguistic perspective, educational institutions produce and reproduce the existing language hierarchies, which results in the social exclusion and educational underachievement of all those who do not speak the majority language.

Studies from different disciplines research how to overcome this reproduction of inequalities (Menken & Garcia, 2010) on a micro-, meso- and macrolevel. Language beliefs are shaped by the macro level of language policies. They determine and regulate the use of language at the meso level of educational institutions and affect the micro level of individual linguistic practices (Spolsky, 2004). According to the findings on Language Policy Making (Shohamy, 2010), language policy measures are important to initiate transformation processes on the educational language market. However, a number of open and covert top-down and bottom-up mechanisms become effective and can restrict or favour the implementation of the new language policies. Menken and García argue that "at each level of an educational system, from the national ministry or department of education to the classroom, language education policies are interpreted, negotiated, and ultimately (re)constructed in the process of implementation" (Menken & Garcia, 2010: 1). In this perspective, the course leaders of the presented professionalization programmes (section 2) play an important role: as actors at the interface between top-down policy making and language practices they act as *de facto policy makers* (Shohamy, 2010). They can function as ideology brokers who circulate new, multilingual language ideologies allowing for multilingual practices. One such practice could be, for example, translanguaging: This pedagogical concept suggests that teachers and students can use all available language resources to allow for language and cognitive transfer as well as social cohesion (García & Wei, 2014).

At the backdrop of the presented literature on international teachers' access to education, the significance of language policies within this process, and the role of course leaders as *de facto policy makers*, the following questions arise: What are the language beliefs of the course leaders? How do they perceive the language resources of the international teachers, and what language policies and practices do they endorse?

Research Design and Methodology

The data was gathered through semi-structured interviews with course leaders in Sweden and in Germany. We chose the instrument because the guide ensures that all important aspects for answering the research question are mentioned. On the other hand, the wording and the order of the questions are not binding. This favours an open and natural situation and helps to assess participants' language beliefs (Witzel & Reiter, 2012). Finally, additional open questions give interviewees the opportunity to respond accordingly to their individual interests: First, the interviewees were asked what language requirements the course participants (international teachers) should meet in order to participate in the programme. If not mentioned, more concrete questions followed on which languages are relevant in the context of the project and professional practice. If the interviewees did not mention languages of the participants here either, the explicit question followed: *To what extent does multilingualism (foreign languages, family languages) of the participants play a role in the teacher training course and in everyday school life?* Interviews were conducted in a place chosen by the interviewees and lasted from 30 to 70 min.

The data corpus consisted of 13 interviews and is presented in Table 5.1. All of the participants were programme actors: university lecturers, project coordinators and supervisors at schools. The university lecturers were recruited in one Swedish and four German universities. School supervisors as well as project coordinators were contacted and asked if they could consider participating. All interviews took place in 2018 in the participants' work places. We recruited them because at the backdrop of the presented literature review these persons act as de facto policy makers – at the interface between language policy and actual practice.

The first step of the Swedish and German data analysis process was the transcribing of the interviews and the organizing of the different data according to central topics. In the second step, we applied comparative analysis to find repeating threads and patterns (Nohl, 2010). In the coding process, we made a list of topics, which were repeated in the interviews. In the third step, the topics were assembled into

Table 5.1 Overview of the participants in Sweden and Germany

Name of the interviewed person, pseudonymised[a]	Position within the programmes
Sweden	
Eva	Language lecturer
Riba	Language lecturer
Astrid	Subject lecturer
Vera	Subject lecturer
Helena	Subject lecturer
Karin	Project manager/coordinator
Anders	Supervisor at school
Inga	Supervisor at school
Germany	
Ms. Zielonka	Project coordinator and subject lecturer
Mr. Thiel	Language lecturer
Mr. Funke	Project coordinator
Ms. Lenz	Project coordinator
Mr. Peters	Project manager and subject lecturer

[a]In Germany, the program coordinators and course leaders were addressed as "Herr/Frau" following their surname, whereas in Swedish interviews, first names were used. This is reflected in the chosen pseudonyms

several themes (DeCuir-Gunby et al., 2011). This allowed us to reduce the scope, organize the data and finally, answer the research questions about language beliefs, multilingualism and language diversity management in the professional training of immigrant teachers. After establishing the respective findings of the Swedish and German data analysis, we compared them in terms of similarities and differences in the individual topics.

Findings and Discussion

The interview analysis revealed three major themes: official language requirements, monolingualism as a norm and multilingualism as a resource on different levels. In this section, we will present the findings following these themes and focus on similarities and differences between the Swedish and the German contexts. To allow insights into the data, the presentation will include direct quotes and paraphrases of the most concise examples from the interviews with course leaders. However, the qualitative data allows us to extend the analysis beyond the quoted examples.

Official Language Requirements

The most fundamental difference between the programmes in Germany and in Sweden are the language requirements at the national level. In Germany most course leaders consider the German language to be essential even within the programmes. This importance is often not argued for or explained, but stated as self-explanatory. In comparison, no such norm was stated by the interviewees in Sweden.

Following Shohamy, the official language policy on the macro-level of federal ministries frames beliefs and practices of individual actors. As in Sweden, the top-down-policy on teacher professionalization expects universities to open courses to all participants without specific language requirements, thus resulting in the use of several languages, Arabic, Swedish and English. Yet, a deeper insight into the data reveals that course leaders' perception of these practices differs, as we will show in the next section.

Monolingualism as a Norm

In the German programmes, three interviewees emphasise the importance of German language courses in the re-professionalization programmes. They consider a high level of language command as a premise for professional teaching and regard German as the predominant school language:

It makes sense for participants to take this test because, of course, it also provides information about whether they can keep up with the course that we will then take with them and then also acquire these degrees, these B2 and then also the C1 degree, from us in this period of time at all.

Mr. Funke, as well the other two interviewees, supports the language requirements. Only in the context of the training for heritage language courses, they perceive languages other than German as relevant, which can be interpreted as a monolingual belief. This belief is also reflected in the Swedish data. Although no language requirement is made on the level of policy making, and in spite of the resulting multilingual practices of everyday instruction, these practices are perceived as problematic. The course leaders consider the language issue as a great challenge for the participants. Even if the course is in Arabic and Swedish, the course leaders would like the participants to use Swedish predominantly:

> Today when the participants presented their group assignment, four out of the five groups spoke Swedish. But, of course, it was not all of them [group members] that spoke or even understood Swedish. They had chosen the one [group member] who could speak in Swedish. And sometimes I can sense that there is too much focus on Arabic because there are only Arabic speaking participants. They need everyday Swedish language in order to communicate out in the schools.

Although four of the five groups chose the Swedish language to present the assignment, the line of argumentation reveals a deficit-oriented perspective on this practice. The achieved result of the group work – the successful presentation in Swedish relying on all the language resources of the participants – is restricted: "But of course, not all of them spoke". The following intensification in Eva's argument – through the statement "or even understood" – reinforces her perceived lack of the skills on the part of the course participants. The subsequent summary, "They had chosen the one", underlines the primary focus on Swedish, on the one hand, and the denial of this skill in the majority of the course participants, on the other. The use of multilingual practice is not argued for learning purposes in terms of translanguaging (see García & Wei, 2014). Rather, it is perceived as the result of the varying levels of Swedish among the group: The "focus on Arabic" is argued and explained only in relation to the lack of knowledge in the majority language. Finally, this deficit-oriented perspective results in the perception of Arabic as a limitation and as "too much". This limitation is stated not only with regard to participants' Swedish language learning in the course but also as an obstacle for interaction with pupils or teachers "in the school".

This deeper insight in the line of argumentation from the course leaders reveals the usefulness of qualitative data analysis. Monolingual practices – the choice of the majority language over the language resources of the course participants – come not from a negative attitude towards some languages or language speakers, but are the result of a genuine concern for the future well-being of the immigrant teachers outside of the professionalization programme. It can be interpreted not as an individual attitude but as an institutionally structured ideology about the role of certain languages in terms of Blommaert (1999), which the course leaders circulate as *ideology brokers*.

Further data from our corpus, in both the German and the Swedish context, support this finding. Concerning the weekly practice experience at schools, the course leaders emphasize how difficult it is for the participants to communicate with their teacher colleagues and the students. Anders, one of the supervisors, points out:

> To send someone here who does not understand anything and only sits there is not good, as I see it. She cannot understand, cannot talk and cannot ask any questions. I cannot use her competence in class, and I wish it had been possible to do so. And the reason for this is that she doesn't speak a word of Swedish.

Anders's remark concerning the participant's deficiencies in the majority language is representative of many of the programme actors, especially in the schools. Most of the course leaders in the Swedish case highlighted that a certain level of Swedish is necessary. Their arguments vary between Swedish being "beneficial" and an "indispensable language in both the course and the school context". This line of reasoning can be interpreted as the result of monolingual ideology on the linguistic market of educational institutions (see Bourdieu, 1990). Speaking Arabic is perceived in contrast to, or even at the cost of, speaking Swedish and not as the starting point of cognitive or linguistic transfer within the language learning process following translanguaging (see García & Wei, 2014). And finally, Arabic is not perceived as a capital course participants can bring to the school as future teachers.

Multilingualism as a Resource

At the same time, data also reveal that some actors do perceive the family languages of the participants as a capital for the work at school, on a social level and in class.

For the Work at School

In Germany, three of the five interviewees emphasise the importance of the participants' family languages as a resource for the work in education. The project manager and subject teacher Mr. Peters points out:

> It is […] very interesting for the labour market to have people who speak the languages, people who are involved with social work, pedagogy, school. This is an important resource, but it is so much more. […] It's also interesting for the labour market to have these languages, which unfortunately aren't trained here, but rather acquire them like that.

This statement reveals a perception of the participants' family languages as a resource for a professional activity in educational settings. The cue "unfortunately" underlines the positive perception of this resource and the need for it in Germany today. Further data support this finding. Mr. Thiel and Ms. Zielonka see the languages of the participating teachers as advantageous and necessary to recognise as a second teaching subject. At school, this would benefit not only the students, but also the immigrant teachers and allow to facilitate teachers' integration into the labour market. In this context Ms. Zielonka, who is project coordinator and leader of one of the subject courses, pleads that the languages of the participating teachers should be offered to all pupils as regular school foreign language subjects:

> So, here would be the possibility to say, Okay, then, let us try to support the people and develop a curriculum which will be valid for this generation or for the next one here. [...] But the debate is not open at all. [...] I was told that Polish and Russian would be available later, from the seventh grade onwards. Why not Arabic, too? At this level as a foreign language, which is offered…

This example can be interpreted as a perception of multilingualism as a capital (see Bourdieu, 1990), and not only for the immigrant teachers themselves. Some course leaders underline how important it is, to include migrant-related multilingualism in the school system, arguing that this would allow for a shift in the discourse on what is considered as relevant. We found similar patterns in further statements with a focus on languages hierarchies and the potential to fundamentally upgrade language hierarchies in society. In terms of the presented literature reviews, this line of argumentation is particularly important: Some course leaders not only have a positive attitude towards immigrant languages and multilingual practices for the individuals, their development, or their learning process, but they also criticise the existing language policy in today's Germany, which privileges some languages over the others.

In contrast, the languages of the immigrant teachers in Sweden are not perceived as a resource for access to the labour market. As compared to the German data, course participants do not encourage the use of Arabic, unless they have a specific background as Arabic teachers. This could be the result of the experienced top-down policy: The goal of the program and its official emphasis is on utilising the teachers' specific subject knowledge. Another tentative explanation of why course participants do not mention participants' skills in Arabic language teaching can be linked to the low status of heritage language teachers on the social level in Sweden, e. g. with lower salaries and no formal education requirements.

On a Social Level

However, on the social level in both Sweden and in Germany, the teachers' multilingualism is perceived as a resource, for example, in dealing with pupils and parents with a migration background, as stated by Helena:

> And the third impulse is, of course, that there are also a lot of newly arrived students at the schools, and, of course, the teachers can communicate on equal terms with these students, if they have already had the same experience.

Helena sees the resource on the social level, as course participants have similar experiences of migration as the "newly arrived students". She expects that "these" students will be happy to have someone who understands their family language. Consequently, the linguistic and cultural background is seen as having the potential to generate intercultural competence and facilitating the role of mediators. This expectation can be often found in literature review on "role model" or "bridge builders" (see Bräu et al., 2013; Goltsev et al. in this volume). In Germany, the interviewed course leaders were concerned that schools could reduce the teachers to the role of language mediators, thus overlooking and neglecting their professional competence. Therefore, Ms. Zielonka pleads for dealing with linguistic diversity as a cross-sectional task of the school.

In Class

As presented in the section "Monolingualism as a norm", some course leaders in the Swedish Fast Track stated that although the concepts of translanguaging worked well during the theoretical courses, it collided with the monolingual norms at the workplace. Yet, the views differ. Inga, for example, stated:

> In some learning contexts, it is very good that there will be many languages. The participant can help many students who speak many languages, sometimes more than two. We need more languages in school.

Inga points out the family language of the participant may become a resource for the newly arrived students in need of "help". We also found this resource-oriented perspective in the interview with Vera. Like Helena, she attaches lower importance to the majority language, Swedish, in the training course. Instead, she sees the entire linguistic repertoire of the participants as helpful for communication purposes. In Germany, however, the use of languages beyond German in the program depends primarily on language beliefs of individual actors working as lecturers. As the language teacher Mr. Thiel explains, he selectively takes the more prestigious Romance languages and English as being an advantage for the acquisition of German in the context of language-contrastive work in the German lessons. However, he does not seem to consider the family languages as a resource in his language course. This may stem from the lack of appropriate methodological-didactic knowledge to include the languages, which he himself does not master. Conversely, Ms. Zielonka and Mr. Peters reveal a resource-oriented attitude towards multilingualism, which also refers to the family languages of the teachers. Ms. Zielonka emphasises the multilingual teachers' potential to reflect on languages, which may result from multilingualism. According to her, their meta-linguistic-awareness can be a great asset as a language support for newly immigrated students in the schools. In general, she attaches great importance to family languages for further language acquisition:

> [The] first language is very important, especially for pronunciation, when you know where the sounds in Arabic come from, while the German language is located a little bit more in the front.

She further explains that teachers should also consider the family languages of the students, as the languages would be "mostly linked together". Because the family languages of the teachers have no place in the official concept of the programme, she herself initiates workshops (for instance, pronunciation) where the family languages of the participating teachers serve as a foundation in the acquisition of

German. Also Mr. Peters explicitly wants the participants to use their family languages for exercises in his own courses:

> And in these international comparisons, we tell the students who you already speak Arabic, that we would like to learn something about the education system in Syria. They look for documents and introduce us to the texts and then we discuss with them and discuss the differences in the education and social system with them. So, where the language is also necessary for the study. And of course that would also be beneficial, if I could speak Arabic or Russian, but well, it's also an interesting situation that they explain it to me.

He adds that the entire linguistic repertoire of the participants is very helpful for communication purposes in class. This description can be interpreted as a translanguaging (see García & Wei, 2014). As mentioned above, this language practice reveals the perception of multilingualism as a capital, and serves to value the participants' language as an asset. Both Mr. Peters and Ms. Zielonka seem to attach lower importance to a high level of German as they do not perceive it as being the only legitimate language within the educational context (in the training programmes and at schools).

Conclusions and Implications

In times of increasing migration, teachers with international qualifications are in the focus of both political and scientific debate. Yet, their presence is extremely scarce, as teachers from other countries are rarely integrated into the national school systems. Professionalization programmes constitute an important move as they allow for integration and access to education. The professional integration of immigrant teachers helps, at the same time, to prevent the chronic underemployment of immigrants. However, this potential strongly depends on the language beliefs of those who initiate and implement these professionalization programmes, as we have shown in the literature review and theoretical framework. The qualitative analysis of data from thirteen interviews allowed us to reconstruct the line of argumentation, and thus the logic and the underlying perception of multilingualism, with a specific focus on language policies and language practices. The in-depth examination of the data from Sweden and Germany reveals both differences and similarities concerning: the official language requirement, multilingualism as a norm and multilingualism as a resource for access to a professional activity, on a social level and in the classroom. In Sweden, no specific knowledge of a language is required for participation in the course. However, the interviews with course leaders reveal a perception of this practice as a problematic issue. The predominance of Arabic is perceived as hindering for the learning progress and for Swedish language acquisition. Moreover, the course leaders perceive the lack of Swedish as an obstacle for interaction with pupils or teachers in the school. Furthermore, the workplace practice is perceived as a difficult period for the participants of the Fast Track course as the multilingual policy in the programme collides with the monolingual norm in schools.

Yet, the results also show that course leaders in both contexts emphasize the participants' family languages as an asset for the interaction in schools. The qualitative data reveal a resource-oriented view towards multilingualism in both educational and social terms. In theoretical courses, the course leaders consider multilingual practices as important, and include them as a pedagogical method.

The two contexts – Sweden and Germany – represent two different approaches: top-down versus bottom-up language policy making. Yet, our analysis shows that monolingual practice can still prevail despite the official multilingual top-down-policy, as is the case in Sweden. Course leaders play an important role in this process. As has been shown, the actual language practices in both Sweden and Germany are negotiated in everyday teaching: While some course leaders include the languages of the participants, others take no account of them, independent of the official language policy. And even those course leaders who consider multilingualism as a resource on a social level still opt for monolingual practices in the course. On the other hand, even in those cases where multilingualism is not supported by official top-down policies, as has been shown for Germany, there are course leaders who reveal multilingual beliefs and integrate languages other than German into their teaching. By doing so, they act as de facto language policy makers (Menken & Garcia, 2010). Thus, our findings suggest that the two approaches – top-down and bottom-up – do not work when implemented separately. This, however, can change, when the course leaders are aware of the family language role for learning processes and the languages themselves are ascribed an important value in programs' structure through top-down policies. These findings suggest that processes on both levels are necessary to overcome the monolingual mindset. This, in turn, would require professionalization programs that acknowledge family languages, while including the course leaders in the process of policy making and simultaneously raising their language awareness.

These two cases are interesting as they approach the re-professionalization of immigrant teachers in different ways. In Sweden, the programs are the result of a political measure, whereas in Germany, they result from bottom-up initiatives. The findings suggest that top-down as well as bottom-up approaches are necessary to reconstruct monolingual beliefs. For the professionalization programs this includes that course leaders are aware of family language role for learning processes and the languages themselves are ascribed an important value. This, in turn, would require more research on multilingual practices in teacher training programs.

References

Bauder, H. (2003). 'Brain abuse,' or the devaluation of immigrant labour in Canada. *Antipode, 35*(4), 699–717.

Blommaert, J. (1999). The debate is open. In J. Blommaert (Ed.), *Language ideological debates* (2010th ed., pp. 1–38). De Gruyter.

Bonoli, G. (2012). Active labour market policy and social investment: A changing relationship. In N. Morel, B. Palier, & J. Palme (Eds.), *Towards a social investment welfare state? Ideas, policies and challenges* (pp. 181–204). Policy Press.

Bourdieu, P. (1990). *Was heißt sprechen? Die Ökonomie des sprachlichen Tausches.* Braumüller.

Bräu, K., Georgi, V. B., Karakaşoğlu, Y., & Rotter, C. (2013). Einleitung. In K. Bräu, V. B. Georgi, Y. Karakaşoğlu, & C. Rotter (Eds.), *Lehrerinnen und Lehrer mit Migrationshintergrund. Zur Relevanz eines Merkmals in Theorie, Empirie und Praxis* (pp. 7–14). Waxmann.

Collins, J., & Reid, C. (2012). Immigrant teachers in Australia. *Cosmopolitan Civil Societies: An Interdisciplinary Journal, 4*(2), 38–61. https://doi.org/10.5130/ccs.v4i2.2553

DeCuir-Gunby, J., Marshall, P., & McCulloch, A. (2011). Developing and using a codebook for the analysis of interview data: An example from a professional development research project. *Field Methods, 23*(2), 136–155.

Ennerberg, E. (2017). *Destination employment? Contradictions and ambiguities in Swedish labour market policy for newly arrived migrants*. Lund University.

Fürstenau, S., & Gomolla, M. (2011). *Migration und Schulischer Wandel: Mehrsprachigkeit*. VS Verl. für Sozialwiss.

García, O., & Wei, L. (2014). *Translanguaging: Language, bilingualism and education*. Palgrave Pivot.

Krüger-Potratz, M. (2013). Vielfalt im Lehrerzimmer. Aktuelle bildungspolitische Entwicklungen unter der Frage von Kontinuitäten und Diskontinuitäten. In K. Bräu, V. B. Georgi, Y. Karakaşoğlu-Aydın, & C. Rotter (Eds.), *Lehrerinnen und Lehrer mit Migrationshintergrund: Zur Relevanz eines Merkmals in Theorie, Empirie und Praxis* (pp. 17–36). Waxmann.

Liboy, G.-M., & Mulatris, P. (2016). Enseignants non immigrants et enseignants immigrants: convergences et divergences autour de la relation entre école et familles immigrantes. *Alterstice, 6*(1), 91–104.

Menken, K., & Garcia, O. (Eds.). (2010). *Negotiating language policies in schools: Educators as policymakers*. Routledge.

Nohl, A.-M. (2010). Narrative interview and documentary interpretation. In R. Bohnsack, N. Pfaff, & W. Weller (Eds.), *Qualitative analysis and documentary method in international educational research* (pp. 195–217). Budrich.

Putjata, G. (2018). Immigrant teachers' integration and transformation of the linguistic market in Israel. *Language and Education, 21*(2), 38–56.

Putjata, G. (2019). 'Und da wurde mir klar, ich bin doch nicht dumm!' – Stimmen eingewanderter Lehrkräfte. In B. Hasenjürgen & M. Spetsmann-Kunkel (Eds.), *Kulturalisierungsprozesse in Bildungskontexten* (pp. 177–190). Nomos.

Remennick, L. (2002). Survival of the fittest: Russian immigrant teachers speak about their professional adjustment in Israel. *International Migration, 40*(1), 99–121.

Santoro, N. (2013). The drive to diversify the teaching profession: Narrow assumptions, hidden complexities. *Race Ethnicity and Education, 18*(6), 858–876.

Shohamy, E. (2010). Cases of language policy resistance in Israel's centralized educational system. In K. Menken & O. Garcia (Eds.), *Negotiating language policies in schools: Educators as policymakers* (pp. 182–197). Routledge.

Spolsky, B. (2004). *Language policy*. Cambridge University Press.

Terhart, H., Putjata, G., Bak, R., & Schnitzer, A. (2018). Bildungsangebote für neu zugewanderte Menschen zwischen Teilhabe und Ausschluss. In E. Feyerer & W. Prammer (Eds.), *System. Wandel. Entwicklung* (pp. 374–380). Klinkhardt.

Terhart, H., Elshof, A., & Preuschoff, S. (2020). Programm für geflüchtete Lehrkräfte in Köln. In G. Kremsner, M. Proyer, & G. Biewer (Eds.), *Inklusion von Lehrkräften nach der Flucht: Über universitäre Ausbildung zum beruflichen Wiedereinstieg* (pp. 207–216). Klinkhardt.

Witzel, A., & Reiter, H. (2012). *The problem-centered interview*. SAGE.

Galina Putjata is Professor for Multilingualism and Migration in Educational Science at the Goethe University Frankfurt, Germany. After having earned her PhD on multilingual development at the University of Dresden, she led several projects on multilingualism in education at the University of Münster, Université de la Réunion, the Université du Québec à Montréal, and the Research Centre on Bilingualism in Bangor. Her research interests are multilingual pedagogies, transnational education, minority teachers as well as teacher training. Currently, she enjoys working with participatory research approaches.

Catarina Economou is Doctor of Philosophy in Subject Matter Education and works as a Senior lecturer of Swedish, Swedish as A Second Language with a Didactic Perspective at the Faculty of Education and Society, Department of Culture, Language and Media, Malmö University. She is also a legitimized teacher in Swedish, Swedish as A Second Language and English. She is has been a researcher of "Snabbspåret" (the Fast Track) for newly arrived teacher trained immigrants.

Elin Ennerberg holds a PhD in Sociology from Lund University, Sweden where she wrote her dissertation on labour market and integration policy. She currently holds a research position at the Faculty of Education and Society, Department of Society, Culture and Identity, Malmö University, where she researches labour market measures for newly arrived teachers.

Jana Arnold obtained her Master of Education degree from the University of Münster, Germany. Her Master thesis investigated the multilingualism-education nexus. She worked as a language Assistant at the University Pablo de Olavide in Seville for the German Academic Exchange Service and currently works as a teacher at a European high school in Düsseldorf.

Open Access This chapter is licensed under the terms of the Creative Commons Attribution 4.0 International License (http://creativecommons.org/licenses/by/4.0/), which permits use, sharing, adaptation, distribution and reproduction in any medium or format, as long as you give appropriate credit to the original author(s) and the source, provide a link to the Creative Commons license and indicate if changes were made.

The images or other third party material in this chapter are included in the chapter's Creative Commons license, unless indicated otherwise in a credit line to the material. If material is not included in the chapter's Creative Commons license and your intended use is not permitted by statutory regulation or exceeds the permitted use, you will need to obtain permission directly from the copyright holder.

Chapter 6
"After Building Relationships, Language Is No Longer a Barrier": Two Bilingual Mathematics Teachers' Growth Through Student Teaching Experiences

Ji Yeong I and EunJin (E. J.) Bahng

Abstract We followed the journeys of two bilingual mathematics teachers during their student teaching experiences. Both bilingual teachers initially expressed the high anxiety they experienced when speaking English as a Second Language speakers during their student teaching. As they interacted with supportive co-operating teachers, along with culturally and linguistically diverse students, both teachers showed how they underwent a crucial shift in their thinking from deficit views to asset-rich views in terms of their own cultural and linguistic identities. The results of this case study suggest that teacher preparation programs should integrate ways of supporting bilingual teachers to help foster a positive cultural identity and to bring enriching linguistic backgrounds into future classrooms.

Introduction

In the U.S., among all public school teachers during the 2015–2016 school year, only 9%, 7%, and 2% were Latinx, Black, and Asian teachers, respectively (Taie & Goldring, 2017), which is clearly disproportionate to students' populations, which are 15% Black, 27% Latinx, and 6% Asian/Pacific Islander (National Center for Education Statistics, 2017). Additionally, there has been a consistent shortage of bilingual or multilingual teachers in K-12 classes (Hollins & Guzman, 2005). This stubborn shortage of bilingual/multilingual teachers from diverse backgrounds is highly discrepant with respect to the student population in the U.S. In fact, according to the National Center for Education Statistics (2017), multicultural students comprise more than 50% of the U.S. school population, including 10% of Emergent Bilinguals (EB; a.k.a. English language learners) in 2014. Indeed, it has been noted

J. Yeong I (✉) · E. (E. J.) Bahng
Iowa State University, Ames, IA, USA
e-mail: jiyeongi@iastate.edu

© The Author(s) 2023
M. Gutman et al. (eds.), *To Be a Minority Teacher in a Foreign Culture*,
https://doi.org/10.1007/978-3-031-25584-7_6

that "this mismatch is seen as problematic for the learner and for the teacher as navigating cultural and linguistic diversity is complex" (Guerra et al., 2014, p. 78).

Teachers from marginalized groups often leave their teaching careers due to the feelings of inadequacy (Clark & Flores, 2001). The complexities involving the rapid change of student demographics, combined with a shortage of bilingual teachers in all subject areas, suggest the need for an in-depth analysis of diverse teacher candidates to identify their needs and challenges in teacher preparation programs. However, little is known about the experiences of and supports put in place for bilingual teacher candidates whose native language is not English, especially during their field experience when they interact with students with whom they may or may not share similar cultural or racial backgrounds.

This study aims to examine the unique challenges linguistically and culturally diverse teacher candidates encounter while teaching within U.S. public schools and seeks ways to support the development of their cultural identity as a teacher in a view of sociocultural approach (Moschkovich, 2002). The sociocultural view allows us to see teacher education as a space of teacher identity development and learning as a sociocultural construction (Clarke, 2008; Morgan, 2004). We pursue these goals by following two bilingual preservice teachers during their one-semester student teaching period. The research questions that drove this research are (1) what challenges and supports do Asian and Latina bilingual mathematics teacher candidates experience during their student teaching? and (2) how do they develop their cultural identities as teachers through their student teaching experience that is paired with mentoring from their university advisor?

Theoretical Perspectives

Research supports the importance of teachers from ethnically minoritized groups as role models for diverse student populations (Zirkel, 2002). Moreover, equitable ethnic representation and distribution among teachers in school have a positive impact on student achievement (Meier et al., 1999). However, teacher shortages exist in areas critical to minoritized students' success, specifically in bilingual education, special education, mathematics and science education (Flores et al., 2007).

Among teachers of color, the shortage of Asian American teachers has not drawn much attention because of the model minority myth—the pervasive belief that Asian Americans academically excel, especially in mathematics (Kim & Cooc, 2020). A few studies focused on Asian American students found that these students are not uniformly doing well, and doing well does not necessarily mean well-being (e.g., Ng et al., 2007; Wing, 2007). To undermine the model minority myth, which is often used to reinforce the narratives of White Supremacy, and to rethink Asian American students' achievement and well-being, it is crucial to recruit and retain Asian American teachers.

In fact, the recent review of Kim and Cooc (2020) on Asian American Pacific Islander (AAPI) teachers emphasizes the important role they play in education by indicating four reflective areas that have emerged from AAPI teachers' practices and contributions: (1) challenging the curriculum and developing students' critical consciousness of Eurocentrism, (2) engaging with diverse youth, (3) valuing students' cultures, and (4) drawing on a shared background. Specifically, in Subedi's (2008) study, an Indian teacher transformed and transcended her own experiences of being treated as a foreigner into her desire to intervene and challenge her students' verbal practices of using prejudicial comments and excluding their peers. Similarly, Rodriguez and Cho (2011) described a Korean American teacher who drew from her background as a language learner to support bilingual students in the complex challenges of heritage language learning and identity building. Both Asian immigrant teachers self-reflected and incorporated their own experiences of being racialized into their teaching practices.

Latinx teachers are another group that is evidently disproportionly lacking representation in the classroom compared to the student population. Despite the high demand for Spanish-English bilingual teachers, a study about Latinx teacher identity found Latinx teachers often remained silent, distanced themselves, or internalized the values and perspectives of the school and its teachers to navigate school discourse (Aguilar et al., 2003). To ensure success of Latinx teacher recruitment, Calderón and Díaz (1993) have made the following recommendations: (a) early recruitment; (b) a well-defined support structure; (c) field-based experiences with mentor teachers; and (d) a support system for novice teachers.

This study draws from a sociocultural approach to understand how two bilingual teacher candidates of color see themselves as mathematics teachers of quality while also being aware of their cultural identity in practice. From this sociocultural perspective, learning is a situated process that occurs through social interaction, negotiation, and collaboration. For instance, teacher identity can be developed through various levels of complex and continued learning processes that involve the self, family, community, and school (Miller-Marsh, 2002). The identity of culturally and linguistically diverse teachers is even more complex partially due to their multiple social and political identities.

Research has shown that teachers of color often define their personal experiences within a cultural framework, drawing on family and community values, and expressing deeper cultural consciousness (e.g., Clark & Flores, 2001; Galindo, 1996). Galindo (1996) referred to this practice as a "bridging identity," whereby teachers of color draw from their cultural experiences to inform their view of the role and purpose of schooling. The awareness and development of teachers' cultural identity is important because cultural factors may shape teacher decision-making in instruction (Evans, 1989). Furthermore, the cultural biographies embodied by teachers of color lead them to counter the rigid and standardized curriculum being enforced in public schools (Apple, 1992). To conclude, we focus on cultural identity, defined as "significant way(s) in which a person is defined or defines oneself as connected to culture" (Berry & Candis, 2013, p. 45). We also emphasize the importance of cultural identity because it interrelates with one's self-concept, which indicates how an individual sees or values themselves (Clark & Flores, 2001).

Context and Methods

This study was initiated when two mathematics teacher candidates (MJ and Ana, both pseudonyms) approached the first author and disclosed their fears and concerns about teaching native-English speaking students as non-native English speakers themselves. To support their growth as educators, we followed and shadowed their student-teaching journeys, observed what challenges they faced, and how they coped with these challenges. The student teaching course was a semester-long and lasted for 16 weeks at one school site. Specifically, during the student teaching period, the first author mentored them both formally (once a month, face-to-face) and informally (e.g., texting, emails). The mentoring sessions were audio-recorded and later analyzed, along with the second author, through multiple compare-contrast discussion sessions focused on the individually coded themes that emerged.

MJ was an Asian international student (she came to the U.S. several years after graduating from college) and a mother of two elementary-age daughters. When MJ started her teacher preparation program, pursuing a secondary mathematics license, she already had a master's degree in statistics. English was her second language, and Korean was both her native and home language. She often shared her anxiety about speaking English in a classroom full of native English speakers, even before she started student teaching. For this reason, she chose to complete her student teaching at a high school embedded within a large metropolitan area that has a racially and linguistically diverse student population.

Ana's family moved from Mexico to California when she was in middle school. At that time, she was identified as an ELL [EB] by her school district. She then majored in mathematics at a four-year college and moved to a small city in the Midwest to enroll into a teacher preparation program where she could also earn her master's degree. Ana's prior teaching experiences before entering the teacher preparation program included working with middle and high school students at a public high school and a private institution in California. Before starting student teaching, she also shared her anxiety related to teaching native English speakers because she had a traumatic encounter during her tutoring experience when high school students laughed at her accent, and the classroom teacher did not chime in to support her. Moreover, while completing her teacher preparation program, she failed the practicum course (a pre-student teaching field experience course that requires class observations and a few assignments of classroom teaching) in which she did not feel connected to the cooperating teachers and the students in the White-dominant rural school where she completed the course.

We focused on student teaching because this is when teacher candidates are first immersed into full-day teaching and face the realities of the classrooms before they develop the practical skills and knowledge needed to handle such real situations. We developed a storyline for each of their student teaching experiences based on the monthly mentoring sessions. The monthly meeting sessions between the first author and MJ were conducted through online conference calls and were video recorded because MJ's student teaching site was out of state. The meetings with Ana were audio recorded because her school site was in town, so she could attend the meetings in person.

We listened and watched the collected data several times and spent at least 12 h in our iterative compare-contrast data analysis sessions. First, when reviewing the two bilingual teacher candidates' stories, we identified three phases: the beginning phase, the middle phase, and the ending phase. Consequently, each phase within MJ's and Ana's stories were analyzed using three analytical dimensions: (a) Anticipation (what concerns they had beforehand), (b) Challenges (what difficulties they encountered), and (c) Navigation (how they responded to and grew from the challenges). Each of their storylines was sent to the corresponding bilingual student teacher for member check (Creswell, 1994). The finalized stories are provided below, each written in chronical order to emphasize their growth as their student-teaching journey evolved.

Research Findings

MJ's Story

MJ's student teaching site was at a 9th grade-only high school whose population breakdown was as follows: approximately 88% Hispanic students, 77% at-risk students, 92% economically disadvantaged students, and 27% Emergent Bilinguals (EBs). At her school, Black teachers (42%) and White teachers (36%) were the most dominant groups, and there were no Asian teachers. Her cooperating teacher was a White male who was bilingual in English and Spanish. Most students spoke Spanish, and they translated each other's sayings and ideas between Spanish to English.

The Beginning Phase

Since MJ and many of her students were not native English speakers, sometimes it became difficult to communicate in English. However, she pointed out how she felt more comfortable working with them than with students who were native English speakers, as she explains in the following excerpt from her first interview:

> Teaching is fine… but interact[ing with students] is challenging, not only English is a problem… Yes. English *is* the problem. When I watched the cooperating teacher, he created a good atmosphere by making a joke… this kind of thing [having casual conversations with students] is more difficult than teaching.

As for teaching, she disclosed her disagreement with the teaching practices used at the school because neither the school professional learning community (PLC) nor her cooperating teacher incorporated problem-solving aspects into the lessons, but instead implemented a traditional lecture-style teaching approach. In the beginning of her student teaching, MJ's ideas and suggestions regarding the use of problem-solving aspects/approaches were not seriously considered and often went ignored. The following excerpt sheds light onto how her ideas were rejected:

> I wanted to make my lesson fun, but my co-op teacher just seeks a handout. I think they [the school math teachers] don't have experience with problem solving. I wanted to use problem solving/activit[ies] and student presentation[s], but it's hard here.

The cooperating teacher, however, was supportive and confident in MJ's level of English proficiency. For example, when MJ shared her high anxiety and concerns about her English, the cooperating teacher encouraged her by explaining that her English is okay for teaching and communication, and he even suggested that she think about how to immediately provide appropriate responses to her students.

To complement her English-speaking skills, MJ practiced pronouncing her students' names by recording the school's Spanish teacher's pronunciation. She understood how frustrated the students were when someone would pronounce their names incorrectly since she often experienced this as well. Moreover, MJ shared her discomfort concerning students giggling when she spoke English. At first, she thought they were making fun of her English. Later, though, she decided to ask the students why they were giggling and discovered the giggles were not directed toward her. MJ felt that she was gradually overcoming her *English anxiety* while also resolving her cognitive biases, such as the one described above. Her cooperating teacher also provided her with practical advice, such as writing any key words on the board, especially when she struggled to pronounce them, and spelling out words rather than using acronyms.

Although MJ liked the united environment and appreciated how teachers cared about her, she sometimes felt that having a conversation amongst these members was still difficult because she could not understand some of the teachers' jokes, and even when she did understand some of them, MJ was not sure how to respond in a culturally appropriate way. As a result, she had no choice but to cultivate a mainly official and professional relationship with other members of the teaching staff since it was hard for her to have personal conversations.

The Middle Phase

Despite MJ's effort to speak clearly, the act of questioning or responding to questions in English remained to be a challenge for her. She did say, though, that "it's getting better", as she describes below:

> My students are getting familiar with my [accent]. After building a relationship, I think English is not a problem. My co-op teacher said, English is not a problem in teaching. I know I still have flaws in my English pronunciation, but there are many EBs in my classes, anyway. Now [the] relationship has been built, so they [students] can ask me multiple times [when they do not understand what I say].

Her strategies to interact and build a relationship with her students had improved, as her excitement concerning the forging of these new connections is clearly present in the following statement:

> I realized showing interest and caring is important. When students were absent, I asked why you were absent and showed how I cared about their personal life. Absence is common in this school, I said to them I missed you, and then talked with them using cheering comments. I first thought students might ignore me, but it worked!

She also shared her success stories about her teaching. When she explained what a slope was using the English word, *steep*, she soon realized many students were not familiar with this word. She looked up the corresponding Spanish word and applied it to the lesson, then students understood. Her cooperating teacher supported her idea to use Spanish as a tool to both learn English and teach mathematics, and she noticed that her students liked when she incorporated the use of their first language.

MJ again confirmed that her bonding with the school's teachers was improving and now she felt as if she was part of the community because the teachers and school staff started to share informal and personal information with her. One significant change noted during this time was that MJ started to openly express and share her cultural identity as both a foreign and Asian teacher in both positive and negative ways. It was interesting because she only shared her anxiety regarding her lack of English proficiency at the beginning of her student teaching during her interviews. Now, she found that she could use her racial and cultural identity as a way to build relationships with students who share the same or similar racial backgrounds. For example, one girl from Nepal approached MJ and expressed how hard she was trying to be successful in her class, and MJ noticed how this student opened up to her with ease. However, there were still some concerns with being a foreign teacher that MJ self-identified. During her interviews, she often said, "There are problems [with being] a foreign teacher" regarding the relationships she cultivated with both her colleagues and students, which she describes further in the following excerpt:

> One good thing about being a foreign teacher is that students think I am different. They see me as friendly. There is another new teacher, a White female, but workers here are mostly Hispanic and they are friendlier to me than her. … I have stress about language, though. I need to watch YouTube videos and other online sources to memorize English expressions. I have to do an additional study that other teachers don't have to do.

Because she felt she needed to work more and harder as a foreign teacher, her coping strategies even included her dress code. The other student teacher at the school wore an attire to school that was somewhat casual, but MJ felt she needed to wear a formal attire because she was a foreigner, so she wanted to complement her "handicap" (as mentioned by her) by dressing professionally.

At the same time, MJ started noticing that she had an advantage when it came to developing an awareness of EBs' learning experiences. She found that she could easily identify effective strategies for EBs that her cooperating teacher tended not to notice. For example, when they used a video in class, MJ thought turning on the Spanish captions would be helpful, but the cooperating teacher had not thought of this as a needed support. In addition, she could create quality language objectives that the school required for all teachers to write on the board. Her well-written language objectives garnered the attention of other teachers who would come over to see her objectives.

The Ending Phase

Towards the end of her student teaching, MJ revealed that disciplining students was the most challenging task she faced as a student teacher. In the beginning, she did not know what to say when behavior problems occurred: "I thought it's because I was inexperienced, but there was some language issue[s,] too." MJ struggled to address students' misbehavior because she could not think of an appropriate response *immediately*. Consequently, she tried to memorize what her cooperating teacher said in response to these kinds of discipline-related situations.

With her expanding emphatic approach to students, MJ started to see how the students were not supported appropriately by other teachers and pointed out the following:

> Teachers work hard but don't care about students' lives. I saw patterns, students laying down and disappearing. I asked why and students explained to me their reasons. When I talked to my co-op teacher, he was surprised that I cared about this. … I think listening to students is worthwhile because I can build a good relationship and because of this, when I had observation [from the student teaching supervisor], my students were cooperating very well. One boy directly told me he would do well for my observation.

MJ felt that having a student ally could be a sign of success in building a positive relationship with her students, especially with those who struggled because of family-related and/or personal reasons. She believed that the trusting relationship she had built with her students was fostered due to her conscious efforts in genuinely caring about her students' lives outside of school. MJ also discovered that her status as a non-native English speaker was valuable as it encouraged the EBs in her class to speak more. When her cooperating teacher—a native English speaker—asked them to express their thinking, they were reluctant to respond or did not answer. However, when MJ encouraged these same EBs to speak or make a presentation in class, they usually responded well to her questions and directions.

At the end of her student teaching, MJ reflected on her student teaching experience by comparing the classroom to what she experienced during her practicum (a mandatory four-week field experience before student teaching):

> In that White school [MJ's assigned practicum site], students didn't ask [for] help and didn't show their work and didn't say hi… To be honest, no single student asked me for help. Here [MJ's student teaching site], they [the students] asked me for help so much and talked to me. I tried very hard there [at the practicum site], but the teacher simply wrote I have a language problem on the report [without any support]. I think I did really well in teaching and prepared a lot, but I got this comment and it was shocking to me. But here, all teachers said English is not a big problem. I earned confidence here. I want to go diverse schools where they need me.

Ana's Story

While she was repeating the practicum course at different school sites, Ana learned the importance of "asking for help and having a conversation with a cooperating teacher in the areas that she needed help." She expressed later that she had been uncomfortable to ask others to help her because she thought this action might make others underestimate her abilities as an educator. With this mindset, Ana started her student teaching at a middle school in a small rural town with a high Hispanic population. This school district runs a Spanish bilingual program, which provides several Spanish-only classes, including Spanish mathematics classes, until the 6th grade.

The Beginning Phase

During Ana's first visit, her cooperating teacher, who was White male, was teaching the last part of his mathematics class. While she was observing his teaching, Ana brightened up thinking, "*Oh, I like this teacher,*" as she could tell that he would be open and flexible. In line with her expectations, her cooperating teacher did treat her as a trustworthy colleague and valued her bilingualism as her asset rather than a deficit, which she highlights in the following excerpt:

> He always gave me an opportunity to see his lesson PowerPoint or lesson plans and let me make changes to whatever I want. I don't know, I felt like we know each other for a longer period of time. He's always talks about his likes/family [with] me, something outside the classroom. I feel that is a connection because we don't talk only about school, but about my personal life, too. That makes a good relationship. I have a good teacher.

At this time, Ana's biggest anxiety was classroom management. She had a similar concern as MJ, worrying that she might "not be able to say the right words about the behavior on the spot." Her cooperating teacher encouraged her to give disciplining her students a try because she would never know how students would react to her classroom management style unless she tried to develop one. It was noticeable when Ana discovered that her ability to speak Spanish helped with her classroom management, as well as when she realized she could express her identity more authentically when she utilized her first language:

> I spoke to them [Latino students] in Spanish. It worked better than when I spoke English. When I speak Spanish, it's more me. I wish when I speak English it's me, too, but I'm working on it. When speaking Spanish, I can say so [many] more things. I talked to them in Spanish and they listened and worked. I feel that if I did the same to other students in English, I couldn't have the same impact. I can use more words with more inspiration in Spanish, but in English I feel limited in my vocabulary. When I speak Spanish, it's [the] real me.

Ana's own experience as an EB helped her guide the bilingual students in the class. For example, although the students understood English, they responded in Spanish, and Ana said this was what she would do when she was a young EB herself.

The cooperating teacher expressed his support by saying "if it's more comfortable, let them speak Spanish and focus on understanding math concepts." Ana also had enough confidence to be transparent about her English skills. For example, when Ana introduced herself to the students, she explained that English is not her first language, so they should feel free to ask her to repeat anything she said if they did not understand. Indeed, at times, some students approached her and asked her to repeat what she had said. Ana revealed her amusement about this, explaining, "I liked that. It didn't make me feel bad but good because it means I am building a relationship with them!"

Because Ana thought her cooperating teacher was an exemplary teacher, she carefully observed every action and comment he made when he was working with his students. After a month of observation, she realized a misconception she previously had and learned how important building relationships is to the teaching of her students, which she reveals in the following comment:

> I felt that the students have more respect towards my cooperating teacher, not because he's male, but because they've established a relationship. Sometimes some students told me "thank you", and I do think that if I don't have a close relationship with other students [, it's] because we haven't spent enough time to build a relationship. I don't think it's because of gender, but in practicum, I thought the gender was the issue, but now… there's many students making connections with me.

During her practicum, she thought the students did not approach her because they did not trust her mathematical ability due to the stereotypes attached to her gender and race. Ana finally found that building a strong relationship is the key to receiving respect from students and not her gender or racial backgrounds.

The Middle Phase

In the middle of the semester, Ana said she "noticed so much improvement" in her teaching and classroom management. This reflection on her improvement was based on the strengthening of her relationships with her cooperating teacher and her students. She now realized her bilingualism and gender can be an asset that supports her teaching and the connections she builds with students, which she explains further in the following excerpt:

> With those two EB students, I can see they trust me. I can see that it's complicated because their teacher doesn't speak Spanish. I can see explaining in Spanish is a big connection, and another connection is I'm female, so other female students can make connections with me. …. I can see that the students talk to me about their home, friends and their ethnicity. Most students are Spanish speakers, so we make conversations about anything. It's interesting to see that.

In addition to building a relationship with her students, Ana found that her attitude related to her students asking questions had changed since the beginning. She initially felt that the students treated her as if she did not know mathematics well or how to solve mathematics problems, but after they interacted with her and asked her about mathematics, they began to see and trust her as a mathematics teacher. She even strategically did not give explanations, not because she did not know the answer, but because she wanted her students to find their own solutions. "I can see students trust me", she said, explaining that "if something went wrong, if I make mistakes, they tell me and show me the mistake. It's a good feeling because I [now] have a good connection with my students."

The Ending Phase

Around the end of her student teaching semester, Ana set goals to refine her English in order to improve her classroom management skills, which was the most challenging aspect of teaching for her, as she describes below:

> Sometimes when I talk to students, I feel I use the same words all the time, I can't find other words, so I'm trying to work on expanding my vocabulary. They [my words] need to be respectful, especially on the spot. Sometimes, I think ahead, but when it actually happens... My teacher does a great job [with] that. He said it's experience [rather than language]. This is your actual first experience working with students daily, so it's okay.

Again, Ana thought her English was a "problem", but her cooperating teacher said, "it's okay" and reassured her that she would be doing well when she had gained enough experience. He did not see Ana's English as a deficit. Rather, he treated it as something she can improve on with experience. Ana appreciated his view related to her challenge and revealed that she trusted her cooperating teacher, saying, "Sometimes, I said how I'm feeling [about my lack of vocabulary]. He said it's [about] years of experience, and he had that feeling, too... He didn't say you need to work on your English. I really appreciate [that] he didn't say it."

As a final remark, Ana shared her wish to work at a school with a diverse student population, noting, "No matter what school, I can make [an] impact, but I feel that for diverse schools, those connections will be [at a] greater scale with those students."

Discussion, Conclusions and Implications

The two bilingual teacher candidates in this study shared a common anxiety, as well as similar challenges and patterns of navigation. Both had high anxiety related to teaching in English within English-only classrooms but gradually found that their racial, cultural, and linguistic diversities could be used as (1) assets in their teaching practices, (2) assets in their efforts to interact with students, and finally (3) assets in the formation of positive cultural identities, which ultimately looped back to empower them.

Moreover, the two teachers' cultural identities seem to play a crucial role. Our findings agree with Clark and Flores (2001)'s study that stresses the role of identities and experiences as marginalized people "become central to how they define and comport themselves with others in their occupation" (p. 74). For instance, MJ and Ana showed significant changes in noticing and verifying the embedded strengths in their own cultural identities and then translating them into their teaching practice. Consequently, these changes-in-practice led the two teachers to build positive self-images as bilingual teachers.

Specifically, in the beginning, they perceived their cultural, racial, and linguistic identities to be deficit, despite their high content knowledge in mathematics, because they thought their ethnic and linguistic status might make them look unqualified as teachers. Then, overtime they began to see how their backgrounds could become cultural, social, and navigating capitals when making connections with diverse students, and even when gaining and building relationships even with students who displayed behavioral problems. To sum up, both MJ and Ana shifted their perceptions regarding their cultural identities from a deficit-based view to an asset-rich view that asserts bilingualism, biliteracy, and biculturalism can be forms of cultural capital or cultural wealth.

This study suggests that the teacher candidates of color were influenced by meaningful others, especially cooperating teachers and students. How their cooperating teachers and students treated them as qualified teachers seemed to make a significant impact on their identity development. For instance, the two co-operating teachers in this study actively supported the bilingual student teachers with their asset-rich views, regardless of any differences in race and gender. Both MJ and Ana voiced that their co-operating teachers' support was crucial, and their student teaching experiences were further maximized when they were placed at diverse schools. Therefore, deliberate care should be taken during both the student-teaching placement process and training to build generative relationships among all participants involved.

Our results shed light on the importance of design field experiences that support bilingual teachers of color for developing positive identity that empowers them. Teacher education programs should include the fostering and enhancement of positive cultural identity development of its teachers. We suggest that teacher education programs, which rarely recognize the critical roles that bilingual teachers play in the U.S. education system, should include a training component for promote a positive cultural identity that will guide the people involved in teacher education, such as program administrators, supervisors, and co-operating teachers, in how to best promote a positive cultural identity amongst student teachers.

González's study (1997) found that satisfaction, retention, and completion of the teaching program of teacher candidates from minoritized groups was deeply related to (1) academic support and skill development, (2) caring mentors and a supportive network, (3) nurturing environment, (4) cohort design, (5) setting of educational goals, (6) volunteer work, (7) high academic standards, and (8) mediators for navigating and accessing university structure. We advocate a teaching program that cultivates caring mentors and a supportive network as well as one that promotes nurturing environment for bilingual immigrant teacher candidates. and found the important role of these factors. The findings of this study provide teacher educators with insight into the critical importance of relationship-building when supporting bilingual preservice teachers, especially within content areas such as mathematics.

This case study of two bilingual mathematics teachers will impact future studies about teachers with diverse racial and linguistic backgrounds whose stories are often unheard. We suggest further studies of novice and experienced teachers with nondominant backgrounds, such as teachers of color, immigrant teachers, and non-native speaker teachers in STEM. The studies can investigate how teachers from nondominant groups develop their teacher identities, what obstacles they experience in schools, and what resources and support effectively help them overcome challenges they encounter. This line of study may contribute to increasing the diversity in the teacher population.

References

Aguilar, J. A., MacGillivray, L., & Walker, N. T. (2003). Latina educators and school discourse: Dealing with tension on the path to success. *Journal of Latinos and Education, 2*(2), 89–100. https://doi.org/10.1207/S1532771XJLE0202_3

Apple, M. W. (1992). Do the standards go far enough? Power, policy, and practice in mathematics education. *Journal for Research in Mathematics Education, 23*(5), 412. https://doi.org/10.2307/749562

Berry, T. R., & Candis, M. R. (2013). Cultural identity and education: A critical race perspective. *Educational Foundations, 27*, 43–64.

Calderón, M., & Díaz, E. (1993). Retooling teacher preparation programs to embrace Latino realities in schools. In R. E. Castro & Y. R. Ingle (Eds.), *Reshaping teacher education in the Southwest (A forum: A response to the needs of Latino students and teachers)* (pp. 53–68). Tomás Rivera Center: A National Institute for Policy Studies.

Clark, E. R., & Flores, B. B. (2001). Who am I? The social construction of ethnic identity and self-perceptions in Latino preservice teachers. *The Urban Review, 33*(2), 69–86.

Clarke, M. (2008). *Language teacher identities. Co-constructing discourse and community*. Multilingual Matters.

Creswell, J. W. (1994). *Research design: Qualitative & quantitative approaches*. Sage.

Evans, R. W. (1989). Teacher conceptions of history. *Theory & Research in Social Education, 17*(3), 210–240. https://doi.org/10.1080/00933104.1989.10505590

Flores, B. B., Clark, E. R., Claeys, L., & Villarreal, A. (2007). Academy for teacher excellence: Recruiting, preparing, and retaining Latino teachers through learning communities. *Teacher Education Quarterly, 34*(4), 53–69. JSTOR.

Galindo, R. (1996). Reframing the past in the present: Chicana teacher role identity as a bridging identity. *Education and Urban Society, 29*(1), 85–102.

González, J. M. (1997). Recruiting and training minority teachers: Student views of the preservice program. *Equity & Excellence in Education, 30*(1), 56–64. https://doi.org/10.1080/1066568970300108

Guerra, N., Castro-Villarreal, F., Cheatham, N., & Claeys, L. (2014). Problem identification and task engagement using the LIBRE problem solving tool: A case study of three bilingual teacher candidates. *Journal of Education and Training Studies, 2*(3). https://doi.org/10.11114/jets.v2i3.396

Hollins, E. R., & Guzman, M. T. (2005). Research on preparing teachers for diverse populations. In AERA Panel on Research and Teacher Education, M. Cochran-Smith, & K. M. Zeichner (Eds.), *Studying teacher education: The report of the AERA Panel on Research and Teacher Education* (pp. 477–548). Lawrence Erlbaum Associates.

Kim, G. M., & Cooc, N. (2020). Teaching for social justice: A research synthesis on Asian American and Pacific Islander teachers in U.S. schools. *Teaching and Teacher Education, 94*, 103104. https://doi.org/10.1016/j.tate.2020.103104

Meier, K. J., Wrinkle, R. D., & Polinard, J. L. (1999). Representative bureaucracy and distributional equity: Addressing the hard question. *The Journal of Politics, 61*(4), 1025–1039. https://doi.org/10.2307/2647552

Miller-Marsh, M. (2002). The shaping of Ms. Nicholi: The discursive fashioning of teacher identities. *Qualitative Studies in Education, 15*(3), 333–347.

Morgan, B. (2004). Teacher identity as pedagogy: Towards a field internal conceptualization in bilingual and second language education. *International Journal of Bilingual Education and Bilingualism, 7*(2 & 3), 172–188.

Moschkovich, J. N. (2002). A situated and sociocultural perspective on bilingual mathematics learners. *Mathematical Thinking and Learning, 4*(2 & 3), 189–212.

National Center for Education Statistics. (2017). *Racial/ethnic enrollment in public schools*. https://nces.ed.gov/programs/coe/indicator_cge.asp

Ng, J. C., Lee, S. S., & Pak, Y. K. (2007). Contesting the model minority and perpetual foreigner stereotypes: A critical review of literature on Asian Americans in education. *Review of Research in Education, 31*(1), 95–130. https://doi.org/10.3102/0091732X07300046095

Rodriguez, T. L., & Cho, H. (2011). Eliciting critical literacy narratives of bi/multilingual teacher candidates across U.S. teacher education contexts. *Teaching and Teacher Education, 27*(3), 496–504. https://doi.org/10.1016/j.tate.2010.10.002

Subedi, B. (2008). Fostering critical dialogue across cultural differences: A study of immigrant teachers' interventions in diverse schools. *Theory & Research in Social Education, 36*(4), 413–440. https://doi.org/10.1080/00933104.2008.10473382

Taie, S., & Goldring, R. (2017). *Characteristics of public elementary and secondary school teachers in the United States: Results from the 2015–16 national teacher and principal survey first look (NCES 2017-072)*. National Center for Education Statistics. https://nces.ed.gov/pubsearch/pubsinfo.asp?pubid=2017072

Wing, J. Y. (2007). Beyond Black and White: The model minority myth and the invisibility of Asian American students. *The Urban Review, 39*(4), 455–487. https://doi.org/10.1007/s11256-007-0058-6

Zirkel, S. (2002). Is there a place for me? Role models and achievement among White students and students of color. *Teachers College Record, 104*(2), 357–376.

Ji Yeong I is an Associate Professor in mathematics education at Iowa State University, USA. She holds a master's degree in mathematics and a doctorate degree in mathematics education as well as a Teaching English for Students of Other Language (TESOL). Her research has a clear trajectory to seek an effective mathematical pedagogy for culturally and linguistically diverse learners, especially Emergent bilingual students and preparing teachers to support Emergent Bilinguals in mathematical learning. Her research/community work has been published in national and international journals and presented at both practitioner and research conferences. Before she found her passion for mathematics education research, she taught mathematics and science at middle and high schools in California as a foreign immigrant bilingual teacher.

EunJin (E. J.) Bahng is an associate Professor in the School of Education at Iowa State University, Ames, Iowa, U.S.A. She has worked as a classroom teacher and has backgrounds in both Life Sciences and Educational Technologies. His scholarship involves facilitating the professional development of new and in-service science teachers through a number of different mentoring programs (e.g., online and/or hybrid mentoring programs using virtual worlds).

Open Access This chapter is licensed under the terms of the Creative Commons Attribution 4.0 International License (http://creativecommons.org/licenses/by/4.0/), which permits use, sharing, adaptation, distribution and reproduction in any medium or format, as long as you give appropriate credit to the original author(s) and the source, provide a link to the Creative Commons license and indicate if changes were made.

The images or other third party material in this chapter are included in the chapter's Creative Commons license, unless indicated otherwise in a credit line to the material. If material is not included in the chapter's Creative Commons license and your intended use is not permitted by statutory regulation or exceeds the permitted use, you will need to obtain permission directly from the copyright holder.

Chapter 7
"Crossing the River by Feeling the Stones": Understanding Chinese Minority Teachers' Transnational and Transitional Experiences

Pei-Ying Wu

Abstract This chapter focuses on 6 minority teachers who were raised and trained in China and traveled transnationally to the U.S. as non-immigrants on J-1 Visas which allowed them to teach in the U.S. for up to 5 years. The central theme of the chapter is that teaching in a foreign culture is analogous to crossing a river by feeling the stones. The great differences between Chinese and American cultures and educational traditions presented unique challenges to these minority teachers. Such differences, especially those in conflict with their original professional norms, demanded that the minority teachers observe and imitate what other American teachers do, explore and test the new norms in their classrooms, and wrestle with and possibly adjust their habitual pedagogy to better meet the foreign culture's expectations. As part of a larger study, this present chapter utilizes interview data collected from six Chinese teachers during their first or second year in U.S. public elementary schools. The findings illustrate a number of shared personal and professional challenges encountered by newly-arrived minority teachers in their initial transitions to life and work in the U.S. The challenges include the unfamiliarity with U.S. public schools, inadequate teaching materials, a heavy teaching load, and other teaching-related issues.

Introduction

The effect of globalization in conjunction with the trend of teacher migration created a unique set of circumstances for studying minority teachers. With such a backdrop, this present chapter focuses on six Chinese minority teachers with the purpose of exploring their transnational and transitional experiences during their early years in the U.S. public elementary schools.

P.-Y. Wu (✉)
California State University, Fresno, CA, USA
e-mail: peiwu@mail.fresnostate.edu

In an increasingly globalized world where the flow of information, capital, and people across national borders is without limits, exchanges across cultures are accelerated. One form of exchange is teacher migration around the world. Twenty-first century technological advancements have made it easier for national governments to seek teachers beyond the confines of the nation-state. Assisted by new technologies, school districts in the U.S. have begun to recruit overseas-trained educators for reasons of diversifying the teaching force and solving some teacher shortage problems.

Since the beginning of the twenty-first century, foreign teacher recruitment increased dramatically. During 2000–2010, more than 100,000 oversea-trained international teachers were sought by U.S. schools (Bartlett, 2014). These teachers are being hired to teach different content areas, usually serving the needs of foreign language education (Fee, 2011). The continued acceleration of teacher migration to the U.S. can be attributed to several "push and pull" factors. Within the U.S., growing teacher shortages in the public school system have become the primary factor that draws international teachers into the U.S. (American Federation of Teachers (AFT), 2009; Hutchison, 2005). Qualified international educators who can teach academic subjects in addition to foreign languages and with the potential to play roles as cultural ambassadors, seem destined to become ideal transnational teacher candidates. Other advantages, such as their strong work ethic and the opportunity to diversify the teaching force, contribute to the view of international teachers as an asset to U.S. schools (Cook, 2000). From the perspective of the teachers, those from relatively poor or less industrialized countries may seek opportunities to migrate to the U.S. in order to obtain higher salaries and better living conditions. Others may simply want to experience American culture or improve their English (Cook, 2000; Hutchison, 2005). Yet another contributing factor to this growing number of transnational teachers is the experience of value-added international teaching that will benefit those who return home.

Although the purported reason for international teachers to come to the U.S. is to teach, this paper is premised on the belief that, as they teach, they also acquire knowledge about education in the U.S. which may call their previously held pedagogical beliefs and practices into question. Based on this premise, this paper seeks to illustrate the challenges minority Chinese teachers encountered when teaching students in another socio-cultural context.

Literature Review and Research Objective

Teaching is a culturally constructed activity and involves complex mental and behavioral processes. Any alteration of circumstances in teaching can bring challenges to teachers or require them to change those processes. Given the fact that this study's participants experienced major changes and adjustments in their teaching careers, a relevant review of literature that provides information related to challenges of teaching in different contexts is conducted.

So far, research that addresses the issues emerging in the transnational contexts of migration largely pertains to children or families (Moskal, 2015; Moskal & Sime, 2015; Suárez-Orozco & Suárez-Orozco, 2013). There is a general lack of empirical research on transnational teachers. However, four that particularly pertain to this study are: Bailey's (2013) phenomenological study on eight Jamaican immigrant teachers in the New York City Schools; Dunn's (2013) qualitative case study on four Indian teachers' transnational teaching experiences (one in middle school and three in high schools); Finney et al.'s (2002) work on Spanish exchange teachers in South Carolina public schools; and Hutchinson's (2005) book about international teachers at a private school in the South. Although some news reports and journal articles address issues about recruiting foreign teachers overseas, this is still "an underexplored territory" (Smith, 2009, p. 111). Furthermore, no study has selected newly recruited transnational teachers from China as subjects and examined their early teaching experiences in U.S. public elementary schools.

Challenges of Teaching in Transnational Contexts

Literature has shown that transnational teachers are likely to experience different practical challenges related to educational issues from culture shock to language barriers, which all increase the level of difficulty for them during their induction years. Within the classroom context, Huang (2009) illustrated three areas of culture shock that Chinese graduate students are likely to experience: different classroom teaching styles, different student-teacher relationships, and different teacher expectations. Although Huang did not focus on transnational teachers, her study of Chinese adults' experiences in U.S. schools reveals some fundamental differences between Chinese and U.S. culture. These kinds of differences may also generate Chinese transnational teachers' discomfort and disorientation when they bring such different educational perspectives to U.S. classrooms. The language barriers may become another source of frustration if it impedes transnational teachers from communicating clearly and effectively with school principals, American colleagues, parents and other stakeholders within the school community.

Finally, so-called "pedagogical shock" (Hutchison, 2005, p. 24) is usually the most direct challenge to their teaching careers in the United States. This means not being familiar with policies, expectations, operations and procedures concerning ordering supplies, school duties, paperwork, interaction with parents and students, classroom management strategies and discipline referral systems, academic standards and curriculum, teaching styles and methods, and assessment methods and grading systems (Cook, 2000; Dunn, 2011, 2013; Finney et al., 2002; Hutchison, 2005). Overall, the lack of preparation for U.S. schools that may contribute to transnational teachers' struggles during their induction years and likely impedes their success in U.S. schools.

As evidenced from the literature reviewed above, teaching in a foreign culture is analogous to crossing a river without proper equipment or prior experience. Feeling your way across a river just using your feet is unnerving. Given the great differences between Chinese and American cultures and educational traditions, the American educational context presents challenges to minority teachers from China. Such challenges, especially those in conflict with their original professional norms, demand that the minority teachers observe and imitate what other American teachers do, explore and test the new norms in their classrooms, and wrestle with and possibly adjust their habitual pedagogy to better meet the foreign culture's expectations. This article seeks to address the following question: What experiences did the six Chinese minority teachers have in their initial transition to the new life and career in the U.S.?

Context of Research

The present chapter is part of a larger study that was situated in a broader context of a rapid globalization of education and the rapid popularity of learning Mandarin in the United States. The "expansion boom" of Mandarin Chinese immersion programs in the U.S. began in 2007 due to the rising power of China. The growth rate of U.S. Mandarin immersion programs from 2007 to 2014 was 336% (Weise, 2014). An initiative announced by former President Obama in 2015, called "1 Million Strong" aimed to increase the total number of stateside learners of Mandarin Chinese from approximately 200,000–1 million by the year 2020 (Allen-Ebrahimian, 2015; Billings, 2015). This initiative was a compelling illustration of the relationship between U.S. global politics and the practices in foreign language education.

Although the Trump administration's restriction on immigrant visas makes it harder for schools to hire and retain qualified international teachers, the popularity of learning Mandarin in many U.S. schools and the demand for native Chinese teachers are still evident. The current restrictions are exacerbating a predicament not only for schools but also for teachers who already face difficult transitional issues and now have to consider their long-term employment possibilities. This educational direction and socio-political attitude create an opportunity to better understand a myriad of challenges that the minority teachers face inside and outside school.

The original study took place in a southeastern state that has been experiencing rapid growth in its Chinese population and equally rapid growth in the number of Chinese Mandarin language programs. Consistent with state aims to produce globally competitive graduates, over 100 dual language immersion programs have been offered across the state (State Board of Education, 2016). Private agencies assist such schools in recruiting, training and assisting transnational teachers with placement-related activities, generally for fees ranging from $11,000–$12,500 per teacher. The provision of post-arrival orientation that addresses cultural, logistical, and teaching issues is also provided by recruitment agencies. In this chapter the focus is on six minority teachers who were raised and trained in China and were recruited to the U.S. on J-1 Visas to teach for up to 5 years. After 5 years, they were required to go back to their home country and stay for at least 2 years. They were employed across four public elementary schools (Table 7.1).

Table 7.1 The host schools demographic profiles of four elementary schools with Chinese immersion programs

School name	Miller elementary	Arnold elementary	Central elementary	Thomas elementary
Geographic status of the school[a]	Rural-fringe[c]	Rural-fringe	Rural-distant[d]	City-large[e]
Title I school	No	No	Yes	Yes
Grades	K-5	PK-5	PK-5	K-5
Size of the school (no. of students)	1128	608	691	532
Cultural diversity	White 54% Asian 19% Hispanic 6% Black 16% Other 5%	White 73% Asian 16% Hispanic 3% Black 4% Other 4%	White 37% Asian 3% Hispanic 14% Black 40% Other 6%	White 31% Asian 4% Hispanic 24% Black 36% Other 5%
Average class size(K-3)	21	19	21	21
Chinese immersion program[b]				
Years of implementation	1	4	3	2
No. of classes at each grade	K:2 1st:2	K:1 1st:1 2nd:1 3rd: 1	K:2 1st:2 2nd:2	K:2 1st:1
Transnational Chinese teachers as % of classroom teachers	5%	15%	20%	13%

[a]Based on a southeastern state's locale code file
[b]At the time of this study
[c]Rural, Fringe: Census-defined rural territory that is less than or equal to 5 miles from an urbanized area, as well as rural territory that is less than or equal to 2.5 miles from an urban cluster (Phan & Glander, 2008)
[d]Rural, Distant: Census-defined rural territory that is more than 5 miles but less than or equal to 25 miles from an urbanized area, as well as rural territory that is more than 2.5 miles but less than or equal to 10 miles from an urban cluster
[e]City, Large: Territory inside an urbanized area and inside a principal city with population of 250,000 or more

Miller Elementary School Miller Elementary is the largest school in this study and is located in the smallest school district in this study. Its students come from a wealthy neighborhood that is close to (less than or equal to 5 miles) an urbanized area in the state and over half of them are white. In the fall of 2015–2016 school year, Miller Elementary launched a Chinese language immersion program in both kindergarten and first grade. It had two classes per grade level (4 Mandarin classes in total) and the school initially hired four Chinese teachers (1 Chinese teacher per class). Miller Elementary was the only school not to adopt the co-teaching model.[1] According to the program overview posted on the school website, the decision of launching this program seemed to be based on the benefits of language immersion

---

[1]Chinese immersion programs that have two Chinese teachers—one lead teacher and one co-teacher—and the co-teaching pair might divide the instructional content into parts or by subject.

education, which include "increase[ing] cognitive skills, higher achievement in other academic areas and higher standardized test scores".

Arnold Elementary School Arnold Elementary is half the size of Miller Elementary with the highest percentage of white students in this study. It is in the wealthiest school district in this study and also in a wealthy neighborhood that is close to (less than or equal to 5 miles) an urbanized area in the state. The Chinese immersion program began in 2012 with one kindergarten class. One grade level was added each year as the students matriculated. As of 2015–2016, there were four lead teachers and two co-teachers in the K-3rd grade Chinese immersion programs. One co-teacher supported instruction in the kindergarten and first grade classes; and the other co-teacher supported instruction in the second and third grade classes.

Central Elementary School Central Elementary is about the same size as Arnold Elementary and is located in a rural area that is 5–25 miles from an urbanized area in the state. It is a Title I school (43% received free lunch) with 40% black students and 37% white students. Central Elementary is in a district that serves the largest military base in the world, so there are many military-connected students in this school. In the 2013–2014 school year, a Chinese language immersion program was launched at the kindergarten level. It had two classes initially and added one grade level each year. As of 2015–2016, there were six lead teachers and three co-teachers hired for the Chinese classes. Two co-teachers supported instruction in two kindergarten classes; one co-teacher supported instruction in two first grade classes; another co-teacher supported instruction in two second grade classes.

Thomas Elementary School Thomas Elementary is a Title I school (54% received free lunch) in a large city in the state. It is also the most culturally diverse school with 31% white, 24% Hispanic, and 36% black students and is located in the poorest district in this study. In the 2014–2015 school year, a Chinese language immersion program began with one kindergarten class; the following year when that kindergarten class went up to first grade, an additional kindergarten class was added (for a total of two kindergarten classes and one first grade class). As of 2015–2016, there were three lead teachers and three co-teachers hired for the program. Two co-teachers supported instruction in the two kindergarten classes; one co-teacher supported instruction in the first-grade class.

Each of the four schools[2] had Mandarin immersion programs that began during the Kindergarten year and were, at the time of this study, at various stages of development: three of the four schools had 2 kindergarten Mandarin classrooms; all included 1st grade; two schools had 2nd grade classrooms; and only one school had a 3rd grade classroom.

---

[2] Pseudonyms are used to insure confidentiality of school sites and study participants.

Methodology

As part of a mixed method study investigating Chinese minority teachers' experiences in the U.S. elementary schools, the present chapter uses the narratives of 6 kindergarten minority teachers to illuminate their transitional and transnational experience in the U.S. These participants' stories were gathered from in-depth semi-structured interviews administered for supporting and specifying the results from a questionnaire. Interview data serves as rich source of information for understanding the shared experiences among the participants and the unique insights of each individual. The semi-structured interviews were conducted and analyzed in Chinese in order to capture rich narratives data and probe the meaning of discourse. For the publication purposes, the results were then translated into English.

Data Analysis

Data were analyzed using a thematic approach (Creswell & Poth, 2016). In the first phase of coding, I developed a list based on the literature as a guide and developed codes relevant to each category inductively while reading and coding the data. Once the data was saturated with base-level codes, I began the next phase of analytic process which was focused on categorizing base-level codes and the themes that hold across 6 minority teachers' stories were extracted. As the data analysis process proceeded, sub-categories under each theme were added, refined and grouped until no revisions were needed. I then summarized themes and used the corresponding passages that emerged from the interview data to answer the research questions.

Participants

These six minority teachers shared some similarities while also reflected the diversity in terms of their teacher preparation, college major, teaching certification, and previous teaching experience in China. They were in their late twenties to early thirties and were all hired as lead teachers. One of the first year teachers, Zach, was a male teacher, and the rest of them were females. Two of the experienced teachers were married and lived with their spouses in the U.S. (Table 7.2).

Table 7.2 Six kindergarten teachers' professional background

Teacher	School	Cohort	College major	Teaching certification	Previous teaching experiences in China
Linda	Arnold	2nd	Early childhood education	ECE	Private PreK-K 4 years
Sandy	Thomas	2nd	Teaching Chinese as a foreign language	Language teaching (Any grade level)	Public elementary 3 years Public high 3 years
Zach	Thomas	1st	Education in the English language	High school (English)	Public elementary 2 years Public high 3 years
Wanda	Central	2nd	Education in the English language	High school (English)	Public PreK-K less than 1 year Public elementary 1 years
Flora	Miller	1st	Teaching Chinese as a foreign language	Elementary	Private PreK 1 year Private elementary 1 year
Maya	Miller	3rd	Teaching Chinese as a foreign language	Elementary	Public elementary 2 years College 2 years

Findings and Discussion

New Life in the U.S.

In spite of the fact that these 6 Chinese minority teachers resided in four different U.S. public elementary schools, they shared a number of common transition experiences with regard to domestic/neighborhood housing arrangements, personal lives, and collegial activities at work. Most of them teachers decided to find housing with access to local Chinese restaurants and supermarkets, although few of their neighbors were of Chinese descent. Most of them got together with their Chinese colleagues after work. Having access to the food and language from home in their respective places of residence seemed to offer these teachers a sense of cultural continuity. The fact that they spent most of their time after work with other Chinese colleagues hinted at their need for proximity to the Chinese communities. While these things provided a sense of familiarity and comfort, still many things remained problematic in the lives of newly arrived minority teachers. Some of them reported experiencing culture shock, communication difficulties and homesickness. Others reported some problems with racial discrimination and economic difficulties. These challenges outside the work environment were common to many international teachers, as noted in the literature. It seemed that the preliminary support and preparation for teachers were not enough for teachers to avoid experiencing these difficulties (Dunn, 2013).

Challenges Encountered at Schools

When these teachers began their professional careers in U.S. public schools, one common problematic area was their unfamiliarity with U.S. public schools, including the philosophy, structures, procedures, policies, rules, classroom setup, and assessment and grading systems. Some of them described facing major challenges of inadequate teaching materials, heavy teaching loads resulting in insufficient prep time, and lack of spare time.

In terms of the challenges related to teaching, the participants reported some difficulties in three broad areas: (1) how to work with individual students (rather than the whole class); (2) classroom management; and (3) pedagogical content knowledge. In the first area, the teachers reported having trouble interacting with and motivating American students, especially slow learners; determining learning levels of students; and paying attention to individual differences and addressing individual learning and behavioral problems. With regard to classroom management, the teachers expressed struggling with managing the whole class's behavior. As for the pedagogical content knowledge, the teachers felt they had insufficient subject matter knowledge to plan lessons and encountered challenges using different teaching methods effectively and assessing student work.

Chaotic First Month One of the kindergarten teachers—Zach—expressed no complaints about the challenges during his transition to the U.S. school. In fact, he described the experience as "a mix of chaos, novelty, and worrisome". His female colleagues, however, were not so sanguine or satisfied. The five (female) kindergarten teachers were particularly open about their struggles during the first month in U.S. public schools. Not only was the transition challenging in a general sense, but three teachers vividly remembered their feelings of being left on their own during their first month in U.S. schools. A first-year teacher, Flora, quoted a Chinese saying, 'crossing the river by feeling the stones', to describe the risks and uncertainties of her acclimation process. An experienced teacher, Linda, noted that in her first year, the school did not give new transnational teachers any time to adjust. Instead, they were expected to be able to teach in their U.S. classroom upon arrival. Common coping strategies mentioned by all six of the kindergarten teachers (Zach included) were to ask a lot of questions of their American colleagues or an experienced Chinese minority teacher, or to simply imitate their practices, sometimes after peeking into other classrooms.

The specific early transition challenges were described at length by individuals. The same teachers who felt that they were 'on their own' also reiterated their unfamiliarity with the U.S. school system, noting that "no schedule was given for the first week," "didn't know hallway rules, where to drink or to have lunch, and dismissal procedure" (Flora); "no idea about open house, A-sub system, or how to take attendance" (Maya); and "didn't know IEP, 504, and all kinds of special documents that need to be filled out" (Linda). In terms of classroom setup issues, Flora, Linda and one other (Sandy) kindergarten teacher said they were given an empty classroom upon arrival, with little assistance in setting up a culturally appropriate learning environment. Several teachers mentioned the lack of resources, and Flora was particularly troubled, as she noted, "[By the end of] the 1st month, I [still] had no computer, no security card, no salary." She was also the only teacher who spoke candidly about resorting to using a limited array of teaching techniques due to insufficient preparation time.

As for the issues of insufficient subject matter knowledge, Linda admitted that she knew nothing about Common Core; Maya and Flora were also confused about the U.S. way of teaching math to young children. Flora was especially critical. "I can't stand the way American teachers teach math, too complicated." She thought she knew a much better way. "Why bother using a number line when you can give students a simpler way to do addition?" Another issue raised by several kindergarten teachers, when asked about early challenges, was that of lesson planning—especially given the program requirements of meeting students' level and learning styles. Sandy and Wanda shared examples of their struggles: Sandy said that "besides knowing the basic second language teaching contents such as 1,2…,10, I did not know how broad a topic should be extended and how deep I should go." Wanda not only "had no idea how to do projects or hands-on activities." She also defended her lack of knowledge because she "did not have relevant experience in China."

We Do Things Differently in China When talking about experiences in the U.S., six teachers constantly used their Chinese teaching and learning experiences as a reference. Many of them were aware of some or major differences with regards to the two cultures' elementary school operating systems, educational philosophies, definitions of good students, interpretations of good teaching, methods of assessing student learning, and class management (See Table 7.3). They also pointed out differences in teacher workloads and attitudes toward low-performing students.

With regard to Chinese ways, the six teachers' descriptions were like different pieces of a puzzle, and by putting them together, they actually reveal a contour of a Chinese cultural model. For example, every teacher except Sandy described "imparting knowledge" as a primary responsibility of Chinese teachers. Four of these teachers (Linda, Wanda, Flora and Zach) described rote instruction as a habitual approach of teaching in China because of its power for promoting test scores. Sandy and Flora added nuance to this description of teaching, pointing out that the act of teaching in China has been contextually bounded by the lengthy historical background of the testing system. Furthermore, a "good Chinese teacher," in Sandy and Zach's views, knows how to break up whole group instruction into chunks and can differentiate assignments by students' learning outcomes. As for a 'good student'—within the Chinese cultural-educational context, as noted by Wanda, Maya and Zach, the qualities of good students include being obedient, earning good grades, and exhibiting a serious attitude toward studying.

Compared to these teachers' overall consensus about the Chinese ways of teaching, their personal interpretations of good students and effective teaching in U.S. kindergartens reflected more subjective opinions about various and multiple parts, making it difficult to construct a complete picture of U.S. elementary

Table 7.3 Six Chinese minority teachers' elaborations on differences in educational contexts between China and the U.S.

Differences between China and the U.S. regarding:	China	The United States
School operating system	Excessive administrative control over teacher and teaching in China Bigger class size School-wide regularized and regulated temporal structure of classes China has a longer school day Chinese elementary students go home for a lunch break	Less administrative control over teacher and teaching in US Smaller class size Teacher-designed elastic temporal structure of classes US kindergarten schedule is fast-paced
Educational philosophy (Ideologies)	China's collectivistic orientation in education The hardship inherent in the path of education Education and knowledge can change fate and lead to better living Less personal freedom is allowed in Chinese education Questioning is subdued in Chinese education Exam- or result-oriented education Learning content information is more important than thinking about it Values academic performance	US's individualistic orientation in education Education comes naturally to American children Education can increase world view and lead to better opportunities Greater personal freedom is allowed in US education US education values creativity Standards and curriculum guide teaching and learning Value holistic development
Definition of good student	Obedient Having good grades Serious attitude	Independent thinking and unique ideas
Definition of good teaching	Imparting as much knowledge as possible Rote learning and rote knowledge that can promote test scores Break up whole group instruction into chunks Differentiate assignments by learning outcome	Emphasize comprehension More guided and exploratory learning Student-centered teaching and cooperative learning A variety of pedagogical strategies are used
Methods of assessing student learning	Standardized written test at regular intervals as the predominant mode of assessment End-of-semester report card records test scores has teacher comments	More forms of classroom assessment Common core standards as assessment criteria Report cards is based on predetermined criteria and designed by the school district to records performance levels

(continued)

Table 7.3 (continued)

Differences between China and the U.S. regarding:	China	The United States
Class management	Chinese teachers control the class through exhibition of personal authority Classroom management signaled by the use of furniture Use of sticker or reward chart Call parents is the ultimate solution to students' negative behavior	Various strategies of classroom management Sit cross-legged on carpet area is the norm Use of online behavior management system
Teacher workload	Chinese teachers teaching classes in their subject is more professional and effective The work of teachers in China is easier	US elementary head teachers' heavier workload and ineffective teaching The work of teachers in US is harder
Low-performing students	Tend to give up low-performing students	Lower-level students receive attention and support

education. This is not surprising given their limited experience in the U.S. Of the six teachers, only Linda and Maya noted that good students in the U.S. were expected to display the characteristics of thinking independently and having unique ideas. In terms of their perceptions of what is considered good teaching in the US, Linda, Sandy and Zach (separately) shared their observations that U.S. teachers used a variety of pedagogical strategies. Zach also added that U.S. teachers emphasized comprehension and implemented more guided and exploratory learning. Wanda regarded student-centered teaching and cooperative learning as highly valued by U.S. teachers.

Conclusions and Implications

Like other novice American teachers teaching in new school contexts, the participants reported feeling unfamiliar with school operations and stressed about learning new rules, procedures, and school cultures in a short period of time. None of the participants were formally assigned a mentor, although they all worked with American colleagues to learn how to develop lesson plans in alignment with the state and local curriculum standards. Based on reports of minimal peer observations, it appears that study participants had limited access to American teachers' expertise. Given the importance of "guided participation" and "participant observations" as ways in which novices learn within cultural context, the teachers' lack of such interactions with more knowledgeable colleagues actually constrained their learning of particular U.S. values and practices (Rogoff, 2003, pp. 10, 284).

Adding to the difficulties experienced in Chinese minority teachers' personal and professional transitions, including language barriers and homesickness, the "pedagogical shock" resulting from their growing recognition of differences between the U.S. and Chinese cultural models of teaching further compounded their adjustment to the U.S. (Hutchison, 2005, p. 24). Given the great number of challenges discussed above, it is no wonder that Linda recalled her first month of teaching at Arnold Elementary as "simply trying to survive."

This chapter suggests the need for better preparation for host school communities. They can reach out to the newcomers before their arrival to solicit their questions and invite them to share their cultural model of teaching and learning. Such school-centered professional development could allow American administrators and teachers to anticipate differences, to identify ways in which the newcomers could contribute to as well as learn from the larger school community, and to foresee where they might need support.

The participants of this study had additional recommendations, including the need to arrive early enough (e.g. at least 3 weeks before the school year begins) to become familiar with their working contexts, have time to set up their classrooms, and meet and develop collegial relationships with their new colleagues. Given the demands and pace once the school year begins, it is better to have a team of experienced American teachers who can offer help and guidance to the new minority teachers beforehand.

Advanced preparations and increased time for the transition into a new culture can only do so much. Even when school begins, the minority teachers' needs for both pedagogical and non-pedagogical support remain. The findings suggest the need for multiple and diverse opportunities for minority teachers to build relationships and work closely with other educators. Possible ways to achieve that goal include (1) formally assigning mentors or pairing one new and one experienced Chinese teacher with one or two experienced American teachers and allowing regular consultation time so that Chinese teachers might be able to help American teachers understand some of the early cultural confusion and conflicts; (2) offering more frequent peer observations, e.g. Lesson studies (Dudley, 2015) followed by meetings focused on peer feedback, self-reflection, and improvement plans; (3) providing ongoing professional development on illustrating aspects of the U.S. cultural models of teaching, e.g. why and how to implement differentiated instruction based on student needs, and the potential of the Chinese cultural model of teaching, e.g. how to teach math; and (4) providing a variety of collaborative opportunities between Chinese and American teachers.

Given the current and projected shortage of foreign language teachers in the United States, the need for more teachers from other countries seems self-evident. However, a lack of empirical research on minority teachers in U.S. school settings has created what Dunn (2013) referred to as an "erroneous assumption…that there are no or few differences between teaching abroad and teaching in U.S. urban schools…if there are differences, the assumption is made that they are not enough to merit specialized discussion and preparation for working in a new environment" (p. 36). The findings reported in this chapter support this concern by highlighting many challenges faced by newly arrived minority teachers. Thus, in order to help the minority teachers have smooth initial transitions into U.S. schools, as well as to ensure that the school communities are culturally responsive to the newcomers, improved preparation and ongoing support need to be provided. The challenges include the unfamiliarity with U.S. public schools, inadequate teaching materials, a heavy teaching load, and other teaching-related issues. This chapter has not only contributed to increased understanding regarding minority teachers from China and their experiences in the U.S. educational context, but has also revealed some implications for the study of teacher development and culturally responsive in-service minority teacher education.

In light of the rapid increase of teacher migration to the U.S. and the promotion of a diverse teaching force in U.S. schools, the findings of this chapter highlight challenges faced by newly arrived minority teachers. Thus, in order to help minority teachers have smooth initial transitions into U.S. schools, as well as to ensure that the school communities are supportive to the newcomers, additional investigation is needed into the differences and challenges associated with teaching in a new cultural context and in-service teacher education that emphasizes extensive, culturally appropriate and inclusive professional development content.

References

Allen-Ebrahimian, B. (2015). Can 1 million American students learn Mandarin? *Foreign Policy*. Retrieved from http://foreignpolicy.com/2015/09/25/china-us-obamas-one-million-students-chinese-language-mandarin/?wp_login_redirect=0

American Federation of Teachers. (2009). *Importing educators: Causes and consequences of international teacher recruitment*. ERIC Clearinghouse.

Bailey, E. K. (2013). From cultural dissonance to diasporic affinity: The experience of Jamaican teachers in New York City schools. *The Urban Review, 45*(2), 232–249.

Bartlett, L. (2014). *Migrant teachers: How American schools import labor*. Harvard University Press.

Billings, E. (2015). *Obama announces new program to dramatically expand U.S. Mandarin learning*. Retrieved from http://100kstrong.org/2015/09/25/obama-announces-new-program-to-dramatically-expand-u-s-manadarin-learning/

Cook, S. (2000). Foreign teachers find a place in US schools. *Christian Science Monitor, 92*(190), 18.

Creswell, J. W., & Poth, C. N. (2016). *Qualitative inquiry and research design: Choosing among five approaches*. Sage.

Dudley, P. (2015). *Lesson study professional learning for our time*. Routledge.

Dunn, A. H. (2011). Global village versus culture shock: The recruitment and preparation of foreign teachers for US urban schools. *Urban Education, 46*(6), 1379–1410.

Dunn, A. H. (2013). *Teachers without borders? The hidden consequences of international teachers in U.S. schools*. Teachers College Press.

Fee, J. F. (2011). Latino immigrant and guest bilingual teachers: Overcoming personal, professional, and academic culture shock. *Urban Education, 46*(3), 390–407. Retrieved from https://auth.lib.unc.edu/ezproxy_auth.php?url=http://search.ebscohost.com/login.aspx?direct=true&db=eric&AN=EJ920668&site=ehost-live&scope=site

Finney, P. B., Torres, J., & Jurs, S. (2002). The South Carolina/Spain visiting teacher program. *The Clearing House, 76*(2), 94–97.

Huang, J. (2009). What happens when two cultures meet in the classroom? *Journal of Instructional Psychology, 36*(4), 335.

Hutchison, C. B. (2005). *Teaching in America: A cross-cultural guide for international teachers and their employers*. Springer.

Moskal, M. (2015). 'When I think home I think family here and there': Translocal and social ideas of home in narratives of migrant children and young people. *Geoforum, 58*, 143–152.

Moskal, M., & Sime, D. (2015). Polish migrant children's transcultural lives and transnational language use. *Central and Eastern European Migration Review, 4*(2), 1–14.

Phan, T., & Glander, M. (2008). *Documentation to the NCES common core of data public elementary/secondary school locale code file: School year 2005–06 (NCES 2008-332)*. Retrieved from Washington, DC: http://nces.ed.gov/pubsearch/pubsinfo.asp?pubid=2008332

Rogoff, B. (2003). *The cultural nature of human development*. Oxford University Press.

Smith, K. (2009). Transnational teaching experiences: An under-explored territory for transformative professional development. *International Journal for Academic Development, 14*(2), 111–122.

State Board of Education. (2016). *Language diversity in North Carolina*. Retrieved from

Suárez-Orozco, C., & Suárez-Orozco, M. (2013). Transnationalism of the heart: Familyhood across borders. In L. C. McClain & D. Cere (Eds.), *What is parenthood? Contemporary debates about the family* (pp. 279–298). New York University Press.

Weise, E. (2014). *A parent's guide to Mandarin immersion*. Chenery Street Press.

Pei-Ying Wu is an Assistant Professor in the Early Childhood Education Program and the Fansler Chair leading the Joyce M. Huggins Early Education Center at California State University, USA. Wu was born and raised in Taiwan and has extensive cross-cultural/international teaching, researching and coaching experiences across multiple educational settings. Her personally informed cross-cultural studying, international teaching and comparative research experiences have contributed to a growing awareness of the cultural nature of education including beliefs and practices about teaching and learning.

Open Access This chapter is licensed under the terms of the Creative Commons Attribution 4.0 International License (http://creativecommons.org/licenses/by/4.0/), which permits use, sharing, adaptation, distribution and reproduction in any medium or format, as long as you give appropriate credit to the original author(s) and the source, provide a link to the Creative Commons license and indicate if changes were made.

The images or other third party material in this chapter are included in the chapter's Creative Commons license, unless indicated otherwise in a credit line to the material. If material is not included in the chapter's Creative Commons license and your intended use is not permitted by statutory regulation or exceeds the permitted use, you will need to obtain permission directly from the copyright holder.

Chapter 8
Research on Minority Teachers in Germany: Developments, Focal Points and Current Trends from the Perspective of Intercultural Education

Lisa Rosen and Drorit Lengyel

Abstract This chapter presents a meta-analysis of studies on ethnic minority (prospective) teachers in Germany and German-speaking countries. Starting with "pioneer studies", current research trends and research foci from the perspective of intercultural education are elaborated: intersectional perspectives on the professional self-concepts of minority teachers, discrimination and anti-Muslim racism experienced by prospective minority teachers, language and multilingualism as a relevant social category of difference and inequality in the context of (prospective) minority teachers and comparisons between (prospective) minority and majority teachers with a focus on the effects of representation of (prospective) minority teachers. Finally, it is argued that in Germany an inclusive perspective on minority teachers, embracing recently immigrated and refugee teachers, is needed to overcome the ethnicised attributions of professional competence and to focus on the discriminatory structures of the German education system, including teacher education.

Introduction

When we started our studies on ethnic minority teachers in 2010,[1] research was still emerging. As one German researcher puts it: "Research on minority teachers in Germany is just as hard to find as the minority teachers themselves" (Strasser,

---

[1] In the following, we simply refer to "minority teachers" instead of "ethnic minority teachers".

L. Rosen (✉)
RPTU - University of Kaiserslautern-Landau, Landau, Germany
e-mail: lisa.rosen@rptu.de

D. Lengyel (✉)
University of Hamburg, Hamburg, Germany
e-mail: drorit.lengyel@uni-hamburg.de

© The Author(s) 2023
M. Gutman et al. (eds.), *To Be a Minority Teacher in a Foreign Culture*,
https://doi.org/10.1007/978-3-031-25584-7_8

2013).[2] In our eyes, this shortfall in research was quite severe, especially seeing as the discourse in educational policy regarding development of a strategy to recruit more minority teachers has long since moved forward.

Our examination of the topic began with a course of studies at the University of Cologne which we designed especially for minority student teachers. In this empowerment seminar, we focused on a vocational biographical reflection on educational policy and on the addressing of minority teachers as particular teachers (Lengyel & Rosen, 2012a; a similar course was later held at the University of Bremen – see Doğmuş, 2017). We presented and discussed the results of our accompanying academic research during a national lecture series, at international conferences and international symposiums (Lengyel & Rosen, 2011, 2012b, 2013, 2014). Some of the presented papers were published in a special issue of the journal "Tertium Comparationis" (see Lengyel & Rosen, 2015b) to present the state of the art in research on minority teachers and found a rich tradition of studies in the US and the UK stretching back to the start of the 1980s (Lengyel & Rosen, 2015a).

In this chapter, we reconnect to our summary back then. Our goal is to identify different thematic strands in this field that clearly go beyond its initial stage. Such a systematisation seems necessary to us in order to reflect on the development of the state of research, the shifts in the discourse and also future research perspectives. We start with some "pioneer studies" in section "Precursor and pioneer studies on minority (pre-service) teachers in German-speaking countries (up to 2013)" and then move on to the latest studies on minority teachers in section "Recent studies on minority (pre-service) teachers in German-speaking countries", addressing relevant topical distinctions that show how well the field is now established in respect to migration-related, intercultural educational research. In our conclusion in section "Outlook", we look at new developments and trends concerning the position of and possibilities for newly immigrated and refugee teachers in the education system.

Precursor and Pioneer Studies on Minority (Pre-service) Teachers in German-Speaking Countries (Up to 2013)

The study *Diversity in the staffroom* (Georgi et al., 2011), offered the first nationwide overview of minority teachers' self-image, self-efficacy experiences and self-efficacy expectations. Together with the anthology *Teachers with a migration background* (Bräu et al., 2013), these two publications can be described as pioneering works of German-language research (Rosen, 2015), as they explicitly refer to

---

[2] Making up a share of 6.1%, minority teachers were considered to be under-represented in the German school system in 2012; the forecasts from 2016 were pessimistic, as many minority adolescents who grew up in Germany have reservations about the teaching profession (Morris-Lange et al., 2016, p. 10).

the then current educational policy programme for recruiting minority teachers and reflect the educational policy context as well as the public debate on integration. In this section, we focus on the anthology, because it includes a large number of exploratory research papers and provides an insight into the emerging field of research on minority teachers, taking into account different pedagogical areas respectively professional career phases. In this respect, the dissertation projects by Akbaba (2013), Kul (2013) and Wojciechowicz (2013), which reconstruct discrimination experiences of (prospective) minority teachers based on qualitative studies, and the contribution by Schlickum (2013), which shows that minority pre-service teachers also reproduce the monolingual habitus found in German schools (Gogolin, 2008), are relevant. Central to this anthology is also a contribution to the historical (dis)continuities in the debate on diversity in staffrooms: Krüger-Potratz (2013, p. 30) discusses the legal framework such as the so-called "national primacy" of the teaching profession and the associated inferior position of non-German teachers with regard to status and salary. Further researchers analyse education policy regarding the recruitment of minority teachers in political documents from ten federal states and a resolution paper drawn up by the Standing Conference of the Ministers of Education. It has been proven that "thoroughly positive intentions" can have "problematic elements", because educational policy statements are permeated by culturalizations and processes of othering (Akbaba et al., 2013, p. 52). Scepticism about education policy is also advisable if minority teachers are seen as "interculturally competent by nature" (Karakaşoğlu et al., 2013, p. 70); in principle, however, they should be given a high priority in the context of intercultural school development. In this pioneering book also the fact is addressed that differences are generated in academic discourse by distinguishing between "with" and "without a migration background" and associated paradoxes in research practice remain unsolved (Rotter & Schlickum, 2013).

In the anthology, Bandorski and Karakaşoğlu (2013, p. 133) present the findings of a study using a mixed-methods design on the study progress and satisfaction of student teachers which was designed and carried out as migration-sensitive basic research aimed at providing an empirically proven requirements analysis. In the quantitative section, data from 560 student teachers was collected via written questionnaires. Here are some central results of the multivariate analysis: The authors note that the "large majority of student teachers with a migration background [...] do not consider themselves a 'group' with specific characteristics and support needs" and therefore recommend not addressing them as such to avoid any potential stigma (Bandorski & Karakaşoğlu, 2013, p. 147; translation from German by the authors). Bandorski and Karakaşoğlu (2013) interpret the fact that the respondents "with a migration background" are somewhat more strongly motivated by inequality-sensitive pedagogy than those "without a migration background" as "cautiously confirming indications" of education policy (p. 152).

Edelmann (2013) focuses on how minority teachers deal with migration-related heterogeneity. Using interviews conducted in Zurich, Switzerland, she explores the fact that, among those interviewed, young minority teachers in particular favour a 'tacit' recognition of heterogeneity, in which possible differences and similarities remain unspoken (Edelmann, 2013, p. 200). Interestingly, "often due to their own negative experiences during their school years, it is particularly important to them never to address their pupils directly about their origin or even as representatives of a culture" (Edelmann, 2013, p. 200; translation from German by the authors). In the two contributions by Karakaş with Ackermann and by Georgi, the results of the study *Diversity in the Staffroom* from the corresponding monograph from 2011 are presented. The former turn to the experiences of minority teachers with migrant parents. They reconstruct these by analysing the content from five of the 45 narrative interviews. The examples are used to illustrate different "access strategies" to parents (Karakaş & Ackermann, 2013, p. 183; translation from German by the authors). One common feature is that the teachers here "specifically make use of their migration-specific resources to increase the participation of migrant parents in parents' evenings and in discussions with parents" (Karakaş & Ackermann, 2013, p. 183; translation from German by the authors). It can also be seen that they have their own special insights on the deficit-oriented discourse on migrant parents among the teaching staff (Karakaş & Ackermann, 2013, p. 184; translation from German by the authors). Georgi's contribution sheds empirical light on the self-assessments of minority teachers regarding their handling of multilingualism and cultural heterogeneity. According to Georgi, one consistent finding from both the quantitative and qualitative data is that the respondents make less use of their non-German languages as a resource in classroom activities than in extra-curricular interactions (Georgi, 2013b, p. 228, p. 233). The usage contexts of multilingualism in class are broadly diversified: from disciplining minority pupils to building up a relationship of trust with them, as well as for contrastive language work (Georgi, 2013b, p. 228). However, there are also reports of some schools encouraging pupils to distance themselves from their own multilingualism, on the grounds that "German should be spoken in schools as a matter of principle" (Georgi, 2013b, p. 232; translation from German by the authors). These findings lead to the open question of what "resource orientation" for minority teachers might look like in teacher education (Georgi, 2013b, p. 238). This question is also supported by a finding presented by Göbel as the "interim result[s]" (2013b, p. 215) of an exploratory study using statistical evaluation methods. It examines teachers' emotional reactions to "critical incidents" (n = 59) and shows (for the nine minority teachers that were interviewed) that they report "a higher emotional burden" of the critical events and make "rather more complex interpretations" of these situations (Göbel, 2013, p. 217).

While this pioneering work in Germany and other parts of German-speaking Europe deals with (prospective) minority teachers in the education system in a general and also racism-critical manner by exploring their perspectives within the educational policy discussion, the field of research is now being further differentiated thanks to the more recent studies.

Recent Studies on Minority (Pre-service) Teachers in German-Speaking Countries

In the following section, we present the current state of research, largely drawing on the systematization developed by Rosen and Jacob (2021, pp. 2–5).³ We present examples of research foci that not only look more deeply at othering processes and experiences of discrimination, but also link them to other dimensions of inequality and focus on questions of gender, religion and language.

A first line of research concerns studies which illuminate the professional self-concepts of (prospective) minority teachers by going into greater depth using hermeneutic methodologies such as biographical analysis (Mantel, 2017) or documentary method (Rotter, 2014a; Lengyel & Rosen, 2015a) to discover hidden structures of meaning and develop different typologies. These studies show that the participants' professional self-concepts are shaped very differently and that they attach different importance to their own migration background by assigning it great or even no significance at all or by sharply rejecting or even overemphasising the connection between their own professionalism as a teacher with migration experiences (Rotter, 2014a). Similarly, pre-service minority teachers wish to simply be considered members of the staff and not be reduced to the role of integration experts. However, they do feel particularly responsible for shaping the migration society and enabling equal opportunities in education (Lengyel & Rosen, 2015a). Conversely, they also show that teachers are constantly confronted with the challenge of defending their allegiances and identities as well as justifying their sensitivity in dealing with migration-related diversity (Mantel, 2020). Recent research also expands the views of (prospective) teachers on complementary issues by shedding light on the experiences and assessments of their pupils, colleagues and head teachers (Bressler & Rotter, 2017; Rotter & Timpe, 2016; Strasser & Waburg, 2015). Here, too, there are very different evaluations. Interestingly enough, it seems that the pupils in particular attach little importance to the minority status of their teachers, and when they do, then only in certain situations and in connection to other dimensions of difference (e.g., age, gender, class) which carry more weight for the pupils (Strasser & Waburg, 2015). In an international comparative project, Waburg and Strasser (2018) pursue a hitherto unique question by taking an intersectional perspective and asking "whether and how other difference dimensions besides ethnicity become relevant for teachers and their actions" (p. 55; translation from German by the authors). While the interplay between "the two categories of gender and ethnicity/race" in the Anglo-American world was examined with a view to "black male teachers", this "has not yet been taken into account in the German-speaking world" (Waburg & Strasser, 2018, p. 58). Waburg and Strasser assume that "dealing with educational policy expectations is not independent of gender-related attributions" and ask "how

---

³Other systematizations of the state of research distinguish, for example, between pre- and in-service minority teachers (Mantel, 2017, p. 15) or between German and English language research (Rotter, 2014b, p. 119; Georgi, 2013a, p. 92).

female and male teachers with a migration background position themselves and which of the expectations placed on them they try to fulfil and how" (Waburg & Strasser, 2018, p. 55; translation from German by the authors). To this end, they choose an explorative design that uses documentary method to reconstruct hidden orientation patterns surveyed in individual interviews and group discussions with teachers in Germany and Austria. The first results reported in the following are based on two group discussions with three teachers from an Austrian primary school and three teachers from an Austrian grammar school (Waburg & Strasser, 2018, p. 60). The analysis provides indications of the gender-specific positioning of minority teachers in relation to the expectations directed at them: "The women open up, share their own experiences, talk to students and parents, take advantage of the assumed proximity between themselves and migrant parents" (Waburg & Strasser, 2018, pp. 67–68; translation from German by the authors). Communal aspects such as warmth and community orientation, feeling connected and focussing on other people become clear. Male teachers, however, do not open up in the same way: They too share their experiences, but with a focus on being role models and an emphasis on "agency" aspects such as competence, instrumentality and self-assertion. Unlike the female interviewees, they do not mention "that they proactively care for and advise minority pupils and their parents and consciously ensure a positive classroom climate" (Waburg & Strasser, 2018, p. 67; translation from German by the authors). It is not only a gender-specific orientation that becomes visible here, but also gender stereotypes in the professional approaches of teachers which will need to be reviewed in future on the basis of broader studies, especially with regard to specific school forms. In this respect, Waburg and Strasser also point out that the female interviewees work at a primary school and, as class teachers, form a fixed reference person for younger pupils, while the male interviewees work exclusively with older pupils in upper secondary schools and do not have the opportunity to form relationships in a comparable framework because they are working as subject teachers who thus focus on specific academic subjects. In this respect, their emphasis on achievement can also be explained by the school form, whereas the school culture of the primary school is oriented towards the formation of relationships and therefore suggests "communal" aspects (Waburg & Strasser, 2018, p. 68).

A second research focus sheds light on the discrimination and racism experienced by (prospective) minority teachers as well as processes of othering in everyday school life (Akbaba, 2017a, b; Doğmuş, 2016; El & Fereidooni, 2016; Fereidooni, 2016; Karakaşoğlu & Doğmuş, 2016; Karakaşoğlu & Wojciechowicz, 2017). In addition to more or less open forms of racism, it looks primarily at the subtle forms of discrimination, which are related to the addressing of teachers as interculturally competent because of their own or their family's migration biography. Furthermore, it examines paradoxes in school interactions, for example in Akbaba's ethnography and discourse analysis (2017b), which stands out from the multitude of interview studies: While teachers are implicitly requested to capitalize their 'foreignness', they are called upon to do so within reference frames that (threaten to) marginalize them. In the above-mentioned studies, the starting points for processes of othering are various facets of migration-related diversity; however, one dimension that has been rather neglected in this respect so far is religious belonging.

During our literature review, we became aware of two contributions that deal with anti-Muslim discrimination as a specific form of racism in the context of the professionalisation of prospective minority teachers in Germany (Karakaşoğlu & Doğmuş, 2016; Karakaşoğlu & Wojciechowicz, 2017). Firstly, Karakaşoğlu and Doğmuş present explorative findings from two interlinked qualitative research projects "that focus on teacher training programmes in the first and second phase of teacher formation in Germany" (2016, p. 92). Based on the analysis of interviews according to grounded theory and the documentary method, they show how the "stereotypical societal discourse on 'migrants' as 'Muslims'" negatively affects preservice teachers and their academic instructors alike. Mirroring the perspective of the instructor in the first phase who doesn't reflect on this practice of othering in terms of "muslimization" with the perspective of a student teacher who faces othering in this respect, Karakaşoğlu and Doğmuş identify "deeply rooted images of deficient students with a 'migration background' both at university and during in-service training" (2016, p. 98). They explain these "stereotypical and even racist images of 'people with a migration background' as uncivilized 'Muslims'" (Karakaşoğlu & Doğmuş, 2016, p. 92) as the result of a poorly considered reflection of the respective German social discourse. The second article supports this result in that it analyses the complementary perspective of fellow students who are also studying to become teachers (Karakaşoğlu & Wojciechowicz, 2017). The authors reconstruct "openly communicated devaluations and defences in dealing with prospective female teachers wearing Muslim headscarves and with the religious heterogeneity of the school community as a dominant interpretative perspective" (Karakaşoğlu & Wojciechowicz, 2017, p. 513). In addition, they conclude that "the Muslim headscarf is generally assigned a specific, anti-democratic symbolic character and the consideration of Muslim holidays at school has the potential to disadvantage the 'German' student body" (Karakaşoğlu & Wojciechowicz, 2017, p. 524; translation from German by the authors). All three cases analysed in this paper are concerned with "banning all visible religious expressions of Islam that do not comply with those norms considered legitimate or established from everyday school life" (Karakaşoğlu & Wojciechowicz, 2017, p. 524; translation from German by the authors). It can be concluded "that 'Muslim migrants' in their new role as prospective teachers are perceived as challenges for school routines" (Karakaşoğlu & Doğmuş, 2016, p. 99). In this respect, it appears necessary "to integrate content on migration-related religious plurality and attitudes to Muslim religious practice, in particular attitudes with a tendency towards anti-Muslim racism, more strongly than before in the further training of educators and in university teacher training" (Karakaşoğlu & Wojciechowicz, 2017, p. 526; translation from German by the authors).

Compared to the aforementioned research foci, fewer studies have turned to language as another relevant social category of difference and inequality in the context of (prospective) minority teachers and the associated language- or multilingualism-related issues (Döll & Knappik, 2015; Lengyel & Rosen, 2015a; Panagiotopoulou

& Rosen, 2016). To illustrate this third research focus, we present the results of two studies. In our qualitative study (Lengyel & Rosen, 2015a) on minority pre-service teachers and perspectives on the recruitment of minority teachers, we gathered different datasets for specific research foci. Concerning language and multilingualism, we asked pre-service teachers to reflect on how their personal multilingualism might benefit them as teachers, and to think of scenarios in which they might be able to use their languages in a meaningful manner. We analysed the written personal statements from ten pre-service teachers and found three different standpoints: (a) the benefits of multilingualism, (b) the potential of shared experiences, and (c) ambivalence towards the use of personal multilingualism. As far as the benefits are concerned, some of the pre-service teachers addressed the antinomy between wishing to use their languages in the classroom and knowing that the German school system is far away from this ideal. Benefits are also seen in the supposed higher metalinguistic abilities (higher language awareness) of multilinguals that could support classroom and learning activities. Furthermore, the pre-service teachers mention opportunities for cooperation with parents because "cooperation would be more successful if bi-/multilingual communication were possible" (Lengyel & Rosen, 2015a, p. 176). Some of them point out that they are more than ready to adopt the role of an intermediary but not that of an interpreter. Finally, they also address the ability to recognise their students (second) language learning difficulties better than monolinguals due to their own knowledge of other languages. Turning to the second argument of sharing common realities and experiences, the pre-service teachers reflect in detail about the teaching and learning possibilities this offers in the classroom. For instance, they assume that they are better able to understand the process of second language acquisition because of their own experiences. This shared experience, also considering the linguicism that some of them have faced, would help them to build relationships with students who expect them to be more sensitive, empathetic, and understanding towards students who are learning German and may therefore face discrimination. The third argument concerning ambivalent feelings about multilingual language use in the professional field not only focuses on the antinomy of individual multilingualism, e.g., translanguaging practices in the classroom, but also on the monolingual language policy of the educational system. Moreover, some of the pre-service teachers voice their fears of being stereotyped and forced into a special role because of their multilingualism. One student teacher puts it like this: "[A]re you suddenly a stopgap when your colleagues don't know what to do anymore?" (Lengyel & Rosen, 2015a, p. 179).

Another study that focuses on language, tackling different views on dialects and multilingualism among minority pre-service teachers, comes from another German-speaking country, Austria. Döll and Knappik (2015) re-analyse interview data from a project which originally aimed at revealing the linguistic requirements for student teachers during their studies at university. While analysing the 35 interviews, it became apparent that a second analysis was required, concentrating on how the faculty addresses the inclusion and exclusion of minority pre-service teachers. The findings can be summarised as follows: Whereas minority pre-service teachers are either seen as others with "fundamentally imperfect" or "perfect" proficiency (Döll

& Knappik, 2015, p. 192), dialect speakers are not addressed as others and are placed on the dialect–standard continuum, conceding their potential to adopt to the standard over time. Minority pre-service teachers are also put into the role of others when it comes to their responsibilities at school or when teaching German as a subject but the analysis also reveals the faculties dilemma, as, for one thing, they "have to ensure that students in pre-service teacher education acquire all necessary skills to later teach" (Döll & Knappik, 2015, p. 199). However, there are still no analyses of "the specific language proficiency requirements of teaching in Austrian schools" and it is not clear "what level of proficiency in German can be considered as sufficient for teaching" (Döll & Knappik, 2015, p. 200). The authors conclude that this manner of addressing minority pre-service teachers and discussing the language proficiency issue can be understood within the leitmotif of native-speakerism where native speakers are considered superior to other speakers of the same language (Döll & Knappik, 2015, p. 200).

In summary, the results of the study so far illustrate the spectrum in which (future) teachers move with regard to language differentiation: They themselves reflect the conflicting realm of 'multilingual language practices – monolingual institutional policies' in parts and position themselves differently along this spectrum. The underlying linguicism is revealed in the perspectives of the teachers, in native-speakerism, and the related dilemma faced by the faculty itself.

A fourth research focus consists of studies that allow comparisons between (prospective) minority and majority teachers and partly explores the effects of representation of (prospective) minority teachers (Edelmann et al., 2015; Glock & Schuchart, 2020; Höckel, 2020; Kleen et al., 2019; Klein et al., 2019; Rosen & Jacob, 2021; Rotter, 2014b; Strasser & Leutwyler, 2020). In a recent study, Höckel (2020) examines – from an economic perspective – the effect of minority teachers who teach German in secondary schools on the German language performance of pupils. The study looks at teachers who either migrated themselves or have at least one parent who migrated and/or have acquired a language other than German. It uses a large data set from the National Educational Panel Study (NEPS), from grade 5 (context data from $N = 4724$ students and $N = 719$ German teachers). Six percent of teachers in the study are minority teachers, which is comparable with the figures of the Federal Statistical Office. Using OLS regressions, Höckel demonstrates a positive and statistically significant effect of minority teachers on reading comprehension performance in German for all pupils regardless of their origin. If the groups are divided (into minority and majority pupils), the effect is even larger among minority pupils. In order to explain this result, Höckel conducts various in-depth analyses to clarify whether the effect can be explained by a possible linguistic proximity between pupils and teachers or by situations in which the role model effect is significant: the results illustrate that the minority teacher effect "is not driven by specific language matches between foreign origin students and teachers" (Höckel, 2020, p. 19). With regard to the role model effect, the analyses bear out the conclusion that the strong positive effect of having a minority teacher on minority students "can partly be attributed to a role model effect that motivates foreign origin students differently than their native counterparts" (Höckel, 2020, p. 21). Interestingly, the pre-service teachers in our research (Lengyel & Rosen, 2015a) as well as the teachers in the study by Georgi et al. (2011) also address the role model effect and partially agree that they can be role models.

Höckel (2020) also looks for explanations for a positive effect on the German reading comprehension performance of pupils, regardless of their origin. She uses further modelling to investigate the assumption that "conscious competence" (Höckel, 2020, p. 22) leads to better learning outcomes in language teaching. She shows that those teachers, who have acquired another language at home in addition to German, have an even greater effect on the reading comprehension performance of pupils than "foreign origin teachers", especially for monolingual pupils. This result is in line with those regarding the perceptions of pre-service teachers in our research (Lengyel & Rosen, 2015a). The student teachers explicitly referred to their higher language awareness as a result of their experience in acquiring German as a second language, which enabled them to help their pupils during language teaching.

Höckel's study (2020) contrasts the result of a study by Klein et al. (2019) where the general question is raised: "Do migrant students benefit from being taught by a migrant teacher?" Working with a large data-set of more than 9000 9th grade pupils and over 400 teachers, the authors found no statistical effects in their multivariate-analyses looking for performance-related effects among minority teachers. This indicates that studies in specific subjects that allow directed hypotheses are necessary to arrive at less ambiguous findings. Höckel's study (2020), which specifically targets subject teachers and examines effects on a clearly defined area of competence, seems therefore more purposeful. These comparative competence studies also underline the difficulties of carrying out such studies, since the number of minority teachers in the available samples is often too small to be meaningfully included in statistical analyses. This also applies, for example, to further analyses of the question as to whether and to what extent performance-related effects can be linked to the same (ethnic) origin.

Studies that focus on minority teachers' beliefs about minority students can be very illuminating in this context. Teachers' beliefs are seen as a part of their professional competence that may influence the students' performance in general or in a specific way, for example, when teachers have low expectations with regard to the achievement levels of minority students. Turning to minority teachers, the question arises as to whether they have more positive beliefs about minority students compared to those of teachers representing the 'majority', or even whether this effect only shows for minority teachers of a certain ethnic group towards students of the same group (in-group favouritism). In a study using a between-subjects design, Kleen et al. (2019) researched beliefs in terms of the implicit and explicit attitudes of pre-service teachers ($N = 149$). They categorised the pre-service teachers into three groups: Turkish minority pre-service teachers, minority pre-service teachers and 'majority' pre-service teachers. Implicit attitudes were measured using a specific test on cognitive associations between two concepts, whereas for the explicit attitudes, a prejudice beliefs scale was applied (Kleen et al., 2019, p. 879). The authors did not find any significant effect for the explicit attitudes. Yet, the ANOVA shows a significant main effect to the extent that the pre-service teachers from the

Turkish group demonstrate higher values on positive implicit attitudes towards Turkish students compared to pre-service teachers from other ethnic minorities. But even these pre-service teachers show more positive implicit attitudes than those from the majority group (here: English). Kleen et al.'s study (2019) reveals that comparative studies, which may also examine questions about the influences of minority teachers on pupils, should include different characteristics or aspects that are already known (from (teacher) research) to influence school performance and educational success.

Conclusions and Implications

Previously, research has focused on (prospective) minority teachers who belong to the second or third generation of migrants. These are established minorities who, although still affected by social inequalities, have completed their schooling in Germany and have been socialised accordingly. Now, research is being carried out that focuses on the first generation, i.e. on newly immigrated or refugee teachers. Since 2016, qualification programmes have been in place to provide support for the transition to teaching in the German school system, a process characterised by institutional barriers and a lack of recognition of vocational qualifications acquired abroad. These are based in university teacher education and usually specifically tailored to refugee teachers (Purrmann et al., 2020; Terhart et al., 2020; Wojciechowicz & Vock, 2019). The discourses on qualification programmes for refugee teachers, international teacher migration, minority teachers and the internationalisation of teacher education are now increasingly being brought together, as initial publications show (Terhart & Rosen, 2022; Schmidt & Schneider, 2016).

One example of the merging of discourses on minority teachers in Europe, their potential as change agents to transform the monolingual language market in the education system, and the discourse on newly immigrated or refugee teachers is Putjata's (language biographical) interview study (Putjata, 2017, 2018) featuring teachers who immigrated to Israel from Russia after completing their training in their country of origin and having already worked there as teachers. As new policies on teacher absorption and language education policy were launched in Israel in the 1990s, Putjata addresses the question as to how these policies were perceived by the teachers themselves and whether they had noticed any status change in schools as a result of these new policies (Putjata, 2018, p. 3). The results show the importance of policy strategies in integrating newly immigrated teachers into the labour market: The teachers emphasised that the Hebrew courses included in the preparatory measure were particularly important, as integration into the labour market and language learning could take place in parallel, without the acquisition of the national language as a prerequisite (Putjata, 2018, p. 7). Moreover, Putjata showed that the interviewees positioned themselves both as "new immigrant multilingual teachers" as well as part of the educational system in their narratives. By implementing suitable policies that recognise the qualifications and professional experience acquired in the country of origin as relevant in the migration context and for the respective education system, the teachers' perception of themselves and their positioning in the social and educational context also changes. Nevertheless, it also becomes clear that it is problematic if education policy efforts refer only to certain groups and ignores other newly immigrated persons (e.g. those from Ethiopia in Israel), who are accordingly not given the opportunity to use their skills for professional integration into the teaching profession.

The "Refugee Teachers" programmes introduced at some universities, qualification programmes for integration into school practice, as mentioned above, are not, as in the example described by Putjata, positioned at the national policy level in Germany, but at the project level (with limited duration) within individual federal states. Nevertheless, they have put the discussion about a general recognition of 'single-subject teachers', i.e. teachers who have a degree in only one subject, back on the education policy agenda. This is a key question because the recognition of qualifications acquired prior to migration regularly fails in Germany because of the requirement to study two subjects, a regulation which is almost unique in international comparison. However, since the societal orientation towards the (supposed) advantages of training in two subjects is extremely effective in Germany, the opportunities that could arise from migration and international mobility remain largely unused despite a shortage of teachers (see also Putjata, 2019).

If the focus in research in the coming years, and we see this as a perspective, is placed both on the first generation of minority teachers and on established minority teachers of the second and third generation of immigrants, then the formulation of common issues will make it possible to focus more strongly on the discriminatory structures of the German education system, including teacher education. Thus, in future it is possible that the question of the inclusion of minority teachers will no longer be correlated with ethnicised attributions of professional competence or with a "capitalization" (Dunn, 2016) of their transnational (professional) biographies in times of acute teacher shortages. There is a risk that mobility is positively connoted and, in particular, discursively presented as useful, but that a distinction is made between useful and threatening subjects of mobility or between legitimate and illegitimate migrants (Ratfisch, 2015). In this respect, when recruiting internationally trained teachers or minority teachers, educational policy and research should be guided by the argument of their social representation: "it should be a social institution's intention to display our diverse society in order to enable minorities to be socially representative (...) [S]o the aim should rather be to diversify the teaching staff so it mirrors the diversity within our society" (Rotter & Timpe, 2016, p. 98). Thus, the argument often used in the German discourse that minority teachers should prove effective or useful in reducing educational inequalities should be rejected as utilitarian ethnicisation.

The contribution of our study shows that research on minority teachers in Germany is becoming more differentiated, although that there are still desiderata. On the one hand, with the focus on gender and language, other dimensions along which social inequalities emerge are being considered. This seems central to future educational research in order to address migration-related diversity and race in an intersectional rather than one-sided way. On the other hand, established research topics such as racism are further differentiated by specifically examining minority teachers' experiences of anti-Muslim racism. Overall, forward-looking research approaches are highlighted that overcome the ethnicised attribution of professional competence to minority teachers by shedding light on the discriminatory structures of the German education system.

References

Akbaba, Y. (2013). Der Migrationshintergrund im Vordergrund. Gesellschaftliche Differenzordnungen und individuelle Umgangsstrategien einer Lehrerin. In K. Bräu et al. (Eds.), *Lehrerinnen und Lehrer mit Migrationshintergrund. Zur Relevanz eines Merkmals in Theorie, Empirie und Praxis* (pp. 187–196). Waxmann.

Akbaba, Y. (2017a). *Lehrer*innen und der Migrationshintergrund. Widerstand im Dispositiv*. Beltz.

Akbaba, Y. (2017b). Discourse ethnography on migrant other teachers: Turn the stigma into capital! *Zeitschrift für Diskursforschung, 5*(3), 309–326.

Akbaba, Y., Bräu, K., & Zimmer, M. (2013). Erwartungen und Zuschreibungen. Eine Analyse und kritische Reflexion der bildungspolitischen Debatte zu Lehrer/innen mit Migrationshintergrund. In K. Bräu et al. (Eds.), *Lehrerinnen und Lehrer mit Migrationshintergrund. Zur Relevanz eines Merkmals in Theorie, Empirie und Praxis* (pp. 37–57). Waxmann.

Bandorski, S., & Karakaşoğlu, Y. (2013). Macht 'Migrationshintergrund' einen Unterschied? Studienmotivation, Ressourcen und Unterstützungsbedarf von Lehramtsstudierenden mit und ohne Migrationshintergrund. In K. Bräu et al. (Eds.), *Lehrerinnen und Lehrer mit Migrationshintergrund. Zur Relevanz eines Merkmals in Theorie, Empirie und Praxis* (pp. 133–155). Waxmann.

Bräu, K., Georgi, V. B., Karakaşoğlu, Y., & Rotter, C. (Eds.). (2013). *Lehrerinnen und Lehrer mit Migrationshintergrund. Zur Relevanz eines Merkmals in Theorie, Empirie und Praxis*. Waxmann.

Bressler, C., & Rotter, C. (2017). The relevance of a migration background to the professional identity of teachers. *International Journal of Higher Education, 6*(1), 239–250.

Doğmuş, A. (2016). Professionalisierung in Migrationsverhältnissen – Eine rassismuskritische Perspektive auf das Referendariat angehender Lehrkräfte. In N. Dunker, N.-K. Joyce-Finnern, & I. Koppel (Eds.), *Wege durch den Forschungsdschungel. Ausgewählte Fallbeispiele aus der erziehungswissenschaftlichen Praxis* (pp. 119–136). Springer VS.

Doğmuş, A. (2017). Empowerment im Lehramtsstudium. In K. Fereidooni & M. El (Eds.), *Rassismuskritik und Widerstandsformen. (Inter)national vergleichende Formen von Rassismus und Widerstand* (pp. 771–788). Springer VS.

Döll, M., & Knappik, M. (2015). Institutional mechanisms of inclusion and exclusion in Austrian pre-service teacher education. *Tertium Comparationis, 21*(2), 185–204.

Dunn, A. (2016). Searching for the "American Dream": International teachers in the United States. *Bildung und Erziehung, 68*(4), 431–444. In A. Rakhkochkine und H.-G. Kotthoff (Eds.), Internationale Lehrermobilität. Themenheft.

Edelmann, D. (2013). Lehrkräfte mit Migrationshintergrund – ein Potenzial pädagogischer Professionalität im Umgang mit migrationsbedingter Heterogenität. In K. Bräu et al. (Eds.), *Lehrerinnen und Lehrer mit Migrationshintergrund. Zur Relevanz eines Merkmals in Theorie, Empirie und Praxis* (pp. 197–208). Waxmann.

Edelmann, D., Bischoff, S., Beck, M., & Meier, A. (2015). More students with migration backgrounds at universities of teacher education. Theoretical reflections and empirical insights on potential aspects and challenges from the perspectives of pre-service teachers and lecturers. *Tertium Comparationis, 21*(2), 205–224.

El, M., & Fereidooni, K. (2016). Racism experienced by teachers of color in Germany. In C. Schmidt & J. Schneider (Eds.), *Diversifying the teaching force in transnational contexts. Critical perspectives* (pp. 127–138). Sense Publishers.

Fereidooni, K. (2016). *Diskriminierungs- und Rassismuserfahrungen im Schulwesen. Eine Studie zu Ungleichheitspraktiken im Berufskontext*. Springer VS.

Georgi, V. B. (2013a). Empirische Forschung zu Lehrenden mit Migrationshintergrund, minority teachers und teachers of color. In K. Bräu et al. (Eds.), *Lehrerinnen und Lehrer mit Migrationshintergrund. Zur Relevanz eines Merkmals in Theorie, Empirie und Praxis* (pp. 85–103). Waxmann.

Georgi, V. B. (2013b). Selbstwirksamkeitsüberzeugungen von Lehrkräften mit Migrationshintergrund. Empirische Schlaglichter auf den Umgang mit Mehrsprachigkeit und kultureller Heterogenität. In K. Bräu et al. (Eds.), *Lehrerinnen und Lehrer mit Migrationshintergrund. Zur Relevanz eines Merkmals in Theorie, Empirie und Praxis* (pp. 223–241). Waxmann.

Georgi, V.B., Ackermann, L. & Karakaş, N. (2011). Vielfalt im Lehrerzimmer: Selbstverständnis und schulische Integration von Lehrenden mit Migrationshintergrund in Deutschland. Waxmann.

Glock, S., & Schuchart, C. (2020). The ethnic match between students and teachers: Evidence from a vignette study. *Social Psychology of Education, 23*(1), 27–50.

Göbel, K. (2013). Interkulturelle Kompetenz und emotionale Belastung von Lehrkräften mit Migrationshintergrund. In K. Bräu et al. (Eds.), *Lehrerinnen und Lehrer mit Migrationshintergrund. Zur Relevanz eines Merkmals in Theorie, Empirie und Praxis* (pp. 209–222). Waxmann.

Gogolin, I. (2008). *Der monolinguale habitus der multilingualen Schule*. Waxmann.

Höckel, L. S. (2020). *Speaking the same language. The effect of foreign origin teachers on students' language skills*. RWI – Leibniz-Institut für Wirtschaftsforschung.

Karakaş, N., & Ackermann, L. (2013). Erfahrungen von Lehrenden mit Migrationshintergrund mit migrantischen Eltern. In K. Bräu et al. (Eds.), *Lehrerinnen und Lehrer mit Migrationshintergrund. Zur Relevanz eines Merkmals in Theorie, Empirie und Praxis*. Waxmann (pp. 174–185).

Karakaşoğlu, Y., & Doğmuş, A. (2016). Muslimization – "Othering" experiences of students in academic teacher programs. In C. Schmidt & J. Schneider (Eds.), *Diversifying the teaching force in transnational contexts. Critical perspectives* (pp. 89–103). Sense Publishers.

Karakaşoğlu, Y., & Wojciechowicz, A. A. (2017). Muslim_innen als Bedrohungsfigur für die Schule – Die Bedeutung des antimuslimischen Rassismus im pädagogischen Setting der Lehramtsausbildung. In K. Fereidooni & M. El (Eds.), *Rassismuskritik und Widerstandsformen. (Inter)national vergleichende Formen von Rassismus und Widerstand* (pp. 507–528). Springer VS.

Karakaşoğlu, Y., Wojciechowicz, A., & Gruhn, M. (2013). Zum Stellenwert von Lehrerinnen und Lehrern mit Migrationshintergrund im Rahmen interkultureller Schulentwicklungsprozesse. In K. Bräu et al. (Eds.), *Lehrerinnen und Lehrer mit Migrationshintergrund. Zur Relevanz eines Merkmals in Theorie, Empirie und Praxis* (pp. 70–83). Waxmann.

Kleen, H., Bonefeld, M., Glock, S., & Dickhäuser, O. (2019). Implicit and explicit attitudes toward Turkish students in Germany as a function of teachers' ethnicity. *Social Psychology of Education, 22*(4), 883–899.

Klein, O., Neugebauer, M., & Jacob, M. (2019). *Migrant teachers in the classroom. A key to reduce ethnic disadvantages in school?* ResearchGate. https://www.researchgate.net/publication/334528962_Migrant_teachers_in_the_classroom_A_key_to_reduce_ethnic_disadvantages_in_school

Krüger-Potratz, M (2013). Vielfalt im Lehrerzimmer. Aktuelle bildungspolitische Entwicklungen unter der Frage von Kontinuitäten und Diskontinuitäten. In K. Bräu et al. (Eds.), *Lehrerinnen und Lehrer mit Migrationshintergrund. Zur Relevanz eines Merkmals in Theorie, Empirie und Praxis* (pp. 17–36). Waxmann.

Kul, A. (2013). "Jetzt kommen die Ayşes auch ins Lehrerzimmer und bringen den Islam mit." Subjektiv bedeutsame Erfahrungen von Referendarinnen und Referendaren im Rassismuskontext. In K. Bräu et al. (Eds.), *Lehrerinnen und Lehrer mit Migrationshintergrund. Zur Relevanz eines Merkmals in Theorie, Empirie und Praxis* (pp. 157–171). Waxmann.

Lengyel, D., & Rosen, L. (2011, November). *Vielfalt im Lehrerzimmer durch Lehrkräfte mit Zuwanderungsgeschichte – intersektionale Rückfragen an eine bildungspolitische Forderung*. Paper presented at the Forschungsstelle für interkulturelle Studie (FiSt) of the University of Cologne, Cologne.

Lengyel, D., & Rosen, L. (2012a). Vielfalt im Lehrerzimmer?! – Erste Einblicke in ein Lern–/ Lehr- und Forschungsprojekt mit Lehramtsstudentinnen mit Migrationshintergrund an der Universität Köln. In K. Fereidooni (Ed.), *Das interkulturelle Lehrerzimmer. Perspektiven neuer deutscher Lehrkräfte auf den Bildungs- und Integrationsdiskurs* (pp. 71–87). Springer VS.

Lengyel, D., & Rosen, L. (2012b, September). *Diversity in the staff room – Perspectives on the recruitment of ethnic minority teachers by migrant students in teacher education*. Paper presented at the European conference on educational research, Cádiz.

Lengyel, D., & Rosen, L. (2013, September). *Potentials and challenges of diversity in pre-service teacher education – Innovations in three German-speaking European countries*. Organised symposium at the European conference on educational research, Istanbul.

Lengyel, D., & Rosen, L. (2014, September). *Recent studies on minority teachers in (Non-) European education systems*. Organised symposium at the European conference on educational research, Porto.

Lengyel, D., & Rosen, L. (2015a). Diversity in the staff room – Ethnic minority student teachers' perspectives on the recruitment of minority teachers. *Tertium Comparationis, 21*(2), 161–184.

Lengyel, D., & Rosen, L. (2015b). Minority teachers in different educational contexts: Introduction. *Tertium Comparationis, 21*(2), 153–160.

Mantel, C. (2017). *Lehrer_in, Migration und Differenz – Fragen der Zugehörigkeit bei Grundschullehrer_innen der zweiten Einwanderungsgeneration in der Schweiz*. transcript.

Mantel, C. (2020). Being a teacher with a so-called 'immigrant background': Challenges of dealing with social boundaries. *Intercultural Education, 31*(2), 173–189.

Morris-Lange, S., Wagner, K. & Altinay, L. (2016). *Lehrerbildung in der Einwanderungsgesellschaft. Qualifizierung für den Normalfall Vielfalt*. Forschungsbereich beim Sachverständigenrat deutscher Stiftungen für Integration und Migration GmbH.

Panagiotopoulou, A., & Rosen, L. (2016). Sprachen werden benutzt, "um sich auch gewissermaßen abzugrenzen von anderen Menschen". Lehramtsstudierende mit Migrationshintergrund plädieren für einsprachiges Handeln im schulischen Kontext. In T. Geier & K. U. Zaborowski (Eds.), *Migration: Auflösungen und Grenzziehungen – Perspektiven einer erziehungswissenschaftlichen Migrationsforschung* (pp. 169–190). Springer VS.

Purrmann, K., Schüssler, R., Siebert-Husmann, C., & Vanderbeke, M. (2020). "Wir haben so lange auf eine Chance gewartet" – Potentiale und Herausforderungen des Qualifikationsprogramms Lehrkräfte Plus für geflüchtete Lehrkräfte. In G. Kremsner, M. Proyer, & G. Biewer (Eds.), *Inklusion von Lehrkräften nach der Flucht: Über universitäre Ausbildung zum beruflichen Wiedereinstieg* (pp. 217–226). Klinkhardt.

Putjata, G. (2017). 'My teacher had an accent too'. Immigrant teachers' and counselors' role in multicultural development – Perspectives of multilingual Israelis. *Journal of Education, 197*(3), 14–24.

Putjata, G. (2018). Immigrant teachers' integration and transformation of the linguistic market in Israel. *Language and Education, 21*(2), 1–17.

Putjata, G. (2019). 'Und da wurde mir klar, ich bin doch nicht dumm!' – Stimmen eingewanderter Lehrkräfte. In B. Hasenjürgen & M. Spetsmann-Kunkel (Eds.), *Kulturalisierungsprozesse in Bildungskontexten* (pp. 177–192). Nomos.

Ratfisch, P. (2015). Zwischen nützlichen und bedrohlichen Subjekten. Figuren der Migration im europäischen 'Migrationsmanagement' am Beispiel des Stockholmer Programms. *Movements, 1*(1), 1–21.

Rosen, L. (2015). Sammelrezension zu Lehrkräften mit Migrationshintergrund. *Erziehungswissenschaftliche Revue, 14*(6) https://www.klinkhardt.de/ewr/978383092859.html

Rosen, L., & Jacob, M. (2021). Diversity in the teachers' lounge in Germany – Casting doubt on the statistical category of 'migration background'. *European Educational Research Journal*. Epub ahead of print 27 November 2021. https://doi.org/10.1177/14749041211054949.

Rotter, C. (2014a). Kompetent durch Migrationserfahrung? Die Betonung des Migrationshintergrunds als Gefahr einer Deprofessionalisierung von Lehrkräften. *Zeitschrift für interpretative Schul- und Unterrichtsforschung, 3*, 101–114.

Rotter, C. (2014b). *Zwischen Illusion und Schulalltag. Berufliche Fremd- und Selbstkonzepte von Lehrkräften mit Migrationshintergrund*. Springer VS.

Rotter, C., & Schlickum, C. (2013). Lehrkräfte mit Migrationshintergrund als Forschungsgegenstand: Fortschreibung einer Differenzmarkierung? In K. Bräu et al. (Eds.), *Lehrerinnen und Lehrer mit Migrationshintergrund. Zur Relevanz eines Merkmals in Theorie, Empirie und Praxis* (pp. 59–68). Waxmann.

Rotter, C., & Timpe, M. (2016). Role models and confidants? Students with and without migration backgrounds and their perception of teachers with migration backgrounds. *Teaching and Teacher Education, 59*, 92–100.

Schlickum, C. (2013). Professionelle Orientierungen von Lehramtsstudierenden mit und ohne Migrationshintergrund im Umgang mit sprachlicher Vielfalt. In K. Bräu et al. (Eds.), *Lehrerinnen und Lehrer mit Migrationshintergrund. Zur Relevanz eines Merkmals in Theorie, Empirie und Praxis* (pp. 107–117). Waxmann.

Schmidt, C., & Schneider, J. (Eds.). (2016). *Diversifying the teaching force in transnational contexts. Critical perspectives*. Sense Publishers.

Strasser, J. (2013). Diversity in the faculty room: Constraints and affordances of minority teachers' professional action in Germany. *International Journal of Diversity in Education, 12*(3), 131–141.

Strasser, J., & Leutwyler, B. (2020). Differenzerfahrungen von Lehrkräften und ihre Bedeutung für den Umgang mit Vielfalt. *Empirische Pädagogik, 34*(2), 128–143.

Strasser, J., & Waburg, W. (2015). Students' perspectives on minority teachers in Germany. *Tertium Comparationis, 21*(2), 251–274.

Terhart, H., & Rosen, L. (2022). Editorial: Diversification of the teaching profession in Europe and beyond: Ambivalences of recognition in the context of migration. *European Educational Research Journal, 21*(2), 203–213.

Terhart, H., Preuschoff, S., & Elshof, A. (2020). Programm für geflüchtete Lehrkräfte in Köln. In G. Kremsner, M. Proyer, & G. Biewer (Eds.), *Inklusion von Lehrkräften nach der Flucht: Über universitäre Ausbildung zum beruflichen Wiedereinstieg* (pp. 207–216). Klinkhardt.

Waburg, W., & Strasser, J. (2018). Geschlechtsbezogene Muster des Umgangs mit (bildungspolitischen) Erwartungen an Lehrer*innen mit Migrationshintergrund. In E. Breitenbach, T. V. Rieske, & S. Toppe (Eds.), *Migration, Geschlecht und Religion* (pp. 61–76). Barbara Budrich.

Wojciechowicz, A. (2013). 'Kulturelle Differenz' als positionszuweisendes Deutungsmuster von Akteurinnen und Akteuren in der Praktikumsbegleitung von Lehramtsstudierenden aus Einwandererfamilien. In K. Bräu et al. (Eds.), *Lehrerinnen und Lehrer mit Migrationshintergrund. Zur Relevanz eines Merkmals in Theorie, Empirie und Praxis* (pp. 119–132). Waxmann.

Wojciechowicz, A., & Vock, M. (2019). Wiedereinstieg in den Lehrerberuf nach der Flucht mit dem Refugee Teachers Program in Brandenburg. *Die Deutsche Schule, 111*(2), 220–230.

Lisa Rosen is Professor of Education with a focus on intercultural education at the University of Kaiserslautern-Landau (RPTU). As Link Convenor she represents Network 07 "Social Justice and Intercultural Education" of the European Educational Research Association (EERA). Her main areas of research and teaching are intercultural education, multilingual education, pedagogical professionalism, inclusion and social inequalities in migration societies, forced migration and refugee studies as well as intersectional and international comparative educational research.

Drorit Lengyel is Professor of Education with special emphasis on multilingual contexts at the Hamburg University. Her main areas of research and teaching are education in linguistically diverse settings, language education, heritage language instruction and education, (pre-service) teacher professionalization, collective beliefs on multilingualism in educational organisations, linguistic racism/ intersection of language and race, international comparative educational research.

Open Access This chapter is licensed under the terms of the Creative Commons Attribution 4.0 International License (http://creativecommons.org/licenses/by/4.0/), which permits use, sharing, adaptation, distribution and reproduction in any medium or format, as long as you give appropriate credit to the original author(s) and the source, provide a link to the Creative Commons license and indicate if changes were made.

The images or other third party material in this chapter are included in the chapter's Creative Commons license, unless indicated otherwise in a credit line to the material. If material is not included in the chapter's Creative Commons license and your intended use is not permitted by statutory regulation or exceeds the permitted use, you will need to obtain permission directly from the copyright holder.

Chapter 9
Teachers with Migration Background in German Discourse: Insights into Research on Education, Professional Integration and Self-Perception

Evghenia Goltsev, Galina Putjata, and Anastasia Knaus

Abstract This chapter presents the state of the art focusing on the so-called teachers with "migration background" in Germany. Applying the method of the literature review, we summarize current and emerging research trends as well as understudied areas in Germany. The chapter provides the reader with a critical survey of the extensive literature produced in the past decade and a synthesis of current thinking on the topic at hand across disciplines and methodological approaches. The chapter opens up with a concise presentation of the context, objectives and the methodology of the study. These are followed by a critical synopsis of the findings and a closing conclusion. The results of the analysis reveal that a vast amount of research is focusing on the three following domains: Ascriptions and (Self-)perception of minority teachers' role in education such as the responsibility of fostering the linguistic diversity) Minority teachers' role for students and students' own perspectives, e.g. the importance of the multilingual teachers for self-positioning of the students as migration-related multilinguals; as well as professional integration of minority teachers including access to the labour market and teacher education revealing an underrepresentation of minority teachers in schools. In the conclusion we point out new perspectives and areas in need of further research, such as the demand for new approaches on how to constructively include migration-related multilingualism in the course of teacher education.

E. Goltsev (✉) · G. Putjata
University of Regensburg, Regensburg, Germany
e-mail: evghenia.goltsev@sprachlit.uni-regensburg.de

A. Knaus
Mercator Institute for Literacy and Language Education, Köln, Germany

Introduction

In Germany, educational policies ascribe high expectations towards the so-called teachers with "migration background". In this chapter, we will present the state of the art focusing on this group of minority teachers. By means of a literature review, we will summarize current and emerging trends as well as research priorities in Germany. Germany constitutes an important research context as transnational mobility has been and continues to be crucial to the German society on one hand. On the other hand, Germany itself plays a significant role in worldwide transnational trajectories. The chapter will start with a short presentation of our research objectives and methodology. In the main part, we will provide the reader with a critical survey of the extensive literature produced in the past decade and a synthesis of current thinking across disciplines. The chapter will close with new perspectives and point out areas in need of further research.

Minority Teachers in Germany: Objectives and Context of the Research

In this chapter, we focus on minority teachers with a "migration background" within German educational context. The aim is to give an overview of the ascribed and perceived roles, chances as well as obstacles faced by the group of pre- and inservice professionals defined by these characteristics. As a substantial scope of research and literature has been dedicated to this topic, our aim was to conduct a narrative review (see section "Methodology") and present the international public with an extensive synthesis.

The group of minority teachers discussed in German research landscapes are quite heterogeneous with regards to age, gender, teacher status (pre-/inservice) and country of origin (some are born in Germany others migrated from different countries at different ages). Related to the age of arrival, some studies focus on individuals who studied to become teachers in Germany, others received an education in other countries. Studies also differ in their language backgrounds, as some of the teachers started to acquire German as adolescents or adults, others grew up with two or more languages including German. There also might be individuals who only spoke primarily German in the family – e.g. due to parental decisions. The (political) discourse and most of the reviewed studies are based on the ascribed common factor – the "migration background" as it is defined by the Federal Statistical Office of Germany (2018) "*A person has a migration background if he or she or at least one parent does not possess German citizenship by birth*"[1] (p. 4). However, it is worth noticing that some of the sources focus specifically on immigrant or newly arrived teachers.

---

[1] This basically creates a three-level categorization of first-, second- and third-generation migration background based on citizenship and country of birth, going back three generations.

Methodology

To address the aim of the study, we applied the method of a narrative review. This approach, also called a literature review, allows for a broad perspective on a topic area that can be obtained inductively without the need to derive and formulate certain hypotheses (Petticrew & Roberts, 2006, p. 10). In our case, this review type followed five steps (based on Grant & Booth, 2009; Mertens, 2010, p. 89; Ressing et al., 2009):

1. Formulating the topic and the objective;
2. Finding pivot examples of the relevant literature, reviewing it and formulating keywords for the search. Researchers who already work in the respective field and are familiar with the topic oftentimes write stand alone narrative reviews. In these cases, the initial review is used to confirm the existing assumptions regarding the keywords;
3. Defining inclusion criteria i.e. deciding on the characteristics of the studies to be included in the review;
4. Searching for further relevant sources in the databases as well as hand-searching bibliographies and consulting experts for gray literature;
5. Reading, synthesizing, summarizing and writing.

First, the research objective was formulated. Then we specified the main concepts and respective keywords for the search based on our individual expertise, supported by pivotal papers.[2] We also decided to include only literature published in the last 10 years, as the topic is well established. Scientific articles as well as chapters in edited volumes and doctoral theses were included. For the search, we used the databases FIZ, ResearchGate, GoogleScholar, Academia and EBSCO Open Dissertations. The results of this search were expanded by hand searching and literature recommended by other experts. In the following, we synthesize by reviewing and comparing the results of the studies but also interpret the findings.[3]

---

[2] These keywords were used applying AND/OR connectors "*MIGRATIONSHINTERGRUND, LEHRAMTSSTUDENT/STUDIERENDE, LEHRER/LEHRER*INNEN, LEHRKRAFT, LEHRERBILDUNG, PROFESSIONALISIERUNG, MEHRSPRACHIGKEIT, SCHULE, ZUWANDERUNGSGESCHICHTE, MIGRATIONSERFAHRUNG, AUSLÄNDISCHE ABSCHLÜSSE, INTERNATIONAL, TRANSNATIONAL* (migration background, teacher – male, female and gender-neutral form -, teacher education, teacher development, multilingualism, school, immigrant, migration experience, foreign diploma, international, transnational). Since the focus of the chapter is on Germany, we only applied the terms in German.

[3] The aim of the present chapter was to inform the reader on the recent state of the art in German research landscape. Since we incorporated quantitative as well as qualitative research of different types, scopes and disciplines, we did not opt to find standardized evaluation criteria for the critical evaluation of the sources. Thus, the publication does not contain any systematic evaluation of the studies. Further information on the peril of the narrative review approach of being prone to biases towards the prefered hypothesis can be found in Grant and Booth (2009). Yet, as we did not have any working hypotheses, we were not at risk to have one-sided source selection.

Results and Discussion

The results of our analysis reveal a vast amount of research in the last 10 years, in the three following domains: (1) Ascriptions and (Self-)perception of minority teachers' role in education; (2) Minority teachers' importance for students and students' own perspectives; and (3) Professional integration of minority teachers including access to the labor market and teacher education. We will present these domains in the following focusing on recent findings and the underlying argumentation.

Ascriptions and (Self-)Perception of Minority Teachers' Role in Education

Sociological studies in education analyze ascriptions towards the constructed group of teachers with a "migration background" as well as teachers' perception of these ascriptions. The Ministry for School and Education in North Rhine-Westphalia (NRW) regards teachers with "migration background" as "examples for successful rise through education" (MSW NRW, 2007, p. 3). In a current initiative for "gaining them", it is further stated that "with their double competence in the German language and heritage language as well as their experiences in two cultures, they can assume an important mediating function at school and promote intercultural qualification" (MSW NRW, 2007). Further studies of educational policies in official statements and documents confirm that teachers with "immigrant background" are expected to represent the complexity of the society and question societal power relations (Strasser & Steber, 2010). They are also supposed to function as so-called change agents, able to drive change within schools (Lengyel & Rosen, 2015). At the same time, they are seen as cultural bridge builders, mediators, language translators and role models (Akbaba et al., 2013; Georgi et al., 2011).

To begin with, these expectations reveal a number of problematising assumptions: Children and youths with an immigration history would need "examples" and would first have to "rise" through education. Thus, the responsibility for educational success is shifted to students and the complexity of institutionally induced educational inequality is ignored. At the teacher level, these assumptions reveal a number of ascriptions. Here, similar patterns of homogenisation can be found as in the case of children with a "migration background" namely: Regardless of the socio-economic background, the (educational) biography or the language skills, the group of teachers is constructed as having a "migration background". They are to be "gained" as a measure that is specifically aimed at the group of students with a "migration background" and not at the homogenisation strategies of educational institutions. In this way, "the responsibility for shaping education in a way that is sensitive to diversity is delegated to teachers who are positioned as migrants" (Hummrich & Terstegen, 2020, p. 117).

Numerous qualitative studies critically examine the link between professionalization and migration experiences from the perspective of the teachers themselves (Fereidooni, 2012; Akbaba, 2017). Edelmann (2013) conducted interviews with primary teachers, including 15 with "migration background", and has identified several types regarding attitudes towards migration related diversity, from distanced one to cooperative-synergie-oriented.[4] Interestingly, teachers with "migration background" were present in all the types, except for the distanced one, which was interpreted as due to engagement with diversity.

Studies on professionalization in dealing with diversity also include quantitative methods: Based on the COACTIV-model of professional competence, Hachfeld et al. (2012) examined self-efficacy expectations, enthusiasm and prejudices with regard to students with a "migrant background" depending on teachers' "own migrant background" and multicultural beliefs in 433 pre-service mathematics teachers. The authors conclude that teachers with a "migration background" have more pronounced multicultural beliefs, which in turn positively influenced their self-efficacy expectations and enthusiasm and negatively influenced their prejudices.

Finally, Syring et al. (2019) examined whether pre-service teachers "with and without a migration background differ in their attitudes towards dealing with social, ethnic-cultural and academic heterogeneity" (p. 201). Having interviewed 877 students, of which 169 "with a migration background", the authors conclude more favourable attitudes in the latter group: "lower costs and negative emotions, higher intrinsic motivation and perceived competence" (Syring et al., 2019) with regard to all three forms of heterogeneity.

With regard to language, the teachers examined in these studies reproduce monolingual notions of normality and support the German-only-policy in and outside the classroom (Panagiotopoulou & Rosen, 2016; Putjata, 2019a, b, c). This behavior has been explained as following: Being teachers, and thus academics themselves, this group of multilingual teachers who mostly grew up in Germany, have successfully passed through the German school and university system and today, they reproduce the constructed value of the educational language German for the successful educational biography. They have hardly encountered family languages in the school context and have not had the opportunity to acquire the expected multilingual reading and writing skills in the institution of school, since the teaching of family languages in German has so far been an exception (Goltsev et al., 2022). Their own perception of multilingualism is the result of socio-political discourse on multilingualism as reflected on the linguistic market of educational institutions. The way society deals with multilingualism shapes their current ideas of normality: Teachers who have experienced multilingualism as a legitimate part of everyday interaction and as a capital for learning and educational success see migration-related multilingualism as an important resource for their students and for society in general (Putjata, 2018).

---

[4] Edelmann differentiates the following six types: detached-distant type, acknowledging type, individual-language oriented type, cooperative-language oriented type, individual-synergie oriented type, cooperative-synergie oriented type.

Yet, data on teachers' own perception of their expected role reveal rejections and resistance: teachers who grew up in Germany and want to be perceived as such refuse to be reduced to special competences of questionable value like knowledge of 'the heritage language' and 'two cultures' (Georgi et al., 2011). According to a recent study based on biographical methods, even the "spontaneous affinity to the role as integration model and mediator does not mean" that one's own experiences of discrimination in the education system lead "to an inclusion-oriented 'attitude' in the field of school that is critical of power and discrimination" (Schwendowius, 2015, p. 528). This critical attitude requires opportunities for interpretation that would make a reflective processing and re-interpretation of own experiences possible (ibid.).

Minority Teachers' Importance for Students' and Students' Own Perspectives

The second identified research area was the ascribed importance for students' academic development as well as students' own perspectives.

The debate on the existent discrepancy in the academic performance of students with and without a "migration background" – in part triggered by international school performance studies like PISA and TIMSS – has put the demand for teachers with a "migration background" increasingly in the focus of educational policy. The main claim is that teachers with an "immigrant background" have a specific potential for dealing with cultural heterogeneity in their teaching practice (Presse- und Informationsamt der Bundesregierung, 2007). Educational political bodies therefore hope that by employing more teachers with a "migration background" they can obtain a positive effect on the academic performance of students with a "migration background", based on the teachers' own migration experience (MSW NRW Ministry of Education, 2007). As already presented in section "Minority teachers in Germany: objectives and context of the research", this statistically used category "migration background" is highly vague and complex to apply equally to all people in this group. Nevertheless, special competencies with regard to students are being attributed to teachers, derived from their migration background and understood as the result of their biographical experience. These competences include sensitivity in dealing with migration-related heterogeneity in school or a special language assessment competence. Thus, they are assigned to have special access to students with a "migration background" (Rotter, 2014). Since the research interest has primarily focused on teachers themselves, little attention has been paid to the perspective of students. So far, only few studies could support the above-mentioned hopes of educational policies (Rotter, 2015; Strasser & Waburg, 2015). Studies that focused on discussions with different groups of students concerning age, gender and ethno-cultural background provide initial results on the students' perspective.

In her survey from 2015, Rotter examined the perspective of students with regard to the questions whether the "migration background" of teachers is particularly relevant for their students in everyday school life and whether the perception of teachers with a "migration background" differs between students with and without a "migration background". In the group discussions with students from both "categories" at two secondary schools, the ethno-cultural background of teachers did not receive any special attention. The students described their teachers by mainly using other, particularly lesson-related, categories. These included, for example, a good classroom management, the ability of a teacher to present new lesson content in a clear and methodically varied manner as well as an understanding of the interests and concerns of their students (Rotter, 2015, p. 17). Two aspects were particularly important to the students: the teachers' technical competence ('mastery theme') and their student-oriented behaviour inside and outside the classroom ('love theme') (ibid.). Yet, interestingly, the results of this study showed that the "immigrant background" of the students has a positive impact on the description of this characteristic in teachers (ibid.). Rotter (2015), however, states that this influence is not determinative or should be understood in a linear relation. The influence rather depends on other factors like language skills in the German or family languages beyond German as well as one's own relationship to the majority society.

Another study that examined students' perspectives on "minority teachers", (Strasser & Waburg, 2015), comes to the same conclusion. Like Rotter (2015), they conducted group-discussions with students in grades 5, 7 and 9. In order not to bias the students' opinions about their teachers' "ethno-cultural background", the groups were asked about their general experiences at school and concerning all their teachers. The results show that teachers' "minority background" itself did not play an important role in terms of the students' expectations. Their judgements rather focused on teachers' personal attitudes and preferences, assigned to the before-mentioned dimensions 'love' and 'mastery theme': "A good teacher – according to the students – delivers vivid lessons, is knowledgeable in his or her subject, maintains good relationships with students and is fair and just." (Strasser & Waburg, 2015, p. 267). The authors, therefore, conclude that the cultural background of teachers does only become relevant to students when they try to find explanations for a certain behaviour of their teachers, thus assigning this characteristic an explanatory function, or when "they want to differentiate or reassure themselves" (Strasser & Waburg, 2015, p. 266).

At the same time, studies from childhood and youth research show that teachers who use their multilingualism in school practice are noticed by students. A recent study on personality development and identity construction shows that multilingual teachers are important for self-positioning as migration-related multilingual students in society: as part of the imagined community and for the legitimacy of minority languages in formal and informal situations. Having experienced that "my teacher had an accent too" – they do not perceive the accentuated pronunciation of authority figures as an obstacle and consequently see themselves as a legitimate member of a linguistically heterogeneous community (Putjata, 2019c).

Finally, the study by Neugebauer and Klein (2016) addresses the question of whether a stronger presence of preschool teachers with a "migration background" has a positive effect on children with a "migration background" thus helping to compensate ethnic disadvantages and contributing to more equal opportunities in education. In order to examine this question, children with a "migration background" who had teachers with a "migration background" were compared with those, whose teachers had no "migration background". A total of 1082 children from 171 kindergardens were included in the study, which mainly focused on two outcome variables: the cognitive-performance-related components such as the German language, natural sciences and mathematics, as well as childrens' social skills. The results did not confirm the postulated expectations. A positive influence could not be determined in neither of the mentioned competence fields. The analysis even showed the opposite: children with a "migration background" from groups with teachers with a "migration background", achieved poorer scores than those groups only with teachers without a "migration background" (Neugebauer & Klein, 2016).

The presented findings point out that teachers with a "migration background" do not necessarily meet the expectations of German educational policies. Their migrant status and ethno-cultural background, considered by itself, is not a primarily characteristic which is noticed by students and which does not automatically lead to positive effects on students' educational achievement. Thus, the migration background in itself implies no special competence for dealing with "migrant" children and students. It is rather the overall teaching competence than the teachers' cultural background that defines the quality in dealing with children and students. Teacher training must therefore focus on offering appropriate opportunities to all (future) teachers to develop the needed skills in the course of their professionalization regardless of their linguistic and migrational background.

Professional Integration and Teacher Education

In this chapter, we will present findings from the last identified research area: professional integration of minority teachers and teacher education.

Studies with newly immigrated teachers in Germany show that their access to the school education market is severely restricted (Terhart et al., 2018). In the interwoven interplay of economic, social and cultural capital, language in particular is a powerful instrument: although immigrant teachers have the incorporated (pedagogical knowledge and skills) and institutionalised capital (diploma) in Bourdieu's sense, it is not present in legitimate language. Every step of recognition is tied to this symbolic capital. Access to a qualified employment is thus restricted and leads to social relegation and suspension, at most on a fee basis with contracts for special services "[…] these would be awarded especially because of the foreign qualifications of the teachers and result in mother-tongue teachers being rated worse in terms of service and salary and often working with contracts limited to one year" (Kremsner et al., 2020).

However, not only newly arrived teachers face difficulties in their education. The recent statistics and findings of studies that are devoted to questions of representation numbers in specific domains show that students who came to Germany at an early age or have parents or grandparents who migrated to Germany are underrepresented in schools: While for students it is 12,5%, it is only 8% for teachers and in teacher education (Besa & Vietgen, 2017; Berthold & Leichsenring, 2012; DESTATIS, 2018).

The latter aspect – underrepresentation in teacher education – can be attributed to negative school experiences and institutional boundries that prevent the decision and the possibility to enter teacher education as well as inequalities during the education that lead to high drop out rates (ibid.). These can include financial, organisational and language issues[5] (Karakaşoğlu, 2011; Kimmelmann & Lang, 2014; Zerlik et al., 2014; Besa & Vietgen, 2017).

Studies on diversity within the educational system and in particular in teacher education, reveal that within the first and second phase of the training at universities and in schools (so called Referandariat) the students often experience discrimination like lacking sense of belonging, offensive remarks as well as rejection and exclusion by colleagues and trainers (Naumann, 2011; Georgi et al., 2011; Fereidooni, 2016).

Based on the outcomes of the research dealing with the school situation from the perspective of the teachers, it can be assumed that the first aspect – underrepresentation in schools – is the issue of retention. Here, different kinds of discrimination are reported as well (Georgi, 2010). They range from openly uttered pejorative comments on the accent or ethnic-cultural background to more subtle ways of sweeping attributions in regards to the phenomenon of othering and associations with the (alleged) country of origin. At the same time, cases of conscious appreciation or use of multilingualism are hardly ever reported (Georgi, 2010; Naumann, 2011; Rotter, 2014).

As a reaction to the difficulties faced by the newly arrived teachers, programmes and courses have been developed throughout Germany with the goal to "provide language and technical qualifications for refugee teachers in order to facilitate their professional re-entry" (Terhart et al., 2018). Such opportunities for professional integration can result in teachers perceiving their migration-related multilingualism as a resource (Putjata, 2019b). Further initiatives and projects aim for teachers with "migration background" (Karakaşoğlu et al., 2013). To list only a few: the scholarship "Horizonte (horizons)"[6] or mentoring for students with migration background at university Kassel[7]; LehrkräftePLUS Köln (TeachersPLUS Cologne[8]) and so called Refugee Teachers and Social Worker Programs, for example in Bielefeld, Potsdam, Cologne, Münster, Oldenburg or Bremen.

---

[5] Often due to monolingual expectations.

[6] https://www.scholarshipportal.com/scholarship/horizonte-stipendien-fuer-angehende-lehrkraefte-mit-migrationshintergrund

[7] https://www.uni-kassel.de/projekte/mentoring-mig/startseite.html

[8] https://portal.uni-koeln.de/international/studium-in-koeln/academic-refugee-support/lehrkraefteplus-koeln

As already stated, even those teachers who enter teacher education do not automatically act as enforcers of multilingual changes. According to the results from an 'integrative school' in Hamburg, it is not enough to simply rely on multilingual teachers in order to change monolingual sense of normality in educational contexts (Putjata, 2019a). Changes are necessary at various levels, from the level of political decision makers to school development as an overall process. It is for instance imperative that not only those who themselves have migration related experience but all teachers foster these changes (Mantel & Leutwyler, 2013; Stitzinger, 2014; Goltsev & Bredthauer, 2020). These modifications should also include professionalization on dealing with multilingualism: Multilingual teachers must be prepared to endure antinomies and contradictions and to shape their own practice in them (Goltsev et al., 2022). Beneficial approaches might be those that enhance possible potentials of multilingual teachers (Rosen & Lengyel, 2012; Lengyel & Rosen, 2015; Putjata, 2018; Syring et al., 2019). These new directions should be implemented in all stages of teacher education starting with the university. Potential focal points might be diversity sensitive communication, discrmination-critical representations in media, multilingualism in classes, research on controversial developments in educational systems and sociological as well as anthropological knowledge about migration and mobility (Allemann-Ghionda, 2017).

Conclusion and New Research Areas

The presented research shows that the topic of teachers with a "migration background" has developed in a broad research field in Germany: Sociological studies reveal ascriptions associated with the constructed group as "othering" and criticize teachers' positioning as responsible for shaping diversity sensitive educational settings. While interviews reveal denial on the part of teachers themselves, studies on students' perspectives show the perceived importance of teachers who position themselves as multilingual for students' self-perception as a legitimate member of the imagined (multilingual) community. Studies from migration research reveal perceived difficulties to access the labor and education market as well as discrimination at universities and schools for teachers with "migration background" and even more so for those with non-German qualifications. Yet, new programs and courses allow for professional and linguistic integration, which open space for valorization of existing skills and may, on long term, contribute to a shift in perception towards multilingualism and diversity in general.

Biographical research shows that monocultural and monolingual notions of normality are not integral constructs that once formed, remain stable. They are fluid and open to processes of change. These findings underline how important it is to develop further didactic methods that would rely on biographical experiences and their critical reflection as important for all participants in teacher education.

The present state of the art shows that the professional handling of (linguistic) diversity in the migration society is perceived as the task of all teachers in German research. However, the handling of one's own experiences with (language) discrimination should constitute a significant topic of pedagogical professionalism (Hummrich & Terstegen, 2020, p. 118). These reflections should be carried out not in additional measures but in regular teacher training. As a reaction to this research lacuna, more research is needed on how to constructively include migration-related multilingualism in the course of teacher education (see the upcoming Special Issue by Author et al.). In light of ever-increasing transnational and global mobility, new research areas are being developed that underline the significance of the multilingual turn in teacher education and practice which extends far beyond the schooling system. As both, multilingualism and teacher education as well as their interaction are critical aspects in issues of equal opportunities, educational equality and social cohesion, this new topic is framed by questions of language-responsible teaching and equality in education.

References

Akbaba, Y. (2017). *Lehrer*innen und der Migrationshintergrund: Widerstand im Dispositiv* (1st ed.). Beltz.

Akbaba, Y., Bräu, K., & Zimmer, M. (2013). Erwartungen und Zuschreibungen. Eine Analyse und kritische Reflexion der bildungspolitischen Debatte zu Lehrer/innen mit Migrationshintergrund. In K. Bräu, V. B. Georgi, Y. Karakaşoğlu-Aydın, & C. Rotter (Eds.), *Lehrerinnen und Lehrer mit Migrationshintergrund: Zur Relevanz eines Merkmals in Theorie, Empirie und Praxis* (pp. 37–58). Waxmann.

Allemann-Ghionda, C. (2017). Zur Diversitätsgerechten Professionalisierung Angehender Lehrpersonen – Pedocs. *Beiträge Zur Lehrerinnen- Und Lehrerbildung, 35*, 139–151.

Berthold, C., & Leichsenring, H. (2012). *Diversity report. Der Gesamtbericht (A1–D3)*. Retrieved from www.che-consult.de/services/quest/diversity-report/

Besa, K.-S., & Vietgen, S. (2017). Repräsentanz von Studierenden mit Migrationshintergrund in Lehramtsstudiengängen: Eine Analyse anhand der Daten des Nationalen Bildungspanels (NEPS). *Beiträge zur Lehrerinnen- und Lehrerbildung, 35*(1), 195–206.

DESTATIS. (2018, October 2020). *Sonderauswertung Mikrozensus 2017 für den MEDIENDIENST INTEGRATION*. Retrieved from https://mediendienst-integration.de/artikel/vielfalt-ist-eine-aufgabe-fuer-alle.html

Edelmann, D. (2013). Lehrkräfte mit Migrationshintergrund – ein Potenzial pädagogischer Professionalität im Umgang mit der migrationsbedingten Heterogenität. In K. Bräu, V. B. Georgi, Y. Karakaşoğlu-Aydın, & C. Rotter (Eds.), *Lehrerinnen und Lehrer mit Migrationshintergrund: Zur Relevanz eines Merkmals in Theorie, Empirie und Praxis* (pp. 197–209). Waxmann.

Fereidooni, K. (2016). *Diskriminierungs- und Rassismuserfahrungen im Schulwesen. Eine Studie zu Ungleichheitspraktiken im Berufskontext*. VS Verlag für Sozialwissenschaften.

Fereidooni, K. (2012). *Das interkulturelle Lehrerzimmer: Perspektiven neuer deutscher Lehrkräfte auf den Bildungs- und Integrationsdiskurs*. Springer VS.

Georgi, V. B. (2010, October 2020). *Forscherinnen der Freien Universität befragen Lehrkräfte mit Migrationshintergrund in Deutschland*. Retrieved from https://www.fu-berlin.de/presse/informationen/fup/2010/fup_10_281/index.html

Georgi, V. B., Ackermann, L., & Karakaş, N. (2011). *Vielfalt im Lehrerzimmer, Selbstverständnis und schulische Integration von Lehrenden mit Migrationshintergrund in Deutschland*. Waxmann.

Goltsev, E., & Bredthauer, S. (2020). Preparing prospective teachers to promote multilingual literacy: Curricular possibilities in teacher training. In G. Neokleous, A. Krulatz, & R. Farrelly (Eds.), *Handbook of research on cultivating literacy in diverse and multilingual classrooms* (pp. 516–534). igi Global.

Goltsev, E., Olfert, H., & Putjata, G. (2022). Finding spaces for all languages: Teacher educators' perspectives on multilingualism. *Language and Education, 36*(1), 1–14. https://doi.org/10.1080/09500782.2022.2085047

Grant, M., & Booth, A. (2009). A typology of reviews: An analysis of 14 review types and associated methologies. *Health Information and Libraries Journal, 26,* 91–108.

Hachfeld, A., Schroeder, S., Anders, Y., Hahn, A., & Kunter, M. (2012). Multikulturelle Überzeugungen. *Zeitschrift Für Pädagogische Psychologie, 26*(2), 101–120. https://doi.org/10.1024/1010-0652/a000064

Hummrich, M., & Terstegen, S. (2020). *Migration: Eine Einführung* (1st ed.). Module Erziehungswissenschaft. https://doi.org/10.1007/978-3-658-20548-5

Karakaşoğlu, Y. (2011). Lehrer, Lehrerinnen und Lehramtsstudierende mit Migrationshintergrund. Hoffnungsträger der interkulturellen Öffnung von Schule. In U. Neumann & J. Schneider (Eds.), *Schule mit Migrationshintergrund* (pp. 121–135). Waxmann.

Karakaşoğlu, Y., Wojciechowicz, A. A., Bandorski, S., & Kul, A. (2013). *Zur Bedeutung des Migrationshintergrundes im Lehramtsstudium. Quantitative und qualitative empirische Grundlagenstudie und Reflexion von Praxismaßnahmen an der Universität Bremen.* Universität Bremen.

Kimmelmann, N., & Lang, J. (2014). Lehramtsstudierende mit Migrationshintergrund und ihre Schwierigkeiten an der Universität. In J. Seifried, U. Faßhauer, & S. Seeber (Eds.), *Jahrbuch der berufs- und wirtschaftspädagogischen Forschung* (pp. 135–146). Verlag Barbara Budrich.

Kremsner, G., Proyer, M., & Biewer, G. (2020). *Inklusion von Lehrkräften nach der Flucht. Über universitäre Ausbildung zum beruflichen Wiedereinstieg.* Verlag Julius Klinkhardt.

Lengyel, D., & Rosen, L. (2015). Minority teachers in different educational contexts. Introduction. *Tertium Comparationis. Journal für International und Interkulturell Vergleichende Erziehungswissenschaft, 21*(2), 153–160.

Mantel, C., & Leutwyler, B. (2013). Lehrpersonen mit Migrationshintergrund: Eine kritische Synthese der Literatur. *Beiträge zur Lehrerinnen- und Lehrerbildung, 31*(2), 234–247.

Mertens, D. M. (2010). *Research and evaluation in education and pscychology* (3rd ed.). Sage.

MSW NRW. (2007). *Mehr Lehrkräfte mit Zuwanderungsgeschichte. Handlungskonzept.* Ministerium Für Schule Und Weiterbildung Des Landes Nordrhein-Westfalen.

Naumann, I. (2011, October 2020). *Lehramtsstudierende mit Migrationshintergrund an der Universität Kassel. Eine Analyse qualitativer Interviews im Rahmen des Projektes "Mentoring für Lehramtsstudierende mit Migrationshintergrund".* Retrieved from http://www.mentoring-mig.uni-kassel.de/wp-content/uploads/2011/11/Forschungsbe-richt_mentoring_naumann_end.pdf

Neugebauer, M., & Klein, O. (2016). Profitieren Kinder mit Migrationshintergrund von pädagogischen Fachkräften mit Migrationshintergrund? *Kölner Zeitschrift für Soziologie und Sozialpsychologie, 68*(2), 259–283.

Panagiotopoulou, A., & Rosen, L. (2016). Sprachen werden benutzt, "um sich auch gewissermaßen abzugrenzen von anderen Menschen". In T. Geier & K. U. Zaborowski (Eds.), *Studien zur Schul- und Bildungsforschung. Migration: Auflösungen und Grenzziehungen: Perspektiven einer erziehungswissenschaftlichen Migrationsforschung* (pp. 169–190). Wiesbaden. https://doi.org/10.1007/978-3-658-03809-0_10

Petticrew, M., & Roberts, H. (2006). *Systematic reviews in the social sciences: A practical guide.* Blackwell.

Presse- und Informationsamt der Bundesregierung. (Edt.). (2007). *Der Nationale Integrationsplan. Neue Wege – Neue Chancen.* Berlin: Presse- und Informationsamt der Bundesregierung.

Putjata, G. (2018). Delivering multilingual schools – Emergence and development of language beliefs in immigrant teachers. *Applied Linguistics Papers, 2/2018*(25), 53–69. https://doi.org/10.32612/uw.25449354.2018.2.pp.53-69

Putjata, G. (2019a). 'Und da wurde mir klar, ich bin doch nicht dumm!' – Stimmen eingewanderter Lehrkräfte. In B. Hasenjürgen & M. Spetsmann-Kunkel (Eds.), *Kulturalisierungsprozesse in Bildungskontexten* (pp. 177–190). Nomos.

Putjata, G. (2019b). Normalitätsvorstellungen von Lehrkräften im Wandel. Ansätze und Potentiale des Moduls 'Deutsch für Schülerinnen und Schüler mit Zuwanderungsgeschichte'. In M. Gomolla, E. Kollender, C. Riegel, & W. Scharathow (Eds.), *Themenheft 'Diversitäts- und Antidiskriminierungskonzepte im Feld von Schule und Migration – Erfordernisse, Spannungen und Widersprüche', Zeitschrift für Diversitätsforschung und –management* (pp. 81–94). Verlag Barbara Budrich.

Putjata, G. (2019c). Language in transnational education trajectories between the Soviet Union, Israel and Germany. Participatory research with children. *Diskurs Kindheits- und Jugendforschung/Discourse. Journal of Childhood and Adolescence Research, 4*, 390–404.

Ressing, M., Blettner, M., & Klug, S. J. (2009). Systematic literature reviews and meta-analyses: Part 6 of a series on evaluation of scientific publications. *Deutsches Arzteblatt International, 106*(27), 456–463. https://doi.org/10.3238/arztebl.2009.0456

Rosen, L., & Lengyel, D. (2012). Vielfalt im Lehrerzimmer?! – Erste Einblicke in ein Lern-/Lehr- und Forschungsprojekt mit Lehramtsstudentinnen mit Migrationshintergrund an der Universität zu Köln. In K. Fereidooni (Ed.), *Das interkulturelle Lehrerzimmer. Perspektiven neuer deutscher Lehrkräfte auf den Bildungsund Integrationsdiskurs* (pp. 71–88). Springer VS.

Rotter, C. (2014). *Zwischen Illusion und Schulalltag. Berufliche Fremd- und Selbstkonzepte von Lehrkräften mit Migrationshintergrund*. Springer VS.

Rotter, C. (2015). Lehrkräfte mit Migrationshintergrund aus der Perspektive von Schülerinnen und Schülern – Ergebnisse einer qualitativen Studie. *Zeitschrift für Bildungsforschung: zbf, 5*(1), 5–20.

Schwendowius, D. (2015). *Bildung und Zugehörigkeit in der Migrationsgesellschaft* (Zugl. bearb. Fassung von: Wien, Univ., Diss., 2014). Transcript.

Statistisches Bundesamt [Statistical Office of Germany]. (2018, October 2020). *Bevölkerung und Erwerbstätigkeit. Bevölkerung mit Migrationshintergrund – Ergebnisse des Mikrozensus 2017.* Retrieved from https://www.destatis.de/DE/Themen/Gesellschaft-Umwelt/Bevoelkerung/Migration-Integration/Publikationen/Downloads-Migration/migrationshintergrund-2010220177004.pdf?__blob=publicationFile&v=4#page=4

Stitzinger, U. (2014). Bilinguale pädagogische Fachkräfte als vorteilhafte Ressource in der Arbeit mitmehrsprachigen Kindern? In S. Sallat, M. Spreer, & C. W. Glück (Eds.), *Sprache professionell fördern* (pp. 311–317). Schulz-Kirchner Verlag.

Strasser, J., & Steber, C. (2010). Lehrerinnen und Lehrer mit Migrationshintergrund – Eine empirische Reflexion einer bildungspolitischen Forderung. In J. Hagedorn, V. Schurt, C. Steber, & W. Waburg (Eds.), *Ethnizität, Geschlecht, Familie und Schule: Heterogenität als erziehungswissenschaftliche Herausforderung; [Festschrift für Leonie Herwartz-Emden]* (1st ed., pp. 97–126). VS Verl. für Sozialwiss. https://doi.org/10.1007/978-3-531-92108-2_6

Strasser, J., & Waburg, W. (2015). Students' perspectives on minority teachers in Germany. *Tertium Comparationis, 21*, 251–274.

Syring, M., Merk, S., Cramer, C., Topalak, M. C., & Bohl, T. (2019). Der Migrationshintergrund Lehramtsstudierender als Prädiktor ihrer Einstellungen zu heterogenen Lerngruppen. *Zeitschrift für Bildungsforschung, 9*, 201–219.

Terhart, H., Putjata, G., Bak, R., & Schnitzer, A. (2018). Bildungsangebote für neu zugewanderte Menschen zwischen Teilhabe und Ausschluss. In E. Feyerer & W. Prammer (Eds.), *System. Wandel. Entwicklung* (pp. 374–380). Klinkhardt.

Zerlik, J., Vogel, R., & Seidel, P. (2014, October 2020). *Schwierigkeiten von Studierenden mit Deutsch als Fremdsprache in Mathematik(didaktik)klausuren im Grundschullehramt*. Retrieved from https://eldorado.tu-dortmund.de/bitstream/2003/33393/1/BzMU14-4ES-Zerlik-119.pdf

Evghenia Goltsev is a junior professor for Multilingualism and German as an Additional Language at the University of Regensburg. Prior to this position she was a substitute professor for Second Language at the Europa University of Flensburg and a postdoctoral researcher at the University of Cologne. She was a PhD-scholarship holder at the Research Training Group "Frequency effects in language" at the Albert-Ludwig University of Freiburg. The main focus of her research and teaching has been multilingual language acquisition and teaching as well as language attitudes and language perception in a multilingual society. Her current interests include multilingual literacy promotion and multilingualism in teacher education.

Galina Putjata is Professor for Multilingualism and Migration in Educational Science at the Goethe University Frankfurt, Germany. After having earned her PhD on multilingual development at the University of Dresden, she led several projects on multilingualism in education at the University of Münster, Université de la Réunion, the Université du Québec à Montréal, and the Research Centre on Bilingualism in Bangor. Her research interests are multilingual pedagogies, transnational education, minority teachers as well as teacher training. Currently, she enjoys working with participatory research approaches.

Anastasia Knaus works as a research associate at the Mercator Institute for Literacy and Language Education in the project COLD (Competencies of school teachers and adult educators in teaching German as a second language in linguistically diverse classrooms) where she currently is doing her doctorate with a dissertation on teacher's attitudes towards multilingualism. Her fields of research interests are competencies of school teachers, cultural diversity and linguistic heterogeneity in classrooms as well as language attitudes and multilingualism in teacher education.

Open Access This chapter is licensed under the terms of the Creative Commons Attribution 4.0 International License (http://creativecommons.org/licenses/by/4.0/), which permits use, sharing, adaptation, distribution and reproduction in any medium or format, as long as you give appropriate credit to the original author(s) and the source, provide a link to the Creative Commons license and indicate if changes were made.

The images or other third party material in this chapter are included in the chapter's Creative Commons license, unless indicated otherwise in a credit line to the material. If material is not included in the chapter's Creative Commons license and your intended use is not permitted by statutory regulation or exceeds the permitted use, you will need to obtain permission directly from the copyright holder.

Chapter 10
Germany: Professional Networks of Minority Teachers and Their Role in Developing Multicultural Schools

Josef Strasser

Abstract In order to explore the conditions for successfully realizing the supposed positive impact, the paper focuses on the role of the school context on the professional cooperation of minority teachers. It is assumed that minority teachers within a supportive context cooperate more tightly and cohesively. Thereby they may develop a common approach and realize a stronger impact on their school's development. Based on two case studies it is highlighted how such an impact can come about. The implementation of professional networks and learning communities of minority teachers may be a major step in developing multicultural schools. Schools with such communities seem to be open to professional impulses of minority teachers and give them space to develop a "diversity agenda", whereas other schools tend to marginalize them.

Introduction

Although in western societies the issue of minority teachers has been addressed for almost three decades (e.g. King, 1993), in German speaking countries minority teachers were investigated only in recent years (Strasser & Leutwyler, 2020). After international assessment studies revealed an achievement gap of minority students, the need for developing a more culturally sensitive school system was recognized. Recruiting more minority teachers became a popular demand of educational policy and was associated with the hope for a more adequate approach towards cultural diversity in schools (Strasser & Steber, 2010). This hope is based on research's consensus on the potential relevant contribution of teachers from diverse cultural and ethnic backgrounds to American education (Easton-Brooks et al., 2010; Irvine & Fenwick, 2011). The need for teacher educators to become aware of minority teacher candidates' specific potential and problems is particularly emphasized (Kohli, 2009). Hence, there is a wealth of studies that focus on how to recruit and

---

J. Strasser (✉)
RPTU Kaiserslautern Landau, Landau, Germany
e-mail: j.strasser@rptu.de

retain minority teacher candidates (Chen, 2012). Despite the unanimous call for more minority teachers and the abundance of international studies, there is still a limited presence of teachers with diverse cultural, ethnic or linguistic background at schools in German speaking countries. Whilst 37% of students share a migration background, only 8% of teachers are from a minority community (Statistisches Bundesamt, 2018). The under-representation of minority teachers that contrasts with a more and more diverse student body justifies the call for a more culturally diverse teacher faculty from a sheer ethical perspective. Concerning the empirical basis for this call, however, there is still little research that corroborates the expectations. After reviewing the existing research that pertains to minority teachers in the USA, Chen (2012) has to note that the knowledge about minority teachers and their professional strengths is still very limited. The bulk of research focused on teacher candidates and teacher education programs. The actual professional action of teachers within their schools and the conditions for the alleged positive impact is rarely addressed. Concerning German speaking countries studies by Edelmann (2006), Georgi et al. (2011), Mantel (2017), Rotter (2012), Strasser (2013), Strasser and Waburg (2015) and Strasser and Leutwyler (2020) only recently sparked an interest in investigating the specific aspects of minority teachers' professionalism. In contrast to undifferentiated expectations expressed in the sphere of educational policy, existing research does not suggest a general efficiency of minority teachers, as the ethnic background of teachers does not guarantee a general effect (Morris, 2007; Quiocho & Rios, 2000). Nevertheless it is plausible to assume that minority teachers draw on specific experiences that may be useful in overcoming cultural and/or linguistic/language barriers (Irvine, 1989; Rotter, 2012). Their socio-cultural experiences as well as possible multilingual competencies (Nieto, 1998) enable a more deliberate dealing with cultural diversity at schools (Georgi et al., 2011). They may also be helpful in establishing constructive relationships between minority parents and the school system (Irvine, 1989; Meier et al., 1989; Rotter, 2012). The realization of their specific potential, however, depends on certain context-specific conditions like school climate, the existence of an inclusive school program and the support by peer teachers and the heads of the school (Strasser, 2013).

Research Objective

Existing results reveal that teachers' professional action seems to be highly dependent on their experiences within the faculty room (Strasser, 2013). The study's purpose was to explore the interplay of minority teachers' professional cooperation and aspects of their "working context". Starting point for developing the study was the alleged positive impact of minority teachers on diverse schools and classrooms. The conditions under which such an impact may come about, have not yet been investigated up to now. It was assumed that the mere presence of minority teachers not automatically entails culture sensitive practices and routines. This would rather depend on the interaction with other minority teachers and their autochthonous colleagues, and on the specific characteristics of the school and teaching situations and classrooms.

Currently, there is no research about the interrelation of minority teachers' backgrounds, their working contexts and their professional cooperation in the educational system of German speaking countries. The presented study explores this issue.

Context of Research

To inform the study different research areas had to be taken into account: (a) Research that directly addressed minority teachers' role in schools (b) research on cooperation and professional learning of teachers and (c) research on the role of school variables (like school climate) in dealing with diversity issues.

(a) Minority teachers and diversity in schools

Several qualitative studies describe the difficult position of minority teachers and the barriers that hinder a positive impact on school development. As studies on minority teachers in the UK and USA reveal, particularly establishing positive relationships with their colleagues seems to be difficult. They experience more interferences in the communication with their majority colleagues and observe a tendency to avoid diversity issues (Gomez et al., 2008; Kohli, 2009; Wilkins & Lall, 2011). As unexpressed issues often contaminate communication, relationships get strained and minority teachers often feel alienated and marginalized (Feuerverger, 1997; Foster, 1994). Immigrant teachers in Canada shared the experience of being marginalized. They reported strong feelings of being treated like second-class citizens. Despite their high qualifications their strengths were not appreciated by their environment much like the strengths of minority students were not recognized. Marginalization was particularly evident in the communication with colleagues when issues of cultural identity were negotiated (Feuerverger, 1997). Sharing the same ethnic or minority background made it more likely for teachers to develop positive relationships with each other; furthermore the degree of support may vary with the minority status of colleagues (Vance et al., 1989). Such a support seems to be an essential precondition for making a specific contribution to the intercultural development of schools. In the study by Feuerverger (1997) the interviewed teachers determined their professional identity by their desire to contribute to a multicultural and inclusive school climate. As they perceived a gap between schools and minority families, improving the contact with minority students' parents was a major objective of their professional action. A central obstacle to their professional goals was the experience that there was little support by the school system. Feeling alienated from traditional values and goals within educational systems seems to be a common experience of minority teachers that is also described in other studies (Foster, 1994). Many minority teachers believe that majority teachers and representatives of school administration prefer conformity and the maintenance of the status quo. This contrasts with their emphasis on equity, social justice and the transformation of the school system. Due to their own schooling experiences these are important issues for them. Hence, when trying to follow an agenda that leads to more inclusive and just schools, they find themselves in opposition to prevailing attitudes (Feuerverger, 1997; Foster, 1994; Klassen & Carr, 1997). Results as to teachers' anti-racist attitudes and knowledge illustrate this point. Attitudes depend on teachers' minority status and knowledge about the implementation of multicultural policies does vary. It is positively associated with the extent of population diversity and socio-economic status (SES) of the communities surrounding the schools (Forrest et al., 2015; Klassen & Carr, 1997).

In order to bring about the expected positive effects as to intercultural school development, the employment of minority teachers has to be systematically accompanied and evaluated as a Dutch study implies (Ledoux et al., 2000). Schools that explicitly followed an integrative approach facilitated communication and cooperation of minority and majority teachers. When cooperating systematically all teachers adapted the content, procedures and attitudes of their teaching to the demands of intercultural education. They felt responsible for the commonly developed concepts and their implementation. Hence, the continuously supported cooperation of teachers helped to change instructional and institutional practices and to develop a common intercultural agenda. A look at research on professional learning communities of teachers may give some insight on how to facilitate teachers' communication.

(b) Cooperation and professional learning of teachers

That teacher communities foster teachers' professional development is well documented (Borko, 2004; Scheerens, 2010). They seem to be particularly promising in challenging areas that necessitate a common effort (Vangrieken et al., 2017). If teachers are to collaborate and reflect on their instructional and educational practices they need space and time to do so. Together with a shared goal, these are the basic preconditions for developing a professional learning community (DuFour & Eaker, 1998). To foster professional development within such communities a positive learning atmosphere and conversation culture seem to be essential (van Es, 2012). Hence, it does not suffice to bring teachers together, but they must be able to develop a sense of belonging to a community and of being safe in this environment. Therefore, learning communities that take place in the context of cultural diversity have to be facilitated carefully. Research has identified a variety of personal, structural, organizational and process characteristics that foster or hinder the collaboration and development of professionals (Vangrieken et al., 2015). The learning atmosphere and conversation culture proved to be important conditions for successful groups (van Es, 2012). They form the basis for productive collaboration and can be described as 'a trustful atmosphere of learning and exchange, in which critical aspects, as well as critical situations of classroom practice, can be addressed, existing teaching routines can be realized, and alternatives can be suggested without judgments' (Gröschner et al., 2014, p. 276). Developing sustained relationships and a shared commitment to support each other's professional practice and development characterizes such learning communities. Differences in teachers' perspectives, knowledge and routines are appreciated as potential learning resource (Grossman et al., 2001). Such a positive learning atmosphere and conversation culture necessitates shared norms and rules for their interactions. Discourse rules such as listening carefully to each other, respecting different perspectives, or being open for practice alternatives have to be mutually acknowledged (van Es, 2012). The emergence of such a conversation culture not only depends on individual characteristics of team members and on structural qualities of the group but is strongly influenced by variables at an institutional level (Vangrieken et al., 2015).

(c) School climate and diversity

To understand teachers' professional action and their interaction the institutional context has to be taken into account. An important aspect of this context is the so-called school climate. School climate refers to the quality and character of a school, which is shaped by its atmosphere, organizational culture, the resources and networks (Cohen et al., 2009). Such climatic aspects have been focused by school research and proved to be influential factors, affecting teachers as well as students and their parents (Freiberg & Stein, 1999). Concerning teacher's development, these factors influence their professional commitment (Collie et al., 2011) and the emergence of stress and burnout (Grayson & Alvarez, 2008). Effects of the school climate are generally related to four dimensions: (1) physical and socio-emotional safety (2) instructional quality (3) relations and cooperation within school (4) structural elements of the school environment (Cohen et al., 2009). The different aspects of the school climate do not take effect as objective external variables but are dependent on the experience and interpretation of subjects (Collie et al., 2011). As the objectively same context can be experienced differently, the individual perception of a school's climate is a decisive aspect. Teachers' interpretation of the situation contributes to their professional approach and job satisfaction (Klassen & Chiu, 2010; Pas et al., 2012; Taylor & Tashakkori, 1995). Particularly their approach concerning cultural diversity is determined by a school's organizational culture. The extent to which a school and its institutional practices are judged as diversity friendly seems to influence teachers' individual attitudes and actions towards minority students (Horenczyk & Tatar, 2002). Schools that, on the other hand, follow an assimilation-oriented approach, may tend to increase stress for the individual teacher and eventually cause diversity-related burnout. Those educational institutions that were perceived to be assimilationist revealed the highest levels of diversity-related burnout among teachers (Tatar & Horenczyk, 2003). Organizational practices and the institutional approach towards diversity can differ largely between schools. Gutentag et al. (2017) differentiate four possible institutional approaches. The distinguishing feature is an institution's underlying notion of diversity. Diversity may be seen as (1) a resource, that has to be used and fostered, (2) a problem, that hinders the institution in reaching its goals, (3) a challenge that holds a potential capability but is also associated with great effort and risks, (4) a negligible category that should not be emphasized. The institutional approach and individual behaviors and attitudes of teachers seem to go hand in hand with each other and concur. This interaction may be based on a cumulative effect. Hence, the positive or negative aspects of the institutional context can reinforce the positive or negative aspects of teachers' attitudes and professional action. When minority students and cultural diversity are appreciated by an institution and are regarded as a resource and asset, teachers tend to teach in more culturally sensitive ways, are less prone to stress and diversity-related burnout (Gutentag et al., 2017). Correspondingly, the highest level of diversity-related problems and stress have been reported in teachers with assimilative attitudes that teach in assimilative schools (Tatar & Horenczyk, 2003). A school's approach towards diversity is not arbitrary and independent of external factors like the percentage of minority children within a school district. Nevertheless, a school's development towards an adequate approach can be influenced and shaped. Head teachers and school management play a decisive role in framing the process. Building a diverse faculty, fostering cooperation among teachers and the joint development of adequate practices are decisive steps (Strasser, 2021).

Research Question and Assumptions

It was assumed that differences in a school's characteristics, particularly in their integration of minority teachers, are reflected in the cooperation of teachers and the joint development of culturally adequate practices. Objective of the following case study was to explore the conditions that lead to cooperation of minority teachers, their integration in the faculty, foster cooperation among teachers and further their professional learning particularly as to cultural diversity.

Based on the presented research the following questions were addressed:

Are differences between schools (esp. in their approach towards diversity and policy of recruiting minority teachers) associated with differences in

1. the integration of minority teachers?
2. minority teachers' cooperation and use of professional networks?
3. minority teachers' relation to and cooperation with majority teachers?
4. the development of joint efforts in changing institutional practices?

Methodology

An explorative approach relying on mainly qualitative research strategies was chosen. Insights in the questions ought to be found by comparing two exemplary cases. The research agenda consisted of three steps:

1. Identification of schools that followed differing approaches towards cultural diversity
2. Identifying school management's strategies towards minority teachers
3. Investigating teacher's cooperation and professional dealing with diversity

In a first step, schools that differed were identified by analyzing the documented profiles and self-portrayals of schools' web sites in a given Austrian school district. The urban district was selected due to its comparably high levels of minority students. It was analyzed if and in what way cultural diversity was addressed on the schools' web sites. Two schools were selected that seemed to follow contrasting approaches although being confronted with a similar extent of diversity.

Secondly, narrative interviews with the school's head teachers were conducted, to explore the school management's dealing with cultural diversity, particularly its strategies concerning minority teachers. The third step comprised group discussions with minority teachers of the selected schools. The discussions focused teachers' perspective on dealing with diversity at their school and their role as minority teachers. Analyzing their ways of interacting during the discussion should help to understand aspects of their professional cooperation. Group discussions are an established research method and serve to examine "collective orientations including the terms and structures of social worlds" (Schittenhelm, 2010, p. 130). As interview effects are less relevant in discussions than in one-on-one interview situations, the method is considered a valuable instrument in cases where participants and interviewers do not share the same background (Herwartz-Emden, 2000). Successfully conducting group discussions for research purposes presupposes that the groups are pre-existing "real groups", that is, the people involved have to share experiences within a common context. Shared experiences form the basis for collective orientations that are formulated on a group level (Bohnsack, 1995)." The group discussions are conducted in a non-directive manner, thus enabling the group to develop its own reference terms" (Schittenhelm, 2010, p. 130).

Sample

After analyzing the public self-portrayals and profiles of schools, two of them were selected because of their apparently contrasting approaches. The first was an elementary school that characterized itself as a multicultural institution. Opening the school to students and parents of diverse backgrounds and diminishing barriers for intercultural cooperation were addressed as major objectives of the school. The profile described the differing ethnic and cultural heritage of their students as assets and resources. Several projects concerning multicultural issues were delineated at the web site. In contrast to that, the second institution, a secondary school ("Gymnasium"), indicated no specific multicultural agenda and their self-portrayal did not address cultural diversity explicitly. A few projects as to diversity issues, however, were documented. The latter were restricted to the lower grades of the school and concerned with linguistic deficits of migrant students. Both schools had a relatively high percentage of minority students of 58% ("Gymnasium") resp. 63% (elementary school).

Six teachers took part in the group discussions, three teachers of the elementary and three of the secondary school. The first group consisted of female teachers, two of them were second-generation migrants from Turkey, one was a first-generation migrant from Serbia. The group from the second school consisted of male teachers only, two first-generation migrants from Hungary resp. Italy and one first-generation migrant with Hungarian and Romanian background.

Material and Analysis

A qualitative content analysis of interviews with schools' head teachers was conducted, categorizing their main statements.

Analysis of the two group discussions combined quantitative and qualitative measures. For the investigation of the interaction and conversation culture during the discussions, different aspects were assessed:

– General appreciation: Do the group members talk to each other politely, listen to each other, and let each other finish speaking?
– Shared rules: Does the group share collective rules for discourse and feedback?
– Common focus on activities: Is there a common focus on events, activities and strategies in the group's school?
– Dynamic of the discussion: Does the discussion run by itself and are themes brought up by the group autonomously or they guided by the interviewer?

These aspects describe important prerequisites for a positive learning atmosphere in professional teams (Sherin & van Es, 2008). Each category was coded by two independent raters for each unit of analysis based on a five-point Likert scale. A consent validation followed the individual coding process in case of low rater accordance. Thematic segments of the discussion were used as units of analysis. The discussion as a whole was rated as to the category "dynamic of the discussion".

The more qualitative interpretation of the data followed a sequential approach according to the "documentary method" (e.g. Bohnsack, 2010). The documentary method distinguishes between an immanent or literal meaning and a documentary meaning (pre-reflective or tacit knowledge) of any given statement. This methodological differentiation results in two work steps: "formulating interpretation" and "reflecting interpretation". "The basic structure of formulating interpretation is the decoding and formulation of the topical structure of the text. […] The task of the reflecting formulation is […] the reconstruction of the framework of orientation, of the habitus" (Bohnsack, 2010, p. 111). This interpretative step investigates if and how common episodes are narrated. Thereby especially the mode of discourse is assessed. An inclusive discourse may indicate common experiences and a common frame of reference. Repeated comparisons within and between group discussions are an important feature of the documentary method. The following two case studies are the result of these comparisons. Presentation focuses on the main results. Due to space limitations not all interpretative steps that led to these results can be described in detail.

Findings

Interviews with both schools' head teacher revealed that both viewed cultural diversity as a major issue. Both related to the urban context of their institution and the high percentage of minorities. Both perceived a need for recruiting more minority teachers and reported active recruiting strategies. They deemed minority teachers as important due their potential capacity as role models for minority students and as cultural mediators. Hence, they might help to overcome linguistic and cultural barriers. The primary school's management explored several other reasons for recruiting minority teachers. Not only might they relate to minority students' experiences (esp. of exclusion and discrimination), but they might also be able to detect dysfunctional institutional practices. Hence, they should play an important role in intercultural school development. The later was described as a common endeavor in which all teachers ought to take part. To reach this objective, collaboration between teachers regardless of their ethnic background ought to be fostered. The relevance of minority teachers for efforts of school development were not mentioned in the second interview.

Group Discussion 1

Superficial Characteristics of the Discussion

The discussion with Y, V and Gm took about 150 min and its transcript contains 14,321 words. It was rated as being highly indicative of general appreciation ($M = 4.5$), and group members were perceived as sharing collective rules for discourse and feedback ($M = 5$). Raters also agreed that there is a distinct common focus on events, activities and strategies in the group's school ($M = 4.5$). Group members also highly determined the course and dynamic of the discussion as themes were brought up by them autonomously ($M = 5$).

Thematic Course of the Discussion

The discussion starts with a short introduction of each teacher and rather quickly shifts to "instructional challenges" within multicultural classes. Teachers extensively explain their view of potential difficulties and resources in their everyday practice. While discussing they complement and confirm each other's statements. It seems as if they share a common understanding of instructional challenges and common strategies in dealing with them. They later on report that they developed a common approach for highly diverse classes. This approach is centered on acknowledging children's linguistic resources and fostering their mother tongue as well as their German language skills. Teachers describe at length different projects they commonly initiated. These projects aim at bringing together children with differing cultural heritage and avoiding the formation of separated ethnic groups. The projects focus on children's shared interests and try to make use of their specific skills and resources. At least two teachers cooperate in conducting the projects. A common approach is also reported with respect to teachers' work with parents. After extensively discussing minority teachers' advantages in relating to minority students' parents, teachers emphasize the necessity that the school as a whole attempt to create a welcoming atmosphere and brings together minority and majority parents. They describe different network strategies that may help that minority parents become more integrated and share contacts with majority parents. Their efforts culminated in the founding of a parents' club that is to strengthen parents' relation with the school. These efforts seem to be acknowledged by both minority and majority parents.

Teachers talk about their experiences with other schools concerning parent-school relations. They perceive a major difference, as in other schools' communication with parents is mostly restricted to formal occasions. The teachers locate the main reason for these differences in the cooperation in the faculty room and the role of the head teacher. The later would always emphasize the need for cooperation and bring together teachers on various occasions. For instance, she developed a specific program for beginning students that is conducted by three teachers. All three teachers agree that a major characteristic of their school is that teachers are strongly related to each other and cooperate frequently. Cooperation in teams helped them particularly at the beginning of their employment. They describe their professional practice as a common learning endeavor. The atmosphere of mutually helping each other would also be reflected in students' behavior. All teachers, regardless of their ethnic or cultural background, would understand intercultural school development as a common task. Fostering the well-being of students and a positive and accepting school climate was discussed as its main objective. Most of the projects targeting cultural diversity were initiated by majority and minority teachers alike. The group later on explores expectations towards minority teachers. They felt that their specific experiences and linguistic resources were appreciated, but they were not restricted to their cultural background and also recognized as "ordinary" teachers. In their view it was up to school management to provide favorable conditions for minority teachers; conditions that prevent being isolated or restricted to the role of a cultural mediator. Despite their positive experiences within their school they also deemed it important to have strong relations with other minority teachers. All three teachers seemed to be part of rich networks of minority teachers in Austria. They used their connections to discuss experiences and get impulses for school development efforts.

Interpretation of the group discussion revealed a consistently inclusive discourse mode with most episodes being told commonly. Hence, teachers drew on common experiences and seem to have developed a common frame of reference.

Group Discussion 2

Superficial Characteristics of the Discussion

The discussion with P, G and F took about 90 min and its transcript contains 8046 words. Raters perceived that group members showed general appreciation (M = 4.0), and shared collective rules for discourse and feedback (M = 4). Raters also agreed that a common focus on events, activities and strategies in the group's school could often not be discovered (M = 2.5). The course and dynamic of the discussion was rarely shaped by the group as a whole but by individual members or the interviewer (M = 2).

Thematic Course of the Discussion

The first part of the discussion is dominated by teachers' introductions. All three teachers describe their biographical and professional development rather extensively. They tell their stories individually in a sequential manner. When talking about their role as a minority teacher they arrive at a commonly discussed issue: being viewed as a role model for minority students. All three teachers agree that being a role model is an important aspect of their professional practice. They accept this role and the corresponding expectations. Two of them report active efforts to present themselves as positive role models to their students. They actively try to establish positive relationships with students that share the same background by conveying feelings of solidarity and relatedness. Their own experiences ought to motivate students in overcoming deficits and barriers. Institutional or contextual conditions that may impede students' careers are not explored. Consequently, no initiatives or projects to foster an intercultural school development are mentioned. All three teachers, however, have developed specific instructional practices to meet their minority students' needs. The basis for these practices is their own individual experiences. In the discussion, they recognize similarities in their individual approaches and they consider the possibility of developing a regular exchange in the future. Their individual strategies are limited to their classroom. When asked about strategies in working with parents, they attribute a minor relevance to this issue. They report positive relationships with their majority colleagues and have the feeling that they are neither viewed nor treated differently than their colleagues. Colleagues particularly appreciate their bilingual skills and P describes situations in which he helped to translate. The group discusses whether xenophobic attitudes or prejudices against minority students or teachers exist within the faculty. All three agree that there is no explicit xenophobic attitude but some colleagues may prefer to work with fewer minority students. P reports episodes in which he felt "a bit uncomfortable" in the faculty room. Generally, the majority colleagues are perceived as open-minded, in rare occasions some of them might tend to attribute ethnic stereotypes to minority students. These or other multicultural issues are not discussed in the faculty room and no efforts of a common intercultural school development are reported. When asked about challenges for their school and future directions of development, they agreed that language barriers have to be overcome, that parents and their students have to be more motivated and willing to adapt as well as the school has to recognize minority students' potential.

Interpretation of the group discussion revealed segments with an inclusive discourse mode changing with more excluding passages. Narrations of episodes were mainly produced individually while general themes (e.g. xenophobic attitudes) were discussed commonly. Hence, teachers obviously did not share experiences of a common practice. Nevertheless, the experienced similar conditions in their professional career and seem to have developed a common frame of reference.

Comparison of the Two Discussions

The discussion with the first group was considerably longer than the second discussion and it mainly ran by itself. The three teachers seemed to work together as a group and reported a wealth of information on common efforts and projects. They emphasized the role of both their experience and their professional learning within networks as relevant factor for these efforts. The teachers in the second discussion also referred to their (migrational) experiences. The discussion seemed, however, to have been their first occasion to compare notes with their colleagues. They did not yet cooperate on a regular basis and just seemed to get to know each other. Hence, commonly told passages were rare and they only partly determined the thematic course of the discussion. Both groups discuss the expectation of being a role model for minority students. This seems to be an important aspect of the professional identity of teachers in the second group. Their stories of successfully overcoming barriers in their educational barrier is meant to have motivational effects on their minority students. The teachers in the first group relate to this theme (being a role model) only when others bring it up. They emphasize that you actively have to engage in efforts to change existing practices. Relying on role model effects might neglect structural and institutional deficits and restrict minority teachers to a special position. To prevent such a limitation, the systematic and continuous cooperation of all teachers is the main approach in the first groups' school. Professional cooperation and common efforts to learn and develop new strategies is the main topic that pervades the first discussion, whilst it is almost totally absent in the second group. The latter seems to follow a more individualistic approach and cooperation takes place only occasionally. While their minority status is of importance for the teachers in this group, they do not transfer it into efforts of developing common initiatives or projects. Correspondingly, both schools seem to differ in their agendas; while there is an explicit agenda of intercultural school development in the first school, the second group is not aware of something similar at their school. While both groups refer to the support of the school management, and both schools seem to follow a strategy of hiring minority teachers, only the first seems to have implemented practices to foster the professional development and cooperation of majority and minority teachers alike. Aspects like well-being of students and the school's climate were discussed explicitly in the first group and only implicitly present in the second group. Differences between the two groups also exist as to the issue of cooperation with parents. While teachers from the elementary school develop various network strategies to strengthen relations to parents, this seems to be less important for the teachers from the secondary school. Although they would like to see minority parents being more strongly involved with school, they emphasize parents' responsibility for this involvement.

Another topic that is not further discussed by them is communication and exchange with minority teachers from other schools. While teachers in the first group seem to be active member of networks of minority teachers and take advantage of these networks, the second group only mentions casual but no systematic relations with other minority teachers.

Discussion

Caution has to be exercised when interpreting the results of the discussions. The two cases may be illustrative for certain tendencies, the detected differences must, however, not be generalized. These differences may well be attributed to differences in the school form (elementary vs. secondary school) or in gender (female vs. male teachers) (Waburg & Strasser, 2018). Nevertheless, certain tendencies as preliminary answers to the research questions can be highlighted.

Both schools clearly provide a different context for minority teachers. Whilst both are situated in the same urban area and follow an approach of actively recruiting minority teachers, they differ in their general approach towards cultural diversity. Based on the interviews with the schools' head teachers and the corresponding statements in the group discussions, one may conclude that the elementary school followed an approach viewing diversity as a resource, that has to be used and fostered. The second seemed not to follow a consistent approach. While the head teacher referred to diversity mainly as a challenge that holds a potential capability but is also associated with great effort and risks, the teachers also discussed diversity as a problem that hinders the ambitious grammar school ("Gymnasium") in reaching its goals. Some of their majority colleagues seemed to view diversity as a negligible category that should not be emphasized. Obviously, there was no common understanding of nor an explicitly formulated concept as to cultural diversity. Such an understanding presupposes a mutual exchange that takes not only place casually or arbitrarily. An important condition for such a systematic communication process seems to be the initiative and continuous support of school management. In the first school, minority teachers and their colleagues were constantly brought together in different settings. Hence, they cooperated in a variety of projects and on different occasions. Teachers were free to participate in those projects that met their needs and ideas. Hence, they did not have the feeling that cooperation was forced upon them. School management and faculty seemed to understand intercultural school development as a common task. Thus, many teachers took the initiative in developing their own professional learning and school development projects with their colleagues. The continuous cooperation resulted in a common understanding of and approach towards cultural diversity. Accordingly, in the discussion, there was a common focus on events, activities and strategies in the group's school and many episodes were narrated commonly. The minority teachers seemed to be fully integrated in the faculty and no differences in cooperation between minority and majority teachers could be detected. With the faculty trying to find new ways and learn new practices it can be described as a professional learning community. The fact that the three teachers were integrated in professional networks of minority teachers seemed to be rather helpful.

Teachers in the second group in many ways serve as a contrasting example. Although their school followed an active stance in recruiting minority teachers, it obviously lacked an explicit strategy in integrating minority teachers and fostering cooperation. There were no joint efforts concerning intercultural school development. Accordingly, the three teachers began to realize their common understanding and potential for cooperation only during the group discussion. Although they shared certain perspectives (e.g. towards being a role model), they have not yet cooperated on intercultural issues neither with each other nor with their majority colleagues. The school management's passive stance in addressing cultural diversity issues on the faculty and on the classroom level may be consequential for the school climate.

Although it is difficult to infer knowledge on the school's climate from the discussion, it is noteworthy, however, that issues like stereotypes and xenophobic attitudes were brought up by the teachers. As learning atmosphere and conversation culture form the basis for productive collaboration (van Es, 2012) such attitudes may hamper a trustful atmosphere of learning and exchange.

Conclusions and Implications

The two cases underscore the findings of Ledoux et al. (2000): Schools that explicitly follow an integrative approach facilitate communication and cooperation of minority and majority teachers alike. When cooperating systematically all teachers can adapt the content, procedures and attitudes of their teaching to the demands of intercultural education. They tend to feel responsible for the commonly developed concepts and their implementation. Hence, the continuously supported cooperation of teachers helped to change instructional and institutional practices and to develop a common intercultural agenda.

The hope that is associated with the call for more minority teachers is that they can deal with diversity issues more adequately and professionally than their majority colleagues. Not only students, but also the faculty and the school as a whole are believed to benefit from the employment of minority teachers. Following insights from existing research, it is plausible to assume that a more diverse faculty does not automatically entail specific, intercultural relevant practices and positive effects on students and schools. Context factors such as the school climate, prevailing attitudes, goals and values or the cultural diversity in the faculty as well as in the classroom deliver constraints and affordances for teachers' actual performance.

To further understand facilitative conditions for such a development, teachers' wider professional networks and integration in their communities has to be further investigated. The strengthening of such professional networks and the implementation of learning communities of minority teachers may be a major step in developing multicultural schools. Schools with such communities seem to be open to professional impulses of minority teachers and give them space to develop a "diversity agenda", whereas other schools tend to marginalize them (Weinstein et al., 2003).

References

Bohnsack, R. (1995). Auf der Suche nach habitueller Übereinstimmung. In H.-H. Krüger & W. Marotzki (Eds.), *Erziehungswissenschaftliche Biographieforschung* (pp. 258–275). Leske + Budrich.

Bohnsack, R. (2010). Documentary method and group discussions. In R. Bohnsack, N. Pfaff, & W. Weller (Eds.), *Qualitative analysis and documentary method in international educational research* (pp. 99–124). Barbara Budrich Publishers.

Borko, H. (2004). Professional development and teacher learning: Mapping the terrain. *Educational Researcher, 33*(8), 3–15.

Chen, H. (2012). *An investigation of racial and/or ethnic minority teacher candidates' strengths awareness and utilization.* Teaching and Leadership – Dissertations. Paper 237. http://surface.syr.edu/cgi/viewcontent.cgi?article=1238&context=tl_etdn[12.02.2015]

Cohen, J., McCabe, E. M., Michelli, N. M., & Pickeral, T. (2009). School climate: Re-search, policy, practice, and teacher education. *Teachers College Record, 111*, 180–213.

Collie, R. J., Shapka, J. D., & Perry, N. E. (2011). Predicting teacher commitment: The impact of school climate and social-emotional learning. *Psychology in the Schools, 48*, 1034–1048.

DuFour, R., & Eaker, R. E. (1998). *Professional learning communities at work: Best practices for enhancing student achievement.* National Education Service, ASCD.

Easton-Brooks, D., Lewis, C., & Yang, Y. (2010). Ethnic-matching: The influence of African American teachers on the reading scores of African American students. *National Journal of Urban Education & Practice, 3*(1), 230–243.

Edelmann, D. (2006). *Pädagogische Professionalität im transnationalen Raum.* LIT.

Feuerverger, G. (1997). "On the edges of the map": A study of heritage language teachers in Toronto. *Teaching and Teacher Education, 13*, 39–53.

Forrest, J., Lean, G., & Dunn, K. (2015). Challenging racism through schools: Teacher attitudes to cultural diversity and multicultural education in Sydney, Australia. *Race Ethnicity and Education, 19*, 1–21.

Foster, M. (1994). The role of community and culture in school reform efforts: Examining the views of African-American teachers. *Educational Foundations, 8*(2), 5–2.

Freiberg, H. J., & Stein, T. A. (1999). Measuring, improving and sustaining healthy learning environments. In H. J. Freiberg (Ed.), *School climate: Measuring, improving, and sustaining healthy learning environments* (pp. 11–29). Falmer Press.

Georgi, V. B., Ackermann, L., & Karakaş, N. (2011). *Vielfalt im Lehrerzimmer*. Waxmann.

Gomez, M. L., Rodriguez, T. L., & Agosto, V. (2008). Who are Latino prospective teachers and what do they bring to US schools? *Race Ethnicity and Education, 11*, 267–283.

Grayson, J. L., & Alvarez, H. K. (2008). School climate factors relating to teacher burn-out: A mediator model. *Teaching and Teacher Education, 24*, 1349–1363.

Gröschner, A., Seidel, T., Schindler, A., & Kiemer, K. (2014). Facilitating collaborative teacher learning: The role of 'mindfulness' in video-based teacher professional development programs. *Gruppendynamik & Organisationsberatung, 45*, 273–290.

Grossman, P., Wineburg, S., & Woolworth, S. (2001). Toward a theory of teacher community. *Teachers College Record, 103*(6), 942–1012.

Gutentag, T., Horenczyk, G., & Tatar, M. (2017). Teachers' approaches toward cultural diversity predict diversity-related burnout and self-efficacy. *Journal of Teacher Education, 69*(4), 408–419.

Herwartz-Emden, L. (2000). Adressatenspezifität bei Interviews und Gruppeninterviews in der interkulturellen Forschung. In J.-L. Patry & F. Riffert (Eds.), *Situationsspezifität in pädagogischen Handlungsfeldern* (pp. 55–80). STUDIEN-Verlag.

Horenczyk, G., & Tatar, M. (2002). Teachers' attitudes toward multiculturalism and their perceptions of the school organizational culture. *Teaching and Teacher Education, 18*, 435–445.

Irvine, J. J. (1989). Beyond role models. An examination of cultural influences on the pedagogical practices of Black teachers. *Peabody Journal of Education, 66*, 51–63.

Irvine, J. J., & Fenwick, L. T. (2011). Teachers and teaching for the new millennium: The role of HBCUs. *The Journal of Negro Education, 80*(3), 197–208.

King, S. H. (1993). The limited presence of African-American teachers. *Review of Educational Research, 63*(2), 115–149.

Klassen, T. R., & Carr, P. D. (1997). Different perceptions of race in education. *Racial minority and White teachers. Canadian Journal of Education, 22*, 67–81.

Klassen, R. M., & Chiu, M. M. (2010). Effects on teachers' self-efficacy and job satisfaction: Teacher gender, years of experience, and job stress. *Journal of Educational Psychology, 102*(3), 741–756.

Kohli, R. (2009). Critical race reflections: Valuing the experiences of teachers of color in teacher education. *Race, Ethnicity and Education, 12*(2), 235–251.

Ledoux, G., Leeman, Y., & Leiprecht, R. (2000). Von kulturalistischen zu pluriformen Ansätzen. Ergebnisse des niederländischen Projekts "Interkulturelles Lernen". In G. Auernheimer (Ed.), *Interkulturalität im Arbeitsfeld Schule. Empirische Untersuchungen über Lehrer und Schüler* (pp. 177–196). Leske & Budrich.

Mantel, C. (2017). *Lehrer_in, Migration und Differenz. Fragen der Zugehörigkeit bei Grundschullehrer_innen der zweiten Einwanderungsgeneration in der Schweiz*. transcript.

Meier, K. J., Stewart, J., & England, R. E. (1989). *Race, class and education: The politics of second-generation discrimination*. University of Wisconsin Press.

Morris, E. W. (2007). "Ladies" or "Loudies"?: Perceptions and experiences of black girls in classroom. *Youth & Society, 38*(4), 490–515.

Nieto, S. (1998). From claiming hegemony to sharing space. Creating community in multicultural education courses. In R. Chavez-Chavez & J. O'Donnell (Eds.), *Speaking the unpleasant* (pp. 16–31). SUNY Press.

Pas, E. T., Bradshaw, C. P., & Hershfeldt, P. A. (2012). Teacher- and school-level predictors of teacher efficacy and burnout: Identifying potential areas for support. *Journal of School Psychology, 50*, 129–145.

Quiocho, A., & Rios, F. (2000). The power of their presence: Minority group teachers and schooling. *Review of Educational Research, 4*, 485–528.

Rotter, C. (2012). Lehrkräfte mit Migrationshintergrund. Individuelle Umgangsweisen mit bildungspolitischen Erwartungen. *Zeitschrift für Pädagogik, 58*(2), 204–222.

Scheerens, J. (2010). *Teachers' professional development: Europe in international comparison: An analysis of teachers' professional development based on the OECD's Teaching and Learning International Survey (TALIS)*. Office for Official Publications of the European Union; European Commission.

Schittenhelm, K. (2010). School-to-work transitions of young women. An intercultural approach based on group discussions. In R. Bohnsack, N. Pfaff, & W. Weller (Eds.), *Qualitative analysis and documentary method in international educational research* (pp. 125–142). Barbara Budrich Publishers.

Sherin, M. G., & van Es, E. A. (2008). Effects of video club participation on teachers' professional vision. *Journal of Teacher Education, 60*(1), 20–37.

Statistisches Bundesamt. (2018). *Ergebnisse des Mikrozensus 2017. Sonderauswertung für den Mediendienst Integration*. Statistisches Bundesamt.

Strasser, J. (2013). Diversity in the faculty room: Constraints and affordances of minority teachers' professional action in Germany. *The International Journal of Diversity in Education, 12*(3), 131–141.

Strasser, J. (2021). Belastung von Lehrkräften durch interkulturelle situationen in der schule. In T. Ringeisen, P. Genkova, & L.F.T. Leong (Eds). *Handbuch Stress und Kultur*. Springer: Wiesbaden. https://doi.org/10.1007/978-3-658-27825-0_34-1

Strasser, J., & Leutwyler, B. (2020). Differenzerfahrungen von Lehrkräften. Bedeutung für den Umgang mit Vielfalt. *Empirische Pädagogik, 34*(2), 5–20.

Strasser, J., & Steber, C. (2010). Lehrerinnen und Lehrer mit Migrationshintergrund – Empirische Reflexion einer bildungspolitischen Forderung. In J. Hagedorn, V. Schurt, C. Steber, & W. Warburg (Eds.), *Ethnizität, Geschlecht, Familie und Schule. Heterogenität als erziehungswissenschaftliche Herausforderung* (pp. 97–126). Wiesbaden.

Strasser, J., & Waburg, W. (2015). Students' perspectives on minority teachers in Germany. *Tertium Comparationis, 21*, 251–274.

Tatar, M., & Horenczyk, G. (2003). Diversity-related burnout among teachers. *Teaching and Teacher Education, 19*, 397–408.

Taylor, D. L., & Tashakkori, A. (1995). Decision participation and school climate as predictors of job satisfaction and teachers' sense. *Journal of Experimental Education, 63*, 217–230.

van Es, E. A. (2012). Examining the development of a teacher learning community: The case of a video club. *Teaching and Teacher Education, 28*(2), 182–192.

Vance, B., Miller, S., Humphreys, S., & Reynolds, F. (1989). Sources and manifestations of occupational stress as reported by full-time teachers working in a BIA school. *Journal of American Indian Education, 28*, 21–31.

Vangrieken, K., Dochy, F., Raes, E., & Kyndt, E. (2015). Teacher collaboration: A systematic review. *Educational Research Review, 15*, 17–40. https://doi.org/10.1016/j.edurev.2015.04.002

Vangrieken, K., Meredith, C., Packer, T., & Kyndt, E. (2017). Teacher communities as a context for professional development: A systematic review. *Teaching and Teacher Education, 61*, 47–59.

Waburg, W., & Strasser, J. (2018). Geschlechtsbezogene Muster des Umgangs mit (bildungspolitischen) Erwartungen an Lehrer*innen mit Migrationshintergrund. In E. Breitenbach, T. V. Rieske, & S. Toppe (Eds.), *Migration, Religion und Geschlecht: Praktiken der Differenzierung* (pp. 61–76). Barbara Budrich.

Weinstein, C., Curran, M., & Tomlinson-Clarke, S. (2003). Culturally responsive classroom management: Awareness into action. *Theory Into Practice, 42*, 269–276.

Wilkins, C., & Lall, R. (2011). 'You've got to be tough and I'm trying': Black and minority ethnic student teachers' experiences of initial teacher education. *Race Ethnicity and Education, 14*(3), 365–386.

Josef Strasser is a Full Professor for Education at the RPTU Kaiserslautern-Landau, Germany. He is leading the Working Group of Professionalization and Organizational Development. After studies in educational science and psychology at the Universities of Bamberg and Regensburg he earned a master degree and a Ph.D. in education from the University of Regensburg. His research focuses on the challenges for professionals that go along with an increasing cultural diversity in the educational domain. Several of his projects investigated the role of minority teachers within German schools. He is interested in individual, institutional and relational conditions for culturally sensitive school development as well as in ways to foster the professional learning of educational practitioners that is necessary to that end.

Open Access This chapter is licensed under the terms of the Creative Commons Attribution 4.0 International License (http://creativecommons.org/licenses/by/4.0/), which permits use, sharing, adaptation, distribution and reproduction in any medium or format, as long as you give appropriate credit to the original author(s) and the source, provide a link to the Creative Commons license and indicate if changes were made.

The images or other third party material in this chapter are included in the chapter's Creative Commons license, unless indicated otherwise in a credit line to the material. If material is not included in the chapter's Creative Commons license and your intended use is not permitted by statutory regulation or exceeds the permitted use, you will need to obtain permission directly from the copyright holder.

Part II
Migrant and Indigenous Teachers as Minorities in Bilingual and Multilingual Schools

Mary Gutman ⓘ, Wurud Jayusi ⓘ, Michael Beck ⓘ, and Zvi Bekerman ⓘ

Chapter 11
"Welcome to the Club": Palestinian-Israeli Teachers in Bilingual Integrated and in Hebrew Speaking Schools

Wurud Jayusi and Zvi Bekerman

Abstract This chapter contributes to a better understanding of how minority teachers in majority schools experience their work and how their participation in such educational contexts helps shape their sense of ethno-cultural belonging and their sense of self-efficacy. Through comparative work, we gain insights into the context-specific conditions which might help support or undermine minority teachers' inclusion. To do this we compared the reported experiences of Palestinian Israeli teachers working in two somewhat different educational contexts; the Hebrew speaking schools which serve the regular Israeli Jewish population and the bilingual integrated schools which offer the opportunity for the two populations to study under one roof in a society in which schools are mostly segregated. Both these educational contexts include Palestinian Israeli teachers in their faculty. Our findings point mostly at similarities in the way these teachers experience their work at the schools but also some notable differences have been exposed. Both groups of teachers' express satisfaction regarding their work at the Hebrew speaking and the bilingual integrated schools. They are satisfied with their work and feel they belong to a very special 'club' a metaphor that affords them a strong and positive positioning within the school context.

W. Jayusi (✉)
Beit Berl College, Arab Academic Institute, Beit Berl, Israel
e-mail: wurud.jayusi@beitberl.ac.il

Z. Bekerman
The Seymour Fox School of Education, Hebrew University of Jerusalem, Jerusalem, Israel
e-mail: zvi.bekerman@mail.huji.ac.il

© The Author(s) 2023
M. Gutman et al. (eds.), *To Be a Minority Teacher in a Foreign Culture*,
https://doi.org/10.1007/978-3-031-25584-7_11

Introduction

The inclusion of minority teachers in schools that serve, for the most part, the majority population has been, for some time now, appreciated as a potentially positive step towards helping narrow the achievement gap between minority and majority students while helping develop a more culturally sensitive school environment which will benefit both minority and majority students. The first by being allowed to find in the educational setting potential positive figures for identification and the second by coming in contact with minority teachers who would hopefully help them better understand and thus embrace diversity.

Though existing research is not conclusive there seem to be signs that the inclusion of minority teachers in majority schools is helpful in soothing potential conflicts arising from linguistic and cultural barriers between both minority students and the school's teachers and administration and these and minority parents (Atkins et al., 2014; Bekerman, 2016; Cherng & Halpin, 2016; Luke, 2017).

In Israel, we have been involved in trying to understand the role of the Palestinian-Israeli teachers' motivations and experiences while teaching at so-called national Hebrew schools and the rather recently created bilingual integrated schools (Bekerman, 2012, 2016; Jayusi & Bekerman, 2019a, b). More specifically we have tried to better comprehend how their participation in such educational contexts helps shape their sense of ethnocultural belonging and their sense of self-efficacy. Both these educational contexts include Palestinian Israeli teachers in their faculty; the first, as we will soon describe, mostly because of instrumental reasons while the second because of their stated ideology. In this paper, we approach our findings comparatively hoping to offer some insights on the context-specific conditions which might help support or undermine minority teachers' inclusion.

Before drawing this comparison, we will introduce in short the present structure of the Israeli school system and the events which brought about the inclusion of Palestinian Israeli teachers in their faculty. We will then review some of the relevant literature on minority teachers serving in majority schools and following the comparison, and will then draw some conclusions regarding what might be learned from each of the educational contexts compared to better the professional impact of minority teachers.

Israel and the Israeli School System

Space limitations preclude us from doing justice to the conflicting narratives that crowd Israeli historiography. Not only those of Jews and Palestinians, but also the different narratives within groups (for some alternative historical perspectives, see, for example (Golani & Manna, 2011; Heydemann, 1991; Khalidi, 2010, 2020; Khalidi et al., 1992; Masalha, 2012; Morris, 1987; Said, 2001; Shafir, 1996; Shlaim, 1998; Teveth, 1989).

In 1947, the United Nations Special Committee on Palestine, UNSCOP, proposed the creation of two separate and independent states, one Arab and one Jewish (Mock et al., 2014). The plan was voted up by the General Assembly on November 29, 1947 (UN General Assembly Resolution 181) and passed by 33 votes to 13, with 10 abstentions. Immediately afterward, fighting erupted between the Jewish and Palestinian populations, and the State of Israel was declared on May 14, 1948, upon the withdrawal of Britain from Palestine.

The Israeli army prevailed, and at the end of hostilities in 1949, Israel had conquered almost 80% of the territory that had been allotted in the partition plan. The remaining 20%, Gaza and the West Bank were attached to Egypt and Jordan respectively. An even more devastating effect of the war for the Palestinians was that by its end, the great majority of them had been expelled by the Israeli army or had fled their homes and villages, creating what later became known as the refugee 'problem' (Forman & Kedar, 2004).

The 1948 war, called the War of Independence by the Israelis and the Nakba (the Catastrophe) by the Palestinians, was the first open military clash between the Zionist and Arab nationalist movements. This conflict remains the most explosive in Israel, placing the Jewish majority and the Palestinian (primarily Muslim) minority at perpetual odds. Though there is a sharp asymmetry between the communities with regard to the distribution of resources, beliefs on both sides reflect their respective claims to a monopoly on objective truth about the conflict and who instigated it, thereby undermining possibilities for resolution (Bar-Tal, 1998).

According to the Israeli Central Bureau of Statistics (CBS, 2019), at the end of December 2019, Israel's total population was estimated at 9,136,000. Jews amounted for 74.1% (6,772,000), Arabs for 21% (1,916,000), and Others for 4.9% (448,000). It is worth noting that these figures reflect political and ideological decisions about which populations should be counted and in what territories. At present, the CBS count includes Jewish settlers living in Area C of the West Bank, as well as the annexed areas of the Golan Heights and East Jerusalem but does not include Palestinians living in the same areas.

The Jewish population represents not only a variety of ethnic-national groups but is also divided along lines of religious sentiment and affiliation. In 2016 8% were Haredi Ultra-orthodox, 10% National Religious, 23% Masorti (traditionalists, mostly Jews, descended from Mizrachi/Sephardic families), and 40% 'secular' (Malach et al., 2018).

The present Arab Palestinian Muslim population, mostly Sunni, totals 1,636,000 (including Bedouin and Druze Arabs). A smaller, non-Arab Muslim population is represented by the approximately 5000 Circassians. About 2% of the total population is Christian, 77.5% of which are Arab Christians (7.2% of the total Arab population in Israel) (Israel's Central Bureau of Statistics (CBS), 2017).

Israel's educational system is composed of five types of schools: (1) state Hebrew-language schools, attended by the majority of Jewish school-age children; (2) state religious Hebrew-language schools, attended by the majority of the religious Jewish population; (3) state Arab-language schools, attended by the majority of the Arab Palestinian population; these three sectors are fully funded by the state;

(4) state-recognized schools, which are unofficial and only partially state-funded (55% and up), that serve both Arab and Jewish populations and have a greater measure of freedom in all education policy matters. These schools serve mostly the Ultra-orthodox Jewish population and those parts of the Arab population that attend denominational, mostly Christian schools (Israeli Education System, 2015). This segregated reality suggests that children belonging to different ethnic, religious, national sectors of the society do not meet each other. This is mostly true for the Ultra-orthodox, Arab and Jewish populations (Shwed et al., 2014).

According to the CBS (2019), nearly three quarters of the Israeli state education system is devoted to Jewish education, divided into state secular (45.1%) and religious (28.8%) systems, and the Arab education system serves the rest of the children in Israel.

Blass (2014) has shown how Israel's centralized education system effectively controls, unifies, and critiques activity in schools, maintaining unequal education opportunities for the Arab minority through a 'concentration of disadvantages,' meaning that Arab education and Jewish education are unequal in both inputs and outputs. Yet, when schools in a similar socioeconomic segment are compared, the achievements of the Arabic-language schools surpass those of Hebrew-language schools, indicating that the achievement gaps between the two derive primarily from their socioeconomic differences (Ayalon et al., 2019). The PISA exam scores of Israeli students are lower than the overall OECD country average and the gaps between the strongest and the weakest students are the greatest. Closer investigation of these scores reveals a similar pattern to the one just described: while Hebrew-speaking students scored higher than the OECD average in 2018 (506 vs. 487), Arab speakers scored much lower (362 vs. 487) (Blass, 2020).

Added to the achievement gaps mentioned, other researchers (Abu-Saad, 2006; Arar & Abu-Asbah, 2013; Jabareen & Agbaria, 2010), point to multiple challenges that Arab Palestinians face, including, among others, structural and content-related subordination to the Jewish education system (Abu-Saad, 2006); the absence of Arab representatives at policymaking levels including in decisions concerning curriculum; its economic dependence on the Jewish education system; and the constant demand for 'loyalty' in exchange for financial and other support. [Dialogic directions: Conflicts in Israeli/Palestinian education for peace (Bekerman, 2000)].

Palestinian Israeli Teachers in Hebrew Speaking and in Bilingual Integrated Schools

The phenomenon of integrating minority/migrant/international teachers in majority schools is not exclusive to Israel. In the United States, for instance, the issue of integrating people of color has been addressed since the 1970s (King, 1993). Researchers unanimously agree that teachers from diverse cultural and ethnic backgrounds contribute extensively to American education (Easton-Brooks et al., 2010; Irvine & Fenwick, 2011).

In Germany, hiring more minority teachers is considered a promising means of dealing with existing difficulties in diverse schools. Minority teachers draw on specific personal experiences that may be useful in overcoming cultural and/or language barriers (Irvine, 1989; Strasser & Waburg, 2015). Their sociocultural experiences, as well as their potential multilingual competencies (Nieto, 1998), facilitate more deliberate dealings with cultural diversity at schools (Lengyel & Rosen, 2015).

McNamara and Basit (2004), examined the induction experiences of British teachers of Asian and African Caribbean origin and showed that the majority of the teachers find their schools supportive and the induction process valuable and that they feel successful in building bridges between antagonistic communities and feel that they counter prejudice and racism both within schools and the wider community.

Santoro (2007) investigated the experiences of indigenous teachers and ethnic minority teachers in Australian schools. She suggested that the teachers' "knowledge of self" in regard to ethnicity and/or indigeneity and social class enables them to empathize with diverse students from perspectives not available to teachers from the dominant cultural majority.

The inclusion of Palestinian Israeli teachers in schools as a matter of policy is a rather new phenomenon in Israel. As stated Palestinian Israelis suffer from multiple structural obstacles regarding their professional development given the limitations imposed on them by Israel's Jewish centered policies. Palestinians with academic credentials in multiple fields of knowledge cannot occupy positions related in one way or another to the army or security areas (Abu Asba, 2006; Hadad Haj-Yahya & Assaf, 2017). Given the existing constraints, thousands of Palestinian Israeli teachers submit employment requests to the State's Arab-sector schools each year, but because of market limitations, many of them remain unemployed. For the left unemployed the State's Hebrew secular schools and the Bilingual integrated schools constitute a chance to teach out of the Arab education system.

Until 1973 Palestinian-Israeli teachers worked only in schools affiliated with their own sector. In 1973, a government committee recommended, for the first time, that Palestinian-Israeli teachers be incorporated into the Hebrew-speaking educational network (Shohat, 1973). By 1980, some 80 Palestinian-Israeli teachers were teaching Arabic in Jewish schools, a full 10% of the total number of Arabic teachers in the country (Yonai, 1992). In 2013, the Ministry of Education decided to step up the process and incorporated an additional 500 Palestinian-Israeli teachers into Jewish schools.

Since then, the numbers have steadily risen and today Palestinians teach not only Arabic but a variety of other subjects for which the system suffers from a shortage of teachers, such as English, science, special education, and other subjects, at Israeli State secular schools (Merchavim, 2016). Recent indicators show that out of a total of 170,238 teachers in Israel, almost 24% of them are Palestinian-Israeli (Israel's Central Bureau of Statistics, 2017), of which only 0.015% teach in the Jewish secular sector budgeted and supervised by the State and Local Authorities.

All in all, the Israeli Ministry of Education primary aim for the integration of Palestinian-Israeli teachers in Jewish schools relates to the potential this step has to add to today's shortage of highly qualified teaching staff, thus saving the government large sums of money by eliminating the need to train or retrain new teachers; only in second place does it mention the potential to encourage tolerance for diversity among students (Ministry of Education, 2015).

The work of Palestinian Israeli teachers in the bilingual integrated schools is to be seen as a rather unrelated event to the ones related above. These schools are a fairly new development in Israel with the first one being created in 1984. The bilingual integrated schools' area bold and innovative initiative by a relatively small group of people who seek to "make a difference" in the education of children living in the current Middle East conflict through collaboration between Jewish and Palestinian teachers, pupils, and parents. Today eight such schools function in Israel (Meshulam, 2019) all of which are state-recognized and supervised by the Ministry of Education most of them under the auspices of the state Hebrew language schools' section of the Ministry. The student corps of all schools reach 1200 students a small fraction of all Israeli students. These schools are also supported by independent Non-Government Organizations interested in implementing peace initiatives in the context of Israeli society.

The schools use the standard curriculum of the secular State school system, which is supplemented to reflect the schools' ideological commitment to equality and coexistence. A team of in-house teachers, aided by professionals, has drawn up additional programs for bicultural issues such as historical narratives and religious/cultural studies. Most of each group's religious festivals are recognized, together with the groups' respective national narratives. In addition, cultural activities representing all the groups are included in the schools' curricula. Sustaining these commitments such as studying the Palestinian-Arab historical narrative is complex for it might be restricted by the Ministry of Education. The schools have had to seek out creative solutions such as instituting extracurricular activities for the school community in cases where there was concern about the possible reaction of the Ministry of Education (Bekerman, 2004).

The funds from the Ministry of Education are inadequate to provide for the supplementary materials and staff that the integrated bilingual schools require. Accordingly, the schools must charge fees to families who enroll their children. This may account for the fact that the families attracted to the bilingual schools, both Jewish and Palestinian-Arab, are mainly from the middle to upper-middle classes. The children's parents tend to be highly educated (Bekerman & Tatar, 2009).

The co-principal arrangement which characterized the schools from their inception was in recent years abandoned because of budgetary pressures, and now each school has a principal and assistant principal, each from a different ethnic group. One of the central features of bilingual schools, co-teaching (i.e. classes taught simultaneously in two languages by teachers representing each group), is also subject to a variety of contextual factors. The schools' decision to implement co-teaching stemmed from the goal of promoting bilingualism, and the presence of two teachers-one Jewish, one Palestinian--in each class, was expected to further this goal. However, given the current Israeli reality wherein most Palestinian-Arab teachers are, of necessity, fluent in both Arabic and Hebrew but most Jewish teachers speak only Hebrew, it would have been difficult to find enough bilingual Jewish teachers for every class. This, coupled with the high cost of employing two teachers for every disciplinary subject, resulted in the decision to terminate the co-teaching arrangements. Today, the schools have one homeroom teacher per class while trying to ensure that Palestinian-Arab and Jewish teachers are represented equally among the teaching staff (Bekerman, 2016).

Research on Palestinian-Israeli teachers working in State Hebrew-speaking schools is scant. Jayusi and Bekerman (2019a, b) found that Palestinian-Israeli teachers experience a strong sense of self-efficacy, satisfaction, and positive relationships with students, parents, and colleagues. Palestinian-Israeli teachers believe that their work helps reduce prejudice and increases mutual understanding among the groups in conflict. Fragman (2008) shows them having a strong desire to be "ambassadors of good will," offering them an opportunity to break down stereotypes and misconceptions about the Palestinian-Israeli minority. Brosh's (2013) findings indicate that the teachers were unsuccessful in integrating because of a lack of cultural understanding and that it was difficult, even impossible, for them to effectively communicate their knowledge to students. Sion (2014) examined how Palestinian-Israeli teachers appropriated performative identity strategies passing as cultural hybrids to gain acceptance in the schools. She found that despite their efforts, the teachers, for the most part, felt lonely, isolated, and vulnerable.

Our present research is more aligned with research inquiring into the teachers' perspectives and concerns when entering majority schools (Maylor et al., 2006; Strasser, 2013; Wilkins & Lall, 2011). More specifically our concern is with the teachers' experiences regarding stereotypical attitudes of peers, social isolation, their experiences in the faculty room, how they judge their potential contribution to school and students, their need to acculturate or not to the hegemonic culture, their sense of having or not having an opportunity for promotion and progression in the school hierarchy, etc.

Teacher Self-efficacy & Effectiveness

We take teacher efficacy to be the belief that one has capabilities in the areas of student engagement, instructional strategies, and classroom management (Tschannen-Moran & Hoy, 2001). Sachs (2004) suggests that teachers in order to be more effective should exercise attributes related to socio-cultural awareness, interpersonal skills, self-understanding, and risk-taking. For Campbell et al. (2003) teacher effectiveness depends on cognitive outcomes and also on teachers' moral and social well-being, as well as on the establishment of positive relationships with colleagues and parents. Furthermore, Gay (1995) and Sachs (2004) underline that effective teachers tend to demonstrate an enhanced self-understanding, which facilitates the development of a positive ethnic self-identity and self-inquiry into the relationships between fundamental values, attitudes, beliefs, and teaching practices.

Effective teachers afford the creation of trusting educational contexts in which communication and collaboration are enhanced and constructive critiques flourish (Gay, 1995; Guyton & Hidalgo, 1995).

Job satisfaction is conceptualized as the positive or negative evaluative judgment that people make about their job (Weiss, 2002). Skaalvik and Skaalvik (2010) have suggested that the impact of the school context on teachers' satisfaction is mediated through teachers' sense of belonging, indicating that teachers' sense of being accepted by the school leadership and their colleagues plays an important role in their motivation to continue to be affiliated with the teaching profession. Within this context, of no less importance is the research that has shown that a positive and supportive social climate in which teachers maintain positive relations with parents, students, and colleagues is positively related to teachers' satisfaction (Kokkinos, 2007; Scheopner, 2010). Teachers with a strong sense of self-efficacy would have a high level of job satisfaction (Caprara et al., 2006).

Last we should consider that teaching is a profession in which ideologies are of central concern. Kelchtermans and Ballet (2002) argue that understanding teachers' micro-political experiences in the school and the external environment is crucial to understanding how teachers take actions to further their interests through power and influence. Pachler et al. (2008) show how teachers views of professionalism are influenced by both that surpass strictly didactic practices. These ideological aspects are central in our own work for the personal position of the teachers concerning the Israeli Palestinian conflict has consequences for how Palestinian Israeli teachers in Hebrew speaking and bilingual integrated schools attempt to address issues of a socio-political nature.

Method

The data upon which we will be building our arguments were gathered from independent studies the authors conducted in both Hebrew speaking schools and bilingual integrated ones. The studies conducted employed a qualitative method that enabled us to construct a richly detailed depiction of Palestinian-Israeli teachers' varied and multidimensional worldviews, with the aim of trying to understand the teachers' perspectives on the social and cultural contexts within which they evolved (Gay & Airasian, 2003). Most of the data upon which we build our appreciations is derived from interviews we conducted with the teachers. Yet, in both settings, we also conducted fieldwork based on traditional ethnographic methods. The in-depth interviews conducted allowed the interviewer to delve deeply into social and personal matters (Dicicco-Bloom & Crabtree, 2006). Teachers, after being asked to render some biographical background, were asked to talk about their decision to work in the majority-sector schools and to describe the reactions they encountered in response to their choice. They were also asked to describe their relationships with the principals, students, teachers, and parents and to give examples of important events or experiences that they had faced in the classrooms and in other school settings. Inquiries were also made regarding their feelings while working at the schools - what made them feel satisfied and proud and what made them feel sad and angry. With the exception of these few guiding questions, interviewees were encouraged to tell their stories without limiting themselves to any fixed agenda. Those interested in full details regarding the research conducted are encouraged to see (Bekerman, 2012; Jayusi & Bekerman, 2019a, b; Rajuan & Bekerman, 2011).

For the present study and so as to be able to compare the data gathered we analyzed all materials using the thematic analysis method based on that of Braun and Clarke (2006) and of Shkedi (2004). We then coded significant units that were perceived as relevant to the present comparative effort. Last we consolidated the codes and created significant themes, which were reviewed to ensure that the contents matched the themes and to ensure consistency.

The researchers are both from the field of education. The first one is a member of the Palestinian national minority an expert in peace education and minority-majority relations in the educational system. The second researcher is a member of the Jewish-Israeli majority group, intellectually anchored in critical perspectives in the field of education and an expert in minority studies. The interviews were analyzed by both authors together.

Findings

Job Satisfaction

In general Palestinian teachers teaching in the Hebrew speaking schools and in the bilingual integrated ones feel satisfied with their job in the schools.

Those working in the Hebrew-speaking schools reported feeling satisfied with their work. They liked teaching in the Hebrew speaking schools and emphasized their desire to continue working in them. The following excerpts point in this direction.

> *The school for me is like a warm home. I have faced a crisis (divorce) and I needed help and support. The school gave me the support that I needed. I don't know if someday I'll leave ...*
> *The school for me is like a warm home ... The school gives me the support that I need.*

The "home" metaphor used is also referred to when teachers working at the bilingual integrated schools express their feelings towards the institutions with which they work. For them, the school *'is not just a place where we work but it is a home for us'*; *'the school satisfies our personal needs; it is not just a job it is a home'*. They emphasize that the schools fulfill their expectations that *'the place where we work should satisfy our personal needs'* and add that the school must have defined objectives for individual needs and that it should be an environment *'where everyone can feel comfortable'*. The expression, to *'feel comfortable'* is repeated frequently. Being *'comfortable'* with one another creates and sustains their aspiration for coexistence in a community build on trust and respect.

The idea of belonging to a club *'an exclusive and prestigious club'* was also used by teachers teaching in both contexts. This metaphor seemed to illustrate the teachers' sense of a strong and positive positioning within the school context given their sense of connection to all faculty members who provided them with support and encouragement.

Teachers in both groups felt that they were able to create good relationships with all stakeholders (parents, teachers, principals, and students). Their success in developing such good contacts contributed to their sense of job satisfaction and feeling of belonging to the school.

Principals play an important role in helping the Palestinian-Israeli teachers adjust to the Hebrew speaking schools by expressing their belief in a teacher's potential to integrate into the school community and by treating the teacher as an equal among other staff members, by offering support and help, and by establishing and maintaining a trusting relationship.

> *This principal was [like] a second mother to me ... The principal helped and supported me from the inside after accepting me from the outside. It is what makes me continue working here ... She was accepting and supportive of me ...*

In the case of the bilingual integrated schools, a similar sense of comfort is expressed in all that relates to relationships with the principal. Yet this feeling is much less underlined given that the schools (during the first years of their activity) were directed by co-principals (a Palestinian and a Jew) who fully shared responsibilities in line with the school's ideology of structural symmetry.

In both contexts teachers emphasized that achieving a strong sense of belonging to the school community was eased by their expressions of solidarity and empathy in school events and commemorations reflecting the Jewish group history (e.g. Holocaust Day; Independence Day). These expressions of solidarity and empathy, though never easy (especially in relation to Independence Day which mainly focuses on the Jewish historical narrative), seemed to be easier in the context of the bilingual integrated school where there was at least an effort to include in these events and commemorations/celebrations aspects of the Palestinian historical narrative too.

Last we want to mention the confidence the teachers expressed in their ability (as educators) to help change the stereotypes they felt are held by the Jewish stakeholders in the school context. A teacher working at a Hebrew speaking school stated:

> *I think that I succeeded in changing the prejudices of a lot of teachers. The strongest proof of that was from the teacher who had lost her son in the war. She used to give me a very piercing and hateful look at the beginning of my first year at the school. She hated all Arabs ... she noticed that I expressed solidarity with my students and the other teachers by participating in the ceremony for Israel's Memorial Day in my first year. This its effected her and made her rethink of me or of everything ... we are friends now.*

Though it could be assumed that in the bilingual integrated schools these such stereotypes would be absent given the presumed stakeholders' belief in integration one of the teachers stated:

> *They are not all lefties here, you know, but they get to know us as humans and change the way they think of us ...*

In spite of these very positive feelings, we found in both groups' expressions of ambivalence towards their school experiences pointing at the unique challenges they face. At the bilingual integrated schools, one of the teachers expressed herself as follows:

> *... it is full of ups and downs. The work in bilingual schools is much more dynamic, for better and for worse. This is one of the reasons why it's so unique.*

The following excerpt exemplifies the expressions we hear from teachers at the Hebrew speaking schools:

> *Generally, I keep a neutral stance with my colleagues and don't argue with them. I think that I have good relations with them but sometimes surprises happen. I was shocked when I entered the teachers' room hearing one colleague ... Russian ... speaking loudly with other colleagues about the right of Jews living in Israel with our us, the Palestinians. I was angry and couldn't help my peace. I told her that we are on this land, tens of years before Jews came from all over the world.*

It is also worth mentioning that while the teachers at the bilingual integrated schools were also parents of children studying in the same institution, an aspect that added to their sense of strong identification with the school community as well as an expression in their trust in the schools' educational aims; teachers in the Hebrew speaking schools did not consider the option of having their children join the school in which they worked. From their perspective, it was clear that though the school is a *'home'* this home was not homely enough to have their children included, the ideological gaps in the schools functioning (mostly related to a strong emphasis on a Zionist agenda as it expressed itself in school ceremonies and some of its curriculum) was not seen fit as a place where their children should be educated.

Professional Self-efficacy

Teachers in both contexts described their professional role predominantly as pedagogical experts. In the bilingual integrated schools, teachers reported that their pedagogical expertise has a deep involvement in a shared vision of multiculturalism and coexistence. Yet, multiculturalism and coexistence are seen as strongly connected to general educational issues.

> *Multiculturalism is concerned with learning about the "other," as well as with providing for children to reach their own potential according to their unique abilities and interests, to give a place for everyone. Some students are better painters than others, some are better in math, etc.*

For these teachers creating a multicultural school, environment means creating an environment in which pupils can find their unique space and pursue their individual learning goals.

schools should be liberal, let pupils express themselves, multicultural, enabling pupils to learn independently and (achieve) personal development.

Teachers at the Hebrew speaking schools reported using a variety of teaching methods, innovating new strategies, enabling genuine learning, and making the students' learning meaningful. Multiculturalism is part of their agenda even when not officially part of the schools' agenda.

> You can't imagine how successful I am at work. That is one of the reasons that keep me in school. I get a lot of compliments and thank-you letters from students and their parents. I teach in an interesting way. I teach them about the similarity between the three religions and that Islam is very tolerant. This is meaningful learning that helps them internalize and remember what they learned.

All teachers are proud of their pupils' high achievements but at the same time, they emphasize their important role in reducing prejudice among students, parents, and colleagues.

The events they recall as having positive effects particularly in reducing prejudice and overcoming negative perceptions relate to both direct and indirect activities and to formal and informal events. At times, they directly intervened in situations to correct perceived prejudices, and at other times, prejudice reduction is perceived as the outcome of their routinely professional work. Teachers are aware that the wider social context of some of the children might be tainted by prejudice, yet they strongly believe that they are successful in changing students' negative prejudiced perceptions, by explaining things that the children do not see in the media or hear in their immediate surroundings. They do this by offering students information that they believe their students lack, telling students about their society, culture, and religion. Yet, they realize change can only occur gradually.

> I am not only teaching, I deliver all the good things from my culture. I present a nation, so it is important for the Arab teacher to be who he is really and to show the good things.
>
> ... Besides my educational contribution, my presence in the Jewish school makes a difference. My students learned that it is important to know about the "other," not to judge, [but rather]to accept the "other." It is not only in relation to Arabs, [but also] Ethiopians or Russians; there are students of many ethnic origins in the class. I'm sending a message to the students that being different doesn't make the other worthless.

Teachers also consider their work as one which helps build bridges between the two societies and that their work not only succeeds in changing negative stereotypes about the Palestinian society in Israel but also strengthens tolerance and understanding toward alterity in general.

In the Hebrew-speaking schools, some of the teachers lead the "Shared lives" projects organizing mutual visits with Palestinian-Israeli schools.

> I organized several activities, Arabic days, and another language day. I founded and managed an Arabic class. I was responsible for preparing everything in this class including books, stories, activities, and students could come and use them. I also had organized a "Shared lives" project with an Arab school from another town.

It is worth noting that some differences are revealed in the interviews. Differences follow from the declared goals of the bilingual integrated schools which are dedicated to bringing Jewish and Palestinian populations together while working towards coexistence and mutual recognition.

While the regular Hebrew speaking schools, according to the expectations of the parents' body, focus mainly on school achievements; the bilingual schools focus on a dual agenda in which school achievements run parallel and equal to coexistence and multicultural one (at least at the declarative level). Some tensions are created by this double agenda which position pedagogical issues related to value education in opposition to academic achievement in disciplinary subjects that are required and tested by the Ministry of Education. Teachers are aware that the enrolment of children in their schools is dependent upon the school fulfilling the expectations of the parents that may be very different from their own.

> *The question wasn't about our worldview; it was about the bourgeois class. We want to attract pupils. The parents are seen as bourgeois due to their aspirations for their children to succeed and become integrated into the dominant society through achievement-oriented goals of high grades on standardized tests that, ultimately, will allow for continuation in higher education and upward mobility.*

Assessment criteria are directly influenced by the different worldviews that create a dichotomy between grades on standardized texts, as opposed to real-life behavior of the pupils to engage in inter-group relationships during play and recess activities.

> *Incompatibility between what we are measuring (achievements) and what we aim for. We measure areas of knowledge, but we wanted to reach a diverse society. I think in order to measure success we need to see how well we've done socially. It's important to let each child think about his achievements, but we should measure whether we're reaching our goal.*

These teachers encounter difficulties balancing their goals for social integration, tolerance, and recognition and those of the parents, the funding institutions, and the Ministry of Education, who they perceive as more interested in academic success.

Teachers in Hebrew-speaking schools have for the most part one main agenda: to focus on alleviating the tensions just mentioned. The academic success of their pupils and their own success in contributing to their success is their main interest.

The teachers talked about using a variety of innovative teaching methods that enable genuine learning and contribute to making the students' learning meaningful. The teachers made it clear that they believe they are recognized by the schools as excellent teachers and that their students' grades have improved:

> *I feel that I am professionally growing. They respect my work. I am a person who likes receiving attention and I have that in school. I have also a lot of encouragement and praise and that encourages me to give more.*

According to the teachers, self-efficacy is connected also with keeping an open mind, having a strong personality, being proficient in spoken Hebrew, exhibiting friendliness, demonstrating professional skills, creativity, a strong work ethic, and is very motivated to succeed. However, it seems that there is a price of fitting into the existing school culture. Despite the many accounts of collaboration and cohesiveness in the schools, there are also accounts in which personal and/or group affiliations interfere with the status quo and individuals do not feel comfortable expressing themselves as "different". One of the teachers in a bilingual integrated school stated:

> *The cultural context is different, I was raised differently, and it has happened more than once that I came out of a classroom crying because of how someone spoke to me and was later told that I took it too much to heart and it's not that significant.*

Though at times a bit problematic these perceived cultural differences end up being reported as positive events. *'Their mentality is completely different from ours in a positive way'* stated one of the teachers. Another teacher reported that:

> *It seems that I went with the flow. My husband tells me sometimes that I am forgetting that I am an Arab. Now I see more wrong habits in my society, I don't like a lot of things and wish to change them.*

Despite their positive attitude towards their own acculturation process, the teachers who have children and work at the Hebrew speaking schools explained that they do not enroll them in Jewish schools because they fear their children's cultural identity and language skills would be jeopardized.

> *The Jews are very liberated; I don't see this liberation or freedom as a positive thing. I see it as a mess, and I don't like a mess. For example, a 5th-grade student was telling me that she has a boyfriend from another class and they are going to a movie together. This is not acceptable for me. I cannot imagine my daughter in this situation. Life is not only math and English; it is important to keep our culture and language and we have to uphold certain limits.*

Finally, in general, all teachers were very positive about their experiences working in the schools. This becomes apparent in the fact that they strongly recommended that other Palestinian teachers work in Jewish State schools or the bilingual integrated ones. They were ready to encourage this participation not only to teachers lacking jobs in the Arab sector but also to new graduate teachers looking for a first job.

They all thought that teaching in a Jewish school was a good and learning experience for Palestinian-Israeli teachers, one that also affords them the opportunity to change Jews' stereotypical beliefs.

> *I recommend it because we can make a difference in Jewish-Arab relations. An Arab teacher can learn a lot of things there like I did. She can adopt the good things and avoid the inappropriate. I began to understand life better thanks to my experience in school.*

The positive relation between the Palestinian teachers and their Jewish colleagues strengthened by their shared perception of themselves as pedagogical experts and the added value of a sense of ideological commitment to multiculturalism and coexistence strengthens the teachers' sense of belonging to a very exclusive and positive group. All together these appreciations allow for a strong sense of self-efficacy.

Political Positioning

Political conflict often forces its way into the classrooms, especially in times of social and political unrest, such as wars and national days, and other commemorative days. Subjects of tension and conflict from the outside world are brought into the classroom through an "adult" agenda.

Political Tension/War

Teachers at the bilingual integrated schools attempt to create a safe home for themselves and the children in isolation from the harsh reality "outside" the school. The teachers feel they have succeeded in creating a safe home in the school for the children based on friendship and similarity. The school's official goals undoubtedly help in achieving these goals.

> *I asked them if they knew what was happening, and they knew very well, even though they are 2nd graders. They didn't change their usual habits - they separated between what was happening outside and what was happening in the classroom.*
>
> *We had an argument about who was suffering more - the Arab children or the Jewish children (children do not fear to speak about these issues).*

Teachers at the Hebrew-speaking schools understand that students asked political questions because they viewed the Palestinian teacher as representing the whole of the Palestinian people, and especially those in the Palestinian territories and in the Gaza Strip.

> *Some students ask questions, like why do the Arabs in Gaza hate us? Why do they attack us? Why do they try to kill us? I answer their questions. I tell them that it happens because there is a struggle and a war between two groups that are in conflict. I explain that not all of Gaza's citizens are terrorists and they have regular families and children, like people in Israel, and that these children have dreams and worlds of their own. I also tell them that there are children on the other side who live under occupation and shelling and some of them die ... This [change] happens gradually; perceptions aren't changed overnight.*

In a sense, it could be said that the strategy adopted to cope with these conflicting issues is one that tries to create symmetry so as to emphasize similarities (children on both sides suffer) and allow for empathy. The attempt to emphasize the suffering of children from both sides appears also among teachers teaching at Hebrew speaking schools. In the following excerpt, a dilemma is presented in the classroom by one Palestinian teacher. In her role as teacher, she believes it is important to convey to the pupils that children on both sides underwent suffering during the war. She wants each side to understand the suffering of the other side.

However, according to her personal position in relation to the conflict, she believes that the two sides are not "equally" suffering. Unclear in her own mind, she is unsatisfied with the result of the class discussion that fails to make a strong statement of any kind.

> It was hard for the children to accept the suffering of the other side. It was necessary to intervene and say that people on both sides were suffering - we wrote on the board the needs of both sides. It was very difficult ... But as an educator, I wanted to emphasize the parity.

In both cases, the way suffering was experienced by both sides during the war is presented in the classroom according to the personal position of the teacher. It is also an attempt to bring the outside reality of chaos and violence into the classroom in a controlled and manageable way through the resolution of the conflict by way of presenting all the children similarly as victims. The teachers' agenda is to help the children in the classroom feel that Palestinian and Jewish children are all similar to each other and not in conflict. However, in this example, personal and political national identifications conflict with the desire to reach symmetry (Bekerman & Zembylas, 2010).

Again on these issues, differences are to be found. While the teachers teaching at the bilingual integrated schools report that in spite of the difficulties a dialogue of conflictual issues is regularly sustained and supported by the school administration between Jewish and Palestinian faculty; in Hebrew speaking schools such an endorsement does not exist.

A teacher at the bilingual schools related to us the following:

> The war horrified me. But from a professional standpoint, the school coped with the war, with the encounter of Jews and Arabs with murder and killing - very professionally. The teachers met in the morning and evening, for ventilation and to discuss the place of the school. Every day we checked what was done and where we stood. I think we took good care of ourselves, we didn't conceal anything.

Offering a very different perspective a teacher at the Hebrew speaking school stated:

> ... When political issues are raised, as happened recently because of the situation, I am very careful and I try not to become emotional because I might say things that I'll regret later. The policy of the school is not to discuss politics, but sometimes it happens, and I try not to intervene. Yet, at times, they felt they could not but react to political statements.

Still, these teachers do not feel they are totally abandoned; one of them shared with us the following:

> It was a hard time for me [during the war in Gaza]: the principal came to me and told me that it is a hard time for all of us and that if I encountered any difficulties in my work, I should tell her. She also offered to come to my classes and to talk to the students, if I felt it would help.

When considering national commemoration days more differences are found.

At the bilingual integrated schools and as part of their declared goals, ways are found (in spite of the Ministry of Education guidelines) that allow for some equity in the presentation of the Jewish and the Palestinian historical narratives. One of the teachers told us the following:

> ... I have no problem with a common ceremony. I have a problem with Nakbah and Memorial Day together, where the only common thing is pain. It's hard to say. ... if I think of Memorial Day I think of soldiers, who are also people, but they went out and killed people who died in the Nakbah.

For teachers teaching at Hebrew-speaking schools, the situation is a bit more complex. Most of these teachers need to adhere to the traditional dress code adopted by Jewish schools for this day (white shirts), yet emotionally, it is a very difficult day for them. Although they abide by the custom of standing at attention during the sounding of the siren, a moment dedicated to the memory of those who died serving their country, they do so out of respect for their colleagues and students. Two of the interviewees explained that they were unable to hold back their tears during the ceremony because they were thinking about their own narrative at the same time.

> *Obviously, I don't sing the "Hatikva" (the national anthem) with them; I even think about the spirits of our dead. They [the Jews present at the ceremony] know that I am standing because I respect them. I sing the Arabic song "Mawtiny e my homeland" in my heart. I cannot shake off my roots. I don't forget who I am. It is too hard for me on Memorial Day. I used to stand with them, but it was very hard. I cried several times and other teachers hugged me, I explained to them that it hurts for me and for my people …*
>
> *The teachers accepted my decision. However, on Holocaust Remembrance Day, I feel sad for the people who were killed and I want to express solidarity. I don't have any problem attending – or even participating actively – in the ceremony.*

Discussion

Two main interests guided our work. First, we wanted to add to the growing research which contributes to a better understanding of how minority teachers in majority schools experience their work and how their participation in such educational contexts helps shape their sense of ethno-cultural belonging and their sense of self-efficacy. Second, we wanted through our comparative work to gain insights into the context-specific conditions which might help support or undermine minority teachers' inclusion. To do this we compared the reported experiences of Palestinian Israeli teachers working in two somewhat different educational contexts; the Hebrew speaking schools which serve the regular Israeli Jewish population and the bilingual integrated schools which offer the opportunity for the two populations to study under one roof in a society in which schools are mostly segregated. Both these educational contexts include Palestinian Israeli teachers in their faculty; the first mostly because of instrumental reasons while the second because of their ideology.

Our findings point mostly at similarities in the way these teachers experience their work at the schools but also some notable differences have been exposed.

Both groups of teachers express satisfaction regarding their work at the Hebrew speaking and the bilingual integrated schools. They feel at 'home' they say, indicating through this metaphor a strong identification with the institutions within which they work. They are not only satisfied with their work but they also feel they belong to a very special 'club' a metaphor that affords them a strong and positive positioning within the school context. Both groups of teachers sustain good relationships with all stakeholders – students, parents, and colleagues. Last both groups of teachers appreciate their exposure to the majority society and believe that for the most part, this exposure is beneficial to their own understanding of social realities and the need (or not) to help change them. All in all, these aspects together contribute to their sense of job satisfaction and feeling of belonging to the school.

All teachers seem to have developed high professional positions with a strong sense of self-efficacy thanks to their positive experiences and to the school environment (Flores & Clark, 2004). Their professional abilities can promote students' outcomes and success (Tschannen-Moran & Hoy, 2001). The success in taking part in the promotion of students' achievements adds to their sense of satisfaction. Teachers in both educational contexts described their professional role predominantly as pedagogical experts. Teachers also reported professional and social acceptance at work (Erlich et al., 2020). They reported using a variety of teaching methods, innovating new strategies, enabling genuine learning, and making the students' learning meaningful. The strategies implemented, they believe, contribute not only to the students' academic success but also have an important role in reducing prejudice among students, parents, and colleagues. These findings are in line with those of Jennett et al. (2003) and Scheopner (2010), who noted that a positive and supportive social climate helps teachers sustain constructive relationships with all school stakeholders, and it is instrumental for establishing and sustaining their sense of satisfaction and motivation (Scheopner, 2010). Reeves (2009) shows how teachers' positioning of students as individuals who actively cope with relevant pedagogical issues on a daily basis could help teachers reposition themselves in relation to their role as guides, partners, and role models for their pupils. The differences found in the teachers' approaches seem to relate to the educational ideologies sustained by the different educational contexts in which they teach.

While the regular Hebrew speaking schools focus mainly on academic achievements; the bilingual schools focus on a dual agenda in which academic achievements run parallel and equal to coexistence and multicultural one (at least at the declarative level). Moreover, the Hebrew-speaking schools have for the most part no representation of the Palestinian population (not at the administrative level or the students and parents body) while the bilingual integrated schools bring together Jewish and Palestinian populations and try to keep an ethnically balanced faculty.

In the case of teachers teaching at Hebrew-speaking schools, these differences seem to make no difference in terms of their general sense of satisfaction. Moreover, given that regular segregated state schools do not necessarily follow a multicultural policy they see themselves as the bearers of a multicultural agenda, a peculiarity that serves to strengthen their feeling of superiority and perceive their work as an ideological calling, rather than as a regular teaching job even if it began as a solution to not finding a job in the Arab schools.

The teachers at the bilingual schools, on the other hand, sense tensions which impinge on their sense of satisfaction and professionalism. They sense they are the only ones truly defending the double academic success/coexistence agenda. They believe parents for the most part look at the school as a pathway for their children to sustain or to better their present position in the social hierarchies and that they are the only ones who not disregarding the importance of academic success stay attached and struggle to advance the coexistence agenda.

The ideological and structural differences between the school contexts are also reflected in the way the teachers confront political issues. Teachers at the bilingual school seem to find it easier to cope with political questions regarding the Palestinian and Jewish historical narratives as well as to confront questions regarding national commemorative events such as Holocaust Memorial Day and the Day of Independence. The declared ideological foundation of the bilingual integrated schools come to their help and allow them to rather openly talk about very sensitive issues in Israel's conflictual society.

Teachers at the Hebrew-speaking schools find this task much more difficult and many times have a sense that silence is the way to cope with the potential dilemmas created by the historical narratives of the groups in conflict. For the most part, the sense that with the help of their principals they can endure the tensions but the tensions and dilemmas are always present. The teachers easily admit that they try to avoid talking about political events or expressing their own opinion. They explain that, in general, they come to teach, to earn a living, and they do not wish to get involved in anything that might jeopardize their job.

Conclusions and Implications

All in all, it becomes apparent that even when considering the difficulties mentioned there is something positive about the presence of minority teachers in majority Hebrew speaking and bilingual schools. Other than their high professionalism they contribute to a more tolerant and diverse society.

Moreover, our research brings strong support to those theoreticians who have pointed at the utter importance of context-specific conditions (Easton-Brooks et al., 2010; Irvine & Fenwick, 2011; Irvine, 1989; Lengyel & Rosen, 2015; Strasser & Waburg, 2015) and their potential to support or undermine minority teachers' inclusion. This point is also supported by Allport's (1954) contact hypothesis that claims that extensive integration between members of an in-group and an out-group is the best means for achieving social stability and harmony. Yet Allport sets conditions without which contact will not do the expected job of prejudice reduction. The main prescriptions recommended in the contact literature include the following: contact should be regular and frequent; it should involve a balanced ratio of in-group to out-group members while allowing for a genuine "acquaintance potential;" it should occur between individuals who share equality of status; and while being institutionally sanctioned, it should be organized around cooperation towards the achievement of a super-ordinate goal.

At this point, these conditions are met with greater approximation in the bilingual integrated schools. Though it seems difficult, at this point in time, to expect the Ministry of Education in Israel to embrace a stronger multicultural agenda and to support the growth of bilingual integrates schools it becomes clear that the effectiveness of the contribution of Palestinian teachers in majority schools can be widened and better supported by securing stronger institutional support (one not only based on instrumental needs, e.g. lack of Jewish teachers) for multicultural approaches geared to the soothing of social and political conflicts. Teachers serve as role models to the children who feel comfortable with them. The inclusion of Palestinian teachers in regular state schools that strongly support the initiative can become a "real-life experiment" with tolerance and recognition helping all involved overcome the prejudices and conflicts of the present generation. Lived experience may be more significant than ideology. We see in our teachers a potential to be effective agents of social change, by helping their students and colleagues combat racism and prejudice.

In general, the research we conducted has the potential of widening and deepening our understanding of how teachers ideological, social, and political perspectives intersect with their pedagogical practices and believe such research efforts should be encouraged and increased. Moreover, we believe that comparative research on the participation of majority teachers in schools mainly populated by minority populations (e.g. Jewish teachers working in Arab schools in Israel) would be very productive. Similar comparative efforts should be conducted in other countries suffering from persistent conflicts; such research efforts would contribute to us on the context specific understanding of the effects of including minority teachers in majority schools. Finally, we suggest extending research on how different systemic reasons/needs to include minority teachers in majority schools (ideological and/or instrumental), influence the teachers' involvement in these initiatives.

References

Abu Asba, K. (2006, October). The Arab education system and equality. *Mifneh*, 43–50. (In Hebrew).
Abu-Saad, I. (2006). State educational policy and curriculum: The case of Palestinian Arabs in Israel. *International Education Journal, 7*(5), 709–720.
Allport, G. W. (1954). *The nature of prejudice*. Addison-Wesley.
Arar, K., & Abu-Asbah, K. (2013). Not just location: Attitudes and functioning of Arab local education administrators in Israel. *International Journal of Educational Management., 27*, 54–73.
Atkins, D. N., Fertig, A. R., & Wilkins, V. M. (2014). Connectedness and expectations: How minority teachers can improve educational outcomes for minority students. *Public Management Review, 16*(4), 503–526.
Ayalon, H., Blass, N., Feniger, Y., & Shavit, Y. (2019). *Educational inequality in Israel: From research to policy*. Taub Center for Social Policy Studies in Israel.
Bar-Tal, D. (1998). Societal beliefs in times of intractable conflict: The Israeli case. *International Journal of Conflict Management, 9*, 22–50.
Bekerman, Z. (2000). Dialogic directions: Conflicts in Israeli/Palestinian education for peace. *Intercultural Education, 11*(1), 41–51.
Bekerman, Z. (2004). Multicultural approaches and options in conflict ridden areas: Bilingual Palestinian-Jewish education in Israel. *Teachers College Record, 106*(3), 574–610.
Bekerman, Z. (2012). Teachers' 'Contact' at the integrated bilingual schools in Israel. *Policy Futures in Education, 10*(5), 552–562.

Bekerman, Z. (2016). *The promise of integrated multicultural and bilingual education.* Oxford University Press.

Bekerman, Z., & Tatar, M. (2009). Parental choice of schools and parents' perceptions of multicultural and co-existence education: the case of the Israeli Palestinian–Jewish bilingual primary schools. *European Early Childhood Education Research Journal, 17*(2), 171–185.

Bekerman, Z., & Zembylas, M. (2010). Fearful symmetry: Palestinian and Jewish teachers confront contested narratives in integrated bilingual education. *Teaching and Teacher Education, 26*(3), 507–515.

Blass, N. (2014). Trends in the development of the education system. *State of the nation report: Society, economy and policy in Israel* (pp. 347–389).

Blass, N. (2020). Opportunities and risks to the education system in the time of the coronavirus: An overview. *State of the nation report: Society, economy and policy in Israel 2020.* Taub Center for Social Policy Studies in Israel.

Braun, V., & Clarke, V. (2006). Using thematic analysis in psychology. *Qualitative Research in Psychology, 3*(2), 77–101.

Brosh, H. Y. (2013). The implications of the sociopolitical context on Arab teachers in Hebrew schools. *Journal of Arts and Humanities, 2*(1), 1–12.

Campbell, R. J., Kyriakides, L., Muijs, R. D., & Robinson, W. (2003). Differential teacher effectiveness: Towards a model for research and teacher appraisal. *Oxford Review of Education, 29*(3), 347–362.

Caprara, G. V., Barbaranelli, C., Steca, P., & Malone, P. S. (2006). Teachers' self-efficacy beliefs as determinants of job satisfaction and students' academic achievement: A study at the school level. *Journal of School Psychology, 44*(6), 473–490.

CBS – Israel's Central Bureau of Statistics. (2019, 2016, 2010). Retrieved from https://www.cbs.gov.il/en/Pages/default.aspx on January 13, 2021.

Cherng, H. Y. S., & Halpin, P. F. (2016). The importance of minority teachers: Student perceptions of minority versus White teachers. *Educational Researcher, 45*(7), 407–420.

DiCicco-Bloom, B., & Crabtree, B. (2006). The qualitative research interview. *Medical Education, 40*, 314–321.

Easton-Brooks, D., Lewis, C., & Yang, Y. (2010). Ethnic-matching: The influence of African American teachers on the reading scores of African American students. *National Journal of Urban Education & Practice, 3*(1), 230–243.

Erlich, R. R., Gindi, S., & Hisherik, M. (2020). "I'll do business with anyone": Arab teachers in Jewish schools as a disruptive innovation. *Israel Studies Review, 35*(3), 72–91.

Flores, B. B., & Clark, E. R. (2004). A critical examination of nor- malistas' self-conceptualization and teacher-efficacy. *Hispanic Journal of Behavioral Sciences, 26*(2), 230–257.

Forman, G., & Kedar, A. (2004). From Arab land to 'Israel Lands': The legal dispossession of the Palestinians displaced by Israel in the wake of 1948. *Environment and Planning D: Society and Space, 22*(6), 809–830.

Fragman, A. (2008). The integration of Arab native teachers as teachers of Arabic in Hebrew-speaking schools: Intended policy or arbitrary strategy. *The Annual of Language & Politics and Politics of Identity, 2*, 55–80.

Gay, G. (1995). Modeling and mentoring in urban teacher preparation. *Education and Urban Society, 28*(1), 103–118.

Gay, L. R., & Airasian, P. (2003). *Educational research: Competencies for analysis and applications* (7th ed.). Merrill Prentice Hall.

Golani, M., & Manna, A. (2011). Two sides of the coin: Independence and Nakba, 1948: Two narratives of the 1948 War and its outcome. *Institute for Historical Justice and Reconciliation.*

Guyton, E., & Hidalgo, F. (1995). Characteristics, responsibilities, and qualities of urban school mentors. *Education and Urban Society, 28*(1), 40–47.

Hadad Haj-Yahya, N., & Assaf, R. (2017). *Arab society in Israel – A socio-financial situation and future outlook*. Center for Democratic Values and Institutions. Retrieved from https://www.idi.org.il/books/19008 (In Hebrew)

Heydemann, S. (1991). The near and middle east research and training act: Background and current status. *Newsletter (Association for Israel Studies), 7*(1), 11–13.

Irvine, J. J. (1989). Beyond role models: An examination of cultural influences on the pedagogical perspectives of black teachers. *Peabody Journal of Education, 66*(4), 51–63.

Irvine, J. J., & Fenwick, L. T. (2011). Teachers and teaching for the new millennium: The role of HBCUs. *The Journal of Negro Education*, 197–208.

Israel's Central Bureau of Statistics. (2017). Retrieved from http://www.cbs.gov.il/reader/cw_usr_view_Folder?ID=141

Israeli Education System. (2015). *Selected issues in the field of the committee's business, education, culture and sport of the Knesset*. Retrieved from http://www.knesset.gov.il/mmm/data/pdf/m03552.pdf

Jabareen, Y., & Agbaria, A. (2010). *Education on hold. Israeli government policy and civil society: Initiatives to improve Arab education in Israel*. Dirasat, The Arab Center for Law and Policy.

Jayusi, W., & Bekerman, Z. (2019a). Yes, we can! – Palestinian-Israeli teachers in Jewish-Israeli schools. *Journal of Teacher Education, 66*(2), 109–121.

Jayusi, W., & Bekerman, Z. (2019b). Does teaching on the "Other" side create a change. *Teaching and Teacher Education, 77*, 160–169.

Jennett, H. K., Harris, S. L., & Mesibov, G. B. (2003). Commitment to philosophy, teacher efficacy, and burnout among teachers of children with autism. *Journal of Autism and Developmental Disorders, 33*(6), 583–593.

Kelchtermans, G., & Ballet, K. (2002). The micropolitics of teacher induction. A narrative-biographical study on teacher socialisation. *Teaching and Teacher Education, 18*(1), 105–120.

Khalidi, R. (2010). *Palestinian identity: The construction of modern national consciousness*. Columbia University Press.

Khalidi, R. (2020). *The hundred Years' war on Palestine: A history of settler colonialism and resistance, 1917–2017*. Metropolitan Books.

Khalidi, W., Elmusa, S. S., & Khalidi, M. A. (1992). *All that remains: The Palestinian villages occupied and depopulated by Israel in 1948*. Institution for Palestine Studies.

King, A. (1993). From sage on the stage to guide on the side. *College Teaching, 41*(1), 30–35.

Kokkinos, C. M. (2007). Job stressors, personality and burnout in primary school teachers. *British Journal of Educational Psychology, 77*(1), 229–243.

Lengyel, D., & Rosen, L. (2015). Minority teachers in different educational contexts: Introduction. *Tertium Comparationis, 21*(2), 153–160.

Luke, A. (2017). Commentary: On the race of teachers and students: A reflection on experience, scientific evidence, and silence. *American Educational Research Journal, 54*(1_suppl), 102S–110S.

Malach, G., Cahaner, L., & Choshen, M. (2018). *Statistical report on ultra-orthodox society in Israel*. The Israel Democratic Institute.

Masalha, N. (2012). *The Palestine Nakba: Decolonising history, narrating the subaltern, reclaiming memory*. Zed Books Ltd..

Maylor, U., Ross, A., Rollock, N., & Williams, K. (2006). *Black teachers in London*. Greater London Authority.

McNamara, O., & Basit, T. N. (2004). Equal opportunities or affirmative action? The induction of minority ethnic teachers. *Journal of Education for Teaching, 30*(2), 97–115.

Merchavim. (2016). *The Institute for the advancement of shared citizenship in Israel*. Retrieved from http://www.machon-merchavim.org.il. Accessed 15 Nov 2016.

Meshulam, A. (2019). Palestinian-Jewish bilingual schools in Israel: Unravelling the educational model. *International Journal of Educational Development, 70*, 102092.

Ministry of Education. (2015). Retrieved from http://meyda.education.gov.il/files/staj/mishtalvim-ivrit.pdf on January 10, 2018.

Mock, S., Obeidi, A., & Zeleznikow, J. (2014). A brief outline of the Israel–Palestinian conflict. *Group Decision and Negotiation, 23*(6), 1245–1262.

Morris, R. D. (1987). Signalling, agency theory and accounting policy choice. *Accounting and Business Research, 18*(69, Winter), 47–56.

Nieto, S. (1998). From claiming hegemony to sharing space. Creating community in multicultural education courses. In R. Chavez-Chavez & J. O'Donnell (Eds.), *Speaking the unpleasant* (p. 16e31). SUNY Press.

Pachler, N., Makoe, P., Burns, M., & Blommaert, J. (2008). The things (we think) we (ought to) do: Ideological processes and practices in teaching. *Teaching and Teacher Education, 24*(2), 437–450.

Rajuan, M., & Bekerman, Z. (2011). Inside and outside the integrated bilingual Palestinian–Jewish schools in Israel: Teachers' perceptions of personal, professional and political positioning. *Teaching and Teacher Education, 27*(2), 395–405.

Reeves, D. B. (2009). *Leading change in your school: How to conquer myths, build commitment, and get results*. ASCD.

Sachs, S. K. (2004). Evaluation of teacher attributes as predictors of success in urban schools. *Journal of Teacher Education, 55*(2), 177–187.

Said, E. (2001). *The clash of ignorance* (p. 22). The Nation.

Santoro, N. (2007). 'Outsiders' and 'others':'different' teachers teaching in culturally diverse classrooms. *Teachers and Teaching: Theory and Practice, 13*(1), 81–97.

Scheopner, A. J. (2010). Irreconcilable differences: Teacher attrition in public and catholic schools. *Educational Research Review, 5*(3), 261–277.

Shafir, G. (1996). *Land, labor and the origins of the Israeli-Palestinian conflict, 1882–1914* (Vol. 20). University of California Press.

Shkedi, A. (2004). Second-order theoretical analysis: A method for constructing theoretical explanation. *International Journal of Qualitative Studies in Education, 17*(5), 627–646.

Shlaim, A. (1998). *The politics of partition, 1921–1951: King Abdullah, the Zionists, and Palestine*.

Shohat, J. (1973). *The instruction of Arabic in Hebrew schools*. Shohat Committee Report.

Shwed, U., Shavit, Y., Dellashi, M., & Ofek, M. (2014). *Integration of Arab Israelis and Jews in schools in Israel* (Policy Paper No. 2014.12). Taub Center. Retrieved from http://taubcenter.org.il/wp-content/files_mf/e2014.12schoolintegration67.pdf

Sion, L. (2014). Passing as a hybrid: Arab-Palestinian teachers in Jewish schools. *Ethnic and Racial Studies, 37*(14), 2636–2652.

Skaalvik, E. M., & Skaalvik, S. (2010). Teacher self-efficacy and teacher burnout: A study of relations. *Teaching and Teacher Education, 26*, 1059–1069.

Strasser, J. (2013). Diversity in the faculty room: Constraints and affordances of minority teachers' professional action in Germany. *The International Journal of Diversity in Education, 12*(3), 131–141.

Strasser, J., & Waburg, W. (2015). Students' perspectives on minority teachers in Germany. *Tertium Comparationis, 21*(2), 251.

Teveth, S. (1989). Charging Israel with original sin. *Commentary, 88*(3), 24.

Tschannen-Moran, M., & Hoy, A. W. (2001). Teacher efficacy: Capturing an elusive construct. *Teaching and Teacher Education, 17*(7), 783–805.

Weiss, H. M. (2002). Deconstructing job satisfaction: Separating evaluations, beliefs and affective experiences. *Human Resource Management Review, 12*(2), 173–194.

Wilkins, C., & Lall, R. (2011). 'You've got to be tough and I'm trying': Black and minority ethnic student teachers' experiences of initial teacher education. *Race Ethnicity and Education, 14*(3), 365–386.

Yonai, Y. (1992). *Arabic in Hebrew schools. A documentary series*. Ministry of Education and Culture.

Wurud Jayusi is the Head of the Arab Academic Institute - Beit Berl College. She is the former head of the Center for the Advancement of Shared Society at the College. She teaches planning & evaluation for learning at the Education faculty. Her main interests are in the study of peace education, multicultural\multiethnic education, and minority-majority relations in the education system. Her recent work has examined cross-cultural teaching. Wurud has published multiple papers in a variety of academic journals and presented her research at multiple international conferences.

Zvi Bekerman teaches anthropology of education at the School of Education, Hebrew University of Jerusalem (Israel), and is a faculty member at the Mandel Leadership Institute in Jerusalem. He is also an Associate Fellow at The Harry S. Truman Research Institute for The Advancement of Peace. His main interests are in the study of cultural, ethnic and national identity, including identity processes and negotiation during intercultural encounters and in formal/informal learning contexts. He is particularly interested in how concepts such as culture and identity intersect with issues of social justice, intercultural and peace education, and citizenship education. His recent work has examined the intersection between civic and religious epistemologies in educational contexts. In addition to publishing multiple papers in a variety of academic journals, Bekerman is the founding editor of the refereed journal Diaspora, Indigenous, and Minority Education: An International Journal. Among his most recent books: Bekerman, Z., & Zembylas, M. (2017). Psychologized language in education: Denaturalizing a regime of truth, Palgrave Macmillan – Springer; Bekerman, Zvi (2016), The Promise of Integrated and Multicultural Bilingual Education: Inclusive Palestinian-Arab and Jewish Schools in Israel, Oxford University Press; Bekerman, Z. & Michalinos, Z. (2012), Teaching Contested Narratives Identity, Memory and Reconciliation in Peace Education and Beyond. London, Cambridge University Press; C. McGlynn, M. Zembylas, & Z. Bekerman (Eds.) (2013) Integrated Education in Conflicted Societies, Palgrave, Mcmillan; and Bekerman, Z. & Geisen, T. (Eds. 2012) International Handbook of Migration, Minorities and Education Understanding Cultural and Social Differences in Processes of Learning. New York: Springer.

Open Access This chapter is licensed under the terms of the Creative Commons Attribution 4.0 International License (http://creativecommons.org/licenses/by/4.0/), which permits use, sharing, adaptation, distribution and reproduction in any medium or format, as long as you give appropriate credit to the original author(s) and the source, provide a link to the Creative Commons license and indicate if changes were made.

The images or other third party material in this chapter are included in the chapter's Creative Commons license, unless indicated otherwise in a credit line to the material. If material is not included in the chapter's Creative Commons license and your intended use is not permitted by statutory regulation or exceeds the permitted use, you will need to obtain permission directly from the copyright holder.

Chapter 12
Independent Schools in South Africa: Acculturation of Zimbabwean Immigrant Teachers

Tshatiwa Makula

Abstract South Africa, which offers relative political stability and prosperity, has always been a major destination country for a large flow of people seeking better economic and social opportunities. Many Zimbabweans left to flee from poverty as a result of Zimbabwe's political and financial crumble around 2008; thus, this paper aimed at shedding light on Zimbabwean immigrant teachers' experiences of acculturation in independent schools in Johannesburg, South Africa. It also sought to identify educational leadership approaches that promote multiculturalism and acculturation in culturally diverse independent schools. Data which were collected from a purposefully selected sample of six immigrant teachers were transcribed verbatim. The transcriptions were then analysed thematically through critical discourse analysis and content analysis, following open coding which identified and named segments of participants' responses. The findings indicated absence of cultural assimilation. Immigrant teachers are treated differently from their South African peers and they do not blend in easily. Thus, formal academic programmes, induction programmes, and in-service-training should be undertaken to cultivate revolutionary principals who facilitate cultural assimilation. There is need for school policies and practices that are sensitive to cultural differences and a call for all relevant individuals to face head-on the issue of multiculturalism.

Introduction

The past two decades have seen intense scholarly attention on international, regional, and national migration triggered by both voluntary and involuntary causes. Since then, the focus has increased and intensified globally – for example, on how industrialised countries attract highly skilled workers (e.g. Findlay et al., 2017; Lange, 2009; Thomas, 2017). Other scholars have been drawn into the brain drain of international student migration facilitated by globalisation (e.g. Mishchuk et al., 2019),

T. Makula (✉)
University of Johannesburg, Johannesburg, South Africa

and this has raised concern for the welfare of the minority – for example, gender disparities in migration (Sondhi & King, 2017).

This trend is true for Africa, where political unrest has been identified as the major push factor driving people out of their countries. Consequently, African scholars have focused on inter- and intra-African mobility in terms of challenges and prospects (Woldegiorgis & Doevenspeck, 2015) and pull factors influencing outflows to South Africa (Iwara et al., 2018; Kritz, 2013). This has seen a rise in studies documenting the push and pull factors in the mass migration of Zimbabwean teachers (Moyo & Perumal, 2018). However, none of the studies have paid attention to acculturation: how these teachers are integrating into foreign cultures in terms of challenges and opportunities. Currently, there is a gap in the existing literature on how these teachers as minorities are grappling with being integrated into the established cultures. The strong relationship between immigration, culture, and education cannot be ignored; therefore, the co-existence of immigrants and nationals of the host country warrants an investigation. The mutual twinning of immigration and education poses practical problems in unravelling the causal link between them. Pitre (2014) affirmed that it is generally the host country that holds and maintains its dominant social, political, and economic culture and norms which may or may not be in line with the immigrants from other cultures, thus, there is a call for acculturation. While research has been carried out on Zimbabwean immigrant teachers, less is known about the role of school principals in the immigrant teachers' acculturation. According to Moyo and Perumal (2018), most immigrant teachers prefer to teach in independent schools rather than public ones.

It is important to note that the number of immigrant teachers has risen drastically and changed the demographic population of independent schools in South Africa (McKay et al., 2018), justifying an investigation. To be specific, scholars such as Moyo and Perumal (2018) and Crush and Tawodzera (2014) have researched Zimbabwean immigrants' working conditions and their socio-economic experiences, but their experiences of acculturation have not been reported even though issues of diversity are especially salient to immigrants. There is a need to identify culturally competitive leadership – school principals who are able to eliminate cultural barriers and put into place systems that value diversity and promote knowledge about various cultures within their schools.

The South African Schools Act (No. 84 of 1996) recognises two categories of schools: the public and independent. All independent schools charge school fees. On the other hand, public schools are divided into fee-paying and non-fee paying schools. Public schools are run by the government while independent schools are run by individuals, trusts, or companies.

According to the Department of Education, in 2015 there were 566,194 learners in independent schools, which is about 4,5% of 12.8 million learners in grade R-12 (Wiese et al., 2010). Although the number of learners in independent schools serve a relatively small percentage of the country's learners, the increase of learners attending these schools has been alarming (Wiese et al., 2010). This could be an indication that parents are losing faith in public schools. The growth of the independent school industry, especially in Johannesburg central, is driven by the fact that most of these schools' employ highly qualified and experienced immigrant teachers (Makula, 2018). Their fees are low and as a result, their growth may be driven by the growing middle class who want high quality education at a low cost. Wiese et al. (2010) argue that parents take ethnicity into consideration when selecting their children's schools. Therefore, this study focused on these independent schools since most of them have more than 70% immigrant teachers (Makula, 2018). Immigrant parents send their children there, where they believe xenophobia is not likely to exist because of the diversity in learner population.

Acculturation is the intra-generational process where individuals of different cultures encounter a new culture and come into first-hand contact with subsequent changes in behaviour and attitude in the original cultural patterns of both groups (Jandt, 2012), thereby adjusting to contact with a culture other than their own. Sam and Berry (1997) argue that this process consists of confluence among heritage-cultural and receiving-cultural practices, values, and identification of immigrants. It is associated with a number of psychosocial effects. Hence, this study sought to understand Zimbabwean immigrant teachers' experiences of acculturation in independent schools in Johannesburg, South Africa. It adopted Berry's model of acculturation, whose strategies are: assimilation, integration, separation, and marginalisation. It is anticipated that an in-depth understanding of the role of school principals in the acculturation of immigrant teachers could provide data for decision making and policy formulation processes for the education system and inform further and future research.

Aims of the Research

This study aimed at shedding light on Zimbabwean immigrant teachers' experiences of acculturation in independent schools in Johannesburg, South Africa. It was motivated by the desire to explore the social justice experiences of Zimbabwean immigrant teachers in Johannesburg inner-city independent schools and the methods and strategies that the principals employ to bring about culturally competitive leadership in these diverse schools. The legislative framework for post-apartheid education enforces democracy and transformation in an education system that values human dignity, equity, and human rights (Mafora, 2013). Against this backdrop, this study examined how these immigrant teachers are treated in independent schools and if their treatment is aligned with the relevant legal frameworks. The aims prompted the research questions that follow: (1) What are the Zimbabwean immigrant teachers' experiences in regard to acculturation in independent schools in Johannesburg's inner city? (2) Which are the culturally competitive leadership approaches?

To focus on the above research questions, we constructed the following objectives: (1) Explore Zimbabwean immigrant teachers' experiences of acculturation in Johannesburg's inner-city independent schools. (2) Investigate the principals' culturally competitive leadership approaches.

Context of Research

When one moves to another country, the process is fraught with anxiety and tension because of shifts between two environments. At times, such behaviours are incongruent with the culture of the new environment (Hammerstad, 2012). Jandt (2012) posited that one can experience cultural shock due to one's reaction to the new culture and the encountering of difficulties in cross-cultural adjustment. On the other hand, Pitre (2014) revealed that cultural shock is not a setback but normal since it is the body's reaction to that which it fears, as it tries to develop a defensive mechanism. Hammerstad (2012) argued that such experiences help individuals to develop psychologically, hence the process of acculturation happens at four levels: learning a new language, immersion, assimilation, and integration, as will be discussed in detail in the paragraphs that follow.

Language

Zimbabwean immigrant teachers in South Africa face classroom management problems (De Villiers & Weda, 2018). There is usually a struggle in the classroom between students adapting to the immigrant teacher's pronunciation and accent and the teacher trying to navigate their way through classroom practices while striving to adhere to the relevant policies and documents. In Vandeyar et al.'s (2014) study, some learners were concerned that these teachers could not communicate effectively, were not firm on them, and that lessons were chaotic. Learners commented on the teachers' accents and called them *"makwerekwere"*, a derogative name for foreigners in South Africa (Moyo et al., 2014). On top of this, Manik's (2015) and De Villiers and Weda's (2018) studies of Zimbabwean immigrant teachers in KwaZulu Natal noted that staff meetings are held in local languages, which indirectly excludes immigrant teachers. They endure isolation resulting from the fact that they are always in the minority and do not speak most of the South African languages (Crush & Tawodzera, 2014). Berry (1997) refers to this state as the marginalisation strategy, where immigrants feel rejected by the host.

Immersion

The immigrant has to live amidst the people of the new culture and understand the customs, traditions, and acceptance behaviours of these cultures so as to live a comfortable and amicable life in a foreign nation. In his qualitative thesis on issues facing expatriate teachers in Singapore, Vial (2006) contended that the key purpose of education in a culturally diverse society must be to assist individuals to develop a sense of identity and belonging. Moyo et al. (2014) also concurred and revealed the positive social experiences of some immigrant teachers who now have cars and houses, which they could not have afforded had they stayed in Zimbabwe. Thus, both teachers and principals must recognise their own social, cultural, and political identities (Martin, 2015) and be responsive by appreciating and tolerating cultural diversity among their students and colleagues (Santoro & Major, 2012) so that their schools become culturally responsive organisations.

Assimilation

According to Fee's (2011) study, teaching away from home leads to a teacher-academic culture shock. Their curricula and home pedagogy and that of the host country might be different. Fee (2011) stated that in the Unites States of America, Mexican immigrant teachers are expected to teach at high schools, yet they are trained at the primary level. According to Halicioglu (2015), immigrant teachers intending to go to the Middle East are expected to accept censorship in some schools and curricula changes in agreeance with Islamic culture. In South Africa, assessment standards are a surprise to Zimbabwean immigrant teachers as they find it ridiculous that 30% is a pass, yet the student does not know 70% of the work, while others find it farcical that learners are given a scope for an examination (Makonye, 2017). They must accept and work within these assessment standards – Berry's (1997) assimilation strategy – giving up on one's culture and being absorbed and accepting the host's culture. One the other hand, concurring with Berry's (1997) separation strategy (rejection of involvement with the host country), some Zimbabwean immigrant teachers fail to forsake their home cultural pedagogies and classroom practices which makes their new environment difficult to navigate. They fail to stabilise and adapt to the new curriculum and teaching methods (Makonye, 2017).

Integration

During the integration process, individuals maintain their own cultural identity while becoming participants in the host culture (Berry, 1997). The apartheid system branded and categorised people into different social groups and years after the end of this system, many black South Africans are still trying to make sense of this new phenomenon of black immigrants (Crush & Tawodzera, 2014). They do so by plugging them into the *makwerekwere* category creating a new social class. Crush et al. (2015) concurred with this and explain that African immigrants are recognised as "other". Immigrant teachers are bound to feel isolated if they teach in schools and communities that do not embrace diversity or tolerate any forms of differences (De Villiers & Weda, 2018; Vandeyar et al., 2014). Some immigrant teachers claim that outside of their places of work, they suffer harassment at the hands of police officers who always demand proof of their right to live in South Africa, such as permits or asylum papers (Chinomona & Maziriri, 2015; Sibanda, 2010).

Educational Leadership Approaches Aligned to Acculturation and Integration

This study has been conceived and initiated at a time when education leadership in South Africa has an important bearing on the principals' daily operations and actions in transforming schools into democratic sites (Bush et al., 2011; Mafora, 2013; Pitre, 2014).

Cultural Leadership

This body of literature on culture and education has brought attention to subtractive education: the affirmation of the cultural contribution made by supreme and dominant groups at the expense of minority ones (Boske, 2015). Culture-based education models provide a base that prepares leaders to assume responsibilities associated with social justice, leadership, and cultural leadership, which according to Hess and Kelly (2007), focus on community, curriculum, culturally relevant pedagogy, and cultural competence.

Moral/Ethical Leadership

Ethical leadership centres on communication and cross-cultural cooperation that builds an egalitarian society where everyone enjoys a harmony of social rights and opportunities (Shields, 2010). Leadership must be critically educative, evaluating in-depth the conditions people live in and determining how to positively change and improve those (Shields, 2010). This acknowledges a strong link between community issues and people's individual reactions. School leaders must create empathic schools that recognise the need for the interaction and interconnectedness to create a caring, supportive environment in which people feel safe, valued, and respected.

Dialogical Leadership

Shields (2010) asserted that leaders need a dialogical approach that will allow discourse around issues of freedom and supremacy. Leaders must overcome their silence about aspects such as ethnicity and social class (Kose, 2009). Researchers assert that it is the responsibility of a principal to instigate structural transformation and understand the relationships among the students, teachers, and parents and between leaders through conversation and dialogue (Boske, 2015). Such leaders must exercise power and authority that will enable them to work towards creating a society grounded in the struggle for racial democracy.

Curriculum Leadership

Curriculum leadership is a shared experience whereby stakeholders come together to shape the school's activities and design a curriculum that transforms the community (Makonye, 2017). The leaders' behaviours and the school policies must develop the curriculum, establish communication networks, and consult with others to implement the chosen curriculum. Leaders must take risks, develop transparency, communicate, and share a vision with all the stakeholders so that they enact the chosen curriculum. Thus, curriculum leadership calls for principals who develop teachers through activities such as staff development and mentoring. Principals who are curriculum leaders are driven by their passion and values (Bush et al., 2011). Therefore, curriculum leadership is not only concerned with developing an individual, but the society or community too.

Research Design and Methodology

Given that qualitative research is the perfect approach if you want to learn more about human interaction, phenomena, people, actions, and social settings that provide the context for meaning in qualitative research, the researcher investigated the phenomenon, in this study case, acculturation, by perceiving that qualitative research is context-based and explores the life experiences of the participants. Thus, qualitative research was relevant in this study that sought to explore acculturation and integration of Zimbabwean immigrant teachers in Johannesburg's inner-city independent schools. It further identified the culturally competitive leadership approaches.

Sampling and Site Selection

According to Lincoln et al. (2011), purposive sampling selects participants for a specific purpose. Hence, Moyo (2015) emphasised that purposeful sampling enables the researcher to carefully choose participants whom they feel have the greatest potential to yield information rich enough to satisfy their particular requirements. Based on this, we choose Johannesburg's inner-city independent schools. The participants were easily accessible, and it was convenient to visit them in terms of time and travel expenses. The research sites are independent schools and diverse in both learner and staff complement and were purposefully selected for their geographical and diverse demographics. They are all situated in Johannesburg central. Studies argue that Johannesburg is the hub of foreign nationals (De Villiers & Weda, 2018; Makula, 2018; Manik, 2015; Perumal, 2015). The two schools were given pseudonyms: Transformative High School and Vision High School, respectively. Transformative High School was founded in 1998 by two sociologists. Today the school has 40 teachers including the principal. Non-South African teachers form 85% of the teaching staff and the rest are South African citizens. Vision High School is individually owned. The owner-principal resigned from the Department of Education in the early 1990s as the rise of independent schools in the inner city attracted him back to education. The school has 700 students and 27 teachers. The approximate 70% of non-South Africans attached to the school come from Botswana, Ghana, Zambia, Nigeria, and Zimbabwe.

The six Zimbabwean immigrant teachers partially represent ethnicity in Zimbabwe; two are Kalangas, Shonas and Ndebeles, respectively, the major cultural groups in Zimbabwe, which is relevant since acculturation is the phenomenon in this study. All the immigrant teachers are qualified and experienced teachers. This met Wiese et al.'s (2018) argument that parents send their children to independent schools because teachers there are competent. Table 12.1 below gives a summary of the participants.

Table 12.1 Biographic details of participants

Pseudonym	Gender	Highest educational qualification	Years in the profession	Teaching Years in South Africa	Number of years associated with this school	Rank
Rampela	Male	Master's degree in education leadership and management	27	N/A	13	Principal
Nzimande	Male	Advanced certificate in education	23	N/A	8	Principal
Ncube	Female	Bachelor's degree in education	15	7	4	H.O.D Science
Makamure	Female	Diploma in education	18	5	3	English teacher
Malikongwa	Male	Master's degree in educational leadership and management	25	13	10	H.O.D Science
Mtambara	Male	Honours degree in mathematics	14	8	4	Maths teacher
Tshivako	Female	Honours degree in mathematics	15		9	H.O.D Maths

Data Collection Methods

As a form of social enquiry, Merriam (2009) affirmed that qualitative research helps in gaining understanding of the phenomenon from the participants' perspective and their interpretation and construction of meaning within the context of their lives. Qualitative research examines meaning using the interpretivist tradition and employs an inductive approach, working from the bottom up, from the concrete to the abstract, from data to concepts, and themes expressed in words (Yin, 2011). It is further stated that through the inductive process, the researcher converts raw empirical data into understandable themes and topics. This study reflects this stance in that semi-structured interviews were the main data collection methods used, supplemented by pre-interview observations, based on Lincoln et al. (2011) who affirmed that triangulation rests on the belief that one method cannot explore a phenomenon fully.

For validity purposes, the interview schedules were assessed for appropriateness and completeness of the contents in relation to acculturation, integration, and culturally competitive educational leadership. A pilot study was carried out at a workplace under conditions like those anticipated in the main study. Thereafter, the authors sought an application for ethical clearance from the Ethics Committee of the University of Johannesburg.

After permission was granted by the Ethics Committee and by the directorate of both schools, the interviews began. All the participants signed consent forms and they all agreed to audiotaping of the interviews. There were two different interview schedules, one for principals and the other for Zimbabwean immigrant teachers. Semi-structured interviews were conducted over a two-week period at Transformative and Vision schools at times convenient to the participants. The interviews were about 45 min long.

Data Analysis

Data were transcribed verbatim from a voice recorder, although at some point there were difficulties in dealing with intonation, speech elision, incomplete sentences, and determining where to punctuate. The transcriptions were then analysed thematically through Critical Discourse Analysis (CDA) and Content Analysis (CA). The authors examined the interview transcriptions using the following coding steps posited by Neuman (2011); open coding identified and named segments of participants' responses in relation to the title of the research. The segments were: dual labour market, acculturation, integration, and culturally competitive leadership approaches that were identified during summative content analysis. As emphasised by Saldana (2013), one looks for expressions of an idea when using themes. Thus, authors focused on the wording, phrasing consistency, and frequency of the responses in relation to the above segments, then highlighted and coded them.

Findings and Discussion

The social constructivist worldview guided the methodology of this study that aimed at exploring Zimbabwean immigrant teachers' acculturation and integration in independent schools. Further, it highlighted the culturally relevant educational leadership. In this section we present findings and the discussion of culturally competitive schools, culturally competitive leadership, and impact of communication, from the data from the eight participants' responses, in relation to acculturation, integration, and educational leadership. The following themes emerged: culturally competitive schools, culturally competitive leadership, and impact of communication.

Culturally Competitive Schools and Culturally Competitive Leadership

Culturally competitive schools promote diversity, a culture of inclusiveness and acceptance. According to Singh (2013), the recruitment processes in these schools reflect a commitment to diversity. Furthermore, Pitre (2014) informed us that such schools foster the development of staff cultural competence and nurture culturally responsive teachers who employ culturally responsive classroom pedagogies. Such a school facilitates and supports achievement of all learners. The strengths the teachers bring into the school are identified and utilised for the benefit of all. In the section that follows, the above concepts are divided into institutionalised, personal, and instructional dimensions. Each dimension is linked to the participants' responses.

Institutionalised Dimension

This centres on the school's administration, its policies and values, and the community involvement. Asked about how he handles diversity, the principal of Transformative High School, Ramphela said:

> *I teach learners and teachers to develop mutual respectful relationships, teach them about God's love, our constitution – that clause on human rights. I composed a school song and a hymn [available from the researcher] both emphasising the value of diversity. We offer History and Bible studies in our curriculum. These subjects help in making learners understand who we are, why some people are where they are, and they develop love and empathy towards other people.*

Shields (2010) argued that cultural leaders deconstruct and eliminate knowledge frameworks. The excerpt reveals the principal as a culturally competent leader. He aims to develop a new way of imagining the world among both teachers and the students, whereby they examine and adjust their attitudes towards others.

Concurring with Ramphela's sentiments on managing diversity, two out of three teachers from Transformative High School (Ramphela's school) attested to his ability to be inclusive and embrace diversity. One of them, Ncube, said:

> To an extent, he tries to accommodate everyone. We have our own cultural clubs as foreigners. On Speech and Prize-Giving days, our theme is diversity – we therefore have cultural dances and poems as part of entertainment. I remember the principal reminded that when we give learners comprehension passages we must use those that reflect South Africa as a welcoming country that encourages unity.

Consistent with Wang's (2016) argument that affirms cultural leadership, the principal considers cultural differences in his leadership practices. In contrast, at Vision High School the principal fears that if he gives foreign teachers leeway to teach South African children their cultures, he will not be preserving South African culture. This is what Makamure, a teacher from this school said about the principal:

> He doesn't want us to mix with learners much. He says that we will take away their culture and instil ours. I remember a time when he came to observe my lessons; I had a passage for comprehension that centred on a Zimbabwean child who had been awarded a scholarship to the United Kingdom. He criticised me for choosing Zimbabwe instead of South Africa.

The above excerpt shows lack of respect and absolute value of another individual's culture that is necessary for acculturation and integration to take place at school. Thus, in order to empower the teachers as professionals, the principals need to provide orientation, coaching, and staff development aimed at helping Zimbabwean immigrant teachers integrate easily into the South African teaching fraternity.

On issues of policies, laws, and Acts governing recruitment of immigrant teachers, this is what Ramphela had to say:

> The manager reminded me about this Act that it is illegal to employ an immigrant who does not have a work permit, and first preference must be given to South Africans. The school already had more immigrant teachers than locals and I was forced to employ the teacher who had the least score from the interviews, who was not going to produce good results compared to what I hoped the one from Ghana would.

Ramphela admits that there are government policies and school recruitment policies drawn by the Directorate, which do not promote diversity and equity. The principals now have a new role requiring their commitment to Zimbabwean immigrant teachers' personal growth and to the broader society.

Community involvement is also key in acculturation and integration processes. Dialogue therefore becomes central in enabling the critical evaluation and examination of present practices that build a culturally competent community.

Personal Dimension

Self-reflection is an important part of self-development. Teachers must examine their attitudes and beliefs and those of others. Thereafter, they must confront biases and reconcile negative feelings towards any other cultural groups or languages.

This creates an atmosphere of social belonging, trust, and acceptance and it becomes easy for the individual to reach out to students and peers (Wang, 2016).

Individuals must explore their personal history and experiences. This leads to greater understanding of others and higher chances of appreciating differences (Bush et al., 2011). Asked how his personal experiences prepared him in working with immigrants, Nzimande narrated:

> *I was in high school when we moved to Botswana. Students were eager to know why I had moved to Botswana, the teachers too were empathetic and in the first weeks they would always ask how I was coping. Everyone was emotionally attached to me. That is when I noticed the social injustice in Apartheid and justice in Botswana. When I encounter an unjust incident, I feel a strong desire, I should say, a calling to remedy it.*

In this excerpt, Nzimande's personal experiences taught him acceptance and tolerance of different cultural groups. Principals may give immigrant teachers the opportunity to present staff development sessions, involve them in curriculum design, and assign them management responsibilities such as being the head of a department.

Fearing victimisation and xenophobic attacks, most immigrant teachers prefer to stay in low density residential areas or where many foreigners reside. Responding to a question on where he stays, Tshivako had this to say:

> *I was a victim in 2008 in Alexandra where all my property was ransacked. I then sought refuge at my cousin who was at Randburg and discovered that xenophobia was not rife there and decided to settle there. I wanted a quiet place. So when I started looking for a house to buy, those areas were my first choice. I was already familiar with north of Johannesburg.*

Acculturation experiences can help to predict and position ones' social class according to financial and career development. Asked about how the principal distributes the workload, Dewa stated,

> *As teaching staff we have complained that all teaching loads are not balanced. Teachers who are South African have fewer loads because they threatened to sue the school that their work is too much and salary low, so the principal reduced their teaching load and those were distributed among those who do not have a lot of rights, us the foreign teachers.*

The above excerpt reveals characteristics of the secondary sector in the dual labour market theory, marked by unfair distribution of work. Immigrant teachers have heavy workloads compared to the South African nationals which shows stratification. In addition to the above strain, salaries are poor. One teacher, Tshivako, echoed, *"I work from hand to mouth. I am a specialist teacher, but I get salary that is even lower than South Africans who hold matric certificates, ABET, adult certificate in education".*

Unfavourable working conditions are evident at Vision High School. Foreign teachers are not afforded family leave or study leave – the no work no pay rule applies throughout the year. However, in both schools, chances of promotion of foreigners to posts of responsibilities, such as head of department, are high, although there are instances where poorly educated nationals hold better positions than highly educated foreigners, as expressed by Malikongwa. In his response to how he views promotions at his school, he stated:

> *Personally, I have been unfairly treated in terms of promotion. I was told I can hold deputy position, but I cannot because I have a work permit, not South African Identity Document. The deputy is less qualified and inexperienced compared to more than five foreign teachers.*

Given that present school structures inhibit the emancipation of immigrant teachers, they may continue enduring challenges. All the same challenges rising from a lack of recognition compel principals to identify their needs so as to develop support programmes. Principals are strategically positioned to support immigrant teachers and in the long run influence change in society. On the same issue of promotion, Makamba stated;

> *I resent them. The principal does not advertise these posts. Teachers are moved from one post to another without any interview whatsoever. It depends on how close you are to him. If not, no matter how hard you work, you will not be promoted.*

The line, *"it depends on how close you are to him"* implies nepotism, a practice among those in power of favouring family and close associates.

Whilst Mtambara agrees that immigrants are promoted to departmental head posts, he feels that this is done not to empower the immigrant but for the benefit of the school. He remarked:

> *There is bias, high positions are for South Africans and those positions such as departmental head that demand a lot of work are given to immigrant teachers. Our school is part of an organisation that has more than seven schools and all principals, deputies are all South Africans, but we have other people who have better qualifications but are not promoted.*

When recognition centres on one group rather than the other, Wang (2016) noted that this results in tension and dissatisfaction among members. By promoting another group, the principals are dividing staff members. The above excerpts all show that there is no cultural assimilation, that immigrant teachers are treated differently from their South African peers, and that they do not blend in easily. Thus, formal academic programmes, induction programmes, and in-service-training should be undertaken to cultivate revolutionary principals and facilitate cultural assimilation (Kose, 2009). Bush et al. (2011) called for principals' exposure to professional courses that develop intercultural communication competence in diverse organisations.

Some immigrant teachers are not willing to integrate and assimilate into the dominant culture. Makamure is not ready to change her dress code, and she did not take heed of the call from her peers to dress like most South Africans. She reflected her frustrations when she said:

> *I am negatively criticised by my colleagues as to how I dress. The departmental head once approached me and told me that I must dress like the other professionals. My culture insists on long dresses for mature women. I cannot move away from culture. Students laugh at my pronunciation and at times I feel disrespected and feel that my dignity as a teacher has been stripped away from me.*

Thus, immigrant teachers may feel a sense of professional disintegration and marginalisation. In order to reflect on diversity, the principals should create a welcoming and embracing atmosphere where every teacher's contribution, input, and culture is appreciated. In this way, South African teachers may welcome and appreciate Zimbabwean immigrant teachers.

Instructional Dimension

Perumal (2015) argued that if tools of instruction such as resources and teaching pedagogy are incompatible with the marginalised, there will be disconnection within teaching and learning. Thus, schools must be culturally responsive in instruction. Immigrant teachers have to be exposed to professional development activities that reinforce culturally competent classroom practices as advocated by Wang (2016). On his methods of distributing teaching material for teaching and learning, Nzimande stated:

> *These are given to the teachers as per the demands. At times I buy more books for English than Maths depending on the needs of the department. Generally, there is equal distribution except that departmental heads have laptops and other teachers don't, but these are departmental not personal.*

In the above excerpt, the principal reveals himself as a leader who demonstrates fairness in working towards higher learner achievement as demanded from culturally competent leaders, as observed by Boske (2015).

Culturally relevant pedagogy nurtures competitive schools and the curriculum must leverage the environment. Both schools offer history and bible studies, relevant to acculturation where individuals need to know each other's history. Biblical studies, from a Christian perspective, help to develop interconnectedness.

Some immigrant teachers fail to leave behind their home pedagogies and classroom practices which makes their new environment difficult to navigate. They fail to stabilise and adapt to the new curriculum and teaching methods (Makonye, 2017). Perumal's *Critical pedagogies of place: Educators' personal and professional experiences of social (in)justice* revealed the pedagogy challenges that Zimbabwean immigrant teachers face "as a result of relocation to new geographic and political contexts" (2015, p. 25). This is evident in the following excerpt:

> *Classroom management is a challenge most of the times, you have to be careful on the approaches you choose in case you offend children politically, methodology is different, there are SBAs, I find it difficult to handle these.*

These were Makamure's words when asked about the challenges of being a teacher in South Africa. Literature suggests that orientation, coaching, and acculturation for immigrant teachers can help them to fit in (Manik, 2015); in Canada for example, immigrant teachers are required to bridge their professional teaching courses. Principals may not be adequately supported in terms of dealing with immigrant teachers, taking into consideration South Africa's cultural diversity consisting of 11 tribal groups which may all be found in a single school. Hence, principals may need support from regional or provincial education departments on how to deal with teachers from other countries. It is important that all efforts to integrate immigrant teachers are based on eliminating discrimination within the human race.

Conclusions and Implications

The study explored acculturation of Zimbabwean immigrant teachers in Johannesburg inner-city schools and identified culturally competitive leadership approaches. The participants' responses brought us to the conclusion that principals, immigrant teachers, nationals, and students all have a duty and a role to play to establish culturally competitive schools that flourish with acculturation. The study confirms that there is need for school policies and practices that are sensitive to cultural differences and a call for all relevant individuals to deal with the issue of multiculturalism head-on.

Furthermore, the study has highlighted that ethnical composition, institutionalised policies, and policies at a national level play a role in hindering or promoting acculturation. The findings suggest that acculturation patterns in independent schools may allow immigrant teachers to draw on the dominant culture. Thus, principals in diverse schools must perform the crucial role of using multicultural intervention strategies and approaches that are easy to implement and quicker in showing positive acculturation as policies at a national level may take longer to show a positive impact. The research shows that lack of leadership approaches to human rights appeal processes, curriculum, hiring, promotion, retention, and school policies result in unjust practices.

This qualitative study has generated some empirical data that has brought to the fore an enhanced understanding of principals of independent schools' approaches to acculturation. Given the wave of immigrants into South Africa and the importance of laws on immigration, labour laws, and school policies, this study is relevant to policy makers as well as researchers in the field of education and sociology. Future research should focus on cultural diversity on issues such as ethnic composition in public schools.

References

Berry, J. W. (1997). Immigration, acculturation and adaptation. *Applied Psychology, 46*(1), 5–34.
Boske, C. (2015). Preparing school leaders to interrupt racism at various levels in educational systems. *International Journal of Multicultural Education, 17*(1), 121–142.
Bush, T., Kiggundu, E., & Moorosi, P. (2011). Preparing new principals in South Africa: The ACE: School leadership programme. *South African Journal of Education, 31*(1), 31–43.
Chinomona, E., & Maziriri, E. (2015). Examining the phenomena of xenophobia as experienced by African immigrant entrepreneurs in Johannesburg, South Africa: Intensifying the spirit of "Ubuntu". *International Journal, 2*(16), 20–31.
Crush, J., & Tawodzera, G. (2014). Exclusion and discrimination: Zimbabwean migrant children and South African schools. *Journal of International Migration and Integration, 15*(4), 677–693.
Crush, J., Chikanda, A., & Tawodzera, G. (2015). The third wave: Mixed migration from Zimbabwe to South Africa. *Canadian Journal of African Studies, 49*(2), 363–382.
De Villiers, R., & Weda, Z. (2018). Zimbabwean teachers in South Africa: Their needs and advice to prospective migrant teachers. *Journal of International Migration and Integration*, 1–16.

Fee, J. F. (2011). Latino immigrant and guest bilingual teachers: Overcoming personal, professional, and academic culture shock. *Urban Education, 46*(3), 390–407.

Findlay, A. M., McCollum, D., & Packwood, H. (2017). Marketization, marketing and the production of international student migration. *International Migration, 55*(3), 139–155.

Halicioglu, M. (2015, June 5). *Challenges facing teachers new to working in schools overseas* (University of Bath Department of Education working papers series). University of Bath.

Hammerstad, A. (2012). Securitisation from below: The relationship between immigration and foreign policy in South Africa's approach to the Zimbabwe crisis. *Conflict, Security & Development, 12*(1), 1–30.

Hess, F. M., & Kelly, A. P. (2007). Learning to lead: What gets taught in principal-preparation programs. *Teachers College Record, 109*(1), 244–274.

Iwara, I. O., Iwara, V. O., & Kilonzo, B. M. (2018). The push for student migration in Africa in a globalized world: A case study of Nigerians studying at the University of Venda, South Africa. *African Renaissance, 15*(3), 111–124.

Jandt, F. E. (2012). Defining culture and identities. In F. E. Jandt (Ed.), *An introduction to intercultural communication: Identities in a global community* (7th ed., pp. 5–33). Sage Publications.

Kose, B. W. (2009). The principal's role in professional development for social justice: An empirically-based transformative framework. *Urban Education, 44*(6), 628–663.

Kritz, M. M. (2013). International student mobility and tertiary education capacity in Africa. *International Migration, 53*(1), 29–49.

Lange, T. (2009). Return migration of foreign students and non-resident tuition fees. *Journal of Population Economics, 26*, 703–718.

Lincoln, Y. S., Lynham, S. A., & Guba, E. G. (2011). Paradigmatic controversies, contradictions and emerging confluences, revisited. *The Sage Handbook of Qualitative Research, 4*, 97–128.

Mafora, P. (2013). Learners and teachers' perceptions of principals' leadership in Soweto secondary schools: A social justice analysis. *South African Journal of Education, 33*(3), 1–15.

Makonye, J. P. (2017). Migrant teachers' perceptions of the South African Mathematics curriculum and their experiences in teaching in the host country. *SAGE Open, 7*, 1–9.

Makula, T. (2018). *Zimbabwean immigrant teachers' experiences of social justice in South African independent schools: Implications for transformative leadership*. Unpublished master's thesis. University of Johannesburg, Johannesburg.

Manik, S. (2015). Living in liminal spaces: Zimbabwean immigrant teachers' othering in South Africa. *The Oriental Anthropologist, 15*(2), 283–299.

Martin, M. Y. (2015). *Performing social justice in South African education: How teachers negotiate the complexity of teaching in an unequal world*. Unpublished PhD thesis. University of Kwa-Zulu Natal, Durban.

McKay, T., Mafanya, M., & Horn, A. C. (2018). Johannesburg's inner city private schools: The teachers' perspective. *South African Journal of Education, 38*(3), 1–11.

Merriam, S. B. (2009). *Qualitative research: A guide to design and implementation*. Jossey-Bass.

Mishchuk, H., Roshchyk, I., Sułkowska, J., & Vojtovic, S. (2019). Prospects of assessing the impact of external student migration on restoring country's intellectual potential (the case study of Ukraine). *Economics and Sociology, 12*(3), 209–219.

Moyo, Z. (2015). *School leadership and teachers with HIV/AIDS: Stigma and discrimination in Gauteng provincial schools*. Unpublished doctoral thesis. UNISA, Pretoria.

Moyo, Z., & Perumal, J. (2018). Globalisation and the experience of Zimbabwean female migrant teachers. *Journal of Educational Studies, 17*(1), 76–93.

Moyo, I., Nicolau, M., & Fairhurst, U. J. (2014). Trapped in a garden of greener pastures: The experiences of Zimbabwean teachers in South Africa. *Scientific Annals of Alexandru Ioan Cuza – University of Iasi – Geography Series, 60*, 126–142.

Neuman, W. L. (2011). *Social research methods: Qualitative and quantitative approaches* (7th ed.). Pearson/Allyn and Bacon.

Perumal, J. C. (2015). Critical pedagogies of place: Educators' personal and professional experiences of social (in)justice. *Teaching and Teacher Education, 45*, 25–32.

Pitre, A. (2014). *Educational leaders in a multicultural society*. Cognella Academic Publishing.

Saldana, J. (2013). *The coding manual for qualitative researchers*. Sage.

Sam, D., & Berry, J. (1997). Acculturation and adaption: Handbook of cross-cultural psychology. *Social Behavior and Applications, 3*.
Santoro, N., & Major, J. (2012). Learning to be a culturally responsive teacher through international study trips: Transformation or tourism? *Teaching Education, 23*(3), 309–322.
Shields, C. M. (2010). Transformative leadership: Working for equity in diverse contexts. *Educational Administration Quarterly, 46*(4), 558–589.
Sibanda, O. (2010). Social ties and the dynamics of integration in the city of Johannesburg among Zimbabwe migrants. *Journal of Sociology and Social Anthropology, 1*(1–2), 47–57.
Singh, S. K. (2013). Zimbabwean teachers' experiences of xenophobia in Limpopo schools. *Love Thy Neighbours, 7*, 51–66.
Sondhi, G., & King, R. (2017). Gendering international student migration: An Indian case-study. *Journal of Ethnic and Migration Studies, 43*(8), 1308–1324.
Thomas, S. (2017). The precarious path of student migrants: Education, debt, and transnational migration among Indian youth. *Journal of Ethnic and Migration Studies, 43*(8), 1873–1889.
Vandeyar, S., Vandeyar, T., & Elufisan, K. (2014). Impediments to the successful reconstruction of African immigrant teachers' professional identities in South African schools. *South African Journal of Education, 34*(2), 1–20.
Vial, D. G. (2006). *Journeys and border crossings: Emerging issues facing the expatriate teacher: An "Ang Moh" art teacher in Singapore*. Doctoral dissertation. Queensland University of Technology.
Wang, F. (2016). From redistribution to recognition: How school principals perceive social justice. *Leadership and Policy in Schools, 15*(3), 323–342.
Wiese, M., Jordaan, Y., & van Heerden, C. H. (2010). The role of demographics in students' selection of higher education institutions. *Professional Accountant, 10*(1), 150–163.
Woldegiorgis, E. T., & Doevenspeck, M. (2015). Current trends, challenges and prospects of student mobility in the African higher education landscape. *International Journal of Higher Education, 4*(2), 105–115.
Yin, R. K. (2011). *Qualitative research from start to finish*. The Guilford Press.

Tshatiwa Makula is a Ph.D student at the University of Johannesburg in the Department of Education leadership and management, South Africa. She holds a Master's degree in Education Leadership and Management. Her career in education began in 1994 when she enrolled for a Diploma in Education at Hillside Teachers' College in Zimbabwe. In 2000 she was conferred with a B.Tech in Education Management by the Tshwane University of Technology (in South Africa) and in 2018 she completed her Master's degree in Education with the University of Johannesburg. Her interests in research lie in social justice and the marginalized. Presently she is a deputy principal at Basa Tutorial Institute, a private school in Johannesburg.

Open Access This chapter is licensed under the terms of the Creative Commons Attribution 4.0 International License (http://creativecommons.org/licenses/by/4.0/), which permits use, sharing, adaptation, distribution and reproduction in any medium or format, as long as you give appropriate credit to the original author(s) and the source, provide a link to the Creative Commons license and indicate if changes were made.

The images or other third party material in this chapter are included in the chapter's Creative Commons license, unless indicated otherwise in a credit line to the material. If material is not included in the chapter's Creative Commons license and your intended use is not permitted by statutory regulation or exceeds the permitted use, you will need to obtain permission directly from the copyright holder.

Chapter 13
Netherlands: Teachers' Perspectives and Practices in Chinese and Polish Language and Culture Teaching

Sjaak Kroon, Jinling Li, and Agnieszka Dreef

Abstract The Netherlands has a long history of immigration. One of the oldest groups are the Chinese and one of the most recent ones are migrants from Poland. Both groups have created clear infrastructures for functioning in the Netherlands. One element thereof are complementary schools, i.e., community run schools that teach Chinese/Polish language and culture to Chinese/Polish students with a migration background, mainly on Saturdays. The teachers in these schools are generally community members who are not necessarily qualified as language or culture teachers. An ethnographic approach to these teachers' classroom practices and perspectives shows that their professional practical knowledge as reflected in the operational and perceived curriculum domain are oriented more toward highlighting and promoting their home country's national history, identity, ideology and values than to preparing their students for living in the superdiverse society of the Netherlands in which Dutch language and culture, also for many Chinese-Dutch and Polish-Dutch students are dominant.

Introduction

This chapter presents data from a Chinese complementary school in Eindhoven and a Polish complementary school in Tilburg, the Netherlands.[1] Its focus is on the practices and perspectives of Chinese and Polish language and culture teachers, in relation to the broader institutional context in which their teaching takes place. The

---

[1] The origin of this study is a HERA funded research project investigating discourses of inheritance and identity in and beyond educational institutions in England, Denmark, Sweden, and the Netherlands (HERA IDII4MES, 2013).

S. Kroon (✉) · J. Li
Tilburg University, Tilburg, Netherlands
e-mail: s.kroon@tilburguniversity.edu

A. Dreef
Opole University, Opole, Poland

main method used is key incident analysis of classroom events that were selected from ethnographic case studies that we conducted in these two schools. Our analysis draws on contemporary theories on language and culture teaching in an era of globalization and superdiversity, on top-down and bottom-up language-and-culture-in-education policies and on teachers' curricular practices and perspectives. It leads to conclusions about possible (dis)continuities resulting from national languages and cultures becoming the object of heritage language and culture teaching in diasporic contexts.

Languages, Cultures, Policies and Practices

Languages and Cultures

The main ambition of parents with a migration background who send their children to complementary schools, is to make them maintain the language and culture of their country of origin. Ancestral or heritage languages and cultures are the main subject in these schools' curriculum. The way a language is referred to however, depends on the specific (political, social, educational, popular) contexts in which it is used (Kaplan & Baldauf, 1997). What is a national and majority language in Poland or China, becomes an immigrant, ethnic minority or community language in the Netherlands. Students in complementary education however, might at the same time go to mainstream Dutch schools, have Dutch as their dominant language, participate in English on social media and might only at home or in their immigrant community be confronted with their (grand)parents' native language and culture. For a growing number of these students the community's language might even appear as almost a foreign language. The same applies to culture: what was 'normal' and part of mainstream societal behavior in the country of origin, becomes potentially conspicuous or even strange or 'abnormal' in the context of the immigration country.

A question to be asked here, is whether a heritage language can still be taught following the national curriculum of the students' country of origin, i.e. as a language that is acquired in primary socialization, if it is no longer the so-called native language or mother tongue of the students in question. Or whether it would be better to teach it as a second language, a foreign language or as a part of an individual student's linguistic repertoire (Blommaert & Backus, 2013)? The reality of linguistic and cultural superdiversity in an era of globalization and mobility leads to a definition of 'language' as a verb ('languaging') rather than as a noun (Arnaut et al., 2016). From this perspective, people simultaneously use multifaceted language repertoires, consisting of the ensemble of linguistic features and characteristics that stem from their own and others' language resources (Spotti & Blommaert, 2017). At the same time however, language education – in mainstream and complementary schools – still seems to engage in teaching specific, well-defined languages in a fixed form and format. It therefore risks losing its connection to the everyday complex linguistic realities of poly- or translanguaging (Jørgensen et al., 2016; García & Wei, 2013) in which features and elements of all languages that inhabit the linguistic repertoires of their users, are successfully used to make meaning. The same again applies to the way education should deal with culture. According to Kroon (2015, p.168), to be successful, education in times of superdiversity should "develop a critical notion of culture in which culture is primarily seen as the way in which people give meaning to their world. This notion of culture should take into balanced consideration a country's national culture or cultures [as well as] the cultures that are represented in superdiverse classrooms [and] it should focus on students developing cultural resources and repertoires that enable them to engage in 'culturing,' i.e., to participate in a variety of national and international cultural encounters in a globalized world."

This new perspective on language and culture has its consequences for education. It poses a challenge for the one-size-fits-all traditional focus on a one-national-language/one-national-culture approach in mainstream as well as complementary schools. All contemporary educational institutions are fundamentally characterized by the linguistic and cultural diversity of their students. They therefore need to rethink the languages and cultures they teach, their teaching methodologies and their aims.

Policies from Above and from Below

Designing a language and culture curriculum requires making choices. The main choices to be made relate to the language and culture that will be taught as a subject and the language that will be used as a medium of instruction. Such choices can only be made based on a set of ideas or an ideology that guide the policymakers' decisions.

Policies are developed and implemented in continuously changing contexts: choices that may be relevant at one point in time may become less relevant or obsolete sooner or later. Apart from the fact that such choices are always connected to a specific time and place, or chronotopic context, that potentially hampers their effectiveness in the long run (Kroon & Swanenberg, 2020), there is another potentially disturbing aspect, i.e. the top-down-bottom-up divide in policy making. From a bottom-up perspective, it would be the practitioners on the ground who, based on their experience, would select a specific language and culture to be taught and a specific language as a medium of instruction. Johnson (2013, p.10) characterizes such bottom-up solutions as micro-level, covert, implicit and *de facto* policies whereas he characterizes top-down policies as macro-level, overt, explicit and *de jure* policies. Although trying to find a solution to the same problem, bottom-up practices and top-down policies often appear to be very different from each other. As Spolsky (2004) already noted, language policy can take the shape of a top-down policy document but at the same time be reflected in people's language practices and attitudes that do not necessarily coincide with decisions in language policy documents (see also Spotti et al., 2019). Classroom realities of language and culture teaching as shaped by teachers and students, can therefore be considered the meeting place of formal policies and norms from above and informal practices and norms from below.

Teachers' Curriculum Practices

Language and culture teaching practices generally occur within a curricular framework. According to Goodlad et al. (1979), a curriculum can have different manifestations that result from sociopolitical and technical-professional processes of adoption and implementation. Conceptualizing these manifestations, Goodlad and colleagues distinguish five curriculum domains. The *ideological* curriculum is the curriculum that emerges from idealistic planning processes but is hardly ever put into practice in its original form. The *formal* curriculum is the curriculum that gained official approval by the state and school boards, is formally adopted by schools and teachers, and is affirmed and sanctioned in written documents such as curriculum guides. The *perceived* curriculum is a curriculum of the mind. According to Goodlad et al. (1979, pp.61–62), "[w]hat has been officially approved for instruction and learning is not necessarily what various interested persons and groups perceive in their minds to be the curriculum." Apart from parents, the most important group here are of course the teachers and their perceptions. The *operational* curriculum is what teachers actually do, i.e. what "goes on hour after hour, day after day in school and classroom" (p. 63). The *experiential* curriculum finally, is the curriculum as it is experienced by the students based on what they think is happening in their classrooms.

The main issue here are the possible discrepancies that exist between these different curriculum domains and more specifically between the curriculum as a top-down document based on a certain ideology, and bottom-up teachers' classroom practices and perceptions, leading to different "versions" (to borrow from Barnes et al., 1984) of the subject they teach.

Here the concept of 'professional practical knowledge' as introduced by Anderson-Levitt (1987) is relevant. According to Anderson-Levitt teachers seem to have a shared and not necessarily conscious knowledge on teaching, i.e. their "savoir faire or 'know-how': *neither what they think nor what they do, but what they think as they are doing what they do.* Knowledge, then, is a shorthand term for beliefs, values, expectations, mental-models and formulas for doing things which the teacher uses in interpreting and generating classroom events." (p.173; italics in original).

In line with the above theoretical considerations, foregrounding the agency of language practitioners instead of language policies from above, in the following we will concentrate on teachers' practical professional knowledge as emerging in their bottom-up practices in Chinese and Polish complementary classrooms and the versions of Chinese and Polish language and culture teaching that emerge from these practices.

Method and Context

In trying to establish the teachers' versions of Polish and Chinese language and culture teaching, we take a sociolinguistic-ethnographic perspective. It consists of qualitative case studies in a Chinese and a Polish complementary school in the Netherlands. The data collection followed the traditional format of ethnographic fieldwork (Blommaert & Dong, 2020). It included classroom observations, field notes, in-depth interviews with the schools' management, teachers and students, and document analysis. The fieldwork was done by Jinling Li for her PhD in 2010–2011 and Agnieszka Dreef for her MA in 2017–2018. The researchers being of Chinese and Polish origin respectively, were proficient in Chinese and Polish and had no problems in getting access to the schools and in building rapport with the participants. They were both also not really involved in the respective diaspora communities which enabled them to be a 'connoisseur' and keep a critical distance at the same time.

Chinese presence in the Netherlands started in the early twentieth century. The number of Chinese inhabitants of the Netherlands is estimated to be around 150,000 (Li, 2016, p.19). Until 1990 Hong Kong citizens were the largest group within the Chinese-Dutch community. As a result of political and economic changes however, the number of people coming from mainland China strongly increased to over 50%. This is reflected in the history of the Chinese school in Eindhoven that was established in 1978 and originally provided Cantonese lessons to a handful of children of Cantonese origin. The student composition now is ethnolinguistically very heterogeneous, including students of Hong Kong Cantonese, Wenzhounese, Guangdong, Fujianese and Malaysian Chinese background. Most students are born in the Netherlands, are proficient in Dutch and go to mainstream Dutch primary, secondary or higher education. At the time of the study, the school had around 300 students and 25 teachers who teach (as of 2016) only Mandarin in weekly Saturday morning classes from kindergarten to grade 12. In the study curriculum documents were studied and 120 hours of classroom observations and interviews with the head, three teachers and 17 students were recorded (see also Li & Kroon, 2020).

Polish migration to the Netherlands first boomed between 1900 and 1945 when up to 6000 Poles came to work in the mines in the province of Limburg. As of 1990 a new wave of Polish immigrants came as seasonal workers mainly, leading to some 120,000 inhabitants with a Polish migration background in 2017 (Dreef, 2018). The Polish school in Tilburg was established in 1994. Its classes take place every 2 weeks on Saturday morning. The school is attended by children from Polish-only and Polish-Dutch families. Consequently, students differ in terms of place of birth and period of residence in the Netherlands, leading to differences in their Polish language abilities and cultural familiarity. In the Polish school 29 hours of classroom observation were recorded as well as interviews with two management team members, four teachers and seven parents. Also, Polish governmental as well as school related curriculum documents were studied.

The data that will be used here mainly focus on the teachers' professional practical knowledge as emerging from their classroom practices. These practices were analyzed through key incident analysis (Erickson, 1977, 1986; Kroon & Sturm, 2007). According to Erickson (1986), a key incident is key in "that the event chosen has the potential to make explicit a theoretical loading [and] brings to awareness latent, intuitive judgments […] about salient patterns in the data" (p.108). The essence of key incident analysis "is to describe key incidents […] as a concrete instance of the workings of abstract principles of social organization" in order to "see the generic in the particular, the universal in the concrete, the relation between the part and the whole" (Erickson, 1977, p.61). As such, a key incident "is a *re*construction of the tacit knowledge underlying an event" (Bezemer, 2003, p.33), which is presented in what Geertz (1973) called "thick description" by using and triangulating different data sources.

In a process of reading and rereading classroom transcripts and field notes and triangulating our Polish, Chinese and Dutch perceptions of language-and-culture related classroom events, we selected a number of potential key incidents for further analysis to understand what it means to teach Chinese and Polish language and culture in a complementary school environment. Data collection took place with informed consent of the schools' management, teachers and parents and the selected key incidents were discussed with the (anonymized) teachers involved to also get their perspective on what happened in the classroom.

Canonical Texts in Heritage Language and Culture Teaching

Going through the data, mainly focusing on the operational curriculum, i.e. the teachers' practices on the ground, we identified two classroom events that specifically deal with language and culture teaching as the core business of complementary education. In these events, the teachers try to improve their students' heritage language proficiency through a classroom activity in reading comprehension using a traditional folk story in the Chinese case, and a classroom activity aimed at understanding and memorizing a canonical poem in the Polish case. In what follows we will analyze these events that we consider to be key incidents, providing a lens for understanding language and culture teaching in complementary schools in the Netherlands in times of globalization and superdiversity. In our analysis we will also include data from the ideological, formal, perceived and experiential curriculum by using curriculum documents, teaching materials, and interviews with teachers and parents.

'The Song of a Little Brook' in the Chinese School

Classroom observations in the Chinese school showed that in the lower grades the focus was on literacy acquisition through endless repetition of Chinese characters and pronunciation training. In the higher grades, the teacher and students also engaged in discussions on topics occurring in curriculum texts, ranging from traditional folk stories to aspects of contemporary Chinese and Dutch societies.

In November 2010 we observed a teacher-led discussion on a curriculum text in Mrs. Sun's classroom with eight 17-to-20-year-old students. On the first day of the academic year, Mrs. Sun had made it clear that the students were required to only speak Chinese, i.e. Mandarin or Putonghua, in class and in the course of time she further encouraged them to do so. The students who had all native-like proficiency in Dutch, addressed the teacher in Chinese on most occasions but peer talk before, during and after classes was almost exclusively in Dutch.

The text that was discussed, *The song of a little brook*, is a well-known Chinese folk story taken from a textbook series called *Zhongwen* (Chinese) published by Jinan University in 1997 and made available to Chinese complementary schools abroad by the PRC's educational authorities.[2] A glimpse of these teaching materials shows that many folk stories and national fairy tales are included aimed at contributing to the creation of a collaborative memory of Chinese history and culture. The text was published in 1959, the days of the Big Leap Forward campaign of the Chinese Communist Party, striving to transform China into a modern communist society trough industrialization and collectivization. According to Creese et al. (2009) folk stories are productively used as heritage texts in complementary education throughout the world to "endorse traditions, values and beliefs, and to invoke features of the collective memory of community" (p.363). They often have a clear ideological and political message and literacy education in this sense becomes an ideologically laden endeavor. This also applies to *The song of a little brook* that aims at producing and instilling traditional values, collectivity and community in the students.

The text tells the story of a personified little brook that never runs dry but moves through the landscape day and night without stopping, and cheerfully finds its way without ever taking a rest. The brook resists various challenges to take a rest or stop running. It becomes bigger and stronger as other brooks join in, turns into a little stream and ultimately a big river that flows into the sea. The story culminates in the coda "Never stop to take a rest, never stop running!" The growth of the little brook is a metaphor for the socialist revolution and construction of China, praising hard work and collective achievement. It aims at producing and instilling traditional values, collectivism and community in the students. And that exactly is what Mrs. Sun wants her class to get out of the text. Her opening question, how they feel about the

---

[2] See Overseas Chinese Language and Culture Education Online at http://www.hwjyw.com/textbooks/

text, however, leads to an unexpected reaction by student Tao (utterances in Dutch are in italics):

Mrs. Sun	这样一篇文章，大家有什么感受? 涛 涛，你有什么感受? (Such a text, what do you think of it? Tao, how do you feel about this text?)
Tao	我没有什么没感受。(I don't have any feeling.)
Mrs. Sun	没有感受?没有 *gevoel* ?它这样一篇 文章讲的是什么意思?(No feeling? No feeling? Such a text, what does it tell us?)
Xin	没意思。(Nothing.)
Mrs. Sun	没意思啊?他用，就用东西写成人 啊，拟人化，对吧? 拟人，然后写小 溪流呢， 他非常努力。从不休息，从 不停留，直奔大海。其实写得，其实 写得，跟人的一生差不多，是吧?你 自从你生下来到你死，经历地就跟他经历地差不多。懂吗? (Nothing? He personifies things, personification, right? He personifies the brook, the brook works very hard, never takes a rest, running straight to the sea. In fact, it is just like the life of people. From the moment you were born until you die, the experience of our life is just like the brook, understand?)
Tao	不一定。(Not necessarily.)

Upon the teacher's question, the students claim to have no feelings at all about the text and assert that it doesn't tell them anything. Mrs. Sun doesn't give up and explains the context and moral implications of the text. But her point of view is contested.

Mrs. Sun	不一定?他讲的要一生努力，直到你 闭眼睛的那一天，就这意思。不可以 停留，懂吗? (Not necessarily? He tells us that people should always work hard until the day you die. Do not stop, understand?)
Tao	Tao 我不那个 (I don't.)
Mrs. Sun	不 *mee eens? Hehe...* 不同意 我的意见，*ok*, 那你讲你的意见。*Ja*, 你要什么样的生活?你想像荷兰 人一样，舒舒服服的?(Don't agree? Hehe.... don't agree with me, ok, then tell us about your opinions. Yes, what kind of life do you want? You just want to be like the Dutch, have a comfortable life?)
Tao	你做你想做的事。(You do what you want to do.)
Mrs. Sun	(Smiling) 那小溪流也是做想做的 事，想去大海。他跟你意思不一样 吗? (The brook also does what he wants to do; he wants to go to the sea. Doesn't he mean the same?)
Tao	不一样。(Not the same.)
Qiang	但那个小溪流呢，一个朋友都没有， 走个不停，不能停下来去玩。(But that brook, he doesn't have a single friend. He flows without stopping. He can't stop to play.)
Mrs. Sun	谁说没有?他把大大小小的小溪流都 拢在一起，变成河，然后把河又拢成 江。他讲的是志同道合的朋友，懂不 懂? (Who says that he doesn't? He meets various brooks and together they form a stream, and then various streams go together, they form a river. He talks about these friends who have the same interests, cherish the same ideals and follow the same path, do you understand?)

Qiang	没有，只是他自己。(No, he has only himself.)
Mrs. Sun	怎么不一样?它想去大海。他的目标　很明确。他只是把它拟人化。看，看，看，他是能去大海。我们 不知道我们往哪儿走?
	对，那就更难，那就对你来说更难，但是他有一点就是要不断努力，不断 探求，不断探索。这才是你的一生，对不对? (Not the same? He wants to go to the sea. The goal of his is very clear. He is just being personified. Look, look, look, it is going to the sea. But we don't know where we are going. Yes, so it is even more difficult, even more difficult for you, but one point to be stressed is that you should always work hard, pursue and explore. This is how you should lead your life, right?)

Student Tao rejects the teacher's interpretation of the story and the dispute is lifted to an intercultural conflict, with the teacher representing traditional Chinese values and the student constructing a Dutch attitude which is characterized by the teacher as not sufficiently ambitious, only aimed at having a comfortable life. The story, according to the teacher, illustrates how to lead your life, i.e. work hard, pursue and explore. This is questioned by student Qiang who says that in such a life there is no time for friendship or play. Finally, reacting on Mrs. Sun's statement that "the Netherlands absolutely makes people lazy, makes people making no efforts" (我觉得荷 兰太让人不努力了), Tao once again clearly expresses his Dutch-Chinese perspective on the matter, saying that "Dutch people are more efficient than Chinese" (荷兰人比中 国人*efficiënt*. 中国人是没办法) and that different from the teacher's '[his] way of thinking is Dutch' (我的想法是荷兰人的想法). In that contemporary Dutch cultural framework, there is clearly no room for the message of a traditional Chinese folk story.

We can conclude that the classroom discussion culminates in Tao's claim that "his way of thinking is Dutch". The contestations and negotiations on the interpretation of the text reveal the different cultural frameworks the teacher and her students applied in making sense of this old Chinese folk story. While the teacher seemed to believe that teaching language and culture through a traditional folk story was a means of reproducing Chinese identity in the students' minds, the imposition of such Chineseness was explicitly challenged by the students. They assertively considered themselves Dutch citizens fully participating in Dutch culture and society and rejected the deeper metaphorical meaning and moral lesson embedded in the story. In the discussion they however showed a thorough and confident understanding of China and Chinese culture in its historical context. Where the teacher sees the classroom as a site to introduce and reproduce traditional Chinese values to her students, the students contest her imposition and upscale traditional Chineseness into a new diasporic Chineseness that is enriched and complemented by their Dutchness. Tao and his classmates in other words are not merely displaced Chinese subjects but also Dutch youth, born in families with transcultural migration backgrounds, receiving their mainstream education in and through Dutch. As a result, they embrace some Chinese cultural and linguistic resources, and reject others.

'The Polish Child's Catechism' in the Polish School

The Polish school's curriculum is based on a Regulation of the Polish Ministry of National Education on the organization of education for Polish children temporarily residing abroad (Rozporządzenie, 2010). This Regulation aims at helping Polish children abroad to reintegrate in the Polish education system upon their return (Petri, 2010). As a complementary school established by Polish community members, the Polish school in Tilburg is not obliged to adhere to the Regulation; they however do so to ensure the "quality of teaching", as a member of the management team said (Informal conversation Felicja, 4-11-2017).

The school's curriculum does not define the medium of instruction. Mrs. Edyta, a member of the school's management team and a teacher, however said that the school's implicit policy is to use "Polish, Polish only" as a language of instruction and that this is "clearly communicated" to the teachers, because: "When one child starts to speak Dutch, others also start to speak [Dutch] and it is a danger […] it is necessary to remind a child that we are at a Polish School and we speak Polish here. If they don't understand, they can approach a teacher and ask, but in general we speak Polish. It is simply a must." (Interview Edyta, 24-4-2018).

Following the Regulation, the curriculum contains teaching objectives related to Polish language skills with elements of Polish history, geography and culture. An interesting combination of language and culture teaching appeared in a lesson of Mrs. Dorota on 28-10-2017 that we selected as a key incident (Dreef & Kroon, 2020). In that lesson the children, aged 6–8, had to learn the poem *Katechizm polskiego dziecka* (The Polish Child's Catechism) also known as *Kto ty jesteś? Polak mały* (Who are you? A little Pole) written by Władysław Bełza (1847–1913) and published in 1900. Róg and Róg (2017, p.371) indicate that the poems of Bełza "can shape the national identity" of Polish children and that they are "to this day […] very popular, liked by children and, above all, still valid. They discuss the subject of the family, homeland, patriotism, pride of the nation. Therefore, they are close to the hearts of several generations of Poles." According to the Regulation the poem is a compulsory curriculum text (Rozporządzenie, 2010, p.13183). It consists of a series of questions and answers about the identity of a young Pole.

The poem was introduced by Mrs. Dorota by asking the students whether they knew the poem *Kto ty jesteś? Polak mały*. One boy said he did and Mrs. Dorota asked him to tell it to the class. He starts but is unable to do it properly. Because the students are not paying attention, Mrs. Dorota addresses them as follows:

Mrs. Dorota: *Ale słuchamy. Teraz kolega nam mówi wierszyk, którego się musimy nauczyć. Nauczymy się wierszyka, 'Katechizm polskiego dziecka', tak Władysława Bełzy. Ja wam przeczytam na początku cały wierszyk i będziemy powtarzać. OK?* (Listen. Now a friend tells us a poem that we need to learn. We will learn a poem, 'Catechism of a Polish Child', by Władysław Bełza. I will read the entire poem to you first and then we will repeat it. OK?)

Mrs. Dorota reads the poem out loud and the students repeat each line after her. There is no interaction involved. Then she concludes:

Mrs. Dorota: *Dobrze to jest* cały *wiersz, który napisał Władysława Bełza. To jest bardzo stary wiersz, którego uczyły się dzieci i nadal się uczą w polskich szkołach, tak. I my się też jego nauczymy. To jeszcze raz.* (Well, this is the whole poem by Władysław Bełza. This is a very old poem that children have learned and are still learning in Polish schools, yes. And we will learn it too. Let's do it one more time.)

And that is exactly what happens. Mrs. Dorota reads the 20 lines of the poem one more time, line by line, and the students repeat every line in unison. At the end Mrs. Dorota concludes:

Mrs. Dorota: *Pięknie. Dobrze będziemy powtarzać na każdych zajęciach aż się nauczymy na pamięć tego wierszyka, tak.* (Beautiful. We will repeat it in every class until we learn the poem by heart, yes.)

The poem is used at primary schools in Poland to strengthen the national identity of Polish children. In the observed complementary school lesson however, the message of the poem is not transmitted to the students. Furthermore, the vocabulary – including *Gdzie ty mieszkasz? Między swemi.* (Where do you live? Among my own); *Czym zdobyta? Krwią i blizną.* (How was it won? With blood and scars); *A w co wierzysz? W Polskę wierzę.* (And in what do you believe? I believe in Poland); *Coś jej winien? Oddać życie.* (What do you owe her? To sacrifice my life) – and the national symbols (*Czym ta ziemia? Mą Ojczyzną.* (What is that land? My fatherland); *Jaki znak twój? Orzeł biały.* (What is your sign? A white eagle.) – are not explained to them. The class is only expected to repeat the poem after the teacher line by line. The only word that gets extra attention because it causes pronunciation problems is *wdzięczne* (grateful). For the rest, the only clarification the children receive is that they are going to learn the poem by heart because children in Poland do so too.

At the celebration of the 99th anniversary of Poland's Independence Day (11 November 2017) the children recited part of the *Polish Child's Catechism* for their parents in the school's canteen while waving Polish flags. After the recitation, the parents applauded. Someone shouted: 'Great, well done!' (Observation, 11-11-2018).

When we interviewed her, Mrs. Dorota said that she realized teaching this poem at the Polish school in Tilburg is not as easy as it is in Poland. She noticed that it was not really accepted by all children. One student for example said that he "will not sacrifice his life for this country". That made her think "because in Poland, when we learn this poem, everything is obvious to us but here, children cannot identify with the message of the poem." (Interview Dorota, 14-4-2018).

As it turns out also not all parents appreciated the implicit instilling of Polish norms and values by learning the *Polish Child's Catechism* by heart. Parent Gabriela for example said: "I registered my child at this school purely for linguistic reasons to improve my child's language skills but here in this school there are a lot of […] activities that emphasize patriotism and homeland, tradition." Gabriela's main criticism relates to the fact that the poem was not properly introduced and explained to the children. She further doubts whether it was appropriate to teach this poem to rather young children. She is not completely against Polish history at school but, as she stated, "it didn't feel right, such a poem for such children [...] who don't know the basic letters and cannot build a simple sentence yet" (Interview Gabriela, 20-2-2018). According to her, children should not learn a poem just because it is an obligatory poem taught in Poland. Parent Julia adds to this that she also feels that the poem "is very difficult [and] that there is too much, you know, patriotism. My child doesn't feel Polish." (Interview Julia, 19-3-2018).

Polish parents with a migration background want their children to learn some Polish to maintain the language for keeping contacts with their relatives in Poland but they clearly do not want their children to be exposed to examples of a rather nationalist Polish culture. Parent Lidia finally says: "[Teaching my child] Polish culture is my job." (Interview Lidia, 4-4-2018) Lidia indicates that she is cultivating Polish traditions at home and there is no need to do this at school. Parent Julia on the other hand values the Polish school for cultivating Polish traditions because she herself would easily forget about such traditions. Nevertheless, also Julia criticizes the school for being too traditional, "ossified, one sided ... I know it's a Polish school, but I think that not everything must be only Polish." (Interview Julia, 19-3-2018).

This key incident illustrates an attempt by the teacher to construct Polish identity through a canonical Polish poem. The poem however does not appeal to the students as they do not know what they are supposed to learn. The only explanation they get, is that they are obliged to memorize this poem just because this is also done in Poland. By simply teaching a poem that is compulsory in Polish schools, the teacher does not take into consideration that she is teaching in a multilingual and multicultural classroom in the Netherlands where students may not identify with the message of the poem or even not understand it. The key incident shows how the teacher, by making the students learn the poem by heart and reciting it for their parents at Poland's Independence Day celebration, uses language as a vehicle for transmitting Polish identity or even nationalism and patriotism. It is this patriotic perspective that is criticized by the parents since they are very much aware of the inconvenience for their Polish-Dutch children who not necessarily feel Polish, to be taught Polish language intertwined with culture in complementary education.

Discussion and Conclusions

In the above, our focus was on Chinese and Polish teachers' daily teaching practices, i.e. on their operational curriculum. We interpreted these practices taking into consideration the ideological and formal curriculum of both schools, including the *Polish Child's Catechism* that Mrs. Dorota dealt with, and *The Song of a little brook* that Mrs. Sun dealt with. Both canonical texts reflect an ideological curriculum that is closely connected to the ideological position of educational institutions in Poland and the PRC, respectively celebrating national identity and patriotism and collectivism and other communist values.

In subscribing to these ideologies in their classrooms, the teachers, by trying to convince Chinese-Dutch students that the societal system of the PRC is better than the Dutch system and by making Polish-Dutch students memorize a patriotic poem, contribute to (re)establishing continuity between diasporic communities and their countries of origin. Or, in Mrs. Dorota's words: "This is a very old poem that children have learned and are still learning in Polish schools, yes. And we will learn it too." And in Mrs. Sun's words: "We should have a goal, work hard in our life, make efforts, make progress, keep doing this, nonstop."

The classroom behavior of the teachers and their interviews made it clear that there was no real difference between their perception of the language and culture curriculum and the way they put it into practice. Their professional practical knowledge showed full endorsement of the ideological perspective of their teaching. The students in the Chinese case and the parents in the Polish case on the contrary, turned out to be much less convinced of the ideological underpinnings of the operational and ideological curriculum in the schools the children were sent to in order to learn some Chinese or Polish. Their evaluations of the curriculum practices that they experienced, as clearly expressed by Chinese student Tao's remark that "his way of thinking is Dutch" and Polish parent Julia's statement that "her child doesn't feel Polish", are very much alike. They show that people in the diaspora are no longer necessarily adhering to the norms and values of their country of origin that heritage language and culture teaching by means of national canonical texts aims to convey.

The Chinese and Polish teachers' professional practical knowledge shows similarities. First, in their teaching, they both adhere to the top-down official curricular focus on monolingualism regarding the language of instruction. Classroom instruction is consistently given in the heritage language and the students are stimulated to refrain from using Dutch. Second, in their teaching they both adhere to national or even patriotic ideologies and morals that prevail in their country of origin. Such tendencies are ubiquitous in the question-and-answer routine in the *Polish Child's Catechism* and they are also clearly reflected in Mrs. Sun's explanation of the essence of collectivity and community referring to the personified little brook.

Such elements of the teachers' professional practical knowledge are however becoming more and more obsolete in a world that is characterized by globalization and superdiversity and in which Polish-Dutch and Chinese-Dutch students and parents voice their bottom-up perspectives. These voices from below (Kroon, 2013), in much the same way as Heller (1999) found for the French linguistic minority in Canada, present and argue for a new set of norms that allow them "to exploit the linguistic capital they do possess, and to downplay the importance of the cultural capital they do not" (p.14). Or, to once again quote Tao from the Chinese school in Eindhoven: "My way of thinking is Dutch."

Our research into teachers' perspectives and practices in teaching Polish and Chinese in complementary schools in the Netherlands needs as an inescapable complement research into the implicit and explicit language policy in immigrant families. Family Language Policy (FLP) is a strongly growing field of research. Curdt-Christiansen (2018:1) defines explicit FLP as "the deliberate and observable efforts made by adults and their conscious involvement and investment in providing linguistic conditions and context for language learning and literacy development", and implicit and covert FLP as "the default language practices in a family as a consequence of ideological beliefs". To get a broader picture of language maintenance efforts in immigrant communities we need to combine research at the level of families and schools.

References

Anderson-Levitt, K. M. (1987). Cultural knowledge for teaching first grade: An example from France. In G. Spindler & L. Spindler (Eds.), *Interpretive ethnography of education: At home and abroad* (pp. 171–194). Erlbaum.

Arnaut, K., Blommaert, J., Rampton, B., & Spotti, M. (Eds.). (2016). *Language and superdiversity*. Routledge.

Barnes, D., Barnes, D. R., & Clarke, S. (1984). *Versions of English*. Heinemann Educational Books.

Bezemer, J. (2003). *Dealing with multilingualism in education. A case study of a Dutch primary school classroom*. Aksant Academic Publishers.

Blommaert, J., & Backus, A. (2013). Superdiverse repertoires and the individual. In I. De Saint Georges & J. J. Weber (Eds.), *Multiligualism and multimodality. Current challenges for educational studies* (pp. 11–32). Sense Publishers.

Blommaert, J., & Dong, J. (2020). *Ethnographic fieldwork: A Beginner's guide* (2nd ed.). Multilingual Matters.

Creese, A., Wu, C. J., & Blackledge, A. (2009). Folk stories and social identification in multilingual classrooms. *Linguistics and Education, 20*(4), 350–365.

Curdt-Christiansen, X. L. (2018). Family language policy. In J. Tollefson & M. PerezMilans (Eds.), *The Oxford handbook of language policy and planning* (pp. 420–441). Oxford University Press.

Dreef, A. (2018). *From policy to practice: Polish language management at the Polish School in Tilburg, The Netherlands*. MA thesis, Tilburg University.

Dreef, A., & Kroon, S. (2020). From policy to practice: The illusion of polishness in polish immigrant community language and culture education. *Journal of Multicultural Discourses, 15*(4), 370–390. Available at: https://doi.org/10.1080/17447143.2020.1797054

Erickson, F. (1977). Some approaches to inquiry in school-community ethnography. *Anthropology and Education Quarterly, 8*(3), 58–69.

Erickson, F. (1986). Qualitative methods in research on teaching. In M. C. Wittrock (Ed.), *Handbook of research on teaching* (pp. 119–161). Macmillan.

García, O., & Wei, L. (2013). *Translanguaging: Language, bilingualism and education*. Palgrave Macmillan.

Geertz, C. (1973). *The interpretation of cultures. Selected essays*. Basic Books, Inc., Publishers.

Goodlad, J. I., Klein, M. F., & Tye, K. A. (1979). The domains of curriculum and their study. In J. I. Goodlad et al. (Eds.), *Curriculum inquiry: The study of curriculum practice* (pp. 43–76). McGraw-Hill Book Company.

Heller, M. (1999). *Linguistic minorities and modernity. A sociolinguistic ethnography*. Longman.

HERA IDII4MES. (2013). Final report. In *Investigating discourses of inheritance and identity in four multilingual European settings*. HERA.

Johnson, D. C. (2013). *Language policy*. Palgrave McMillan.

Jørgensen, J. N., Karrebæk, M. S., Madsen, L. M., & Møller, J. S. (2016). Polylanguaging in superdiversity. In K. Arnaut, J. Blommaert, B. Rampton, & M. Spotti (Eds.), *Language and superdiversity* (pp. 137–154). Routledge.

Kaplan, R. B., & Baldauf, R. B. (1997). *Language planning: From practice to theory*. Multilingual Matters.

Kroon, S. (2013). Catechistic teaching, national canons, and the regimentation of students' voice. *Anthropology and Education Quarterly, 44*(2), 189–204.
Kroon, S. (2015). Top-down policies and bottom-up practices. Teacher education and superdiversity in Europe. In J. Helmchen, S. Gehrmann, M. Krüger-Potratz, & F. Ragutt (Eds.), *Bildungskonzepte und Lehrerbildung in europäischer Perspektive* (pp. 157–170). Waxmann.
Kroon, S., & Sturm, J. (2007). International comparative case study research in education: Key incident analysis and international triangulation. In W. Herrlitz, S. Ongstad, & P.-H. van de Ven (Eds.), *Research on mother tongue education in a comparative international perspective – Theoretical and methodological issues* (pp. 99–118). Rodopi.
Kroon, S., & Swanenberg, J. (Eds.). (2020). *Chronotopic identity work; sociolinguistic analyses of cultural phenomena in time and space*. Multilingual Matters.
Li, J. (2016). *Chineseness as a moving target: Changing infrastructures of the Chinese diaspora in The Netherlands*. PhD thesis Tilburg University.
Li, J., & Kroon, S. (2020). Chineseness as a moving target. Language and identity transformations in the Chinese diaspora in Eindhoven, The Netherlands. *Journal of Asian Pacific Communication, 31*, 137–158. Available at https://doi.org/10.1075/japc.00062.kro
Petri, K. (2010, September 2). *Rozporządzenie w sprawie organizacji kształcenia dzieci obywateli polskich czasowo przebywających za granicą zostało podpisane*. Retrieved May 11, 2018 from http://www.polska-szkola.pl/index.php/5106-rozporzadzenie-w-sprawie-organizacji-ksztalcenia-dzieci-obywateli-polskich-czasowo-przebywajacych-za-granica-zostalo-podpisane-1770
Róg, M., & Róg, D. (2017). Literatura dziecięca jako element kształtowania poczucia tożsamości narodowej i bezpieczeństwa kulturowego. *Rocznik Stowarzyszenia Naukowców Polaków Litwy, 17*, 358–381. Retrieved June 24, 2018 from http://www.snpl.lt.rocznikT17.php
Rozporządzenie. (2010). *Rozporządzenie Ministra Edukacji Narodowej z dnia 31 sierpnia 2010 r. w sprawie organizacji kształcenia dzieci obywateli polskich czasowo przebywających za granicą*. Dz.U. 2010, Nr 170, Poz. 1143. Retrieved May 11, 2018 from: http://prawo.sejm.gov.pl/isap.nsf/download.xsp/WDU20101701143/O/D20101143.pdf
Spolsky, B. (2004). *Language policy*. Cambridge University Press.
Spotti, M., & Blommaert, J. (2017). Bilingualism, multilingualism, globalization and superdiversity: Toward sociolinguistic repertoires. In O. García, N. Flores, & M. Spotti (Eds.), *The Oxford handbook of language and society* (pp. 161–178). Oxford University Press.
Spotti, M., Kroon, S., & Li, J. (2019). New speakers of new and old languages: An investigation into the gap between language practices and language policy. *Language Policy, 18*(4), 535–551. Available at: https://doi.org/10.1007/s10993-018-9503-5

Sjaak Kroon is an emeritus Professor of Multilingualism in the multicultural society at the Department of Culture Studies at Tilburg University, the Netherlands. His main field of interest is linguistic and cultural diversity, language policy and education in the context of globalization and superdiversity. He has been involved in a number of research projects dealing with linguistic diversity, language policy and literacy in countries in the Global South such as Eritrea, Suriname and East Timor.

Jinling Li obtained her PhD at the Department of Culture Studies, Tilburg University, The Netherlands. Her main research interest is the Chinese diaspora in The Netherlands in times of globalization and digitalization. She has worked as a teacher of Chinese in complementary education. Currently she is employed by Focus Urban Development as international investment director.

Agnieszka Dreef holds a master's degree in English Philology from Opole University in Poland, and a master's degree in Management of Cultural Diversity from Tilburg University, The Netherlands. Her research interest is in linguistic and cultural diversity, and language policy in education in the context of globalization and superdiversity. Currently she is employed in the International Office at Tilburg University.

Open Access This chapter is licensed under the terms of the Creative Commons Attribution 4.0 International License (http://creativecommons.org/licenses/by/4.0/), which permits use, sharing, adaptation, distribution and reproduction in any medium or format, as long as you give appropriate credit to the original author(s) and the source, provide a link to the Creative Commons license and indicate if changes were made.

The images or other third party material in this chapter are included in the chapter's Creative Commons license, unless indicated otherwise in a credit line to the material. If material is not included in the chapter's Creative Commons license and your intended use is not permitted by statutory regulation or exceeds the permitted use, you will need to obtain permission directly from the copyright holder.

Chapter 14
Convergences and Divergences in Career Paths: Recruiting Foreign Teachers in Binational Schools in Argentina

Liliana Mayer and Verónica Gottau

Abstract This chapter seeks to analyze the reasons why binational schools house foreign native speakers' teachers as part of their staff and the reasons that make foreign residents work in binational schools in Argentina. We developed a multiple case design to predict similarities or contrasts based on arguments that explain these differences (Yin, Case study research: design and methods. Sage, Thousand Oaks, 2003) and conducted 15 in-depth interviews with educational agents – teachers and authorities – from binational schools, between 2017 and 2020.

Our findings show that divergences in 'career paths' are marked by different contracting mechanisms: while foreign teachers are recruited through specific networks and enjoy economic privileges similar to diplomatic corps, Argentine teachers receive their salary in the local currency and according to national parameters. From these material advantages other symbolic ones will land. By creating a sense of belonging to an *endogroup*, some foreign teachers have the power to set the values and identities that create meaning within the school. This 'minority though elite' group of teachers finds a fertile soil in the school ethos of binational schools, closely in line with cultural diplomacy. We conclude that binational schools tend to legitimate their added value through the hiring of foreign teachers, and foreign teachers find solid ground for a successful career path, granted by their place of birth, and by the credentials derived from educational paths that have proved to be advantageous for specific institutional projects.

Introduction

Towards the end of the nineteenth century, 65 North American teachers packed their suitcases and left privileged and secure positions to begin their journey to Argentina, within one of the many initiatives that the then Minister of Education Domingo

---

L. Mayer (✉)
University of Buenos Aires, Buenos Aires, Argentina

V. Gottau
Torcuato Di Tella University, Buenos Aires, Argentina

Sarmiento developed, to foster and strengthen the national educational system, which he created with Law 1420[1].

More than 150 years have passed since these ladies accomplished their dream and built a new life. Nowadays, in a much-extended education system that has undergone changes,[2] certain schools continue to receive foreign teachers, but in the private subsystem. However, this is no longer the outcome of a national educational policy, nor the result of the absence of locally trained human resources as it once was. This article seeks to analyze the reasons why binational schools house foreign native speakers' teachers as part of their staff, on the one hand, and on the other, the reasons that make teachers and expatriates, that is, already foreign residents in Argentina, work in schools of their own country of origin.

Where to Work: Binational Schools and Foreign Teachers

Binational schools are among the institutions that most encourage hiring of foreign teachers. With this term, we refer to institutions that besides being located in Argentine territory and belong to the Argentine educational system, are also part of another educational system, mainly from the Europe's most powerful countries.

The latter supports the institutions in financial terms, subsidizing part of their expenditures, on the one hand and taking active part in the Curriculum and its definition, on the other. Binational schools are long-standing institutions, with origins

---

[1] The Law 1420 on General Common Education passed in 1884 established free, public and compulsory education for primary school, while secondary school was reserved for the advantage and privileged sectors of the population, especially urban upper middle-class males. High School enrolment rates started increasing from the 1940s on, in relation to public policies that generated processes of inclusion.

This law was first modified in 1993, with the Federal Education Law that established the compulsory nature of the lower path of secondary school. In 2006, with the currently in force National Education Law, the entire secondary level became mandatory. This expanded state commitment. A large part of the Latin American countries and the Caribbean have undergone similar processes of expansion of compulsory schooling.

At present, Argentina, like many countries of the region, has reached universalization for primary level, but the same doesn't happen with the secondary level. By 2018, Argentina reached a secondary enrollment rate of 88.7%, while 69.7% of students finished High School.

[2] During the post-World War II period, the Argentine State had control over the financing, administrative and pedagogical or educational fields, showing a clear picture of a sort of unchallenged State monopoly over the educational system (Narodowski et al., 2016; Morduchowicz, 2001). The allocation of State subsidies (Law 13.047) to private school provision was first introduced in 1947. Throughout the 1960s, private schools were granted more pedagogical autonomy. Nowadays, 65% of private educational institutions in Argentina are subsidized by the State to some degree. Half a century later, private schools have an enrolment share of 28.7% for 2012 (Narodowski & Moschetti, 2013). The privatization of education in Argentina, which has been the scenario for governed and ungoverned processes, has brought about serious consequences in terms of equity and social cohesion (Tiramonti, 2004; Gasparini et al., 2011).

that can go back more than 100 years (Banfi & Day, 2004; Silveira, 2011). Originally these schools were linked with Argentine immigration processes, to generate integration processes within minority groups of European citizens in exile. In this sense, binational schools initially had a center- diaspora relationship, by endowing the Argentine schooling processes with the cultural heritage of the communities they represented. These schools guaranteed this "differentiated integration", where specific cultural capitals were preserved.

As we said above, these schools correspond to the European, mainly Italian, French, German and English-speaking migrant communities. The institutions within the British community had from their earliest days' policies of greater openness and connection with the local public.

Several works (Mayer & Schenquer, 2014; Mongiello, 2012) show that by the 1980s, these *communitarian* schools had no longer only housed descendants of immigrants, but also diversified their audience. Although some continue to harbor proportions linked to their roots and to children of nomadic or diplomatic families (Resnik, 2012), today they have been converted into *elite* schools. Though we agree with local scholars that the *elites* in Argentina are shaped in different ways than in other countries, we take the importance of this term then as it refers to advantageous sectors of the societies that "bet" on certain schools to consolidate their positions of privilege, power and accumulation of capital intergenerationally (Larrondo & Mayer, 2018). Tiramonti et al. (2008) define elites as those social sectors that combine economic, social and cultural capital in its different forms. In line with Bourdieu (2016), we understand that the elite is neither homogeneous nor monolithic, but rather its heterogeneity is expressed through different interests and behaviors, which is reflected, among other, in schools' choice.

Currently these schools have a diversified curriculum, which includes the national (Argentine) curriculum, but also adding extra loads for learning the language of the foreign educational system to which the institution belongs, and other subjects taught in that language to improve their learning. These schools offer the three education levels stipulated as compulsory by law in Argentina: kindergarten, primary school and secondary school.

Furthermore, in order to facilitate the processes of mobility and internationalization of education they include in their curriculums the high school completion exams typical of their countries, which allow studying abroad (Mayer, 2019; Mayer & Catalano, 2018). The objective of these schools is that their students become bilingual (Banfi & Day, 2004) and also have a high level of English.

The educational field contains different types of schools: as Braslavsky (1985) and Tiramonti (2008) specified, this exceeds the classic public-private division, which also predates the rise of neoliberal discourses in the region (Morduchowicz, 2001). Although between 1940 and 1950 the private sector reached the lowest school enrollment rate in its history, between 1950 and 2015 there was a process of sustained and progressive growth in private enrollment until reaching nowadays 30% points. This process should be analyzed in the light of the new regulations introduced towards the end of the 1940s (Morduchowicz, 2005; Narodowski & Andrada, 2002).[3]

Beyond its scope of management and the public to which it caters, schools are legitimate groups to which certain social actors give - to a greater or lesser extent - a certain entity and specificity. Thus, school institutions are spaces of struggle and power dispute rather than a thoughtless reproduction of current regulations. However, as we will analyze, privately run schools have greater margins of autonomy (Morduchowicz, 2001), where many aspects of decisions are consequences of the specific schools' dynamics, within the frame of national educational policy.

A common feature in all binational schools is the presence of teachers from the second country to which the school belongs. These educational agents have two main mechanisms of access to schools. The first refers to what we will call "career teachers", meaning educational agents who belong to the Network of Schools Abroad in each of these countries. As we will develop later, these teachers are recruited and *sent* to different destinations for certain periods of time, analogously to the diplomatic corps, and often hold managements positions. Then, secondly, and with various heterogeneities within this group, are the residents of those countries in Argentina, who have arrived in the country for various reasons, often unrelated to educational purposes, but for various reasons related to their career paths, they join these institutions. In the third place, there are of course the *local* teachers. These are the Argentineans and Spanish speakers schooling agents, mainly born, raised, and educated in Argentina, by Argentinean pedagogical and scholastics traditions and perspectives (Banfi et al., 2016).

Hence, these private schools hold an heterogenous staff which include foreign and local teachers. Usually, the later are the majority, while the first category, holds sub-categories that consists of fewer schooling agents who only teach in the second language of the school. In other words, while foreigners or international teachers teach on subjects related to the second language or on subjects taught in that tongue, the rest of the subjects take place in Spanish. This *mixture* in nationalities, career paths and biographies bring more heterogeneity to institutional staff to the regular heterogeneity existing in other schools. This heterogeneity within the group of foreign teachers, leads us to propose the term *minority* in the plural, that is, *minorities*. By doing this, this concept allows us to account for the diversity and multiplicity of the agents included, articulated around intersectionality with other social markers that structure the action on the one hand and that allows accounting for different

---

[3] Gamallo (2015) argues that since the 1990s, when the name "publicly run public schools" was incorporated into national legislation, private schools increasingly resemble public ones. There is also a transfer of school management to the provinces in the 1970s and a system of social polarization and educational massification is consolidated, with an increasingly polarized system. The participation of the private subsystem in Argentina isn't the result of educational policy (Morduchowicz, 2001; Ball & Youdell, 2009), but rather the conversion of privately run schools "increasingly similar to public ones" monopolized enrollment, accounting for a sociological component in the population, where migration to the private sector is recorded even in the lowest quintiles of society.

distributions of power within these *minorities* and in their relationship with the majority groups (in numerical terms).

Methodology

To conduct this research, we have developed a multiple case design, which according to Yin (2003) can be used to predict similarities or contrasts based on arguments that explain these differences. Hence, Eisenhardt (1989) conceives a contemporary case study as "a research strategy aimed at understanding the dynamics present in unique contexts". The general objectives are to analyze the ways in which binational schools are structured, as well as their dual membership. From there we derive other objectives related to the institutional agents that inhabit them (teachers and authorities) and the public to which the schools cater: the students.

For this paper, we selected 15 in-depth interviews (Saltalamacchia, 1992) with educational agents -teachers and authorities from both foreign teachers' categories- between 2017 and 2020. The schools selected are 8 binational institutions located in the city of Buenos Aires.

For the analysis of the interviews we used the software Atlas Ti. We applied inductive and deductive techniques on the data obtained searching for patterns or recurring themes. The first encoding was made based on the conceptual criteria extracted from the theoretical framework and the following encodings were made by layers with native categories. Considering that the interviews are based on the narratives of the interviewees, we resorted to cross-examination as a way of reinterpreting the stated and constructed meaning. We tried to go beyond the premise from which the narrative started, understanding that all argumentation constitutes a social construct.

In all the cases interviewed, the narratives were approached comprehensively, that is, considering the specific contexts within which they develop. From our perspective, every social actor produces their own social context through its narration: we agree with Saltalamacchia when he points out that the individual is "a place of knotting" of a determined set of social relations" (1992: 38). In view of this, the interview must be understood as the framework of a joint theoretical elaboration in which total agreements or similar uses will not necessarily arise; but there are interpretations that did not exist before the relationship.

Regarding the analytical categories, and in line with the deductive-inductive technique for data analysis, there are two different types: conceptual, those that derive from the theoretical framework and they refer to the concept of *Minority; Elite, School Autonomy and Cultural Diplomacy,* and those that were constructed or emerged from the analysis of the interviews and they allude to *Native People, Institutional Weight, Internal Hierarchy and Career Teacher*.

Fieldwork included also class observations and analysis of institutional documentation. All the interviews were anonymous, and we have provided fictional names to the extracts of the interviews for confidential reasons. Argentina has 10 binational schools, all situated in the metropolitan region of Buenos Aires, where more than one third of the population resides. In general terms, bilingual school provision is located either in the neighborhoods with the highest purchasing power of the city and/or in the suburban districts of the northern area.

Findings and Discussion

The Working Scenarios and Conditions from the Teachers' Perspective

In one interview with an Italian teacher, she explains how she ended up in Argentina:

> I had been on vacation before and I loved it, but my then husband didn't like it enough to stay. We went back to Italy, where I was working as a journalist. Sometime later, my mother died and I divorced. I had no strings attach and took up the idea of coming to Argentina for a while, being able to keep my job remotely. At the time I started working [at the Italian school] and ended up staying here.

When interviewing a German teacher, she explains that she came to Argentina due to her husband's work. At an embassy event she met a school principal, who hired her, since she is a native speaker. She has never worked in education before and had no degree related. We talked about German and Argentine educational systems:

> Teacher (T): I think it is very cool the way [Argentine] system is, from k-5 till high school graduation, that students don't change institutions.
> Researcher (R): but that's not the way it is. It is in your school, because it's a private one. State school are different: you change from elementary to primary and finally, go to a different high school. You don't stay in the same place.
> T: I didn't know that. I thought it all was the way my school is.

This teacher introduced us to several other international teachers to interview. Before contacting them, she explained:

> There are different situations. I collect very little at school: I have a few hours' dedication and my salary is in the local currency. Others' are in euros, such as Katarina, they have huge salaries! And then there are other teachers, like Peter, which is like an intermediate: since they stayed in Argentina, they get lower salaries, but still better than ours.

Karina, who is also coordinator of the German department, explained her motives and professional path:

> I have always been a teacher. I studied to be one and worked in Germany all my life. My kids are adults, and I returned to the idea of traveling. I searched for opportunities for German teachers abroad and Argentina appeared. I had never been to a Latin country and I found it fascinating. I didn't know a word of Spanish. After 3 years, I still don't speak much. I don't really need it: at school everything is in German and I socialize with most people from my country. With the rest, I use English.

When interviewing another Italian teacher, she describes her working atmosphere:

> The school has many foreign teachers. But with different hiring conditions. There are those who are like me, who looking for a job started working in education. Our salary is like that of the locals, or a little higher, hardly. Then there are those who come from the official teacher system, those are what I call "the viceroys": with salaries in euros and lots of benefits, they are exempt from various tasks and obligations. They are the schools' favorites, the "untouchables", even being very few, they have a special treatment and relevance and a great influence on the authorities.

Career Paths for Foreign Teachers in Binational Schools

In another work (Mayer et al., 2020) we analyzed how Argentina has been nourished from its beginnings by a great cultural diversity, which was conceptually reflected in the "melting pot", although the possibilities of integration were different depending on the origin of the immigrants, often to the detriment of the *native peoples* of the Americas. This is relevant because the specific weights that minorities had -and have- aren't necessarily related to quantitative issues, but to others related to geopolitics and valuation of western values and westernization. As shown in some works, these repertoires are not absent in the educational field, which has always been influenced by the ideas and development of the western educational systems (Beech, 2009).

The literature suggests that due to endogenous issues that exceed the objectives of our article, the Argentine educational system has remained resistant to certain contemporary waves or trends proposed by central and international agencies (Beech & Barrenechea, 2011), even more in the state subsystem (Mayer, 2020). Argentina lacks standardized tests and a high school final exam which enables or not admission to university, which in Argentina is unrestricted. Furthermore, it lacks modalities for *grouping and segregating* students according to their abilities and qualifications, a persistent modality in several of the jurisdictions of the central countries though there are some trends to modify those (Mayer, 2019). Though there is a certain consent in local didactics and pedagogies and within policy makers that the introduction of those approaches would have a negative impact in the classrooms, the private sector shows a certain openness to these discourses and practices but there is usually a lack of professionals to enact those practices (Larrondo & Mayer, 2018). There is also a difference in the modes of insertion of foreign teachers in relation to other countries (Wallace & Bau, 1991) which is processed through the state schools, while in Argentina these spaces are opened from privately run schools, especially, binational ones. Although the private education subsystem is subject to the same regulations as the state one, the former has higher levels of autonomy than the latter (Morduchowicz, 2001, 2005), including hiring its teachers.

The analysis of the narratives of the schooling agents interviewed, allowed us to see that even when foreign "career" teachers are appointed by the central authorities of the networks of binational schools, this is possible due to the high levels of autonomy that these schools have with respect to the State sector. As interview fragments show, foreign "career" teachers have financial and symbolic benefits, ranging from preferential treatment to privileged positions. Most of the teachers in their countries of origin didn't occupy hierarchical positions, so, when becoming part of the teacher networks abroad, they access coordination or leadership positions more easily than if they had remained at home.

Here we see an extra benefit: a quicker promotion possibility, especially for "careers teachers" whose possibilities to reach leading positions are higher mainly because of their nationality which implies a training under the foreigner pedagogical and academic perspectives and trends that are fundamental for binational schools. The promotion seems to be more in line with a specific capital (nationality), unavailable for local teachers and reconfigured for non-careers foreign teachers or expats.

Landing Into the Unknown

The adventurous spirit is also a special issue that stands out in teachers' career path, translated into other concepts. As Blackmore (2014) states, teachers' mobility in their careers should be understood within wider global transformations, considering globalization and mobility processes (Appadurai, 2000; Bauman, 2001; Beck-Gernsheim, 2001), developing and creating skills related to flexibility, new and reflexive identities and adaptable to different international environments (Tran & Nguyen, 2014; Singh & Doherty, 2004). As Ball claims (2016), this professional is flexible and adept in the languages of reform. Rizvi and Lingard (2010) state that travelling teachers need to be understood as territorially situated in global spaces integrated and articulated, in relation to methodological approaches accountable for the complex interchange that takes place between unequally empowered discourses focused on cross-cultural and cross-linguistic terms and conditions that underpin globally interconnected/localized relationships. As one resident teacher claims:

> We learn and they learn from us: for example, we learn about the "mate",[4] and from us about punctuality. Those are big issues!

As another teacher mentions:

> Kids come to this school and realize that Germany isn't only what they thought: here we are not so structured, nor disciplined in terms of popular imagination; we believe in freedom and from there we build the school.

---

[4] Mate is the typical hot drink in Argentina made of green leaves.

The analysis of the interviews shows that foreign teachers usually have little or no knowledge of the society. Not speaking Spanish and lacking specific knowledge related to the development and historicity of the Argentine educational system and its pedagogy are among the main indicators of this situation.

In the case of "career" teachers, we observed that they bring with them their heritage and teaching experience typical of their educational systems, while in the case of expatriates or residents here, lacking specific knowledge of both educational policy and didactics and in pedagogy, they work with students according to their own experience as students. However, this second group is more permeable to education and training, so they usually adapt their teaching strategies to local modes. Different is the case of career teachers, who work according to their own imported criteria in pedagogical matters and are indulged for that:

> They think [pedagogy and didactics] the same way as the Principal. Here things are different, less strict, that I like more. But that helps the Principal to guide a path even if it is with few teachers. But that doesn't mean that we take it.

In this sense, what the fragments show is that the same attribute, the nationality, isn't enough to generate a "community solidarity". Quite the contrary, the heterogeneity of hiring and ways of going through the teaching career, can break or hinder social ties within apparent homogenous groups. Following Bourdieu (1998), foreign teachers are agents who move in a field and within which they occupy certain positions, associated with the unequal distribution of power. Even being a minority, many of these teachers occupy hierarchical or determining positions in the schools, spots that it would take a long time for a local teacher to reach. According to one interviewee:

> If we all get along? No, it's very funny, but at recesses and events, we go to different terraces [referring to her school building, which consists of several formerly familiar houses bought by the school when expanding].

According to Beech et al. (2019), the teaching career in Argentina tends to be "flat", since it has rigid promotion mechanisms and access to hierarchical positions. Although we agree to a certain extent with this, we can also consider how the exogenous mechanisms favor, in particular institutions, this "flatness". If foreign professors -especially those who correspond to the "career" sectors - are those who occupy these positions, the chances of promotion to positions of leadership of agents that are the same or more qualified, decrease due to not having a certain nationality.

In Argentina, teaching in secondary schools requires a teaching degree of 5 years that can be obtained at University or Higher Education Institutions. Training doesn't involve standardized evaluation practices. State schools for example, are subject to strict bureaucratic regulations. In these schools, promotion is based on the accumulation of credits which are acquired though specific trainings endorsed by the State. Private schools, however, deal with promotion, hiring and firing procedures in many ways, since each educational institution has its own legitimacy processes for a career path.

In binational schools, a main factor that legitimates professional progress might be -and actually is- being a foreign citizen. As we have outlined above, schools are institutions that comprise multiple interlocking arenas with front and back stages (Goffman, 1976; Hall, 1996). The front stage refers to the departments, teachers, meetings, among others, and the backstage involves friendship, hidden power mechanisms and legitimacy process.

Between the front and backstage there is a struggle over dissention and competition where teacher training or professional knowledge may not be the best value at stake. So, beyond the endogenous mechanisms that may or may not make the rigidity and "flatness" of the teaching career, we can also analyze concomitant processes that in certain institutions and under certain criteria, are increased by the attributes of career paths in institutions, and together with the material privileges, they collaborate in the "terrace" division that one of the teachers mentioned in her interview.

Building Bridges Through Foreign Teachers

Part of that adventurous spirit to which we refer and the very development of being a teacher abroad, also involves settling either in little-known or familiar places. The "adventurous" or "free spirit" is translated now in benefits for schooling agents in CV terms, and benefits in institutional terms. The flexibility to new and remote environments is associated with the development of "soft" skills, promoted also within students (Mayer, 2019). As Brown (2013) states, within a context of global *social congestion* for quality and good jobs, upper and middle-class professionals interpret and seek to provide access to processes that activate the kinds of 'personal capital' now arguably rewarded by multinational institutions. As Tran and Nguyen (2014) pointed out, the qualities emerging from traveling teachers are various. In the literature, flexibility, physical and professional mobility, variations in destination and the ability to adapt to different environments are highlighted. This is conceived as the adoption of new identities – that García Canclini (1995) calls "hybrids" – that mix the roots with cosmopolitan components (Beck, 2008) where identities are negotiated, made and remade in practice and in the contact with international education (Singh & Doherty, 2004).

Now, whether speaking of career or non-career foreign teachers, this is crucial for schools representing countries pretending to get closer to the local culture, since it brings binational links beyond official ways. Here the concept of cultural diplomacy becomes important (Fierro Garza, 2008): this notion refers to the promotion of the values that nurture a national identity and the history, where the language acquires a central place from two dimensions: it improves language and assumes that teaching and using the language of a country abroad becomes an essential tool to improve the knowledge of the country's politics, economy, society and culture (Djian, 2005; Montiel, 2010; Saddiki, 2009).

The concept of cultural diplomacy implies also public diplomacy, as the set of actions by which governments directly address the population of another country. This perspective differs from the readings regarding education abroad as a "country brand" sales tool (Mongiello, 2012), due to its emphasis on marketing and commerce, but also due to its reductive nature and poor interpretation of the identity of the countries. Cultural and public diplomacy suppose ties of cooperation and interaction between two of them, allowing us to see the different strategies that the State interested in expanding takes not only for each national case, but within it.

In this respect, we observe that most teachers regarded as minority -or minorities- within the staff, constitute a set of actors with a certain power and hierarchy based on credentials that fundamentally "local" teachers cannot have. One of these is nationality. This *capital* is common to all types of foreign teachers who work in the institutions, regardless of whether they have a career or not. Then, there are the credentials derived from the socialization and schooling processes in that country. Finally, there is the pedagogical and didactic dimension, referring, for example but not only, to the lack of final exams and standardized tests that we have described above, where Argentina shows different approaches than western central countries.

In addition to the "bridges" between cultures that teachers weave, they are strategic in the introduction of foreign pedagogical formats and perspectives in the institutional projects, within the frameworks of possibilities established by Argentine educational policy. We understand these "transfers" are not necessarily due to a deliberate or *master* plan, but rather to the extension of their own educational practices beyond conventional (national) limits. Of course, this inclusion of new and often disruptive pedagogical perspectives can bring resistance within the staff and the educational community, but they can also be supported by school authorities. As a teacher says:

> They (career teachers) think like the Dean. They learned pedagogy that way and work as if they were in Italy. Many times, the ways and tradition of this foreign pedagogy is imposed, sometimes it coexists with Argentinean one, and others are negotiated, but for example "competition" between students is very common in this school.

As we have underlined, Argentinean educational policy discourages internal classroom competition. However, many private schools consider it an option or a value to encourage: as we have pointed out (Mayer, 2020), some schools claim particular forms of meritocracy and stand out within local frames, which are often resisted by local schooling agents. So foreign teachers play a fundamental role in introducing these pedagogical trends mixing them up with local boundaries.

In this context, head teachers are key figures that play a vital role in mediating between the external regulations and the internal culture and expectations. It is therefore expected a certain degree of disagreement regarding aims and problem-solving, and that each institution builds its own working conditions and consensus, partly because the stakes of competition are not the same for all the groups. As we have mentioned, this is not accidental, but part of an institutional project. Ball (2016) refers to the processes of "borrowing educational policy" that occur beyond the reforms -or the impossibility of carrying them out, as we argued above- through *policy windows*, where schooling agents take a major place.

Hence, the contributions of institutional agents in binational schools should not be understood only in terms of the contributions to their CV, or to the possibility of bringing two cultures closer together, but also to the ways in which agents incorporate their professional practices in schools. By doing this, they may help in the reconfiguration of teaching practices in binational schools, incorporating exogenous elements to local traditions.

Conclusions and Implication

Throughout the article, we have analyzed the modes of insertion of foreign teachers in binational schools. As we have observed, what at first glance can be understood as native teachers of the second school system to which these institutions belong, are in fact, a cohesive group where solidarity logics prevail. Grounded on a school-based management model, and, due to institutional action, divisions are built based on the material and symbolic benefits that some have to the detriment of others. In other words, it is the school itself that fosters and establishes differences among teachers: by creating a sense of belonging to an *endogroup*, some foreign teachers have the power to set the values and identities that create meaning within the school. One of the findings of this article is, that this cluster doesn't mean homogeneity, since it establishes hierarchies within an apparently homogeneous unit. Thus, this *endogroup* contributes in the delimitation of a minority within minorities, from a group that appears to be homogeneous at first sight, based on a particular capital: nationality. This analysis creates tensions regarding the classic concept of minority, usually associated with sectors that accumulate lesser volumes of power in certain networks which can be examined in additional national contexts in follow-up studies. As we have seen, some foreign teachers have a greater say in their institutions, a fact legitimated not only by nationality, but by their career status and paths. In fact, these international teachers appear as an "elite" within the teaching body. As a consequence, specific forms of knowledge, dispositions and professional paths play a role in the process of a sense of belonging to a particular group, enacting forms of social closure (Van Zanten, 2009).

This 'minority though elite' or minority between minorities group of teachers finds a fertile soil in binational schools. One of the main reasons for this is the school *ethos* which is closely in line with cultural diplomacy and the working conditions that each institution stipulates. Foreign teachers legitimate the position that these schools aim at in the local *spectrum* and help them take distance with other schools. Another reason is that this geo-repositioning of teachers' hierarchy marks some limits to the growth or at least the imagery of growth of the local ones and leaves a disputed but open space for the foreign teachers to land. Where the local teachers find a 'roof' for professional growth the foreign teachers find just a platform for growth.

References

Appadurai, A. (2000). Grassroots globalization and the research imagination. *Public Culture, 12*(1), 1–19.
Ball, S. J. (2016). Neoliberal education? Confronting the slouching beast. *Policy Futures in Education, 14*(8), 1046–1059.
Ball, S. J., & Youdell, D. (2009). Hidden privatisation in public education. *Education Review, 21*(2).
Banfi, C., & Day, R. (2004). The evolution of bilingual schools in Argentina. *International Journal of Bilingual Education and Bilingualism, 7*(5), 398–411.
Banfi, C., Rettaroli, S., & Moreno, L. (2016). Educación bilingüe en Argentina Programas y docentes. *Matices en Lenguas Extranjeras, 3*, 5.
Bauman, Z. (2001). Consuming life. *Journal of Consumer Culture, 1*(1), 9–29.
Beck, U. (2008). Mobility and the cosmopolitan perspective. In W. Canzler & V. Kaufmann (Eds.), *Tracing mobilities: Towards a cosmopolitan perspective* (pp. 25–35). Routledge.
Beck-Gernsheim, E. (2001). Mujeres migrantes, trabajo doméstico y matrimonio. Las mujeres en un mundo en proceso de globalización. In E. Beck-Gernsheim, J. Butler, & L. Puigbert (Eds.), *Mujeres y transformaciones sociales* (pp. 59–76). El Roure.
Beech, J. (2009). Who is strolling through the global garden? International agencies and educational transfer. In R. Cowen & A. Kazamias (Eds.), *International handbook of comparative education* (pp. 341–357). Springer.
Beech, J., & Barrenechea, I. (2011). Pro-market educational governance: Is Argentina a black swan? *Critical Studies in Education, 52*(3), 279–293.
Beech, J., Guevara, J., & del Monte, P. (2019). *Diploma Programme implementation in public schools in Latin America: The cases of Costa Rica, Argentina (Buenos Aires) and Peru*. Documento de trabajo interno.
Blackmore, J. (2014). 'Portable personhood': Travelling teachers, changing workscapes and professional identities in international labour markets. In R. Arber et al. (Eds.), *Mobile teachers, teacher identity and international schooling* (pp. 141–161). Brill Sense.
Bourdieu, P. (1998). *The state nobility: Elite schools in the field of power*. Stanford University Press.
Bourdieu, P. (2016). *La distinction: critique sociale du jugement*. Minuit.
Braslavsky, C. (1985). *La discriminación educativa en Argentina*. FLACSO, Grupo Editor Latinoamericano.
Brown, P. (2013). Education, opportunity and the prospects for social mobility. *British Journal of Sociology of Education, 34*(5–6), 678–700.
Djian, J. M. (2005). *Politique culturelle: la fin d'un mythe*. Gallimard.
Eisenhardt, K. M. (1989). Building theories from case study research. *Academy of Management Review, 14*(4), 532–550.
Fierro Garza, A. (2008). La diplomacia cultural como elemento privilegiado de la política exterior. *Revista Mexicana de Política Exterior, 85*, 23–28.
Gamallo, G. (2015). La "publificación" de las escuelas privadas en Argentina. *Revista SAAP. Publicación de Ciencia Política de la Sociedad Argentina de Análisis Político, 9*(1), 43–74.
García Canclini, N. (1995). *Hybrid cultures: Strategies for entering and leaving modernity*. University of Minnesota.
Gasparini, L., Jaume, D., Serio, M., & Vazquez, E. J. (2011). La segregación entre escuelas públicas y privadas en Argentina. Reconstruyendo la evidencia. *Desarrollo Económico: Revista de Ciencias Sociales*, 189–219.
Goffman, E. (1976). *Estigma. La Identidad Deteriorada*. Amorrortu.
Hall, S. (1996). Who needs identity. *Questions of cultural identity, 16*(2), 1–17.
Larrondo, M., & Mayer, L. (2018). *Ciudadanías Juveniles y Educación: Las otras desigualdades*. Grupo Editor Universitario.

Mayer, L. (2019). Viajar para aprender y aprender viajando. Estrategias educativas de sectores aventajados de Argentina. *Universitas, 30*(1), 41–62. Ecuador.

Mayer, L. (2020). Educación internacional en Argentina: Grandes proyectos para pequeños públicos. In L. En Mayer, M. I. Domínguez, & M. Lerchundi (Eds.), *Infancias, juventudes y desigualdades: experiencias, procesos y espacios*. CLACSO.

Mayer, L., & Catalano, B. (2018). Internacionalización de la educación y movilidad: reflexiones a partir del caso argentino. *Universitas, Revista de Ciencias Sociales y Humanas, 29*, 19–41.

Mayer, L., & Schenquer, L. (2014). Europe outside Europe: Developing a German Jewish citizenship in Argentina. The case of the Pestalozzi Schule. In J. En Galkowski & H. Kotarski (Eds.), *Pragmatics of social and cultural capital*. University of Rzeszow.

Mayer, L., et al. (2020). Desigual y diversa: producción de ciudad y vida urbana entre jóvenes de Buenos Aires. In L. Mayer, J. P. Duhalde, A. A. Ortega, & M. J. Silva (Eds.), *Ciudades x Jóvenes: aportes a la Nueva Agenda Urbana de las Juventudes Latinoamericanas*. CLACSO/CINDE.

Mongiello, E. (2012). *Cambios en la relación escuela y nación. Las escuelas italianas en el exterior: el caso argentino*. Tesis de Maestría en Ciencias Sociales, FLACSO.

Montiel, C. J. (2010). Social representations of democratic transition: Was the Philippine People Power a non-violent power shift or a military coup? *Asian Journal of Social Psychology, 13*(3), 173–184.

Morduchowicz, A. (2001). *Private education: Funding and (de) regulation in Argentina*. National Center for the Study of Privatization in Education Teachers College, Columbia University.

Morduchowicz, A. (2005). Private education: Funding and (de) regulation in Argentina. In L. Wollf, J. C. Navarro, & P. González (Eds.), *Private education and public policy in Latin America*. Partnership for Educational Revitalization in the Americas (PREAL).

Narodowski, M., & Andrada, M. (2002). Nuevas tendencias en políticas educativas: alternativas para la escuela pública. In E. J. Granica (Ed.), *Nuevas tendencias en políticas educativas: estado, mercado y escuela* (pp. 9–28). Ediciones Granica.

Narodowski, M., & Moschetti, M. (2013). The growth of private education in Argentina: Evidence and explanations. *Compare: A Journal of Comparative and International Education, 45*, 47–69. https://doi.org/10.1080/03057925.2013.829348

Narodowski, M., Gottau, V., & Moschetti, M. (2016). Quasi-State monopoly of the education system and socio-economic segregation in Argentina. *Policy Futures in Education, 14*(6), 687–700.

Resnik, J. (2012). The denationalization of education and the expansion of the International Baccalaureate. *Comparative Education Review, 56*(2), 248–269.

Rizvi, F., & Lingard, B. (2010). *Conceptions of education policy. Globalizing education policy*. Routledge.

Saddiki, S. (2009). El papel de la diplomacia cultural en las relaciones internacionales. *Revista CIDOB d'afers internacionals*, 107–118.

Saltalamacchia, H. (1992). *La historia de vida: reflexiones a partir de una experiencia de investigación*. Cijup.

Silveira, M. L. (2011). Territorio y ciudadanía: reflexiones en tiempos de globalización. *Unipluriversidad, 11*(3), 15–34.

Singh, P., & Doherty, C. (2004). Global cultural flows and pedagogic dilemmas: Teaching in the global university contact zone. *TESOL Quarterly, 38*(1), 9–42.

Tiramonti, G. (2004). *La trama de la desigualdad educativa: mutaciones recientes en la escuela media*. Ediciones Manantial.

Tiramonti, G. (2008). As mutações da escola média na Argentina no marco da reconfiguração de um mundo globalizado. *Pro-Posições, 19*(3), 105–129.

Tiramonti, G., Ziegler, S., & Gessaghi, V. (2008). *La educación de las elites: aspiraciones, estrategias y oportunidades*. Editorial Paidós.

Tran, L. T., & Nguyen, N. T. (2014). Teachers' negotiation of professional identities in the 'contact zone': Contradictions and possibilities in the time of international student mobility. In *Mobile teachers, teacher identity and international schooling* (pp. 43–61). Brill Sense.

Van Zanten, A. (2009). The sociology of elite education. In M. W. Apple, S. J. Ball, & L. A. Gandin (Eds.), *The Routledge international handbook of the sociology of education* (pp. 329–339). Routledge.

Wallace, M. J., & Bau, T. H. (1991). *Training foreign language teachers: A reflective approach*. Cambridge University Press.

Yin, R. K. (2003). *Case study research: Design and methods*. Sage.

Liliana Mayer is a sociologist; she holds M.A and Ph. D. in social sciences, Buenos Aires University (UBA), Argentina. She was tenured Researcher Position at CONICET (National Council for Scientific and Technological Research). Currently she is serves as a senior consultant at TECHO Latino America. Her area of research focus on education, youth and a social inclusion

Verónica Gottau is Associate Researcher at Centre for the Evaluation of Evidence at Torcuato Di Tella University, Argentina. She holds PhD in education from the University of San Andrés. Her research relates to educational policies, the privatization of education, the autonomy of school institutions, and family processes of school choice.

Open Access This chapter is licensed under the terms of the Creative Commons Attribution 4.0 International License (http://creativecommons.org/licenses/by/4.0/), which permits use, sharing, adaptation, distribution and reproduction in any medium or format, as long as you give appropriate credit to the original author(s) and the source, provide a link to the Creative Commons license and indicate if changes were made.

The images or other third party material in this chapter are included in the chapter's Creative Commons license, unless indicated otherwise in a credit line to the material. If material is not included in the chapter's Creative Commons license and your intended use is not permitted by statutory regulation or exceeds the permitted use, you will need to obtain permission directly from the copyright holder.

Chapter 15
Argentina: Minority Indigenous Teachers of Bilingual Intercultural Education

Ana Carolina Hecht

Abstract In the province of Chaco (northeastern Argentina) bilingual and intercultural school models emerged to help meet the educational needs of indigenous children. Bilingual intercultural education schools implemented a system in which two teachers coexist in the same classroom: a non-indigenous teacher and a minority indigenous teacher. However, in recent decades, indigenous languages are being displaced by Spanish, which is becoming widespread as a means of daily communication for indigenous families. In this scenario, the role of indigenous teachers is currently focused on linguistic revitalization and the teaching of the indigenous language as a second language. Considering this complex sociolinguistic panorama, this chapter analyzes specific aspects of these new practices among the Toba/Qom teachers whose pedagogical tasks have shifted from teaching the indigenous language to reversing language shift. Additionally, it examines the experiences and knowledge of the native tongue among these minority teachers, who range from fluid bilingual speakers to less competent ones. As a consequence, from an anthropological perspective, the question of Bilingual Intercultural Education is raised because one of its principal objectives (bilingualism) is blurred. The findings are drawn from observations and ethnographic records from fieldwork conducted in 2016/2017 in a school in a Toba/Qom neighborhood in Chaco, and in-depth interviews with thirty-six teachers who identify as Toba/Qom.

Introduction

Argentina is a country that historically since its consolidation has denied and invisibilized its ethnic matrix, despite there being twenty-some indigenous peoples – speakers of at least fourteen languages with heterogeneous types of bilingualism – who statistically represent 2.4% of the total national population

---

A. C. Hecht (✉)
Universidad de Buenos Aires, Buenos Aires, Argentina

Consejo Nacional de Investigaciones Científicas y Técnicas, Buenos Aires, Argentina
e-mail: anacarolinahecht@yahoo.com.ar

(National Institute of Statistics and Censuses [INDEC], 2010). In regard to the rights of ethnically plural populations, only since democratic restitution (1983) has a series of legislative reforms been produced motivated by the activism of indigenous movements and international declarations of specific rights. Thus, through legal regulation, respect for and valuing of Argentina's indigenous peoples has been achieved and, consequently, official discourse has attenuated its historically ethnocentric vision to recognize ethnic plurality. Legislative and academic discourses of political reaffirmation and ethnic revindication call upon the Nation-State to review and include nuances in the treatment of the indigenous question. That is to say, the issue is no longer to deny indigenous otherness as part of the models of Argentine citizenship, but rather to think of alternatives that offer space for its inclusion and recognition within a framework of respect for differences.

The relation between the languages spoken in a jurisdiction and the school system that regulates them is very complex and evokes countless debates in educational management and research. Language policies are closely associated with educational policies, as through educational planning assumptions are expressed as to how it seems feasible to modify, prescribe and hierarchically arrange the asymmetrical relations between languages that coexist in a State. Through the designs of monolingual, bilingual or plurilingual educational policies, the status and positive valuing of certain languages is promoted, while the social visibility of others is reduced, or a balance is simply maintained among a linguistic multiplicity. Of these multiple analytical dimensions, this text contemplates designs for the schooling of those persons (such as indigenous peoples) who speak minority languages other than the official one.

In Argentina, indigenous languages were included in education policies only very recently. Since the Reform of the National Constitution (1994), a shift took place from an integrationist-homogenizing model to another based on inclusion of the right of indigenous peoples to Bilingual Intercultural Education (hereinafter, BIE). Currently, school institutions postulate the modification of their historical bet on linguistic unification in Spanish, shifting to the incorporation of other languages (in addition to the hegemonic-official language) and other intercultural views that question curricular contents, with the aim of overcoming still-present colonialism and settling the historical debt with indigenous peoples.

Contemporary BIE policies promote plurilingualism and the inclusion of the cultural practices and knowledge of indigenous peoples to strengthen their cultures, worldviews and ethnic identities. The recipients of BIE are indigenous children, who tend to find themselves in socio-educational contexts of extreme inequality and poverty. Therefore, for indigenous peoples access to BIE forms part of a broader body of rights whose aim is to guarantee their social inclusion, the self-determination of their peoples and the preservation of their languages and cultural patterns in the contemporary context. In sum, to paraphrase the theoretical contributions of Hornberger (2008), the indigenous population would face the paradox of the transformation of a standardized education, but in the spirit of a "diversification" that would suppose the construction of a multilingual and multicultural national indigenous identity.

BIE schools in Argentina are characterized by a "pedagogical pair" model, i.e., there are two teachers in the classroom (or school): one non-indigenous teacher with a normal educational background and the figure of some indigenous teacher. The indigenous teachers can be defined as the teachers of minorities insofar as they are minoritized/undervalued vis-à-vis the inequality and asymmetry in terms of accessing a series of basic rights, though numerically they represent a significant swath of the regional population. The formative experiences of indigenous teachers are very heterogeneous and differ according to geographical contexts and generations of teachers. Indigenous teachers are charged with teaching the indigenous language and so-called "cultural content," while the normal grade teacher is in charge of teaching Spanish and the other subjects (mathematics, social sciences, natural sciences, literature, etc.). These teacher roles were designed more for the beginnings of BIE and we are currently facing thoroughly diverse scenarios among Argentina's provinces, and among the different indigenous peoples within each province.

Regardless of the different sociolinguistic contexts and regions of Argentina, the impact of school interventions for the maintenance or displacement of indigenous languages is undeniable (Censabella et al., 2013; Hecht, 2014). In other words, the sociolinguistic situations of indigenous languages are impacted by pedagogical interventions in schools. Therefore, the present vitality and status of many indigenous languages are linked to the modes of teaching in schools, the place of indigenous languages in the school curriculum and the indigenous teachers' practices.

Research Objective

From the conceptual framework of educational anthropology and linguistic anthropology, the objective of this chapter is to try to understand current school contexts, based on systematizing the practices of indigenous teachers in relation to the status and management of languages (Toba and Spanish) in classrooms. In other words, this chapter is interested in documenting and understanding the practices of indigenous Toba/Qom teachers for teaching the indigenous language within the framework of BIE schools in Chaco province.

Context of Research

This chapter addresses the particular case of the Toba/Qom people of the province of Chaco (northeast Argentina), which is one of the numerically largest of Argentina (they represent 13.3% of the total national indigenous population). The Toba/Qom belong to the *Guaycurú* linguistic family. Currently there are an estimated 80,000 individuals who consider themselves Toba in the provinces of Chaco, Formosa, Santa Fe and Buenos Aires (National Institute of Statistics and Censuses [INDEC], 2010). Persons who self-recognize as Toba/Qom residents in Chaco, in only three decades, have reversed the predominance of the indigenous language and the hegemonic language in their bilingualism: from dominance of the Toba language to the present supremacy of Spanish (Hecht, 2010; Medina, 2014; Messineo, 2003).

In Chaco province at the end of the '80s, when the specific rights for indigenous peoples began to be generalized, these were embodied in a pioneering, integral Law on the indigenous question (Ley N° 3258/1989). In those years, as regards schooling, the central concerns of indigenous families and of school institutions called for an intervention that facilitated the communication of Toba/Qom children with the teaching staff during their time in school, as for the majority of them the indigenous language was their first language, and their first contact with Spanish took place at school (Messineo, 1989). At that time, the figure of the minority indigenous teacher occupied the key role within BIE because it officiated as translator/mediator between the school, the community and the children given that it was its intervention that sought to bridge that linguistic distance between children – centrally monolingual in Toba – and non-indigenous teachers – speakers of Spanish only.

In recent decades, this scenario changed radically in the province of Chaco. The Toba/Qom language is losing vitality and is no longer the privileged means of communication in families' private settings, but rather Spanish has installed itself as the language of day-to-day life (Censabella, 1999; Hecht, 2012; Medina, 2014; Messineo, 2003). Currently, Toba/Qom children entering school practically do not speak the native language, thus leaving it in a condition of vulnerability. At present, with the aim of teaching the indigenous language, indigenous teachers have special hours dedicated to the subject "Toba language and culture." This class works on writing in the native language and teaches knowledge linked to the indigenous worldview that is considered significant to the people, such as legends, mythology, outdoor resources, traditional music, artisanal products, etc. Given that there is no uniform curricular design as to what content to teach in this space, that which is registered varies greatly according to the minority teachers' profiles, the school institutions' characteristics and the demands or requirements of the indigenous fathers/mothers.

In the case of Chaco, bilingualism was handled in different ways over time: from a transitional model, at the beginning, to the aspiration to an additive model currently.[1] Although promising legislation regulating BIE has emerged in the last thirty years, its application in projects and concrete actions depends exclusively on the will of local governments and even on the initiative of teachers and school administrators or on the demands and claims of indigenous parents (Hecht, 2015, 2020).

---

[1] The bilingual school models within BIE projects can be characterized as being of a bilingualism that is subtractive, of transition or additive (Hornberger, 2014; Skutnabb-Kangas & McCarty, 2008). In the first case, a language is valued more than another and bilingualism ends up being to the detriment of the language of lower status, which is eventually replaced by the dominant one. In the second case, the use of the minoritized language is instrumental, foreseen only at the start of schooling, and gradually the hegemonic language is incorporated, to later foster exclusively its use in the remainder of mandatory schooling. Lastly, in additive bilingualism the two languages are valued equally, and they are developed evenly because bilingualism is considered a cultural enrichment.

Since the implementation of BIE in Chaco (from the late '80s to the present), far from maintaining or increasing the amount of Toba speakers, different sociolinguistic diagnoses performed by specialists and speakers themselves have coincided in indicating that the vitality of this language is in jeopardy (Censabella, 1999; Medina, 2014; Messineo, 2003). That is, an accelerated process of language shift in favor of Spanish is evidenced, most of all in the cities where a large percentage of this population lives and in the majority of daily communicative events in which the children and youth participate (Hecht, 2010). In spite of efforts to value the indigenous language in schools, the social stereotype that denigrates the status of ethno-linguistic minorities' languages continues to predominate, at the same time that the majority language is treated with prestige as the vehicle for social development. Hence, though the BIE models in Chaco have been generalized and consolidated through legislation that promotes the validity of indigenous languages, they are nonetheless "threatened."

The correlation between these sociolinguistics aspects and school practices within the BIE framework still needs to be investigated. This chapter focuses on the repercussions of this change in bilingual communicative practices in the daily experiences of school institutions, surveying first and foremost the role of minority Toba/Qom teachers, and Toba Language status.

Methodology

The general research that I conduct on the Toba/Qom people began in the year 2002. However, during the first fourteen years I took as empirical reference a community in the province of Buenos Aires that is the product of migration from Chaco to the metropolitan area. From 2016 to 2019, I have focused my fieldwork in one school situated in a Toba/Qom neighborhood in the heart of Chaco province. Therefore, while the corpus of this chapter appears to be brief, it bears mentioning that it is part of a further-reaching research trajectory.

The fieldwork is composed of a corpus of thirty-six in-depth interviews with indigenous teachers (men and women between 27 and 60 years old) and more than forty-eight records of observations of classes dedicated to the teaching of the Toba/Qom language in different levels of education. The interviews were mainly oriented to characterize: ideas about the indigenous language, teaching practices, school trajectories and contexts of language use (Toba and Spanish).

Along with the interviews, I conducted class observations in one school, at different school levels and in different subjects, although priority was given to indigenous language classes. The observations focused on: teacher behaviours and activities; linguistic interactions of adults with each other and of adults with children; and ways of teaching in different subjects. All information was recorded on audio and/or video and recorded in field diaries and photographs.

Likewise, I complement this information with that from observations of daily routines in extracurricular contexts, recorded through field notes, which offer contextual information of interest for framing the interpretation of narrative of the interviewees and class records.

In terms of ethics, I worked with the informed consent of all subjects in this research. This ethnographic field material is exhaustive and, although it does not claim to be statistically representative, it brings together a set of situations that account for common aspects in BIE schools in Chaco.

Results and Discussion

To understand the daily bilingual communicative practices at the heart of a BIE school, nothing better than to read ethnographic field notes resulting from observation of a Toba/Qom teacher's class. It bears mentioning that this is not an isolated record, selected for its specificity or originality. Quite the contrary, this record is repetitive, just like many other results of years of observation of classes in which the same questions as will be analyzed below were always surveyed. I agree with Rockwell (2009) in that we see how representative what we survey is, from among things that frequently occur, thanks to prolonged fieldwork which is what allows us to appreciate recurrences. That is why these field notes condense all those recurrences and deserve to be the focus of our analysis:

> I am in the third grade of the Public Primary School of Indigenous Community Management, and in the entrance there is a sign that reads *No'on ra Qarviraxac* (Welcome). Most of the students are from the Toba neighborhood where the school is located; however, there are several *criollo* (non-indigenous) children from adjacent neighborhoods. Inside the classroom there are some posters about oral hygiene in Spanish, about school anniversaries in Qom and some letters of the *acechedario* (Qom alphabet). Sergio, the teacher, is very patient with the children, he gives them ample time for each activity and there is an environment of happiness in the classroom. A constant bustle accompanies the daily work. Sergio does not sit at the head of the class, but rather in the back. As the children work, they come near to show him their progress and in a gentle tone he congratulates them and urges them to continue. All the interactions are in Spanish, and at times there seems to be a stray Qom word uttered by a child telling a joke, as the reactions of the other children are to laugh shyly as accomplices. At one point Sergio says, "Open your mother language workbook, we're going to look at the Qom language." Then on the blackboard he writes an enormous bilingual list with terms of kinship: mother, grandmother, grandfather, father, brother, uncle. The proposal consists of the children copying what is written and reading it collectively under the guiding voice of the teacher. This is the moment in which one can detect the ethnic belonging of some children, whom Sergio personally calls on to participate with phrases like: "Come on, Nayra, your grandfather talks in Qom a lot," "Nicolás, don't laugh, it's our language," and "Look at how well Julia reads and she's not Qom." Spanish predominates even in this subject as the explanations and instructions are given in that language. (Author field notes, June 2017)

The conceptual framework that this research is set in takes up anew the contributions of educational anthropology and linguistic anthropology, insofar as it is interested in the place of linguistic practices as social practices in a specific socio-scholastic context. In this sense, for the analysis of this record I must point out at least two large dimensions that I will analyze separately. Therefore, this section will be divided into three subsections to exhaustively systematize the different aspects that are condensed in this ethnographic record. These are, on the one hand, the teacher's practice in relation to the use and teaching of the Toba language; and, on the other hand, the status of the indigenous language inside the classroom. Lastly, both aspects are linked with the purpose of rethinking the scope of schooling for linguistic maintenance.

Monolingual Teachers for Bilingual Intercultural Education?

The first dimension refers to the practice of the teacher in relation to the use and teaching of the Toba language. In this respect, I can also point out two aspects: one in terms of their role and another with regard to their linguistic competencies. As concerns the former, in many contexts the task of indigenous teachers is to teach the indigenous language to indigenous children who do not speak the language and possess very uneven levels of competence (some understand, others produce isolated phrases, others yet neither speak nor comprehend). Their role has shifted from promoting literacy in the indigenous language to revitalizing, recovering and strengthening the language in children who self-recognize as indigenous, yet who are not speakers.

In that sense, the teachers experience a certain lack of curricular content to be taught because their function is more precisely to raise awareness among students that they are indigenous and the language is inscribed as just another diacritic of that identification. In that regard, it is important to textually quote an indigenous teacher reflecting on their role in the current contexts in which fewer and fewer children speak the indigenous language:

> (Teachers) are the fundamental pillars for teaching children that they are not speakers of their own language. And it is a right and it is an identity. Because we as indigenous teachers can't not teach the language, which with time is disappearing and we're to blame for not teaching the Qom language at school to our indigenous children. (Interview with a teacher, September 2018)

In their role as teachers, the use of the indigenous language as a means of communication of teachers with students is clearly discarded. The teacher-student interactions are in Spanish, and at most one can observe the use of the Toba language in certain abetting conversations among bilingual teachers, though outside the classroom space (as, for example, in the teachers' lounge or in the courtyard). In the "Toba Language" classes the Qom teachers interact with the children in Spanish and the Toba language becomes an object of reference.

Minority teachers shifted from being fluid bilingual speakers to possessing fewer competencies in the indigenous language than in Spanish; thus, their teaching function is no longer to generate literacy in the indigenous language. The minimal linguistic competence in the native language of many teachers becomes rather evident in these classes, as there is a notable constraint on the contents they can teach. Therefore, as specialists have already warned previously (Biord Castillo, 2018; Meek & Messing, 2007; Suina, 2004), the decisions made by teachers while intervening in the use of language can end up undermining the possibility of minority community empowerment and hinder development of communicative competence without achieving a reversal of language replacement.

As I have documented in prior work, one of the most notable characteristics of those currently studying to become indigenous teachers and of recent graduates is their limited communicative competence in the Toba language as opposed to teachers of an older age (Artieda & Barboza, 2016; Enriz et al., 2017; Hecht, 2015; Hecht & Schmidt, 2016). Many Toba/Qom teachers indicate that the basic notions they have of the native language were learned only when they studied to become teachers. That is, these teachers undergo a process of recovery of the native language in their professional training, as in many cases they represent a first or second generation that does not speak Toba as their first language and they have varying levels of competence (some produce simple utterances, others merely comprehend, others manage to pronounce some words and others neither speak nor comprehend).

Teachers who are not speakers of Qom while teaching it tend to develop very limited and simple didactic plans, which greatly adhere to writing and let oral production fall by the wayside. Yet this is not an isolated phenomenon, but rather part of the historical intervention BIE was intended to have in indigenous languages. These teaching perspectives centered on writing conceive of language as a homogenous code and of the purpose of teaching it as the simple fact that the student acquires this code (Rebolledo, 2014). The pedagogy seems to be centered on the code, while in a context of language replacement as that of Toba, a pedagogy that focuses on use would be important (Rebolledo, 2014).

Likewise, as argued by Sichra (2005), worldwide, linguistic policies on indigenous languages have been guided by the objective of the written form of said languages and this has redounded in certain obstacles in day-to-day school activities. In other words, teaching indigenous languages in schools entailed the development of their writing systems (unified and agreed by consensus) and, consequently, a certain discrediting of orality. However, the founded methodological proposals theoretically postulate an oral phase prior to writing in language learning processes, and those considerations are currently being omitted in BIE (López, 2015). Discarding orality in school linguistic planning is an affront against the modes of circulation and use of indigenous languages themselves, which are of an oral tradition. That is, indigenous languages have historically maintained their vitality through orality; therefore, current linguistic ideologies that associate "language maintenance" with "writing" end up jeopardizing their daily use. Communication has always encompassed much more than normalized and written language (Hornberger, 2014).

In the "Toba Language" classes, surveyed through participatory observation, only writing is exercised – some vocabulary from a specific semantic field or greeting formulas – and there is no real communicative context. For example, Figs. 15.1 and 15.2 show what was written by certain teachers during their classes in which

15 Argentina: Minority Indigenous Teachers of Bilingual Intercultural Education

Fig. 15.1 Blackboard with the notes of the class of the teacher Toba/Qom

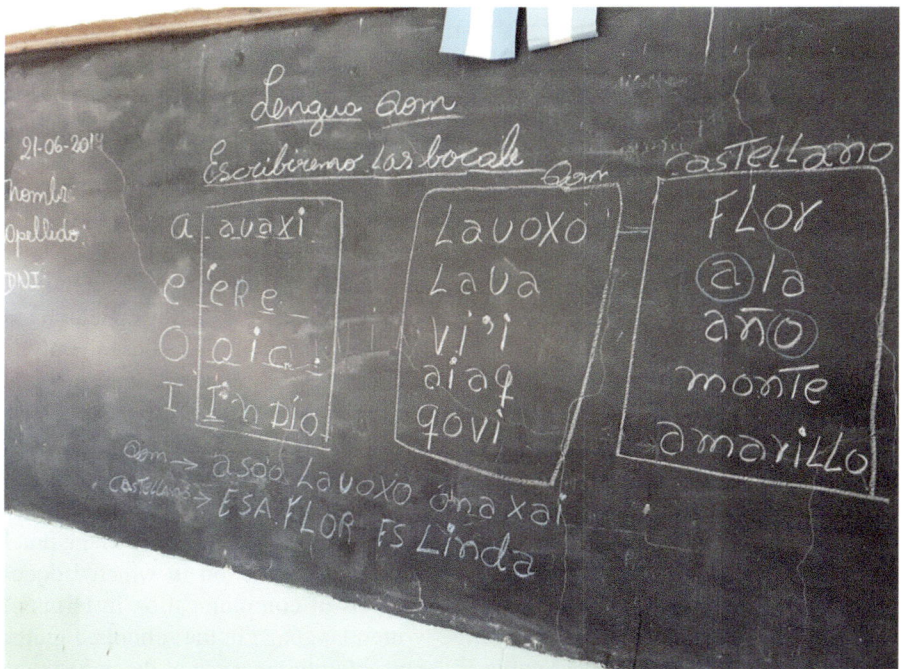

Fig. 15.2 Blackboard with the notes of the class of the Toba/Qom teacher

grammar and lexicon are treated as the central topic. It should be added that this manner of conducting the class is not only constrained by the teacher's scant bilingual competence, but also because no didactic materials exist that the teacher can rely on to fulfill their task. Therefore, the language-teaching planning is dependent on the minority teacher's expertise in their classes, generating great inequality in the type of teaching received by the children based on the linguistic competence of the teacher in charge of the course. The indigenous teachers' practices are conditioned by the contact they have had with the indigenous language in their life experiences (according to their age group, place of birth and/or residence, family of origin, etc.).

Minority Language, from School Subject to Object?

The second analyzed dimension refers to the status of the Toba language in the classroom, which in this case appears to have two senses: one that is associated with its functionality and another that is more symbolic. In the field notes I read that the indigenous language is included as a subject, since a specific curricular space exists that is aimed at teaching the language and aspects of the indigenous culture. While conducting this fieldwork, I have recorded classes in which the "mother language" or "Qom language" or "*qom laqtaqa*" is taught as a separate subject independent of the school curriculum. According to other research on this matter, in the interactional dynamic of these classes there is a prevalence of bilingual uses and a metalinguistic use of the indigenous language that is the object of study, though not necessarily the vehicular language (Censabella et al., 2013). Coincidentally, in the Qom language classes in which I participated, I detected that the interactions and communications were produced in Spanish and Qom was used above all in written form and perhaps in reading aloud. That is, as stated in the field notes, the blackboard was used to write lists of greetings, family-related vocabulary or the names of plants and animals (Figs. 15.1 and 15.2). Teaching of the language is conceived as an isolated lexicon and the pedagogical activity consisted in the children copying what was written and collectively reading it under the teacher's guidance.

In my field experience, I also surveyed that the indigenous language occupies a place as a symbol within school institutions, i.e., although the language is not habitually used by the students, it is invoked as a symbolic resource for identity. In these cases its use is materialized in posters, drawings and the use of greeting formulas or expressions referring to the weather (Figs. 15.3 and 15.4). In contrast with the practices of the minority teachers analyzed in the previous section in which I documented the scarce use of the language as a means of communication in terms of orality, there was an overabundance of the written language in the schools. Figures such as 15.3 and 15.4 are just a sample of the visual omnipresence of the indigenous language writing in institutional contexts. The reified language in written words is a constant presence and an indisputable emblem of BIE schools.

All of those cases present symbolic uses of the indigenous language in the midst of a dominant sociolinguistic exchange in Spanish within the school. These

15 Argentina: Minority Indigenous Teachers of Bilingual Intercultural Education   243

Fig. 15.3 School event with scenery in Toba/Qom language

Fig. 15.4 Bilingual billboard in school (Toba/Qom – Spanish)

situations are clearly exemplified in the fragment of class transcribed and in the reiterated notes compiled in which the children copy indigenous language words into their notebooks (even without understanding their meaning) – for example, what the weather is like (rainy, sunny, cloudy) (Figs. 15.1, 15.2, 15.3 and 15.4). Also very recurrent is the use of the Toba language at the start of all school events in which significant historical anniversaries are commemorated, as a way of marking the indigenous spirit of the event. In my field notes on school events at BIE educational institutions, there are reiterated descriptions of how on those special days the school is decorated with posters offering welcoming messages in the indigenous language and all the events begin with a greeting in the indigenous language, and usually a community or religious authority is invited who tends to give an opening speech in the native language. Such an example appears in Fig. 15.3, in which the flag of the indigenous peoples is accompanied by speeches of referents of the indigenous community, whereby they enter the school and occupy a space that they do not normally have in the school's day-to-day routine.

In synthesis, the status of the Toba language in the classroom is reified and reduced to the formal structure of language, and at most occupies a symbolic place as the patrimonial language of heritage. Thus, coinciding with the assessments of Suina (2004), it seems that native languages have not yet found the place they deserve in schools, especially if we do not begin to question that language is not an abstract identity, but is updated through the practices of its speakers (Vigil, 2011). The Toba language class is reduced and limited to the discursive resources of Spanish. In this regard, we have contributions such as those of Meek and Messing (2007) who have warned us of the dangers of the indigenous/minority language being reduced to the logic of the hegemonic/majority language. In other words, if the dominant language is the matrix for teaching the "endangered" indigenous language, it will be difficult for the latter to be revalued in those communicative routines. The framing of the hegemonic language does nothing but reaffirm the asymmetrical and unequal power relations between the languages and their speakers.

Indigenous Languages Versus the School?

Though schools historically appear to have been the place where non-official languages were banished, currently they present themselves as the space for revitalizing them. Schools are assigned great power of action over languages, both as a result of their negative and positive power: they go from being the instrument for eradicating non-dominant languages, to being the place for their maintenance and revitalization due to their inclusion in teaching programs (Hagège, 2002; López, 2015; Moya, 2012; Suina, 2004). That is, the possible repercussions that school institutions have on the possibilities of linguistic rejection or maintenance due to simply including them in the curriculum is overstated. The mere presence of the minority language in classrooms is potentially necessary though not sufficient for linguistic vitality.

With respect to this last point, the presence of the minority language in the school is not sufficient precisely because it depends on the teachers' daily practices. The teachers exert influence not only through their classes and teaching methods, but rather also in their daily routines related to the use of languages. That is to say, whether or not they speak in the indigenous language with their students and colleagues, whether they identify their ethnic belonging with a certain language, whether they learned the indigenous language during childhood or whether they only developed their linguistic competencies while studying to become a teacher, among other aspects. The reflections on the practices of minority indigenous teachers within the classrooms of BIE schools have not been addressed with the depth that they deserve. Oftentimes, the BIE policies (and even the very indigenous peoples) have conformed themselves with the mere inclusion of the indigenous language in the school curriculum, disparaging the importance and influence of the trajectories and training of the indigenous teachers for the development of those languages.

Furthermore, there are other out-of-school areas of use that should also be stimulated (religious, communications media, domestic, among many others) (Sánchez Avendaño, 2012). Therefore, schools, like any social institution, can contribute to the linguistic maintenance of those languages subjected to hegemonic powers, though not necessarily through pedagogical actions, but rather through the positive effects entailed by their presence in terms of the linguistic-cultural valuing and prestige of that language community.

Conclusions and Implications

This chapter is an approximation to a very complex issue as is the role, the expectations and the challenges of Toba/Qom indigenous teachers in the current sociolinguistic context of Chaco, where it is evident that the dominant bilingualism of Toba has been inverted to Spanish. My review of how change in the scenarios of vitality of indigenous languages impacts teachers' functions has caused multiple questions to arise. Indigenous teachers emerged to address the communicative barriers between indigenous languages and Spanish, though at present this is no longer so because the children's requirements and teachers' profiles have been modified. Even the premise and basic aptitude for every bilingual educator has been challenged, to wit: that they be truly bilingual. Contrarily, I have surveyed complex sociolinguistic competencies of teachers, with diverse bilingual mastery of the indigenous language; therefore, it seems that it is an outstanding debt that such work be in favor of bilingualism.

Minority indigenous teachers charged with teaching the indigenous language are in their majority not speakers thereof because they belong to subalternized sectors that underwent complex processes of social submission and linguistic displacement by Spanish. This is a very complex problem set since it evinces the chasm that exists between what is planned in school legislation and that which can be observed through ethnographic fieldwork in indigenous schools. That is, there is an ostensible distance between what is postulated as part of the design of an educational policy whose aim is to address the linguistic and social needs of Argentina's indigenous peoples and what actually occurs with teachers in the current framework of "bilingual and intercultural" schools.

As is well noted by Acuña (2010), BIE in Argentina, despite its name, has failed to ensure bilingualism itself as it is something that must be planned, built up and not taken for granted. Furthermore, this is especially so in indigenous contexts, where teaching the children's language is not only a pedagogical issue, but is the recognition of a right (Vigil, 2011). Hence, in order to keep 'bilingual' and 'intercultural' from becoming empty or ornamental adjectives for schools in the indigenous education category, it is necessary to contemplate:

> The fundamental role of teachers in implementing any educational innovation (…). Without the support and conviction of teachers, BIE runs the risk of getting stuck in political and academic discourse and, although it may lead to a few interesting actions, it will not effect the radical change that is desired and necessary. Given that its main sphere of application is still schools, this is the place where teachers can contribute to strengthening the processes of social change that the communities are demanding. (Serrudo, 2010, p. 269)

Since the incorporation of indigenous teachers into the educational system, there have been many uncertainties about the requirements demanded of them as educators and, as a result, they have been charged with different interventions over the years, without this having been accompanied by the training received. The training program for indigenous teachers has stayed the same since its creation, impervious to changes in the use of the native language and the expansion of Spanish. For that reason, the teachers find themselves lacking the tools to confront the new sociolinguistic reality that both their students and they themselves face.

At present the revitalization of the patrimonial language is associated with writing and, hence, with school (Hecht, 2012). But the fossilization of writing does not allow to amplify the conception of bilingualism as something dynamic, associated with orality, which emerges in heterogeneous competencies and uses, and in intimate connection with identity. In my case, all that which is related to the orality of indigenous languages is not considered content to be addressed in BIE schools. In the contexts I observed through the ethnographic fieldwork, I can highlight the symbolic presence of the indigenous language (in greetings, signage, school events, formal presentations, etc.) and the reified language as a subject that is alien to the interactional dynamic. The Toba language is not used as a means through which the teachers communicate with the children, but rather as an emblem or diacritic of heritage.

This language conception is not BIE's only currently outstanding debt, but rather it finds itself at a crossroads since it needs to evolve from being a discursive reality to a factual one. To that end, it must redefine its goals and beneficiaries, taking into account the accumulated potential of indigenous movements' experiences, advances in terms of the methodologies for teaching languages and the scope that interculturality is having in relation to quality of education (Biord Castillo, 2018; Hecht, 2014, 2016; Valiente Catter, 2011). BIE must not be understood as an end in itself, but a means to produce changes in society (Dietz, 2012). Therefore, it is fundamental that we rethink BIE as an educational policy, to keep it from being a subordinate project within the official system, but to do so we need not only to answer pedagogical questions, but also political ones (Alonso & Díaz, 2004). As Hornberger (2014) put it, multilingual education is potentially an ample and fortuitous doorway toward the recuperation of oppressed peoples and the overcoming of colonial conditions that have so obstinately pursued us through to our times.

That is, BIE has to be recognized as a field of rights that were fought for and won by indigenous collectives. It is impossible to proceed as if schools were isolated from the historical and socio-cultural context, thus omitting the inferiorization and subordination that affect indigenous groups. This decolonizing focus is important because it allows for a break with colonialist discourses that cancel out differences. Therefore, in future research it is important that the problems to be studied help reverse that socio-educational inequality that affects indigenous peoples and permit collaboration for the maintenance of the linguistic-cultural heritage of their peoples.

References

Acuña, L. (2010). Lenguas propias y lenguas prestadas en la EIB. In S. Hirsch & A. Serrudo (Eds.), *La Educación Intercultural Bilingüe en Argentina. Identidades, lenguas y protagonistas* (pp. 197–222). Novedades Educativas.

Alonso, G., & Díaz, R. (2004). ¿Es la educación intercultural una modificación del statu quo? In R. Díaz & G. Alonso (Eds.), *Construcción de espacios interculturales* (pp. 67–88). Editorial Miño y Dávila.

Artieda, T., & Barboza, T. (2016). ¿Son posibles otras educaciones para indígenas dentro del sistema escolar tradicional? Análisis de un caso en el nordeste argentino. *Nodos y Nudos, 41*(5), 21–34.

Biord Castillo, H. (2018). De la escuela intercultural a la cosmovisión indígena: los escollos del camino. *Pueblos Indígenas y Educación, 65*, 103–119.

Censabella, M. (1999). *Las lenguas indígenas de la Argentina. Una mirada actual*. EUDEBA.

Censabella, M., Giménez, M., & Gómez, M. (2013). Políticas lingüísticas recientes en la provincia del Chaco y su posible impacto en la revitalización de lenguas indígenas. In M. Haboud & N. Ostler (Eds.), *Voces e imágenes de las lenguas en peligro* (pp. 195–200). Foundation for Endangered Languages Found & Pontificia Universidad Católica del Ecuador.

Dietz, G. (2012). Multiculturalismo, interculturalidad y diversidad en educación. Una aproximación antropológica. México DF: Fondo de Cultura Económica.

Enriz, N., García Palacios, M., & Hecht, A. C. (2017). Llevar La palabra. Un análisis de la relación entre las iglesias y la escolarización de niños indígenas tobas/qom y mbya-guaraní de Argentina. *Revista Universitas Humanística, 83*, 180–205.

Hagège, C. (2002). *No a la muerte de las lenguas*. Editorial Paidós.

Hecht, A. C. (2010). *"Todavía no se hallaron hablar en idioma" Procesos de socialización lingüística de los niños en el barrio toba de Derqui, Argentina*. Lincom Europa Academic Publisher.

Hecht, A. C. (2012). Entre silencios presentidos y voces anheladas. Ideologías lingüísticas sobre la vitalidad del toba en un contexto de desplazamiento por el español. *Spanish in Context, 9*(2), 293–314.

Hecht, A. C. (2014). An analysis of intercultural bilingual education in Argentina. *Journal for Multicultural Education, 8*(2), 70–80.

Hecht, A. C. (2015). Trayectorias escolares de maestros toba/qom del Chaco. *Cuadernos del Instituto Nacional de Antropología y Pensamiento Latinoamericano, 24*(2), 1–12.

Hecht, A. C. (2020). Exploraciones sobre Educación Intercultural Bilingüe en Argentina. *Revista del CISEN Tramas/Maepova, 8*(1), 103–113.

Hecht, A. C., and Schmidt, M. (Comps.) (2016). *Maestros de la Educación Intercultural Bilingüe. Regulaciones, experiencias y desafíos.* Editorial Novedades Educativas.

Hecht, A. C., Enriz, N., & García Palacios, M. (2016). Reflections on the concept of Interculturality in the current educational debate in Argentina. *Intercultural Education, 27*(3), 231–244.

Hornberger, N. (2008). *Can schools save indigenous languages? Policy and practice on four continents.* Palgrave Macmillan.

Hornberger, N. (2014). La educación multilingüe, política y práctica: diez certezas. In L. M. Lepe & N. Rebolledo (Eds.), *Educación bilingüe y políticas de revitalización de lenguas indígenas* (pp. 235–261). Editorial Abya-Yala.

López, L. (2015). El hogar, la comunidad y la escuela en la revitalización de las lenguas originarias de América Latina. *Pueblos Indígenas y Educación, 64*, 211–339.

Medina, M. (2014). *Prácticas educativo-lingüísticas en la modalidad de EIB: Una aproximación etnográfica a las clases de qom la'aqtaqa en una escuela periurbana del barrio Mapic (Resistencia, Chaco).* Tesis de Maestría en Antropología Social de la Universidad Nacional de Misiones, Posadas.

Meek, B., & Messing, J. (2007). Framing indigenous languages as secondary to matrix languages. *Anthropology & Education Quarterly, 38*(2), 99–118.

Messineo, C. (1989). Lingüística y Educación indígena. Una experiencia en comunidades tobas de la provincia del Chaco. *Pueblos indígenas y Educación, 12*, 9–27.

Messineo, C. (2003). *Lengua toba (guaycurú). Aspectos gramaticales y discursivos.* Lincom Europa Academic Publisher.

Moya, R. (2012). La escuela: acicate para acceder a la educación superior indígena. *Pueblos Indígenas y Educación, 61*, 83–136.

National Institute of Statistics and Censuses (INDEC). (2010). *National population, household and housing census 2010. REDATAM database: Methodological aspects, Buenos Aires.* National Institute of Statistics and Census. Available at: https://www.indec.gob.ar/indec/web/Nivel4-Tema-2-41-135

Rebolledo Recendiz, N. (2014). Enseñanza de lenguas indígenas y revitalización lingüística. Una aproximación interdisciplinaria. In L. M. Lepe & N. Rebolledo (Eds.), *Educación bilingüe y políticas de revitalización de lenguas indígenas* (pp. 19–40). Editorial Abya-Yala.

Rockwell, E. (2009). *La experiencia etnográfica. Historia y cultura en los procesos educativos.* Paidós.

Serrudo, A. (2010). Indígenas en la escuela: representaciones y tensiones acerca de los docentes indígenas bilingües en Argentina. In S. Hirsch & A. Serrudo (Eds.), *La Educación Intercultural Bilingüe en Argentina. Identidades, lenguas y protagonistas* (pp. 255–272). Novedades Educativas.

Sichra, I. (2005). *Bilingüismo y educación en la región andina: en búsqueda del aporte de la educación al mantenimiento de las lenguas indígenas.* In Encuentro internacional Educación y Diversidad Cultural en la Región Andina.

Skutnabb-Kangas, T., & McCarty, T. (2008). Key concepts in bilingual education: Ideological, historical, epistemological, and empirical foundations. In J. Cummins & N. Hornberger (Eds.), *Volumen 5 of encyclopedia of language and education* (pp. 3–17). Springer.

Suina, J. (2004). Native language teachers in a struggle for language and cultural survival. *Anthropology & Education Quarterly, 35*(3), 281–302.

Sánchez Avendaño, C. (2012). El papel de la escuela en el desplazamiento y en la conservación de la lengua maleku. *Revista Educación, 36*(1), 25–43.

Valiente Catter, T. (2011). Educación Intercultural Bilingüe: visión de una propuesta y realidad de su práctica en la región andina. *Pueblos Indígenas y Educación, 60*, 101–129.

Vigil, N. (2011). *Reflexiones de Invierno.* Tarea Asociación de Publicaciones Educativas.

Ana Carolina Hecht is a leading specialist in Anthropology and Education, and Linguistic Anthropology and has been recognized for advancing social research on intercultural education and linguistic socialization processes in indigenous peoples. She has been directing the research team "Interculturality and Education" at the University of Buenos Aires (Argentina) since 2013 and serves as a co-coordinator of the internationally constituted CLACSO Working Group on Education and Interculturality. She is currently an Independent Researcher at the National Council for Scientific and Technical Research at the National Institute of Anthropology and Latin American Thought and a lecturer at the University of Buenos Aires.

Open Access This chapter is licensed under the terms of the Creative Commons Attribution 4.0 International License (http://creativecommons.org/licenses/by/4.0/), which permits use, sharing, adaptation, distribution and reproduction in any medium or format, as long as you give appropriate credit to the original author(s) and the source, provide a link to the Creative Commons license and indicate if changes were made.

The images or other third party material in this chapter are included in the chapter's Creative Commons license, unless indicated otherwise in a credit line to the material. If material is not included in the chapter's Creative Commons license and your intended use is not permitted by statutory regulation or exceeds the permitted use, you will need to obtain permission directly from the copyright holder.

Part III
Journeys and Identities of International Minority Teacher Educators

Mary Gutman ⓘ, Wurud Jayusi ⓘ, Michael Beck ⓘ, and Zvi Bekerman ⓘ

Chapter 16
The Growth of Minority Supervisors: Supervision of Pre-service Teachers' Field Experiences

Bing Xiao

Abstract The anthropologists are outsiders to the culture who were studying in traditional ethnography. I understand this since I identify as both an insider and an outsider when I instruct, supervise, and advise my American students. I am an "insider" in the teacher education program but an "outsider" of American school culture. I am originally from China, but I am immersing myself in my doctoral studies in the American education system. I instruct teaching methods classes and have served as a supervisor for students' field experiences for around ten years. As a minority educator, I am faced with multiple challenges, especially supervising student teachers. The purpose of this chapter will explore the challenges of the minority supervisors' growth and those influences on pre-service teachers. The research used the video-cued multivocal ethnographic method. I conducted focus-group interviews with university supervisors and the instructors of a teaching methods course. I presented video clips from students' field teaching experience to the interviewees and discussed how videos impact teaching and teacher preparation notions. Additional data comes from my own experience. The chapter expands on Foucault and Bourdieu's work to better understand how power flows in the field experience and how power changes supervisors' and pre-service teachers' habitus and behaviors. It also draws from Latour's Actor-Network Theory (ANT) theoretical lens to investigate how different actors, such as the university, local schools, mentor teachers, supervisors, and pre-service teachers, change their action transforms the field experience.

Introduction

Field experience plays an essential role in the whole pre-service teacher education program wherein they are furthering the professional preparation of teachers, and it is the most powerful learning experience for future pre-service teachers

---

B. Xiao (✉)
Austin Peay State University, Clarksville, TN, USA
e-mail: xiaob@apsu.edu

© The Author(s) 2023
M. Gutman et al. (eds.), *To Be a Minority Teacher in a Foreign Culture*,
https://doi.org/10.1007/978-3-031-25584-7_16

(Darling-Hammond & Bransford, 2005; Hodges & Hodge, 2017; Lawson et al., 2015). Since the 1960s, an increased emphasis on field experience and clinical practice has been considered a way to improve teacher preparation.

University supervisors are uniquely situated to understand the intertwined nature of theory and practice in education. Many teachers have reported that student teaching experience was one of the most crucial aspects of their professional preparation (Hodges & Hodge, 2017; Lawson et al., 2015; Wilson & Ferrini-Mundy, 2001). As the representative of program commitments, the university supervisor helps student teachers synthesize concepts learned during coursework (Cuenca, 2012; Hodges & Hodge, 2017). As Abdal-Haqq (1997) pointed out,

> Both school and university faculty engaged in schoolwork are frequently called "bicultural" or "boundary spanners" in the literature because they cross conventional lines of demarcation between school and university cultures and/or between roles within a particular culture. (p. 22)

Pre-service teachers participate in university course work and practice teaching simultaneously, and supervisors can draw upon fieldwork experiences to help them make connections between theory and practice.

The anthropologists are outsiders to the culture who were studying in traditional ethnography. I can relate to this situation as I identify as both an insider and an outsider when I instruct, supervise, and advise my American students. I am an "insider" in the teacher education program but an "outsider" of American school culture. I am originally from China, but I have been learning and familiarizing myself with the American education system since my doctoral studies in the USA ten years ago. I instruct teaching methods classes of PreK-3 and K-5 programs and have also served as a supervisor for students' field experiences for several years. As a minority educator, I faced multiple challenges from the academic and research success of higher education areas and supervised student teachers at the local schools.

Research Objectives

The importance of supervision work, predominantly minority supervisors' experience, is rarely acknowledged and valued; different ways to think about the nature of supervisors' experience should be explored. Also, the increased use of technology, such as videos, remote observation, online supervision systems for assessment, faced some new challenges; therefore, it is needed to help supervisors identify their roles and responsibility in fieldwork and change the regular supervision and instruction style. Moreover, there seems to be a limited theoretical framework associated with supervision during the student teaching experience to explain the triadic relationship between student teachers, minority supervisors, and mentor teachers.

This study aims to better understand the different expectations the minority educators bring to the teacher preparation program and how their different background influences the pre-service teachers' professional development. First, the chapter will reveal compare to the white supervisors, how cultural factors and backgrounds inform minority supervisors' practices in the field placement. Moreover, there is a discussion about how the challenges and difficulties they faced influence the triadic relationship among minority supervisors, student teachers, and classroom mentor teachers. Finally, the chapter explores how the minority instructor/supervisor can balance instructing and supervision and use their diverse background to prepare their students to be significant future teachers.

Theoretical Frameworks

Foucault, Bourdieu, and Latour did not write about teacher education, but their theories could conceptualize the supervisor's practices. Foucault's and Bourdieu's theory work together to understand how power flows in the field experience and influence supervisors' expectations on pre-service teachers' behaviors. Additionally, Latour's Actor-Network Theory (ANT) theoretical lens investigates how different actors, mentor teachers, minority supervisors, and pre-service teachers, change their actions and relationship in the triadic social network.

Michel Foucault

According to Foucault (1982), "Power relations are rooted deep in the social nexus, not reconstituted 'above' society as a supplementary structure whose radical effacement one could perhaps dream of" (p. 208). In other words, power exists everywhere in society, and it operates in particular social contexts. The power has never been fixed in an actor, and the field placement includes student teachers, mentor teachers, supervisors, the local school, the university, children, parents, and the school district, where both large and small entities exist in a structured relationship and relate to one another.

Pierre Bourdieu

Bourdieu (2000) pointed out that a biological individual occupies a physical and social space position, even simultaneously several physical and social positions. For example, a pre-service teacher's social position is both that of a university student and a temperate teacher in a classroom and cannot be separated from their physical position. Many participants in this research are both instructors of student teachers' teaching method classes and supervisors of their field placements. Their physical and social positions overlap each other.

Bourdieu (1984) explained that the field could provide a framework to explain and understand how pre-service teachers establish their beliefs and then consciously or unconsciously normalize their behaviors. According to Bourdieu's idea, when pre-service teachers enter into the new environment, their field placement has to change their behavior and even tastes to follow the new field's rules. Also, social status and social class are essential parts of cultural capital, and they also impact people's behavior and opinions. Most teachers in America come from a middle-class white culture, the mainstream American culture; therefore, middle-class whites' ideology represents the foundation of teacher education programs' educational courses and the local school's classroom culture. Minority supervisors face the challenges of adapting themselves to the mainstream American culture.

Bruno Latour

Another influential theory dealing with actors in a complicated relationship is the Actor-Network Theory (ANT), which treated objects as an integral part of social networks and explained how material-semiotic networks come together to act as a whole (Latour, 2005). Any actor can be considered linked with other actors, and different actors relate together in a network to form a coherent whole. The classroom is an example of a complicated system containing many components, such as mentor teachers, students, and pre-service teachers, all of which are virtually hidden from the pre-service teacher's view, who deals with the whole class a single object. The relationships among the actors are not two-dimensional or three-dimensional; they are nodes that have as many dimensions as they have connections. For example, the unique background of each pre-service teacher will influence the atmosphere of a classroom. On the other hand, classroom culture also influences pre-service teachers through the social interaction between all actors in the classroom.

Context of Research

Pre-service Teacher, Field Experience, and Supervisor

Pre-service teachers are enrolled in an undergraduate, graduate, or alternative-route university-based teacher education program but have not yet completed training to be teachers. Field experiences are defined as various early and systematic P-12 classroom-based opportunities in which pre-service teachers may observe, assist, tutor, instruct, and conduct research (Capraro & Helfeldt, 2010; Hodges & Hodge, 2017; Lawson et al., 2015). Field experiences are a crucial feature of teacher education programs due to their ability to blend theory and practice, promote reflection, and focus on student learning. It provides a good chance for pre-service teachers to transition from campus to school, from theories to practice, and from professionals in preparation to school reform agents. Sandhotlz (2011) examined writing documents from 290 pre-service teachers enrolled in a combined teacher credential and master's degree program at a public university in Southern California to explore the potential value of preparing pre-service teachers to engage in reflective practice focused on student learning. The researcher demonstrated that field experiences are meaningful for encouraging students' learning, getting compelling teaching experiences, and obtaining critical reflection for pre-service teachers.

Many literary works explore how to be a supervisor in a teacher preparation program and the supervisor's crucial role. Elfer (2012) described the complexities of supervision and stated some troubles, travails, and opportunities he faced when he transformed from a classroom-based teacher to a field-based teacher educator. In his final section, he talked about the "value of collaborative inquiry, dialogue, and program design in the context of developing and problematizing effective field-based supervisory practices" (p. 3). His narrative shows how a new supervisor can mesh his beliefs of teaching with the goal of the institution's program to support student teachers and unpacks ways in which collaborative inquiry and dialogue helped him through this initial experience with supervising student teachers.

Strieker et al. (2016) examined 15 university supervisors' communication approaches with the pre-service teachers enrolled in P-12 clinical experiences. The authors concluded that after 20 h of professional training, these university supervisors primarily used collaborative and nondirective communication approaches to improve pre-service teachers' teaching skills. Through the authors' statements, people have a deeper understanding of supervisors' real situation and their work; simultaneously, the argument makes supervisors rethink their work, communication approaches, and more flexible work methods with student teachers.

Triadic Relationship

Triad relationships between university supervisors, mentor teachers, and student teachers are another hot topic about the student teacher's field experience. Schmeichel (2012) argued that the literature fails to reflect the complex context in which power circulates in the field experience. She drew on her own experiences as a field instructor and teacher educator to explore the use of power imbued in the supervisors' position; the power shifts between the triadic relationship and will benefit each actor. She used Michel Foucault's (1976) theory of power to explore the fluid and mobilized power within the student teaching triad and stated that the supervision spaces are saturated with power dynamics and complexities in which the supervisors can use power and mobilize it toward pedagogical goals. The power circulating in triadic relationships is inherent but fluid. Understanding, exploring, and accepting our power and responsibility might be an excellent way to deal with the conflicts' triadic relationships.

Garrett (2012) introduced psychoanalysis as a theoretical framework to develop the physical and psychical spaces for student teachers' supervision. He stated,

> The 'third space' is simultaneously inside and outside of the normalized conceptions of time and duration; inside in the sense that it is presenting a productive possibility for subjective change, but outside in the way that it goes beyond what has counted as stable knowledge before. (p. 159)

The third space--student teacher, mentor teacher, and supervisor--shifts, and with each of those shifts come different forms of relating and relation. His argument provoked us to rethink the timing and spaces of supervision that might create different possibilities for field-based teacher education.

Field Experience and Course Work

Teacher education programs historically have been criticized for lacking the relation between course work and practical experiences. Real-life in school is often different from the knowledge shared in books. How might instructor/supervisor help the preservice teacher connect their learned knowledge to real teaching is an essential step for their transition from teacher candidate to a real teacher and a crucial part of a university's teacher preparation program?

Zeichner (2010) utilized the concept of "hybridity" and "third space" to make readers rethink the connections between campus courses and field experiences in college- and university-based teacher education. He argued that the old paradigm of university-based teacher education focuses on academic knowledge, which is viewed as the authoritative source of knowledge about teaching but ignores the nonhierarchical interplay between academic, practitioner, and community expertise. He suggested that we create expanded learning opportunities, the "third space" for prospective teachers, and help them enact problematic teaching practices.

Muted Voice of Minority Supervisor

Many literature pieces come from the supervisors' own experience, but the minority supervisor rarely has a voice in recent literacy, especially in the area of P-12 teacher preparation education. Hernández et al. (2009) interviewed ten ethnic minority supervisors about their experience in clinical supervision. They suggested that "making diversity dimensions central to the supervisory process, deepening the exploration of self of therapist and identity issues, and providing more mentorship into the profession (p. 88)" will help minority supervisors deal with the dilemmas. Mcroy et al. (1986) examined racial and power dynamics that affect supervisory relationships for social work education and suggested enhancing learning and communication between supervisors and students in cross-cultural field situations.

Additionally, some literature touches on the topic of minority faculties' experience in higher education. The literature explored the social and economic inequalities, issues of cultural conflicts, dilemmas about teaching in a different culture, and difficulties of the professional work experience the minority faculty faced (Gumpertz et al., 2017; Zambrana, 2015, 2018; Whittaker et al., 2015). The minority instructors and supervisors in this research are also the faculties or doctoral students in higher education settings; they may face the same issues which this literature stated.

Methodology

The chapter used the video-cued multivocal ethnographic methods. The 23 pre-service teachers registered in the Initial Teacher Certification Program in Early Childhood Education participated in this study. Also, there are eight University instructors and supervisors who attended the research. Four are White, and four are Asian. The white instructors' and supervisors' opinions are good comparisons to understand the different expectations on pre-service teachers' performance.

The pre-service teachers must videotape themselves teaching and submit a reflection paper on their teaching and videotaping experience as a part of their teaching methods class coursework. After collecting the videos and reflection papers, the researcher conducted the video-cued focus-group interviews with these pre-service teachers, instructors, and university supervisors. Tobin and Hsueh (2007) applied this method in their study; they claimed that, in this method, "the videos function primarily neither as data nor as a description but instead as rich nonverbal cues designed to stimulate critical reflection" (pp. 77–78). To guide the focus-group interviews, I used scenes from the videos, as they offered a visual aid for the questions, served to stimulate memory, and provoked reflection, placing more attention and scrutiny on the visible aspects of teaching. The interview questions include (1) What are the expectations for becoming an effective teacher? (2) How is video assessment impacting notions of teaching and teacher preparation, both positively and negatively? (3) How do you think about the importance of embodied aspects of teaching? This method is highly applicable to research on people's multiple perspectives from different groups and may have various assumptions on the topic being discussed. In this study, each participant is both an insider and an outsider. She/he not only a person who was studied, videotaped, or interviewed but also an essential informant for the research and an expert on her/his practice.

The data for this study is videos and focus-group interviews. As has been mentioned already, I used the videos for the video-microanalysis and as cues for focus-group interviews. I used a camera and a sound recorder to record each interview and transcribed all of the interviews. I coded the results of the content analysis of the interviews in an Excel table and used a color-coding strategy to sort the data according to its relevance categories: expectations on the effectiveness of teacher; embodied aspect of teaching; video assessment, and others.

Position of the Researcher

There is still ambiguity about the nature of preparation for supervisors; in fact, supervisors need some powerful tools to understand their role and work. Ritter (2012) showed us an excellent example of using self-study as a powerful methodological tool to understand further being a university supervisor. The author first described the complex nature and aims of teacher education, and then she traced the origins of self-study, clarifies its meaning, and explains some typical motivations that drive teachers to study their practice. Ritter argued the pre-service teachers bring their biographies into the field, so it is difficult to build a model of learner-centered instruction within the student teaching triad; however, self-study is a potential method to develop and enact a pedagogy of supervision to response the varying contexts where clinical experiences take places. In this chapter, I also share some my personal experience to support the discussion in later.

In this research, I have had the opportunity to situate myself as an insider and an outsider. I was an instructor for the 23 participants and supervised them when they were placed in the local schools to complete their field experiences. As an "insider" in this early childhood education program, I have had the chance to participate extensively in major-related courses with pre-service teachers. Also, talking and working with the other instructors, professors, faculty members, staff, and other program supervisors has allowed me to know the program more intimately. Moreover, I have known and understood the real challenges and conflicts that take place in the field through my observation and discussion with pre-service teachers as their supervisor. Lastly, I have witnessed and taken part in the plans, decisions, and deliberations in adjusting the program and curriculum in teaching methods courses to adopt new changes in the program.

However, I am also an "outsider" in another sense. As an immigrant, I have had to familiarize myself with the American education system in my doctoral studies. The training methods and evaluating new teachers are quite different in the US and in my country (China), which allows me to bring a different perspective into the discussion. Moreover, I am outside of the pre-service teachers' social group. Most of the time, the pre-service teachers do not see the supervisors as their peers; a supervisor is a person who may be evaluating them at any time. Supervisors and pre-service teachers belong to different roles and hold different views and preferences. Observing the pre-service teachers and interacting with them as their instructor and supervisor, I developed an insider's perspective as part of the program; on the other hand, I stayed on the pre-service teachers' periphery group as an outsider.

Results and Discussion

Different Expectations on Students' Performance

The following two scenarios reveal people from different cultures have different explanations for students' performance. The first scenario shows the different understanding of embodied teaching from American students and their Asian supervisors. These different points of view influence they choose a different strategy to manage students' behavior. The second scenario shows the different expectations on students' engagement between white supervisors and Asian supervisors.

Scenario One-Embodied Aspects of Teaching

One interview question is, "how do you think about the importance of embodied aspects of teaching?" The use of touch is an aspect of teaching young children that varies by gender, class, race, and culture. When I introduced touch as a classroom management strategy, some pre-service teachers in this cohort of mostly white middle-class were confused, as they carried the implicit belief that touching children was inappropriate. In the focus-group interview with supervisors, two Asian field supervisors were surprised by the pre-service teachers' hesitation to use touch. A Korean supervisor said:

> When I was a teacher, actually especially for young kids, touching is a very, very usual habit as a teacher but when I came here [to the US], I just think about it, is it true, Asian teachers' body strategy? When I look back at my student video, yeah, it's a little weird. Even though they sit closely, my students, they didn't show much about the touching strategy and just gently called the boys' names if they got distracted. They didn't use many touching strategies. If a boy or a girl is so distracted, I hold him or her on my knee and just continue to teach with the group. But in this culture, in our students' videos, I cannot see that kind of moment.

A Chinese supervisor built on her respond,

> I feel like these teachers in our program are very disembodied because this idea of using your body—how they use their hands, gestures, and gazes—has never been, like, strange to me when I was still a student teacher... Even as a student teacher, even in the planning process, if we are going to teach a lesson by our self, we spend a lot of time to think about materials, bodies, and children.

We need to be sensitive to cultural, racial, gendered, and social class differences in bodily techniques. As Mauss pointed out in his 1934 essay, the body's techniques are characteristic of genders, professions, classes, countries, and cultures. For example, in traditional Anglo-Saxon culture, avoiding eye contact usually portrays a lack of confidence or certainty, whereas in Japan and many other cultures, people often lower their eyes when speaking to a superior as a gesture of respect (Moran, 2007), and prolonged eye contact may be a sign of anger or aggression. I understand why the two Asian supervisors felt surprised because I also came from Asian; however, the cohort I studied was relatively culturally homogeneous; the different cultural backgrounds influence their understanding of their minority supervisors' expectations.

Scenario Two-Student's Engagement

When we talk about student engagement, a white instructor remarked, I'm sitting here, I'm rocking the whole time. I can't physically sit still, and so I'm always moving, but I'm actually engaged—I'm listening—and they were like, "You need to quit moving, you need to quit rocking, or fiddling."

Along with others, this instructor suggested that the pre-service teachers needed to get better at observing and interpreting students' behaviors. These novice teachers tended to direct too much of their attention to misbehavior and problems during teaching, causing them to give less attention to their lesson and children who were well behaved. Another white instructor commented,

> The thing that always makes me nervous is that they use their videos as evidence as of what the kids are doing wrong. Like, "I couldn't get them to sit down, they wouldn't listen, they're not listening." No, wait. She is listening to everything you're saying and she just answered all your questions, so what does it mean to be engaged? What is engagement?

If I just arrived in the USA, I will be surprised by their responses. In Asian culture, the students all need to sit still and not move around during class time or do their works, which shows their engagement to the lesson or task. However, I saw several times at a local school classroom, the kids sit on the rocking chair during a teacher's lecture or doing classwork.

According to ANT, everything is an agent that can influence itself and other actors, so supervisors' behaviors and expectations also shaped and affected pre-service teachers' performance and beliefs in the classroom network. As the minority supervisor, she/he has to mesh his/her beliefs of teaching with the goal of the program and unpacks ways in which collaborative inquiry and dialogue with student teachers.

Creating a Field for Symbolic Interaction

Foucault's idea of power is helpful to explore how the power shifts within the complicated triad relationship. In the classroom, mentor teachers have much power over pre-service teachers, especially when pre-service teachers are just beginning to access the field; they do not even have much authority over students. As time goes by, pre-service teachers get more power from mentor teachers and gain authority over students. On the other hand, power is productive and constitutive. Supervisors gain power from their previous experiences and background; in fact, their previous position and experiences confer their constructive comments to pre-service teachers. Also, a faculty member's current role and position in a university program bring them new power. Especially when they go into the field for observation, they have much more power than mentor teachers. On the other hand, they are powerless when they go into a classroom as a stranger.

I taught and worked with the 23 participants in the same teaching methods class. Every week in this class, we discussed the issues they met within their fields and the concerns about their teaching, their students, and the course works. These experiences played a crucial role in mediating our interactions and scaffolding their collaborative growth as teachers. In Bourdieu's terms, this creates a "field" where their practices came into virtual contact. As Bourdieu (2000) wrote:

> The field is the space of a game where thoughts and actions can be effected and modified without any physical contact or even any symbolic interaction, in particular in and through the relationship of comprehension. (p. 135)

According to Bourdieu's idea, when pre-service teachers and supervisors walk into a specific school, they have to follow that school's culture. Different local schools have different cultures. Some local schools are traditional; even as they partner with the university and accept the interns, they still keep distant from the university. Nevertheless, some local schools have more friendly relationships with the university's people. When a new person, supervisor, or pre-service teacher goes into a school with a relatively loose relationship with the university, they have to be very careful because they are guests in their classroom. While when a new person goes into a school with a close relationship with the university, they can walk in at any time and feel like they are a part of the school or classroom. Therefore, when going into local schools, supervisors and pre-service teachers have to pay attention to principals and teachers' attitudes, school culture, and implicit rules, and then they have to adjust themselves to the new environment, to build a good relationship with them and adapt to the new field. When the supervisor is a minority, this complicated situation may become worse, because the supervisor is not only outside of the school culture but also an outsider of this country's culture.

One of the advantages of thinking in terms of actor-networks is that we may get rid of "the tyranny of distance" or proximity. As Latour (1996) pointed out, elements which are close when disconnected may be infinitely remote if their connections are analyzed; conversely, elements which would appear as infinitely distant may be close when their connections are brought back into the picture (p. 4).

That is to say, actor-networks can transcend spatial limitations and relationships, which provides people with a notion of space that includes all types of relationships—both physical and social. I often have pre-service teachers, working in different field placements and with different mentor teachers and students, but encountered the same issues, had similar concerns and therefore had empathy for each other's situations. When we are in the same program and course, we could share similar feelings, which creates a field in which pre-service teachers and I could engage in symbolic interaction. The actor-network theory explores the idea that a minority supervisor who is unacquainted with mainstream American culture enters the school. She/he feels remote from others because of the differences in our cultures, positions, beliefs, attitudes, and experiences. However, she/he may be spatially close with the student teachers because they are staying in the same program for several semesters.

Growth as Both Instructor and Supervisor

As Bourdieu (1984) stated, "Academic capital is in fact the guaranteed product of the combined effects of cultural transmission by the family and cultural transmission by the school" (p. 23). Teacher education programs reinforce this kind of mainstream academic capital in their courses to cater to the atmosphere of current society and the school system. A person who comes from mainstream US culture more readily accepts the cultural capital and transfers it to the others; however, a person who comes from a different culture and class needs to spend some time learning and adapting to the cultural capital. I think it is dangerous if the teacher education program reinforces the mainstream academic capital to their students. They will find it challenging to meet all kinds of children's needs and feel frustrated when they meet some cultural conflict in the field. Therefore, one crucial element of my teaching philosophy is helping students become sensitive to and appreciative of cultural differences and diversity. After they graduate, many of my students will teach children from different countries, cultures, social statuses, and backgrounds. I always encourage students to share personal experiences and present non-judgmental comparisons among different lifestyles, cultures, and school systems. For example, in a teaching method course, I shared my experience as an immigrant parent and asked my students what they know about different families they have met. This type of discussion allows learners to connect their previous knowledge to "new" or "unknown" cultural backgrounds. I take great care to ensure that students feel comfortable in class and are not intimidated in any way. I strive to create a comfortable and respectful environment in the classroom and respond to each question thoughtfully and encouragingly to gradually become more confident and readier to face diversity issues.

In the focus group interview, the different background instructors and supervisors shared different ideas about using video as a tool for reflection and video-cued practice. One instructor suggested that the pre-service teacher and her instructor watch videos of her teaching together, identify examples of effective and ineffective teaching strategies, and practice practical techniques. Another instructor asked his students to share their videos with the whole class, talked about each video's practices, and encouraged classmates to offer their feedback. In this study, some participants said that their classmates' suggestions during role-play and reviewing the video were very beneficial. The videotaping assignment was a useful tool for facilitating communication between pre-service teachers and their instructors. Supervisors and pre-service teachers might ordinarily miss some of the details captured on video, but when a lesson is recorded, they can sit down together to review the video and discuss the lesson's issues. Also, the pre-service teachers can explain the context and share their thoughts about the lesson and their students with their supervisors, which can facilitate rethinking their lesson's meaning. As one instructor commented, but just practicing with each other. They get the sense of their own voice, they get the sense of their own tone. When they address interact they get sense of how important eye contact is. And where their presence is, where their bodies are in space. Where their bodies probably their bodies can come in the presences or come in the attention or engage, so I think it's (videos) really helpful.

Keeping the above considerations in mind, teacher educators need to make a serious effort to consider both the challenges and the productive applications of different pedagogical tools, such as video in teacher preparation. I learned a lot through different people's sharing, which helped me expand my knowledge about the teaching profession, discover new teaching technologies, and add innovative ideas to develop new courses and curricula in the future.

Conclusions and Implications

Creating new roles for supervisors and finding out ways to bring academic, practitioner, and community-based knowledge together in the teacher education process is a timely topic in higher education. Building on Foucault and Bourdieu's work, can better understand how power changes supervisors' and pre-service teachers' behaviors in field-based learning and field supervision. Additionally, it draws from Latour's Actor-Network Theory (ANT) theoretical lens to investigate how different actors, such as cultural factors, the university, the local schools, mentor teachers, supervisors, pre-service teachers, and their different background change their action to transform field experience. This chapter aims to bring minority supervisors' voices in exploring the impacts on pre-service teachers' professional development. These voices must be given a hearing in the current context because the minority faculty can advocate for cultural equality in the school settings. The implications for understanding issues and difficulties of minority educators encountered and how to most effectively implement strategies to use their diverse backgrounds and views to help future teachers.

Even bring different cultural backgrounds to go into the field may bring different expectations on the pre-service teacher's performance, minority supervisors can reexamine their roles and work responsibilities and cultivate dialogic spaces and interactive relationships in the supervision of student teachers. Additionally, as the university and program representative, the supervisor can create a useful field for symbolic interaction with their student teachers and add congruence between them and teacher preparation program goals. As the bridge between university and field, supervisors play a vital role in this process. Last but not least, as both instructor and supervisor, can scaffold pre-service teachers' learning from their field practices and help them make authentic connections—to the different class environments, to each other, to their community, and to themselves—is facilitated by being purposeful and present-focused, as well as well-informed and non-judgmental regarding processes of learning and teaching.

As a fieldwork supervisor, I have spent much time with students in schools, helping them work through problems and difficulties in their school settings. I can encourage them to apply what they have learned in the university as much as possible to the classroom's real world. Pre-service teacher's learning is best stimulated in situations that require a new perspective. Students should step into unfamiliar territory in the classroom by participating in a wide variety of in-class activities that may require them to move around the room, make impromptu presentations, or approach a debate topic from a viewpoint other than their own.

In this study, all the research participants and the researcher were in the same program at the same university. This specific location is a context that undoubtedly shaped the participants' and the researcher's experiences and ideas. Therefore, more experience and more research are needed to help determine the most effective way for instructors and supervisors to help students draw out their field experiences' most significant benefit. Teacher preparation programs also call for more practical and useful research, such as case studies or self-study, to deal with the problem between field experience and course work in the future.

References

Abdal-Haqq, I. (1997). Student learning and inquiry. In *Professional development schools: Weighing the evidence* (pp. 31–43). Corwin Press, INC.

Bourdieu, P. (1984). *Distinction: A social critique of the judgement of taste*. Harvard University Press.

Bourdieu, P. (2000). *Pascalian meditations*. Stanford University Press Polity Press.

Capraro, M. M., Capraro, R. M., & Helfeldt, J. (2010). Do differing types of field experiences make a difference in teacher candidates' perceived level of competence? *Teacher Education Quarterly, 37*(1).

Cuenca, A. (Ed.). (2012). *Supervising students teachers: Issues, perspectives and future directions*. Sense Publishers.

Darling-Hammond, L., & Bransford, J. (2005). *Preparing teachers for a changing world*. Jossey-Bass.

Elfer, C. J. (2012). Becoming a university supervisor. In *Supervising student teachers* (pp. 3–19). Sense Publishers.

Foucault, M. (1982). The subject and power. In H. L. Dreyfus & P. Rabinow (Eds.), *Michel Foucault: Beyond structuralism and hermeneutics* (pp. 208–226). The Harvester Press.

Garrett, H. J. (2012). Rethinking the spaces of supervision: Psychoanalytic considerations. In *Supervising student teachers* (pp. 157–168). Brill Sense.

Gumpertz, M., Durodoye, R., Griffith, E., & Wilson, A. (2017). Retention and promotion of women and underrepresented minority faculty in science and engineering at four large land grant institutions. *PLoS One, 12*(11), e0187285.

Hernández, P., Taylor, B. A., & McDowell, T. (2009). Listening to ethnic minority AAMFT approved supervisors: Reflections on their experiences as supervisees. *Journal of Systemic Therapies, 28*(1), 88–100.

Hodges, T. E., & Hodge, L. L. (2017). Unpacking personal identities for teaching mathematics within the context of prospective teacher education. *Journal of Mathematics Teacher Education, 20*(2), 101–118.

Latour, B. (1996). On actor-network theory. A few clarifications plus more than a few complications. *Dinish Philosophy Journal, 25*(3), 47–64.

Latour, B. (2005). *Reassembling the social: An introduction to actor-network-theory*. Oxford University Press.

Lawson, T., Çakmak, M., Gündüz, M., & Busher, H. (2015). Research on teaching practicum – A systematic review. *European Journal of Teacher Education, 38*(3), 392–407.

McRoy, R. G., Freeman, E. M., Logan, S. L., & Blackmon, B. (1986). Cross-cultural field supervision: Implications for social work education. *Journal of Social Work Education, 22*(1), 50–56.

Moran, R. T., Harris, P. R., & Moran, S. V. (2007). *Managing cultural differences: Global leadership strategies for the 21st century*. Managing Cultural Differences.

Ritter, J. K. (2012). Personal examples of self-study as a means of developing and enacting a pedagogy of supervision. In *Supervising student teachers* (pp. 139–155). Sense Publishers.

Sandholtz, J. H. (2011). Pre-service teachers' conceptions of effective and ineffective teaching practices. *Teacher Education Quarterly, 38*(3), 27–47.

Schmeichel, M. (2012). Good teaching? An examination of culturally relevant pedagogy as an equity practice. *Journal of Curriculum Studies, 44*(2), 211–231.

Strieker, T., Adams, M., Cone, N., Hubbard, D., & Lim, W. (2016). Supervision matters: Collegial, developmental and reflective approaches to supervision of pre-service teachers. *Cogent Education, 3*(1), 1251075.

Tobin, J., & Hsueh, Y. (2007). The poetics and pleasures of video ethnography of education. *Video research in the learning sciences*, 77–92.

Whittaker, J. A., Montgomery, B. L., & Acosta, V. G. M. (2015). Retention of underrepresented minority faculty: Strategic initiatives for institutional value proposition based on perspectives from a range of academic institutions. *Journal of Undergraduate Neuroscience Education, 13*(3), A136–A145.

Wilson, S. M., Floden, R. E., & Ferrini-Mundy, J. (2001). *Teacher preparation research: Current knowledge, gaps, and recommendations*. Center for the Study of Teaching and Policy.

Zambrana, R. E. (2018). *Toxic ivory towers: The consequences of work stress on underrepresented minority faculty*. Rutgers University Press.

Zambrana, R. E., Ray, R., Espino, M. M., Castro, C., Douthirt Cohen, B., & Eliason, J. (2015). "Don't leave us behind" the importance of mentoring for underrepresented minority faculty. *American Educational Research Journal, 52*(1), 40–72.

Zeichner, K. (2010). Rethinking the connections between campus courses and field experiences in college- and university-based teacher education. *Teacher Education., 61*(1–2), 89–99.

Bing Xiao is an associate Professor of Early Childhood Education of the Department of Teaching and Learning, Martha Dickerson Eriksson College of Education at Austin Peay State University (USA). She has been teaching in the Early Childhood program at high education since 2012 and taught a variety of ECE and Education courses. Xiao completed an M.A. in Psychology at Peking University and received her PH. D. in Early Childhood Education from the University of Georgia. Xiao maintains an active research agenda focusing on Early Childhood Education, Teacher Education, and Educational Technology. She has published articles in the Journal of Early Childhood Teacher Education, International Journal of Social Policy and Education, and The National Social Science Journal. One of her publications awarded the Taylor & Francis 2019 Journal of Early Childhood Teacher Education (JECTE) Outstanding Journal Article of the Year Award on a top-ranked peer-reviewed journal. She has also published the book, *Effective online teaching: Strategies, resources, technologies, and approaches as the first author*. Xiao is the director of Ready! for Kindergarten project for the Children's Reading Foundation and has served as a reviewer for several international and national journals, grants, and conferences.

Open Access This chapter is licensed under the terms of the Creative Commons Attribution 4.0 International License (http://creativecommons.org/licenses/by/4.0/), which permits use, sharing, adaptation, distribution and reproduction in any medium or format, as long as you give appropriate credit to the original author(s) and the source, provide a link to the Creative Commons license and indicate if changes were made.

The images or other third party material in this chapter are included in the chapter's Creative Commons license, unless indicated otherwise in a credit line to the material. If material is not included in the chapter's Creative Commons license and your intended use is not permitted by statutory regulation or exceeds the permitted use, you will need to obtain permission directly from the copyright holder.

Chapter 17
Foster Child of the Family: An Autoethnography of an International Minority Teacher Educator in a U.S. University

Yiting Chu

Abstract In this chapter, I used critical autoethnography to document my experiences as a minority teacher educator in a predominantly White institution (PWI) of higher education in the United States and examined how my intersectional identities as a foreign-born, non-White, non-native English speaking, teacher educator of Asian descent had influenced my practices as a multicultural educator and researcher. I used tenets of the critical race theory (CRT) and Asian critical theory (AsianCrit), in particular counterstorytelling and intersectionality, as analytic lens to frame my explorations of what it meant to be a minority educator in a foreign cultural and institutional context. Data in the form of reflective narratives drawn from my lived experiences and documents were analyzed and presented as counternarratives to explicate my intersectional identities and navigational strategies used to negotiate my position and practices in the often-limiting, PWI academic space. I ended the chapter with a call for more inclusive CRT and AsianCrit frameworks to understand the unique transnational lives and identities of minority educators in an increasingly global world. By sharing my autoethnographic recollections and counternarratives, I hope this chapter will serve as an empowering invitation for international minority scholars to join the collective endeavor to advance the conversation and transform higher education towards a more diverse, inclusive, and equitable space.

Introduction and Objective

I was born in China and came to the United States for graduate studies in education. I am part of the majority ethnic group and culture, the Han Chinese, the largest by population among the 56 officially recognized ethnic groups in China (Joniak-Luthi, 2017). Therefore, one of my first encounters in the U.S. was to (un)learn the

Y. Chu (✉)
University of Louisiana Monroe, Monroe, LA, USA
e-mail: chu@ulm.edu

privileged perceptions and experiences that I was not aware of until then as a member of the dominant ethnic and cultural group in my home country. While I did not have to view myself through a racial or ethnic lens being a member of a group that made up more than 90% of the Chinese population, similar to the experiences of many White Americans in the U.S. (DiAngelo, 2018), and did not consciously self-identify as Asian, coming to the United States meant a transition from majority to minority mindset with the assigned Asian (American) identity (Lee & Ramakrishnan, 2020) and the racial/ethnic minority and people of color labels, both of which were novel to me.

I learned in graduate school about the racist history and racial relationships in the U.S. and its racialized understandings of citizenship that permeated across social institutions, including education (Brodkin, 1998; Jacobson, 1999; Ladson-Billings, 2004), and started developing a racial consciousness both in my professional work and my daily life as I was *Asianized* (Iftikar & Museus, 2018). Similar to what many minority scholars have reported, while I have chosen to accept such labels as "Asian American" or "minority" as formal descriptions in public settings, they are "loose garments" that can be readily removed in private life (Hernandez et al., 2015). Therefore, while I will check the box of "Asian (American)" when filling forms unless "International" or "Non-U.S." is an option, I certainly am not an Asian American in the legal, citizenship sense and do not have a strong "Asian American" identity. Nor can I say that I understand what it means to be an Asian in the U.S. despite the many cultural values and practices and memories that I share with this diverse group (Lee, 2009).

Upon completion of my doctoral study in a research university in the Pacific Northwest, I was fortunate enough to accept a tenure-track faculty position in a mid-size public university in a Southern state. While the city the university is located has a Black-majority population and is geographically close to several of the most racially and linguistically diverse cities in the country, the institution itself is comprised of mostly White students, faculty, staff, and administrators. Therefore, I am a minority not only in the cultural and legal senses as a non-citizen in a foreign country, but also in the institutional sense as a non-White faculty of color who is "foreign" to a predominantly White institution (PWI).

Because I was raised and primarily socialized outside the United States until graduate school, my experiences and knowledge as an educator are not typically represented or even expected in the U.S. higher education contexts. Additionally, literature documenting the stories of foreign minority faculty members vis-à-vis domestic minority faculty remains limited (Hernandez et al., 2015; Mamiseishvili, 2010). Therefore, in this chapter I used autoethnographic narratives and reflections to explicate my experiences and intersectional identities as a foreign-born, non-White, non-native English speaking, pre-tenure teacher educator and researcher in a PWI in the United States. Adopting a critical race theory framework, I analyzed how the overlapping "foreign/minority" status shaped my practices and explained the strategies I used to navigate and resist the White-dominant academic and institutional norms. I hope that sharing my experiential knowledge and counternarratives will empower and invite minority educators facing similar racialized experiences and struggles in foreign cultural and educational settings to join the collective transformation endeavors.

Theoretical Framework

I draw on critical race theory (CRT) and two related constructs, intersectionality and Asian critical theory (AsianCrit), in framing my analysis. The CRT framework centers analysis on race and racism while recognizing the intersectional relationships among racism and other forms of oppression, such as sexism, classism, and nativism, across contexts (Crenshaw, 1991; Delgado & Stefancic, 2017). AsianCrit builds on and expands the CRT framework to examine White supremacy, systemic racism, and other forms of subordination as they manifest among the Asian American lives and experiences (Museus & Iftikar, 2014). All three constructs are helpful to illuminate my racialized experiences and identities as a minority educator of Asian descent in a foreign context intersecting on race, language, immigration, and professional status.

Critical Race Theory

The critical race theory framework purports that racism is pervasive and endemic in the United States to the extent that White-centrism and -dominance are often considered as the social "norm" and "ordinary." CRT also recognizes the intersection of racism with other forms of oppression that operate in such dimensions of gender, social class, and language (Crenshaw, 1991; Solórzano & Yosso, 2002) and challenges the research paradigm and practices that privilege the experiences and perspectives of the dominant social groups (Ladson-Billings, 1998; Ledesma & Calderón, 2015). CRT thus values the experiential knowledge and counternarratives of people of color and other minoritized groups that are historically excluded and marginalized from the dominant, master narratives (Aronson et al., 2020; Brown & Au, 2014; Solórzano & Yosso, 2002).

Ladson-Billings and Tate (1995) first introduced the CRT framework to the study of education from legal studies where it originated (Bell, 1980; Crenshaw, 1991; Delgado, 1989). The CRT framework has thereafter been applied in examining White supremacy and racism as they pertain to educational policies, programs, and practices, and impact on the learning opportunities, experiences, and outcomes of individuals from minoritized and marginalized groups in K-16 education settings (Annamma et al., 2013; Brayboy, 2005; Gillborn et al., 2018; Ledesma & Calderón, 2015; Milner, 2013; Solorzano & Yosso, 2001; Yosso, 2005).

Delgado and Stefancic (2017) offer a set of essential tenets of CRT, two of which are in particular relevant to this chapter: counternarrative and intersectionality. Counternarrative, or counterstorytelling, empowers people of color to challenge the dominant, White-centric perspectives and majoritarian interpretations of issues and events with their own voices and stories (Delgado, 1989; Solórzano & Yosso, 2002). This notion of counterstorytelling is important for minority educators and scholars to disrupt the White-dominant academic spaces and ways of knowing by elaborating their struggles and complex identities that are often silenced and marginalized. Intersectionality, as explained in depth below, refers to the ways in which racism intersects with other forms of structural oppression and discrimination, such as sexism, homophobia, and classism (Crenshaw, 1991). This orientation compels me to ask how my intersected experiences of race, nationality, gender, and language have shaped my position and informed my practices as a minority educator in foreign cultural and institutional contexts.

Intersectionality

Intersectionality contends that discrimination and marginalization based on socially and culturally constructed categories, such as race, ethnicity, language, social class, sexual orientation, gender, and nationality, do not operate in isolation. Instead, these forms of oppression intersect with one another to collectively constitute systems of prejudice, stereotype, suppression, and exclusion that render the lives of certain individuals and groups subordinated across different social and institutional contexts, such as women living in poverty and LGBTQ people of color (Collins & Bilge, 2016; Crenshaw, 1991; Ladson-Billings, 1998). While the intersectionality framework was originally created to conceptualize the lives of Black women, it has been applied to examine the racialized and gendered experiences of other minoritized and marginalized groups, including male of color, and the intersected systems of oppression they face (Griffin et al., 2014). The intersection of my nation of origin/citizenship, race, and non-native English-speaking status contextualizes how I negotiate my identities and how I am perceived as a minority educator and researcher in a PWI in the U.S.: while I am an insider of the academia in the sense of having earned graduate degrees and becoming a college professor, my foreign origin, non-White presence, and non-native English accent inevitably signal me as an outsider to the dominant U.S. society as a "forever foreigner" (Tuan, 1998). Intersectionality is thus a helpful construct to analyze the overlapping function of racism, nativism, and xenophobia that collectively affect my experiences as a minority educator of color in a foreign country and in the predominantly White and English-dominant culture of the U.S. universities (Stanley, 2006).

Asian Critical Theory

Iftikar and Museus (2018), building on the CRT scholarship, propose an AsianCrit framework with seven interrelated tenets:

- *Asianization* as a result of White supremacy and racialization that positions Asian Americans as perpetual foreigners, yellow perils, model and deviant minorities, emasculated men, and hypersexualized women;
- *Transnational contexts* that situate Asian American experiences affected by racism and White supremacy within broader socio-economic and -political structures at the global level;
- *(Re)constructive history* aims to foreground Asian American voices in the process of reconstructing historical narratives in the United States;
- *Strategic (anti)essentialism* reiterates the argument that race is socially constructed and challenges the ways in which Asian Americans are essentialized as a monolithic group with their inter- and intra-group diversities being reduced into a singular set of racialized characteristics;
- *Intersectionality* examines the intersecting forms of oppression that shape the Asian American experiences and identities;
- *Story, theory, and praxis* highlight the lived experiences and experiential knowledge of Asian Americans as alternative epistemological perspectives to the dominant, White narratives that can inform the development of transformative theories and praxis;
- Commitment to *social justice* aims to end all forms of oppressions, exploitation, and dehumanization.

Similar to the original CRT and derived frameworks, such as LatCrit (Solorzano & Yosso, 2001) and DisCrit (Annamma et al., 2013), AsianCrit bears a "methodological nationalism" standpoint (Shahjahan & Kezar, 2013) that is primarily situated within the U.S. context and centers on the lives and oppression of Asian *Americans*. As such, much AsianCrit scholarship falls short of examining the complex experiences of foreign-born immigrants/non-U.S. citizens who are (and perceived as) of Asian descent and subject to the many stereotypes, prejudice, and discrimination resulting from the ways in which Asian Americans are racialized in the United States (Lee, 2009). Nor does this framework fully take account of the exclusion and alienation based on markers that are unique and perhaps more salient to their identities, such as language, immigration status, and religion.

Iftikar and Museus (2018) recognized the limitations of the AsianCrit framework in attending to the impact of language and the differences between Asian Americans born and raised in the U.S. and recent international Asian immigrants. A few studies have also problematized the U.S.-centric orientation of the CRT scholarship and started applying the CRT framework in analyzing racialization and racism in global histories and transnational contexts (Busey & Coleman-King, 2020; Yao et al., 2019; Zhu et al., 2019). Yet our understandings of non-U.S.-domestic minority teachers' lives and trajectories in a foreign cultural, linguistic, and educational context remain limited. Therefore, I shared in this chapter my experiences as an Asian, non-native-English-speaking, minority educator in a PWI setting in a foreign (the U.S.) culture with the hope of advancing the conversation and pushing the CRT and AsianCrit frameworks to be more inclusive and equitable.

Methodology

This chapter is a critical autoethnography (Chang, 2008) that primarily draws from my reflective narratives and lived experiences. Autoethnography is both a qualitative research method through which researchers collect and analyze their autobiographical data and the product this process creates (Hughes & Pennington, 2017). Similar to other qualitative inquiries, autoethnography focuses on the experiences and perspectives of the participants, i.e., the researchers themselves, so that meanings are constructed out of the researchers' lived experiences and presented from their emic point of view (Chang, 2008). The ethnographic orientation of autoethnography allows researchers to situate their personal experiences within the cultural communities and practices of which they are members and to illuminate various aspects of a culture through embodied and affective narratives (Ellis et al., 2010). Critical autoethnography works well with the CRT framework as they both empower me to critically reflect on and convey my lived experiences and intersectional identities in the form of counternarratives (Solórzano & Yosso, 2002) as a minority educator negotiating foreign cultural and institutional contexts. As such, I hope to provide an account that not only has meanings for my own reflection and growth but also challenges the pervasive White-centric norms and narratives ingrained in the U.S. cultural and academic spaces.

I followed the conventions of autoethnographic research by collecting written narratives as the primary data sources (Chang, 2008; Ellis et al., 2010). The narratives were drawn from an ongoing, reflective journal I have been writing since 2017, with the purposes of recording critical incidents at work that were of significance to my practices and identities as a teacher educator, as well as my emotions and reflections in making sense of these events. Additional reflective writing was created for the purpose of this research when I reviewed my journal in preparing for this chapter. I also added explanatory notes and memos to some of the original observations and interpretations in the process of re-reading and reflecting. This activity added an initial analytic layer to my documented personal experiences and narratives (Ellis et al., 2010).

I used an inductive, iterative approach to coding the data and building meanings from the narratives across time and incidents, adopting the techniques of qualitative data analysis (Miles et al., 2019). When reading my writings, I paid attention to incidents that had shaped my experiential understandings (Delgado, 1989) of race, ethnicity, language, and gender in the U.S. and the intersectional systems of oppression that positioned me as a minority teacher in a foreign country/culture and a PWI context. Open codes were created and constantly refined and later clustered under three emerging categories (Miles et al., 2019): teaching, research, and service. Categorizing data in this way prompted me to see the multifaceted impact of the "minority" status on my practices and identities as a teacher educator and researcher as I navigated the dominant academic and institutional spaces, leading to common themes across categories (Chang, 2008; Miles et al., 2019).

The validity of autoethnographic accounts is established by illuminating how others might experience similar personal and cultural experiences. That is, relating the self to others and gaining cultural meanings out of personal understandings, which is the ethnographic nature of autoethnography (Chang, 2008; Ellis et al., 2010). Ladson-Billings (2014) also cautions against writing about personal stories that are merely "vent or rant or be an exhibitionist regarding one's own racial struggle." Instead, Ladson-Billings argues that principled arguments should be made in order to "advance larger concerns or help us understand how law or policy is operating" (2014, p. 42). Therefore, I strove to situate my personal narratives and unique experiences within the CRT-informed literature about the challenges and struggles of minority and international educators throughout my data analysis and presentation of findings (Ellis et al., 2010).

Findings and Discussion

I this section, I presented findings around the three areas identified from the inductive analysis and most relevant to my work as a university faculty member, teaching, research, and service, with a focus on the first. I explored the tensions arising from me being a minority, multicultural teacher educator and researcher practicing within a foreign and PWI context. I am simultaneously invisible and highly visible, though often for different reasons and under different circumstances: in a national context where education is locally grounded, my non-citizen status and most of my non-- U.S. experiences are not valued as legitimate sources of knowledge unless when conversation about cultural diversity is evoked or when an "international" perspective is requested, which then makes my presence super visible. In a PWI in the U.S. South where the White bodies and White ways of knowing are the norms, my mere presence as a minority/international *other* and my non-White pedagogy are constantly scrutinized and even questioned by my colleagues and students, despite my expertise and qualifications as an educator and researcher. In addition, the majority of the (White) faculty members either receive at least one degree from or spend decades teaching in the university. This institutional context adds yet another layer of foreignness that positions me as a "minority" outsider who is new to the institution as a junior, non-tenured faculty member of color. While nobody ever comes out declaring that this is a White territory, it soon becomes clear that I am, as one White senior colleague once told me, the "foster child" of the family, who allows me to temporarily enter *their* space, the *White* space.

Teaching

The first task I was charged as a new faculty member was to develop and teach an undergraduate course in cultural diversity and education, which was my research area and was something I was very passionate about. This course was needed for accreditation purposes per the diversity requirements of the accrediting agency and would be a required course for all teacher education major students. Therefore, my background in multicultural education became visible to my colleagues and valuable to fulfill this task. Meanwhile, this expectation also constituted a particular kind of recognition of my expertise that simultaneously placed specific limits on the kind of work and identity options available to me. I was given detailed instructions on what to be included in the curriculum and what the department considered the most relevant topics to be taught. I listened carefully and passionately added curricular and pedagogical ideas I thought were important to the state histories and local contexts. I remember negotiating with my senior colleagues and administrators on including challenging topics and counternarratives, such as slavery and racist legacy of the South, a local celebrity and his family's anti-LGBTQ comments, environmental and health equity, and the ongoing refugee and immigration crises. I eventually learned to keep silent in many occasions after these ideas and my non-White ways of knowing were repeatedly interrupted or even dismissed and after being told how high the stakes were for this course. In other words, while my qualifications as a diversity scholar, i.e., a Ph.D. in multicultural education, was generally recognized, my embodied professional knowledge was rendered illegitimate and irrelevant in this specific context (Delgado & Stefancic, 2017). Instead, I was asked to observe a colleague's classroom that supposedly showcased the desired ways of teaching and classroom management that to me were reproducing and reinforcing the dominant curricular narratives (Brown & Au, 2014) and power hierarchy between teachers and students. As a non-citizen, pre-tenure junior faculty member new to the institution, I had no choice but to comply with and reinforce the departmental and institutional expectations that were oppressing and punitive in nature. However, rather than enforcing institutional norms and majoritarian policies and succumbing to the dominant culture of teaching, I managed to integrate social justice issues in my teaching and invited guest speakers and community members knowledgeable about local histories. I also encouraged students to voice their interests and contribute to class policies, assignments, and activities as counternarratives (Solórzano & Yosso, 2002) so that they could feel that they legitimately owned and took responsibility for their learning. As such, I actively carved space for powerful yet subtle resistance, or "wiggle room"—tailoring practice within the parameters of the local circumstances (Erickson, 2014)—so that I could keep true to my pedagogical beliefs and enrich student learning without overtly defying university policies.

In addition to this multicultural education course, I designed all my courses as vehicles through which students were prompted to see the relevance and significance of cultural diversity, social justice, and (in)equity in education and educational research. I consciously embedded in my teaching multicultural experiences, marginalized and oppressed perspectives, and counternarratives, which students might not otherwise be invited to think had the courses been taught by members of the dominant group. I adopted a pedagogy I called teaching with and for multiple perspectives that not only incorporated different viewpoints in teaching materials and activities but also empowered students with diverse backgrounds to share their points of view in an equitable and empowering learning environment (Gay, 2013). I engaged students to read multicultural authors and analyze research featuring marginalized groups so that they developed understandings of schooling opportunities and outcomes from a variety of standpoints (Clarke & Whitney, 2009; Marcus & Stoddard, 2009). I used my own lived experiences as an entry point to introduce issues related to immigration, linguistic diversity, and the internationalization of higher education and invited students to share their own experiential knowledge and community cultural wealth (Solórzano & Yosso, 2002; Yosso, 2005). Students learned to listen to one another's opinions, debate with evidence and respect, and deliberate for solutions in a civic manner (Hess & McAvoy, 2014). The active participation and collaboration allowed my students to develop not only the cognitive ability to interpret issues and concepts from multiple points of view but also an empathic faculty to relate to and appreciate diverse experiences, fostering the much-needed cross-cultural competencies in a multicultural society and global world (Banks, 2017). While I was able to push the curricular and pedagogical boundaries and challenge the institutional "norm" through my praxis, I often received student comments, via both informal channels and official end-of-course evaluation, suggesting that some of the required readings and activities were "not relevant" or "biased" because they exposed White privilege and racial oppression.

As a minority teacher, I have to endure constant gaze from colleagues and students and make the challenging decisions associated with how to present myself in the classroom. That is, do I teach as an authoritative instructor that is closer to the dominant image of college professor or teach in ways that are built on authentic relationships with students that would break the power hierarchy in classroom while supporting student learning? Would the second choice compromise my authority and place me in a position at odds with my colleagues? This feeling of estrangement escalates as my English accent is constantly judged, both explicitly and implicitly, by my colleagues and students. Being perceived as a foreigner and non-native-English speaker, my authority as a professor has already been questioned by some students. In my undergraduate class, some students were evidently surprised to see an Asian man teaching an education course in the U.S. South. During office hours, I was frequently asked "Where are you from?" Coming across this question so many times, I knew exactly what they meant and what answer they expected to hear. "Seattle," I would say, quickly adding "I received my Ph.D. from the University of Washington, Seattle." "But where are you *originally* from?" was often the next question, which was a constant reminder of me being perceived as a "forever foreigner" (Tuan, 1998) whose legitimacy and legality of presence, intersecting with my ethnic and linguistic identities, required frequent interrogation in the White dominant professional and institutional spaces (Museus & Iftikar, 2014; Yoon, 2019). Evidently, I am required to explicitly define "what I am" and how I stand with regard to immigration or citizenship status as if my degree and experiences alone are insufficient to establish my credibility as a college professor.

Research and Service

In many U.S. universities, conducting research and publishing research works are critical to faculty members' promotion and tenure consideration. While the "publish or perish" pressure in the teaching-focused institution where I work is not as strong as in research universities, there is an unambiguous emphasis on research projects leading to external funding, which shapes the kind of research projects faculty members are expected to pitch for (Belgrave et al., 2019). As a multicultural educator, I center my research on issues surrounding power relationships in knowledge construction that challenges the established paradigms of knowing (Banks, 1993). My research also has a strong focus on equity and social justice, which requires me to spend time with my participants in the communities, building trusting relationship with them so that they feel safe to share with me their experiences. This is important for me as a social justice-oriented qualitative researcher (Solórzano & Yosso, 2002). I also carry out my work in close collaboration with educators at the ground level and integrate my research with practitioner knowledge through partnership with schools and school districts. The deep participant engagement and investment in the communities come at a price as it takes longer to produce research outputs, which is at odds with the institutional expectations on the number of grants and publications valuable for tenure considerations.

While I do not necessarily share the same experiences as Asian Americans, the model minority myth (Lee, 2009; Ng et al., 2007) can work to my advantage by positioning me as someone with academic excellence and as a high-achieving researcher among my colleagues. However, my Asian presence in the school was often unexpected, if not suspicious, in a (White) place where virtually nobody looked like me (Museus & Iftikar, 2014; Tuan, 1998). When I was conducting research in local schools, I would be introduced by my White female colleagues to the school leaders, teachers, and staff. Even weeks into the project, I would still be questioned "How can I help you?" by random school staff when I was walking in the hallway or waiting for my informants in a classroom. I was also often asked by students if I was the father of one of the students, who was Japanese American and the only student of Asian descent in that rural school. Yoon (2019) characterized similar haunting experiences when she was conducting research in the field as an Asian American woman. This incidence of "being the only one" and seeing "nobody like me" in the classroom, in the research site, and in university meetings has been the norm for me most of the time.

Minority faculty members in higher education are often called upon to carry heavy service loads (Guillaume & Apodaca, 2022; Martinez & Welton, 2017). They also feel a need to mentor minority students who have to go through similar challenges in the academia (Acevedo-Gil & Madrigal-Garcia, 2018; Griffin et al., 2014). I was placed, within the first month into the job, on the diversity committee of the department that was chaired by a White female colleague. I again became highly visible and *Asianized* (Iftikar & Museus, 2018) and my presence seemed desirable and even essential whenever there was a need for "diversity," such as a culturally responsive teaching workshop for teacher candidates or diversity seminar for college instructors. My fellow White colleagues would turn to me and expect me to speak as a "representative" of the "minority" or "international" community. I have also been asked to serve on many other committees in order to be shown as living evidence of how diverse the faculty is, often for recruiting and marketing purposes, both of which are of prime interests to the school (Bell, 1980). I am frequently sought by racial minority and female students who are less familiar with the conventions of academia and bring with them less, quoting one of my graduate students, "cultural capital" (Yosso, 2005). I feel a sense of responsibility to mentor these students who similarly find it challenging to see someone who look like them and share their struggles in the White dominant institutional space.

Epilogue

When I was preparing for the first draft of this chapter in June 2020, I attended an event at my institution that aimed to promote diversity, equity, and inclusion amid the aftermath of the murder of George Floyd and in response to the outrage invoked by two faculty members' racist posts found in social media within a week. University leaders gathered together with students, faculty, staff, alumni, and community members to reaffirm the institution's commitment to embracing diversity, deemed as "one of the university's core values." The event started and ended with ceremonies that were associated with one particular religion to which I did not subscribe. Everyone was invited to stand up and participate. I was, once again, reminded that I was the foster child who had yet to be part of the family.

I share my journey and reflections in this chapter as I continue to work as a pre-tenured, minority educator in foreign national, cultural, and institutional contexts. While my experiences are similar to what scholars called "perpetual foreigner" facing many Asian Americans (Ng et al., 2007; Tuan, 1998), my perspectives are unique to my positionality as a foreign-born, English-learning, immigrant educator who had to navigate the majority-turned-minority status in addition to the racialized Asian American label. While the AsianCrit framework recognizes the transnational experiences and memories of Asian Americans due to immigration and colonial histories (Iftikar & Museus, 2018; Yoon, 2019), expanding the framework is necessary given the increasing presence of international minority teachers in K-16 education settings and the internationalization of higher education around the world (Dolby & Rahman, 2017; Dunn, 2011). An expanded framework that attends to the transnational trajectories and intersectional identities of educators within and across divergent contexts will add the needed complexity to the CRT scholarship and help advance the CRT-informed praxis in a global world (Busey & Coleman-King, 2020; Ledesma & Calderón, 2015).

Minority teachers contribute to the diversity at schools and serve as role models for minority students (Jayusi & Bekerman, 2019). In an era of globalization and transnational migration (Banks, 2017), it is an imperative to pay greater attention and respond to the struggles of minority teachers living and practicing in foreign cultures. While minority educators are often expected to assimilate to the majority cultural and educational settings, transformative policy changes at the institutional level need to be made to structurally include them. It is also important for minority teachers from all spectrum of experiences and contexts to engage in critical studies that collectively add to the repertoire of counter narratives. I hope that sharing my stories can help other international minority teachers feel empowered to claim their voices and to fight towards more diverse, inclusive, and socially just spaces in educational institutions through transformative and engaged praxis.

Findings of this chapter call for more inclusive Critical Race Theory (CRT) and AsianCrit frameworks to recognize the unique perspectives and lived experiences of international minority educators. An expanded framework that attends to the transnational trajectories and intersectional identities of educators within and across divergent contexts will add the needed complexity to the CRT scholarship and help advance the CRT-informed praxis in a global world. I hope this chapter will serve as an empowering invitation for international minority scholars to contribute to the collective counter narratives and to transform education towards a more diverse, inclusive, and equitable space through transformative scholarship and engaged praxis.

References

Acevedo-Gil, N., & Madrigal-Garcia, Y. (2018). Mentoring among Latina/o scholars: Enacting spiritual activism to navigate academia. *American Journal of Education, 124*(3), 313–344. https://doi.org/10.1086/697212

Annamma, S. A., Connor, D., & Ferri, B. (2013). Dis/ability critical race studies (DisCrit): Theorizing at the intersections of race and dis/ability. *Race Ethnicity and Education, 16*(1), 1–31. https://doi.org/10.1080/13613324.2012.730511

Aronson, B., Meyers, L., & Winn, V. (2020). "Lies my teacher [educator] still tells": Using critical race counternarratives to disrupt whiteness in teacher education. *The Teacher Educator, 4*, 1–23. https://doi.org/10.1080/08878730.2020.1759743

Banks, J. A. (1993). The canon debate, knowledge construction, and multicultural education. *Educational Researcher, 22*(5), 4–14.

Banks, J. A. (Ed.). (2017). *Citizenship education and global migration: Implications for theory, research, and teaching*. American Educational Research Association.

Belgrave, F. Z., Moore, M. P., & Douglas-Glenn, N. E. (2019). Barriers and assets to external funding for African American faculty. *International Journal of Qualitative Studies in Education, 4*, 1–20. https://doi.org/10.1080/09518398.2019.1659443

Bell, D. A. (1980). Brown v. Board of education and the interest-convergence dilemma. *Harvard Law Review, 93*(3), 518–533. https://doi.org/10.2307/1340546

Brayboy, B. M. J. (2005). Toward a tribal critical race theory in education. *The Urban Review, 37*(5), 425–446. https://doi.org/10.1007/s11256-005-0018-y

Brodkin, K. (1998). *How Jews became white folks and what that says about race in America*. Rutgers University Press.

Brown, A. L., & Au, W. (2014). Race, memory, and master narratives: A critical essay on U.S. curriculum history. *Curriculum Inquiry, 44*(3), 358–389. https://doi.org/10.1111/curi.12049

Busey, C. L., & Coleman-King, C. (2020). *All around the world same song: Transnational anti-Black racism and new (and old) directions for critical race theory in educational research*. Urban Education. https://doi.org/10.1177/0042085920927770

Chang, H. (2008). *Autoethnography as method: Developing qualitative inquiry*. Left Coast Press.

Clarke, L. W., & Whitney, E. (2009). Walking in their shoes: Using multiple-perspectives texts as a bridge to critical literacy. *The Reading Teacher, 62*(6), 530–534. https://doi.org/10.1598/rt.62.6.7

Collins, P. H., & Bilge, S. (2016). *Intersectionality*. Polity.

Crenshaw, K. (1991). Mapping the margins: Intersectionality, identity politics, and violence against women of color. *Stanford Law Review, 43*(6), 1241–1299. https://doi.org/10.2307/1229039

Delgado, R. (1989). Storytelling for oppositionists and others: A plea for narrative. *Michigan Law Review, 87*(8), 2411–2441. https://doi.org/10.2307/1289308

Delgado, R., & Stefancic, J. (2017). *Critical race theory: An introduction* (3rd ed.). NYU Press.

DiAngelo, R. (2018). *White fragility: Why it's so hard for white people to talk about racism*. Beacon Press.

Dolby, N., & Rahman, A. (2017). Research in international education. *Review of Educational Research, 78*(3), 676–726. https://doi.org/10.3102/0034654308320291

Dunn, A. H. (2011). Global village versus culture shock: The recruitment and preparation of foreign teachers for U.S. urban schools. *Urban Education, 46*(6), 1379–1410. https://doi.org/10.1177/0042085911413152

Ellis, C., Adams, T. E., & Bochner, A. P. (2010). Autoethnography: An overview. *Forum Qualitative Social Research/Sozialforschung, 12*(1), 10. https://doi.org/10.17169/fqs-12.1.1589

Erickson, F. (2014). Scaling down: A modest proposal for practice-based policy research in teaching. *Education Policy Analysis Archives, 22*(9), 1–11. https://doi.org/10.14507/epaa.v22n9.2014

Gay, G. (2013). Teaching to and through cultural diversity. *Curriculum Inquiry, 43*(1), 48–70. https://doi.org/10.1111/curi.12002

Gillborn, D., Warmington, P., & Demack, S. (2018). Quantcrit: Education, policy, 'big data' and principles for a critical race theory of statistics. *Race Ethnicity and Education, 21*(2), 158–179. https://doi.org/10.1080/13613324.2017.1377417

Griffin, R. A., Ward, L., & Phillips, A. R. (2014). Still flies in buttermilk: Black male faculty, critical race theory, and composite counterstorytelling. *International Journal of Qualitative Studies in Education, 27*(10), 1354–1375. https://doi.org/10.1080/09518398.2013.840403

Guillaume, R. O., & Apodaca, E. C. (2022). Early career faculty of color and promotion and tenure: The intersection of advancement in the academy and cultural taxation. *Race Ethnicity and Education, 25*(4), 546–563. https://doi.org/10.1080/13613324.2020.1718084

Hernandez, K.-A. C., Ngunjiri, F. W., & Chang, H. (2015). Exploiting the margins in higher education: A collaborative autoethnography of three foreign-born female faculty of color. *International Journal of Qualitative Studies in Education, 28*(5), 533–551. https://doi.org/10.1080/09518398.2014.933910

Hess, D., & McAvoy, P. (2014). *The political classroom: Evidence and ethics in democratic education*. Routledge.

Hughes, S. A., & Pennington, J. L. (2017). *Autoethnography: Process, product, and possibility for critical social research*. SAGE.

Iftikar, J. S., & Museus, S. D. (2018). On the utility of Asian critical (AsianCrit) theory in the field of education. *International Journal of Qualitative Studies in Education, 31*(10), 935–949. https://doi.org/10.1080/09518398.2018.1522008

Jacobson, M. F. (1999). *Whiteness of a different color: European immigrants and the alchemy of race*. Harvard University Press.

Jayusi, W., & Bekerman, Z. (2019). Yes, we can! Palestinian-Israeli teachers in Jewish-Israeli schools. *Journal of Teacher Education, 71*(3), 319–331. https://doi.org/10.1177/0022487119849869

Joniak-Luthi, A. (2017). *The Han: China's diverse majority*. University of Washington Press.

Ladson-Billings, G. (1998). Just what is critical race theory and what's it doing in a nice field like education? *International Journal of Qualitative Studies in Education, 11*(1), 7–24. https://doi.org/10.1080/095183998236863

Ladson-Billings, G. (2004). Culture versus citizenship: The challenge of racialized citizenship in the United States. In J. A. Banks (Ed.), *Diversity and citizenship education: Global perspectives* (pp. 99–126). Jossey-Bass.

Ladson-Billings, G. (2014). Critical race theory—What it is not! In M. Lynn & A. D. Dixson (Eds.), *Handbook of critical race theory in education* (pp. 34–47). Routledge.

Ladson-Billings, G., & Tate, W. F. (1995). Toward a critical race theory of education. *Teachers College Record, 97*(1), 47–68.

Ledesma, M. C., & Calderón, D. (2015). Critical race theory in education: A review of past literature and a look to the future. *Qualitative Inquiry, 21*(3), 206–222. https://doi.org/10.1177/1077800414557825

Lee, S. J. (2009). *Unraveling the "model minority" stereotype: Listening to Asian American youth* (2nd ed.). Teachers College Press.

Lee, J., & Ramakrishnan, K. (2020). Who counts as Asian. *Ethnic and Racial Studies, 43*(10), 1733–1756. https://doi.org/10.1080/01419870.2019.1671600

Mamiseishvili, K. (2010). Foreign-born women faculty work roles and productivity at research universities in the United States. *Higher Education, 60*(2), 139–156. https://doi.org/10.1007/s10734-009-9291-0

Marcus, A. S., & Stoddard, J. D. (2009). The inconvenient truth about teaching history with documentary film: Strategies for presenting multiple perspectives and teaching controversial issues. *The Social Studies, 100*(6), 279–284. https://doi.org/10.1080/00377990903283957

Martinez, M. A., & Welton, A. D. (2017). Straddling cultures, identities, and inconsistencies: Voices of pre-tenure faculty of color in educational leadership. *Journal of Research on Leadership Education, 12*(2), 122–142. https://doi.org/10.1177/1942775115606177

Miles, M. B., Huberman, A. M., & Saldaña, J. (2019). *Qualitative data analysis: A methods sourcebook* (4th ed.). SAGE.

Milner, H. R. (2013). Analyzing poverty, learning, and teaching through a critical race theory lens. *Review of Research in Education, 37*(1), 1–53. https://doi.org/10.3102/0091732x12459720

Museus, S. D., & Iftikar, J. S. (2014). Asian critical theory. In M. Y. Danico (Ed.), *Asian American society: An encyclopedia*. SAGE.

Ng, J. C., Lee, S. S., & Pak, Y. K. (2007). Contesting the model minority and perpetual foreigner stereotypes: A critical review of literature on Asian Americans in education. *Review of Research in Education, 31*(1), 95–130. https://doi.org/10.3102/0091732x07300046095

Shahjahan, R. A., & Kezar, A. J. (2013). Beyond the "national container": Addressing methodological nationalism in higher education research. *Educational Researcher, 42*(1), 20–29. https://doi.org/10.3102/0013189x12463050

Solorzano, D. G., & Yosso, T. J. (2001). Critical race and LatCrit theory and method: Counter-storytelling. *International Journal of Qualitative Studies in Education, 14*(4), 471–495. https://doi.org/10.1080/09518390110063365

Solórzano, D. G., & Yosso, T. J. (2002). Critical race methodology: Counter-storytelling as an analytical framework for education research. *Qualitative Inquiry, 8*(1), 23–44. https://doi.org/10.1177/107780040200800103

Stanley, C. A. (2006). Coloring the academic landscape: Faculty of color breaking the silence in predominantly white colleges and universities. *American Educational Research Journal, 43*(4), 701–736. https://doi.org/10.3102/00028312043004701

Tuan, M. (1998). *Forever foreigners or honorary whites?* Rutgers University Press.

Yao, C. W., George Mwangi, C. A., & Malaney Brown, V. K. (2019). Exploring the intersection of transnationalism and critical race theory: A critical race analysis of international student experiences in the United States. *Race Ethnicity and Education, 22*(1), 38–58. https://doi.org/10.1080/13613324.2018.1497968

Yoon, I. H. (2019). Hauntings of a Korean American woman researcher in the field. *International Journal of Qualitative Studies in Education, 32*(5), 447–464. https://doi.org/10.1080/09518398.2019.1597211

Yosso, T. J. (2005). Whose culture has capital? A critical race theory discussion of community cultural wealth. *Race Ethnicity and Education, 8*(1), 69–91. https://doi.org/10.1080/1361332052000341006

Zhu, G., Peng, Z., Hu, X., & Qiu, S. (2019). Extending critical race theory to Chinese education: Affordance and constraints. *Compare: A Journal of Comparative and International Education, 49*(5), 837–850. https://doi.org/10.1080/03057925.2019.1602966

Yiting Chu is an Assistant Professor of Curriculum and Instruction at the School of Education, University of Louisiana Monroe. Yiting earned his Ph.D. in Multicultural Education from the University of Washington, Seattle. His research is grounded in the intersections of cultural diversity, social justice, and teacher education, with the goals of preparing and sustaining culturally responsive and equity- and justice-oriented teachers in and for minoritized and marginalized communities.

Open Access This chapter is licensed under the terms of the Creative Commons Attribution 4.0 International License (http://creativecommons.org/licenses/by/4.0/), which permits use, sharing, adaptation, distribution and reproduction in any medium or format, as long as you give appropriate credit to the original author(s) and the source, provide a link to the Creative Commons license and indicate if changes were made.

The images or other third party material in this chapter are included in the chapter's Creative Commons license, unless indicated otherwise in a credit line to the material. If material is not included in the chapter's Creative Commons license and your intended use is not permitted by statutory regulation or exceeds the permitted use, you will need to obtain permission directly from the copyright holder.

Chapter 18
Pedagogical Challenges of Immigrant Minority Teacher Educators: A Collaborative Autoethnography Study

Xuexue Yang and Byungeun Pak

Abstract Oftentimes, novice teacher educators need to navigate social and institutional context when they transitioned from teachers to teacher educators. This is particularly true for minority teacher educators. To date, studies on pedagogical challenges that minority teacher educators encountered when teaching in a dominating foreign culture are understudied. This paper concerns pedagogical challenges of two novice teacher educators teaching in a transcultural context where their home languages and cultures are marginalized relative to the U.S. mainstream culture. Using collaborative autoethnography, we investigated our own pedagogical challenges related to language, culture, and power structure through the notion of third space. In a teacher preparation program at a mid-western university, we as doctoral students taught white teacher candidates in courses of world language and elementary mathematics methods, respectively. We position ourselves as immigrant MTEs from China and South Korea. The study focuses our reflection on teaching practices as novice teacher educators in the U.S. and the relationships of these practices to personal and professional life experiences in home countries. We collected the data by interviewing each other with topics, such as our teaching practices and pedagogical challenges. We analyzed the data by coding inductively and deductively. To increase the reliability and creditability of our analysis process, we did a cross check by examining each other's selected interview excerpts and codes that we labeled. We presented three findings on pedagogical challenges pertaining to language, culture, and sociopolitical dimensions and how we negotiated our perspectives of teaching and learning. This study has implications on supporting minority teacher educators and the pedagogy of teacher education.

X. Yang (✉)
The State University of New York at Oneonta, Oneonta, United States
e-mail: xuexue.yang@oneonta.edu

B. Pak
Dixie State University, St. George, UT, USA

Introduction

In this paper, we regard *foreign-born* teacher educators like ourselves as immigrant *minority teacher educators* (hereafter, MTEs). We attend to how MTEs navigate their challenges in a new and foreign sociocultural context in the U.S. They have to deal with enormous challenges, which are caused largely by differences in language and cultures, broadly speaking. Research has thus far paid attention to the complexities of teacher educators' teaching practices and learning (Knight et al., 2014). However, MTEs' teaching and learning practices are still one of the understudied research areas (Goodwin et al., 2014; Korthagen, 2016; Hordvik et al., 2020). Rare research attends to the pedagogical challenges that MTEs encounter while teaching in a dominating *foreign culture*, which indicates specifically how MTEs perceive a U.S. mainstream culture.

This collaborative autoethnographic study aims to uncover the complexities of MTEs' teaching practices through investigating their pedagogical challenges. We examine how we as immigrant MTEs from China and South Korea, negotiated our perspectives of teaching and learning. Specifically, this study was guided by the following research questions:

1. What are the pedagogical challenges that the MTEs have encountered when teaching undergraduates in a teacher preparation program in the U.S.?
2. How do the MTEs negotiate their pedagogical challenges when they teach in a "*foreign culture*" context in the U.S.?

Literature Review

Complexities of Becoming Teacher Educators

Becoming teacher educators is a complicated process (Ritter, 2007). Teacher educators not only need to enact pedagogy by teaching undergraduates and supervising student teaching, but also need to coordinate multiple duties and reform themselves via reflections on their own teaching (Erickson et al., 2011; Wei & Maddamsettti). In particular, novice teacher educators need to navigate new social and institutional contexts when transitioned from the role as a teacher to a teacher educator (William et al., 2012). In the meantime, it is not uncommon for novice teacher educators to encounter tensions and conflicts in the process of negotiating their professional identity and pedagogy (William et al., 2012).

Given the complexities of becoming a teacher educator, several researchers have tried to uncover pedagogical challenges that teacher educators might encounter. The specific challenges that teacher educators encountered include maintaining "authenticity" in teaching which refers to a negotiation of personal values and the situation values (William et al., 2012; Murray & Male, 2005), a negotiation of personal voices within the structures of the institution and curricula (Bullock, 2007), uncertainty of teaching, and concerns of students' perceptions to novice teacher educators due to teacher educators' strive for perfectionism (Hordvik et al., 2020).

Research also shows a difference in pedagogical challenges that novice teacher educators encountered based on their experiences as school teachers (e.g., William et al., 2012). Novice teacher educators with less experiences as classroom teachers tend to advocate traditional teaching methods in their college teaching. They need to navigate both their teaching practices and belief and the institutional context when they face pedagogical challenges in their course teaching. On the other hand, novice teacher educators with more experiences as classroom teachers tend to be more comfortable and confident about their teaching practices and belief in the context of university teaching, and instead they focus on navigating the institutional context as they encounter pedagogical challenges.

Complexities and Challenges of Becoming MTEs

In addition to the aforementioned complexities of becoming a teacher educator, MTEs encounter more challenges while negotiating their pedagogies that they brought from their home country and those mainstream pedagogies in the U.S. In the section below, first we review literature on tensions and challenges that MTEs encountered. Then we review literature on how MTEs transformed their pedagogical practices in a dominating *foreign culture*.

Tensions and Challenges of MTEs' Pedagogical Practices

The first challenge comes from MTEs' feelings and concerns of being perceived as "less competent" when teaching in a "*foreign culture*" context. These feelings and concerns have been reported by MTEs in multiple studies (Mayuzumi, 2008; Liao & Maddamsetti, 2019; Dao & Bian, 2018; Mayuzumi, 2008). For example, Dao & Bian (2018) reflected that they were concerned about students perceiving them as less capable teachers. Sometimes the MTEs felt "captive" because students' evaluation showed a hesitant attitude toward their teaching due MTEs' international background (Dao & Bian, 2018, p. 144).

The second challenge that MTEs encountered is that students may perceive them as "lack of language proficiency and culture references" (Liao & Maddamsetti, 2019, p. 9). For example, Skachkova (2000) found that instructors with an accent tended to receive negative feedback on their teaching. The accent, oftentimes, was regarded as a distinct marker between immigrants and non-immigrants, and between white and non-white (Mayuzumi, 2008). In addition, MTEs themselves also perceived them as lacking English proficiency, which caused barriers for them to use certain activities as a tool to support student learning. For example, Liao & Maddamsetti (2019) work showed that MTEs encountered challenges of having a full understanding of certain game activities (e.g., Barnga) due to a limited English vocabulary related to the card game. As a result, the game activities were not implemented well. Because of worries about students' perception, MTEs can show more anxieties when they are planning lessons and interacting with students in the U.S. In addition, those pedagogical challenges that MTEs encountered may lead MTEs to doubt their quality of teaching in the U.S. as a teacher educator (Liao & Maddamsetti, 2019).

The third challenge that MTEs encountered is associated with the teacher authority in classrooms. According to Rong (2002), minority educators, particularly the Asian American female educators, who were perceived as permissive, tended to receive aggression from students and thus faced a difficult classroom situation.

The last challenge is about tensions caused by MTEs' teaching and learning experiences from their home sociocultural context versus expectations and norms in the new sociocultural context. When MTEs planned lessons and activities drawing on the training that they received in their home countries, it may cause tensions with expectations in the new teaching context. For example, an MTE expressed that he used to want to be "knowledgeable" in front of students because of his teaching and learning experiences in his home country; however, it turned out that students were easily getting bored although he had planned for almost every minute for his lesson when teaching in the U.S. as a teacher educator (Liao & Maddamsetti, 2019).

MTEs' Pedagogical Transformation

Although MTEs faced various challenges in forming a professional identity and pedagogical practices because of their marginalized status in the new sociocultural context of teaching (Kostogriz & Peeler, 2007; Lee & Tucker, 2018), they did not end up staying at the stage of struggling. Instead, MTEs negotiated their pedagogical practices constantly after learning new knowledge in the new teaching context.

As the aforementioned case in Liao and Maddamsetti's (2019) study showed, the MTE started to seek help and looked for suggestions from his American colleague after he noticed the tension between his initial expectation of being "knowledgeable" in front of students and the institutional expectation of teacher educators being a facilitator. Then, he switched to step back and tended to be "co-learner" in his class. Since then, the situation got improved and the MTE felt more comfortable to work with his students.

MTEs also made sense of their pedagogical practices in the U.S. via perceiving their home cultural backgrounds and autobiography as an asset. For example, MTEs used their cultural backgrounds as a tool to create space for students to learn things from different perspectives (Dao & Bian, 2018; Liao & Maddamsetti, 2019). In turn, positive feedback from students could help to build MTEs' confidence when they explored and negotiated "best" pedagogical practices in a new teaching context.

Theoretical Framework

This study draws on the notion of third space to examine MTEs' pedagogical challenges and their negotiation of the challenges. Conceptualized by Bhabha (1996), third space refers to a transformative space created by contrasting cultural experiences. This "in-between" transformative space is not a physical space (Lee & Tucker, 2018). Instead, it is created by the reciprocal interaction between the first and second spaces (Soja, 2004). In our study, the *first space* refers to teaching in the sociocultural context of MTEs' home country; while the *second space* refers to teaching in the sociocultural context of a new country. When the teaching practices from a sociocultural context meet teaching practice in another sociocultural context, a third space was created. Within this hybrid space, teachers negotiate their teaching practices in different sociocultural contexts and may produce "new" pedagogies.

In our study, a third space has multiple dimensions given that pedagogical challenges and negotiation can be complicated to understand due to their multidimensionality (Hordvik et al., 2020; Goodwin et al., 2014). According to Gee (1999), teachers will encounter multiple sets of discourse with language practices and non-language practices, such as thinking, feeling, and acting while they teach at local communities. Those multiple discourses can be implicit and explicit, and pose myriad challenges for teachers (Wang, 2016).

To uncover the complexities of MTEs' pedagogical challenges, we examine how MTEs negotiate their teaching practices in a third space from three dimensions: culture, language, and sociopolitical dimension (Fig. 18.1).

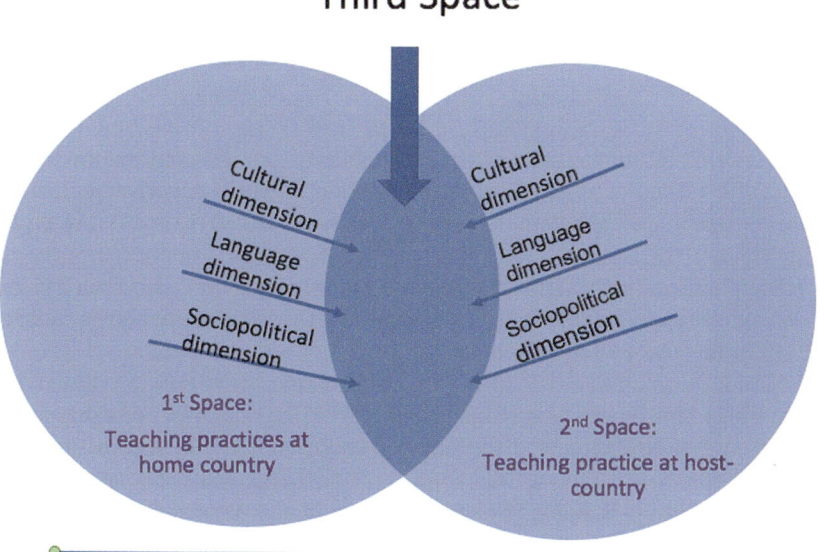

Fig. 18.1 MTEs teaching in a "foreign" culture

First, the language dimension indicates teachers' verbal and non-verbal language to communicate with students and to plan and deliver their instructions. English language proficiency has been identified as a common challenge that MTEs face when teaching transnationally (Dao & Bian, 2018; Faez, 2010; Liao & Maddamsetti, 2019; Mayuzumi, 2008). In addition to English, we extended the connotation of the language dimension, and included non-verbal communication, such as body language and facial expressions into this study.

Second, drawing on ideas from Garson (2005), we define "culture" as values, norms, attitudes, assumptions and expectations when teaching in different sociocultural contexts. Culture, including religion, history, politics, and physical surroundings, shapes people's thinking, feeling and behaviors (Garson, 2005). Since teaching is a social and cultural behavior, MTEs' pedagogies are hardly isolated from their life experiences in different contexts. Cultural experiences in different contexts cause MTEs to encounter various pedagogical challenges related to, for example, respect for educators (Hoare, 2013), teacher authority in classrooms (Dao & Bian, 2018), and student-centered versus teacher-centered approaches (Slethaug, 2007).

Third, we define the sociopolitical dimension as power dynamics between MTEs and students and between MTEs and colleagues in different teaching contexts. Research shows a recurring theme that minority teachers' sense of marginalization received more and more attention pertaining to the sociopolitical dimension (Wang, 2016). Teaching in a transcultural context, minority teachers might feel isolated because of their languages, ethnicity and home culture (Lee & Tucker, 2018; Dao & Bian, 2018; Liao & Maddamsetti, 2019). We are interested in how MTEs' may or may not feel marginalized because of the power structures and how they negotiate the power dynamics within the third space.

Methodology

Our study draws on collaborative autoethnography as research methodology (Lapadat, 2017; Chang et al., 2013). Collaborative autoethnography is "collaborative", "autobiographical" and "ethnographic" (Chang et al., 2013, p. 17). We chose this methodology for two reasons. First, this methodology has gained attention among researchers and educators who may be marginalized and who seek MTEs' voices as insiders (Lapadat, 2017; Ngunjiri et al., 2010). As minority teacher educators. We think this methodology helps us find ways to voice our pedagogical challenges. Second, this methodology allows for contributions of multidimensional and multidisciplinary lens on research (Chang et al., 2013; Lapadat, 2017). In this study, both authors are from different disciplinary backgrounds (language for the first author and mathematics for the second author). As such, this methodology can open a space for both authors to listen to each other deeply and delve into MTEs' pedagogical challenges in different disciplines.

Context and Participants

The context of our experiences was at a teacher preparation program at a midwestern university in the U.S. Two authors were the participants in this study. In the program, we as doctoral students taught white teacher candidates in courses of world language and elementary mathematics methods, respectively. We position ourselves as immigrant MTEs from China and South Korea. We speak Chinese and Korean as mother tongues, respectively. The level of our English as the instructional language is fluent enough to pass a speaking test administered by the university. Xuexue Yang (hereafter XY), the first author, has relatively less experiences being a classroom teacher in China. Byungeun Pak (hereafter BP), the second author, has 13 years of classroom teaching experience as an elementary school teacher in South Korea. Both participants did not have experience of teaching abroad before working as a teacher educator in the U.S.

Data Collection

In this study, we focus on MTEs' reflections on teaching practices as teacher educators in the U.S. and the relationships of these practices to personal and professional life experiences in their home countries. In particular, we collected interviews as our primary data source. While recalling teaching and learning stories at our home country, we also reflected on our teaching practice as MTEs in the U.S. By recalling stories and digging into our past experiences, we aim to make better sense of our teaching practices and pedagogical challenges in the context of the U.S.

We collected the interview data in two parts. In each part, we conducted two rounds of interviews in which we took turns to interview each other each time. In the first part, we collected participants' personal and professional stories and background information. We used a semi-structured interview protocol (see Appendix A). This protocol includes questions to explore our teaching and learning experiences in China and South Korea, reasons for being a teacher educator in the U.S., and the strengths and weaknesses of being MTEs. Each interview was audio recorded and lasted around 45 min. We transcribed these two interviews with a purpose to read through it and prepare our probing questions for the next step.

In the second part, we collected data related to participants' pedagogical practices and challenges while we taught undergraduates in the U.S. We used another semi-structured interview protocol for this interview (see Appendix B). Similar to the first interview, each virtual interview lasted around 45 min and was audio recorded. In total, we have 180-min interview transcripts.

Data Analysis

To analyze the interview transcripts, we conducted both deductive and inductive coding. For deductive coding, we coded our interview data guided by the three dimensions of our theoretical framework (linguistic, cultural, and sociopolitical dimension). To avoid potential subjectivity, we took a closer examination on each other's interview transcripts looking for excerpts including cues on pedagogical practices relevant to these three dimensions. For example, we looked for excerpts with cue sentences, such as "I have limited proficiency", "I think language first" and "I have lots of pedagogical challenge, so [the] first [is] language." We then compiled all the selected interview excerpts and categorized them into cultural dimension, language dimension and sociopolitical dimension. For inductive coding (Strauss & Corbin, 1998) to find emerging themes and patterns, we first conducted open coding by labeling codes sentence by sentence. For example, we labeled sentences as codes, such as "language proficiency and authority", "language and position, "communication with students/colleagues." Then we looked for broader themes via discussing the labeled codes and comparing similarities and differences across our experiences. For example, we grouped some codes such as "communication with students" and "communication with colleagues" into a broader category "quality of teaching." Overall key codes that we obtained via the inductive and deductive coding were presented in Table 18.1 below. Finally, after getting all those codes, both authors wrote memos on their analysis of the interview excerpts; then discussed how to make sense of the memos during a Zoom meeting.

Table 18.1 Key codes of pedagogical practices and challenges

Language dimension	Culture dimension	Sociopolitical dimension
Quality of teaching	Teachers' role in classrooms	Lesson/ curriculum co-planning
Language proficiency and teacher authority	Cultural relevant expectations on respect	
Language proficiency as barrier of communication with students, thus affecting teacher-student relationships	Less active learning vs active learning philosophy	Power dynamic in co-planning and teaching
	The role of teacher in classrooms and teacher authority	Feeling of subordinate and marginalized in collaboration
Negotiation of language proficiency as a barrier in teaching	Negotiation of respect and authority issues	
	Classroom culture	Students' perception of power differences
	Encouraging and motivating learning environment in the U.S. and less active learning in South Korea	
	Negotiation of cultivating a learning environment that give students more freedom	Building students' trust in MTEs
	Lack knowledge of U.S. local context Knowledge in local schools and teaching norms	Balance of authority and giving trust to students

To increase the reliability of our analysis process, we did a cross check by examining each other's selected interview excerpts and codes that we labeled. The purpose of the cross check is to challenge each other's perspectives and to ensure that we interpret each other's interviews accurately (Chang, 2013).

Findings

In this section, we present three findings as a result of the analysis to capture how each of the three dimensions reveal our pedagogical challenges in third space.

Language Dimension

First, we pointed out language as a cause of pedagogical challenges, even though we were qualified by the university for teaching courses for undergraduate students. XY, the first author, suggested that language was a crucial determinant to high quality teaching in her World Language Methods courses. For example, she said, "I see the language can be a barrier to prevent me from establishing a deeper relationship with my students." She perceived her oral language proficiency to be not as good as she expected, which constrained a deeper relationship between her and her students. In her interview, she also took body language, such as hand gesture or eye contact, as examples of the language-as-a barriers. "I felt like my hand gesture or eye contact affected how my students perceived me. They might see me as a less confident or assertive teacher educator." In this excerpt, she described her perception of non-verbal language as pedagogical challenges in her classrooms. What she talked about in the excerpt reveals her perception of a conflict between her teaching behaviors and more confident instructional style. Her body language is inseparable from the way she was raised and educated in her country. In the U.S., she perceived that she was expected by her students to be more confident and aggressive.

BP, the second author, explained this relationship between his mother tongues and English as an instructional language in his courses. In the second-round interview, he mentioned,

> I felt like my accent and pronunciation prevented my students from understanding what I was trying to say. Because my accent and pronunciation are what I cannot change easily even though I know I need to speak the way Americans do. Even though I speak in English to teach my students, I felt like what I bring with me in terms of accent and pronunciation does not help me teach well.

In this excerpt, BP perceived accent and pronunciation as the other language-as-barriers to support his students in learning to teach mathematics. His accent and pronunciation are shaped deeply by how he speaks Korean language. In his course teaching, his unique accent and pronunciation does not help him teach well. As such, it is possible to think about a pedagogical challenge in a third space where his speaking habits in Korean language was in conflict with English as an instructional language.

To deal with the language-related pedagogical challenges, both teacher educators create their ways. For example, XY coped with these challenges, in the beginning of the semester, she often invited her students to ask questions for clarification. BP took additional time to correct his accent and pronunciation for terms or words he had to say before the class.

Cultural Dimension

Second, we perceived cultural differences in teaching as causing us to encounter pedagogical challenges. What we brought to the U.S. classrooms was related to our professional teaching culture we had experienced as a K-12 learner and as a teacher in our home country classrooms. Both authors mentioned differences in teaching philosophy and practices. XY expressed pedagogical challenges she experienced in her course teaching. In this excerpt from the first-round interview, she talked about how she perceived the differences between teacher-centered teaching culture that she experienced in China and student-centered teaching culture in the U.S.

> I kind of like to compare which kind of teaching methods or teaching philosophy… I didn't say I kind of only value the U.S. teaching, but instead I make a balance in my class. So for example I know many people have critiqued lecture-based teaching methods in China or the Asian culture. I want to highlight [that] I still perceive some good stuff by using lecture-based teaching methods. I feel like [teaching] it's quite flexible in the U.S. classroom. Especially in higher education when I learned to be a teacher educator, it's always flexible for you to talk or to debrief about the articles. So for me I appreciate those flexibility and the freedom for every teacher educator to share their perspective in terms of how to prepare teachers or what's your perspective about teaching or kind of education. But at the same time, I feel sometimes I still want the instructor or professor in the classroom to share their views or their feelings about these the article explicitly, like [using] a summary, or using a diagram.

In this excerpt, she described a pedagogical challenge that came from conflict between different teaching practices. This challenge results from some part of her uncomfortableness for "flexibility and the freedom for every teacher educator." In her country, teacher educators tend to lecture what their students need to know. By lecture, they guide students to be able to achieve a clear understanding. As a result, she had negotiated her practices between lecture-based teaching that she still valued the teaching approach of giving students more freedom to learn in the U.S. Then she created a third space where she valued a mixed use of both types of teaching methods flexibly in classrooms.

BP emphasized that being a teacher educator means to continue to negotiate cultural differences between his home country context and the U.S. context. He often felt that his cultural backgrounds shaped the way he made sense of his interaction with students. In his second interview, he talked about his perception of instructors being respected differently by their students.

> I needed myself to lower my expectations in relation to getting respect as much as Korean professors are getting from their prospective teachers. So I needed to adjust my expectations in the U.S. classrooms. Very often I feel uncomfortable when I interact with my students in my courses. So, the way I deal with them with uncomfortableness was expressing my uncomfortableness to them in a very respectful manner.

This excerpt shows a pedagogical challenge related to low respect that he experienced in his course teaching. As a teacher educator, he received high respect from his college students in South Korea. From his experiences, it was true for the other instructors in his country. But he felt receiving low respect when he interacted with his U.S. students in his course teaching. To deal with this pedagogical challenge, he tried to lower his expectations in relation to getting respect "as much as Korean professors are getting from their prospective teachers." By lowering his expectations, a third space was created for him to perceive his pedagogical challenges.

Sociopolitical Dimension

Third, power and authority played out in interactions and relationships with students in our course teaching. XY frequently mentioned that her students seemed to position her as an instructor in a lower status than her co-instructor. In her second interview, she described her perception of the power and authority differences. "Even though I co-taught with a professor, I felt an imbalance about the power because I could sometimes feel the students perceived me kind of like a teaching assistant, while they perceived the professor as a core instructor." This excerpt shows that students' reactions suggested to her an unequal power difference. This positioning was important for her because how her students see her may shape building trust with students.

She talked about the power differences emerging from her lack of enough knowledge of U.S. local and school context. "You have to make a lot of efforts for them to trust you, such as lesson planning and also including some knowledge beyond those courses or some knowledge about the U.S. schools." She thinks that this kind of local contextual knowledge caused her students to position her as an MTE in a lower status than her co-instructor. Thus, she negotiated the power differences by adjusting her position to be a learner learning from the professor that she worked with. BP talked about his sense of being subordinated and marginalized and how his sense was related to his pedagogical challenges. He felt marginalized when he worked with prospective teachers. For example, in his first-round interview, he mentioned how his students responded differently to his request when his U.S. colleagues asked students to close their electronic devices in class time.

> I was always thinking about how I could make my prospective teachers learn to teach mathematics. Sometimes prospective teachers in my course were off task or they were playing with a phone and device. That off-task behavior was annoying. Some prospective teachers responded to my request to stop using electronic devices differently from my co-instructor. When something like that happened, it made me think about the differences in authority as an instructor.

This excerpt shows a pedagogical challenge related to his perception of lower authority different from U.S. instructors. As mentioned above in the cultural dimension, he felt he received lower respect from his students in the U.S. In his country, he was "not trying to be like an authority in the classroom" and he was trying "not to be strict to students." His perception of low authority caused him to navigate ways to negotiate his authority in his course teaching, which created a third space.

Discussion, Conclusions and Implications

This study provides a picture of how multiple dimensions may interfere with MTEs' teaching practices. In this study, we extend the concept of pedagogy and include MTEs' interaction with colleagues such co-planning and co-teaching. We found that three dimensions (language, culture, and power structure) often constrained our teaching practices.

First of all, both participants perceived language proficiency as a challenge for them to communicate and to deepen relationships with students, which echoed existing literature (Liao & Maddamsetti, 2019; Dao & Bian, 2018; Faez, 2010; Mayuzumi, 2008). It seemed that both participants held a high expectation to their teaching quality. Yet, because of the limited oral language proficiency, both participants might not achieve the teaching outcome that they expected. BP commented on his battle between his accent that was shaped by his home languages and the instructional language as norms in classrooms. He chose to correct his accent and pronunciation as a way to cope with the pedagogical challenge of communication with students. XY, another participant, decided to be open to her students and invite students to ask clarification questions. Even though with those teaching strategies, both participants were concerned that students perceived them as "less competent" instructors. Thus, the finding may suggest that when preparing a novice teacher educator in higher education, it is important for the institution or teacher preparation program to provide MTEs with professional development opportunities in instructional language, as well as strategies of dealing with the difficult situation caused by language barriers in classes. This suggestion is also connected to Liao and Maddamsetti's (2019) study, where it calls for support provided to develop MTEs' language proficiency.

In addition, findings in this study also bring about tensions of MTEs' body language that were shaped by their home culture versus the body language expected in the U.S. cultural context. Unfortunately, the study did not show explicit evidence on how the two participants negotiated their body languages in the third space. Future study can further illustrate how body language plays a role in MTEs' pedagogical challenge and how they negotiated it.

Second, this study shows MTEs encountered a pedagogical challenge in negotiating respect in classrooms. There has been a long history of respecting teachers in the Confucius culture. The sayings such as "day as a teacher, life fatherhood", has shown the status of teachers, and the relationship between students and teachers. Thus, it is not surprising that BP held a high expectation on respect from his students. However, the cultural norms on a teacher's role in classrooms, as well as relationships between students and teachers in the U.S. are different. It was not surprising that BP felt uncomfortable after noticing less respect from students than he assumed. Drawing on the tension between his assumption on respect from students and the reality of teacher-student relationship in U.S. classrooms, BP created a third space and he adjusted his pedagogy. Findings on the expectation of "respect" and the role of teachers in classrooms inform us a need to adopt multiple and comparative perspectives when preparing MTEs.

Third, regarding pedagogical challenge in the sociopolitical dimension, both participants mentioned that they felt being marginalized and subordinated while co-planning and co-teaching lessons with American colleagues. In addition, they felt that students perceived them as having less authority than their colleagues. Those feelings of being marginalized and having less authority figures are consistent with previous studies (Rong, 2002; Dao & Bian, 2018; Wang, 2016). Yet, both participants did not talk much more about how they used their home language and cultural background as a powerful tool to support their teaching and student learning. This can be associated with their deficit views when talking about their pedagogical practices in a new sociocultural context. Unlike non-MTEs, MTEs may get vulnerable more easily because they need to navigate both the U.S. institutional context and pedagogical practices, and beliefs at the same time, no matter they are experienced teachers and less experienced classroom teachers before becoming a teacher educator.

Conclusions and Implications

Drawing on collaborative autoethnography approach, we explored our own pedagogical challenges through the notion of third space while teaching in a *foreign culture* context. This study showed the sources of MTEs' pedagogical challenges and ways for them to negotiate the challenges. Findings in this study added insider perspectives to what we know about MTEs' pedagogical challenges to the existing literature. We found that the language, culture, and power structure often constrained our teaching practices. Findings across the three dimensions reveal that one of the biggest resources responding for MTEs' concerns is students' perception and satisfaction. Negative feedback, either verbal or nonverbal, seemed to affect MTEs' confidence in exploring most suitable teaching practices for them. In addition, two participants show sincere care about building relationships and trust with students.

However, a lack of language proficiency and cultural reference may prevent them doing so. This study is suggestive for teacher preparation programs as institutions. Building on this study, teacher education programs may begin to think about how to support MTEs to develop their teaching practices in relation to language, culture, and power structure, not just to survive in a *foreign culture*.

Appendices

Appendix A

Sample Interview Questions

1. Can you introduce your experiences of working as a school teacher in your home country?
2. Tell me about your experiences of becoming a teacher educator.
3. What kind of teacher educator would you like to be? Why do you want to pursue being a teacher educator in the US?
4. Have you encountered any tensions or conflicts when learning to become a teacher educator in the US?

    (a) If yes, could you describe what happened? How did you address the tensions or conflicts?

Appendix B

Sample Interview Questions

1. How do you perceive yourself when teaching in the US? Will you perceive yourself as a minority teacher educator? If yes, why?
2. Have you seen any strength or vulnerability of being a minority teacher educator in the US?
3. What is the biggest pedagogical challenge in your experiences of learning to be a teacher educator?

    (a) Can you specify what aspects are the most challenging?

References

Bhabha, H. K. (1996). Culture's in-between. In S. Hall & P. D. Gay (Eds.), *Questions of cultural identity* (1st ed., pp. 53–60). SAGE.

Bullock, S. M. (2007). Finding my way from teacher to teacher educator. In T. Russell & J. Loughran (Eds.), *Enacting a pedagogy of teacher education values, relationships and practices* (pp. 77–94). Routledge.

Chang, H. (2013). Individual and collaborative autoethnography as a method. In S. H. Jones, T. E. Adams, & C. Ellis (Eds.), *Handbook of autoethnography* (pp. 107–122). Left Coast Press.

Chang, H., Ngunjiri, F., & Hernandez, K. A. C. (2013). *Collaborative autoethnography*. Left Coast Press.

Dao, V., & Bian, Y. (2018). International novice teacher educators navigating transitional Sel(f)ves in multicultural education teaching. In E. Lyle (Ed.), *Fostering a relational pedagogy* (pp. 139–151). Brill Sense.

Erickson, L. B., Young, J. R., & Pinnegar, S. (2011). Teacher educator identity: Emerging understandings of person, positioning, roles, and collaborations. *Studying Teacher Education, 7*(2), 131–132.

Faez, F. (2010). Linguistic and cultural adaptation of internationally educated teacher candidates. *Canadian Journal of Educational Administration and Policy, 100*, 1–20.

Garson, B. (2005). Teaching abroad: A cross-cultural journey. *Journal of Education for Business, 80*(6), 322–326.

Gee, K. S. K. H. (1999). A new approach to teaching and learning in journal club. *Medical Teacher, 21*(3), 289–293.

Goodwin, A. L., Smith, L., Souto-Manning, M., Cheruvu, R., Tan, M. Y., Reed, R., & Taveras, L. (2014). What should teacher educators know and be able to do? Perspectives from practicing teacher educators. *Journal of Teacher Education, 65*(4), 284–302.

Hoare, L. (2013). Swimming in the deep end: Transnational teaching as culture learning? *Higher Education Research & Development, 32*(4), 561–574.

Hordvik, M., Mac Phail, A., & Ronglan, L. T. (2020). Developing a pedagogy of teacher education using self-study: A rhizomatic examination of negotiating learning and practice. *Teaching and Teacher Education, 88*, 1–11.

Knight, S. L., Lloyd, G. M., Arbaugh, F., Gamson, D., McDonald, S. P., & Nolan, J., Jr. (2014). Professional development and practices of teacher educators. *Journal of Teacher Education, 65*(4), 268–270.

Korthagen, F. A. J. (2016). Pedagogy of teacher education. In J. Loughran & M. L. Hamilton (Eds.), *International handbook of teacher education* (pp. 311–346). Springer.

Kostogriz, A., & Peeler, E. (2007). Professional identity and pedagogical space: Negotiating difference in teacher workplaces. *Teaching Education, 18*(2), 107–122.

Lapadat, J. C. (2017). Ethics in autoethnography and collaborative autoethnography. *Qualitative Inquiry, 23*(8), 589–603.

Lee, H., & Tucker, S. I. (2018). Living and teaching in two worlds: Professional identity development in transnational dual language immersion teachers. *Journal of Education and Practice, 9*(1), 72–80.

Liao, W., & Maddamsetti, J. (2019). Transnationality and teacher educator identity development: A collaborative autoethnographic study. *Action in Teacher Education, 41*(4), 287–306.

Mayuzumi, K. (2008). 'In-between' Asia and the west: Asian women faculty in the transnational context. *Race Ethnicity and Education, 11*(2), 167–182.

Murray, J., & Male, T. (2005). Becoming a teacher educator: Evidence from the field. *Teaching and Teacher Education, 21*(2), 125–142.

Ngunjiri, F. W., Hernandez, K. A. C., & Chang, H. (2010). Living autoethnography: Connecting life and research. *Journal of research practice, 6*(1), 1–17.

Ritter, J. K. (2007). Forging a pedagogy of teacher education: The challenges of moving from classroom teacher to teacher educator. *Studying Teacher Education, 3*(1), 5–22.

Rong, X. L. (2002). Teaching with differences and for differences: Reflections of a Chinese American teacher educator. In L. Vargas (Ed.), *Women faculty of color in the white classroom* (pp. 125–145). Peter Lang.

Skachkova, P. (2000). *The ethnic teaches back: Identity formation and academic status of foreign-born women academics in the US*. [Accession No. 9958308]. State University of New York at Buffalo.

Slethaug, G. E. (2007). In G. E. Slethaug (Ed.), *Teaching abroad: International education and the cross-cultural classroom* (Vol. 1). University Press.

Soja, E. (2004). *Postmodern geographies: The reassertion of space in critical social theory* (2nd ed.). Verso.

Strauss, A., & Corbin, J. (1998). *Basics of qualitative research*. Sage Publications.

Wang, F. (2016). *Narrative inquiry into competing pedagogies: Chinese international students' learning to teach in the US* (Accession No. 10164577). [Doctoral thesis, University of Minnesota]. Pro Quest Dissertations Publishing.

Williams, J., Ritter, J., & Bullock, S. M. (2012). Understanding the complexity of becoming a teacher educator: Experience, belonging, and practice within a professional learning community. *Studying Teacher Education, 8*(3), 245–260.

Xuexue Yang is an Assistant Professor in the Department of Elementary Education and Reading at The State University of New York at Oneonta. Her interests include teacher education, language and literacy, and immigrant and ELL/Bilingual Education. Over the past five years, Xuexue has worked with pre-service and in-service teachers in the world language, elementary childhood education, literacy, and bilingual education. Her research has been published in peer-reviewed journals such as International Multilingual Research Journal and Foreign Language Annals.

Byungeun Pak is an Assistant Professor in the Department of Education at Dixie State University, Utah. He studied teachers' teaching practices with an emphasis on elementary mathematics at Michigan State University. He currently works with prospective teachers in mathematics methods courses for K-8 teachers and general education courses, such as multicultural education courses for aspiring teachers. His research interest is in understanding novice teachers' mathematics teaching practices. He is an active member of American Educational Research Association (AERA). He was born and educated in South Korea. His home town is very traditional and famous for traditional Korean food. Before studying abroad in the U.S., he had worked as an elementary school teacher with 13 years of teaching.

Open Access This chapter is licensed under the terms of the Creative Commons Attribution 4.0 International License (http://creativecommons.org/licenses/by/4.0/), which permits use, sharing, adaptation, distribution and reproduction in any medium or format, as long as you give appropriate credit to the original author(s) and the source, provide a link to the Creative Commons license and indicate if changes were made.

The images or other third party material in this chapter are included in the chapter's Creative Commons license, unless indicated otherwise in a credit line to the material. If material is not included in the chapter's Creative Commons license and your intended use is not permitted by statutory regulation or exceeds the permitted use, you will need to obtain permission directly from the copyright holder.

Chapter 19
Linguicism in U.S. Higher Education: A Critical Autoethnography

Hyesun Cho

Abstract This critical autoethnography discusses the emotional and cognitive dissonance encountered by the author, an international faculty member, during her professional journey at a large public research university in the United States. Despite being recognized for her scholarship as a promising researcher in the field of TESOL (Teaching English to Speakers of Other Languages), she has still encountered covert *linguicism* (Skutnabb-Kangas, 2012), a phenomenon ubiquitous in the English-dominant higher education context. This chapter discusses the ways in which the linguistic discrimination has shaped the author's professional identity and how she exerts her agency as a teacher educator-researcher through critical reflexivity to promote legitimacy and self-efficacy in her professional community. By unpacking and problematizing the dominant discourse, such as native speakerism (Holliday, 2015), in English language teaching, this study aims to provide a nuanced understanding of the lived experience of a bilingual faculty member in a teacher education program in the United States.

Introduction

As I write this chapter in the summer of 2020 in Lawrence, Kansas in the United States, I cannot help but thinking about the current xenophobia and racism explicitly endorsed by the Trump administration with the recent order against international students in higher education.[1] On July 6, U.S. Immigration and Customs Enforcement (ICE) released a directive regarding fall 2020 enrollment for F-1 students in the Student and Visitor Exchange Program (SEVP). The directive made it clear that if

---
[1] According to Open Doors, 1,095,299 international students were studying in the United States in 2018/2019. There was an increase of 0.05% over the prior year in the number of international students (Institute of International Education, 2019).

H. Cho (✉)
University of Kansas, Lawrence, KS, USA
e-mail: hcho@ku.edu

all of an international student's fall 2020 classes are online, they cannot remain in the U.S. and must leave the country.

As a former F-1 visa student, I was deeply concerned about the ramifications of this directive on the future of the colleges and universities in the country. In the midst of the COVID-19 pandemic, many higher education institutions, including my own, were attempting to address the numerous questions and concerns among the international student community by holding virtual town hall meetings. Harvard and Massachusetts Institute of Technology took further actions by filing a lawsuit against ICE. On July 14, a federal judge declared the order rescinded, but its negative repercussions of the policy continue to impact international students and faculty. Despite the Biden administration's significant shifts in immigration and federal higher education policies, the illegitimization of "foreigners" in U.S. society and schools persists through with the rhetoric of the mutually exclusive notion of "us versus them" (Aneja, 2016; Flores, 2013). In general, public discourse and sentiment regarding immigrant populations, both legal and illegal, is highly racialized and negatively charged in the United States.

Research Objective

This chapter discusses the challenges I have encountered in my professional trajectory as a "foreign" teacher educator in U.S. higher education. By using a critical autoethnography, this chapter also illustrates ways in which I enact and perform my multifaceted identities as an international faculty member in the U.S. teacher education context where I work with teacher candidates in the TESOL (Teaching English to Speakers of Other Languages) program. Despite being recognized for my scholarship in the field, I have still encountered linguicism (Skutnabb-Kangas, 2012), historically dominated in English-only U.S. higher education settings. By unpacking the dominant discourse in relation to linguicism, such as *native speakerism* (Holliday, 2015), this study provides a nuanced understanding of the lived experience of a "non-native English speaking teacher (NNEST) (Kumaravadivelu, 2016) in higher education. Ultimately, the chapter aims to raise critical questions about academia and the education of future teachers. As an educator and scholar advocating for social justice, I believe that it is of utmost importance to problematize the taken-for-granted assumptions about power imbalance inextricably inherent in education and academia.

Conceptual Framework

The following section briefly discusses the two theoretical constructs that undergird this chapter—*linguicism* and *performativity*. While the first represents the ideology deeply drenched in academia and society, the latter foregrounds my enactment of teacher identity to challenge such linguistic discrimination in U.S. higher education.

Linguicism

Linguicism refers to "ideologies, structures, and practices which are used to legitimate, effectuate, regulate, and reproduce an unequal division of power and resources (both material and immaterial) between groups which are defined on the basis of language" (Skutnabb-Kangas, 1988, p. 13). This linguistic discrimination, profoundly coupled with racism, is prevailing not only in K-12 education through the form of deficit thinking (Valencia, 2010) but also in higher education in the United States. Phillipson (1992, 2009) conceptualized this phenomenon as 'linguistic imperialism' in which English had been imposed as the primary language of communication, including the dissemination of knowledge in the academy through publications and presentations. Language proficiency or background is often "used as a euphemism to mask race-based" (Mahboob & Szenes, 2010, p. 348) discrimination among its members. As Da Costa (2020) asserts, linguistic racism is exacerbated when a speaker is bi/multilingual and shuttles between languages because her ability to translanguage (Li, 2018) is seen as a liability, rather than an asset.

I would concur with Kubota and Lin (2006) that language must be a focus of investigation in the discussion of racism as linguicism and racism are inherently intertwined. In particular, linguistic and racial discriminations permeate as leading orientations to language and race in teacher education research and practice in the United States (Milner et al., 2013).

Performativity in Language Education

Drawing on Butler's (1990) performativity theory of identity from a poststructuralist perspective, Morgan (2004) has called for teacher identity to be reconceptualized as a pedagogy in language education. This poststructural perspective views that language is interconnected with power relations marked by race, ethnicity, gender, social class, and sexual orientation in ways that result in social inequity (Luke, 2009). It also recognizes the fluid, dynamic, and discursive nature of identity. Morgan argues for the contingent and relational processes through which teachers negotiate their varying roles and identities in the classroom. From this view, teacher identity should be used for pedagogical purposes by harnessing her personal and professional lives in classroom instruction to disrupt ascribed beliefs and assumptions about language learning and teaching. In other words, the multifaceted, dynamic, and relational nature of teacher identity is highlighted as a strategic performance of a teacher.

Context of Research

As Yoo (2020) poignantly described in her autoethnography as a struggling mother-researcher in higher education, a neoliberalist university culture makes academia into an increasingly unwelcoming space in which "workers" are forced to comply to a hectic productivity schedule. Central to understanding how social justice and diversity are manifested in institutions of higher education are the experiences of female faculty from racial groups underrepresented in higher education. Furthermore, due to the hegemony of English in the geopolitics of scholarly publishing (Canagarajah, 2002), faculty members, particularly at a research university, have no choice but subscribe to the culture of "publish or perish" entirely in English (Curry & Lillis, 2018).

Methodology

Autoethnography as a Research Method

In this chapter, I use autoethnography with a critical event focus (Webster & Mertova, 2007) to address linguicism in the U.S. higher education context. Autoethnography is an established qualitative research method to analyze a researcher's own life as data. Autoethnography as a research method can shed light on the personal nature of the intersection of language, race, and gender that is institutionalized across society including teacher education (Zuniga et al., 2019). It centers "the researcher as a site of cultural inquiry within a cultural context, breaking open the dichotomous notions of the self/other within empirical traditions (Hughes et al., 2012, p. 210). Further, Richards (2008) views autoethnography as emancipatory discourse since "those being emancipated are representing themselves, instead of being colonized by others and subjected to their agendas or relegated to the role of second-class citizens" (p. 1724).

In a similar vein, Yazan (2019) asserts that autoethnography allows a researcher to assert agency to narrate his or her own lived experiences and enact identities without allowing others' interpretation (Canagarajah, 2012). This approach contests canonical ways of conducting research and representing others (Spry, 2001) and treats research as a socially-conscious act (Ellis et al., 2011). Critical autoethnography aims to make unheard voices heard and invisible faces visible by revealing the lived experiences of the minoritized people from their own perspectives (Marx et al., 2017a, b). Critical autoethnographers are interested in positionality that requires researchers to recognize both marginalization and privilege through reflexivity (Boylorn & Orbe, 2017). A critical take on my autoethnography allows me to tell the typically inaudible story to the audience while acknowledging my own privilege as a tenured professor at a Research One university in the United States. The primary data source for this chapter is my reflective journals that I have recorded throughout my academic journeys, both in Korea and the United States.

Findings and Discussion

My Language Background

Born in Busan, South Korea's second largest city, I was a monolingual speaker of Korean until I learned English when I entered middle school. At that time, Korean students officially began to learn English language from the first year of middle school (i.e., grade 7) and continued it through the last year of high school (i.e., grade 12).[2] Unlike many of my classmates who learned the alphabet and basic greetings in English before middle school, I had no prior knowledge in English. Korean teachers taught English vocabulary and grammar exclusively in Korean in decontextualized manners. I still remember repeating the teacher mindlessly, saying "I am a boy. You are a girl" in class. With much 'drill or kill' practice and rote memorization of endless lists of vocabulary without any accompanying example sentences, English was not a tool for communication but a subject matter to learn by heart for tests. My middle school English teachers made students memorize the entire textbook to get ready for the midterms and finals with multiple-choice items. There were no speaking and no writing tests. Things were not that different at my high school until I joined an English Conversation club where we were introduced to a few basic 'communicative' games, such as bingo and jigsaw activities.

I had never had a native English-speaking teacher until I entered a private university in Seoul which was well-known for English language education in the country. Despite my initial excitement about having a native speaker for the first time as an instructor, I was soon disappointed by the lack of opportunities to interact with him partly because of the class size and his teaching styles. He taught a class of 35 students in "English Communication" where speaking and listening were supposed to be taught. My biggest disappointment stemmed from the fact that his teaching was not different from the Korean teachers I had before. In my imagined classroom with a native speaking teacher who presumably speaks "perfect English," I expected to have ample opportunities to use English as a communication tool, not merely to memorize words and phrases from the textbook. Communicative activities were minimal not just because of the class size, but his lack of teaching experience with EFL college students.

Admittedly, I subscribed to 'native-speakerism,' a term coined by Holliday (2006, 2018). It refers to a widespread ideology perpetuated in the English Language Teaching (ELT) profession whereby those perceived as "native speakers" of English are considered to be better language models and embody a superior western teaching methodology than those perceived as "non-native speakers" in the periphery. Native speakerism, underpinned by the assumption that privilege and marginalization are categorically experienced across contexts, has served as the dominant

---

[2] Since 2007, English has been taught from 3rd grade in Korean elementary schools. Students receive 1–2 h of instruction a week in grades 3–6, 2–4 h a week in grades 7–9 and 4–5 h a week in grades 10–12.

paradigm in applied linguistics and TESOL (Phillipson, 2009). This idealized native speaker serves as "the universal linguistic and cultural target for acquisition, use, and instruction regardless of language teaching and learning context" (Rudolph et al., 2015, p. 28). The "ideal native speaker" norm continues to reify monolingualism and the competence of monolingual speakers (Ricento, 2013). The binary notion of native speaker and non-native speaker and the privilege of native speakers have been normalized in the field.

When I was junior in college, I decided to study abroad in Australia for 4 weeks to attend an extensive language program over the winter break. It was my first time traveling outside Korea and I was thrilled to use the English language in the "real-world" with native speakers. Despite my concern about the lack of my English proficiency, I did not have much trouble getting my meaning across with other international students and Australians around me. Despite a few miscommunications due to the phonological differences between Australian English ("Aussie English") and American English that I was accustomed to hearing during my schooling in Korea, this short-term study abroad experience improved my confidence, making me think that my English from grammar-based textbooks was not completely useless after all. Before graduation from the college of education, I passed a highly competitive national exam to become a public-school English teacher in Seoul. During my teaching in secondary schools, I enforced the English-only policy in my classroom because of the TESOL knowledge I gained from my BA studies in English language education. I was instructed to provide my Korean students with the maximum exposure to the target language as they do not have much exposure outside the classroom in an English as a foreign language (EFL) environment. Although I taught my classes entirely in English with some codeswitching to Korean, I felt my 'non-nativeness' would not facilitate my students' progress in English. I had a sense of inadequacy, a feeling of being 'imposters' pretending to be what I was not (Bernat, 2008; Llurda, 2015). As with Yazan (2019) who described his life story as an EFL teacher in Turkey, I have grappled with the notion of "nativeness" in my English learning and teaching experiences.

Another instance of native speakerism was from my English teaching experience at a middle school in Seoul. As the youngest (and probably most proficient) teacher at school, I was assigned to work with a native speaker who had no teaching credentials and experiences. She was a white female in her mid-20 s and studied piano at a college in Canada. Under the name of globalization in the mid-1990s (Jeon, 2009), the Korean government hired native speakers from the so-called "Inner Circle" countries (Kachru, 1990) and assigned them to teach English in K-12 classrooms with no to very little training in teaching (Jenks, 2017). The ideology of the native speaker as "the ideal English speaker" and even "the ideal English teacher" was readily adopted by the Korean government and the public (Jeon, 2009). As a result, all the NES teachers I worked with had no knowledge and skills necessary to teach EFL in the secondary classroom. Although I loved teaching middle school students, I was thirsty for more advanced knowledge in ELT while aspiring to the level of legitimacy of native speakers (Llurda, 2015). I studied TOEFL and GRE after work and during the weekends and applied for several graduate programs in the United

States after teaching for almost 6 years in Korean schools. To my delight, I was awarded a U.S. federal government scholarship to pursue my graduate studies at a university which was known as the top program in applied linguistics.

My Experience in U.S. Higher Education

I was beyond excitement when I first entered the United States to pursue a master's degree in TESOL. I felt as if I was in the right place to be, finally. However, my initial excitement was soon replaced with distress and anguish due to my struggles in the graduate program. Despite my prior teaching experience as an EFL teacher and my educational background in English language teaching, I was rendered inaudible (Miller, 2003) during my MA studies. I found that the cultural capital afforded to me did not necessarily translate into positive learning experience in the graduate program. I took endless pages of notes before class while making sense of the SLA theories, mostly from cognitive perspective. It took me a much longer time to get ready for class discussion than my native English-speaking classmates. I even recorded my voice to prepare for class discussion so that I could rehearse it before class. My notebooks were always filled with what I wanted to say to the class related to the topics at hand. However, it was a daunting challenge for me to compete for the floor as native speakers dominated the class discussion. It was more challenging for me to contribute as a legitimate member in the classroom when some white professors in the program did not acknowledge my previous EFL teaching experience and discounted my experience as anecdotal and not evidence-based (Cho, 2018). This was the first time in my life that I felt marginalized. Even when I was in a graduate seminar with other students from East Asian countries, it was my perceived lack of English proficiency that inhibited my full participation in class discussion. Some professors in my graduate courses did not even remember my name although each class size was relatively small. Again, I felt invisible and inaudible.

The significant turning point for my academic identity was my first conference presentation at an international conference, where I discussed the challenges of Korean EFL education from a teacher perspective. To prepare for the presentation, I wrote an entire script for my 20-min presentation and practiced it for countless hours and days. I even rehearsed it in front of my faculty advisor so he could give me feedback not only on the language choice and tone but on non-verbal communication skills, such as eye contact and hand gestures. It was a major milestone for me because it was my first-time conference presentation in my life. I had never made a presentation in my schooling even in Korean, so it was an undoubtedly memorable moment in my professional life.

Despite this successful, well-received presentation during my master's program, I felt that I was not ready to teach a class full of native speakers in my first year as a doctoral student in teacher education in the U.S. Midwest. I felt nervous about teaching white, native English-speaking undergraduate students. I spent numerous days to prepare for class and even recorded myself to find any mistakes in the video.

In retrospect, what made me feel nervous and insecure about teaching was not only my perceived lack of English proficiency but my lack of knowledge about U.S. school systems and educational culture. As I did not have any teaching experience in the U.S., especially in the Midwest, I lacked the tactic knowledge that my preservice teachers were learning from their education courses.

Academic writing was another challenge for me as with many other international students from Kachru's (1990) "Expanding Circle" countries, such as China and Japan. The cultural deficit theories suggested by L2 writing scholars has been engrained in my mind that I do not possess the linguistic resources that are required to construct abstract academic texts. While reading numerous journal articles and books, I learned to appropriate the academic writing that I needed for research papers and class presentations. My confidence about academic writing grew thanks to my fellow classmates with whom I studied for our first doctoral seminar in the Ph.D. program. They assured me that my writing was clear, even powerful, during our study group. With this affirmation of my writing ability in English, I kept writing but adhered to the conventional academic writing that appeared in most journal publications. As Maguire (2011) observed in her graduate seminars with international students, I experienced conflicts derived from the power imbalance between the authoritative discourse of scholars and my own internally persuasive discourses as an authoring self (Bakhtin, 1981).

After I was hired as a new faculty member in TESOL, I taught teaching methods for graduate students. Once a linguistics graduate student in my TESOL methods course was surprised that I corrected his grammatical errors in his paper and did not hide his surprise in the office hours when we discussed his draft. However, the most disheartening experience in relation to linguicism in my work environment was from interactions with a colleague in faculty meetings. They did not acknowledge what I had to say several times until another colleague, who was a native speaker like them, reiterated my comments. They turned to me and said, "Was that what you meant? Oh, I am sorry. I did not know that." It did not feel like an apology to me. Rather, it felt like covert discrimination based on my language background although I had more experience in teaching and research than that colleague. Oftentimes, linguicism is manifested in a more subtle manner. Another colleague complimented my English in a meeting, saying "Sometimes, I forget you're not a native speaker" and another asked me, "How come you don't have accent?" as an ostensibly compliment. These anecdotal instances have become naturalized in me as they often occur in my interaction with colleagues in the department as well as across campus.

Performing my Identities as a Teacher Educator and Researcher

As Yazan (2019) argues, teacher educators leverage their teacher identities for their legitimacy as teachers of preservice teachers by constructing their identities through their prior experience. Because of my previous experience as an international student with a difficult first name to pronounce for my white professors (Cho, 2018), I wanted to use naming practice as an icebreaker activity in my first day of class. Names are elements of one's identity that has complicated social implications (Thompson, 2006). I did not change my Korean first name, Hyesun, to an American name which is not uncommon for Korean immigrants to position themselves as a "cosmopolitan" as De Costa (2011) described in his case study of a Korean woman, Joanne ("Hye Ran"). Alternatively, I use my name as a means for engaging my students in a conversation about the value of naming practice in the education of emergent bi/multilingual students in school (García, 2009). My first day of class typically starts the meaning of my name both in Korean and Chinese.[3] I tell the class that my name based on the Sino-Korean means "to benefit others" and "offer help to others" and that's why I become a teacher. And then I ask my students about the meanings of their names. What I find interesting was that my white preservice teachers usually do not know the exact meaning of their names while my students of color, including international students, are aware of the meaning of their names and eager to share them with the rest of the class. These identity-maintenance efforts impact my investments as an integral part of my teacher educator identities.

Using my identity as a mother of two bilingual children in my TESOL courses is another way to "claim desirable subjectivities" (Mirzaee & Aliakbari, 2018, p. 34). I often take my experience as a parent of children in U.S. public schools as an example in class discussion. For instance, I shared my daughters' frustration with the state standardized testing for English language learners they had to take because I wrote Korean as a home language in the survey when they first entered the elementary school. As with Marx (2017) for her Hungarian-American bilingual children, I did not know until later that that a non-English language listed on the home language survey mandates English language evaluation. I considered (still do) their Korean as an asset, not a liability, something that I am proud of rather than a point of concern.

Not only did I express my concern with the English placement test and the home language survey, but I also shared both optimal and inapt practices that my daughters' teachers showed in the elementary classroom. As an immigrant parent, I did not have K-16 schooling experiences in the United States, but possessed the cultural and linguistic capital as a college professor who specializes in bilingual education to express my concern and ask questions during parent-teacher conferences, something that many other immigrant families do not have. My children's schooling experiences have allowed me to recognize the pitfalls of English service provided by school districts as well as the predicaments that immigrant parents encounter without appropriate bilingual support for them to communicate with their children's teachers throughout the school year.

Another way that I perform my identity as an immigrant mother of Korean American children is to promote Korean as a community language in the local community where I reside. In collaboration with a few Korean mothers, I developed Korean Storytime at the public library in the community. Korean and non-Korean

---

[3] Typical Korean names include Chinese characters (*hanja*) and their accompanying meanings.

families participated in this monthly event where children and their parents learned about Korean language and culture, read Korean picture books, and created Korean artifacts such as traditional fans and cards. Furthermore, I conducted research regarding Korean mothers' practices and beliefs about heritage language maintenance with a colleague who was the principal of a Korean Saturday school in the community (Cho et al., 2019b). Using my networking in Korea, I also co-founded a faculty-led study abroad program for American student teachers to teach English in high schools in Korea over the summer (Cho & Peter, 2017).

My research interest in teacher education made me conceptualize my practices as a teacher educator inseparable from my research. I share my take on language teacher identity with my students that NNEST advocacy efforts need to use a conceptual lens that views privilege and marginalization as fluidly experienced by teachers without positioning them as categorically and universally marginalized or privileged (Rudolph, 2016). The majority of my preservice teachers in a TESOL methods course are white, most of them are women who admit that they do not have much experience with bilingualism or multilingualism while growing up. In my graduate courses, I have a more diverse student body which includes international students from China, Korea, Japan, and the Middle East.

My teaching in a teacher education program also incorporates the use of autoethnography in two main ways: First, I have students write their language/literacy autobiography in the beginning of the semester to reflect on their first, second or third language learning experiences. The goal of this course assignment is for them to reflect on their own language/literacy learning experiences while exploring in some depth their attitudes and assumptions about language learning and teaching. This is also my attempt to center experiential knowledge in the course where students expect to learn content knowledge and pedagogical knowledge in TESOL. Second, I have them interview an English language learner or emergent bilingual (EB) (Garcia, 2009) to better understand their experiences in and outside of the classroom. By listening to EB learners' stories, teacher candidates have developed empathy and self-efficacy thereby becoming advocates for EB students (Cho & Guelly, 2017, Cho & Adams, 2018; Cho et al., 2019a).

With a critical awareness of linguistic discrimination in higher education, I purposefully give the floor to language minority students in class by asking them about their experiences pertaining to the topics at hand. By sharing their experiences and perspectives, I acknowledge them as creators of knowledge rather than merely recipient of knowledge from the western-based literature. I often share my struggles as a former international student who did not learn academic literacy until the MA program when I first learned how to cite references in APA format. My minority students frequently mentioned to me that my story resonated with them. For instance, a female Native American graduate student in my Language and Identity class stated in her final reflection that she was constantly encouraged to get her voice heard in my seminar, rather than remaining silent like the way she chose to do in her graduate program. A Fulbright scholar from India who audited my class wrote a letter to the Dean, stating that "I really applaud the personal touch

Dr. Cho lends to her class, how she uses her own experience as once a foreign student in the USA to connect with her foreign students. Personalized examples, I feel helps a teacher bond with her students better and this is exactly what Dr. Cho does: she builds a rapport with each leaner, making the learning experience so meaningful."

My passion and advocacy for international students in teacher education has led me to form a student group that focuses on the issues and needs of international students in the school of education. I collaborated with a few international students to conduct research on the topics of socio-academic identities of international graduate students in teacher education programs. My positioning as a former international student put me at an advantage because of my familiarity with my students and our shared lived experiences as students of color and bi−/multilingual scholars. This common ground facilitated our discussions and assisted our understanding of ourselves. Rather than the deficit mindset of international students regarding academic literacy, we as co-researchers embraced the multifaceted, fluid, and dynamic nature of international students' social identity that was afforded by our intercultural knowledge and experiences. In the cognitive research paradigm of second language acquisition, non-native speakers still remain inferior to the "native speaker" as the norm. Despite the current multilingual shift that has given way to the emergences of theoretical and pedagogical perspectives, such as translanguaging (Garcia & Lin, 2017; Li, 2018) and translingual practices (Canagarajah, 2013) in applied linguistics and TESOL, the status of bi−/multilingual scholars in the English-dominant U.S. high education context is lower than the monolingual, monocultural white faculty. Codemeshing in academic writing (Canagarajah, 2011) is not widely accepted in publications and standardized English is the desired medium for all scholars regardless of their language backgrounds.

Conclusion and Implications

Using a critical autoethnography, this chapter has illustrated my journey within ideological discourses that attempt to frame "linguistically qualified" against the intersectionality of race, gender, and country of origin. The amalgamation of privileges possessed by native-English speaking faculty members in the United States is often taken as a given and their "foreign" and "non-native English speaking" counterparts have not been closely examined in the literature. This chapter particularly elucidates the dissonance I have experienced in navigating the academy that imposes the English-only policy on faculty and students. This chapter sheds light on the hyphenated identities minoritized faculty members from other countries in the U.S. higher education context inhabit. Recently, systematic racism has been intensively discussed both in the public and education in the United States and around the world, but linguicism has not been the focus of such discussion. A commitment to diversity, equity, and inclusion is one of the top priorities of American higher education. Yet, it must be much more than simply having a token representation of faculty of color, particularly in teacher education.[4]

Linguicism is so entrenched that pedagogical changes alone will not challenge the linguistic hierarchies among members in U.S. higher education (Austin, 2009). By providing a space for faculty and students to critically reflect on their own language learning practices and identities that challenge the universalizing rhetoric of linguicism, faculty and students can become part of a larger institutional critique of linguicism, along with racism. As a Korean-mother-former EFL teacher-researcher-teacher educator, I view the world from the nexus of my multifaceted identities and negotiate the hyphenated identities on a daily basis. It is a struggle to challenge and destabilize the idealized, static, and monolithic constructs of 'language,' 'culture,' and 'identity' (Rudolph et al., 2020). I hope this story will resonate with some scholars and educators in higher education who are interested in learning more about the ways subtle linguistic discrimination can serve to incrementally disadvantage "foreign" teachers and ways in which teacher educator identity can be performed to contest such discriminatory practices.

References

Aneja, G. A. (2016). Rethinking nativeness: Toward a dynamic paradigm of (non) native speakering. *Critical Inquiry in Language Studies, 13*(4), 351–379. https://doi.org/10.1080/15427587.2016.1185373

Austin, T. (2009). Linguicism and race in the United States: Impact on teacher education from past to present. In *Race, culture, and identities in second language education: Exploring critically engaged practice* (pp. 252–270). https://doi.org/10.1080/13613324.2016.1150827

Bakhtin, M. M. (1981). *The dialogic imagination: Four essays* (C. Emerson & M. Holquist, Trans; M. Holquist, Ed.). University of Texas Press. https://doi.org/10.2307/2497064

Bernat, E. (2008). Towards a pedagogy of empowerment: The case of 'impostor syndrome' among pre-service non-native speaker teachers in TESOL. *English Language Teacher Education and Development, 11*(1), 1–8.

Boylorn, R. M., & Orbe, M. (2017). *Critical autoethnography: Intersecting cultural identities in everyday life*. Routledge. https://doi.org/10.4324/9781315431253

Butler, J. (1990). *Gender trouble: Feminism and the subversion of identity*. Routledge. https://doi.org/10.1353/esc.2015.0070

Canagarajah, A. S. (2002). *A geopolitics of academic writing*. University of Pittsburgh Press. https://doi.org/10.2307/j.ctt5hjn6c

Canagarajah, S. (2011). Codemeshing in academic writing: Identifying teachable strategies of translanguaging. *The Modern Language Journal, 95*(3), 401–417.

Canagarajah, A. S. (2012). Teacher development in a global profession: An autoethnography. *TESOL Quarterly, 46*, 258–279. https://doi.org/10.1002/tesq.18

---

[4] When I argued for diversifying the teacher education faculty at my university at a school assembly, the dean briefly agreed but said that Asians are not a "minority" group like Blacks and Latinos in higher education. After my initial dismay, I realized that the prevailing assumptions about Asians as "model minority" obscure the heterogeneity in the diverse population (Iftikar & Museus, 2018).

Canagarajah, A. S. (Ed.). (2013). *Literacy as translingual practice: Between communities and classrooms*. Routledge. https://doi.org/10.4324/9780203120293.
Cho, H. (2018). *Critical literacy pedagogy for bilingual preservice teachers: Exploring social identity and academic literacies*. Springer. https://doi.org/10.1007/978-981-10-7935-1
Cho, H., & Adams, D. (2018). Service-learning as a means for preparing preservice teachers to work with English language learners. In T. Meidl (Ed.), *Service-learning initiatives in teacher education programs*. IGI Global. https://doi.org/10.4018/978-1-5225-4041-0.ch004
Cho, H., & Gulley, J. (2017). A catalyst for change: Service-learning for TESOL graduate students. *TESOL Journal., 8*(3), 613–635. https://doi.org/10.1002/tesj.289
Cho, H., Johnson, P., & Somiari, S. (2019a). Service-learning as authentic practice for teacher candidates to work with English language learners. In C. Lenkaitis & S. Hilliker (Eds.), *Engaging teacher candidates and language learners with authentic practice* (pp. 35–54). IGI Global. https://doi.org/10.4018/978-1-5225-8543-5.ch003
Cho, H., & Peter, L. (2017). Taking the TESOL practicum abroad: Opportunities for critical awareness and community-building among preservice teachers. In H. An (Ed.), *Efficacy and implementation of study abroad programs for P-12 teachers*. IGI Global. https://doi.org/10.4018/978-1-5225-1057-4.ch009
Cho, H., Song, K., & Lee, J. (2019b). (Reprinted). Korean immigrant parents' involvement in children's biliteracy development in the U.S. context. In Management Association, I (Ed.), *Immigration and refugee policy: Breakthroughs in research and practice* (pp. 171–186). IGI Global. https://doi.org/10.4018/978-1-5225-8909-9.ch010
Curry, M. J., & Lillis, T. (2018). *Global academic publishing: Policies, perspectives and pedagogies*. Multilingual Matters. https://doi.org/10.3138/jsp.49.4.07
De Costa, P. (2011). Cosmopolitanism and learning English: Perspectives from Hye Lan Alias Joanne. *Journal of Second Language Acquisition and Teaching, 18*, 55–76.
De Costa, P. I. (2020). Linguistic racism: Its negative effects and why we need to contest it. *International Journal of Bilingual Education and Bilingualism, 23*(7), 833–837.
Ellis, C., Adams, T. E., & Bochner, A. P. (2011). Autoethnography: An overview. *Historical Social Research, 36*(4), 273–290. https://doi.org/10.12759/hsr.36.2011.4.273-290
Flores, N. (2013). Silencing the subaltern: Nation-state/colonial governmentality and bilingual education in the United States. *Critical Inquiry in Language Studies, 10*(4), 263–287. https://doi.org/10.12759/hsr.36.2011.4.273-290
García, O. (2009). Emergent bilinguals and TESOL: What's in a name? *TESOL Quarterly, 43*(2), 322–326. https://doi.org/10.1002/j.1545-7249.2009.tb00172.x
García, O., & Lin, A. M. (2017). Translanguaging in bilingual education. *Bilingual and multilingual education*, 117–130.
Holliday, A. (2006). Native-speakerism. *ELT Journal, 60*(4), 385–387. https://doi.org/10.1093/elt/ccl030
Holliday, A. (2015). Native-speakerism: Taking the concept forward and achieving cultural belief. In *(En) countering native-speakerism: Global perspectives* (pp. 11–25).
Holliday, A. (2018). Native-speakerism. *The TESOL Encyclopedia of English Language Teaching*, 1–7. https://doi.org/10.1002/9781118784235.eelt0027
Hughes, S., Pennington, J. L., & Makris, S. (2012). Translating autoethnography across the AERA standards: Toward understanding autoethnographic scholarship as empirical research. *Educational Researcher, 41*(6), 209–219. https://doi.org/10.3102/0013189X12442983
Iftikar, J. S., & Museus, S. D. (2018). On the utility of Asian critical (AsianCrit) theory in the field of education. *International Journal of Qualitative Studies in Education, 31*(10), 935–949. https://doi.org/10.1080/09518398.2018.1522008
Institute of International Education. (2019). International student enrollment trends, 1948/49–2018/19. *Open Doors Report on International Educational Exchange*. Retrieved from https://opendoorsdata.org/
Jenks, C. J. (2017). Race and ethnicity in English language teaching: Korea in focus. *Multilingual Matters*. https://doi.org/10.21832/JENKS8422

Jeon, M. (2009). Globalization and native English speakers in English Programme in Korea (EPIK). *Language, Culture and Curriculum, 22*(3), 231–243.

Kachru, B. B. (1990). World Englishes and applied linguistics. *World Englishes, 9*(1), 3–20. https://doi.org/10.1080/07908310903388933

Kubota, R., & Lin, A. (2006). Race and TESOL: Introduction to concepts and theories. *TESOL Quarterly, 40*(3), 471–493. https://doi.org/10.2307/40264540

Kumaravadivelu, B. (2016). The decolonial option in English teaching: Can the subaltern act? *TESOL Quarterly, 50*, 66–85. https://doi.org/10.1002/tesq.202

Li, W. (2018). Translanguaging as a practical theory of language. *Applied Linguistics, 39*(1), 9–30. https://doi.org/10.1093/applin/amx039

Llurda, E. (2015). Non-native teachers and advocacy. In M. Bigelow & J. Ennser-Kananen (Eds.), *The Routledge handbook of educational linguistics* (pp. 105–116). Routledge.

Luke, A. (2009). Race and language as capital in school reform. In R. Kubota & A. Lin (Eds.), *Race, culture, and identities in second language education: Exploring critically engaged practice* (pp. 286–308). Routledge. https://doi.org/10.1.1.493.9396

Mahboob, A., & Szenes, E. (2010). Linguicism and racism in assessment practices in higher education. *Linguistics and Human Sciences, 3*(3), 325–354. https://doi.org/10.1558/lhs.v3i3.325

Marx, S. (2017). Intercultural manifestations of racial, language, and class privilege in schooling: An autoethnographic tale. *International Journal of Multicultural Education, 19*(1), 24–40.

Marx, S., Pennington, J. L., & Chang, H. (2017a). Critical autoethnography in pursuit of educational equity: Introduction to the IJME special issue. *International Journal of Multicultural Education, 19*(1), 1–6. https://doi.org/10.18251/ijme.v19i1.1270

Marx, S., Pennington, J. L., & Chang, H. (2017b). Critical autoethnography in pursuit of educational equity: Introduction to the IJME special issue. *International Journal of Multicultural Education, 19*(1), 1–6. https://doi.org/10.18251/ijme.v19i1.1393

Maguire, M. H. (2011). A missing dimension in multiculturalism in higher education: The marginalization of international students' voices and writing identities. *Canadian Issues, 35*.

Miller, J. (2003). *Audible difference: ESL and social identity in schools* (Vol. 5). https://doi.org/10.1075/aral.26.2.10ham

Milner, H. R., Pabon, A., Woodson, A., & McGee, E. (2013). Teacher education and black male students in the United States. *Multidisciplinary Journal of Educational Research, 3*(3), 235–265.

Mirzaee, A., & Aliakbari, M. (2018). "They now respect me and send me to the best schools!": Identity construction of an Iranian EFL teacher. *Critical Inquiry in Language Studies, 15*(1), 21–42. https://doi.org/10.1080/15427587.2017.1327794

Morgan, B. (2004). Teacher identity as pedagogy: Towards a field-internal conceptualisation in bilingual and second language education. *International Journal of Bilingual Education and Bilingualism, 7*(2–3), 172–188. https://doi.org/10.1080/13670050408667807

Phillipson, R. (1992). *Linguistic imperialism*. Oxford University Press. https://onlinelibrary.wiley.com/doi/10.1002/9781405198431.wbeal0718.pub2

Phillipson, R. (2009). *Linguistic imperialism continued*. Routledge. https://doi.org/10.4324/9780203857175

Ricento, T. (2013). Language policy, ideology, and attitudes in English-dominant countries. In R. Bayler, R. Cameron, & C. Lucas (Eds.), *The Oxford handbook of sociolinguistics* (pp. 525–543). Oxford University Press. https://doi.org/10.1093/oxfordhb/9780199744084.013.0026

Richards, R. (2008). Writing the othered self: Autoethnography and the problem of objectification in writing about illness and disability. *Qualitative Health Research, 1*, 1717–1728. https://doi.org/10.1177/1049732308325866

Rudolph, N. (2016). Negotiating borders of being and becoming in and beyond the English language teaching classroom: Two university student narratives from Japan. *Asian Englishes, 18*(1), 2–18. https://doi.org/10.1080/13488678.2015.1132110

Rudolph, N., Selvi, A. F., & Yazan, B. (2015). Conceptualizing and confronting inequity: Approaches within and new directions for the "NNEST Movement". *Critical Inquiry in Language Studies, 12*(1), 27–50. https://doi.org/10.1080/15427587.2015.997650

Rudolph, N., Selvi, A. F., & Yazan, B. (2020). Introduction: The complexity of identity and interaction in language education. In N. Rudolph, A. F. Selvi, & B. Yazan (Eds.), *The complexity of identity and interaction in language education*. Multilingual Matters.

Skutnabb-Kangas, T. (1988). Multilingualism and the education of minority children. In T. Skutnabb-Kangas & J. Cummins (Eds.), *Minority education: From shame to struggle* (pp. 9–44). Multilingual Matters. https://doi.org/10.1177/0016549298060001003

Skutnabb-Kangas, T. (2012). Linguicism. *The encyclopedia of applied linguistics*, 1–6. https://doi.org/10.1002/9781405198431.wbeal1460

Spry, T. (2001). Performing autoethnography: An embodied methodological praxis. *Qualitative Inquiry, 7*(6), 706–732.

Thompson, R. (2006). Bilingual, bicultural, and binominal identities: Personal name investment and the imagination in the lives of Korean Americans. *Journal of Language, Identity, and Education, 5*(3), 179–208. https://doi.org/10.1207/s15327701jlie0503_1

Valencia, R. R. (2010). *Dismantling contemporary deficit thinking: Educational thought and practice*. Routledge. https://doi.org/10.4471/ijep.2012.15

Webster, L., & Mertova, P. (2007). *Using narrative inquiry as a research method: An introduction to using critical event narrative analysis in research on learning and teaching*. Routledge. https://psycnet.apa.org/doi/10.4324/9780203946268

Yazan, B. (2019). Toward identity-oriented teacher education: Critical autoethnographic narrative. *TESOL Journal, 10*(1), e00388.

Yoo, J. (2020). An autoethnography of mothering in the academy. *The Qualitative Report, 25*(8), 3173–3184.

Zuniga, C. E., Lachance, J. R., Aquino-Sterling, C. R., & Guerrero, M. D. (2019). Preparing the "linguistically qualified" bilingual teacher: Self/auto ethnographies of bilingual teacher educators. *Teacher Education Quarterly, 46*(3), 3–11.

Hyesun Cho is an Associate Professor of TESOL in the Department of Curriculum and Teaching at the University of Kansas, USA. Her previous teaching experience includes teaching EFL in Korea and working as an instructor in the Hawaii State Department of Education. Her research interests include heritage language education, language teacher identity, critical literacy, critical pedagogy, and teacher education for social justice. She received the 2008 Outstanding Dissertation of the Year Award from the Second Language Research SIG at the American Educational Research Association. Her monograph on critical literacy pedagogy for pre-service teachers was published by Springer in 2018. She is the recipient of the KU School of Education Faculty Achievement Awards for Research (2018) and Diversity, Equity, and Inclusion (2022).

Open Access This chapter is licensed under the terms of the Creative Commons Attribution 4.0 International License (http://creativecommons.org/licenses/by/4.0/), which permits use, sharing, adaptation, distribution and reproduction in any medium or format, as long as you give appropriate credit to the original author(s) and the source, provide a link to the Creative Commons license and indicate if changes were made.

The images or other third party material in this chapter are included in the chapter's Creative Commons license, unless indicated otherwise in a credit line to the material. If material is not included in the chapter's Creative Commons license and your intended use is not permitted by statutory regulation or exceeds the permitted use, you will need to obtain permission directly from the copyright holder.

Chapter 20
Science Teacher Education in Canada: Addressing Diversity by Living and Teaching Intersectionality

Lydia E. Carol-Ann Burke

Abstract As a Black woman of Caribbean heritage, born and raised in England, my own school science experience was focused on learning the tricks that teachers presented as intuitively graspable. I was used to pushing through and ignoring the 'outsider' feelings that I possessed. As a science teacher and science teacher educator, I came to understand that there are many students for whom the acquisition of science knowledge means compromise to their sense of selfhood, either because they are members of groups for whom Western modern science is not a central tenet of understanding or because of the esoteric mode of science instruction. In this chapter, I identify four critical incidents that have occurred during my professional experience as a science teacher educator. I explore the implications of these incidents by examining them through the equity lens of intersectionality to highlight broader concerns in science teaching and science teacher education. The analyses reinforce the need for science teachers to allow themselves and their students to be open and reflective about their own positionings in the field of science education as well as the need to acknowledge the historical and philosophical contexts of Western modern science as a body of knowledge. I hope that this chapter will be used by science teacher educators to stimulate dialogue and provide an artifact around which constructive and meaningful conversation foments in the many spaces of science teacher education.

Introduction

My fundamental professional concern is the quality of the educational experiences gained by children and youth. I worry about what and how our children are learning. As a former science teacher who transitioned to become a teacher educator in a city that has one of the most diverse populations in the world, I recognize that population

L. E. C.-A. Burke (✉)
Department of Curriculum, Teaching and Learning, Ontario Institute for Studies in Education, University of Toronto, Toronto, ON, Canada
e-mail: carolann.burke@utoronto.ca

diversification often mobilizes an array of biases, discriminations, and prejudices in society. Therefore, I consider it a priority that pre-service and in-service teachers are intentional in their response to the diversity of children and youth in K-12 classrooms. In my role as a science teacher educator and researcher, I care about the skewed demographic profile of people who represent science practice and science education; this is what drives my objective of finding ways to broaden participation in science education. My research focuses on science inclusion by exploring how science is presented to school students and how teachers position themselves and their students as scientific knowers. I have no interest in approaches that focus on 'fixing' the children of minoritized groups so that they are more compliant within a system of inherent biases.[1] In this chapter, I examine my own experience to critically probe diversification initiatives and policies. I recount significant incidents in my academic career when my racial, ethnic, and/or gender identities were foregrounded. Using an intersectionality framework, I explore my positioning as an expatriate science teacher educator, and how this has influenced notions of diversity for my teacher candidates and colleagues.

Who Teaches Our Teachers and What Are they Learning? Diversity in Canadian Higher Education Policy

Major cities in North America are increasingly reflecting the demographic trends seen in Toronto. According to Toronto's 2016 census, approximately 50% of the city's residents belong to a 'visible minority' group, with the same proportion being 'foreign-born' (Statistics Canada, 2017). In 2017, Universities Canada—the organization representing institutions of higher education across the country—published a set of 7 *Inclusive Excellence Principles*, promoting equity, diversity, and inclusion across the higher education sector (Universities Canada, 2017).[2] Among the 7 principles was a focus on broadening faculty diversity. The *Principles* also described a

---

[1] Throughout this paper, I use minoritized or minoritization (as opposed to minority) to signify a process of societal structuring that supports the subordination of people and silencing of voices, irrespective of their actual numerical representation in the population.

[2] Although the terms equity, diversity, and inclusion are often conflated into a single abbreviation, EDI, in this chapter I have used each of the three terms with intentionality to render significant the distinction between and relatedness of the terms. I situate equity within the notion of fairness but not necessarily sameness; the concept calls for systems of power to make judgments based on justice as a right of personhood over protocol or technicality, combatting bias and discrimination. The term diversity is commonly used (euphemistically) to signify difference relative to the dominant category of people but I use it to suggest variance in a population in any one or more of a range of dimensions including race, class, ethnicity, ability, language, gender, religion, etc. Inclusion is one of the most problematic of terms in this triad as it can be used to suggest assimilation of minoritized persons and groups, but I use it to connote processes of providing access and voice whereby participation can be freely chosen (or not) by individuals from historically minoritized groups.

commitment to continued consultation with groups that are under-represented in Canadian university settings—identified in the Universities Canada communication as women, racialized individuals, Indigenous peoples, persons with disabilities, LGBTQ2+ peoples, and men in women-dominated disciplines. These objectives were underlined in the *Principles* by an opening statement affirming the belief that "universities are enriched by diversity and inclusion" (Universities Canada, 2017). Tamtik and Guenter (2019) explained that additional pressures exerted by funding bodies such as the Canada Research Chair Program (Government of Canada, 2018), have incentivized universities to create action plans and policies to publicly demonstrate their commitment to and progress with equity, diversity, and inclusion. The fact that there has been a need for these policies suggests that there is a problem regarding minoritization of students and faculty across the various institutions, but also that there is hope that this problem is enough of a priority to promote real change. Even though I was hired before the introduction of these diversification policies, I see myself as a participant in the *Inclusive Excellence* project, not merely because I am minoritized in a profession that is dominated by White middle-class men, but because the responsibility for enlivening these policies rests on all educators.

Commenting on the diversification agenda of universities in North America, James (2017) stated that academics of colour are often positioned as the individuals in the faculty who "deal with issues of 'diversity' – from counselling students of colour, to covering issues of race and ethnicity in courses, to conducting research in related areas" (p. 155). James continued by explaining that without a critical understanding of race and racialization (and prejudice more broadly), as embedded in social structures and norms, the components constituting the complex intersectionality of racialized and otherwise minoritized lives will be inappropriately read as distinct and equivalent units of oppression. This reductionist view of diversity encourages inclusion strategies that focus on increasing the representation (in terms of sheer numbers) of minoritized faculty and students, and helping minoritized students to navigate university structures. Rather than changing the fundamental structure of systems, and challenging the dispositions of individuals, these approaches serve to maintain the bounds of exclusion for minoritized students. In response, I remain concerned about how critical understandings of diversity will be incorporated into the education of teacher candidates, and what messages those teacher candidates will take into schools.

It is time for teacher educators of all backgrounds to embrace and embody the spirit of the *Inclusive Excellence Principles* so that Canadian teacher candidates may utilize pedagogical approaches and philosophical stances that are not only focused on doing no harm to the students in their care, but which actively confront, disrupt, and seek to combat prejudices and biases. Sleeter (2016) pointed out the error of many teacher educators who assume that their well-qualified and intellectually astute teacher candidates will readily grasp, or passively assimilate, an ability to recognise and confront prejudices such as racism. Speaking of the overwhelming whiteness of teacher education, Sleeter described the generative space created when teacher candidates' knowledge about discriminatory conceptions, such as race, exposes inherent tensions. The challenge to expose and explore prejudice is even more acute when we prepare teacher candidates to teach the ostensibly objective subject matter of science.

The Sociocultural Context of Science Education

There appears to be some resistance to engaging with issues of power and social injustice in the field of science teacher education. It is common to teach about the benefits and challenges of intervention strategies and student-centred modes of teaching and learning for students who are marginalized in science, but teacher candidates are rarely asked to examine how achievement gaps in science arise in the first place; such an examination would lead to exposure of the potential for teachers' complicity in the maintenance of achievement gaps (Le & Matias, 2019). This inattention to deconstructing dominant narratives can leave teacher candidates inadequately prepared to teach students who are marginalized in the science education context (Underwood & Mensah 2018), which can lead to further disenfranchising of already ill-served students. Underwood and Mensah (2018) went further in saying that science teacher candidates need to uncover and examine their own biases, stereotypes, and prejudices with respect to the discipline they teach and the students in their classrooms.

The history of national systems of education in what we euphemistically call the West, combined with the positivist European origins of Western modern science have reinforced the notion that science education is the property of White middle-class men (Mensah & Jackson, 2018). Borrowing from Shizha's notion of science as "a culture for the privileged" (Shizha, 2007, p. 305), Mensah and Jackson (2018) described science as White property, stating that the Eurocentric heritage of science tends to "reify a White, male ownership of science" (p. 9). Mensah and Jackson went on to explain that this conceptualization of science as White property "limits the teaching and learning of science as a right for students of color or other marginalized groups, such as women, students of poverty, and students in low-resourced urban and rural areas" (p. 9). Indeed, Le and Matias (2019) cited data from the USA National Science Foundation asserting that "over 70% of the science workforce are White, and as such, many science faculty at college and university settings are also White". Figures are similar in Canada where fewer than 25% of full-time university science teachers are women (CAUT, 2018). A further complication is seen in science pedagogy where science is presented as an objective knowledge that is used by all developed societies such that anyone who disregards science is deemed ignorant (does not know enough) or backward (their thinking is fundamentally flawed).

The complicated history of science as motivation and mechanism of colonisation has left a legacy in 'Western' and once-colonised nations as a knowledge of the powerful (Burke & Wallace, 2020); hence, there is an incentive for students to capitulate with the science teacher, for fear of being further marginalized in society.

This means that our work, as science teacher educators, starts from a baseline that needs to be intentionally and deliberately unsettled. It is not enough to focus on helping students of colour or students who are otherwise marginalized to navigate the prevalent system of science education, nor is our work done when we call out oppressions in science education. We also need to resist and mitigate further oppressions by helping all teacher candidates to understand the origins and maintenance strategies of oppressions in science education; as asserted by Le and Matias (2019), all educators need to understand the insidious nature of prejudice in science education in order to "unmask unintentional oppression" (p. 21). As minority teachers, we need to start seeing our positions as opportunities to influence the mindsets of present and future generations. As my embodied self, I see opportunities to support the fundamental education of my teacher candidates, as I perform the dual task of combatting the personally draining stereotypes about me and people like me that the preservice teachers may bring to the learning context, while pushing for change and growth of our teacher candidates and the institution. This should be a work of all science teacher educators, not just those for whom the work is the most harrowing.

In this chapter, I explore how my minoritization, as a teacher educator, can be combined with approaches taken by colleagues in more dominant social positions to progress a more critical reading of Canada's higher education diversity agenda for our pre-service teachers. Given the significant social positioning of teachers in society, we cannot wait for the recruitment profile of teachers to shift before progress is made with respect to how diversity is 'dealt with' in schools. Our existing teachers and teacher candidates need to be supported as they develop a more critical appreciation for the socially unjust positionings that many of our school children occupy in contemporary society.

Theoretical Framework: Viewing Educational Inequities Through the Eyes of Intersectionality

Crenshaw (1989) utilized the term intersectionality to describe the compounded subordination of people who experience more than one category of societal marginalization. As an analytic framework, intersectionality has the potential to challenge and confront unidimensional explanations for the skews and imbalances observed in various social contexts. The framework asserts that oppressions based on race, gender, ability, ethnicity, and other dimensions of discrimination interact and result in different levels of political, structural, and representational minoritization. The relationship between categories is historical, socially constructed, and overlapping in ways that are not simply additive. One overwhelming strength of intersectionality (which also represents, perhaps, its greatest challenge as an analytic tool) is its confrontation of dichotomies and its resistance to reductionism (Jordan-Zachery, 2007). As a cautionary note, Rodriguez and Freeman (2016) warned against interpretations of intersectionality that allow distinct prejudices to go unnamed under the guise that 'diversity' is part of the complexity of contemporary living; in these instances, intersectionality is inappropriately invoked to distract from a specific social injustice, so that those in more privileged positions can share in experiences of marginalization. To combat this perspective, just as intersectionality highlights multiple oppressions, its focus on positioning and power dynamics can be used to illuminate compounded layers of privilege. As educators who represent those who have the social advantage of educational capital, we must leverage this aspect of our personas to exert pressure for social change on behalf of countless children who have the potential to get lost in the field that we fight so hard to support.

Methodology: Using Intersectionality to Interpret Critical Incidents

Drawing on various works of Kimberlé Crenshaw and Patricia Hill Collins, Christensen and Jensen (2012) explored the analytic strength of intersectionality, suggesting that a starting point for analysis can be "life-story narratives and the analysis of everyday life" (Christensen & Jensen, 2012, p. 109). In this chapter, I use a selection of my own professional life events (critical incidents) as points of reference from which an analysis of ways forward can be derived. Based on Flanagan's (1954) description of critical incident analysis, Butterfield et al. (2005) identified five phases to the methodology: (i) determining the research objectives and focus; (ii) setting parameters for incidents included in the study; (iii) gathering data (incidents); (iv) analyzing the data based on a pre-determined/emerging schema or framework; (v) interpreting the data and producing a report.

As identified above, the aim of this chapter, and the focus of the incidents selected and analyzed below, is to explore how my positioning, as a minoritized teacher educator, can be used to support colleagues and teacher candidates to adopt a more critical interpretation of Canada's higher education diversity agenda. In selecting which aspects of my story to share in this chapter, I first recounted the top-of-mind work-based experiences that I have found myself relating to friends and colleagues who are insiders to my professional activities and to broader aspects of my life story. These are incidents that have positively or negatively impacted how I think about and perform my professional role, and which have caused me to assess and adjust my perceptions and practices in the workplace. This incident selection approach aligns with Butterfield et al.'s (2005) assertion that critical incidents "help promote or detract from the effective performance of some activity or the experience of a specific situation or event" (p. 483). The incidents selected are analyzed based on the oppression/privilege dynamic of the intersectionality framework described above. It is my hope that, through analysis, these incidents can be used in positive ways to help me, and colleagues in similarly marginalized situations, navigate professional contexts that, at times, can feel less than inviting of our presence.

Findings and Discussion

Below, I recount four incidents (presented in narrative form in italics). After each incident, an analysis is presented where power relations are explored, as described in the oppression/privilege dimensions of the intersectionality framework. I end the chapter with some implications for teacher educators in all strata of society.

Must Some Parts of Me Be Silenced for Others to Thrive?

At the outset of each of my university courses, I share a short biographical profile with my students. I include details of my background as a school science teacher, my perspective on science as a discipline, aspects of my philosophy of teaching, my research background of using postcolonial theory to critique science education, and my focus on broadening participation in science. My aim is to illustrate how my perspective on science education has been shaped by the many life experiences that have influenced every aspect of who I am and how that influences how I teach. I explain that there are many elements of my identity that make this educational journey novel for me and my students. I identify myself as a Black woman from England of Caribbean heritage and I invite my students to journey through the course, exploring with me what the positioning of a teacher might mean for students in various educational settings. I always address aspects of identity because I want my teacher candidates to question and challenge what it means to interact with others as their full selves, acknowledging the various biases that such interactions may reveal. I was caused to reflect on this introduction when at the end of one course, a student confided that she and her peers were initially worried about what the course would be like when I first spoke about 'race and all that' but she was pleased to report that her concerns had not been borne out, and they had all enjoyed the course.[3]

My student's congratulatory tone suggested that she had shared this comment as a compliment but, to me, it highlighted a fundamental issue of a desire for colour-blindness (at least held at the outset of the course) so that the teacher candidate is protected from the discomfort that critical, race-related conversations can evoke. I have long understood that my social positioning as a Black woman might cause others around me to question my 'fit' (and, perhaps, fitness) as a science teacher and science teacher educator. As discussed by Mensah and Jackson (2018), speaking from a United States perspective, "there are tangible aspects of life that White people claim as their own" and from which 'people of colour' are excluded (Mensah & Jackson, 2018, p. 7); science seems to be one of those areas. Although I am a

---

[3] Throughout this chapter I have made approximations of conversations based on my recollections.

Black woman, when I am outside of the British context, my positioning becomes more ambiguous; I occupy a professional role that is usually classified as prestigious, and I carry an accent that suggests my European birth (which would align me with the knowledge system within which I work). I speak of *carrying* an accent and *suggesting* my origins because the lines of questioning that I face in North America reveal that what was previously read as a standard 'home counties' British accent is often read as affect (as if the various facets of my life are not already incongruent enough that I would seek to affect an accent). Asher (2006) referred to such identity disjunctures as interstitial locations, "dynamic spaces between identifications and cultures" (p. 176). The enigmatic nature of my presence in my professional role presents me with many personal challenges, but this ambiguous positioning provides numerous opportunities for me to be an impactful influence on the lives of teacher candidates with whom I work.

Solomon et al. (2005) referred to their numerous encounters with "the level of discomfort that is experienced on the part of the candidates when discussions of oppression, marginalization, colonization, racism, etc., are initiated" (p. 154). They caution that "in attempting to engage discussions of whiteness among white teacher candidates, teacher educators must remain aware of the ways in which the anger, frustration and general sense of uneasiness among participants can lead to the opposite effect" (p. 156). This is likely to be true when discussing discrimination with any group of socially privileged individuals, as is often the case with graduate teacher education programs such as the one within which I teach. Although I am intentional in my teaching approach, I do not have a specific agenda to 'tackle' race, ethnicity, and gender issues with my teacher candidates. I am just trying to prepare them for teaching science to all children; so, diversity cannot be ignored. For me, these are just natural considerations, not forced or laboured, just the reality of contemporary science education in Canada. As identified by Solomon et al. (2005), the unique vantage point that membership of a racialized group brings provides "multiple lenses through which the world is seen" (p. 152). The authors describe this as providing access to the double-consciousness described by DuBois (1973). While the situation of understanding the professional culture of the dominant while having the privilege of cultural connections with the marginalized may be read as somewhat disjointed, I believe it is a position from which we are well equipped to support our teacher candidates as they grapple with the various disparities we see in science education. This includes helping teacher candidates to move beyond meritocratic explanations in order to explain the complexities associated with differential achievement in our school communities; understanding these complex issues starts with examination of our own histories and positionings, rather than the 'diversity' of school students (Le & Matias, 2019). I appreciate that, while I model this examination at the outset of my courses, I need to provide my teacher candidates with explicit opportunities to conduct such self-examination.

The Embodied Self Can Signify Hope

Each year, I attend one of the graduation ceremonies for our range of degree programs. A couple of years ago, I had the opportunity to be a faculty participant during the convocation ceremony for our graduating teacher candidates. As is often true of university graduation ceremonies, the occasion was an elaborate event with strict dress codes, precision timing, and an array of Latin utterances. The students were in positive and jovial mood. So much so that, despite warnings to the contrary, several of them brushed past the flowers and the ceremonial mace on the stage to hug their professors. At the end of the ceremony, a Black woman, who was part of the officiating team at the event, came over to me and whispered "I have been noticing who comes over to hug you, you are doing an important job here!" I smiled politely, thanked her for her encouragement, and felt somewhat energized but, in that moment, I did not grasp what she had meant. Later, when I reflected upon the events of the day, I recalled that most of the students who had defied protocol to come and hug me were students from racially minoritized groups.

A body of literature has established a positive correlation between the academic performance of minoritized students and being taught by teachers who have similar backgrounds (E.g., Dilworth & Coleman, 2014; Easton-Brooks, 2015; Villegas & Davis, 2008). In addition, Brown (2014) cited numerous studies confirming the idea that teachers of color do not just see themselves as role models for minoritized students, they also seek to be transformative change agents. Nevertheless, being taught by a Black teacher educator, particularly in science education, may be unexpected for most teacher candidates in Canada, particularly those for whom racial and ethnic diversity of educators has not been a significant feature of their prior educational experience.

For the minoritized student trying to navigate through their introduction to the teaching profession, Brown (2014) explained that preservice teachers of colour often identify their teacher education programs as lacking in knowledge that is socioculturally relevant, critical, and humanizing. I find that students from racially minoritized groups will often find ways to spend time with me, discussing issues and taking my elective courses that will provide spaces for them to openly express concerns about science education that have been brewing for some time. Students tell me that there are few places where they can discuss some of the oppressions they have faced in their own science education, and some come to a realization that they are not personally to blame for much of the negativity they have encountered while receiving a science education. I hope that, by providing such spaces to intellectually engage with challenges experienced as racially minoritized students, my teacher candidates are able to echo the comments made by 'pre-service teachers of colour' in the study conducted by Mensah and Jackson (2018): "I was able to find my voice and place in science education" (p. 25), "I had a teacher I was able to relate to … and this made me a lot more comfortable during the semester" (p. 24), and "I see myself as a science teacher" (p. 25). More importantly, I hope that my teacher candidates, irrespective of their ethno-racial background, can create science classroom climates for their own students so that the science classroom will be an inviting, engaging, and inclusive space of learning for all students; this is unlikely to happen if my teacher candidates are afraid to participate in challenging conversations about bias and social positioning in science education.

Challenging and Confronting Without Uttering a Word

A few years ago, during a teacher candidate group presentation, an incident occurred which shifted the entire tone of the class, and my subsequent approach in the course. The group member leading the presentation, advanced the slides to reveal a monochrome image of a flock of caged birds being liberated by a single bird. The presenter used the image to illustrate the teacher's role in science education. Unfortunately, the liberating bird was white, and the encaged birds were black. As soon as the presenter appreciated the potential interpretation of the image as being racially loaded, he paused, seemingly very conscious of my presence, and started apologizing for the image, stating that they had not previously thought about other connotations that the image might have beyond the idea of children being free to express themselves. As the composure of the teacher candidate (usually very calm, collected, and in control) started to unravel, the apology continued; he explained that when they picked the image they had not thought about the colours and now they feel terrible that the bird in charge of liberation is a white bird acting as 'savior' to the black birds. He referred to my research using a postcolonial framework and, as the explanation went on, I remember trying to avoid any display of emotion, I could see that the student was in evident discomfort and I felt my own level of frustration rising. I realized that, had my body not been in that room, that teacher candidate would not have had that moment of confrontation; a moment when, what was taken for granted was confronted with different/imagined perspectives because I was sitting in front of him and my approval would influence his grade. I resolved to be more intentional about approaching and deconstructing challenging ideas as they present themselves in class.

Reflecting on the incident above, I wondered if my teacher candidates would second guess themselves in the same way if they had made a similar representational faux pas in front of a classroom full of school children. Would there be the same level of consciousness about subliminal messages in the pedagogies they employ in their own classrooms? It was important for me to follow up with questioning and constructive challenging that would model approaches they could use in their own classrooms. We needed to add some additional elements to our community agreement. I encouraged the students to identify and try to eliminate euphemisms such as 'diverse students' from our conversations. We spoke about challenging the indeterminate 'they' when referring to a marginalized group, prompting each other to clarify meanings when such comments are made. Finally, we spoke about the power of labelling and explored noun placement in descriptions of groups (as with my own work with children from low-income communities, as opposed to low-income children). It is important for teacher candidates to see how their own social positioning influences the messages they send about science education to their students. As Banks (2001) stated, teacher candidates "must be helped to critically analyze and rethink their notions of race, culture, and ethnicity and to view themselves as cultural and racial beings" (pp. 11–12). Banks also went on to speak about seeing how these concepts position the teacher socially, economically, and politically. A greater awareness of these positionings may help teacher candidates to be more cognizant of how their actions and attitudes can serve to maintain achievement gaps that are highlighted in the academic literature.

All Educators Need to Engage Authentically with the Work

I am disheartened when I reflect on so many instances when I have voiced equity concerns to my colleagues, only for those issues to be devalued or simply ignored. Sometimes I think that I may be too indirect in my approach as I am often acutely mindful of the potential to elicit responses that are based on emotional defensiveness rather than reflective engagement. One such example of this occurring was when, in casual conversation, I referred to the teacher candidate presentation incident above to make the point that our teacher candidates are not used to being challenged to think beyond their own positions of privilege. I suggested that the absence of peers of colour, particularly Black teacher candidates, meant that confrontation of deficit ideologies about race were not common. My concern was met with a response of bewilderment from a senior faculty member who stated, "How can that be? I thought we put a Black teacher candidate in each cohort!".

My colleague's assertion reinforces the belief that gaining a complex understanding of diversity that challenges prejudices and biases will occur passively, just by association. My colleague might as well have said: "How can that be? Each teacher candidate has a Black friend!". Framed in that way, the absurdity of the comment becomes clearer. It suggests that explicit and intentional work (beyond the academic examination of literature about diversity) is not required since all teacher candidates are being exposed to diversity in their teaching cohorts. This, indirectly, places the onus on teacher candidates who identify as marginalized to educate their peers into a state of critical consciousness. This expectation, even if common, is unsupported by the literature which states that "teacher candidates of color report high levels of alienation, a disconnection from the larger program community and a sense of not 'seeing themselves' in their programs" (Brown, 2014, p. 334). With such alienation, the pressing matter at hand is self-preservation rather than education of peers. In addition, Le and Matias (2019) indicated that the way diversity and inclusion are addressed in teacher education tends to emphasize a "safe multiculturalism" (p. 18) that neglects specific naming of oppressions and critical examination of complicity, leaving personal perspectives unchallenged. According to Le and

Matias, these approaches to teacher education keep minoritized teachers and teacher candidates silenced. The silencing of already minoritized teacher candidates was described by Sleeter (2016), where she referred to a study conducted by Amos (2016) explaining that:

> White teacher candidates enacted whiteness (such as joking about racist remarks, and avoiding learning by claiming to already understand another culture) in a class taught by a professor of color, and how these enactments silenced the few teacher candidates of color in the class who worried about consequences of confronting White peers not only in class, but also later on in schools where they might be hired. For candidates of color, this prevalent whiteness was agonizing, even terrorizing (Sleeter, 2016, p. 1066).

Not only did prominent White students try to silence the teacher candidates of colour, they were described as preying on the minority instructor. This emphasizes the fact that the work is not just for teacher educators of colour, indeed, it cannot be carried out by us alone as we are often unable to validate our own voices. If there are no benign positions in systems of education, then we are all doing something to either confront or maintain inequity and discrimination.

Conclusions

Returning to the focus of Universities Canada's *Inclusive Excellence Principles*, it is all to easy to see how the policy document might be used superficially to ensure that representation (in terms of the numbers) of faculty of colour in teacher education positions might be used to mitigate 'bad press' or litigation (as discussed in Henry et al., 2017). This focus can, at times, obscure a true commitment to the work of deconstruction that undergirds social justice initiatives; consequently, there is a need for institutional structures and mechanisms where new faculty hires are made on the basis of faculty being equity minded, and not just equity seeking. There needs to be a drive for shifting the profile of dispositions of institutional members; this will impact the expectations placed on our teacher candidates and, ultimately, will be carried into schools by the new generation of teachers. We cannot afford to relax when the demographic profile of teacher candidates in our teacher preparation programs starts to approximate the diversity of the given population, since oppression is a matter of power, not numbers. If the hard work of confronting deeply embedded deficit ideologies goes unchecked, particularly in teacher education, then we are using a band-aid to fix a heart attack in our education systems. The responsibility for promoting equity and inclusion sits with everyone in our teacher education programs: all teacher educators and all teacher candidates. This is particularly important when we consider the history of oppressions associated with the field of science education.

In this chapter, I have suggested that using critical interpretations of diversity (as are facilitated by the intersectionality framework) can support a more complex reading of diversity for faculty and teacher candidates. I want my teacher candidates to own that they, just as I, carry assumptions about people based on their backgrounds, accents, appearance, etc. I want them to be able to acknowledge this and continue to second guess themselves, asking the "what if I'm wrong" question. The physical trigger of a minoritized faculty member can support the process and provide important support for difficult conversations but all faculty members must face the issue of discrimination with humility so that learning can occur at all levels within the university institution. As illustrated in Crenshaw's (1989) discussion of the complexity of employment policies and laws in addressing the rights of Black women, the embodied intersectionality of minoritized instructors in teacher education can support students as they start to contextualize diversity and facilitate consideration of "how different social categories mutually constitute each other as overall forms of social differentiation or systems of oppression" (Christensen & Jensen, 2012, p. 110). The somewhat enigmatic nature of a Black woman in science education could be a means of stimulating conversation that begins to challenge stereotypes.

Difficult conversations challenge the White property status of science education, but those conversations need to start with an understanding of science in relation to its history and what that means for who is included in the field of science education. When teacher educators ask science teacher candidates to question the meritocratic strength of systems of education, the teacher candidates are often defensive because they feel that they have worked hard to get to where they are today, they feel that they have earned their academic accolades and, if we challenge the system, it calls into question their hard work. There is often a visceral response to such confrontations which can manifest itself as hostility towards the instructor. Solomon et al. (2005) reminded teacher educators that sometimes, merely attempting to engage in such challenging conversations with teacher candidates can shut down and reverse attempts to broaden perspectives. Nevertheless, if only to support teacher candidates of minoritized social groups, all teacher educators must commit to the task of working to disrupt this knee-jerk response to ethical discomfort; as described by Sleeter (2016), "given the many studies of whiteness in teacher education extending back at least 20 years, teacher educators cannot claim ignorance about White candidates collectively victimizing peers (and faculty) of color." (p. 1066).

For minoritized faculty members, this is painful work. Although pain is never welcome, it is important that the pain of prejudice does not get so normalized that we fail to recognize it or, worse, start to accommodate it. As recounted by Nina Asher, who identifies as a South Asian woman academic in North America, "at least, over time, I have acquired some where withal to deal with such shocks ... I have not become numbed to the pain. Because, if I were 'unable to feel the pain, unable to make it conscious,' then, of course, I would be 'unable to engage the possibility of transformation'" (Asher, 2006, citing her previous work Asher, 2003). I sometimes marvel at the fact that the pain does not get any less acute; perhaps I should start to see this as a blessing.

References

Amos, Y. T. (2016). Voices of teacher candidates of color on white race evasion: 'I worried about my safety!'. *International Journal of Qualitative Studies in Education, 29*(8), 1002–1015.

Asher, N. (2003). Engaging difference: Towards a pedagogy of interbeing. *Teaching Education, 14*(3), 235–247.

Asher, N. (2006). Brown in Black and White: On being a South Asian woman academic. In G. Li & G. H. Beckett (Eds.), *"Strangers" of the academy: Asian women scholars in higher education* (pp. 163–177). Stylus Publishing.

Banks, J. A. (2001). Citizenship education and diversity: Implications for teacher education. *Journal of Teacher Education, 52*(1), 5–16.

Brown, K. D. (2014). Teaching in color: A critical race theory in education analysis of the literature on preservice teachers of color and teacher education in the US. *Race, Ethnicity and Education, 17*(3), 326–345.

Butterfield, L. D., Borgen, W. A., Amundson, N. E., & Maglio, A.-S. T. (2005). Fifty years of the critical incident technique: 1954-2004 and beyond. *Qualitative Research, 5*(4), 475–497.

Burke, L. E. C., & Wallace, J. W. (2020). Re-examining postcolonial science education within a power-knowledge framework: A Caribbean case study. *Science & Education, 29*(3), 571–588.

CAUT [Canadian Association of University Teachers]. (2018). *Underrepresented & underpaid: Diversity & equity among Canada's post-secondary education teachers*. Retrieved from: https://www.caut.ca/sites/default/files/caut_equity_report_2018-04final.pdf

Christensen, A. D., & Jensen, S. Q. (2012). Doing intersectional analysis: Methodological implications for qualitative research. *NORA-Nordic Journal of Feminist and Gender Research, 20*(2), 109–125.

Crenshaw, K. (1989). Demarginalizing the intersection of race and sex: A Black Feminist critique of antidiscrimination doctrine, feminist theory and antiracist politics. *University of Chicago Legal Forum, 1989*(1), 139–167.

Dilworth, M. E., & Coleman, M. J. (2014). *Time for a change: Diversity in teaching revisited*. Retrieved from http://hdl.handle.net/10919/84025

DuBois, W. E. B. (1973). *The education of Black people: Ten critiques, 1906–1960*. University of Massachusetts Press.

Easton-Brooks, D. (2015). Bridging the gap and diversifying teaching education. In L. D. Drakeford (Ed.), *The race controversy in American education: Volume 1* (pp. 259–280). ABC-CLIO.

Flanagan, J. C. (1954). The critical incident technique. *Psychological Bulletin, 51*(4), 327–358.

Government of Canada. (2018). *Open letter from the Canada Research Chairs Program management to institutional presidents*. Retrieved from https://www.chairs-chaires.gc.ca/whats_new-quoi_de_neuf/2018/letter_to_presidents-lettre_aux_presidents-eng.aspx

Henry, F., Dua, E., Kobayashi, A., James, C., Li, P., Ramos, H., & Smith, M. S. (2017). Race, racialization and indigeneity in Canadian universities. *Race Ethnicity and Education, 20*(3), 300–314.

James, C. E. (2017). "You know why you were hired, don't you?" Expectations and challenges in university appointments. In F. Henry, E. Dua, C. E. James, A. Kobayashi, P. Li, H. Ramos, & M. S. Smith (Eds.), *The equity myth: Racialization and indigeneity at Canadian universities* (pp. 155–170). UBC Press.

Jordan-Zachery, J. S. (2007). Am I a black woman or a woman who is black? A few thoughts on the meaning of intersectionality. *Politics & Gender, 3*(2), 254–263.

Le, P. T., & Matias, C. E. (2019). Towards a truer multicultural science education: How whiteness impacts science education. *Cultural Studies of Science Education, 14*(1), 15–31.

Mensah, F. M., & Jackson, I. (2018). Whiteness as property in science teacher education. *Teachers College Record, 120*(1), 1–38.

Rodriguez, J., & Freeman, K. J. (2016). 'Your focus on race is narrow and exclusive': The derailment of anti-racist work through discourses of intersectionality and diversity. *Whiteness and Education, 1*(1), 69–82.

Shizha, E. (2007). Critical analysis of problems encountered in incorporating indigenous knowledge in science teaching by primary school teachers in Zimbabwe. *Alberta Journal of Educational Research, 53*(3), 302–319.

Sleeter, C. (2016). Wrestling with problematics of whiteness in teacher education. *International Journal of Qualitative Studies in Education, 29*(8), 1065–1068.

Solomon, R. P., Portelli, J. P., Daniel, B. J., & Campbell, A. (2005). The discourse of denial: How white teacher candidates construct race, racism and 'white privilege'. *Race Ethnicity and Education, 8*(2), 147–169.

Statistics Canada. (2017). *Toronto, C [Census subdivision], Ontario and Canada [Country]* (table). *Census Profile*. 2016 Census. Statistics Canada Catalogue no. 98–316-X2016001. Statistics Canada. Retrieved from https://www12.statcan.gc.ca/census-recensement/2016/dp-pd/prof/index.cfm?Lang=E

Tamtik, M., & Guenter, M. (2019). Policy analysis of equity, diversity and inclusion strategies in Canadian Universities–How Far Have We Come? *Canadian Journal of Higher Education, 49*(3), 41–56.

Underwood, J. B., & Mensah, F. M. (2018). An investigation of science teacher educators' perceptions of culturally relevant pedagogy. *Journal of Science Teacher Education, 29*(1), 46–64.

Universities Canada. (2017). *Universities Canada inclusive excellence principles*. Universities Canada. Retrieved from https://www.univcan.ca/wp-content/uploads/2017/10/equity-diversity-inclusion-principles-universities-canada-oct-2017.pdf

Villegas, A. M., & Davis, D. E. (2008). Preparing Teachers of Color to confront racial/ethnic disparities in educational outcomes. In M. Cochran-Smith, S. Feiman-Nemser, D. J. McIntyre, & K. E. Demers (Eds.), *Handbook of research on teacher education, third edition* (pp. 583–605). Routledge.

Lydia E. Carol-Ann Burke is an Associate Professor of Science Education in the Department of Curriculum, Teaching and Learning at the Ontario Institute for Studies in Education (OISE), University of Toronto. Prior to embarking on a career in research, she worked for 15 years as a full-time science teacher in school and college contexts. Her research focuses on broadening participation in science by exploring the factors that marginalize youth from engagement with science education in formal and informal settings. Through this research, she is dedicated to supporting educators as they develop meaningful and relevant learning experiences for their students.

Open Access This chapter is licensed under the terms of the Creative Commons Attribution 4.0 International License (http://creativecommons.org/licenses/by/4.0/), which permits use, sharing, adaptation, distribution and reproduction in any medium or format, as long as you give appropriate credit to the original author(s) and the source, provide a link to the Creative Commons license and indicate if changes were made.

The images or other third party material in this chapter are included in the chapter's Creative Commons license, unless indicated otherwise in a credit line to the material. If material is not included in the chapter's Creative Commons license and your intended use is not permitted by statutory regulation or exceeds the permitted use, you will need to obtain permission directly from the copyright holder.

Chapter 21
White College Students' Cognitive Dissonance When Taught by Immigrant Professor of Color

Amani Zaier and Faith Maina

Abstract This study investigated whether White college students experience cognitive dissonance when taught by immigrant professors of color and if so, how do they restore harmony and balance in order to complete the course successfully. Cognitive dissonance refers to feelings of discomfort that arise when a person's behavior or attitude is in conflict with the person's values and beliefs, or when new information contrary to their beliefs is presented to them. The participants in this study were 321 preservice teachers who were enrolled in a culturally and linguistically diversity course and a bilingual education course at a large, predominantly White university in the southwestern United States Using three archival instruments including anonymous questions, a guessing activity, a mid-term and end-of-semester evaluations, the students manifested dissonance by "othering" the professor through cultural and racial profiling, questioned the professor's qualification, professionalism and credentials, and expressed anger and anxiety towards the course. These processes have significant implications for the career trajectory of the immigrant professor of color, while at the same time impacting the knowledge access for White college students.

Background Story

Being an immigrant professor of color is an interesting academic status that reflects a controversial façade of academe. It brings pride and acknowledgement as well as doubt about credibility and competence. The way teachers of color have been historically perceived and evaluated supports this claim. For example, African American teachers have been portrayed as incompetent and powerless (Fultz, 1995). From another perspective, Walker (2001) provided a historiography of African American teachers between 1940 and 1960 who had a strong sense of commitment and determination to make a difference, despite all odds. These African American

---

A. Zaier (✉) · F. Maina
College of Education, Texas Tech University, Lubbock, TX, USA
e-mail: Amani.Zaier@ttu.edu

© The Author(s) 2023
M. Gutman et al. (eds.), *To Be a Minority Teacher in a Foreign Culture*,
https://doi.org/10.1007/978-3-031-25584-7_21

teachers in the South did not consider themselves victims of their environment, despite the harsh and unfair conditions they had to navigate (Walker, 2001).

Other teachers coming from diverse racial and ethnic backgrounds share similar experiences in their teaching career, regardless of their trajectories and teaching approaches. They are usually reminded of their foreignness and questioned about their competencies (Creese, 2019; Dumlao & Mengorio 2019; Eros, 2016; Hutchison, 2006; Kuhn, 1996). Kim and Cooc (2020) reviewed 37 peer-reviewed research studies on the beliefs, experiences, and practices of Asian American and Pacific Islander teachers in relation to social justice work within U.S. schools. Their analysis of teacher diversity shed light on teacher practices that disrupt whiteness in schools. The results showed that these teachers of color questioned whiteness by adopting a set of beliefs and pedagogical practices that celebrate difference, value multiple perspectives, and empower marginalized voices. As a remediation strategy, Kim and Cooc (2020) urged school policies and culture to "affirm and sustain the belonging of teachers with diverse cultures and languages regardless of their country of birth or official citizenship, to uphold diversity as an asset to the overall learning environment" (p. 10).

In academe teacher pedagogical competence is transferable and transportable. Teachers carry their competence and experiences wherever they move as part of their teaching journey either from urban to rural cities or across international borders. Thus, it is assumed that foreign teachers as well bring with them competence from prior experiences. It is evident that teacher hiring is based on strong qualifications and promising competencies. This is indeed applicable to international teachers. When they move to a foreign country to teach, they carry their acquired competencies and experiences, along with pride and ambition for professional growth.

I came from Africa to the United States as a Fulbright scholar to teach at an institution of higher education. This award is highly competitive, and is given to scholars who demonstrate outstanding achievement and potential, and who represent the diversity of their societies (Council for international Exchange of Scholars – CIES, n.d). In the succeeding years, I kept seeking various opportunities for growth. I gradually enhanced my competence and expertise by earning additional graduate degrees, certificates, attending trainings, and teaching in diverse contexts within the United States. I was always cognitively, emotionally, and academically prepared to advance and grow professionally; equipped with qualifications, enthusiasm, and passion for teaching. However, it was not until the last 4 years that I began teaching specific courses related to diversity and methods of teaching diverse learners; it was then that I started to notice a consistent pattern of questioning and resistance from some students. The questions they asked at the beginning of every course were not about the intellectual discourse, but rather, about my racial and cultural background. They wanted to know more about my qualifications, teaching competency, and expertise. Some of the questions were outright intrusive and by the time I got my mid and end-of-semester evaluations, I knew something was not right. During informal conversations with other professors of color, I heard similar complaints about the inquiries they were receiving from students and the hostile end of semester evaluations. These conversations sparked my motivation to conduct this study as a way of investigating possible reasons for this kind of behavior and learning about White college students' attitudes towards immigrant professors of color. The purpose of the study is to understand why White students experience cognitive dissonance when they are taught by a foreign professor. For this reason, this study adopted the action research attitude (Johnson & Christensen, 2019) as an approach to understand students 'beliefs and attitudes with the goal to create a positive learning environment for all. Data was primarily collected from one professor's classes, while a second research expert, who is also a female professor of color, helped with data analysis.

Conceptual Framework

When White college students first enter a college classroom, they expect to find a professor who looks like them. It therefore comes as no surprise that they experience cognitive dissonance when they find an immigrant professor of color (DiAngelo, 2012; Kowal et al., 2013). Cognitive dissonance is defined as that state in which people have a core belief and when they are presented with evidence that works against that belief, the new evidence cannot be accepted (Fanon, 1967). Since it is very important to protect the core belief, people will rationalize, ignore, and even deny anything that does not fit with the belief (Fanon, 1967). Cognitive dissonance refers to feelings of discomfort that arise when a person's behavior or attitude is in conflict with the person's values and beliefs, or when new information that is contrary to their beliefs is presented to them. According to Festinger et al. (1955), people desire consistency and want assurance that their values and beliefs have always been right. They want to act in ways that align with their beliefs. When the beliefs are challenged, it creates a dissonance which might be manifested though stress, anxiety, regret, shame, embarrassment, or feelings of negative self-worth (Festinger et al., 1955).

Loosing Balance & Harmony

According to McFalls and Cobb-Roberts (2001), an individual can experience psychological tension or dissonance when new knowledge or information is incongruent with previously acquired knowledge. Therefore, White college students experience feelings of mental discomfort when they find an immigrant professor of color in their classroom and they may seek to alter their attitudes, beliefs or behaviors to reduce the discomfort and restore balance. This type of behavioral disequilibrium is expected especially in predominantly white serving institutions. Students are used to be taught by professors they can associate with and with them they share common characteristics. When exception happens and they are presented with a professor who does not fit into their existing schema, they may experience some type of discomfort and unbalance. They are later forced to assimilate the new reality and expand their mental effort to adjust and accommodate with the new experience.

Restoring Balance & Harmony

However, restoring the balance and harmony is not always easy. Festinger et al. (1955) found the danger of cognitive dissonance lies in the fact it is much easier to make excuses than to make changes. This leads people to self-justification and a search for arguments that reinforce their viewpoint:

> We have all experienced the futility of trying to change a strong conviction, especially if the convinced person has an investment in his belief. We are familiar with the variety of ingenious defenses with which people protect their convictions, managing to keep them unscathed through the most devastating attack (Festinger et al., 1955, p. 1).

Literature Review

Boatright-Horowitz et al. (2013) conducted a study to investigate whether White college students would change their attitudes about racism after being exposed to a list of White Privileges (McIntosh, 2001). This was after the acknowledgement that campus social climates were racist and many White students failed to acknowledge the problem. Indeed, more than 70% of Black college students felt "they were viewed as lacking academic competence by faculty and others on campus" (Boatright-Horowitz et al. 2013, p. 699) and 65% experienced verbal and racial harassment. Even though 50% of the White college students in this study admitted to exhibiting open dislike (e.g., name-calling, physical violence, negative facial expressions) towards others because of their race, being exposed to the White Privilege (McIntosh, 2001) list resulted in hostile, anti-diversity, sexist and insulting responses from some students. Similarly, Clark and Zygmunt's (2014) study on implicit bias resulted in disregard and rationalization when teachers' core beliefs and attitudes were challenged. Teachers were exposed to the Implicit Association Tests (IATs) instrument, which measured their preference for European American and light skin against Black skin. Even though 96% of the teachers indicated a preference for European American and light skin, some disregarded the results and rationalized the results. One participant in the study argued that "the results of the IAT did not seem accurate to me. It stated that I had a strong preference for White people but I don't agree with this. I almost felt like it was a trick" (Clark & Zygmunt, 2014, p. 152). The pattern of complete dismissal, denial, and devastation at the thought of possessing a hidden bias resulted in the teachers failing to acknowledge race as a social construct, "moving them to consider their personal role in advancing equitable education for all" (Clark & Zygmunt, 2014, p. 158). College students in the Kinney (2013) study experienced a moment of "awkwardness" when they were exposed to a barrage of negative tweets towards a Black character in a film. The bone of contention was that the beloved character in the book from which the film was derived bore perceived White characteristics and viewers felt betrayed when a Black person was cast in the film. The White audience was therefore angry and experienced a moment of "cognitive dissonance between imagined impression of the character and the way she was represented in the film" (Kinney, 2013, p. 47). Prior to discussing the angry tweets, students in this class had rejected the notion of White privilege and subscribed to "we are different and should celebrate our differences as equals" (Kinney, 2013, p. 41). The purpose of the activity was, therefore, to engage the students and show them "how common sense hegemonic narratives are created, produced, reproduced and contested through popular culture" (Kinney, 2013, p. 41). DiAngelo (2012) argues that most of "White superiority is internalized and unconscious" (p. 175), such that any address of racism and privilege elicits responses that include "anger, withdraw, emotional incapacitation, guilt, argumentation and cognitive dissonance" (p. 183). DiAngelo (2012) refers to this phenomenon as "White fragility," in which even a minimal amount of racial stress becomes "intolerable, triggering a range of defensive moves" (p. 183). White fragility limits the ability to build cognitive or affective skills to develop the stamina and allow for constructive engagement across racial divides and when faculty of color raise race issues: "they are seen as a problem and accused of being racist towards whites for suggesting that racism is present" (DiAngelo, 2012, p. 184). Consequently, faculty of color find themselves in a double bind: "they either have to endure racism or be penalized for trying to change it" (DiAngelo, 2012, p. 184). To restore balance and harmony, Whites modify their existing beliefs and values so that "white privilege is not a factor because we do not see color anyway, we see each person as unique individual" (DiAngelo, 2012, p. 174) and thus, "categories such as race have no meaning and provide no more or less opportunities" (p. 175). Kowal et al. (2013) introduce the concept of "reflexive anti-racism" in reference to diversity training because even motivated anti-racist trainers are prone to negative emotions such as "discomfort, distress, guilt, fear, anxiety, inaction and withdrawal" (p. 318), and this disjunction may arise "between anti-racist ideas and unconscious feelings, thoughts and behaviors that reflect racist social norms" (Kowal et al., 2013, p. 318). By engaging in reflexive anti-racism, Kowal et al. (2013) argue that White people would shift their thinking of racism from something that is "individual malicious, overt, to seeing it as pervasive reality that they themselves have a responsibility to address" (p. 321). This sentiment was equally expressed by Kinney (2014), who noted that the "cloak of color blindness frequently renders whiteness invisible" (p. 147) and therefore, "they need to recognize how they benefit from privilege without becoming mired in guilt and anxiety (Kowal et al., 2013, p. 325). White college students are prone to experience cognitive dissonance when they realize their professor is an immigrant of color. This study therefore was guided by two questions: (1) How is cognitive dissonance manifested in White college students' beliefs and attitudes in my course? and (2) How do they restore their balance and harmony in order to be successful in the course?

Methodology

Research Approach

This study followed an action research design to investigate how cognitive dissonance is manifested in White college students when taught by an immigrant professor of color and how they restore their balance and harmony in order to succeed in the course. In action research, the teacher is the main investigator and the intent of the inquiry is to inform and improve the instructional practices or understand a specific student behavior. In this particular study, the intent of the researcher is to understand the cognitive processing behind students' perceptions and expectations of their immigrant professor of color. This research was carried out within the context of the professor's environment. Implicit in the term *action research* is the idea that teachers will begin a cycle of posing questions, gathering data, reflection, and deciding on a course of action. Action research emphasizes the involvement of teachers in problems in their own classrooms and has as its primary goal the in-service training and development of the teacher, rather than the acquisition of general knowledge in the field of education (Metler, 2013). Johnson & Christensen (2019) mentioned that "action research starts with you and your place of work, and it is used to address what you believe is important to address" (p. 56). In congruence with this assumption, the researchers in this study adopted the action research attitude to improve their teacher-student relationship by identifying the sources of cognitive dissonance. "This attitude asks you to be both reflective and forward thinking and to be a good observer" (p. 56).

Context of Study

The study took place in a large, predominantly White university in the southwestern United States. Even though the university has reached a 25% Hispanic population, thus earning a Hispanic Serving Institution (HIS) status, the teacher education program where I taught has majority White middle-class female students. For the last 4 years, I have been teaching diversity and bilingual courses required for students in the teacher education program to become certified teachers in PreK-12.

Participants

The participants in this study were preservice teachers enrolled in both my culturally and linguistically diversity course or/and bilingual education course. These preservice teachers go through a rigorous teacher education curriculum that is focused on students' learning and intensive clinical experiences. The implementation of the field practice is intended to better prepare these preservice teachers to the teaching profession. Upon the completion of the program they become certified teachers in preK-12. A total of 321 preservice teachers provided information for this study. There were 278 females and 43 male preservice teachers who were predominantly white.

Data Sources

Three archival data sources were used in this study: (1) anonymous direct questions and guesses on sticky notes, (2) mid-semester student feedback, and (3) end of semester official students' evaluations.

Anonymous Direct Questions and Guesses on Sticky Notes Over the last 4 years, I developed a habit of starting off the first day of class with an ice breaker activity. I pull a pack of sticky notes and move around the class, providing each student with a sticky note. I then ask them to write three questions related to the course or the instructor. I give them few examples such as "Do we need a textbook?", "Are we going to have a final exam or final project?" They are also encouraged to make three guesses such as" I guess this course requires group work and discussions", "I guess you love dogs". I finally remind them not to write their names on the sticky notes. Once they are done, I ask them to stick their notes on the board. With no exception, this introductory activity has always been a great ice-breaker. I intentionally use a few jokes to encourage students to make guesses and ask questions. Their attention usually peaks when I start responding to their questions. While conducting this activity, students indirectly get a fair picture of who I am and about the course. Students have repeatedly asked about my academic background, teaching experience, teaching philosophy, my origin, and family. We also cover a big portion of the syllabus and course expectations. Depending on class size, this activity usually takes about 45 min. Right after, we move to students' introductions, followed by clarification of the syllabus. I usually have about 20 students in each section. After 4 years, I have collected 321 sticky notes from my undergraduates' preservice teachers enrolled in both my diversity course and bilingual classes.

Mid-Semester Students' Feedback At mid-semester, I collect informal and anonymous feedback from my preservice teachers. The purpose of collecting this feedback is twofold. First, is to measure students' satisfaction with the course content, method of delivery, and usefulness. Second, is to gather suggestions for improvement. Students are encouraged to critique the course and instructor by responding to questions such (1) Which aspect of the course is most helpful to you? (2) Which aspect of the course is least helpful to you? (3) Are there any suggestions you would like to make about how to improve the course? (4) If I could change one thing about this course, it would be?

End Semester Official Students' Evaluations This set of data is gathered by the institution. They are the formal course and instructor evaluations that students complete at the end of each academic semester. These are the standard approach used by most educational institutions to rate course and instructor effectiveness. In most cases, these are the sole variables used to evaluate teaching effectiveness and have implications for tenure, promotion, and personnel decisions. Only the comments section of the evaluations was used in this study.

Data Analysis

After eliminating missing and redundant data, the final data set included 321 sticky notes, 73 feedback forms, and 21 formal evaluation comments. We followed open and axial coding for data analysis. We first used open coding, looking for emergent themes guided by Strauss and Corbin (1990). We read through the questions and guesses written on the 321sticky notes. We had a total of 963 questions and 640 guesses collected over the course of 4 years. We separately created tentative labels for each chunk of data that corresponded to either perception or expectation. We initially color-coded the questions that fit into the same category to establish properties for each code, such as origin, academic qualifications, and course requirements. In a second phase, we used axial coding (Strauss, & Corbin, 1990; Scott, & Medaugh, 2017; Vollstedt, & Rezat, 2019) to identify relationships among the open codes. By axial coding, we investigated the relationships between the emerging concepts and categories that have been developed in the open coding process. The coding paradigm simply went through breaking the data in the process of open coding, and then joined together by axial coding pulling out the categories and their subcategories.

Findings

In analyzing the data, three major themes emerged: (a) cultural and racial profiling – othering the professor, (b) competencies, professionalism and credentials questioned, and (c) expressed anger and anxiety towards the diversity and bilingual courses.

Cultural and Racial Profiling – Othering the Professor This theme emerged primarily from the analysis of the anonymous direct questions and the sticky notes guesses. The commonly asked questions evolved around my origin, culture, language, ethnicity, and race. This was evident as soon as I enter the classroom, students immediately made a mental note that I was a foreigner. While this curiosity could be extended to any professor on the first day of class, the invasiveness in which some of questions were framed indicated a certain level of intrusiveness on the professor as a person (e.g., "Do you plan to go back home one day?", "At what grade did you start learning English?"). The physical appearance urged some students to make inaccurate guesses centered around the geographical origin based on visible physical attributes such as skin color, hair type, and the English accent, (e.g., "I guess you are from Puerto Rico" or "I assume you are from…", whichever country where my physical features could stereotypically fit). When going through the guesses students made about the instructor, we found out that they all, without exception, made a clear assumption that the professor is of a foreign origin. This conclusive observation is derived from the preconceived assumptions students have about what physical traits people from a foreign background have. It was, therefore, not surprising that the multilingual status became a factor in determining the effectiveness in teaching as shared by one student (preservice teacher, spring, 2019):

> This class was a valuable learning experience; the teacher was knowledgeable and available. My comment is for the Bilingual program: Why this course, which was supposed to prepare me to teach English language learners is taught by professor who speaks English as a third language? This does not make sense.

The same sentiment of "othering" the professor was expressed by another participant (preservice teacher, fall, 2018) who shared:

> She was phenomenal in cultivating a safe environment for controversial conversations. She was very respectful, kind, and was eager to pass along her knowledge and share experiences with us; however, I do not understand why this course is taught by a professor who is not from here.

Despite the acknowledgement that teaching was effective and the professor had the indicators of a successful educator, being an "other" challenged the sensibilities of the participants in this study especially when the diversity course addressed sensitive topics related to race, racism, and white privilege.

Competencies, Professionalism and Credentials Questioned This second theme was derived from the Mid-semester students' feedback and the final evaluations. Some students questioned the professor' competency, professionalism, and credentials right on day one of the course. They wanted to know my academic qualifications, whether I had experience teaching in the college or K-12 environment in the United States or if I had a teaching philosophy. It did not take long for the students to confirm their doubts by mid-term evaluations with comments about the diversity course such as "So far, I did not find much benefit in this class. I do not understand why we are taking this course about diversity, how this can prepare me to teach, I felt like it was a waste of time and money" (preservice teachers, mid-term evaluations). Others claimed the bilingual course was redundant, as they had already picked up the skills in other courses and one thing they would change about the course was to have another teacher "from here", with experience teaching in K-12 in the US. One student wrote: "She is teaching us how to differentiate instruction for diverse students in high school and not how to control them. She has no clue how to deal with their problems and behaviors because she had never taught at high school" (mid-term evaluation). This sentiment was expressed by yet another student (preservice teacher, mid-term evaluation) who said,

> You have told us in the first day of class that you did not attend K-12 school here and you have only college level teaching experience, therefore, you really do not know how hard it is to deal with students with diverse backgrounds here.

Some students questioned the pedagogical approaches used in the classroom, such as peer-review and micro-teaching. They perceived these student centered practices which put more responsibility on the students about their own learning as irrelevant. One student shared (end of semester evaluation):

> A lot of microteaching was done and at times was ineffective. I'm paying for a class where a professional is going to teach me, not my fellow peers. She is a fine teacher, but the structure of the class was ineffective and not a valuable learning experience. I Wish I learned more about the theory behind ESL.

This sentiment was further reinforced by another student (end of semester evaluation) who said:

> She is a sweet lady and is a kind professor. When it comes to this course though, I do have a different opinion. The way that she laid out this course or this course was designed was not really effective. She had students teach every class time. Which to an extent I can get that, but when we are teaching ourselves the content I don't really feel like there is a need to show up for class. We each had a micro lesson that we had to teach and so I felt like we are all teaching each other information. I don't feel as though I learned as much as I could have if we had just been lectured to and taught by our professor rather than being taught by other students. Again, I don't have anything negative to say about her., she was nice and was respectful.

A similar sentiment was expressed by a student (end of semester evaluation) who shared:

> She made us teach the class this semester, which I can understand from an educator perspective as being helpful. I'm very disappointed that my money has been spent on me teaching myself the material or having a peer do it.

References to being "sweet" "nice", "kind", "respectful", and so forth premises the scathing criticism which follows, akin to saying, "am not racist" but this person is not qualified for the job.

Expressed Anger and Anxiety Towards the Diversity and Bilingual Courses This third theme stemmed from the mid-term and final course evaluations. Teaching diversity and bilingual courses to students who are predominantly white raises anxiety even in the best of circumstances. Being taught by an immigrant professor of color may have brought an added layer of anger. Even before the course began, students had assumed that the professor would be harder on them in terms of meeting expectations and even in their classroom behavior. They wanted to know whether "absenteeism, tardiness, or late submission" of assignments would impact their grades, exuding some level of anxiety. By mid-term evaluation, students had begun to show higher level anxiety about grades and class assignments as shared (end of semester evaluation):

> Her class was a valuable learning experience; however I felt that some lesson did not have adequate instructions to help us understand what it was that we were supposed to be doing for an assignment. When contacted for clarification she would respond quickly and she would give clarification. I feel that if more explanation was given on some assignments students would be more successful in completing assignments to the proper standards.

This sentiment was reinforced further by a student (end of semester evaluation) who said:

> when I would speak with her in class she would come off as if she didn't care what I was asking and would not answer my questions clearly. Her assignments were not clear and if you didn't do them correctly she gave you points off, which didn't make sense due to the fact that the rubric didn't clearly state that's what was to be done for the assignment. Having clearer instructions would have helped make this course run smoother.

Even though anger and frustration about lack of communication were expressed only by a few students, we decided to still include them in the analysis. This may be interpreted as the approach these students used to restore their balance and harmony by using teacher's perceived lack of good communication as evidence to justify their low scores. Beyond the anxiety observed about grades and assignments, pre-service teachers also expressed fear and anxiety when it comes to meeting the needs of diverse learners at the pre K-12 environment. For instance, during the topic concerning differentiated instruction for culturally and linguistically diverse learners, students argued that the specific differentiated instructional strategies they were practicing would not be impactful during their teaching practice. Instead, they preferred to be taught skills on managing diverse students' behavior and maintaining control in the classroom. It was undeniable that preservice teachers see diverse students as an extra challenge added to their teaching duties.

Discussion and Conclusions

In this study, we questioned whether White college students experienced cognitive dissonance while taught by an immigrant professor of color, and if they did how they restored balance and harmony in order to be successful in the course. We argue that cognitive dissonance is manifested by the White college students in this study through processes such as "othering" the professor, questioning their competencies and expressing anger and anxiety towards the course through macroaggressions. These findings have significant implications. One, there is the danger of impeding the professional growth of the immigrant professors of color or reducing the ability to thrive in their career. Official student evaluations are used by many administrators as the only tool to measure teaching effectiveness and are determinants of tenure, promotion, and other personnel decisions. Preservice teachers in this study are aware of the weight that is carried by these evaluations in higher education and therefore, directly questioned the wisdom of those charged with responsibility of staffing this position (e.g., Why is this course, which was supposed to prepare me to teach English language learners, taught by professor who speaks English as a third language?) This is a direct message to the employer to reevaluate the services of this person in order to eliminate the mental discomfort of the student. Secondly, preservice teachers use a mental block to emotionally drop out from participating in their own learning. Pedagogical approaches, such as peer- review and micro-teaching that are used widely in the profession become a barrier to their own learning. This self-sabotage to accessing knowledge results in negative comments (e.g., "this course was a waste of money"). Thirdly, opportunities for reflexivity are lost because of the emotions of anger and anxiety directed towards the course. Since some preservice teachers harbor these unconscious biases, they are unable to productively engage with the professor in the process of problem-solving, where much learning takes place. We therefore recommend that colleges intentionally prepare White students for intellectual engagement with diverse professors. Preservice teachers and students in general need to build cognitive and affective skills to develop the stamina that would allow for constructive engagement across racial divides (DiAngelo, 2012; Kasztalska, 2019; Ramjattan, 2019). It is possible they will find jobs in diverse work places or themselves become foreign teachers in different parts of the world: therefore, they need to be prepared for success in such positions and contexts. More primary data should be directly collected from students to further investigate what can be done to mitigate and fully understand the phenomenon of cognitive dissonance in White college students when taught by immigrant professors of color. Likewise, the voice of faculty of color can provide further insights on how conductive environments for teaching and learning can be created in diverse classrooms.

The purpose of this study was to investigate how White college students manifest their cognitive dissonance when taught by immigrant professors of color and how they restore balance and harmony in order to successfully complete the course. Cognitive dissonance is a state of mental discomfort leading to an alteration of attitudes, beliefs or behaviors to reduce the discomfort and restore balance. Students in this study developed a mental note as soon as I entered the classroom that I was an "other". During an ice-breaker activity in which they were asked to anonymously ask questions and make guesses, they framed the questions in terms of cultural and racial profiling with comments indicative of attacks on my personhood. They clearly questioned my qualification, professionalism and credentials, wondering how I would manage the course given my multilingual background and foreignness. Students expressed fear and anger towards the diversity course and harshly judged the impact it would make to their overall practice as teachers.

White college students experience cognitive dissonance when taught by immigrant professors of color, which is manifested through the processes of othering the professor through cultural and racial profiling, questioning competencies, qualifications and credentials, and expressed direct anger and anxiety towards the course. The danger of these processes is that they threaten the career trajectory of the immigrant professor of color, impede intellectual growth of the students, and make the learning environment hostile and stressful. Given the diverse environment in which the students will be seeking employment, colleges have the challenge and responsibility to prepare students to engage constructively with people from diverse racial backgrounds.

Limitations of the Study

We used archival data for analysis of this study, which means that it was collected for other purposes and later found to be relevant to the investigation of this phenomenon of cognitive dissonance. It is therefore possible that it may not accurately answer the specific questions raised in this study. The findings may therefore have to be interpreted with caution. But even with that limitation, the study has yielded significant findings. The preservice teachers in this study experienced cognitive dissonance described by McFall and Cobb-Roberts (2001) as a state of psychological tension or dissonance when new knowledge or information is incongruent with previous acquired knowledge. Typically, college White students expect to find a professor who looks like them when they enter the classroom. On entering the classroom and finding that their professor is an immigrant of color, they did what Festinger et al. (1955) describe as the danger of cognitive dissonance where making excuses become easier than making changes. This leads people to self-justification and a search for arguments that reinforce their viewpoint. Preservice teachers quickly created a mental memo that the professor did "not belong"; thus, consequent intrusive attacks on my personhood concur with Boatright-Horowitz et al. (2013) on college White students exposed to the notion of "White Privilege" (McIntosh, 2001). Rather than change behavior towards their fellow students of color, they responded in hostile, anti-diversity, sexist, and impertinent comments. Similarly, teachers in the Clark and Zygmunt (2014) study noted disregard and rationalization when their core beliefs and attitudes were challenged during an implicit bias training. Likewise, students in this study questioned the professor' qualification, professionalism, and credentials, but vehemently denied it was anything to do with race. Indeed, they described their professor as being "sweet, nice, respectful, helpful, knowledgeable, and loved her" but had not yet reached the threshold of an effective professor. This is the kind of awkwardness described by Kinney (2013) about the "imagined impression of the character and the way she was represented in the film" (p. 47) when a Black person was cast in what the White audience perceived to be White characteristics based on the book where the film was derived. The professor did not fit the imagined impression of a college professor, so that visible physical attributes such as skin color, hair type, and accent become the central focus in order to trivialize any feelings of discomfort. The way students in this study questioned the qualifications, professionalism, and credentials could correspond to what DiAngelo (2012) refers to as "White fragility" (p. 183). Being taught by an immigrant professor of color caused racial stress, which triggered a range of defensive moves such as questioning the competencies and conspiratorially questioning the wisdom of those who put this professor in that position in the first place (e.g., "I do not understand why this course is taught by a professor who is not from here" [preservice teacher, Fall, 2018]).

References

Boatright-Horowitz, S. L., Frazier, S. Y., Harps-Logan, Y., & Crockett, N. (2013). Difficult times for college students of color: Teaching white students about White Privilege provides hope for change. *Teaching in Higher Education, 18*(7), 698–708. https://doi.org/10.1080/13562517.2013.836092

Clark, P., & Zygmunt, E. (2014). A close encounter with personal bias: Pedagogical implications for teacher education. *The Journal of Negro Education, 8*(3), 147–161.

Corbin, J. M., & Strauss, A. (1990). Grounded theory research: Procedures, canons, and evaluative criteria. *Qualitative Sociology, 13*(1), 3–21.

Creese, G. (2019). "Where are you from?" racialization, belonging and identity among second-generation African-Canadians. *Ethnic and Racial Studies, 42*(9), 1476–1494.

DiAngelo, R. (2012). What makes racism so hard for whites to see? In what does it mean to be white? Developing white racial literacy. *Counterpoints, v*(398), 167–189.

Dumlao, R. P., & Mengorio, T. (2019). From inland to outland: Experiences of non-native expatriate teachers teaching in a foreign context. *Journal of English Education, 4*(1), 24–37.

Eros, J. (2016). "Give me a break—English is not my first language!" experiences of linguistically diverse student teachers. *Journal of Music Teacher Education, 26*(1), 69–81.

Fanon, F. (1967). *Black skins, white masks*. Grove Press.

Festinger, L., Riecken, H. W., & Scatchter, S. (1955). *When prophesy fails*. University of Minnesota Press.

Fultz, M. (1995). African American teachers in the South, 1890–1940: Powerlessness and the ironies of expectations and protest. *History of Education Quarterly, 35*(4), 401–422.

Hutchison, C. B. (2006). Cross-cultural issues arising for four science teachers during their international migration to teach in US high schools. *School Science and Mathematics, 106*(2), 74–83.

Johnson, R. B., & Christensen, L. (2019). *Educational research: Quantitative, qualitative, and mixed approaches* (6th ed.). Sage.

Kasztalska, A. (2019). International teaching assistants in the composition classroom: From world Englishes to translingualism and beyond. *Journal of Language, Identity & Education, 18*(3), 161–175.

Kim, G. M., & Cooc, N. (2020). Teaching for social justice: A research synthesis on Asian American and Pacific Islander teachers in US schools. *Teaching and Teacher Education, 94*, 103104.

Kinney, R. J. (2014). "But I don't see race". Teaching popular culture and racial formation. *Transformations: The Journal of Inclusive Scholarship and Pedagogy., 24*(1 & 2), 40–55.

Kowal, E., Franklin, H., & Paradies, Y. (2013). Reflexive antiracism: A novel approach to diversity training. *Ethnicities, 13*(3), 316–337.

Kuhn, E. (1996). Cross-cultural stumbling block for international teachers. *College Teaching, 44*(3), 96–100.

McFalls, E., & Cobb-Roberts, D. (2001). Reducing resistance to diversity through cognitive dissonance instruction: Implications for teacher education. *Journal of Teacher Education, 52*, 164–172. https://doi.org/10.1177/0022487101052002007

McIntosh, P. (2001). White privilege and male privilege: A personal account of coming to see correspondences through work in women's studies (1988). *Race, class, and gender: An anthology*, 95–105.

Ramjattan, V. A. (2019). Racist nativist macroaggressions and the professional resistance of racialized English language teachers in Toronto. *Race Ethnicity and Education, 22*(3), 374–390.

Scott, C., & Medaugh, M. (2017). Axial coding. *The International Encyclopedia of Communication Research Methods*, 1–2.

Vollstedt, M., & Rezat, S. (2019). An introduction to grounded theory with a special focus on axial coding and the coding paradigm. *Compendium for Early Career Researchers in Mathematics Education*, 81–100.

Walker, V. S. (2001). African American teaching in the South: 1940–1960. *American Educational Research Journal, 38*(4), 751–779.

Amani Zaier is an Associate Professor of practice at the Department of Educational Psychology at Texas Tech University (USA). She enjoys training future educators and working with diverse population of learners. Her current research interests focus on Culturally Responsive Teaching, teacher self-efficacy beliefs and addressing the psycholinguistic needs of culturally and linguistically diverse students.

Faith Maina is a Professor in the department of Curriculum & Instruction at Texas Tech University (USA). Faith Maina is a teacher educator with special emphasis on Action Research and culturally relevant pedagogy. Her research interests include cultural and language diversity in the classroom, issues of culturally responsive teaching and preparing diverse learners for the STEM career pipeline. Her research also interests include culturally relevant diverse pedagogies as a way of increasing access to knowledge for diverse learners.

Open Access This chapter is licensed under the terms of the Creative Commons Attribution 4.0 International License (http://creativecommons.org/licenses/by/4.0/), which permits use, sharing, adaptation, distribution and reproduction in any medium or format, as long as you give appropriate credit to the original author(s) and the source, provide a link to the Creative Commons license and indicate if changes were made.

The images or other third party material in this chapter are included in the chapter's Creative Commons license, unless indicated otherwise in a credit line to the material. If material is not included in the chapter's Creative Commons license and your intended use is not permitted by statutory regulation or exceeds the permitted use, you will need to obtain permission directly from the copyright holder.

Part IV
Ethnic Minority Teachers as a Cultural Mediators

Mary Gutman ⓘ, Wurud Jayusi ⓘ, Michael Beck ⓘ, and Zvi Bekerman ⓘ

Chapter 22
Kurdish Teachers in Turkey Within the Context of History Education

Fatih Yazıcı

Abstract The relationship between Turks and Kurds, two peoples who have lived together for nearly a thousand years, has become tense with the nation-building policies that have been implemented in Turkey for over a century. The imposition of a singular identity based on Turkishness on a wide range of national/ethnic differences ranging from the constitution to educational policies has caused limitations in Kurds' living their own identities along with other minority communities. Due to its close relationship with national identity, history courses are among the areas of education that tend to ignore ethnic/cultural differences in Turkey. Kurdish teachers of history, who have to teach a content organized with such an understanding, are trapped between the truths of official history and the truths of their own identities, as well as the identity problems they face in the social and political field. In this study, interviews were conducted with Kurdish teachers of history of different religious/sectarian, political and sexual identities and their relations with their students, colleagues and educational bureaucracy and the meaning of history lessons for them were revealed. Thus, it was tried to understand what it means to be a Kurdish teacher of history in Turkey.

Introduction

Densely populated in specific areas of Turkey, Iraq, Iran, and Syria, Kurdish people are the fourth largest community in Middle East region following Turks, Arabians, and Iranians (Kurubaş, 2008). In addition to these political boundaries, Kurds also display socio-cultural differences such as religion/sect and language (Yılmaz, 2015). The tribal structure prevented Kurds living even in the same country from being a socio-economic whole (Kurubaş, 2008). As Van Bruinessen (2011) pointed out, therefore, Kurds give the impression of a community formed by the clusters of different ethnic groups rather than being a single ethnic group in terms of economic,

---

F. Yazıcı (✉)
Tokat Gaziosmanpasa University, Tokat, Turkey
e-mail: fatih.yazici@gop.edu.tr

political and cultural criteria. However, the consciousness of common destiny brought about by historical developments brings Kurds into a whole (Kurubaş, 2008). Different theories have been put forward that Kurds, one of the ancient peoples of Mesopotamia, are of Med, Armenian, Arab, Persian or Turkish origin (Dündar, 2009; Eröz, 1982; Hennerbichler, 2012; Limbert, 1968; Nikitin, 2002).

The Kurds, who are a minority within the political boundaries they are divided into in the Middle East, have made various political and cultural claims against the majority culture, bringing with them a number of "problems" for countries that are determined to maintain their unitary structure, such as Turkey. It would be useful to examine the history of Turkish/Kurdish relations in order to understand this complex and multidimensional situation, which is called the "Kurdish problem" in Turkey.

The first meeting between Turks and Kurds dates back to the Middle Ages (Biçer, 2013a, b). With the arrival of Turks in Anatolia and the Middle East, first conflict and then a consensus due to sharing the same religion determined the fate of the relationship between the two communities. The institutionalization of this relationship took place in the fourteenth century when the Ottoman empire significantly dominated the Middle East geography, where the Kurds were densely populated. During this period, a vassal relationship was established between the Ottoman sultans and the local Kurdish beys and an autonomous structure was defined for the region (Koçal, 2014; Yeğen, 2014). In return, the Kurds, who are mostly Muslims, recognized the political presence of the sultan, who was also the Caliph of Islam.

The end of nearly five centuries of peaceful period in Turkish/Kurdish relations and the definition of Kurdishness as a 'problem' encounters the period of modernization of the Ottoman Empire (Yeğen, 2014). The struggle to liquidate the 'loose' relationship that became a structural feature of the relationship between Kurds and central power in the nineteenth century has caused the first clashes between local Kurdish beys and Ottoman central rule (Koçal, 2014). However, these conflicts, which are considered as the emergence of the Kurdish problem, are distinguished reactions not related to the identity demand of the masses, but based on the demands for the continuation of the autonomy of local/traditional authorities against the Ottoman process of centralization. As a matter of fact, since the social structure based on the tribe delayed the development of a common ethnic/national identity among Kurds, identity-based conflicts took place more during the Republican period, when nation-building policies were strictly followed.

The Republic of Turkey was built on the ideology of the nation-state with emphasis on Turkishness by rejecting the multilingual, multi-religious, multi-ethnical heritage of the Ottoman Empire due to the influence of the internal political conditions of the period (Altun, 2013). For the founding staff, "Turk", the name of a nation, was also the name of the citizenship identity of the Republic and no distinction was made between both. A citizenship identity built on ethnic foundations meant a process of assimilation or ignoring for non-Turkish communities that did not have the same ethnic references. Kurds were the most affected and most reacting to this process of assimilation and denial due to their demographic density (Yazıcı, 2015). Indeed, during the first years of the Republic, Kurds were defined in the

Turkish Language Dictionary as " a community name, most of whom are Turks who have changed their language and speak a broken Persian..." (Beşikçi, 1986). Because of this approach, Kurds are not defined as a minority community in international texts such as the Treaty of Lausanne, which determines the status of minorities in Turkey.

On the other hand, the secular quality of the newly established state and the citizenship identity it was trying to build has reduced the cooperation of Kurds, who are mostly Muslims, with the Republic (Yazıcı, 2015). Unable to position themselves within the kind of identity that the nation-state is trying to build, the Kurds followed an opposing line that highlighted their differences (Aktay & Kızılkaya, 2014). The Kurdish uprisings, an example of this reaction, have become the founding staff's greatest endeavor in domestic politics. As Tunçay (1981) noted, only one of the 18 incidents that could have been described as an uprising between 1924 and 1938 did not take place in Eastern Anatolia (Kurdish population region). What is taking place in the East, except for the Nasturî Uprising, is directly related to the Kurds.

The rise of nationalism in Europe in the 1930s (Aktoprak; 2010) brought significant limits to experience cultural/ethnic differences in Turkey as well as in different countries. The shaping of nation-building in the fields of culture, history and language during this period also led to non-Turkish citizens being forced to speak Turkish both privately and publicly (Yıldız, 2010). Avoiding cultural demands of Kurds with such bans shows that the expressions of cultural identity by Kurds, who have the second largest population, are perceived as a potential risk to the integrity of the Republic (van Bruinessen, 2008).

The Kurdish reaction to the singular citizenship identity imposed by the Early Republican Era began to become visible from the 1950s onwards. Doubtlessly, Turkey's new democratic structure by transition to multiparty system had an effect on this situation (Yazıcı, 2015). In addition, factors such as migration waves from rural areas to cities, the development of transportation and communication tools in the same period have made various identities more visible. Moves such as representation in right-wing and especially left-wing political parties have also ensured that Kurdish ethnic and cultural demands are constantly on the agenda (Altun, 2013).

With the 1980 military coup, the liquidation of the political space in Turkey and the human rights violations that followed have been an important breaking point in Turkish/Kurdish relations. Kurdish groups in the left spectrum of politics have formed the PKK (Kurdistan Workers' Party), launching an armed struggle that will last for decades from this period (Feridun, 2016). Since the beginning of the armed struggle in 1984, approaching the issue as security, not an identity problem, has prevented Turkey from producing permanent solutions to the "Kurdish problem". Moreover, the armed actions of the PKK, which peaked in the 1990s, fed Turkish prejudices against Kurds, while human rights violations caused during the fight against the PKK supported the negative image of Kurds about Turks (Alkan & Yazıcı, 2020).

In the early 2000s, Turkey's willingness to join the European Union (EU) positively influenced the approach to Kurdish identity because recognition of Kurdish identity and cultural rights have been issues that the EU has been meticulously focusing on in the Progress Reports during this process. Eu harmony laws enacted between 2000 and 2004 abolished bans such as speaking, teaching and broadcasting in local languages other than Turkish (Ergin, 2010; Nal, 2010; Oran, 2010; Tacar, 1996). Despite these positive developments, it continues to be highlighted in the EU Progress Reports that restrictions on minority rights in Turkey are still ongoing, the language, culture and fundamental rights of minorities should be respected, tolerance should be increased and a more inclusive approach should be taken (Yazıcı, 2015).

As all these historical developments have shown, Turkey continues to significantly ignore the Kurdish problem today, rather than learning about the civil-democratic ways to deal with it. Most human rights violations in Turkey are related to the Kurdish issue (Sambur, 2008). A significant number of its citizens who share this identity believe that they are subjected to various discriminations and cannot maintain their own identity freely (Altun, 2013). The relevant research shows that Kurds think that they are most pressured and excluded among the different ethnic communities living in Turkey because of the way they define themselves (Aktay & Kızılkaya, 2014). Therefore, ethnic belonging, which should be considered natural, has been transformed into a heavy burden for Kurds.

The state's policy of ignoring the issue makes its presence felt in education as in many areas. In fact, it can be expressed that education is one of the areas where claims of different ethnic communities are embodied. For example, the most fundamental demand on the Kurdish question focused on education in mother tongue/ mother tongue education (Kaya, 2012). This shows that Kurdish families in Turkey are concerned about providing their children with an education that will convey their language and culture (Çayır, 2014). On the other hand, it is not officially accepted that children starting school can have a mother tongue other than Turkish, and educational practices are not included to ensure the adaptation of bilingual or not Turkish speaking students to school. This causes student-teacher miscommunication, behaviors of grade-repetition and leaving school, stigma and alienating violence for Kurdish students within the education system (Coskun et al., 2010). In the first phase of education, Kurdish children realize that knowing the official language in school, not their own mother tongue, is a privilege and entitled feature and feel the weight of their identity from a young age. On the other hand, students from the majority culture are deeply unaware of who the people they live with are.

Although discriminatory statements and rights violations about differences in textbooks have decreased relatively in the last 20 years, the fundamental mentality problem remains. Textbooks still continue to produce content that excludes/ignores differences. So much so that Kurds are not mentioned even in the Kurmanci, Zazaki elective textbooks, and moreover, the books contain statements that see citizens with different religions, languages and ethnicity as a threat (Çayır, 2014). This shows that education continues to be a power apparatus in order to legitimize the denial of a social reality called Kurdish.

Research Objective

In this research, it was tried to reveal what it means to be a Kurdish teacher of history working in Turkey. In this context, answers to the following questions were sought:

For a Kurdish teacher of history

1. How does her/his ethnic identity affect her/his relationships with her/his students?
2. How does her/his ethnic identity affect her/his relations with colleagues, the school administration and the education bureaucracy?

Context of Research

National or ethnic identities need common memories to strengthen co-ordnance and belonging among community members (Smith, 1991). History responds to this need of nation-states by producing a number of symbols, memories, customs, habits, values and beliefs (Bilgin, 1999; Korostelina, 2008). History teaching, on the other hand, achieves the purpose of disseminating "we", which is built through a common memory (Pamuk, 2014). All kinds of values, images, positive and negative judgments that are desired to be included in social memory are transferred to students through textbooks in a planned and programmed way (Yıldırım, 2016). Thus, history education becomes a instrumental quality around the idea of basing the nation-state on a homogeneous society (Parlak, 2005).

Republic of Turkey's experience in teaching history is an example of the nation-state's close interest in teaching history. Since it was seen as a political duty to write and teach history after the proclamation of the Republic, active political people have undertaken this mission (Ersanlı, 2006). History teaching has been re-established with a secular nationalism approach with drastic changes made since the 1930s (Yıldırım & Şimşek, 2015; Kabapınar, 1992). With the effects of nation-building weakening in the following years, the secular dimension of national identity has been liquidated (Copeaux, 1998; Yazıcı, 2011), however, an ethnically singular identity continued to be conveyed through history courses.

As a result of some developments in favor of differences in the last decade, some ethnic and religious claims within the education system has affected history courses. In this sense, compared to previous years, it can be stated that there has been a relative improvement in discriminatory statements and rights violations in history textbooks. However, problems remain over ignoring differences or discrimination (Çayır, 2014). This affects Kurds along with other minority communities. While Kurdish students have to learn a history in which they have been ignored, the situation is even more interesting for Kurdish history teachers because they have to teach the history, which they are not a part of, belonging to a society they are a part of to both Kurdish and Turkish students. The dilemma of these teachers whose knowledge collides with what they have to teach from time to time is the starting point of this research.

Methodology

Critical qualitative research method was used in the study to understand what it means to be a Kurdish teacher of history in Turkey. In this context, preliminary interviews were conducted with 47 history teachers who defined their ethnic identity as Kurdish, had different political tendencies, religious/sectarian identities, and served in middle or high schools in different parts of Turkey. In these interviews, the participants were explained the purpose and scope of the research. Although they were guaranteed that their identities would be kept secret, many of the participants did not want to take part in this research because they felt that it was dangerous for their professional careers due to Turkey's political climate. In the final phase, interviews were conducted with 12 history teachers who volunteered for the study and had the same demographic characteristics as the pre-interviewed group. The names of these participants were changed while they are used in findings.

An open-end and semi-structured interview form was used to collect data in the research. Interviews conducted online due to pandemic conditions have been recorded digitally. The recordings of the interviews, which were between 34 and 57 min, were transcribed verbatim. The document obtained in this way has been examined through content analysis. In this context, participant responses were categorized, citations found to be suitable for the purpose of the research and highly representative were determined and converted into research findings.

Results & Discussion

Relations of Kurdish History Teachers with Students from Majority Culture

It is one of the important objectives of this research to reveal the relationship that Kurdish history teachers have with their students from the majority culture. In this context, participants were first asked if they shared their ethnic identity with their students. Participants' views at this point show that Kurdish history teachers tend not to share their ethnic identity with their students for the most part. Some participants are very clear about this (*"no, no, no, I don't share at all"*, P3), some participants prefer not to share their identities with their students as much as possible or unless asked directly. P1's statements are an example:

> In terms of my own teaching ethics, my professional ethics, I try to give my students this: When it comes to it, when they ask, they have nothing to do with my marital status, ethnic

identity, political identity, etc., except for my educational identity, just my educational identity. I'm trying to teach them not to ask anyone. Ask about the books I read, ask about the faculty I graduated from, what you should read, that is, here are the books I will recommend... every question is free within the framework of education... Of course, the children are falling for their curiosity, and they ask a lot of questions socially. When asked, I do not avoid expressing it in any way. I never hid my identity. But I've never lived my identity in the foreground because identities are temporary and variable.

P1 thinks that it is not suitable for teaching ethics to share not only the ethnical identity but all of the collective identities as well. The reference to the approach of P4, which expresses that it does not "take a choice" from sharing its ethnic identity with its students when "asked" in the same way as P1, is religious: "*I am part of the Sunni sect, and I have never bragged about what God has given us, nor has there been any shame in them.*"

But is there any differentiation in the relationship between the students of the teacher who shares his ethnic identity in some way? P1 answers this question:

I describe myself as a successful, good teacher. I'm loved by the student. It initially amazes them that someone they love so much, someone they admire, has an identity that is so often referred to as problems, but once they know that identity, I have not yet witnessed their respect or love for me diminished.

Many of the other participants in the study similarly stated that they did not have a problem with their students because of their ethnic identity. However, the view of cultural differences in the education system and society in which students are raised can also cause some teachers to worry about the future:

After the children grow up from that point of view, I wonder if they get into that med and judge me like that, it's going to be a huge trauma. Of course, it creates a sadness when the person you know and care about changes and gives you a role and imposes on you through super identity, even though he knows you. But I'm telling you again, that sadness is temporary. Because it's a shortcoming in him that he doesn't accept you for who you are (P2).

In some cases, you may not be able to hide your ethnic identity even if you want to. For example, if you were born in a predominantly Kurdish city identified with Kurdish identity like Diyarbakir, you can't hide your ethnic identity from your students or their parents, even if you want to. P5's statements make this clear:

Of course, they knew. When you are already from Diyarbakir, you have a different position in the thinking of students or parents. Say it or not, you're from Diyarbakir, then you're Kurdish. That's why, at first, most parents approached me with prejudice. They stated that I should not take students' classes because I could lead their children to different thoughts. But because they later found that the information we gave the students was useful, the parents' approach towards me was also very different. I only had half a semester of trouble there. After that, the parents and students accepted me.

If you are a Kurdish teacher and teach a course that directly appeals to students' identities, such as history, it is possible to be met with a bias by your students or their parents. As can be seen from K5's statements, in this case, you need to prove yourself to students or their parents with your success in your profession and eliminate prejudices with your own efforts unlike a Turkish teacher.

Relations of Kurdish History Teachers with Majority Cultural Colleagues and Education Bureaucracy

While most participants stated that their ethnic identity was not a determinant in their relationship with their students, the participant's answers may differ when it comes to the relationship they have with their colleagues. In this differentiation, it can be stated that the perception of the participants' own ethnic identity and the relationship they established with the majority culture were effective. For example, participants who stated that they did not experience the cultural characteristics of their ethnic identity too much or that their different collective identities, such as religious identity, took precedence over their ethnic identity, stated that they did not have any problems due to their ethnicity in the relations they established with their colleagues. However, the situation is different for participants who try to experience the cultural characteristics of their ethnic identity in their social life or shape their worldview through this identity.

P6, who is working in a predominantly Kurdish region, is trying to experience the cultural characteristics of her/his ethnic identity in school, which can cause problems with Turkish teachers:

> I, for example, speak Kurdish all the time in the teachers' room. There was a Turkish teacher, and we were very friendly. There was an argument with me about 'why do you speak Kurdish, why do you speak Diyarbakir dialect with students in class?' etc. I said look, you can't interfere with my class, I'll talk whatever I want. Because I said my Turkish is not very strong, so I can't speak Istanbul Turkish, which is none of your business.

According to some of the participants, it is not their own ethnic identity, but the way teachers from the majority culture position themselves in the face of this identity or establish a hierarchical relationship between the two identities is a problem. P2's statements embody this situation:

> When there are Turkish teachers who are trying to impose Turkish identity on the issue of being a senior identity, we can fall into discussion with them. But other than that, we have sincere Turkish teacher friends who act only with teaching qualifications… Presenting and imposing now are two separate things. So you distinguish that. It is ok to present, I can accept or not but if you impose, you get the reaction. I am one of the most intimate with Turkish teachers in school right now. It doesn't mean we're a consensual on ideas, but we can have very comfortable relationships humanly. I must tell you that if there is no imposing, I mean the Turkish teachers don't impose their own systematic on us, we don't have problem.

P1's statements also show that it is difficult to make a generalization of the relationship of Kurdish teachers with teachers from the majority culture. However, she/he also states that she/he encounters colleagues who "ideologically approach" her/his identity from time to time and at this point feels discrimination:

> They're wary at first, but I'd say I exist in my own character. If I don't have a positive with my character, I wouldn't accept… Here's how I want to sample ideologically approaching people; On October 10th, you know, there was a huge massacre…There was an explosion in the heart of Ankara…Many friends were on the weekend course…It's already the weekend of the explosion. A lot of our friends say that 'they were going to be there; I wonder

what happened.' Well, our friends had emotional moments, they cried. Some of them, those I call approaching this ideologically… state that 'but they were there', so if they're there, they deserve it, there's nothing we can do… So it doesn't make much of a change if they're P1 or someone else… There are people who I feel are very clear that their ideology prevents them from approaching me when there are so many things that maybe they can share, maybe chat with.

Similarly, in the relations established with the school administration, rather than systematic discrimination, the world view of the administrator and whether it reflects this in his profession is decisive:

I didn't have any problems with the principals I worked with earlier, but I had trouble with the last principal. In the first month of his arrival, the principal called all the teachers at the school to his own room and warned them not to walk around with P2 and not to share information. When the teachers asked why, he/she said, 'K2 is from Diyarbakır, she/he is Kurd. It's not right for you to be with him/her, it's not right for you to share'. Of course, after I heard about it, it went to different dimensions, so can you imagine? Being from Diyarbakir, being Kurdish, identify you with divisiveness, they call you a member of a terrorist organization, that's how they see it. But they also ignore this: After all, I'm an employee of national education. If the National Education has awarded me this task and sent me away, then there is no problem. I've been with these teacher friends for four or five years before the principal even got here. They are my colleagues, and the friends have already expressed it to the principal in the same way, so far, we have never encountered such a divisive identity of P2. They had some rhetoric against the principal like we don't expect this problem from P2.

P2's problem with the school administration due to its ethnic identity grows in the future and moves to the district national education directorate. Then, both P2 and the principal with which she/he had problems are assigned to different schools in the same province or, as P2 says, "banished." However, P2 considers that at this point he/she has been discriminated by the education bureaucracy because of his/her ethnic identity:

They banished me from K. to S. County, and where I went, grey wolves[1] were the majority. I had officially fallen into the grey wolves, and the situation made me think differently. I thought, "Why me here?" For example, you could have sent me to K, but S is the county where the grey wolves are the majority. I'm in the middle of it, and I was confronted by a student's threats. He said, "teacher," and he said, "we heard you were from Diyarbakir." I said, "Yes, I'm from Diyarbakir." He said, "We had a neighbor, he was hiding that he was from Diyarbakir." I said, "What happened?" 'My brothers beat them up well after they found out he was from Diyarbakir'. I said, "What do you mean?" 'Now that your brother found out I'm from Diyarbakir, he's going to come and beat me up the same way?' He said, "You never know." I mean, I worked in a place like this. The way I've been in these situations obviously makes me think that I'm not facing the goodwill of national education. I mean, I think they discriminated.

Discrimination by the school board or the education bureaucracy may not always be so pronounced. Sometimes the admiration they expect in vain due to their

---

[1] They are associations operating in the form of youth branches of the Nationalist Movement Party in Turkey.

performance is also associated with their ethnic identity by Kurdish teachers and described as discrimination:

> In 11 years, I have worked with many administrators. Although they experienced their ideology very prominently, I did not have problems with people who lived without adding it to their profession. But there are some administrators that I had problem with. For example, there are activities in the school, ceremonies required by our branch, special days… Although you have put forward a much better, much more vocal, much more beautiful work, I have come across approaches that, as a result of ethnic identity or the union of which you are a member, have been praised, given the value they deserve, even if they are mentioned.

The events in schools related to national days in Turkey are mostly organized by history teachers, as these days are also of historical importance. As can be seen from the above statements of P1, ethnic identity may cause the appreciation that the teacher expects not to be shown by the school administrators. At this point, it is also possible to open a special parenthesis to national days because while these days have the potential to be integrate for national identities, they can be discriminatory for cultural differences within society or for minorities. In Turkey, it is possible to encounter examples that meet both conditions. National ceremonies or events according to P2:

> It's got to be distinguished. Like which can be imposition? National Oath[2] is an imposition according to me. But is the Independence Anthem an imposition? It is not because the Independence Anthem is the anthem of the whole nation, the anthem of all Turkey. Yes, it has a more unifying feature of Turks. But you don't have a problem with the Independence Anthem. But when you look at the content of National Oath, look at the lyrics of the Independence Anthem, so the two are very different, but National Oath is an imposition, but Independence Anthem is not. Situations in which the state should have, which exists in many countries.

Conclusions and Implications

Anatolia, on which Turkey is founded, has hosted different civilizations since the ancient ages of history and has been a geography where different cultures live together. This cultural diversity was also significantly preserved with the Seljuk and Ottoman states founded after the arrival of Turks in Anatolia. However, the policies of centralization and nationalization, which were tried to be implemented since the end of the eighteenth century, have caused great damage to this cultural variety. The first clashes between Kurds and the state, along with many minority groups living in Anatolia, began during this period.

---

[2] Although it has made some changes since its first application in 1933, National Oath begins as *I am Turk, I am right, I am hardworking*, and ends with *my existence is a gift to Turkish existence, how happy is the one who says I'm a Turk*. Until it was removed from practice in 2013, all elementary students (including Kurdish students) would disperse into their classrooms every morning after repeating this oath together.

The republic of Turkey, built on an imperial heritage, was determined to continue its nation-building policies that already started in the last period of the Ottoman Empire, which caused the conflict between Turks and Kurds to increase. Some groups politicized around the cultural rights of Kurds until the 1980s began terroristized armed acts after this date, deepening the conflict between both communities. Although there have been some important improvements regarding cultural rights in Turkey since the 2000s, Kurds still face the forms of being the other such as being ignored, discriminated against and marginalized, and not being able to live their own identity freely.

As can be understood from their answers, the ethnic identity of the participants is not an important determinant in their relationship with their students. Considering that the age range of students in middle and high school in Turkey varies between 12 and 19, it can be stated that the collective identity orientation of the students has not yet been fully shaped. However, it is not the same for parents. It is understood from the participants' statements that some parents approach Kurdish history teachers with prejudice, and that teachers should do more to eliminate these prejudices and prove themselves compared with Turkish teachers. Parents' prejudices can affect students, albeit in rare examples.

It is not very possible to talk about systematic discrimination in the relations established by Kurdish history teachers with colleagues or the school administration in their professional lives. However, the fact that some participants carry their cultural characteristics to school, even if they are only From Southeast, can pose a problem for some teachers and administrators from the majority culture. This means that even if there is no systematic discrimination within the education bureaucracy, there is no legal means to prevent discrimination.

When the statements of the participants in the study are evaluated as a whole, it is seen that they have very different or even opposite views on the same subject. It can be stated that although all participants are Kurds, this is due to the difference in how they approach this identity. Although it may be misleading to make a generalization about this issue, the participants' statements show us that Kurdish history teachers feel that they are being discriminated against within the education system to the extent that they want to experience the cultural characteristics of their ethnic identity or put these identities first. If he/she does not bring these characteristics to the forefront or does not have a problem with the role assumed to his/her own ethnic identity in history lessons, there is no discrimination for him/her.

The discrimination that Kurdish history teachers feel they are subjected to is not unique to them. Kurds in different professional groups in Turkey or in different areas of social life may be subjected to similar forms of otherization. However, for minority groups such as Armenians, Greeks and Jews, whose proportions in the population are much smaller compared to Kurds, the burden of being otherized can be much more severe. Therefore, in Turkey, which inherits the legacy of an empire of different cultural/ethnic elements, the understanding that a singular identity arising from nation-building policies is imposed in everything from the constitution to social life continues to threaten turkey's multicultural structure.

As can be seen, teaching the past plays an important role in shaping ethnic or national identities and the relations between these identities (Anderson, 2006; Korosteline, 2008; Pamuk, 2014; Yıldırım, 2016). But as a result of the paradoxical nature of collective identities (Kılıçbay, 2003), attempting to create a sense of "we" among those who share the same identity also serves the purpose of legitimizing and disseminating the "other". On the other hand, the ignoring of diversity in society in history lessons by the nation-states to create a sense of national identity further feeds this distinction (Stradling, 2003). That is because in such a historical understanding of education, students from the majority culture cannot comprehend that cultural and ethnic differences are a natural feature of the society in which they live and cannot react to these differences as it is expected. Students with ethnic differences have trouble seeing themselves as part of society.

References

Aktay, Y., & Kızılkaya, A. (2014). *Hepimiz ötekiyiz*. Tezkire Yayınları.
Aktoprak, E. (2010). *Bir "kurucu öteki" olarak: Türkiye'de gayrimüslimler*. İnsan Hakları Çalışma Metinleri:XVI. https://insanhaklariizleme.org/vt/yayin_view.php?editid1=1498 25.02.2021.
Alkan, M. F. & Yazıcı, F. (2020). Teacher educators' perceptions of terrorism and the role of education: A qualitative inquiry. *ie: Inquiry in Education, 12*(1), 1–20.
Altun, N. (2013). Modern Türkiye'de kimlik: Kürt kimliğinden Kürt sorununa. *Akademik İncelemeler Dergisi, 8*(2), 45–67.
Anderson, B. (2006). *Imagined communities: Reflections on the origin and spread of nationalism*. Verso.
Beşikçi, İ. (1986). *Türk tarih tezi ve Kürt sorunu*. Dengê Komal.
Biçer, B. (2013a). Selçuklular ve Kürtler. *The Journal of Academic Social Science Studies, 6*(2), 165–202.
Biçer, B. (2013b). Ortaçağda Kürtler ve Türkler. *The Journal of Academic Social Science Studies, 6*(6), 231–261.
Bilgin, N. (1999). *Kolektif kimlik*. Sistem Yayıncılık.
Copeaux, E. (1998). *Türk tarih tezinden Türk-İslam sentezine*. Tarih Vakfı Yurt Yayınları.
Coskun, V., Derince, S., & Uçarlar, N. (2010). *Dil yarası: Türkiye'de eğitimde anadilinin kullanılmaması sorunu ve Kürt öğrencilerin deneyimleri* [A wound on the Tongue: The Issue of the Use of the Mother Tongue in Education in Turkey and Experiences of Kurdish Students]. DİSA.
Çayır, K. (2014). *"Biz" kimiz? Ders kitaplarında kimlik, yurttaşlık, haklar*. Tarih Vakfı Yayınları.
Dündar, S. (2009). *Kürtler ve azınlık tartışmaları*. Doğan Yayıncılık.
Eröz, M. (1982). *Doğu Anadolu'nun Türklüğü*. Ötüken.
Ersanlı, B. (2006). *İktidar ve Tarih: Türkiye'de "Resmi Tarih" Tezinin Oluşumu (1929–1937)*. İletişim Yayınları.
Feridun, M. (2016). Impact of education and poverty on terrorism in Turkey: An empirical investigation. *Applied Research in Quality of Life, 11*(1), 41–48.
Hennerbichler, F. (2012). The origin of Kurds. *Advances in Anthropology, 2*(02), 64.
Kabapınar, Y. (1992). Başlangıcından günümüze Türk Tarih Tezi ve lise tarih kitaplarına etkisi. *Çağdaş Türkiye Tarihi Araştırmaları Dergisi, 2*(1), s.143–s.178.
Kaya, N. (2012). Türkiye'nin Eğitim Sisteminde Azınlıklar ve Ayrımcılık: Kavramsal Çerçeve ve Temel Sorunlar. In K. Çayır ve, & M. A. Ceyhan (Ed.), *Ayrımcılık: Çok boyutlu yaklaşımlar içinde*. İstanbul Bilgi Üniversitesi Yayınları.

Kılıçbay, M. A. (2003). Kimlikler okyanusu. *Doğu Batı Düşünce Dergisi, 23*, 155–159.
Koçal, A. V. (2014). Osmanlı-Türkiye modernleşmesinin sosyo-ekonomik temelleri ve aktörleri bağlamında 'Türk'-Kürt ikileminin doğuşu ve kaynakları. *Tarihte Türkler ve Kürtler Uluslararası Sempozyumu*, 9–11.
Korostelina, K. (2008). History education and social identity. *Identity, 8*(1), 25–45. https://doi.org/10.1080/15283480701787327
Kurubaş, E. (2008). Etnik grup-devlet ilişkilerinin sorunsallaşması ve aktör tutumlarındaki açmazlar: Türkiye'deki Kürt sorunu örneği. *Liberal Düşünce Dergisi, 50*, 19–53.
Limbert, J. (1968). The origins and appearance of the Kurds in pre-Islamic Iran. *Iranian Studies, 1*(2), 41–51.
Nal, S. (2010). *Avrupa İnsan Hakları Sözleşmesi hukukunda azınlık hakları*. Nobel Yayın Dağıtım.
Nikitin, B. (2002). In Çev. H. Demirhan, C. Süreyya (Ed.), *Kürtler: Sosyolojik ve tarihi inceleme*. Deng Yayınları.
Oran, B. (2010). *Türkiye'de azınlıklar*. İletişim Yayınları.
Pamuk, A. (2014). *Kimlik ve tarih kimliğin inşasında tarihin kullanımı*. Yeni İnsan Yayınevi.
Parlak, İ. (2005). *Kemalist ideolojide eğitim*. Turhan Kitabevi.
Sambur, B. (2008). Liberal açıdan kürt sorunu. *Liberal Düşünce Dergisi, 50*, 91–108.
Smith, A. D. (1991). *National identity*. Penguin Books.
Stradling, R. (2003). *20. Yüzyıl Avrupa tarihi nasıl öğretilmeli* [Teaching 20th-century European history]. Tarih Vakfı Yayınları.
Tacar, P. (1996). *Kültürel haklar dünyadaki uygulamalar ve Türkiye için bir model önerisi*. Gündoğan Yayınları.
Tunçay, M. (1981). *Türkiye Cumhuriyeti'nde tek-parti yönetimin kurulması*. Yurt Yayınları.
van Bruinessen, M. (2008). *Kürtlük, Türklük, Alevilik etnik ve dinsel kimlik mücadeleleri* [Being a Kurd, a Turk, an Alevi: Ethnic and religious identity struggles]. İletişim Yayınları.
van Bruinessen, M. (2011). *Kurdish ethno-nationalism versus nation-building states: Collected articles*. Gorgias Press.
Yazıcı, F. (2011). Cumhuriyet Dönemi tarih ders kitaplarında tarih yazımı. In Vahdettin Engin ve Ahmet Şimşek (Ed.), *Türkiye'de tarih yazımı*. Yeditepe Yayınevi.
Yazıcı, F. (2015). *Azınlık okullarında tarih eğitimi ve çokkültürlülük*. Yeni İnsan Yayınevi.
Yeğen, M. (2014). *Müstakbel Türk'ten sözde vatandaşa: Cumhuriyet ve Kürtler*. İletişim Yayınları.
Yıldırım, T., & Şimşek, A. (2015). "The narrative of religion" in the high school textbooks of the early republican period in Turkey. *Education & Science, 40*(179), 323–340.
Yıldırım, T. (2016). *Tarih ders kitaplarında kimlik söylemi*. Yeni İnsan Yayınevi.
Yılmaz, A. (2015). Kürt milliyetçiliğine eleştirel bir bakış: Kürt mülteciler ve Kürdistan milliyetçiliği. *Mülkiye Dergisi, 39*(1), 37–56.
Yıldız, A. (2010). *"Ne mutlu Türküm diyebilene" Türk ulusal kimliğinin etno-seküler sınırları (1919-1938)*. İletişim Yayınları.

Fatih Yazıcı is an associate Professor at the Department of Social Sciences Education, Tokat Gaziosmanpasa University in Turkey. Yazıcı conducts research on multiculturalism, multicultural education, minority rights, identities, and patriotism in the context of History Education.

Open Access This chapter is licensed under the terms of the Creative Commons Attribution 4.0 International License (http://creativecommons.org/licenses/by/4.0/), which permits use, sharing, adaptation, distribution and reproduction in any medium or format, as long as you give appropriate credit to the original author(s) and the source, provide a link to the Creative Commons license and indicate if changes were made.

The images or other third party material in this chapter are included in the chapter's Creative Commons license, unless indicated otherwise in a credit line to the material. If material is not included in the chapter's Creative Commons license and your intended use is not permitted by statutory regulation or exceeds the permitted use, you will need to obtain permission directly from the copyright holder.

Chapter 23
"They Respect Me as a Person Who Can Help" Roma Teaching Assistants in the Czech Republic

Zbyněk Němec

Abstract In the Czech Republic, where Roma represent the largest ethnic minority, Roma teaching assistants have been an irreplaceable form of support for the education of socially disadvantaged students for more than two decades. This chapter draws on experience from various research projects that took place from 2012 to 2019, and focuses on the benefits of the work of Roma teaching assistants in the education of socially disadvantaged Roma students; data were obtained through semi-structured interviews and subjected to a thematic analysis, using basic elements of grounded theory. According to research, the main responsibilities of Roma assistants include assisting teachers in the education of socially disadvantaged Roma students during lessons, tutoring Roma students, providing psychosocial support for these students, organising leisure activities for these students, and supporting communication between the school and the Roma students' families. Having a deep knowledge of Roma students, their needs and cultural specifics, Roma assistants can also represent an important information resource for teachers; the ethnicity of Roma assistants can also be beneficial in overcoming language barriers – if both the Roma assistant and the students or their parents speak Romani, the assistant can translate and interpret for teachers and other school staff. At a general level, cooperation of Roma assistants and non-Roma teachers can serve as a model for relations between Roma and non-Roma students and thus remove prejudices and barriers in society.

Introduction

The Roma represent the largest ethnic minority in many European countries; international institutions estimate that nowadays there are approximately 10–12 million Roma living in Europe (European Commission, 2020). However, the Roma are also one of the most vulnerable and discriminated ethnic minorities – research has shown

---

Z. Němec (✉)
Faculty of Education, Charles University, Prague, Czech Republic
e-mail: zbynek.nemec@pedf.cuni.cz

that most Roma in Europe live in significantly sub-average living conditions, at least one third of Roma children live in conditions of absolute poverty and many young Roma are not involved in formal education (European Union Fundamental Rights Agency, 2017). The inclusion of the Roma minority is thus one of the important tasks of contemporary European society.

The situation regarding the education of Roma students is also serious in many respects. Across Europe, approximately one in ten Roma children of the age of compulsory education do not attend school – the most critical situation is in Romania, where every fifth Roma child does not attend elementary school, or in Greece, where almost a third of Roma children don't attend elementary school (European Union Fundamental Rights Agency, 2017). Various researchers also point to the persistent segregation of Roma students in non-mainstream schools – in many Central and Eastern European countries, Roma students receive lower levels of education in classes and schools attended mainly by Roma students, separated from their non-Roma peers (Arabadjieva, 2016; Messing, 2017; Rostas & Kostka, 2014). Therefore, there is a strong need to focus on any support measures that could facilitate the inclusion of Roma students into regular mainstream schooling.

In the Czech Republic, the current number of Roma is around 250,000, which represents approximately 2.2% of the country's total population (Government Council for Roma Minority Affairs, 2019). Within the European Union, the Czech Republic thus represents a state with a relatively significant proportion of Roma – only in Bulgaria, Slovakia, Romania and Hungary does the Roma minority represent a higher percentage in the total population of the state. As in various other countries, in the Czech Republic Roma face many problems relating to housing and education: approximately 50% of Roma live in socially excluded areas and many students from these localities attend segregated schools (Government Council for Roma Minority Affairs, 2019). In elementary education, where Roma children account for approximately 4% of all students, a lot of Roma students struggle with language barriers, lack of motivation and insufficient support from their parents (MEYS, 2017; Šotolová, 2011).

In order to support Roma inclusion and increase the quality of education for Roma students, especially for those coming from socially disadvantaged settings, many schools and professionals focus on seeking and implementing effective educational tools and measures – and one of the most recommended is the introduction of Roma teaching assistants (Council of Europe, 2000).

The History and the Present of Roma Teaching Assistants in the Czech Republic

In the Czech Republic, Roma teaching assistants have been part of the educational system since the early 1990s (Němec et al., 2014b). In these years, shortly after the so-called Velvet Revolution and the transition from a socialist to a democratic state, the Czech Republic was inspired by the British model of ethnic assistants. Assistants who assisted teachers in educating socially disadvantaged Roma students and who were themselves Roma were first introduced unofficially on the initiative of some experienced school headteachers[1] (Němec et al., 2014a).

At the official level, the Ministry of Education established the profession of "Roma assistant" in the school year 1997/1998 and, during the following years, these pedagogical workers became a very useful source of support in schools with higher ratios of Roma students. The main responsibilities of the Roma assistant were defined as: *"helping teachers during their educational activities in communication with Roma children, taking an individual approach to students and eliminating educational obstacles, helping with extra-curricular activities of the class and school, cooperating with students' parents, and cooperating with the Roma community in the school neighbourhood"* (MEYS, 1998). It is also worth noting the relatively rapid increase in the number of workers in this profession: in the Czech Republic, where high Roma unemployment was and still is a significant problem, the number of Roma assistants in schools increased from twenty in 1998 to more than two hundred in 2001 (Bartoňová, 2003). This reliably proves not only the interest of Roma in working in education but also the interest of schools in the work of Roma pedagogical staff. Professional training of Roma pedagogical assistants, provided by non-profit organisations, was set at 80 h of theoretical study of the basics of pedagogy and psychology and 40 h of practice (Šotolová, 2003).

From its inception in the 1990s, the role of the assistants, who were Roma themselves, focused on removing barriers arising from the different distribution of cultural and social capital – In the Czech Republic, sociological studies describe a strong link between the school environment and the cultural capital of the white majority; children from culturally different and socially disadvantaged minorities, especially the Roma, thus encounter a certain "clash of cultures" when entering school (Havlík, 2007). Therefore, the position of Roma assistant was and is intended as a certain bridge between the majority culture and the minority culture of Roma students.

The first significant change in the profession took place in 2001, when the Ministry of Education decided to rename the position "educator – teaching assistant". Following this new designation, the profession continued to focus on supporting socially disadvantaged students but was no longer strictly tied to Roma ethnicity – although one of the main tasks of these workers still remained *"cooperating with the Roma (or another) community in the school neighborhood"* (MEYS, 2001). The profession was changed to its current form in 2004, when the position of assistants working with socially disadvantaged students was merged with the position of assistants working with students with disabilities – a unified position of teaching assistant was created in the new Education Act (Němec et al., 2014b).

---

[1] A well-known example is the "Přemysl Pitter Parochial Primary and Nursery School" in Ostrava where the position of Roma assistant was established in 1993.

At present, teaching assistants in the Czech Republic are legislatively defined by the Education Act as a "support measure" in the education of students with special educational needs[2] (Czech Republic, 2004a). Their number, with the development of inclusive education, is growing rapidly – while in 2011 there were less than six thousand teaching assistants, in 2018, schools already employed more than twenty-one thousand teaching assistants (MEYS, 2019). In recent years, another group of workers in the field are the so-called "school assistants", whose work is covered by ESF-funded projects; even these assistants have the primary task of supporting the education of students in need[3] (Němec et al., 2014a). Unfortunately, official statistics do not record how much work assistants (whether teaching assistants or school assistants) do with socially disadvantaged Roma students, or how many of the assistants are themselves Roma; in these respects, it is therefore necessary to rely on qualitative research and practical experience of schools.

As regards qualification requirements, the Act on Pedagogical Staff distinguishes between two levels in the teaching assistant profession – at the higher level, assistants provide more qualified support to teachers and must have a secondary education with a graduation exam, at the lower level, assistants provide only auxiliary educational work and must have completed their elementary education; at both levels, however, assistants must have a pedagogical education, at least in the form of a 120-h qualification course (Czech Republic, 2004b). According to the valid legislative definition, teaching assistants provide activities such as: teacher support in the education of students with special educational needs, assistance to students in learning and in preparation for learning, auxiliary educational and organisational activities in working with students, assistance in communicating with parents/legal representatives of students and the community from which the students come, and the necessary assistance of students in relation to self-care and mobility (Czech Republic, 2004a, 2016). Some of these tasks are particularly important for assistants working with socially disadvantaged Roma students – researchers mainly emphasise their irreplaceable role in facilitating communication between the school and students' families (Drotárová, 2006; Bartoňová & Pipeková, 2008).

---

[2] According to the valid decree, "students in need of support in education due to different cultural and living conditions" are also considered students with special educational needs (Czech Republic, 2016) – a significant number of socially disadvantaged Roma students are also included in this category.

[3] Compared to "teaching assistants", the work of "school assistants" is more focused on supporting cooperation between school and family and on supporting extracurricular training for socially disadvantaged students; in many other respects, however, the two positions are comparable. In practice, some assistants move from the position of teaching assistant to the position of school assistant over the years and vice versa, or combine both jobs. For the purposes of this text, the positions are therefore considered to be identical.

Methodological Note

The following text draws on experience from various projects that took place from 2012 to 2019. Two of those were research projects: The first one[4] took place between 2012 and 2014 and included semi-structured interviews with 40 teaching assistants from 25 elementary schools; the second one[5] took place between 2017 and 2019 and was based on interviews with 59 teaching assistants from a large number of different schools. Another two projects[6] were primarily applied but contained evaluation research as a part of their realization; being implemented in the years 2012 to 2014/2016 to 2018, these projects established and managed the positions of sixteen assistants in six schools situated in socially excluded areas. In all these projects, data were obtained through semi-structured interviews with teaching assistants (or school assistants), teachers, headteachers and sometimes even students with various special needs. Interviews with pedagogical staff were recorded and then converted into written form. All the data were subjected to a thematic analysis, using basic elements of grounded theory. The quotes in the following text come exclusively from Roma assistants. In order to maintain anonymity, the names of the assistants were changed.

Findings

Roma Assistants and Their Support in the Education of Socially Disadvantaged Students

According to research[7], Roma assistants provide a number of support services in schools with a significant number of socially disadvantaged Roma students. The most important forms of their support include: (a) assisting teachers in the education of socially disadvantaged Roma students during lessons; (b) supporting teachers in understanding Roma students and their needs; (c) providing psychosocial support for Roma students; (d) tutoring Roma students; (e) organising leisure activities for socially disadvantaged Roma students; (f) supporting communication between the school and Roma students' families.

---

[4] A. "The Quality of an Interpersonal Relation as a Determinant of the Effectiveness of Pedagogical Assistance "(supported by the Grant Agency of Charles University, No. 663512)

[5] B. "The Preconception, Construction and Reconstruction of the Teaching Assistant's Professional Identity" (supported by The Czech Science Foundation, No. 17-07101S)

[6] C. "Chances of success: systematic support for socially disadvantaged students in education" (supported by ESF, No. CZ.02.3.61./0.0/0.0/15_007/0000226) and

D. "The School Assistant – An Instrument Consolidating Equal Opportunities for Children and Students in the Central Bohemia Region" (supported by ESF, No. CZ.1.07/1.2.33/02.0022)

The designations of projects A to D are also used in the following text for quotes – to specify which project which verbatim quote comes from.

[7] For more details, see also Němec et al. (2015, 2018, 2019).

Assisting teachers in educating socially disadvantaged Roma students during lessons is a key part of the work of Roma assistants. It significantly helps to individualise the education process, and, in many cases, it seems to be the basic factor in the success of Roma students.

> Magdalena (D): *"I'm in a class where there are over 20 students and each one of them is different and it is not in the teacher's powers to manage everything. If the children are absent for a month or two or if they come from home unprepared, I think that at that moment I am very useful, and I can see the progress. I know that the teacher wouldn't have time to go back with them to do a lesson from a month or two months before. So I say 'Let's go and look at it' and I can see that although they have missed some classes, they already know some letters, they can read, well 'read' in inverted commas, they can't read as fast as their peers, but they can manage a bit, and counting too."*

The presence of an assistant and the possibility of individualised support help many socially disadvantaged Roma students to become more focused, more self-confident, and therefore more successful during classes.

> Laura (D): *"...the teacher always says, 'Laura, he is always so happy that you sit next to him, that you help him, he is always looking forward to you working with him, but when you leave he is totally desolate.', but when there's time, the teacher also sits with him because he is still very unsure of himself, he doesn't know how to do things..."*

From the perspective of many socially disadvantaged Roma students, Roma assistants represent both a formal and an informal authority, which is sometimes even more important than the teacher's authority. Therefore, in some cases, Roma assistants provide significant support to teachers in maintaining students' discipline.

> Adam (A): *"...then there are even teachers who teach well but do not get much respect from the children, so then I go there, for example, because the children do respect me..."*

Especially in classes with heterogeneous collectives, which include Roma as well as non-Roma students, it is important to emphasise that Roma assistants should also work with non-Roma students and so enable the teacher him/herself to pay more attention to disadvantaged Roma students. Thus, the teacher and the Roma assistant can work with different groups of students and take into account their special educational needs as much as possible.

> Lada (B): *"Reading itself was very useful because we really have a big problem with reading, so I take a couple of children aside, maybe three or four, and we read separately, it pays off. Or we have learning centres, for working in those centres we divide kids into groups ..."*

Another important part of the Roma assistants' work is **supporting teachers in understanding Roma students and their needs**. Sometimes this 'understanding' is meant literally – some Roma students come from families where Romani language or the so-called 'Romani ethnolect of Czech'[8] are spoken, so they encounter numerous barriers in communication with the teacher. In some cases, Roma students also prefer communication in Romani, which the teacher does not understand.

---

[8] The Romani ethnolect of Czech is defined as a variety of the Czech language in which there are significant influences of the original Romani language (Bořkovcová, 2006).

In these and many other situations, an assistant who knows the communication specifics of Roma students can promote mutual understanding between the students and the teacher.

> Monika (C): "*... children from the seventh and eighth grades cursed each other in Romani, they spoke rudely, but the teacher did not understand them, so she did not solve it. I told the boys to stop and I told the teacher what they were talking about. Since then, she has been paying attention to it.*"

At a more general level, assistants can support teachers in understanding the overall behavior and needs of socially disadvantaged Roma students – the Roma teaching assistants often have good knowledge of the students' family and social environment, of their cultural traditions and customs, and so they can become advisers for teachers in this area.

> Lada (B): "*Because the Roma assistant has that experience and knowledge, we can give our own advice to benefit of the teacher ... I understand that the parents do not work and do not have financial resources, but it it's sometimes hard to understand why it really is that way. And the teachers hear it from the assistants who have the possibility of going to those families and who know the situation.*"

Roma assistants often work with students from socially excluded areas, with students living in an environment with a significantly low socio-economic level, with students affected by the lack of some of the basic necessities of life; and so the understanding of the students' living conditions is, from the perspective of Roma assistants, considered to be a basic precondition for both their own work and the work of the teacher.

> Magdalena (D): "*Both the children and the teachers say, 'She just sits there and looks out of the window.' Well, no wonder she looks out of the window, when in [the socially excluded area] they are dealing with whether they can continue to live there or not, that they live in such a dump, sometimes they have nothing to eat and so on, so she's looking out of the window and thinks... and I know exactly why that is, because there's nothing nice waiting for her at home.*"

During schooling, Roma assistants can also be a particularly important source of **psychosocial support for socially disadvantaged Roma students**. The ability of assistants to listen to their students, to pay attention to their worries and needs, helps to compensate for any lack of attention from the students' parents and improves the psychological balance of the students. The presence of an assistant who is "theirs" can be also an important factor for Roma students in identifying themselves with the school environment.

> Laura (D): "*There are many Roma children in this school. So, it's great because I know if there was a Czech teacher or assistant, the Roma children would not form such an attachment to her. That's the way it is. When, for example, some parents had a problem, the class teacher explained it to them, but they didn't listen. When I told them, it was different. And it's the same with children because when I came here for the first time, they were all excited and asked me 'Are you Roma or Czech? Where are you from?' and so on. And when they saw that I'm in the lessons, they were delighted and I must say that they are still happy that I'm there, that I work with them there.*"

Both Roma assistants and Roma students are convinced that an assistant who is him/herself Roma can better identify the needs of students who also belong to the Roma minority.

> Magdalena (D): "*However different I am from them, I am the same – I don't mean that every Roma is the same, but I have an idea what the people have in their heads, what they experience and what leads them to it. I also probably understand them better and they themselves hope that a Roma will understand them better, I think.*"

Especially in schools with a high number of Roma students coming from socially excluded localities, Roma assistants can also serve as role models – students whose parents are often poorly educated and long-term unemployed can see the assistant as a role model who "belongs to them" but who is at the same time educated, employed and respected by the majority. As a member of a minority, the assistant is more likely to influence the future educational and professional motivation of socially disadvantaged Roma students.

> Andrea (C): "*… in some way to guide these kids all over again… I first encountered here that they say: 'I'm going to be here until I turn fifteen and then, because I have asthma, I'm going to ask for a disability pension.' That's the way they think, or the girls: 'Me, in eighth grade, I'll give birth to children.' That's the struggle I've been talking about, for a long time, a long journey, gradually, slowly, so they just do not think this way … here every change, every little thing counts, when a boy comes to me and he wants to study at a building school, and he goes to the secondary vocational school, or he'll be a chef.*"

A very important part of teaching assistants' work is represented by **tutoring socially disadvantaged Roma students**. This tutoring is much needed due to the lack of educational support that many Roma students have in their families – many parents themselves do not have sufficient knowledge to be able to help their children with school preparation, so, for some socially disadvantaged Roma students, assistants are the only possible source of help in preparing for school.

> Laura (D): "*Tutoring is important, at least they do their homework with me and they know that they do it right. That is the advantage, that even in maths or in the Czech language they do the homework right. I know that Helena has just been here, she's in fourth grade and she had her maths homework after a long time and her teacher was surprised that she had done it and she said she did it during the tutoring.*"

The tutoring of socially disadvantaged Roma students provided by assistants usually focuses on subjects in which students have the most significant problems – in addition to mathematics, it is most often Czech and foreign languages. Proof of the importance of tutoring in the work of Roma assistants is also the fact that students are interested in this form of support and regularly attend tutoring.

> Andrea (C): "*… I think even if there was nothing else, so at least I managed this tutoring successfully and everyone here will tell you that this tutoring gives a certain order to the kids, they come, even wait for an hour here. Nobody would believe me that if they have a one-hour break, yeah, and they will have to wait – the big kids for example, their classes end at half past twelve and I have the smaller kids first, then I have these six, seventh graders – they wait for an hour here for the tutoring. I think it's a success to have built this in them.*"

The tutoring usually takes place in the school building, but in some cases Roma assistants also provide tutoring in students' families, in their households. The advantage of tutoring in the family can be that the assistant can also involve the student's parents and thus show these parents how they should carry out school preparation with their child.

> Ilona (D): "...*I do this with Honza because his parents are older and have no other children, just him, so they sit down with us and I tell them that they have to do this and that...*"

In addition to tutoring, another important form of assistants' support is **organising leisure activities** for socially disadvantaged Roma students. These activities often take place in the school environment and create opportunities for spending time meaningfully even for those disadvantaged Roma students who are not able to take part – usually due to financial barriers – in leisure activities in other institutions. In some cases, the assistants manage to organise these activities in cooperation with teachers, following the joint tutoring of students.

> Jana (C): "*We made an activity for children who don't go to the club so that they can get involved as well. So, we play there, listen to fairy tales or tell stories, read fairy tales and go for walks. Then we have a club. When the teacher comes, we learn for 45 minutes, then we play for 45 minutes, and then we wait to for the parents to come.*"

The involvement of assistants in the organisation of the leisure activities for socially disadvantaged Roma students is important for several reasons: it is another form of developing students' knowledge and skills, but it is also a form of preventing undesirable ways of spending afternoons in the bleak environment of excluded localities, and finally, it is a tool that strengthens the students' positive attitude to school. Some Roma assistants also appreciate the fact that in leisure activities and tutoring they can get to know their students better and become more sensitive to their needs.

> Magdalena (D): "...*I have leisure time activities during the school year and again during the holidays. For me it's great, it definitely is – I do tutoring with the kids, I go to their homes, I know them from school and then I can have another perspective as an assistant, to see them when they are completely relaxed, under no pressure; they draw, cook, dance, sing.*"

For many teachers, Roma assistants also represent a powerful instrument to **support communication between the school and the Roma students' families**. Especially in socially excluded localities, parents of Roma students often distrust the institutions of the majority society and avoid contact with the school – in such cases, a Roma assistant can often represent the only possible link between the school and the students' families.

> Lada (B): "...*but above all, it is work with socially disadvantaged children in this area because we actually live in the 'Bronx' of* [name of the city], *so it is my biggest job to work with the family.*"

In practice, the Roma assistants communicate with the Roma parents using all possible opportunities to get in touch – e.g. via telephone contact, addressing parents in the school environment but often also by attending the households of students' families.

> Jana (C): "*I am ok with being in class every day only for the first two hours, then I have time to go around the families, according to what my teachers give me. It will take me another part of the morning to walk through town and get back again...*"

Some Roma assistants are very personally involved in their work, so they also devote part of their personal free time to contact with the students' parents.

> Monika (C): "*... I always manage to visit the families. If it sometimes isn't possible to reach them in the afternoon, then I do some work at home and then I visit them in the evening. I will definitely communicate with the family that day.*"

Unlike teachers, Roma assistants often have the advantage when contacting the parents of socially disadvantaged students in that they know the habits of these parents well and know where to look for them.

> Eva (C): "*Once I couldn't find a mother, and because I know where all these parents meet, I went to the bar in the evening. She was quite surprised and begged me "don't embarrass me here", and the next day she finally came to school.*"

When communicating with students' parents, **the ethnicity of Roma assistants also has an incredibly significant positive effect**. As mentioned in the introduction to this text, the Roma are among the most discriminated minorities, and therefore many of them do not trust the representatives of the majority society. An assistant who is Roma him/herself can gain the trust of students' parents so much easier.

> Ilona (D): "*It is certainly an advantage that we understand them better when something happens, and they surely confide in us more than they otherwise would because... I'm the one who is equal to them, even though we might live differently, but I'm an equal. But if a Czech comes, it is like a supervisor that has come to look at them and that will check them. From me they accept it, I will talk to them as usual and they will take it as usual. But when a Czech comes and says, 'You should do this and that' it's as if they ordered them to do it, 'And now do this.' And I think that some Czechs... they are not all the same... but they come and just the way they look at them, the Roma notice it immediately. Yes, I'm Roma, so I sense that look. I go there as normal and I know what they live like, even though some of them live in terrible conditions, but I talk to them normally.*"

Thanks to good contacts with students' parents, Roma assistants even have the chance to obtain – and subsequently pass on to teachers – important information that would not otherwise reach the school.

> Martin (A): "*Because I am a Roma myself, and we have Roma children here... I must therefore appreciate that I have very good communication with the parents, whatever the problem, so if the teachers need something, maybe just to resolve a minor issue, I will intervene spontaneously before any inconvenience occurs ... If Roma parents see their children have a problem, they are a little bit reluctant to talk about it with the teacher. I seem to have a greater possibility to ask the parents about everything, so I sometimes have more insight.*"

The ethnicity of Roma assistants can also be beneficial in overcoming language barriers when communicating with students' parents – if both the Roma assistant and the student's parent speak Romani, the assistant can translate and interpret information for teachers and other school staff.

Lada (B): *"I'm lucky that they are rather positive, that most of my parents respect me as a person who can help the family, and even if they do not want to say something directly to the teacher, they tell me in Romani and I interpret it for the teacher ..."*

Discussion, Conclusions and Implications: 'They Respect Me as a Person Who Can Help'

Many research studies prove that the position of Roma teaching assistant has a significant positive effect on the education of socially disadvantaged Roma students. For example, it has been shown that the presence of an assistant – in relation to Roma students – increases the likelihood of meeting the requirements of a standard educational program and decreases the risk of reducing educational content (Gabal & Čada, 2010).

It is also clear that the teaching assistants' affiliation to an ethnic minority plays an important role. The assistant, who is Roma him/herself, understands the needs of Roma students (Miškolci et al., 2017), can adequately take these needs into account in education, and can even train other teachers in the specifics of working with Roma students (Open Society Fund Prague, 2018). Roma assistants contribute to the fact that Roma students consider the school environment to be safe (Pape, 2007) and they can also act as a work and study model for Roma students – research shows that even parents of socially disadvantaged Roma students prefer the assistant to be Roma, precisely so that s/he can set an example for their children (Kaleja, 2011). Having knowledge of Romani, the assistant can facilitate communication with Romani-speaking families (Public Defender of Rights, 2018).

Roma teaching assistants also can – through their own example – show Roma and non-Roma students an effective model of cooperation between the minority and the majority society (Pape, 2007). Due to their affiliation with an ethnic and cultural minority, assistants can also help teachers as partners in the implementation of multicultural education (Šotolová, 2003). And, by working with Roma and non-Roma students, as well as Roma and non-Roma parents, assistants contribute to mutual understanding and the removal of prejudices and barriers in society (Moree, 2019).

On the other hand, it is also necessary to be aware of certain risks, which – although not exactly described by Roma assistants in the research analyzed above – have been precisely specified by other researchers and could significantly affect assistants' work. First, research shows that in many schools, assistants are used exclusively as support for students with special educational needs, who, however, are then often dependent on an assistant and do not have sufficient professional teacher support (Giangreco, 2010). It is therefore necessary to ensure that assistants work with all students in the class, thus helping more qualified teachers to gain opportunities for individualised work with students with special educational needs. Second, in terms of ethnicity, researchers also point to the risks associated with the emergence of segregation, both between schools and within the schools themselves – the presence of a Roma assistant can motivate parents of Roma students to place their children in the school where the assistant works, therefore, there is a risk of a higher concentration of Roma students in particular schools; within the school, higher frequency of communication between the assistant and the parents of socially disadvantaged Roma students can paradoxically lead to a reduction in the intensity of communication between the teacher and these parents (Starčević et al., 2016). Therefore, it is desirable to support the employment of Roma teaching assistants in a larger number of schools and in practice to ensure that socially disadvantaged Roma students and their parents are supported as much as possible by both Roma assistants and non-Roma teachers.

In summary, there is already much evidence of the benefits of Roma teaching assistants – they can facilitate work with socially disadvantaged Roma students, they can help with communication between school and Romani students' families, and they can help teachers understand Romani culture and language. Their cooperation with non-Roma teachers can also be a model for relations between Roma and non-Roma students and thus support the multicultural atmosphere of schools. As Lada, Roma assistant, said – the parents of the students she works with "*respect me as a person who can help*". And that is it: respect, respect between parents and educators, respect between Roma assistants and non-Roma teachers, that is what our society needs. Roma teaching assistants thus contribute not only to increasing the academic success of socially disadvantaged Roma students but also to improving relations and mutual understanding between the majority society and the Roma minority.

The Roma represent the largest ethnic minority in Europe; statistics also show that even in the twenty-first century many Roma children live in poverty and are not sufficiently involved in education. The involvement of Roma students in education is thus a very important issue. Our research projects pointed to the main responsibilities of Roma assistants including assisting teachers, tutoring Roma students, helping them to overcome language barriers, providing psychosocial support and organizing leisure activities for Roma students, supporting communication between the school and the Roma students' families.

Building on these findings, it would be valuable in future research to further investigate the cultural context of the deployment of ethnic minority assistants, as well as the possibility of professional growth from Roma assistants to Roma teachers.

References

Arabadjieva, K. (2016). Challenging the school segregation of Roma children in Central and Eastern Europe. *International Journal of Human Rights, 20*, 33–54. https://doi.org/10.1080/13642987.2015.1032266

Bartoňová, M. (2003). Strategie a přístupy k efektivnějšímu vzdělávání romského etnika [Strategies and approaches to the effective education of Roma ethnicity]. In M. Vítková (Ed.), *Integrativní školní (speciální) pedagogika* [Integrative school (special) education] (pp. 204–218). MSD.

Bartoňová, M., & Pipeková, J. (2008). Asistent pedagoga v přípravné třídě základní školy [The teaching assistant in preparatory classes of primary schools]. In M. Vítková & M. Bartoňová (Eds.), *Vzdělávání žáků se speciálními vzdělávacími potřebami II* [The education of students with special educational needs II] (pp. 229–244). Paido.

Bořkovcová, M. (2006). *Romský etnolekt češtiny* [Romani ethnolect of Czech]. Signeta.

Council of Europe. (2000). *Recommendation R. 2000. 4 of the Committee of Ministers 'On the education of Roma/Gypsy children in Europe'*. Council of Europe.

Czech Republic. (2004a). Act No. 561/2004 Coll. on Preschool, Primary, Secondary, Higher Professional and Other Education (Education Act). *Collection of Laws of the Czech Republic*, No. 190. As amended.

Czech Republic. (2004b). Act No. 563/2004 Coll., on Pedagogical Staff. *Collection of Laws of the Czech Republic*, No. 190. As amended.

Czech Republic. (2016). Decree no. 27/2016 Coll., on the education of students with special educational needs and talented students. *Collection of regulations of the Czech Republic*, No. 10. As amended.

Drotárová, L. (2006). *Asistent pedagoga – stav v ČR 2006* [The teaching assistant – The situation in the CR 2006]. Institut pedagogicko-psychologického poradenství ČR.

European Commission. (2020). *Roma integration in the EU* [Online, cit. 2020-03-09].

European Union Fundamental Rights Agency. (2017). *Second European Union Minorities and Discrimination Survey (EU-MIDIS II) Roma – Selected findings*. Publications Office of the European Union. https://doi.org/10.2811/469

Gabal, I., & Čada, K. (2010). Romské děti v českém vzdělávacím systému [Roma children in the Czech educational system]. In P. Matějů, et al. (Eds.), *Nerovnosti ve vzdělávání. Od měření k řešení* [Inequalities in education. From measurement to solution]. Sociologické nakladatelství.

Giangreco, M. F. (2010). Utilization of teacher assistants in inclusive schools: Is it the kind of help that helping is all about? *European Journal of Special Needs Education, 25*, 341–345. https://doi.org/10.1080/08856257.2010.513537

Government Council for Roma Minority Affairs. (2019). *Zpráva o stavu romské menšiny v České republice za rok 2018*. [Report on the State of the Roma Minority in the Czech Republic in 2018]. The Government Council for Roma Minority Affairs [cit. 2019-11-05].

Havlík, R. (2007). Rovnost k přístupu k vyššímu vzdělání jako sociologický problém [Equality of access to higher education as a sociological problem]. In H. Radomír & K. Jaroslav (Eds.), *Sociologie výchovy a školy* [Sociology of education and school] (pp. 81–94). Portál.

Kaleja, M. (2011). *Romové a škola versus rodiče a žáci* [Roma and school versus parents and students]. Ostravská univerzita v Ostravě.

Messing, V. (2017). Differentiation in the making: Consequences of school segregation of Roma in The Czech Republic, Hungary and Slovakia. *European Education, 49*, 89–103. https://doi.org/10.1080/10564934.2017.1280336

MEYS: The Ministry of Education, Youth and Sports, Czech Republic. (1998). *Informace o zřízení funkce romského asistenta základní a zvláštní škole* [Information on the establishment of the RTA position in primary and special schools]. In MEYS. Bulletin of the Ministry of Education, Youth and Sports of the Czech Republic, 6/1998.

MEYS: The Ministry of Education, Youth and Sports, Czech Republic. (2001). *Metodický pokyn MŠMT ke zřizování přípravných tříd pro děti se sociálním znevýhodněním a k ustanovení funkce vychovatele – asistenta učitele* [Methodical Instruction of MŠMT to establish preparatory classes for socially disadvantaged children and to establish the position of educator – Teaching assistant]. In MŠMT. Bulletin of the Ministry of Education, Youth and Sports of the Czech Republic, 1/2001.

MEYS: The Ministry of Education, Youth and Sports, Czech Republic. (2017). *Zpráva ke zjišťování kvalifikovaných odhadů počtu romských žáků v základních školách ve školním roce 2016/2017* [Report on the investigation of qualified estimates of the number of Roma students in elementary schools in the school year 2016/2017]. MEYS Czech Republic. http://www.msmt.cz/file/39658/

MEYS: The Ministry of Education, Youth and Sports, Czech Republic. (2019). *Statistické ročenky školství – Výkonové ukazatele* [Statistical yearbooks of education – Performance indicators] [cit. 2019-06-05]. http://toiler.uiv.cz/rocenka/rocenka.asp

Miškolci, J., Kubánová, M., & Kováčová, L. (2017). *Who really wants the inclusion of Roma children in education? Mapping motivations of various school stakeholders in Slovakia*. Slovak Governance Institute [cit. 2020-06-10]. http://www.governance.sk/wp-content/uploads/2017/06/0-4.pdf

Moree, D. (2019). *Cesty romských žáků ke vzdělávání. Dopady inkluzivní reformy* [Ways of Roma students to education. The impacts of inclusive reform]. Nadace Open Society Fund Praha.

Němec, Z., et al. (2014a). *Asistence ve vzdělávání žáků se sociálním znevýhodněním* [Assistance in the education of socially disadvantaged students]. Nová škola o.p.s.

Němec, Z., Šimáčková-Laurenčíková, K., & Hájková, V. (2014b). *Asistent pedagoga v inkluzivní škole* [A teaching assistant in an inclusive school]. Karolinum.

Němec, Z., Šimáčková-Laurenčíková, K., Hájková, V., & Strnadová, I. (2015). 'When I need to do something else with the other children, then I can rely on her': Teaching assistants working with socially disadvantaged students. *European Journal of Special Needs Education, 30*, 459–473. https://doi.org/10.1080/08856257.2015.1035904

Němec, Z., Hájková, V., Květoňová, L., & Strnadová, I. (2018). The role of teaching assistants in the education of students from ethnic minorities in The Czech Republic. In L. Goméz Chova, A. López Martínez, & I. Candel Torres (Eds.), *ICERI2018 proceedings (11th international conference of education, research and innovation)* (pp. 8407–8413). IATED Academy.

Němec, Z., et al. (2019). *Systematická podpora sociálně znevýhodněných žáků ve vzdělávání* [Systematic support of socially disadvantaged students in education]. Nová škola o.p.s.

Open Society Fund Prague. (2018). *Rovný přístup k předškolnímu vzdělávání v Ostravě* [Equal access to pre-school education in Ostrava] [cit. 2020-06-02]. http://osf.cz/cs/publikace/rovny-pristup-k-predskolnimu-vzdelavani-v-ostrave/

Pape, I. (2007). *Jak pracovat s romskými žáky. Příručka pro učitele a asistenty pedagogů* [How to work with Roma students. A handbook for teachers and teaching assistants] (p. 21). Slovo.

Public Defender of Rights. (2018). *Doporučení veřejné ochránkyně práv ke společnému vzdělávání romských a neromských dětí* [The Ombudsman's recommendations on the joint education of Roma and non-Roma children]. The Office of the Public Defender of Rights. Doc. Nr. 86/2017/DIS/VB.

Rostas, I., & Kostka, J. (2014). Structural dimensions of Roma school desegregation policies in central and Eastern Europe. *European Educational Research Journal, 13*, 268–281. https://doi.org/10.2304/eerj.2014.13.3.268

Šotolová, E. (2003). Vzdělávání romských dětí v ČR se zaměřením na přípravné třídy a romské pedagogické asistenty [Education of Roma children in The Czech Republic with a focus on preparatory classes and Roma teaching assistants]. *Pedagogika: Časopis pro vědy o vzdělání a výchově, 52*, 79–83.

Šotolová, E. (2011). *Vzdělávání Romů* [Roma education] (4th ed.). Karolinum.

Starčević, J., Dimitrijević, B., & Macura Milovanović, S. (2016). Rethinking the role of pedagogical assistants: Establishing cooperation between Roma families and schools in Serbia. *Center for Educational Policy Studies Journal, 6*, 73–90.

Zbyněk Němec is an associate professor at the Faculty of Education, Charles University in Prague (Czech Republic). In his research and education activities, he is engaged in the work of teaching assistants and issues related to the education of students from ethnic minorities or socially disadvantaged backgrounds. He co-authored the publications as "Teaching assistant in inclusive school", "Assistance in the education of socially disadvantaged students", "Teaching assistant: profession created in dialogue" and "'Raise your hands who will go to places where they do not feel recognized': On the segregation of Roma students in education". Since 2015, he has been a member of the Czech Society for Inclusive Education. For more than 8 years he has also collaborated with the New School association (NGO), which supports Roma students and students from socially excluded localities.

Open Access This chapter is licensed under the terms of the Creative Commons Attribution 4.0 International License (http://creativecommons.org/licenses/by/4.0/), which permits use, sharing, adaptation, distribution and reproduction in any medium or format, as long as you give appropriate credit to the original author(s) and the source, provide a link to the Creative Commons license and indicate if changes were made.

The images or other third party material in this chapter are included in the chapter's Creative Commons license, unless indicated otherwise in a credit line to the material. If material is not included in the chapter's Creative Commons license and your intended use is not permitted by statutory regulation or exceeds the permitted use, you will need to obtain permission directly from the copyright holder.

Chapter 24
South Africa: Desegregated Teaching, Democratic Citizenship Education and Integrating of Ethnic Minority Teachers

Nuraan Davids

Abstract Much of the debates on South Africa's recently desegregated schools centre on intersectional tensions between access/participation; external inclusion/internal exclusion; and assimilation/integration – as it pertains to minority-group learners. Limited attention has been given to the experiences of minority group teachers, as they struggle to find professional and personal inclusion in historically prohibited schools. Yet, not only do minority group teachers experience untold professional undermining within majoritarian schools, but they are often subjected to prejudicial scrutiny by parents and learners, as will be highlighted in this chapter. Leaning on a narrative inquiry, this chapter centres on the experiences of a first year, 'black' female teacher, Slindile, at a historically advantaged ('white') school in South Africa. The narrative inquiry brings to the fore her dialectical experiences, while simultaneously revealing the normative discourses which have thus far remained intact at the school. Underscored by a discursive synchronicity between presumptions of privilege and prejudice, the findings reveal a powerful, yet painful social reality. Firstly, a construction of 'black incompetence' is necessary for the preservation of 'white competence'. Secondly, perceptions of Slindile's 'black' body lends itself to an intersectional tension, which provides for deep considerations on how whiteness reduces the other to the extent of erasure. Thirdly, assigning blame for racism and discrimination to institutional cultures ensures the avoidance of individual accountability. Lastly, minority group teachers are not the only ones at risk. The less diverse a teacher corps is, the less capacitated schools are in advancing democratic citizenship education.

N. Davids (✉)
Stellenbosch University, Stellenbosch, South Africa
e-mail: nur@sun.ac.za

Introduction

One of the key expressions of South Africa's remarkable transition from an apartheid to a democratic state, in 1994, is the desegregation of public schools. Prior to 1992, public schools were defined by stark racial and ethnic segregation – entrenching not only differentiated schooling, but normalising unequal opportunities and expectations. The subsequent opening of all schools to all learners suggested a break from a dehumanising past, intent upon integrated teaching and learning, with the objective of cultivating the grounds for a shared and equitable citizenship. Given the enormous disparities in terms of resources and infrastructure between historically ('white') advantaged and historically ('black', 'coloured' and 'Indian') disadvantaged schools, the exodus from the latter to the former was expected. Learner migratory patterns adopted different tropes. A significant number of 'Indian', 'coloured' and 'black' learners flocked to historically 'white' schools; a number of 'white' learners left public for private schools; the country saw a surge in the number of faith-based schools as well as home-schooling options. While some parents equated desegregation with a drop in the quality of education, others simply did not want their children learning and interacting with different racial, ethnic, cultural, and religious groups. Not only has South Africa's desegregated schools given rise to new forms of separation – as is evident in the proliferation of new kinds of educational spaces – but desegregated schools have not been without their own sets of exclusionary tensions and controversies.

The result is a burgeoning body of literature on the experiences of learners, as they struggle to find their sense of belonging amid historically constructed identities and practices, which remain resistant to other forms of being and acting. The heightened attention on learners – albeit with good reason – has, in most cases not taken account of the teachers' experiences at schools, where they constitute the minority. Part of the reason for this neglect is an assumption that teachers might encounter more professional settings and relationships within schooling environments, and therefore be less prone to any forms of discrimination, marginalisation, and racism. Another reason resides in teachers' reluctance to participate in research or conversations, which attempts to look at the specific experiences of minority-group teachers. This reluctance stems from a fear of further victimisation, alienation, or non-promotion, despite assurances of research confidentiality and anonymity. As revealed by one such teacher, who is enrolled in my BEd Hons class, there is no point in raising her experiences as a matter of concern, the situation simply is what it is; it is the way society operates. When probed as to what the situation is, she responded, with a wry smile on her face: the Head of Department (HOD) regularly sitting in her classes for the purposes of lesson observation, without any prior notification or discussion, and never allowing her to set any examination papers. The HOD justified her actions on the fact that the teacher was new and needed guidance. Yet, according to the teacher, she had been in the post for 4 years at the time of the latter explanation, and no guidance has ever been forthcoming. In the interest of "not rocking the boat", she decided not to raise any further questions or complaints about how she was being treated.

In the ensuing discussion I will commence by bringing into contestation the idea that all desegregated schools in South Africa are conducive and open to diverse teacher identities, or teaching practices. This discussion will shed some light not only on the internal barriers within schools, but also the role of parents in ensuring that minority-group teachers are kept to the minimal both in terms of representation and participation in schools. I follow this with an in-depth narratival account of the experiences of a first-year 'black' teacher at a historically advantaged ('white') school. Her narrative sheds profound light on the intersectional complexities and discourses, which led to her eventual departure from the school. In concluding, I turn my attention to what the implications are for democratic citizenship, if schools act as barriers to pluralist teacher identities, and persist in a preservational ethos of maintaining schools, which is closed to diversity and difference.

Schools as Closed Off Spaces

Although not as widespread, teacher migratory patterns from historically disadvantaged schools to historically advantaged schools, are driven by the same imperatives as those for learners. These include better resourced schools, smaller classes, more opportunities, safer school environments, more learning support services and, in some instances, a higher salary, augmented through the SGB (Davids & Waghid, 2015). The deep-seated disparities which continue to characterise South African schools, despite substantive educational reform, have put into play not only particular patterns of movement away from historically disadvantaged schools (for those who can afford it), but has entrenched the latter as deficient spaces of teaching and learning. Dyadically, historically advantaged schools, by virtue of their well-resourced spaces and opportunities, benefit from associated perceptions of quality education and academic achievement. That these perceptions might neither be fair nor true, has done little to stem the tide of attraction presented by historically advantaged schools. The debilitating effects of poor socio-economic communities, coupled with high levels of violence, vandalism, substance abuse, poor learner attendance, and restricted or compromised parental support, hold dire emotional, psychological and physical consequences for teachers.

There are two points worth noting. Firstly, the decision by 'black' teachers to leave historically disadvantaged schools, is not solely due to adverse school conditions. This decision is influenced by nodes of socio-economic despair, coupled with disillusionment in what has become political rhetoric about equal, equitable and democratised schools. On the one hand, teachers should not have to work in schools, without electricity, running water, inadequate sanitation facilities, limited or no resources, and unacceptable levels of violence. On the other hand, teachers should have the right to teach in schools, which are representative of their society's diversity and pluralism. Inasmuch as South African schools have desegregated, most have retained their historically designated teacher and learner demographics. While learner migratory patterns have been more significant than that of teachers, the majority of teachers in South Africa continue to seek employment in schools, which are aligned to their historical racial category. Moreover, even where schools have shifted entirely in its learner demographics, the teacher body does not necessarily reflect this change, with the historical composition often remaining intact. It is therefore not unusual to find diverse school environments in terms of learner demographics taught by a teacher corps, which does not reflect this diversity.

Debates and concerns about the experiences and under-representation of minority-group teachers are certainly not new. In the United States, for example, it has long been an issue of national importance, with numerous scholars and commentators arguing that there is a growing mismatch between the degree of racial/ethnic diversity of the school learner demography and the teaching corps (Ingersoll et al., 2019). What sets the South African context apart, firstly, is its dual erosions of colonialism and apartheid, which have entrenched not only racial hegemonies and segregation, but a kaleidoscopic infiltration into other intersectionalities of ethnicity and culture. The second factor is the society's relative newness to desegregated educational spaces and diverse teaching corps. And third is a misplaced assumption that either teachers are not sharing similar experiences of marginalisation and exclusion as learners, or that they are better equipped to respond to it.

Yet, the reality that learners are likely to encounter only one kind of teacher – as in schools retaining their historically designated racial identities – holds particular implications not only for teaching and learning, but for the democratic responsibility of schools. In examining teachers' responses to integration, Vandeyar (2010) found inherent notions and practices of racial discrimination and cultural bias. Despite having a class of diverse learners, "a white Afrikaans-speaking teacher" taught "as if she was teaching to a class of Afrikaans-speaking students" (Vandeyar, 2010, p. 354). According to Vandeyar (2010, p. 354), teachers' responses to school integration involved a suppression of seeing difference (colour-blindness), and focusing instead on "sameness", thereby dismissing the "power and structural dimensions of racism".

There are immense benefits to learners, as well as teachers and parents, if a school's teaching cohort reflects that of a learner body and is representative of society. In this regard, a "demographic parity" (Ingersoll et al., 2019) or a "democratic imperative" (Achinstein et al., 2010, p. 71) to counter the disparity between the racial and cultural backgrounds of learners and teachers, is equally important for minority and majority group learners. In turn, "demographic parity" provides the context for "cultural synchronicity", which allows for minority-group teachers to relate to the life experiences and cultural backgrounds of minority-group learners due to "insider knowledge" (Ingersoll et al., 2019, p. 3), and possibly promote culturally responsive teaching (Achinstein et al., 2010, p. 72). Sleeter (2001), for example, posits that although a large proportion of 'white' pre-service students anticipate working with children of another cultural background, as a whole, however, they bring very little cross-cultural background, knowledge, and experience. Proponents of a "democratic imperative", according to Achinstein et al. (2010,

p. 72), cite an emerging body of research, which suggests that minority-group teachers can produce more favourable academic results on standardised test scores, attendance, retention, advanced-level course enrolment, and college-going rates for minority-group learners than white colleagues.

Often because of personal experiences with a culturally disconnected curriculum, or the under-resourced conditions of their own schooling, assert Kohli and Pizarro (2016), minority-group teachers have a heightened awareness of educational injustice and racism. In comparison with 'white' teachers, minority-group teachers have more positive views of minority-group learners, including more favourable perceptions of their academic potential and higher expectations of their learning potential (Kohli & Pizarro, 2016). This argument does not necessarily infer that 'white' teachers cannot be effective teachers of minority-group learners, or that only minority-group teachers can effectively teach minority-group learners. The contention, however, is that the demographic discrepancy between the racial and cultural backgrounds of teachers and learners may contribute to the democratic failure to provide minority-group learners not only with opportunities to learn (Achinstein et al., 2010), but with experiences of inclusion and belonging.

'Whiteness' as De-democratization

To scholars like hooks (1992), Giroux (1997) and Yancy (2008), race is a social construction, without a referent in the natural world. In an interview with Michael Peters, Yancy states:

> Despite the fact that race is not a natural kind, it has tremendous social ontological power; the concept is a powerful organizing social vector that functions as if it cuts at the very joints of reality. The concept of race constitutes our institutional spaces, our political forms of arrangement, our perceptions, our bodily comportment in space, our organization of lived space and lived experience... While the concept of race is unreal qua natural kind, the concept of race has served to create rigid social binaries and used to oppress, to dehumanize, to murder, to render disposable (Peters, 2019, p. 664).

Although democratic South Africa has seen the replacement of explicit racialised discourses and exclusion with more subtle murmurings of 'competence' – the ensuing tensions, however, remain the same. Minority-group teachers, who pursue employment at historically advantaged schools are subjected to vague descriptors and criteria of 'competence' or 'standards', which could include any feature from qualifications and experience, to religion and accent (Davids & Waghid, 2015). Framing this multi-faceted construction of 'competence' or 'standards', most often, is a 'whiteness', which on the one hand, "benefits all whites regardless of their class or gender status" (Leonardo, 2009, p. 70), and on the other hand, is used for no other reason but oppression.

'Whiteness', by its very nature, explains Yancy, is binary and hierarchical. While 'whiteness' establishes itself as the thesis, racialized groups that are not white are deemed "different, deviant, that is, the antithesis" (Peters, 2019, pp. 663–4). As "a structural, ideological, embodied, epistemological and phenomenological mode of being", 'whiteness', explains Yancy (Blasdel, 2018) "is predicated upon its distance from and negation of blackness"; neither 'whiteness' nor 'blackness' are based on objective, biological facts, but are "sites of lived meaning" (Yancy & Del Guadalupe Davidson, 2016, p. 8). To Yancy, 'whiteness' "is a master of concealment; it is insidiously embedded within responses, reactions, good, intentions, postural gestures, denials, and structural and material orders…Whiteness as a form of ambushing is not an anomaly. The operations of whiteness are by no means completely transparent" (2008, p. 229). So embedded is the condition of 'whiteness' that it has not been subjected to the same level of scholarly scrutiny and analyses as 'blackness' (Giroux, 1997, p. 379).

Although invisible, the presumptuous presence of 'whiteness' asserts and sustains its dominance through judgements not only on itself, but on others. Whatever is inferred by and associated with 'whiteness' cannot equate to that of 'blackness'. Reflecting from this hegemonic framework, are trivial tributaries – identities and modes of being which are approached as less-than in terms of value, and hence, 'competence'. How these tributaries take effect, varies from context to context, and reveals a spectrum of racialised thinking, which cuts across a 'black'/'white' binary. 'Black' schools appoint 'white' principals, while 'coloured' schools refuse to appoint 'black' principals; 'black' teachers are not only excluded from 'white' schools, they are also excluded from 'coloured' and 'Indian' schools (Makhetha, 2017; Simelane, 2017).

Notably, while all schools ('black', 'Indian', 'coloured' and 'white') are prepared to appoint 'white' teachers or principals, all schools are not prepared to appoint teachers of all other races – suggesting two key considerations. Firstly, that 'whiteness' is as Yancy (Blasdel, 2018) describes, a "transcendental norm", which means that 'whiteness' goes unmarked – "As unmarked, white people are able to live their identities as unraced, as simply human, as persons". Secondly, not only is 'whiteness' is generically allied with a presumptive privilege and competence, but notions of competence should not be misunderstood as a judgement of excellence. Instead, what the use of 'competence' seeks to do is to re-assert a hegemony of 'whiteness', which is diametrically dependent on a perception of 'blackness' as 'incompetent'.

The imposition of a deficit pertains not only to 'incompetence' in terms of teaching, subject content knowledge, or classroom management skills, but to the very identities of teachers. On the one hand, it is commonplace for 'black' teachers to be subjected to 'mentoring processes', which is seemingly not applicable to other staff members. Other times, they are actually not allowed to teach their subject specialisation – as was the case with a 'black' teacher, who had applied for the post of a mathematics teacher but was instead only allowed to teach mathematical literacy (Davids & Waghid, 2015). On the other hand, attempts by teachers to bring their diverse backgrounds and identities into an existing ethos, assert Kohli and Pizzaro (2016), are met with resistance, which makes it difficult for them to engage holistically with their peers and learners. While manifested differently, the same fields of tensions, which are used to keep minority-group learners out of historically advantaged schools, are used to keep minority-group teachers at bay. Once appointed, and granted external access, minority-group teachers face continuous struggles and barriers to be included and recognised – rendering the challenge of remaining within these schools, greater than trying to get appointed in the first place. In one instance, a teacher faced endless complaints from parents, on behalf of their children, that they could not understand his 'Indian' accent. His eventual decision to leave was precipitated when the principal mistook him for being Muslim, when he was in fact, Hindu (Davids & Waghid, 2015).

As debilitating and dehumanising as the infliction of 'whiteness' can be on the lives and experiences of minority-group teachers, these experiences become even more nuanced and harmful for minority-group teachers, who are not male. Practices and experiences of oppression can seldom be understood or explained in relation to a single categorical axis. To do so, following Crenshaw (1989), would be to erase the particular experiences of minority group women, as it fails to take into account the intersectionality of discrimination and oppression. To Crenshaw (1989, p. 140), the intersectional experience is greater than the sum of racism and sexism:

> Black women sometimes experience discrimination in ways similar to white women's experiences; sometimes they share very similar experiences with Black men. Yet often they experience double-discrimination – the combined effects of practices which discriminate on the basis of race, and on the basis of sex. And sometimes, they experience discrimination as Black women – not the sum of race and sex discrimination, but as Black women.

Following the above, the ensuing case study discussion centres on the experiences of a first year, 'black' female teacher at a historically advantaged ('white') school in South Africa. The case study leans on a narrative inquiry, which allows for the unfleshing and exploration of her experiences in the context of a particular sociality. Her identity as a 'black' woman lends itself to an intersectional phenomenon and tension, which provides for deep considerations and contemplations on how whiteness reduces the other to the extent of erasure.

Methodology: Narrative Inquiry as Disrupting the Centre

To Connelly and Clandinin (1990), knowledge of the self and of the self in relation to others and one's context provide a powerful lens through which to construct educational research. In this regard, a narrative inquiry brings theoretical ideas about the nature of human life as lived to bear on educational experience as lived. The key difference between more traditional uses of didactic and strategic narrative, and narrative inquiry, elaborates Conle (2000), is the open-endedness and empirical nature of the latter, since the story must be open to being re-told. Narrative, explain Connelly and Clandinin (1990, p. 2), is both phenomenon and method – "Narrative names the structured quality of experience to be studied, and it names the pattern of inquiry for its study." Hence, their assertion that "people by nature lead storied lives and tell stories of those lives, whereas narrative researchers describe such lives, collect and tell stories of them, and write narratives of experience". (Connelly & Clandinin, 1990, p. 2). As a methodology, they continue, narrative inquiry allows for a rich description of experiences, as well as an exploration of the meanings that the participants derive from these experiences. It amplifies voices that may have otherwise remained silent. To use narrative inquiry methodology is to adopt a particular view of experience as phenomenon under study. (Connelly & Clandinin, 2006).

It is essential, state Connelly and Clandinin (1990, p. 4), that the participant gets to tell her story first, so that she, "who has long been silenced in the research relationship is given the time and space to tell his or her story so that it too gains the authority and validity that the research story has long held". They maintain that by galvanising the voice of the participant, the two narratives of the researcher and the participant evolve into a shared narrative construction and reconstruction through inquiry (Connelly & Clandinin, 1990). Any particular narrative inquiry, state Clandinin and Connelly (2000, p. 54), is defined by a three-dimensional space: "studies have temporal dimensions and address temporal matters: they focus on the personal and the social in a balance appropriate to the inquiry: and they occur in specific places or sequences of places." By working within this three-dimensional inquiry space, narrative inquirers or researchers can begin their inquiries either with engaging with participants through telling stories or through coming alongside participants in the living out of stories (Connelly & Clandinin, 2006). Narrative inquirers cannot bracket themselves out of the inquiry but rather need to find ways to inquire into participants' experiences, their own experiences as well as the co-constructed experiences developed through the relational inquiry process. As such, narrative inquirers are part of the metaphoric parade and are complicit in the world they study (Clandinin & Connelly, 1998).

Central to narrative inquiry is the space and potential for the debunking of perceptions, myths, stereotypes, and normative discourses while simultaneously bringing to the centre voices and stories, which ordinarily might have been marginalised and lost. In this regard, narrative inquiry allows for the construction of new stories and new social realities.

Findings

While born into the promise of democracy, Slindile's story is atypical to most young 'black' people in South Africa. After completing her primary education, she attended one of the most prestigious schools in South Africa and attained her undergraduate degree and postgraduate teaching diploma at the University of Cape Town. Her entire education had been attained via historically 'white' and advantaged institutions. While completing her teaching diploma, she completed a learnership at the same historically advantaged primary school she had attended as a young girl. Upon graduating, she was offered a teaching post at this same school. Other than one other 'black' teacher, who was responsible for teaching isiXhosa, Slindile was the first 'black' class teacher in the history of school's 125-year existence. What started as "a dream come true to teach at a school that has played a vital role in shaping" her, soon became short-lived, described by her as "a painful period during my tenure at the school. Being told to resign or face disciplinary action shook me to my core."

During her first meeting with the parents of her grade 5 class Slindile was questioned about where she had qualified and whether she could show proof of her qualifications. It became apparent that a number of parents were unhappy about having their children taught by her. Soon thereafter she became aware of online chat groups among parents, who discussed her suitability to the ethos of the school. After just a few weeks into the new academic year, she was called to a meeting with the principal, deputy principal, HOD, as well as a parent representative from the School Governing Body (SGB). Slindile was informed that her performance was "not up to scratch", and that she would be subjected to a "quality assurance plan", which involved an "eight-point plan". This plan, which was never discussed with her, consisted of a list of instructions and requirements. She was required to submit detailed weekly and daily lesson plans, including assessment practices; she would receive daily classroom visits at any given time by various members of the School Management Team (SMT); her marking and use of teaching resources would be monitored; and she should ensure "an energised and enthusiastic attitude when presenting lessons". When she queried why she was the only newly appointed teacher being subjected to an "eight-point plan", she was merely told that she required "mentoring". She was never made aware of the specific issues being raised about her, or what had led to concerns about "poor performance". Slindile described her "mentorship programme" as leaving her "more traumatised that supported". She described her "discrimination as subtle, yet so painful" – "I was the only the teacher who had to make additional lesson plans for everything that I taught. I was the only teacher to whom a mentor could come any time of the day and teach my class on my behalf".

The daily classroom visits created great anxiety for Slindile. From her perspective, she was neither experiencing any difficulties with her teaching, nor with managing her class. She did not know when the visits would occur, who would be coming, what was being observed, or what was being discussed about her teaching. The daily visits did not only involve observations of her teaching and interaction with learners, it also involved the 'mentor' simply interrupting her teaching and taking over her role as a teacher. As the days passed, Slindile became aware that the undermining of her pedagogical authority in the classroom had begun to lead to a loss of credibility with her learners. One morning, while taking register, she was informed by one of her learners that an absent learner had in fact left the school. She found this surprising as she had not been notified by the learner, her parents, or the school administrator. When Slindile followed up on the matter with the principal, she was told that the parent "was so unhappy that she decided to take her daughter out of my [her] class to be home-schooled and only to return to the school next year". When she sought clarity on what the parent was unhappy about, she was told that "it wouldn't be appropriate" for her to know.

By the time the first school term concluded, Slindile had begun to experience deep alienation from her colleagues and members of the SMT. She remain uninformed about the complaints being levelled against, and there was no engagement with her as to how she could improve her "'poor performance". Matters came to a head, when a 'white' parent wrote to the principal, complaining about the parents' remarks about Slindile; the hostility and prejudice being presented by the school; as well as a widely shared question, posed by a grade 5 learner: "Are black teachers real teachers?" At a subsequent meeting, again with the principal, deputy principal, as well as two parent representatives from the SGB, Slindile reported, "I was told that I needed to resign or face disciplinary action. If I did face disciplinary actions, it was going to ruin my reputation, so I opted to resign. I was scared, I felt that I was put under pressure to make a decision. The school made my job intolerable and treated me in a discriminatory manner".

Nine months after being appointed, Slindile resigned. In a newsletter to parents, the principal indicated that she had resigned due to "personal reasons". Given the historical 'white' status of the school, and the fact that she had been the school's first appointed 'black' class teacher, a number of parents expressed their dismay at Slindile's sudden departure and demanded to know what had led to this decision. Amid a significant outcry from the parent body (across racial lines), one parent encouraged Slindile to seek legal assistance. The matter attracted widespread media attention, with renewed questions being asked about the pace of transformation in South African schools – not only in terms of learner demographics and inclusion, but teachers as well.

Slindile's lodged a grievance with the Commission for Conciliation, Mediation and Arbitration (CCMA). The school defended its decision to ask for her resignation by citing that parents had threatened to remove their children from the school. The school denied Slindile's version that she was unaware of the details of the complaints made against her, and instead maintained that they had had regular meetings and interventions with her, as well as provided support. They could not, however, provide any written proof of providing her details of the complaints, of issuing her warnings, or of the content and purpose of the "mentorship programme". After the initial CCMA hearing the school made her an offer that she could return as a learnership teacher. She refused and demanded compensation for the way she had been treated. The CCMA found that the school had indeed acted in a discriminatory fashion, that she had, in fact, been constructively terminated, and should receive an apology and compensation. In adhering to this instruction, the school's SGB stated: "As an SGB we have recognised that the school's institutional culture does not fully reflect the diversity of South Africa and we have publicly committed to changing this. It is a priority".

While this particular case had an eventual just outcome, the harm experienced by Slindile is experienced by many minority-group teachers. As noted by her, "the apology from the school does not acknowledge the truth of what actually happened". These experiences are often endured in silence for fear of reprisal – whether in the form of further discrimination and marginalisation, non-promotion, or as has been seen in Slindile's case, termination. Moreover, Slindile received significant support from a group of parents, who mobilised around her case and ensured that she could act against the school. It is doubtful that she would have gone to the

CCMA without this support. It is exceptionally difficult for teachers, who experience discrimination or racism to act against these entrenched practices – not only because of their fear of reprisals, but because these practices are often deceptively disguised in a discourse of 'competence', which is used to systematically break down the self-esteem of teachers.

Analysis and Discussion

The narrative inquiry assisted Slindile in reflecting upon a deeply troubling experience. What became especially evident through the study is her subjection to certain practices and requirements, because of the way she had been objectified as a 'black' woman. As she moved between her past and her present, she began to become aware of the disjuncture between her perception of herself as a 'black' woman, and how she was perceived as a 'black' woman. Slindile had assumed that her attendance at a historically advantaged high school and university, as well as her attendance at the very primary school, where she would later be appointed, would secure her an unhindered pathway into her career. She had mistakenly thought that her economic privilege and social capital would allow her inclusion across racial lines. What she experienced and learnt, however, is that her racially construed identity presents an impenetrable barrier not only to being seen as qualified and competent, but to being seen as equally human.

Despite reporting on her deep sense of humiliation, marginalisation and alienation at the school, neither the principal, nor the SGB accepted responsibility for the harm they had inflicted on her. Seemingly, the barrier which renders Slindile's 'blackness' to less-than is the same one which retains the preservation of 'whiteness'. The refusal by the principal and the SGB to accept responsibility for what Slindile had experienced, meant not only a refusal to acknowledge that she had indeed been subjected to racism and discrimination, but that they had been the perpetrators of that racism and discrimination. The decision therefore to issue a statement which assigns blame to an institutional culture is misleading. On the one hand, it suggests an abdication of any accountability, as if institutional culture exists in isolation from those, who instil and cultivate it. On the other hand, it is a manifestation of the capacity of 'whiteness' to conceal itself – "insidiously embedded within responses, reactions, good, intentions, postural gestures, denials, and structural and material orders…" (Yancy, 2008, p. 229). In this regard, the narrative inquiry brings to the fore the dialectical experience of Slindile, while simultaneously giving voice to the normative discourses which have thus far remained intact at the school. While identified as an institutional culture that "does not fully reflect the diversity of South Africa", this culture is retained through a presumptive privilege, which, in turn, is mutually contingent on constructing Slindile as incompetent. She cannot be allowed to succeed at being competent. If she does, she not only debunks the myth of 'black' incompetence, she also disrupts the hegemony of 'whiteness'.

Emanating from this discussion is the synchronous relationship between a presumptive privilege and a presumptive prejudice. 'Whiteness' presumes a privilege, which is sustained through prejudice. The prejudice is evident in Slindile's first encounter with the parents of her learners, who question her about her qualifications. But the question has little to do with her acquired qualifications. Her 'black' skin has already disqualified her, if not as a 'competent' teacher, then as a teacher 'competent' enough to teach 'white' children. What the question confirms, is that judgment on Slindile has already been passed. Next, follows a series of prejudices – from the presumptive occupation and teaching of her class, without prior or post deliberation; the removal of a learner and the "inappropriateness" for Slindile to know the reason why; to the question by a grade 5 learner as to whether 'black' teachers are "real teachers", and of course, the threat by the principal "to resign or face disciplinary action".

Underscoring all of these encounters is a presumptive prejudice, which takes for granted the right to treat Slindile as if she has no voice, no equality, and no right to a dignified treatment. When she dared to question any of it – as she did when trying to understand why a learner had been removed from her class – the response she received had nothing to do with her right to access to certain knowledge; it had to do with her "inappropriate" conduct in having the impudence to ask the question in the first place.

Conclusions and Implications

As I conclude this chapter, it is worth considering why teachers from diverse identities and backgrounds are so critical to teaching and learning, schools and the cultivation of a democratic society. Firstly, teacher diversity allows for the inclusion and articulation of different life-worlds and perspectives, which stands to benefit all learners, teachers, as well as the parents, and hence, society. Secondly, teachers from different backgrounds provide points of resonance and aspiration for minority-group learners. Thirdly, the more learners are able to engage and learn from those, who are different to themselves, the greater and deeper their preparation for engaging with difference, not only at school, but later, as citizens in a pluralist society. Concomitantly, the less diverse a teacher corps is, the greater the risk of a perpetuation of existing hegemonies, stereotypes and prejudices.

The entire point of schooling and education is to prepare young people for their roles as citizens. Schools cannot shy away from the knowledge and obligation that while schooling is temporary, education is not. Schools ought to provide the space and ethos where democratic practices are not only made visible in the inclusion of diverse learners and teachers, but where the very ideals of democratic citizenship – that is, equal recognition, inclusion, respect – are preserved. It matters therefore what learners are taught, and it matters who teachers are. Stated differently, young people learn not only by *what* and *how* they are taught, they also learn from *whom* they are taught. It is often not enough for learners to learn about different ways of being and acting; they have to be able to participate in those differences. It is only when learners witness and participate in diverse and dissenting contexts that they learn about themselves and others; they learn that they do not have to be and act like others in order to find a sense of belonging.

References

Achinstein, B., Ogawa, R., Sexton, D., & Freitas, C. (2010). Retaining teachers of color: A pressing problem and a potential strategy for "hard-to-staff" schools. *Review of Educational Research, 80*(1), 71–107. https://doi.org/10.3102/0034654309355994

Blasdel, A. (2018). *Is white America ready to confront its racism? Philosopher George Yancy says we need a 'crisis'*. Retrieved from https://www.theguardian.com/world/2018/apr/24/george-yancy-dear-white-america-philosopher-confront-racism

Clandinin, D. J., & Connelly, F. M. (1998). Stories to live by: Narrative understandings of school reform. *Curriculum Inquiry, 28*(2), 149–164.

Clandinin, D. J., & Connelly, F. M. (2000). *Narrative inquiry: Experience and story in qualitative research*. Jossey-Bass.

Conle, C. (2000). Narrative inquiry: Research tool and medium for professional development. *European Journal of Teacher Education, 23*(1), 49–63. https://doi.org/10.1080/713667262

Connelly, F. M., & Clandinin, D. J. (1990). Stories of experience and narrative inquiry. *Educational Researcher, 19*(5), 2–14. https://doi.org/10.3102/0013189X019005002

Connelly, F. M., & Clandinin, D. J. (2006). Narrative inquiry. In J. L. Green, G. Camilli, & P. Elmore (Eds.), *Handbook of complementary methods in education research* (3rd ed., pp. 477–487). Lawrence Erlbaum.

Crenshaw, K. (1989). Demarginalizing the intersection of race and sex: A black feminist critique of antidiscrimination doctrine, feminist theory and antiracist politics. *University of Chicago Legal Forum, 1989*(1), Article 8, 139–167.

Davids, N., & Waghid, Y. (2015). The invisible silence of race: On exploring some experiences of minority group teacher at South African schools. *Power and Education, 7*(2), 155–168. https://doi.org/10.1177/1757743815586518

Giroux, H. A. (1997). White squall: Resistance and the pedagogy of whiteness. *Cultural Studies, 11*(3), 376–389. https://doi.org/10.1080/095023897335664

Hooks, b. (1992). *Black looks: Race and representation*. South End Press.

Ingersoll, R., May, H., & Collins, G. (2019). Recruitment, employment, retention and the minority teacher shortage. *Education Policy Analysis Archives, 27*(37), 1–37. https://doi.org/10.14507/epaa.27.3714

Kohli, R., & Pizarro, M. (2016). Fighting to educate our own: Teachers of color, relational accountability, and the struggle for racial justice. *Equity & Excellence in Education, 49*(1), 72–84. https://doi.org/10.1080/10665684.2015.1121457

Leonardo, Z. (2009). *Race, whiteness and education*. Routledge.

Makhetha, T. (2017). *School racism row: Parents don't want a black principal*. Retrieved from www.iol.co.za/news/south-africa/gauteng/school-racism-row-parents-dont-want-a-black-principal-10458915

Peters, M. A. (2019). Interview with George Yancy, African-American philosopher of critical philosophy of race. *Educational Philosophy and Theory, 51*(7), 663–669. https://doi.org/10.1080/00131857.2018.1498214

Simelane, B. C. (2017). *Another Gauteng school embroiled in a principal appointment row*. Retrieved from https://www.dailymaverick.co.za/article/2017-12-05-another-gauteng-school-embroiled-in-a-principal-appointment-row/#.WsoO4ohuZPY

Sleeter, C. E. (2001). Preparing teachers for culturally diverse schools research and the overwhelming presence of whiteness. *Journal of Teacher Education, 52*(2), 94–106. https://doi.org/10.1177/0022487101052002002

Vandeyar, S. (2010). Responses of South African teachers to the challenge of school integration. *South African Journal of Education, 30*, 343–359. https://doi.org/10.1080/13613320500110501

Yancy, G. (2008). *Black Bodies, White Gazes: The continuing significance of race*. Rowman & Littlefield Publishers.

Yancy, G., & Del Guadalupe Davidson, M. (2016). Thinking about race, history, and identity: An interview with George Yancy. *The Western Journal of Black Studies, 40*(1), 3–13.

Nuraan Davids is Professor of Philosophy of Education in the Department of Education Policy Studies in the Faculty of Education at Stellenbosch University. Her research interests include democratic citizenship education; Islamic philosophy of education; and philosophy of higher education. She is a fellow of the Center for Advanced Study in the Behavioral Sciences at Stanford University (2020–2021). She is the Co-Editor-in-Chief of the Journal of Education in Muslim Societies; Associate Editor of the South African Journal of Higher Education, and an Editorial Board Member of Ethics and Education. Her most recent publications include Out of Place: An autoethnography of postcolonial citizenship; Teaching, friendship & humanity (Springer, 2020; with Y. Waghid); Teachers Matter: Educational Philosophy and Authentic Learning (Rowman & Littlefield – Lexington Series, 2020; with Y. Waghid); The Thinking University Expanded: On Profanation, Play and Education (Routledge, 2020, with Y. Waghid); Democratic Education and Muslim Philosophy: Interfacing Muslim and communitarian thought (Palgrave-MacMillan, 2020, with Y. Waghid).

Open Access This chapter is licensed under the terms of the Creative Commons Attribution 4.0 International License (http://creativecommons.org/licenses/by/4.0/), which permits use, sharing, adaptation, distribution and reproduction in any medium or format, as long as you give appropriate credit to the original author(s) and the source, provide a link to the Creative Commons license and indicate if changes were made.

The images or other third party material in this chapter are included in the chapter's Creative Commons license, unless indicated otherwise in a credit line to the material. If material is not included in the chapter's Creative Commons license and your intended use is not permitted by statutory regulation or exceeds the permitted use, you will need to obtain permission directly from the copyright holder.

Chapter 25
"Why Are We Only Learning About White People?" The Role of Identity in the Curricular and Pedagogical Considerations of One Latino Educator

Kelly R. Allen

Abstract This chapter focuses on the perspectives of Ricardo, a Latino educator, and his experience with navigating identity as he made curricular and pedagogical considerations in his practice. The chapter begins by reviewing the literature on the experiences of minoritized educators in education, asking: How do minoritized educators navigate the complexity of their identity as a minoritized individual *and* educator working within predominantly white concepts of knowledge and behavior construction? This chapter analyzes a collection of focus groups, individual interviews, and curriculum artifacts as a means of approaching and analyzing Ricardo's experiences. This analysis illuminates, (1) how language and hybrid classroom discourse was used to connect with students, and (2) the deep responsibility Ricardo felt to create bridges to the curriculum for his students. The findings of this chapter underscore the need for teacher education programs to better support minoritized educators in navigating the complex positions they assume, as educators and as minoritized individuals, and the ways that these two identities intersect in their practice.

Introduction

It was a sunny spring day when I went to Ricardo's classroom for the first time. School had just released for the day and Ricardo met me at the school doors to help navigate me through the extensive, winding halls of the school. Upon greeting me, Ricardo was approached by a student who excitedly greeted him in Mexican Spanish. On our walk to his classroom, we were stopped by four students along the way, with each student conversing with Ricardo in Mexican Spanish. Knowing that

K. R. Allen (✉)
Department of Research, Counseling, and Curriculum, College of Education and Human Development, Augusta University, Augusta, GA, USA
e-mail: KALLEN8@augusta.edu

© The Author(s) 2023
M. Gutman et al. (eds.), *To Be a Minority Teacher in a Foreign Culture*,
https://doi.org/10.1007/978-3-031-25584-7_25

my Spanish comprehension is minimal, Ricardo translated for me along the way. One student stopped to tell Ricardo "thank you" for helping him with an assignment, two others stopped to talk about soccer, and one just wanted to wish Ricardo a good evening. Along the way, I noticed other teachers – all white – going about their end-of-day tasks uninterrupted by students. I observed the walls of the hallways lined with trophy cases featuring pictures of notable alumni of the school, all of whom were white. When we got to Ricardo's classroom, however, it seemed like his classroom was the antidote to the whiteness in the hallways of the school. The walls of Ricardo's classroom were splattered with facts about Latino history, and featured pictures of notable, yet marginalized, individuals throughout history.

Observing Ricardo's classroom and his interactions with his students made me question: How do racially minoritized educators navigate the complexity of their identity as a person of color *and* educator working within predominantly white concepts of knowledge and behavior construction? Throughout this chapter, I seek to illuminate, (1) how language and hybrid classroom discourse was used by Ricardo to connect with students, and (2) the deep responsibility Ricardo felt to create bridges to the curriculum for his students. The findings of this chapter underscore the need for teacher education programs to better support minoritized educators in navigating the complex positions they assume, as educators and as minoritized individuals, and the ways in which these two identities intersect in their practice.

Understanding the Identity Development of Minoritized Educators

In the United States, racial disparities between teachers and students, as well as broader disparities in education testing, access, and achievement, have led to calls to diversify the teacher workforce (Milner, 2006; Neena, 2018; Nevarez et al., 2019). However, there is little discussion and understanding around how to support educators of color as they enter the white majoritarian field of education (Montecinos, 2004; Sleeter, 2001). Research has shown that individuals' complex racial identities and lived experiences shape their professional identity (Al-Khatib & Lash, 2017; Gilpin, 2005; Hasberry, 2019; Kayi-Adyar, 2019; Sparks, 2018). However, minoritized educators experience conflicts in forming their professional identity. These conflicts arise because their identity as a racialized, gendered and cultured beings differs from the professional identity they are expected to assume inside of school (Agee, 2004; Gilpin, 2005; Olitsky, 2020; Singh, 2019). Similarly, minoritized educators are forced to grapple with the proliferating constructs of whiteness and racialized gender constructs that have infiltrated the formations of their personal and professional identities (Burant et al., 2002; Gilpin, 2005; Ramanathan, 2006; Smith Kondo, 2019, Warren, 2020). Further complicating the development of professional identities for minoritized educators is the fact that they embody multiple complex and weaving identities that cannot be separated (Crenshaw, 1995).

This understanding of teacher identity is critical if we seek to understand the ways that minoritized educators approach pedagogy and curriculum decision making in their practice. While research has shown that teacher education programs play a role in shaping teacher identity (Alsup, 2006; Britzman, 1986; Clarke, 2009), there is a hyper focus on preparing white teachers to teach students of various cultural backgrounds that has often left minoritized educators on the margins of professional and pedagogical development in teacher education programs (Gay, 2000; Milner, 2006; Sleeter, 2001). Despite examples of exemplar pedagogy implemented by minoritized educators (Milner, 2006, 2010, 2012a; Vickery, 2016) research continues to show that some minoritized educators struggle to implement pedagogical strategies that are responsive to their students (Coffey & Farinde-Wu, 2016; Ullman & Hecshb, 2011) and continue to lack professional support (Castaneda et al., 2006; Gay, 2000; Mabokela & Madsen, 2003). For example, the structure of many multicultural education courses in teacher education programs addresses race in relation to whiteness and discusses pedagogical considerations in a way that is geared towards the development of white teachers (Agee, 2004; Gorski, 2009). This reality is especially problematic for teachers of subjects like social studies, where issues of race/ism and whiteness permeate the curriculum (Marri, 2003; Rains, 2003), curricular standards (Branch, 2003; Eargle, 2016; Marshall, 2003), and textbooks (Craig & Davis, 2015; Gay, 2003; Shear, 2015).

Methodology

This chapter focuses on the experiences of Ricardo,[1] a Latino male social studies teacher. Ricardo was a participant in a larger study that sought to understand urban (see Milner, 2012b) social studies teachers' self-efficacy in enacting culturally responsive and sustaining pedagogy. The study included four social studies educators who were all prepared at an institution that focuses on urban education in the United States Midwest. The four educators engaged in a series of focus groups and individual interviews that sought to illuminate their experiences as culturally responsive and sustaining pedagogues. Of the four educators involved in the study, two educators identified as white women, one educator identified as a white male and one educator, Ricardo, identified as a Latino male.

Throughout the course of the study it became clear that Ricardo's curricular and pedagogical decision making was deeply informed by his lived experiences and identity as a Latino. As I continued data analysis for the larger study, it became apparent that the white educators did not leverage their cultural capital (Yosso, 2005) in the same way that Ricardo did when making curricular and pedagogical decisions in their practice. As the difference in Ricardo's perspective became more

---

[1] Ricardo is a pseudonym self-selected by the participant.

salient, I recognized that deeper inquiry into Ricardo's experience and identity was necessary. This chapter is the result of my inquiry into Ricardo's experience.

To begin this examination, I started with the following research question: How do minoritized educators navigate the complexity of their identity as a minoritized individual *and* educator working within predominantly white concepts of knowledge and behavior construction? In this following section, I will outline the context of the research described in this chapter, the guiding theoretical perspective of this research, as well as the methods of data collection and analysis.

Context

Ricardo is a high school social studies teacher in an urban emergent (see Milner, 2012b) school district. While the teacher demographic data for Ricardo's school is unavailable, 70% of the teachers in the school district that Ricardo teaches in are white, while only 12% of the students in the school district at large identify as white (DPI, 2018). Ricardo's school district has a long history of racial segregation and educational disparities within the district's schools. This mirrors the contentious atmosphere around race that has led to widespread residential segregation and various economic and social inequities throughout the city. At Ricardo's school, 50% of the students identify as Hispanic/Latino, 28% of students identify as Black or African American, 15% of students identify as Asian, 4% of students identify as white, 2% of students identify as two or more races, 0.5% of students identify as American Indian or Alaskan Native, and 0.1% of students identify as Native Hawaiian or Other Pacific Islander (DPI, 2019). In describing his upbringing, Ricardo describes that he grew up in the neighborhood that his students currently live. In fact, he even went to the high school that he is currently teaching at and remembers the "white" social studies curriculum, which he says has influenced his approach to teaching today. Though Ricardo recalls his experiences throughout this chapter as a Latino teacher teaching predominantly Latino students, the shared racial identity that he and his students possess is still set within an educational system that is dominated by whiteness through the prevalence of white faces, policies, practices, and perspectives.

Theoretical Perspective

The research for this chapter is grounded in a post-positive realist conception of identity. A post-positivist realist conception of identity acknowledges connections between an individual's lived experiences, social location and cultural identity (Mohanty, 2000; Moya, 2000; Gilpin, 2006). In acknowledging this, it is believed that "understanding emerges from one's past and present experiences and interactions as interpreted in sociopolitical contexts" (Gilpin, 2006, p. 10). Because of this,

"Understanding, then, is relative to one's experiences as a raced, gendered, classed, nationalized, and so forth, being" (Gilpin, 2006, p. 10). A post-positivist realist conception of identity also assumes that knowledge gained through oppressive experiences influences identity formation (Mohanty, 2000; Moya, 2000). In the context of this study, a postpositivist realist conceptualization of identity is employed to understand how Ricardo's curricular and pedagogical considerations are influenced by his experiences as a racialized, gendered, classed, and marginalized being.

Gilpin (2006) outlines four tenets of postpositivist realist theory to include the understanding that "(1) identities are both constructed and real, (2) identities are mediated through cognitive and social processes, (3) knowledge garnered in the context of oppression should be afforded epistemic privilege, and (4) the power of individual and collective agency should be part of discussions of identity" (p. 13). The first tenet, which conceptualizes identities as both constructed and real, draws from the understanding that the racial identities are constructed through various aspects of society, though society's construction of various racial identities are not all encompassing of oneself as a racial, ethnic, cultural, or other being (Gilpin, 2006). This is to say that parallels may be drawn within and across racially constructed groups, with the understanding that the totality of oneself does not exist within the confines of the racially constructed group you are categorized within. Similarly, the second tenet, which states that identities are mediated through cognitive and social processes, draws from the understanding that an individual's experience is shaped by the identity categories they are placed within (Gilpin, 2006; Mohanty, 2000; Moya, 2000). The third tenet asserts that "knowledge garnered in the context of oppression should be afforded epistemic privilege." This tenet is imbedded in the understanding that the knowledge and identities that one possesses work together "in constructing an understanding of the world that is uniquely valid" yet "intertwined with the understandings of those whose share elements of [their] historical positions and social group memberships" (Gilpin, 2006, p. 12). Through this understanding, the lived experiences and perceptions of individuals are used to not only understand themselves, but others who they interact with. The fourth tenet, which focuses on agency, is predicated on the understanding that individuals have agency and that this agency must be conceptualized through an understanding of "individuals, the groups to which the individuals belong, and the location of those groups within larger sociopolitical contexts" (Gilpin, 2006, p. 15). Throughout this chapter, I use a post-positivist realist conception of identity to analyze how Ricardo finds power and agency as a racially minoritized individual within a white majoritarian space.

Data Collection and Analysis

The data collection for this research is nested within the larger study, noted above. The methods included a semi-structured focus group interview, individual interviews, and the collection of curriculum artifacts over a 1 year period. Due to the shared experiences the educators had in their teacher preparation program, a semi-structured focus group interview was conducted with all of the educators involved in the study (Wilson & McChesney, 2018). Semi-structured individual interviews (Rubin & Rubin, 1995) were also conducted with the participants to elicit rich details about their teaching experiences. At one of the interviews, each educator brought a collection of self-selected curriculum artifacts they felt demonstrated their approach to teaching. These curriculum artifacts were discussed and collected by whom and for what?. Further, a series of phenomenological conversational interviews occurred with Ricardo to elicit understanding of his identity construction both personally and professionally.

The interviews were voice recorded, transcribed, and analyzed using a three-step inductive to deductive analysis process (Sipe & Ghiso, 2004). Through this approach to analysis, which first included a close read of the data followed by an inductive to deductive coding scheme, themes around language, identity, and curricular agency emerged. After the identification of these themes, line by line coding according to these themes was conducted. Through this line by line coding, 28 excerpts that discussed Ricardo's curricular and pedagogical considerations in relation to language, identity and curricular agency were selected. The 28 excerpts were then analyzed using a post-positivist realist approach to discourse analysis that considered Ricardo's positioning, experiences, and agency as a Latino male in a white majoritarian educational space. Drawing from perspectives on critical discourse analysis (Gee, 2011), the following questions were asked of each of the 28 excerpts:

1. What understanding of Ricardo's identity does this piece of language elicit?
2. What activity is Ricardo's identity being used to enact?
3. What identity or identities is this piece of language attributing to others and how does this help Ricardo enact his own identity?
4. How does this piece of language connect or disconnect Ricardo from other aspects of his identity?
5. How does this piece of language privilege certain aspects of Ricardo's identity? Are there any parts of Ricardo's identity that this piece of language minimizes or pushes aside?

The emerging themes within the answers to the above questions were analyzed with a postpositivist frame. This postpositivist realist approach to analysis illuminates Ricardo's words and experiences in a way that would not be possible if analysis was conducted through a solely white majoritarian perspective.

Findings

Of the 28 excerpts I analyzed using a post-positivist realist conception of identity, I highlight three of them here to demonstrate how Ricardo felt a strong responsibility to create bridges to the curriculum for his students, and how his language and hybrid classroom discourse was used as a means to make this connection.

Language Usage

> Language carries culture…at the end of the day, it can help and can contribute to the way that you teach.

In considering the prominent use of Mexican Spanish in his practice, Ricardo recalled the above sentiment in one of our conversations. Throughout my interactions with Ricardo, I noticed that he almost solely used Mexican Spanish when speaking with his Latino students. Further, his use of Mexican Spanish was structured throughout his lessons.

Throughout our conversations, Ricardo shared that his approach to teaching is rooted in the respect, understanding and sustainment of his Latino students' cultural ways of knowing and being. For Ricardo, his usage of Mexican Spanish becomes a critical pedagogical tool that he uses with his Latino students because he is able to discuss concepts and ideas shrouded in whiteness through a lens more familiar to the students. Within the constructs of whiteness that permeate the schooling for his students, Ricardo explains that this shared language usage is an anomaly that becomes something the students gravitate towards as a beacon of cultural sustainment and affirmation in the classroom setting. Ricardo explained that this shared language usage became a means of cultural resiliency and sustainment, not only for his students but for himself, in a space where they are largely forced to conform to white norms. Because of the cultural resiliency and sustainment that Mexican Spanish provided for him and his students throughout the teaching and learning process, Ricardo drew on their shared use of Mexican Spanish to establish norms for hybrid classroom discourse.

Hybrid Classroom Discourse

> I think at first they step back like, 'Woah!' they didn't see that coming. They think that teachers, people who are professionals, just come from a good socioeconomic background, have good family values, and were never exposed to the type of experiences that I was.

The use of Mexican Spanish in Ricardo's practice gave way to a number of natural conversations on Latino identity, culture and history. In the above excerpt, Ricardo reflects on how hybrid classroom discourse allowed him to engage with his students as a dialogic participant. This dialogic exchange allowed Ricardo to not only understand his students and their perspectives, but allowed his students to understand Ricardo and his perspective as well. Hybrid classroom discourse merges multiple forms of discourse into one space (Barton & Tan, 2009). For example, Ricardo and his students engaged in the use of conversational Mexican Spanish within a white, English dominated educational space. The use of hybrid discourse for students and teachers of color is seen as a form of resistance to dominant white, English discourse methods traditionally seen in educational spaces (Dyson, 1999).

Seeing how these conversations allowed him to understand his students' lived experiences and understandings of their shared Latino identity more fully, Ricardo structured his classes to have a dialogic basis. Every class period began with a dialogic circle which provided the basis for learning. The students could elect to answer a question, or not, from a set of questions that Ricardo curated for the day which included questions like:

1. Tell us about a time in your life when you experience injustice.
2. Tell us about a time in your life when you experienced justice.
3. What change would you like to see in your community? What can you do to promote that change?

This use of hybrid classroom discourse allowed Ricardo to build deeper relationships with his students, understand their lived experiences, and make connections between the lived experiences they shared with the course curriculum.

However, Ricardo struggled to balance sharing aspects of his identity with his students, with the professional identity he was being asked to conform to. Ricardo noted a number of times throughout his first years of teaching where students felt a sense of closeness to him because he shared aspects of his identity that resonated with their own. Ricardo contended that it's often hard for students to balance his professional identity with his Latino identity because the pervasive whiteness in education creates a reality where students see these identities as two separate identities that are never to intersect. Therefore, it is hard for them to imagine how one's Latino identity and identity as a professional educator can coexist.

Responsibility to Bridge Curriculum to Students

> I don't see people of color in the curriculum and that to me is a huge problem...If you aren't teaching them about their history and their ancestors and stuff like that, it's easier for the white man to establish their culture and their values upon you. They have become so used to it that they never have fussed about it or said, "Well, why are we only learning about white people?"

In a conversation about how he approaches curriculum development, Ricardo expressed the above sentiment as his reasoning behind implementing Mexican Spanish language usage and hybrid classroom discourse into his practice. Throughout our multiple conversations, Ricardo expressed that his desire to bridge curriculum to his students was cultivated by his own realization that the history that he was taught himself was whitewashed. He explained that the content that he currently teaches his students, which is focused on the histories of minoritized populations, was not something he learned in his K-12 education or his teacher preparation program. Ricardo lamented the fact that he struggled to go beyond the confines of his teacher preparation curriculum and learn about these histories himself. Ricardo admits that his sentiment that "it's easier for white men to establish their culture and values" upon individuals who do not understand their racial and cultural history stems from his realization of this occurring within himself, both personally and professionally. This process of sociohistorical discovery and reclamation for Ricardo filters into his professional identity, where it emerges as a deep responsibility to bridge the social studies curriculum he presents to the identities of his students.

Discussion

The findings show how Ricardo's approach to language usage, hybrid classroom discourse, and his desire to connect curriculum to his students' lived experiences is informed by, and deeply intertwined with the complex personal identities he holds. For example, Ricardo and his students drew on shared language usage as a means of cultural resiliency and sustainment within a space where they are largely forced to conform to white norms. Throughout his teaching, Ricardo drew on shared language usage to build relationships and forge deeper meaning in the curriculum with his students. Through this demonstration of resistance capital (Yosso, 2005), Ricardo was able to actively resist the constructs of whiteness that persisted throughout various levels of the broader school context that he and his students operated within. While the use of shared language has been documented throughout educational research to be a great relationship building strategy (Stevenson et al., 2019) and correlates with increased academic and socioeconomic success for students (Carreira, 2007; Delgado-Gaitain & Trueba, 1991; Walqui, 2000), teacher preparation programs fail to support educators of color in recognizing and activating their various forms of resistance capital – like shared language usage- as a means of cultural and professional sustainment (Castaneda et al., 2006; Gay, 2000; Mabokela & Madsen, 2003).

Similarly, Ricardo reflected on how hybrid classroom discourse allowed him to engage alongside his students as a dialogic participant, which allowed him to not only understand his students and their perspectives, but allowed his students to understand him and his perspectives. Once again, Ricardo expressed tension in finding balance between sharing this dialogic space with his students, which allowed him to engage with his students around their shared Latino identity, and the expected operationalization of his professional identity within the classroom. While educational philosophy and research has evaluated the merits of shared dialogue in the classroom (Dewey, 1938; Emdin, 2016; Freire, 1998), Ricardo's struggle to implement this strategy in his practice reflects the prevalence of a theory-practice gap in Ricardo's teacher preparation program around the use of shared dialogue as a pedagogical strategy. Further, it illuminates the fact that many teacher preparation programs privilege white educational norms that fail to acknowledge the professional development needs of teachers of color (Castaneda et al., 2006; Gay, 2000; Mabokela & Madsen, 2003). In the same vein, Ricardo vehemently expressed that his desire to share Latino histories in his curriculum was cultivated by his own realization that the history education he received was whitewashed. In explaining this realization,

Ricardo lamented the fact that the whitewashing of history was not a topic that was critically addressed in his teacher preparation program.

The salience of Ricardo's Latino identity throughout various aspects of his pedagogical and curricular considerations in the classroom, and the degree to which this was not addressed in his teacher preparation program, leads me to question how the role of identity in the pedagogical and curricular decision making process is discussed and addressed in teacher preparation programs and professional development. To this end, this research underscores the need for teacher preparation programs to attend to the specific needs of minoritized educators (Souto-Manning & Cheruvu, 2016). While everybody involved in education must understand and consider the role of identity in the pedagogical and curricular considerations of teachers, this task is especially relevant for teacher preparation programs due to the role they play in shaping teacher identity (Alsup, 2006; Britzman, 1986; Clarke, 2009).

Conclusions and Implications

Ricardo's experience with language and identity as a Latino educator, and how his multiple identities intersect and influence the curricular and pedagogical considerations he makes in his practice are not necessarily generalizable. Instead, they reflect his experiences and perceptions as a uniquely racialized and gendered being.

However, the considerations he makes in his practice may provide insight to the way other minoritized teachers approach curricular and pedagogical decision making in their practice. The findings of this chapter underscore the need for teacher education programs to better support minoritized educators in navigating the complex positions they assume, as both educators and as minoritized individuals, and the ways in which their multiple identities intersect in their practice.

This chapter highlights a case study of a Latino educator's pedagogical and curricular decision making. Findings demonstrate how the educator felt a strong responsibility to create bridges to the curriculum for his students, and how his language and hybrid classroom discourse was used as a means to make this connection. The findings of this research underscore the need for teacher preparation programs to attend to the specific needs of minoritized educators in navigating the intersectionalities of their personal and professional identities by explicitly discussing and demonstrating how to fuse identity, language and pedagogy in practice.

I contend that we must analyze how teacher education programs can assist teachers in navigating the intersectionalities of their personal and professional identities, which is especially pertinent for educators of color (Gutierrez et al., 2019; Prabjandee, 2020). A part of this must include discussions and demonstrations of how to fuse identity, language and pedagogy in educators' practice, and scaffolded support as they navigate this process. This is especially pertinent considering that research shows that minoritized educators struggle to implement pedagogical strategies that are responsive to their students (Coffey & Farinde-Wu, 2016; Ullman & Hecshb, 2011) and continue to lack professional support (Castaneda et al., 2006; Gay, 2000; Mabokela & Madsen, 2003).

References

Agee, J. (2004). Negotiating a teaching identity: An African American teacher's struggle to teach in test-driven contexts. *Teachers College Record, 106*(4), 747–774.

Al-Khatib, A. J., & Lash, M. J. (2017). Professional identity of an early childhood Black teacher in a predominantly White school: A case study. *Child Care in Practice, 23*(3), 242–257.

Alsup, J. (2006). *Teacher identity discourses: Negotiating personal and professional spaces*. Lawrence Erlbaum Associates, Inc.

Barton, A. C., & Tan, E. (2009). Funds of knowledge and discourses and hybrid space. *Journal of Research in Science Teaching, 46*(1), 50–73.

Branch, A. J. (2003). A look at race in the national standards for the social studies: Another bad check. In G. Ladson-Billings (Ed.), *Critical race theory perspectives on social studies: The profession, policies and curriculum* (pp. 99–120). Information Age Publishing.

Britzman, D. (1986). Cultural myths in the making of a teacher: Biography and social structure in teacher education. *Harvard Educational Review, 56*, 442–456.

Burant, T., Quiocho, A., & Rios, F. (2002). Changing the face of teaching: Barriers and possibilities. *Multicultural Perspectives, 4*(2), 8–15.

Carreira, M. (2007). Spanish-for-Native-Speaker matters: Narrowing the Latino achievement gap through Spanish language instruction. *Heritage Language Journal, 5*(1), 147–171.

Castaneda, C., Kambutu, J., & Rios, F. (2006). Speaking their truths: Teachers of color in diaspora contexts. *The Rural Educators, 27*(3), 13–23.

Clarke, M. (2009). The ethico-politics of teacher identity. *Educational Philosophy and Theory, 41*(2), 185–200.

Coffey, H., & Farinde-Wu, A. (2016). Navigating the journey to culturally responsive teaching: Lessons from the success and struggles of one first-year, Black female teacher of Black students in an urban school. *Teaching and Teacher Education, 60*(1), 24–33.

Craig, R., & Davis, V. (2015). "The only way they knew how to solve their disagreements was to fight": A textual analysis of Indigenous peoples of North America before, during and after the Civil Rights Movement. In P. T. Chandler (Ed.), *Doing race in social studies: Critical perspectives* (pp. 89–125). Information Age Publishing.

Crenshaw, K. W. (1995). Mapping the margins: Intersectionality, identity politics, and violence against women of color. In K. Crenshaw, N. Gotanda, G. Peller, & K. Thomas (Eds.), *Critical race theory: The key writings that formed the movement* (pp. 357–383). The New Press.

Delgado-Gaitan, C., & Trueba, H. T. (1991). *Crossing cultural borders: Education for immigrant families in America*. Palm.

Department of Public Instruction. (2018). *2017–18 equitable teacher distribution plan*. Accessed at https://dpi.wi.gov/sites/default/files/imce/wi-equity-plan/_files/milwaukee.pdf

Department of Public Instruction. (2019). *School district accountability report cards*. Accessed at https://apps2.dpi.wi.gov/reportcards/home

Dewey, J. (1938). *Experience and education*. Free Press.

Dyson, A. H. (1999). Coach Bombay's kids learn to write: Children's appropriation of media material for school literacy. *Research in the Teaching of English, 33*, 367–402.

Eargle, J. (2016). The dominant narrative of slavery in South Carolina's history standards. *The Journal of Social Studies Research, 40*(4), 295–307.

Emdin, C. (2016). *For White folks who teach in the Hood...and the rest of Y'all too: Reality pedagogy and urban education*. Beacon Press.

Freire, P. (1998). *Pedagogy of the oppressed*. Rowman & Littlefield.

Gay, G. (2000). *Culturally responsive teaching: Theory, research, and practice*. Teachers College Press.

Gay, G. (2003). Deracialization in social studies teacher education textbooks. In G. Ladson-Billings (Ed.), *Critical race theory perspectives on social studies: The profession, policies and curriculum* (pp. 123–147). Information Age Publishing.

Gee, J. P. (2011). *An introduction to discourse analysis: Theory and method*. Routledge.

Gilpin, L. (2005). Storying and de-storying Black teacher identities. *Teacher Education and Practice, 18*(2), 215–230.

Gilpin, L. (2006). Postpositivist realist theory: Identity and representation revisited. *Multicultural Perspectives, 8*(4), 10–16.

Gorski, P. C. (2009). What we're teaching teachers: An analysis of multicultural teacher education coursework syllabi. *Teaching and Teacher Education, 25*(1), 309–318.

Gutierrez, M. V. A., Adasme, M. A. N., & Westmacott, A. (2019). Collaborative reflective practice: Its influence on preservice EFL teachers' emerging professional identities. *Iranian Journal of Language Teaching Research, 7*(3), 53–70.

Hasberry, A. (2019). Self-acceptance in Black and White. *Education in Science, 9*(143), 1–20.

Kayi-Aydar, H. (2019). A language teacher's agency in the development of her professional identities: A narrative case study. *Journal of Latinos and Education, 18*(1), 4–18.

Mabokela, R. O., & Madsen, J. A. (2003). Crossing boundaries: African American teachers in suburban schools. *Comparative Education Review, 47*(1), 90–111.

Marri, A. R. (2003). Race, social studies, and the world wide web. In G. Ladson-Billings (Ed.), *Critical race theory perspectives on social studies: The profession, policies and curriculum* (pp. 247–269). Information Age Publishing.

Marshall, P. L. (2003). The persistent deracialization of the agenda for democratic citizenship education. In G. Ladson-Billings (Ed.), *Critical race theory perspectives on social studies: The profession, policies and curriculum* (pp. 71–97). Information Age Publishing.

Milner, H. R. (2006). The promise of Black teachers' success with Black students. *Educational Foundations, 20*, 89–104.

Milner, H. R. (2010). *Start where you are but don't stay there: Understanding diversity, opportunity gaps, and teaching in today's classrooms*. Harvard Education Press.

Milner, H. R. (2012a). Challenging negative perceptions of Black teachers. *Journal of Educational Foundations, 26*(1), 27–46.

Milner, H. R. (2012b). But what is urban education? *Urban Education, 47*(3), 556–561.

Mohanty, S. (2000). The epistemic status of cultural identity: On beloved and the postcolonial condition. In P. Moya & M. Hames-Garcia (Eds.), *Reclaiming identity: Realist theory and the predicament of postmodernism* (pp. 29–66). University of California Press.

Montecinos, C. (2004). Paradoxes in multicultural teacher education research: Students of color positioned as objects while ignored as subjects. *International Journal of Qualitative Studies in Education, 17*(2), 167–181.

Moya, P. (2000). Postmodernism, "realism," and the politics of identity: Cherríe Moraga and Chicana feminism. In P. Moya & M. Hames-Garcia (Eds.), *Reclaiming identity: Realist theory and the predicament of postmodernism* (pp. 67–101). University of California Press.

Neena, B. (2018). Effects of teacher-student ethnoracial matching and overall teacher diversity in elementary schools on educational outcomes. *Journal of Research in Childhood Education, 32*(1), 94–118.

Nevarez, C., Jouganatos, S. M., & Wood, J. L. (2019). Benefits of teacher diversity: Leading for transformative change. *Journal of School Administration Research and Development, 4*(1), 24–34.

Olitsky, S. (2020). Teaching as emotional practice or exercise in measurement? School structures, identity conflict, and the retention of Black women science teachers. *Education and Urban Society, 52*(4), 590–618.

Prabjandee, D. (2020). Narratives of learning to become English teachers in Thailand: Developing identity through a teacher education program. *Teacher Development, 24*(1), 71–87.

Rains, F. V. (2003). To greet the dawn with eyes: American Indians, White privilege and the power of residual guilt in the social studies. In G. Ladson-Billings (Ed.), *Critical race theory perspectives on social studies: The profession, policies and curriculum* (pp. 199–227). Information Age Publishing.

Ramanathan, H. (2006). Asian American teachers: Do they impact the curriculum? Are there support systems for them? *Multicultural Education, 14*(1), 31–35.

Rubin, H., & Rubin, R. (1995). *Qualitative interviewing: The art of hearing data*. Sage.

Shear, S. (2015). Cultural genocide masked as education: U.S. history textbooks' coverage of indigenous education policies. In P. T. Chandler (Ed.), *Doing race in social studies: Critical perspectives* (pp. 13–40). Information Age Publishing.

Singh, M. V. (2019). Refusing the performance: Disrupting popular discourses surrounding Latino male teachers and the possibility of disidentification. *Educational Studies: Journal of the American Educational Studies Association, 55*(1), 28–45.

Sipe, L., & Ghiso, M. (2004). Developing conceptual categories in classroom descriptive research: Some problems and possibilities. *Anthropology and Education Quarterly, 35*(4), 472–485.

Sleeter, C. (2001). Preparing teachers for culturally diverse schools: Research and the overwhelming presence of whiteness. *Journal of Teacher Education, 52*(2), 94–106.

Smith Kondo, C. (2019). Front streeting: Teacher candidates of color and the pedagogical challenges of cultural relevancy. *Anthropology & Education Quarterly, 50*(2), 135–150.

Souto-Manning, M., & Cheruvu, R. (2016). Challenging and appropriating discourses of power: Listening to and learning from early career early childhood teachers of color. *Equity & Excellence in Education, 49*(1), 9–26.

Sparks, D. M. (2018). The process of becoming: Identity development of African American female science and mathematics preservice teachers. *Journal of Science Teacher Education, 29*(3), 243–261.

Stevenson, A. D., Gallard Martínez, A. J., Brkich, K. L., Flores, B. B., Claeys, L., & Pitts, W. (2019). Latinas' heritage language as a source of resiliency: Impact on academic achievement in STEM fields. *Cultural Studies of Science Education, 14*(1), 1–13.

Ullman, C., & Hecshb, J. (2011). These American lives: Becoming a culturally responsive teacher and the 'risks of empathy'. *Ethnicity and Education, 14*(5), 603–629.

Vickery, A. (2016). "I worry about my community": African American women utilizing communal notions of citizenship in the social studies classroom. *International Journal of Multicultural Education, 18*(1), 28–44.

Walqui, A. (2000). *Access and engagement: Program design and instructional approaches for immigrant students in secondary schools*. Center for Applied Linguistics.

Warren, C. A. (2020). Meeting myself: Race-gender oppression and a genre study of Black men teachers' interactions with Black boys. *Race Ethnicity and Education, 23*(3), 367–391.

Wilson, S., & McChesney, J. (2018). From coursework to practicum: Learning to plan for mathematics. *Mathematics Teacher Education and Development, 20*(2), 96–113.

Yosso, T. J. (2005). Whose culture has capital? A critical race theory discussion of community cultural wealth. *Race Ethnicity and Education, 8*(1), 69–91.

Kelly R. Allen is an Assistant Professor of Curriculum Studies at Augusta University. Informed by her experience as a high school social studies teacher, her current research interests focus on issues of equity and race/ism in social studies education.

Open Access This chapter is licensed under the terms of the Creative Commons Attribution 4.0 International License (http://creativecommons.org/licenses/by/4.0/), which permits use, sharing, adaptation, distribution and reproduction in any medium or format, as long as you give appropriate credit to the original author(s) and the source, provide a link to the Creative Commons license and indicate if changes were made.

The images or other third party material in this chapter are included in the chapter's Creative Commons license, unless indicated otherwise in a credit line to the material. If material is not included in the chapter's Creative Commons license and your intended use is not permitted by statutory regulation or exceeds the permitted use, you will need to obtain permission directly from the copyright holder.

Chapter 26
China: Decolonization and Teaching: An American Professor's Experience at Yunnan University

MaryJo Benton Lee

Abstract This chapter describes the experiences of an American Sociology professor who taught Chinese Education students at Yunnan University, People's Republic of China, in 2017. The author explains how she structured the teaching of two classes, Qualitative Research Methods and Writing for the Social Sciences, to show respect for the collective history and cultures of her Chinese graduate students. The chapter illustrates how curriculum (what is taught) and instruction (how it is taught) can be rethought to avoid overreliance on Western examples to the neglect of local context. The methodology used is autoethnography, which has been described as research and writing that connects the autobiographical and personal to the cultural and social. The author discusses how an understanding of Southern theory, as it has been developed by Australian sociologist Raewyn Connell, shaped her work. Connell makes a distinction between two types of theorizing. The first, Northern theory, privileges the perspectives of metropolitan society (the former imperial powers) while presenting itself as universal knowledge. The second, Southern theory, is an alternative way of thinking about the world from the viewpoints of the global periphery (the former colonized world). The chapter concludes with three concrete pedagogical tips—on experiential education, on cooperative learning and on mutual learning—for academics considering a teaching experience beyond their own national borders.

Introduction

China's premier sociologist of all time, Fei Xiaotong, like most of his contemporaries in the early 1900s, was educated largely by renowned Western academicians such as Professor Robert Park of the University of Chicago. Reflecting later on his education, Fei (Fei & Zhang, 1945, p. viii) wrote, "We learned from books about Chicago gangs and Russian immigrants in America, but we knew very little or nothing about the Chinese gentry in the town and the peasants in the village, because

M. B. Lee (✉)
South Dakota State University, Brookings, SD, USA

these were not in the books." Seventy plus years later, in 2017, I walked on to the Yunnan University campus, in the far southwest of China, to teach in the very place where Fei had chaired the Sociology department in the 1940s. Dr. Fei and his words have profoundly shaped my teaching—of Sociology, as a Fulbright U.S. Scholar to the People's Republic of China (PRC)—and my scholarly work since then as well.

Objectives

In this chapter, I will outline how I structured the teaching of two classes, Qualitative Research Methods and Writing for the Social Sciences, to show respect for the collective history and cultures of my Chinese graduate students. I will illustrate how curriculum (what is taught) and instruction (how it is taught) can be rethought to avoid overreliance on Western examples to the neglect of local context.

Context

I came to China as a Fulbright scholar following 10 years of teaching and 12 years of working as a clinical sociologist at South Dakota State University (SDSU). I had co-founded, with two colleagues at the Flandreau Indian School, a college preparatory program for American Indian high school students. The FIS-SDSU Success Academy program that I directed increased by 100 fold the number of Indian School seniors going to college at SDSU (Lee, 2013, p. 154). A similar jump was seen in FIS seniors intending to pursue post-secondary education elsewhere. Fundamental to the success of the program was its foundational principle, that ethnicity matters in education (Lee, 2006). While the leap from working with American Indian high school students at South Dakota State University to teaching graduate scholars at Yunnan University's Research Institute of Higher Education seems great, the transition actually occurred through a series of small steps that had begun 25 years earlier. Together with my husband, Journalism professor Richard W. Lee, I spent the spring semester of 1991 teaching at Yunnan Normal (Teachers) University, part of an SDSU-YNNU faculty exchange program. In 1997, after completing my course work in Sociology at SDSU, we returned to YNNU. Then I was a visiting scholar, collecting data for my doctoral dissertation on ethnic minority education (Lee, 2001). Yunnan is the country's most ethnically diverse province, with one third of its population comprised of minorities. Twenty-five of China's 55 officially recognized minority groups live within Yunnan's borders.

My interests as a sociologist in education, race and ethnicity drew me back to Yunnan. I applied to the Fulbright Scholar Program, which sends about 500 U.S. academics to 125 countries around the world each year. Certain universities in each country are designated as eligible to accept Fulbright lecturers, and Yunnan University where I was placed is one of these. It is the next-door neighbor of Yunnan

Normal University where Dick and I had been twice before. Both universities are located in Kunming, the provincial capital of Yunnan. (Fulbright provides a generous allowance that enables spouses to travel with grantees. Dick and I shared with each other all three of our teaching/research experiences in Kunming—in 1991, in 1997 and in 2017.)

Methodology

I will use a methodology called "autoethnography." Qualitative researcher Carolyn Ellis defined "autoethnography" as "research, writing and method that connect the autobiographical and personal to the cultural and social" (Denizen, 2006, p. 419). In this chapter, the "autobiographical and personal" refer to my practice day-to-day as a Fulbright lecturer at Yunnan University. The "cultural and social" refer to my efforts to dismantle the hegemony of European values in the teaching of research methods and academic writing. To reflect on my experiences, I turned to the daily journal I kept while in Yunnan and to my teaching materials, such as class syllabi and student assignments.

Methodology cannot be discussed separate and apart from theorizing. I will refer to the work of Australian sociologist Raewyn Connell (2007) who has made a distinction between two types of theorizing. The first is "Northern theory," which privileges the perspectives of metropolitan society (or the former imperial powers) while presenting itself as universal knowledge. The second is "Southern theory," an alternative way of thinking about the world from the viewpoints of the global periphery (or the former colonized world). Throughout the chapter I will explain more explicitly how an understanding of Southern theory shaped my teaching in China. But first, to be clear, China was not colonized, except for a brief period between the first Opium War in 1842 and the Japanese occupation in 1937. "Decolonization," as I will use it in this chapter, is "a movement to eliminate, or at least mitigate, the disproportionate legacy of white European thought and culture in education…It also means dismantling the hegemony of European values and making way for the local philosophy and traditions" (Nordling, 2018). "Social Science has been Eurocentric throughout its institutional history," Immanuel Wallerstein (1997, p. 21) reminded us.

Findings and Discussion

Rethinking Curriculum: Qualitative Research Methods Class

This was a class, for master's and doctoral students in Education. About 35 students were enrolled, approximately one-quarter male and three quarters female. Most had worked as school teachers or administrators for several years after receiving their undergraduate degrees. I have taught Qualitative Research Methods both at my home institution, South Dakota State University, and at my Fulbright host school, Yunnan University. The class, as described in the syllabus, "is designed to make students into confident qualitative researchers in Education by improving their observation, interviewing and data analysis skills." In their book, *Knowledge and Global Power: Making New Sciences in the South* (Collyer et al., 2019, p. 10), the authors referred to the process of "extraversion" that they defined as the way "knowledge workers in the periphery are oriented to, and become dependent on, the institutions, concepts and techniques of the metropole." When I have taught Qualitative Research Methods in the United States, the examples I have used have been largely drawn from the metropole. I have had students read such American classics as *Street Corner Society* by William Foote Whyte (1943) and *Stranger and Friend* by Hortense Powdermaker (1966). These texts and authors, however, seemed inappropriate for a class in China. Consequently I tried consciously to "co-construct a decolonial curriculum" (Watkins et al., 2018, p. 319). In the following sections I will illustrate what I mean.

Giving Priority to Locally Created Knowledge: The Yunnan Ethnographies

The texts I used for my Yunnan University class were four studies of Chinese communities, all done in the once remote and inaccessible Yunnan Province between 1936 and 1943. The four world-renowned anthropologists and sociologists who produced these community studies came to Yunnan from Northern China, England and the United States. For the most part they worked in isolation, each knowing little to nothing about the others' endeavors. Laboring under the most challenging wartime conditions, they produced four community studies, all published as books in English and in Mandarin and all still in print today. Their writings significantly shaped worldviews of China as it existed before the Communist Revolution in 1949.

This was an incredibly rich archive of qualitative work, done by four recognized scholars—Fei Xiaotong and Zhang (1945), Xu Langguang (1948), C. P. FitzGerald (1941) and Cornelius Osgood (1963). Yet few of the excellent students in my class, enrolled in one of China's top-ranked universities, were aware that these studies existed, much less that they had been conducted literally in the front yard of Yunnan University.

My students were astonished that I had read numerous texts by Fei long before I came to China—and they were surprised that I said "good morning" to Dr. Fei's picture, which hung in the foyer of our teaching building, each day when I came to work. (A story about my semester at Yunnan University appeared on the front page of the campus newspaper and mentioned prominently my daily greeting to Dr. Fei!) I assigned each student to read one of the four community studies, either in Mandarin or in English. Then, working in groups, they discussed how the authors had used, in their work nearly 80 years earlier, the same qualitative techniques—observation, interviewing and data analysis—that the students themselves were currently learning in our class. The students reflected together on the challenges the scholars had faced while conducting research in wartime China and how they overcame these while doing fieldwork. Each group reported back to the class as a whole on its findings.

The students spent tens of hours dissecting the community studies, far more time than I required. Most students found the studies compelling to read and were moved by what they learned. Speaking for her group during its final oral report, one student said: "In the case of escaping Japanese bombers, Fei Xiaotong and Zhang Zhiyi (Fei's co-researcher) were brave, hard-working, strong-willed and vigorous. They made great things. This is the spirit of knowledge and scholarly attitude. Because of this, this book reflects its eternal value, flashing its immortal light." The students, through their scholarship, taught me much about fieldwork in wartime China that I had not known before. They did this both inside of and outside of the classroom, as I will discuss in the next section.

University Beyond the Walls: Field Trip to Kuige

"How do we enable our students to re-visit the past histories of their countries through a foreign eye," Joyce C. H. Liu (2020, p. 1168) recently asked. Liu (2020, p. 1169) says that "curricular decolonization" often occurs beyond "pedagogical tasks in the classroom," that is, beyond the university walls.

I later took another group of Qualitative Research Methods students to the Yunnan Station for Sociological Research in Chenggong (about an hour's drive from Kunming). The research station was where Fei, Xu and their colleagues fled in 1940 when the Japanese air raids over Kunming had become too frequent. The scholars set up shop there in Kuige, a crumbling nineteenth century tower built to honor the God of Literature. (The research station subsequently was called "Kuige," for the tower in which it was housed.). Some dozen manuscripts (including those by Fei and Xu that the students read for class) were produced at Kuige. Kuige became a refuge during the Anti-Japanese War (World War II) for some of China's most distinguished anthropologists and sociologists. In 1938, they had been forced to leave the country's top universities (Beida, Qinghua and Nankai), all in the North, which the Japanese first occupied and later destroyed.

After the war, Kuige was abandoned when the scholars returned home. All of the Kuige researchers, with the exception of Xu, remained in China after the Communist Revolution in 1949. Two years later Sociology was eliminated as a subject from China's university curricula. All of the Kuige scholars dropped out of sight. From the late 1950s to the early 1970s, some were criticized and removed from their posts. Others were arrested and jailed. Inside of China, the Kuige scholars were disgraced. Outside of China, they were forgotten for more than a century. Today Kuige, which sat in disrepair for decades, has been restored. A monumental sculpture, of the eleven scholars who worked at Kuige during the war, has been erected in the courtyard. The figures are posed around a table, frozen in time, as if they are participating in one of Fei's seminars.

In 2000, Fei and others gathered at Kuige for a triumphant reunion. As with the Yunnan ethnographies, my students and most others I met in Kunming had no idea what Kuige was, where Kuige was or why that mattered. That changed the day we went to Kuige. The students touched Dr. Fei's desk. They posed next to his picture, in the same spot where he had stood 80 years before. They roamed the rooms where the researchers had lived in the most challenging conditions and had produced some of China's finest social science between 1939 and 1946. Finally, the students climbed into the sculpture, gathered around the table, with Fei, Xu and the others, and took a photo—China's scholarly past joined with China's promising future.

Critical educator Paulo Freire (1970) coined the term "conscientization," which means "developing a critical awareness of one's social reality through reflection and action" (Freire Institute, 2020). "Conscientization" also has been explained as a process through which people realize that *their own cultural values and histories are legitimate and worth maintaining*. The students realized just that the day we went to Kuige. That day was my best ever in my life as a teacher.

Summing up the last two sections, I maintain that it is important for students to see cultures and histories from their own society reflected in the curriculum. It is also important for students to see strong positive role models of practitioners, with backgrounds like their own, doing qualitative research in settings outside the university. This I will illustrate in the next section.

Decolonizing the Mind: Teacher-Researchers at Daguan Kindergarten

Preschool in Three Cultures (PSin3C), published in 1989, was a landmark study of education, an exploration of the different ways that preschoolers are taught in China, Japan and the United States (Tobin et al., 1989). One of the three preschools studied was the Daguan Kindergarten in Kunming. A follow-up study of Daguan and the other two schools was conducted in 2002, and the results published in 2009 (Tobin et al., 2009). Luckily for me, my close friend and colleague, Professor Li Hong of Yunnan Normal University, was part of lead author Joseph Tobin's team that conducted the follow-up study. Because of Li Hong's connections, I have visited the Daguan Kindergarten several times. I have gotten to know the educators there who truly are teacher-researchers in the best sense of the word. They were co-researchers with the Tobin team for both *PSin3C* books, and they have participated in the ongoing studies at Daguan since then.

During my semester teaching Qualitative Research Methods at Yunnan University, I introduced students to the work of Tobin and his co-researchers. (They used a qualitative technique called "video-cued multivocal ethnography.")

The students and I then spent the better part of a day at the Daguan Kindergarten, located a short distance from the university.

My students, all majoring in Education, were captivated by seeing a day in the life of the famous preschool, considered by most to be one of Yunnan Province's best. After our school tour, we viewed, with principals and teachers, a video on the research that resulted in the publication of *PSin3C*. Students learned, firsthand from practitioners, what "teacher research" is. It is "intentional, systematic inquiry by teachers with the goals of gaining insights into teaching and learning" (National Association for the Education of Young Children, 2020).

In an article on "decolonizing the mind," researcher Wanga Zembe-Mkabile, has discussed the problem of "invisibility" for African women aspiring to become social scientists (Nordling, 2018). There are relatively few African women in social science disciplines with whom she and others can identify. By immersing my class in the ongoing research at the Daguan Kindergarten—and by introducing the class to those who are conducting this research—I hoped to break down some of the barriers that separate students from professionals. I also hoped that students would begin to envision their own possible futures as Chinese researchers engaged with public education.

Rethinking Instruction: Writing for the Social Sciences Class

Writing for the Social Sciences was a course I developed specifically for my Chinese students, unlike Qualitative Research Methods, which I had taught elsewhere. So I will begin this section by discussing my rationale for this class and the content of the course. In the remainder of this section I will focus on pedagogy. More specifically, I will discuss three instructional techniques that I found useful while teaching in China and that others may find useful as well. I will give examples of what each looks like in practice. Since I used all three techniques in both classes I taught, some of the examples will be from the Writing for the Social Sciences class and others will be from the Qualitative Research Methods class.

To this point I have been discussing the decolonization of the curriculum for the Qualitative Research Methods class. In other words, I have been focusing on *what* I taught. In this section I will switch to writing about the decolonization of instruction, that is, *how* I taught. Fulbright lecturers are chosen for their teaching excellence in American classrooms. Moving to classrooms in other countries challenges us to consider our audiences in different ways. It requires us to move away from Western-centric ways of seeing, knowing and communicating that may be inappropriate for students with vastly different backgrounds and cultures than our own. How this might be accomplished will be discussed below. But first, some background on the Writing for the Social Sciences class.

The Rationale: Knowledge Production and China

"Western research has achieved a monopoly through protectionism that inhibits global knowledge developments, especially in non-Western countries," said Connell (2007, as cited in Tierney, 2018, p. 400). For example, while China has reached parity with the United States in terms of submissions to journals considered to be globally recognized, China's rates of acceptance (and those of other non-Western countries) lag far behind (Tierney, 2018, p. 400).

Scholars in China and other Southern countries are working hard to gain power in knowledge production, that is, in research and publication. In 2017 the Chinese government announced a list of 42 institutions that were designated to become "Double First-Class Universities" by 2049, the PRC's 100th anniversary. Yunnan University where I taught is one of the 42. Double First-Class Universities receive strong financial and policy support from both the central and local governments, support to help them achieve the ambitious "knowledge production" goals set for them. Here is an example of one of these goals: "Yunnan University will have at least five disciplines entering the top 1% in the Essential Science Indicators database." (ESI surveys 11,000 journals worldwide in order to rank authors, institutions, countries and periodicals, based on publication and citation performance.)

Course Content: Decolonizing Knowledge Production

The title of my Fulbright project statement was "Training the Next Generation of China's Educational Researchers." I envisioned the class I proposed, Writing for the Social Sciences, as a small start at the decolonization of knowledge production at my host university. My goal was to teach students how to report on social science research, using a wide range of writing styles. I wanted my Chinese students to become comfortable writing and speaking before professional peers and international audiences. As I wrote in the syllabus, upon the completion of the course, I hoped students would:

- Be able to write effective scholarly papers, theses/dissertations, journal articles and book chapters;
- Master such practical skills as writing curricula vitae, developing grant proposals and delivering conference presentations; and
- Become familiar with topics ranging from networking to mentoring that are seldom discussed in textbooks, but are essential for professional advancement in research and publishing.

Collyer et al. (2019, p. 11) acknowledged that an inequitable "international knowledge economy" currently exists that prioritizes English. It is important long-term to dismantle that system. But it is fundamental now for Chinese graduate students, preparing for life in academe, to be able to write and present effectively in English. All Chinese undergraduates are required to pass the national College English Test in order to receive their degrees. (For this reason, most Fulbright lecturers in China, like me, teach in English.) Students in my class were competent English writers and speakers, but they had little knowledge of how to write for academic audiences or how to get published in respected journals. That was the intent of the class. (I will add that, in my experience, many American graduate students are in dire need of such training as well.)

Pedagogy Tip #1: Experiential Education

A Eurocentric stereotype, which many Western teachers hold about Asian students, is that they are passive learners who sit quietly in huge lecture halls, recording verbatim their professors' words. At Yunnan University, I found quite the opposite. My students were curious and engaged. They eagerly embraced the hands-on, learning-by-doing approach that I used in both the writing and the research class.

The American philosopher, John Dewey, is famous for his advocacy of hands-on learning or, as it is also called, experiential education. Dewey travelled through China in 1919, gaining "superstar" status, with people flocking to his lectures and reading translations of his talks (Braendel, 2019). His philosophies of education were widely applied throughout China then and still are today. The colleague who I mentioned earlier, Professor Li Hong of Yunnan Normal University, is currently engaged in a 5-year training program for 10,000 school principals. Their assigned reading? Six books by John Dewey.

In-class Social Sciences Conference Students in the Writing for the Social Sciences course could choose to write either a 10-page scholarly paper or a 10-page thesis or dissertation proposal. With my help, students then planned a day-long social sciences conference, during which they presented their work. The audience included professors in our Research Institute and guests from other universities. They gave feedback to the students at the end of the day.

We tried to make our conference as "real" as possible. Participants registered when they arrived and received nametags and copies of the conference program. Students were coached beforehand on professional dress and came suitably attired.

Each conference session had three presenters, a chair and a discussant. Presenters were required to have PowerPoints, notecards and handouts. Presentations could be no more than 10 min long, and points were deducted for exceeding the time limit. After each presentation, time was allowed for reflections by the discussant and questions from the audience.

Because there were 30 students in the class, some sessions were concurrent. Attendees moved from room to room between sessions. A break, with tea and refreshments, midway through the conference, allowed attendees to mingle. Networking at professional meetings was a skill that had been covered in class earlier in the semester.

In evaluating the course, students declared the in-class social sciences conference a high point of the semester. Most had not attended an academic conference before. Our conference gave them the opportunity to try on the professional identity of "scholar," in essence, to picture themselves in the role for which they were preparing. After class ended, a few of the students had the opportunity to present at an international conference, and they reported that their "dry run" in our writing course had built their confidence.

Pedagogy Tip #2: Cooperative Learning

Dewey believed that the best learning occurs through experience and involves hands-on activities directly related to students' lives. In my research methods class, students learned how to do field observation, intensive interviewing and data analysis. I created three major assignments to be completed outside of class, experiences designed to encourage students to practice these skills.

Dewey maintained that experiences, in and of themselves, are not learning. Students also must have an opportunity to reflect meaningfully upon their experiences in order for true learning to occur. I needed to find the best ways for this kind of reflection to happen. Teaching in China, I soon came to realize that cooperative group activities are more in keeping with Chinese culture than individualized projects that emphasize competition. Chinese civilization is rooted in the philosophy of Confucius, the great educator-sage who lived about 500 BCE. Confucianism encourages collectivism over individualism. The rights of the individual are subordinated to those of the general good.

Early on in the semester, I was impressed with just how cohesive my two classes of students were. Though the students had known each other for only a few months, they were kind and caring to each other in ways that I had seldom seen before as a teacher.

Student-Led Seminars In the Qualitative Research Methods class, after each assignment—observation, interviewing, data analysis—students prepared 10-page reports on that experience. During the next class, I divided them into work groups, of five students each, to discuss their research experiences. Because I wanted the groups to be composed of different class members for each of the three assignments, I divided the students randomly by having them choose colored M & M's out of a hat (indicating membership in the green group, in the red group and so forth). The groups separated themselves, spreading out through our teaching building and its courtyards. (Yunnan has the best weather in all of China.) Each group chose a leader, a scribe and a presenter. I distributed some guide questions to assist the groups in organizing their discussions. The questions were designed to help the students focus on the challenges and the successes that they had experienced out "in the field." The groups had about 90 min to work before reporting back to the class as a whole.

Our class's "seminar sessions" were patterned deliberately after Fei's work with his colleagues at Kuige. "Regular seminars were held at Kuige. Fresh ideas developed as new observations were brought back by field workers," Fei (Fei & Zhang, 1945, p. xi) wrote. I had taught students in both of my classes the technique of "mind mapping" (Buzan & Buzan, 1996) early in the semester. (Mind maps are diagrams used to visually organize information.) On seminar days, I gave each group a large piece of poster paper and a set of colored markers. Students delighted in making mind maps to summarize their group discussions and to report back, with an audiovisual aid, to their classmates. The groups tried to outdo each other in the colorfulness and creativity of their mind maps.

Pedagogy Tip #3: Mutual Learning

Confucius's educational thought has been compared to that of contemporary critical educators such as John Dewey and Paulo Frieire, and many common threads have been found (Zhao, 2013, p. 9). "Among any three people, there must be one who can be my teacher," Confucius wrote in the *Analects* in the fifth century BCE. Similarly, Freire (1998), in his last book, *Pedagogy of Freedom,* wrote "Whoever teaches learns in the act of teaching; and whoever learns teaches in the act of learning."

Colleagues as Co-teachers Mutual learning occurred throughout my semester in China in many ways, and I benefitted greatly from it. Associate professor and dear friend, Dr. Wu Mei, of the Research Institute of Higher Education, agreed to be my co-teacher for both the writing and the research classes. Mei earned her doctorate in Education at the University of Idaho and shortly thereafter wrote a book using qualitative methods to study ethnic minority education in China (Wu, 2013). In our classroom, she translated into Chinese concepts that were hard for the students to grasp in English. Just as importantly, she supplied examples, from the Chinese context, that enriched both the students' and my understanding of research work and scholarly writing.

Three junior scholars, all teaching in the Research Institute, regularly sat in on both of my classes. They were actually teachers of my students in classes other than mine. These colleagues provided valuable role models for the students. Through my friendship with these scholars, I gained a far better understanding of higher education in China, both its challenges and its rewards, than I had previously. One of these colleagues was Dr. Fan Hua, an assistant professor in the Research Institute. As with Mei, I got to know Fan well both inside of and outside of the classroom. (We had an interesting trip, with students, to the local Super Walmart, where we purchased a washing machine for my apartment and carried it back to campus in his small car.)

In 2018 and 2019, Mei organized two international research conferences, held at the Research Institute and funded by the Double-First Class University initiative. An outgrowth of those conferences has been a writing partnership between Mei and me that has thus far produced two papers. In addition, I am a core member of Fan's research group, studying interdisciplinary education worldwide, under a grant from China's National Science Foundation. Mei and Fan exemplify for me what Collyar et al. (2019, p. 173) have described as "busy, creative people, who have built institutions, careers and research agendas" in the Global South. Their work illustrates what Collyar et al. (2019, p. 173) called efforts to close a gap in the "global knowledge economy dominated by the most privileged countries, institutions, and social groups." I feel honored to be a participant in Mei and Fan's research, and I continue to learn much from them in the process.

Finally, Dean Dong Yunchuan of the Research Institute gave me two "gifts" when I began my teaching. First, he asked three of his doctoral students to enroll in both of my classes, despite the fact that they did not need these classes to complete their programs. The master's students enrolled in my classes greatly respected these hard-working doctoral students and tried diligently to do work that was "up" to their standards. The doctoral students, for their part, had to perform as the "role models" that the younger students expected them to be. Both groups benefitted, another example of mutual learning.

Second, Dr. Dong assigned to me not one, but four, graduate assistants to help with my classes at the Institute and with my life outside of school. These four young women had all been trained as teachers and had worked for several years before returning to graduate school. They had a way of making all things possible, both inside of and outside of the classroom. They began as my helpful teaching assistants and became my cherished friends, particularly after my husband, Dick, returned home unexpectedly midway through the semester due to health concerns. As the days and weeks of the semester unfolded, my graduate assistants and I shared with each other countless details of our lives that transcended our student-teacher relationship. I came to see them as my teachers, and I still do, as we continue to communicate almost weekly via WeChat (a Chinese messaging app).

From knowing them and the others I have mentioned, I now realize that insight comes from contrast. By learning about others' lives in China, I came to understand more about the United States; by learning about my life in the United States, they came to understand more about China. An American friend and professor, just returned from China, put it this way: "It is impossible to understand one culture. You must be familiar with at least two to understand one."

Teaching and Learning Outside the Classroom

The next three subsections, while not specifically about the "decolonization of teaching," do relate closely to the book's overall focus "on being a minority teacher in a foreign culture." Fulbright scholars are selected, in part, for their ability to be "cultural ambassadors" while serving abroad. Much of the teaching about one's own culture and learning about others' cultures happens outside of the classroom.

Home and Family The family is at the foundation of Chinese civilization. Ancestor worship dates back 3500 years. A central tenet of Confucianism is "filial piety" or respect for one's ancestors, parents and elders. Because Chinese family bonds are exceptionally strong, naturally my students wanted to learn about my family, as I wanted to learn about theirs. My husband, Dick, and I, lived in university-owned housing, across the street from the campus gate. Our sunny, airy apartment had a living room, kitchen, bathroom and bedroom. A wall of pictures—of our house, our university, our friends, our children and even our kitten—was a glimpse into our American life. We hosted several gatherings, like one for Easter, complete with egg dyeing, Easter baskets and an egg hunt. Students and faculty friends reciprocated, with a celebration of my birthday at a colleague's apartment and with a farewell party at my dean's home.

Food and Relationships Food is an important part of daily life for the Chinese. They believe eating good food can bring harmony and closeness to the family in particular and to relationships more generally (EthnoMed, 2020). Dick and I ate lunch each weekday in the faculty dining room with professors and staff from my department and others. Food was served buffet style, with perhaps 20 or 25 different, truly delicious dishes each day. The cost for a meal, paid by the university, was seven yuan (about one dollar). People sat at round tables, making conversation easy. Faculty occasionally invited students to join them for lunch. In our apartment building's courtyard there was a family-operated restaurant called the New Earth Café. It was a comfortable place to meet, eat and drink with students and colleagues.

Gift-Giving and Books The Chinese idiom, *li shang wang lai*, taken from *The Analects* of Confucius, translates as "for the sake of propriety, people must engage in social intercourse" or "giving and repaying is the thing attended to" (Chang, 2016). The modern idiom that evolved from this means "a gift (or favor) given must be returned." My Fulbright appointment was a life-changing gift. I reciprocated, in part, by giving about 200 books to the Research Institute of Higher Education where I taught. We shipped these books—on qualitative methods, on academic writing and on ethnic minority education—to China for my use in teaching. Some were purchased with Fulbright funds, others with my own. Many books came from my personal library. They were kept in my office, available for checkout. The collection is now called the Fulbright Scholar Library and is a source of information on topics not well covered in the university library's general collection.

Conclusions and Implications

A "power differential between 'core' and 'peripheral' culture" (Xu, 1999, p. 231) was apparent from the very first teaching of Sociology in China. Fei Xiaotong and his classmates were required to learn about Chicago gangs to the neglect of the Chinese gentry. More recently, Yogesh Atal wrote that Sociology in Asia remains a relatively young discipline. "No doubt we quite often hear the call for indigenization, but we have not gone beyond articulating our reaction against the intellectual kit that we borrowed from the West," Atal (1986, p. 304) said.

As a Fulbright lecturer at Yunnan University, I tried to take the "intellectual kit" I carried with me, trained as an American sociologist, and repack it with "academic tools" more appropriate for teaching in China. In redesigning curriculum and rethinking pedagogy, I attempted, in one small classroom in Yunnan Province, to "southernize" the teaching of Sociology, "to extend its gaze and horizons beyond the North Atlantic world" (Carrington et al., 2019, p. 163). Whether I was successful or not is for others to decide.

"Decolonization," as I use this term in my chapter, describes "a movement to eliminate, or at least mitigate, the disproportionate legacy of white European thought and culture in education…It also means dismantling the hegemony of European values and making way for the local philosophy and traditions," writes South African journalist Linda Nordling. Future research in the scholarship of teaching and learning could build on this idea, extending the scope of my work, done in China, to other national and international contexts.

Acknowledgements I wish to thank my mentors and dearest friends, Professor Emerita of Sociology Diane Kayongo-Male and Professor Emeritus of Journalism Richard W. Lee (1934–2018), of South Dakota State University, for their confidence in me and for all I have learned from them about teaching.

References

Atal, Y. (1986). Sociology and the future. *International Social Science Journal, 38*(2), 303–310.
Braendel, C. (2019, June 7). A century later, John Dewey's travels to China influence a new generation. *UChicago News*. https://news.uchicago.edu/story/century-later-john-deweys-travels-china-influence-new-generation
Buzan, T., & Buzan, B. (1996). *The mind map book: How to use radiant thinking to maximize your brain's untapped potential*. Penguin Group.
Carrington, K., Dixon, B., Fonseca, D., Rodriguez-Goyes, D., Liu, J. H., & Zysman, D. (2019). Criminologies of the Global South: Critical reflections. *Critical Criminology, 27*, 163–189.
Chang, X. (2016). Reciprocity (*lishang-wanglai*): A Chinese model of social relationships and reciprocity—State and villagers' interaction 1936-2014. *Journal of Sociology, 52*(1), 103–117. https://doi-org.excelsior.sdstate.edu/10.1177/1440783315589151
Collyer, F., Connell, R., Maia, J., & Morrell, R. (2019). *Knowledge and global power: Making new sciences in the south*. Monash University Publishing.
Connell, R. (2007). *Southern theory*. Polity.
Denizen, N. K. (2006). Analytic autoethnography, or déjà vu all over again. *Journal of Contemporary Ethnography, 35*(4), 419–428.
EthnoMed. (2020). *Chinese food cultural profile*. https://ethnomed.org/resource/chinese-food-cultural-profile/
Fei, X., & Zhang, Z. (1945). *Earthbound China: A study of rural economy in Yunnan*. University of Chicago Press.
FitzGerald, C. P. (1941). *The tower of five glories: A study of the Min Chia of Ta Li, Yunnan*. The Cresset Press.

Freire, P. (1970). *Pedagogy of the oppressed*. Penguin Books.
Freire, P. (1998). *Pedagogy of freedom: Ethics, democracy and civic courage*. Rowman and Littlefield.
Freire Institute. (2020). *Concepts used by Paulo Freire*. https://www.freire.org/paulo-freire/concepts-used-by-paulo-freire/
Lee, M. B. (2001). *Ethnicity, education and empowerment: How minority students in Southwest China construct identities*. Ashgate.
Lee, M. B. (2006). *Ethnicity matters: Rethinking how Black, Hispanic, and Indian students prepare for and succeed in college*. Peter Lang.
Lee, M. B. (2013). *Success academy: How Native American students prepare for college (and how colleges can prepare for them)*. Peter Lang.
Liu, J. C. H. (2020). Beyond borders: Trans-local critical pedagogy for inter-Asian cultural studies. *Educational Philosophy and Theory, 52*(11), 1162–1172.
National Association for the Education of Young Children. (2020). *What is teacher research?* https://www.naeyc.org/resources/pubs/vop/about-teacher-research
Nordling, L. (2018). How decolonization could reshape South African science. *Nature, 554*(7691), 159–162. https://www-nature-com.excelsior.sdstate.edu/articles/d41586-018-01696-w
Osgood, C. (1963). *Village life in old China: A community study of Kao Yao, Yunnan*. The Ronald Press.
Powdermaker, H. (1966). *Stranger and friend: The way of an anthropologist*. W.W. Norton.
Tierney, R. J. (2018). Toward a model of global meaning making. *Journal of Literacy Research, 50*(4), 397–422.
Tobin, J., Wu, D. Y. H., & Davidson, D. H. (1989). *Preschool in three cultures: Japan, China and the United States*. Yale University Press.
Tobin, J., Hsueh, Y., & Karasawa, M. (2009). *Preschool in three cultures revisited: China, Japan and the United States*. The University of Chicago Press.
Wallerstein, I. (1997). Eurocentrism and its avatars: The dilemmas of social science. *Sociological Bulletin, 46*(1), 21–39.
Watkins, M., Ciofalo, N., & Jones, S. (2018). Engaging the struggle for decolonial approaches to teaching community psychology. *American Journal of Community Psychology, 62*, 319–329.
Whyte, W. F. (1943). *Street corner society*. The University of Chicago Press.
Wu, M. (2013). *Higher education for China's ethnic minorities: The influence of cultural and linguistic backgrounds on social and academic adjustment*. Scholar's Press.
Xu, L. (1948). *Under the ancestors' shadow: Chinese culture and personality*. Columbia University Press.
Xu, B. (1999). Anxiety of translation and abdication of the translator: A case of Sino-postcolonialism in the 1990s. *Postcolonial Studies, 2*(2), 231–245.
Zhao, J. (2013). Confucius as a critical educator: Towards educational thoughts of Confucius. *Frontiers of Education in China, 8*(1), 9–27.

MaryJo Benton Lee is an adjunct Assistant Professor of Sociology and Rural Studies at South Dakota State University (USA) and an honorary Professor of the Research Institute of Higher Education at Yunnan University, Kunming (People's Republic of China). She was a 2016–2017 Fulbright U.S. Scholar to China. Her first work in China was in 1991, when she was an exchange Professor at Yunnan Normal University. She returned there in 1997 as a visiting scholar. From 2000 to 2012 she was co-founder and coordinator of the Flandreau Indian School-South Dakota State University Success Academy, an early and intensive college preparatory program for Native American high school students. She is the author of two books and the editor of a third, on race, ethnicity and education. She holds bachelor's and master's degrees in Journalism from the University of Maryland-College Park, and a Ph.D. in Sociology, with a minor in Asian Studies, from South Dakota State University.

Open Access This chapter is licensed under the terms of the Creative Commons Attribution 4.0 International License (http://creativecommons.org/licenses/by/4.0/), which permits use, sharing, adaptation, distribution and reproduction in any medium or format, as long as you give appropriate credit to the original author(s) and the source, provide a link to the Creative Commons license and indicate if changes were made.

The images or other third party material in this chapter are included in the chapter's Creative Commons license, unless indicated otherwise in a credit line to the material. If material is not included in the chapter's Creative Commons license and your intended use is not permitted by statutory regulation or exceeds the permitted use, you will need to obtain permission directly from the copyright holder.

Chapter 27
Finland and Sweden: Muslim Teachers as Cultural Brokers

Inkeri Rissanen

Abstract This chapter focuses on the experiences and perspectives of Muslim teachers, who serve informally as "cultural brokers" in Finnish and Swedish schools. It begins by reviewing research on minority teachers and their roles as cultural mediators, as well as on Muslims in European public education. After that, the contexts, methodology and results of a case study are presented. The data includes semi-structured interviews with 14 "cultural broker" teachers. The results present the tasks of cultural brokering, as well as teachers' perceptions of what makes a good cultural broker and how this role should be developed. The chapter includes a critical discussion on what is expected of minority teachers; they are not a homogenous group and their willingness to take on the tasks of cultural brokering depend on the nature of their jobs. The simplistic view of cultural broker teachers as role models for minority students is scrutinized, likewise the ways of outsourcing "all things multicultural" in the school to them.

Introduction

Diversifying the teaching staff in culturally diverse schools by recruiting minority teachers is promoted in many European countries for several reasons. For instance, increasing "parent-teacher ethnic match" is considered an important means to develop parents' trust in the school and achieve higher parental involvement (Mantel, 2020; Calzada et al., 2015). Minority teachers are regarded as important "role models" for minority children yet the assumptions and implications of what it means to act as a role model are sometimes criticized as vague and simplistic (Carrington & Skelton, 2003). In any case, having higher proportions of ethnic minority teachers has been found to correlate positively with ethnic minority students' educational achievement (Lindahl, 2007).

I. Rissanen (✉)
Tampere University, Tampere, Finland
e-mail: inkeri.rissanen@tuni.fi

The common focus on minority teachers as intercultural mediators includes a risk of increasing stereotypical images of teachers as "ethnic professionals", and of recognizing their competencies only in urban-immigrant neighborhoods. On the other hand, many teachers of immigrant background willingly assume the role of mediator: they wish to be of use particularly in such contexts through their language skills and experiences attached to their personal histories. However, naïve assumptions of minority teachers as a homogeneous group are common, and more research is needed on the experiences of teachers from different minority groups in various contexts (Mantel, 2020; Santoro, 2015).

Apart from the question of whether minority teachers want to tie their professional identity to their ethnic/racial/religious positioning, the need for intercultural mediators in school communities has been recognized. "Cultural broker" is a descriptor, which in the educational research literature has been assigned to intermediaries who in different ways help to bridge the gap between the worlds of minority families and school. They may be teachers, instructional aides, family members, staff in community programs, or different kinds of project workers. Their role as intermediaries can be officially recognized, or they may informally mediate in various negotiations between members of the school community over and above their principal work duties. Cultural brokering is used as an umbrella concept for a wide array of tasks, such as translating and interpreting language, helping immigrant parents to navigate the school system, serving as advocates of minority parents and integrating and affirming their cultural values, educating school staff about the cultures of the families and generally helping disparate social systems to adapt to each other on both micro- and macro levels (Cooper et al., 1999; Martinez-Cosio & Iannacone, 2007; Yohani, 2013; Ishimaru et al., 2016).

The role of cultural brokers in schools may be recognized as important and valuable, but often their work is not without tensions. Acting simultaneously as advocates of parents and as institutional agents means that cultural brokers, on the on hand, are part of and reproduce the existing order, and on the other hand, expose forms of structural injustice in it. This means they may receive credit in the school from the more superficial bridging activities (e.g. organising cultural activities), but encounter resistance when exposing the privileges of the dominant group or calling for extra resources to fight against existing inequalities (Martinez-Cosio & Iannacone, 2007). This article presents the results from a study that explored Muslim teachers' perspectives and experiences of serving as cultural brokers in Finnish and Swedish schools. Since the vast majority of Muslims in Finland and Sweden are of immigrant background, the focus is mostly on the role of cultural brokers in supporting the inclusion of immigrant Muslims. The research questions are:

1. What tasks are involved in cultural brokering?
2. What makes a good cultural broker?
3. How do cultural brokers perceive their role and how would they like to see it evolve in the future?

Muslims in European Public Education

The reason to focus research on Muslim cultural brokers stems from the relevance of questions concerning Islam and Muslims in European public education systems. European Muslims are a heterogeneous group and categorize themselves in various ways, but identification as a Muslim rather than identification through ethnic identities, and the construction of collective Muslim identities have been rising trends, powered by common experiences of exclusion (Hopkins & Blackwood, 2011; Tinker & Smart, 2012). However, failure to understand the "diverse diversity" of Muslims stemming from e.g. different schools of law, cultural factors and different identity strategies in the West is mirrored in the perception that there are two kinds of Muslims – "good Muslims" who share "our" modern liberal lifestyles, and "bad Muslims" who are non-modern and difficult (Mamdani, 2002).

The majority of young European Muslims are educated in public (i.e. not faith-based) schools. The accommodation of Muslim identities in compulsory schooling has raised debates that reflect the wider renegotiation of the public role of religion in contemporary European societies. The failures experienced in Muslim inclusion in public schools have increased the willingness to found Islamic schools in many European countries. Muslim parents' reasons for prioritizing faith schooling relate to concerns about the general well-being of their children – developing a positive sense of identity and belonging – and fears and experiences of discrimination in public schools (McCreery et al., 2007). In Finland and Sweden, for example, Somali parents feel that teachers assume parents do not know what is in their children's best interests (Haga, 2015).

Much is known of the high impact of socio-emotional factors and teacher-student relationships on learning. Thus, the mis/recognition of students' identities in school as well as negative teacher attitudes may play a role in explaining the differences in students' educational achievements. Immigrant pupils from Islamic countries may be outperformed by other immigrant students, and these differences are not fully explained by socio-economic background, characteristics of the school or education system (Dronkers & van der Velden, 2013). However, research on the inclusion of immigrant Muslims in education has been somewhat polemic – either Muslims have been posited as a social problem or teachers have been accused of racism and Islamophobia (Niyozov, 2010). The focus of this study on the experiences and perceptions of Muslim cultural brokers is one attempt to overcome this polemic.

Contexts of the Study: Finland and Sweden

Finland and Sweden are Nordic welfare countries with majority populations that can be described as "secular-Lutheran", but they are becoming increasingly multicultural, Finland a little later and at a slower pace than Sweden. Muslims in Sweden account for approximately 5% of the population, while the corresponding figure in

Finland is 1% (Larsson., 2015; Pauha, 2018). The Muslim population in both countries is heterogeneous. The state and municipal school systems in both countries offer instruction in pupils' mother tongue and Finland provides religious education (RE) "according to students' own religion". Islamic religious education (IRE) has been offered in Finnish schools since the mid-1980s, and currently it is the second largest form of RE with 2.2% of students participating in it – Lutheran RE still dominates in Finnish schools (Sakaranaho & Rissanen, 2021). In both countries, the vast majority of pupils study in mainstream (not faith-based) schools; however, in Sweden there also are Islamic schools.

Both Finland and Sweden have been ranked as countries of "strong multiculturalism policy" (Multiculturalism Policy Index, 2010), and have included efforts to recognise and support minority cultural identities in their public education systems, but Sweden has experienced a backlash in multiculturalism policies with the state taking less responsibility for immigrants' cultures (Zilliacus et al., 2017). In Finland there seems to be a gap between the multiculturalist policies and the everyday realities. For instance, attitudes toward Muslims are exceptionally negative when compared to those in other countries in Western Europe (Pew Research Centre, 2018), and teachers' attitudes mirror this general tendency (Rissanen et al., 2015). School cultures in Finland and Sweden are commonly based on trust, democratic leadership and low power distance (Rissanen, 2018). School-home collaboration is regarded as important and actively pursued. In the face of increasing cultural diversity new forms of collaboration as well as parental education have been developed; however, there are also reports of immigrant parents being treated by their children's teachers in a manner which they find alienating, paternalistic or even discriminatory (Mohme, 2017; Haga, 2015). Earlier research has described how the "secular normativity" of Finnish and Swedish schools indicates that non-religious positions tend to be regarded as "normal" or "neutral", while religious positions, and particularly Islam, are seen to be contradictory to modern, rational and independent thinking (Berglund, 2017; Rissanen, 2018, 2020, 2021).

In both countries, the number of students with immigrant background entering into teacher education is slowly increasing. There are also more ways for teachers with foreign degrees to complement their studies and achieve eligibility for teaching in Finnish/Swedish schools. However, teachers with immigrant background and without proficiency in the local language are often recruited for positions where they mainly teach immigrant students – for instance, as native-language support teachers, language teachers or RE teachers (Käck et al., 2018; Virta, 2015; Hahl & Paavola, 2015). School leaders in both countries emphasize the importance of hiring teachers with migrant backgrounds as a strategy to develop multicultural schools, and often take for granted teachers' ability and willingness to serve as cultural interpreters (Rissanen, 2021; Jönsson & Rubenstein Reich, 2006; Lahdenperä, 2006, 10). However, immigrant teachers themselves may want to emphasize their professional role as teachers even though they also are willing to mediate relations between home and school. They struggle for professional respect and see their position as marginalized and insecure, often face discrimination and sometimes feel their background is seen as a handicap (Colliander, 2017; Virta, 2015; Lefever et al., 2014).

Methodology

This study is part of a larger qualitative research project concerned with the inclusion of Muslims in Finnish and Swedish schools. In this project, principals of Finnish and Swedish urban multicultural schools (n = 10 in each country) as well as Muslim parents and teachers/other staff members (n = 8 in each country), were interviewed. For the present article, the perspectives and experiences of the Muslim teachers (of religious education, languages or social sciences) (total n = 16) were analysed. They all were self-identifying as Muslims and served informally as cultural brokers in their school communities. Eight of the interviewees were female and eight male; apart from two native Finns, they were first-generation immigrants (from Iraq, Iran, Malesia, Morocco, Senegal, Somalia and Turkey). They were fluent in Finnish, Swedish or English and the interviews were conducted in these languages.

Semi-structured interviews were conducted with the informants in the spring of 2016. The interviews lasted from 50 to 90 min. They were recorded and transcribed verbatim. The data were analysed by means of inductive qualitative content analysis (Elo & Kyngäs, 2007). Condensed meaning units were formed of the parts of the interviews that related to the research questions. The condensed meaning units were then coded and the codes categorized. In this article, the results for each research question are reported in their own respective sections and the categories appear in bold face and in italics in the text. Previous analyses on the data of the project have focused on schools as the arenas for negotiations on Muslims' inclusive citizenship (Rissanen, 2018), principals' diversity ideologies in supporting the inclusion of Muslims (Rissanen, 2021) as well as School-Muslim parent collaboration and the role of parental cultural capital (Rissanen, 2020).

Findings and Discussion

What Tasks Are Involved in Cultural Brokering?

Serving as Information Banks for Other Teachers, School Leaders, Parents and Students Previous research on cultural brokers often highlights their role in educating minority families about the dominant culture and its school system (Ishimaru et al., 2016; Cooper et al., 1999). The brokers of this study also reported these tasks but often put more emphasis on their role in providing information for other teachers as well as school leaders about Islam, Muslims, and the realities of Muslim immigrant families. Through this they challenged teachers' eurocentric views, increasing understanding on the internal diversity of Islam and tackling prejudices. Sometimes Muslim parents' or students' prejudiced views of teachers as racists also needed to be challenged by giving them information about the Finnish/Swedish educational culture. Furthermore, the brokers were educating both teachers and parents about the different cultural styles of communication in order to reduce friction. All this was done informally through everyday interactions with the different members of the school community. The cultural brokers who worked as teachers of all students (as class teachers or subject teachers), mostly wanted to confine their brokering tasks to providing information and avoid a role where they would be seen as the allies of minority students:

> F3 (Finnish Islamic Religious Education-teacher): It's more like… a teacher comes to me before the meeting (with Muslim parents) to ask why it is that they want this and that, like informally we discuss the issue and I can explain what I think the problem is and the interpretations (of religious matters) some families have. They come to me for information, I am a Finn so I understand their view and I work at the school, but I also understand the families' views and why some want to obey certain rules a bit more strictly. Rarely do I participate in those meetings because I would be in a very uncomfortable position, I work at the school but I'm also a Muslim, I would have to choose sides, which would be uncomfortable, so consciously we have tried to avoid these situations.

Serving as Advocates and Support Persons of Parents and Students However, cultural brokers who mainly taught minority students also served as advocates and support persons in school for Muslim families, which meant they positioned themselves more openly as their allies and as minority members themselves. According to them, Muslim parents contacted them with a much lower threshold than they did other teachers, asking for help in matters concerning the accommodation of their children's culture- or religion-based needs in the school:

> S6 (Swedish teacher of social studies): When I have had Muslim students, their parents seem to trust me, like oh, ok, so you will understand that my child cannot eat pork in school… and these kinds of small things we talk about, they trust me.

Furthermore, they talked about how Muslim students often long for an adult who understands both their religion and their everyday realities, and sometimes even trust cultural brokers with their most difficult issues.

Serving as Role Models Efforts at diversifying teaching staff in many countries are often based on the "role model" argument (Carrington & Skelton, 2003), but the cultural brokers in this study rarely participated in this discourse of minority teachers as role models for minority students; they deemed it more important to model and represent Islam to non-Muslim teachers and students. Only the Finnish IRE teachers talked about themselves as role models for Muslim students in the sense of combining identities as Finns and as Muslims. The idea of Muslim girls needing role models met with criticism:

> S8 (Swedish language teacher): Each time I got hired, I encountered the discourse of being…they thought that it was good for the school to get a role model of a veiled Muslim woman, who has an academic background. So… I mean for me, that's fine, but… why people don't realise that Muslim women with hijab, with a veil, can be educated?

Because in Indonesia, in Iran or Iraq, they are members of the parliament, in Indonesia, they do work in universities, they are like you, you know— but the thing is that... we should be role models for the Muslim girls but the Muslim girls KNOW that women can get educated. So it's like, they (teachers and principals) have the...the idea that these girls belong to a closed world... that these girls think that because you are a Muslim and you have hijab you cannot succeed in life, so here's a teacher to show you. But these girls live in a Muslim environment, they KNOW...

Mediating Conflicts If there were conflicts between the members of the school community – these were reported between parents from different ethnic backgrounds, between Muslim students and non-Muslim teachers, parents and school leaders, and among Muslim students – the cultural brokers were often asked for help. Sometimes they helped in resolving conflicts even in other schools or outside the school:

> F2 (Finnish Islamic Religious Education teacher): For example, last week in one school one kid's parents came to me and told me that the kid had been bullied outdoors. They did not want to go to the principal since the quarrel seemed to have been between Muslim kids and Finnish kids. So they asked if I could take care of the situation and maybe also talk to the principal.

Even though conflicts are often trivial, cultural brokers regard it as important to work to resolve them by increasing mutual understanding. They also talked about how the problem often is not in a lack of cultural knowledge but failure to listen or respect and, for instance, principals' authoritative ways of managing issues or giving up on collaboration. However, they also reported on seeing how through dialogical practices the need for cultural brokers as mediators diminishes.

Serving as Interpreters Very commonly, the cultural broker teachers served as interpreters in the school, even though some of them also talked about the importance of simultaneously encouraging parents to practice their Finnish/Swedish skills in the school and communicate without an interpreter. However, when negotiating difficult issues the cultural brokers wanted to help with the language since they felt that immigrant parents were often in a weaker position and not respected as intelligible equal adults due to their lack of Finnish/Swedish skills, even though entirely able to express themselves in other languages.

Influencing Practices and Structures in the School and Municipality Some of the cultural brokers also reported efforts to exert influence at the structural level. They had taken an active role in developing an inclusive school culture, but had also been involved in different committees designing municipality-level solutions and suggestions. Resistance was reported but also successes: one of the cultural brokers had designed a whole new model for hiring assistants from different language backgrounds for schools, and now worked as their supervisor.

What Makes a Cultural Broker?

A Good Understanding of the Majority Society and Sufficient Commitment to Its Norms All the cultural brokers wanted to emphasize that having certain ethnic or religious background is never a sufficient condition for successfully serving as cultural broker. A good understanding of the majority society and sufficient commitment to its norms was considered vital. The brokers deplored some principals' lack of interest in what teachers new to the society (and sometimes hired without formal qualifications) actually taught and the models they provided for minority children. Even though cultural brokers need not share all the values and ways of thinking common in the dominant cultures, they had to understand them – and make them understandable to others. A profound understanding also made it possible to promote immigrant minorities' matters constructively:

> F6 (Finnish mother tongue teacher) [...] For religious reasons, people feel they have to be polite and express gratitude. But AFTER that, these problems have to be intelligently faced [...] you always have to remember the histories of things and people, get to know them, to remember that you are from Somali culture and how to effectively communicate there and how here, also to know the history and culture of Finland.

Being Seen as an Insider in Minority Cultures and Knowing Enough About Them On the other hand, cultural brokers also felt a need to be seen as insiders among the minority groups. Mere recognition as a Muslim is sometimes enough to create trust in Muslim parents, but most informants regarded familiarity with the minority culture and religion (and their internal diversity) essential for their brokering tasks. They talked about the problems that occurred if all Muslim teachers were assumed to be able to serve as experts and mediators in issues related to religion; IRE teachers could be expected to possess this kind of knowledge. Nevertheless, being members of minorities enabled the cultural broker teachers to discuss sensitive issues with families:

> F6 (Finnish mother tongue teacher): The kind of conversations I have (with the parents), it is impossible for Finns to have, they will be called racists. But I can have those conversations, and I can be blamed for being westernized, but I have the benefit that I KNOW the field, and they know me and that I am a well-intentioned person, I just want people to see things from both sides.

Developing Networks Outside the School Some of the informants reported that their success as cultural brokers was heavily based on their networks and relationships outside the school, which they had consciously cultivated. The IRE teachers in particular reported creating a position where they enjoy the trust of Muslim families from very different backgrounds had required a lot of footwork among the ethnic and religious communities. However, the brokers had very varying views on this and the networks were regarded as important mostly by those teachers who themselves mainly taught minority students: those who had a teaching position where they taught majority and minority students alike actually considered it harmful to be associated with minority communities and tried to keep their distance.

Knowing the Limits of Cultural Brokering The need to critically reflect their role and be aware of the limits of appropriate cultural brokering was discussed:

> F4 (Finnish Islamic Religious Education teacher): I also want to question this role of a consultant, there are some pitfalls in it. Like…a typical question to the Islamic religious education teacher is, what is appropriate clothing for Muslim girls in the P.E. lessons? You know, I am not a fatwa-bank. What is important is that they have separate clothing for sports and are able to take care of their personal hygiene, I mean I don't issue scarf measures. Or tell them how much ankle they can show. It is an erroneous idea to put RE teachers or mother tongue teachers in this kind of position, where we actually would violate equity and freedom of religion. I am not going to dictate how people can practice their religion, that is not my job as a teacher, as a public servant.

According to this broker, some Muslim teachers did not understand that it was not their job to standardize religious practice, and this undermined the autonomy of families.

How Do Teachers Perceive Their Role as Cultural Brokers and How Would They Like to See It Evolve in the Future?

Experiences of Cultural Brokering as a Rewarding and Respected Position The brokers talked about seeing the everyday problems Muslim students and their families face in the school and feeling the urge to help. As already discussed, their willingness to profile themselves as cultural brokers varied, but some had purposefully sought to be employed in schools where their background and cultural/religious expertise could be of use. They talked about big differences in how they were seen by other teachers and principals: many brokers worked in several schools and reported difficulties in receiving respect in some of them, but being regarded as "key persons" and "treasures" in others. Principals who valued their contributions as cultural brokers occasionally organized substitute teachers for their lessons so that they could use their time on brokering tasks.

Experiences of Frustration However, experiences of frustration and exhaustion were also reported. Much of the frustration was caused by the fact that the brokers were given a lot of responsibility, but little power. Many of the issues they tried to handle – for example, problems in school-family collaboration – would require more structural level changes to be truly resolved, but the brokers' endeavors to influence school level or municipality level decision-making were often met with resistance and even hostility. Occasionally brokering felt like continuously cleaning up the messes other teachers or principals had made through their ignorance or insensitive communication. Sometimes the immigrant teachers felt caught between two fires – being accused of being "too westernized" by the immigrant Muslim families, and being seen as difficult or "reluctant to integrate" in the professional community. Also the students' might "test" them, as described by this broker:

> S8 (Swedish language teacher): when I had a conversation with one student, she told me this is SWEDEN here, and she told me in that tone you know, this is SWEDEN [...] And they like to test me, in the class, like what do you think about gays, so well, you know, I don't really care. If I didn't tolerate gays I would live somewhere else... so they test me. I don't know how it goes with other teachers but I suppose that I get... It might be little more difficult for me to handle the group, to build the relationship with the group as a teacher. And then I get all the immigrant kids who try to, "ok, you speak Arabic so you are our friend". No, I represent Swedish values and, you know... So no, I don't speak Arabic. And I get, ok, it's haram, it's haram, from some students who always try to drag me into these conversations, but I avoid it, systematically.

According to the brokers, many immigrant Muslim parents were afraid of raising any issues in the school for they fear their children would be seen in a negative light, but needed a channel to express the feelings of frustration they sometimes had behind the polite and grateful façade. Here is how one cultural broker described efforts at negotiating issues related to organising IRE in schools:

> F6: (Finnish mother tongue teacher): They (parents and teachers) lean on me in all kinds of questions, but I don't have any answers to them. I have sought guidance from the education division of the city administration, but everyone just evades the issue. Nobody wants to take responsibility. [...] I am constantly in contact with the city administration and ask them to come up with guidelines, but the answer is that this is the law and we live by it. But I think this is not responsible. And I take flack because of this but I don't care. As long as I know I'm doing the right thing. Somebody has to raise these issues.

Furthermore, open communication on the part of other teachers was sometimes prevented by fears of being regarded as racist. Thus, cultural brokers served as filters for concerns and emotions from different sides.

Perceptions of the Continuous Need for Cultural Brokering at All Levels of the Public Education System In order to avoid segregation in the public educational system, cultural brokers called for public schools to be developed as arenas where the inclusion of different groups in society was continuously negotiated, and saw the role of cultural brokers in this as also relevant in the future. They did not consider the need for cultural brokers to be an interphase: in multiculturalizing societies, negotiations on inclusion are contextual and continuous. School cultures have to reflect the changing realities and local populations, and cultural brokers are needed as "continuous problem solvers", as described by one of the informants.

Perceptions of the Need to Help Minority Members to Take Agency in Society When talking about the changes they would like to see in the educational system and society, none of the brokers considered this as something that could be expected to arise from the majority society: they emphasized the agency of active minority members such as themselves to push unflaggingly through resistance by acting like model citizens and finding new ways to exert influence. They wanted to believe that relentless work on correcting misconceptions and increasing mutual understanding through knowledge would have the desired effect.

Conclusions and Implications

This study analyzed the experiences of Muslim cultural broker teachers in Finnish and Swedish schools. There are limits to the interpretations that can be made on the basis of this case study sample, which is by no means representative. The study does not aim to cover the whole variety of experiences of Finnish and Swedish Muslim cultural brokers and it makes no claim of generalizability. Furthermore, it is likely that some differences in the brokers' views may have been linked to their respective background factors such as nationality, but making interpretations of these correlations on the basis of individual representatives of different nationalities in this data would be mere speculation. However, the data enabled tentative interpretations on the links between teachers' orientations to cultural brokering and their job descriptions (whether or not teaching mainly minority students). Previous studies have demonstrated how minority teachers are sometimes stereotyped and their professional competence is reduced to being "professional ethnic", which serves to narrow their career paths and professional prospects. Professional respect for minority teachers may suffer if their background is seen as the reason for their recruitment (Santoro, 2015; Wilkins & Lal, 2011; Carrington & Skelton, 2003). On the other hand, they may have very different orientations: while some want to be assimilated into the dominant professional community of teachers, others seek to be employed in urban-immigrant neighborhoods and want to use their language skills, cultural competences and experiences to negotiate issues related to the inclusion of minorities (Mantel, 2020). The cultural brokers in this study also seemed to have different orientations, which were linked to their professional roles. All teachers who mainly taught minority students (RE teachers or mother tongue teachers) were strongly committed to cultural brokering and took up a wide variety of brokering tasks. Those whose job description was not mainly focused on teaching minority students wanted to avoid being profiled as the advocates of minorities; however, they, too, wanted to serve as cultural brokers by advising their colleagues.

The "role model" argument, according to which minority teachers are primarily needed as role models for minority students, has been criticized for its vagueness (Carrington & Skelton, 2003) and the brokers in this study also criticized the often simplistic views of Muslim girls in particular being in need of role models. They saw the barriers to inclusion in the fixed attitudes and misconceptions of majority teachers and principals rather, and challenged assumptions of ignorance and lack of academic motivation among Muslim minority members. Even though minority teachers are often recruited to teach minority students, the thinking and professional practices of their colleagues and principals may also change through collaboration with these teachers (see Rissanen, 2020, 2021). This study demonstrated the strong agency of cultural broker teachers: their professional role was not limited to the expectations and tasks assigned to them from outside, but much shaped by their own active way of getting involved in matters where they believed their contribution might be needed.

According to the findings of this study, policies that enable developing some formal recognition and resourcing of the informal tasks of cultural brokers are to be recommended. The results reveal the quantity of the work cultural broker teachers continuously accomplish informally in addition to their "normal" workloads. Sometimes this work extends outside school hours and school premises. Much of the work is invisible to the professional community, and meagre resources are allocated to it. Furthermore, cultural brokers are often asked to address problems at the grassroots level, which in their view would need more structural level solutions. The mismatch between the problems they are asked to resolve and their lack of power to influence their root causes creates frustration. Thus, another policy recommendation is to increase cultural brokering at all levels of the education system and educational decision-making.

Furthermore, the challenges encountered by cultural brokers demonstrate the need to cultivate all teachers' cultural responsiveness. Sometimes cultural brokers are given complete power and responsibility to deal with "minority issues" without any support or interest from principals or other teachers: this is experienced as indifference towards developing inclusive schools. Thus, even though many Finnish and Swedish principals affirm the value of cultural broker teachers in schools (Rissanen, 2021; Jönsson & Rubenstein Reich, 2006; Lahdenperä, 2006, 10), the common assumptions that they can outsource "dealing with minorities" to cultural broker teachers and that all minority teachers are willing to assume this role are decidedly problematic and based on perceptions of one-way inclusion. Instead of giving cultural brokers responsibility for "all things multicultural", culturally responsive teaching and efforts to promote inclusion, equality and social justice are the responsibility of all teachers (see Santoro, 2015).

References

Berglund, J. (2017). Secular normativity and the religification of Muslims in Swedish public schooling. *Oxford Review of Education, 43*, 524–535.

Calzada, E. J., Huang, K. Y., Hernandez, M., Soriano, E., Acra, C. F., Dawson-McClure, S., Kamboukos, D., & Brotman, L. (2015). Family and teacher characteristics as predictors of parent involvement in education during early childhood among Afro-Caribbean and Latino immigrant families. *Urban Eeducation, 50*(7), 870–896. https://doi.org/10.1177/0042085914534862

Carrington, B., & Skelton, C. (2003). Re-thinking 'role models': Equal opportunities in teacher recruitment in England and Wales. *Journal of Education Policy, 18*(3), 253–265. https://doi.org/10.1080/02680930305573

Colliander, H. (2017). Building bridges and strengthening positions: Exploring the identity construction of immigrant bilingual teachers. *International Journal of Bilingual Education and Bilingualism.*

Cooper, C., Denner, J., & Lopez, E. (1999). Cultural brokers: Helping Latino children on pathways toward success. *The Future of Children, 9*(2), 51–57. https://doi.org/10.2307/1602705

Dronkers, J., & van der Velden, R. (2013). Positive but also negative effects of ethnic diversity in schools on educational achievement? An empirical test with cross-national PISA data. In M. Windzio (Ed.), *Integration and inequality in educational institutions* (pp. 71–98). Springer.

Elo, S., & Kyngäs, H. (2007). Qualitative content analysis. *Journal of Advanced Nursing, 62*(1), 107–115.

Haga, R. (2015). Freedom has destroyed the Somali family. Somali parents' experiences of epistemic injustice and its influence on their raising of Swedish Muslims. In M. Sedgwick (Ed.), *Making European Muslims: Religious socialization among young Muslims in Scandinavia and Western Europe* (pp. 39–55). Routledge.

Hahl, K., & Paavola, H. (2015). "To get a foot in the door": New host country educated immigrant teachers' perceptions of their employability in Finland. *Australian Journal of Teacher Education, 40*(3). https://doi.org/10.14221/ajte.2014v40n3.3

Högskola (University Collage). (2006). Working paper. 1.

Hopkins, N., & Blackwood, L. (2011). Everyday citizenship: Identity and recognition. *Journal of Community & Applied Social Psychology, 21*, 215–227.

Ishimaru, A. M., Torres, K. E., Salvador, J. E., Lott, J., Williams, D. M. C., & Tran, C. (2016). Reinforcing deficit, journeying toward equity: Cultural brokering in family engagement initiatives. *American Educational Research Journal, 53*(4), 850–882. https://doi.org/10.3102/0002831216657178

Jönsson, A., & Rubenstein Reich, L. R. (2006). En yrkesidentitet i förändring? Invandrade lärares möte med den svenska skolan. [An occupational identity in transformation? Immigrant teachers meeting with the Swedish school]. *Pedagogisk Forskning i Sverige, 11*(2), 81–93.

Käck, A., Männikkö Barbutiu, S., & Fors, U. (2018). Unfamiliar ways of thinking and practising in teacher education: Experiences by migrant teachers. In M. Sablic, A. Skugor, & I. Durdevic Babic (Eds.), *Proceedings of the 42nd ATEE annual conference 2017 in Dubrovnik, Croatia: Changing perspectives and approaches in contemporary teaching* (pp. 219–235).

Lahdenperä, P. (2006). *Intercultural leadership in school environments*. Södertörns.

Larsson. (2015). Sweden. In O. Scharbrodt, S. Akgönül, A. Alibašić, & J. Nielsen (Eds.), *Yearbook of Muslims in Europe* (pp. 549–561). Brill.

Lefever, S., Paavola, H., Berman, R., Guðjónsdóttir, H., Talib, M.-T., & Gísladóttir, K. R. (2014). Immigrant teachers in Finland and Iceland: Successes and challenges. *International Journal of Education for Diversities, 3*, 65–85. http://blogs.helsinki.fi/ije4d-journal/volume-3-2014/

Lindahl, M. (2007). *Gender and ethnic interactions among teachers and students: Evidence from Sweden* (No. 2007: 25. Working Paper). IFAU-Institute for Labour Market Policy Evaluation.

Mamdani, M. (2002). Good Muslim, bad Muslim: A political perspective on culture and terrorism. *American Anthropologist, 104*(3), 766–775.

Mantel, C. (2020). Being a teacher with a so-called 'immigrant background': Challenges of dealing with social boundaries. *Intercultural Education, 31*(2), 173–189. https://doi.org/10.1080/14675986.2019.1702291

Martinez-Cosio, M., & Iannacone, R. M. (2007). The tenuous role of institutional agents: Parent liaisons as cultural brokers. *Education and Urban Society, 39*(3), 349–369. https://doi.org/10.1177/0013124506298165

McCreery, E., Jones, L., & Holmes, R. (2007). Why do Muslim parents want Muslim schools? *Early Years: An International Research Journal, 27*(3), 203–219.

Mohme, G. (2017). Somali swedes' reasons for choosing a Muslim-profiled school – Recognition and educational ambitions as important influencing factors. *Journal of School Choice, 11*(2), 239–257. https://doi.org/10.1080/15582159.2017.1302256

Multiculturalism Policy Index. (2010). Retrieved from http://www.queensu.ca/mcp/

Niyozov, S. (2010). Teachers and teaching Islam and Muslims in pluralistic societies: Claims, misunderstandings, and responses. *Journal of International Migration and Integration, 11*(1), 23–40.

Pauha, T. (2018). Finland. In O. Scharbrodt, S. Akgonul, A. Alibašić, J. S. Nielsen, & E. Račius (Eds.), *Yearbook of Muslims in Europe* (Vol. 9, pp. 232–247). Brill.

Pew Research Center. (2018). *Being Christian in Western Europe*. http://www.pewforum.org/wp-content/uploads/sites/7/2018/05/Being-Christian-in-Western-Europe-FOR-WEB1.pdf

Rissanen, I. (2018). Negotiations on inclusive citizenship in a post-secular school: Perspectives of "cultural broker" Muslim parents and teachers in Finland and Sweden. *Scandinavian Journal of Educational Research, 64*(1), 135–150. https://doi.org/10.1080/00313831.2018.1514323

Rissanen, I. (2020). School–Muslim parent collaboration in Finland and Sweden: Exploring the role of parental cultural capital. *Scandinavian Journal of Educational Research.* https://doi.org/10.1080/00313831.2020.1817775

Rissanen, I. (2021). School principals' diversity ideologies in fostering the inclusion of Muslims in Finnish and Swedish schools. *Race Ethnicity and Education, 24*(3), 431–450. https://doi.org/10.1080/13613324.2019.1599340

Rissanen, I., Kuusisto, E., & Tirri, K. (2015). Finnish teachers' attitudes to Muslim students and Muslim student integration. *Journal for the Scientific Study of Religion, 54*(2), 277–290.

Sakaranaho, T., & Rissanen, I. (2021). Islamic religious education in Finland. In L. Franken & B. Gent (Eds.), *Islamic religious education in Europe: A comparative study* (pp. 112–127). Routledge. https://doi.org/10.4324/9780429331039-7

Santoro, N. (2015). The drive to diversify the teaching profession: Narrow assumptions, hidden complexities. *Race Ethnicity and Education, 18*(6), 858–876. https://doi.org/10.1080/13613324.2012.759934

Tinker, C., & Smart, A. (2012). Constructions of collective Muslim identity by advocates of Muslim schools in Britain. *Ethnic and Racial Studies, 35*(4), 643–663.

Virta, A. (2015). "In the middle of a pedagogical triangle" – Native-language support teachers constructing their identity in a new context. *Teaching and Teacher Education, 46*, 84–93. https://doi.org/10.1016/j.tate.2014.11.003

Wilkins, C., & Lal, R. (2011). You've got to be tough and I'm trying': Black and minority ethnic student teachers' experiences of initial teacher education. *Race Ethnicity and Education, 14*(3), 365–386.

Yohani, S. (2013). Educational cultural brokers and the school adaptation of refugee children and families: Challenges and opportunities. *Journal of International Migration & Integration, 14*, 61–79. https://doi.org/10.1007/s12134-011-0229-x

Zilliacus, H., Paulsrud, B., & Holm, G. (2017). Essentializing vs. non-essentializing students' cultural identities: Curricular discourses in Finland and Sweden. *Journal of Multicultural Discourses, 12*(2), 166–180.

Inkeri Rissanen is a docent (associate professor), and university lecturer at the Faculty of Education and Culture at the Tampere University, Finland. Her fields of expertise include multicultural education, religions and worldviews in education, teachers' intercultural competencies, and growth mindset pedagogy.

Open Access This chapter is licensed under the terms of the Creative Commons Attribution 4.0 International License (http://creativecommons.org/licenses/by/4.0/), which permits use, sharing, adaptation, distribution and reproduction in any medium or format, as long as you give appropriate credit to the original author(s) and the source, provide a link to the Creative Commons license and indicate if changes were made.

The images or other third party material in this chapter are included in the chapter's Creative Commons license, unless indicated otherwise in a credit line to the material. If material is not included in the chapter's Creative Commons license and your intended use is not permitted by statutory regulation or exceeds the permitted use, you will need to obtain permission directly from the copyright holder.

Chapter 28
Ethnic Identity as a Cultural Mediator in Teaching: An Autoethnography of a Latinx Teacher

Jennifer M. Barreto

Abstract In this chapter, the author examines her experience of education as a Latinx in the United States, first as a student, and then as a teacher, through the intersectionality of language bias, racism, and elitism. Producing autoethnographic research acknowledges and validates her Latinx presence and draws attention to her marginal position inside the dominant structures of education. This autoethnography puts the critical focus on her experiences within the broader context of education (Denzin NK, Interpretive ethnography: ethnographic practices for the 21st century. Sage, 1997). This personal narrative (Bochner AP, Narrat Inq 22:155–164, 2012) employs the theoretical frameworks of critical race theory and Latinx critical race theory (CRT; Delgado R, Stefancic J, Critical race theory: an introduction. University Press, 2001) to explore the tensions of being Latinx in the United States education system. This cultural analysis considers personal, social, and culturally constructed identities. The author discusses the everyday negotiations between Latinx culture and teaching in an elementary school. Centering the critical framework, the author interrogates how society shapes our narratives, identities, and lives (Kehly MJ, Gend Educ 7:23–31, 1995) through culture, power, and language.

Introduction

I am an anomaly in education—an elementary school teacher from a working-class, Puerto Rican family, and a first-generation college student. This exceptional advantage point leads me to examine how—despite the forms of oppression I experienced as a student and despite the lack of representation of Latinx educators—my Latinx ethnic identity played a role in my choice to become a teacher and to teach in an elementary school in the United States.

Researchers in the field of education have documented scarcity in recruiting and retaining Latinx and other marginalized teachers in the United States (Bristol &

J. M. Barreto (✉)
Eastern Michigan University, Ypsilanti, MI, USA
e-mail: jbarreto@emich.edu

© The Author(s) 2023
M. Gutman et al. (eds.), *To Be a Minority Teacher in a Foreign Culture*,
https://doi.org/10.1007/978-3-031-25584-7_28

Martin-Fernandez, 2019; Goldhaber et al., 2019; Irizarry & Donaldson, 2012), despite the student population in the United States becoming increasingly more culturally, ethnically, and linguistically diverse, with Latinx students identified as the largest minority (National Center for Educational Statistics [NCES], 2018). In contrast with these diverse demographics of students, 80% of teachers are white and only 9% are Latinx (NCES, 2018). How does the field of education become diversified when historically it has suppressed the narratives of Latinx students and other non-dominant groups (Yosso, 2005) and has excluded the insightful experiences of Latinx teachers (Goldhaber et al., 2019)?

Highlighting the marginal positions in which Latinx people live in dominant institutions of education, Lamar (2019) describes her teaching experience in the United States as excluding her ethnic and cultural identities. Lamar felt devalued in education, and ultimately, she left teaching. In their study of a Latina pre-service teacher, Gomez and Rodriguez (2011) found that she relied on her ethnic and cultural background when working with students. They reported she reflected critically, strategically considering ways to find representation so students would see themselves reflected in their learning. While the results of such studies are encouraging, more work must be done in the field of education to elevate Latinx and diverse voices. The benefits of sharing Latinx stories include encouraging teachers to use their cultural/linguistic experiences to help diverse students. Viewing culture as another resource for all students to learn, Latinx teachers recognize the importance of celebrating—not devaluing—a student's native language.

Sharing my story by examining the intersections of language bias, racism, and elitism as both a Latinx student and as a teacher in the United States can help address educational inequities. Educators have underscored the crucial role of attending to multicultural lived experiences in the classroom, and how these experiences inform classroom pedagogy (Yazan, 2019). Bartolomé (2004, 2008) argues that teachers must understand how their ideological orientation shapes their students' views and influences their teaching. In thinking about my ethnic identity, my beliefs, ideas, and language impacted my classroom decisions. Vellanki and Prince (2018) found that in U.S. classrooms teacher educators had a singular understanding of the multicultural context that excluded the stories of multicultural students and teachers; they identified the need for further research in multicultural teacher stories in education.

Limited research exists on Latinx educators finding their voice as role models in an oppressive environment. Coker and Cain (2018) state the importance of marginalized teachers as uniquely positioned to empathize with students who are also marginalized. By examining my tensions in the classroom as a Latinx teacher dealing with different forms of oppression, including language bias, racism, and elitism, my goal is to continue the conversation of representation. I aim to address this missing link by examining the intersections of who I am. In this chapter, I would like to create a roadmap of my thoughts, experiences, and reflections as a minority K–12 educator. I am using critical autoethnography as a method to understand my personal experience to contribute to our knowledge of power and social inequality in the education system.

Theoretical Framework

Framing My Ethnic Identity in Education

Being Puerto Rican guides my ethnic, cultural, and linguistic identity. The theories I used to examine my ethnic identity include critical race theory (CRT) and Latinx critical race theory (LatCrit). LatCrit stems from CRT building on critical race theorists (Delgado & Stefancic, 2001; Solórzano & Yosso, 2001), who examine social justice through an empowering and liberating framework to show inequalities (Bell, 1995). LatCrit considers the historical oppression of ethnicities and cultures. This framework highlights the Latinx experience of ethnicity, language, culture, and the oppressions this group encounters (Covarrubias & Lara, 2014; Yosso, 2005), "beyond the limitations of the black/white paradigm" (Iglesias, 1997, p. 178). The framework of CRT and LatCrit in this chapter adds to this dialogue, highlighting the experiences of Latinx educators.

I draw on the CRT tenet of storytelling or counter-storytelling as one way of contextualizing the importance of culture (Bernal, 2002). LatCrit scholars in education have relied on storytelling to document and share how Latinx culture influences the educational experience. Storytelling provides me with a path toward understanding how my Latinx identity empowered me to navigate power dynamics within schools. My narrative and knowledge production are symbiotic; hence, these stories are personal and essential in education (Clanindin & Connelly, 2000). In this chapter, I focus on the centrality of my experience to understand how ethnicity functions in society. Through sharing my experiences, I use my culture as a mediator when teaching. Solórzano and Yosso (2002) state that CRT is "a set of basic insights, perspectives, methods, and pedagogy that seek to identify, analyze, and transform those structural and cultural aspects that maintain subordinate and dominant racial positions in and out of the classroom" (p. 25). Sharing my counter-story centers my Puerto Rican self through a type of narrative that goes beyond the status quo to empower other Latinx teachers to share their stories and continue my commitment to social justice.

LatCrit scholars document and analyze counter-stories intentionally to highlight varied and persistent oppression. To challenge dominant stories, this way of data collection and analysis focuses on the diverse and persistent nature of inequalities of Latinx lived experiences that are often silenced (Solórzano & Yosso, 2002). Through the sharing of one's story, there is an opportunity for healing as others find similarities from their own experiences (Delgado & Stefancic, 2001).

Methodology

Narrative as Inquiry

I use narrative research to explore my ethnic identity connected to my identity as a teacher in Florida and to interrogate how these intersections impacted my pedagogy. Producing autoethnographic research acknowledges and validates my Latinx presence and draws attention to my marginal position inside dominant structures of education, "a topic of investigation in its own right" (Ellis & Bochner, 2000, p. 733). Autoethnographic work allows storytelling to be at the center. It is powerful in that it "can be used as a springboard to explore a myriad of issues related to identity and belonging, as well as curricular matters and teaching in ways that are explicitly antiracist" (Aveling, 2006, p. 266–67). My choice of autoethnography focuses on my lived experience as a route to illuminate aspects of my culture or society (Bochner, 2012). The interrogation of my ethnic identity transforms from a noun to a verb through my lived experiences (Heath & Street, 2008); the examination of my ethnic identity as both a student and teacher in the United States is not stagnant but is instead an action to propel what is needed in future research and schools.

Creating an "autobiographically oriented narrative" illuminates issues of oppression that I "have suffered in silence for too long" (Bochner & Ellis, 1996, p. 24). My aim is to immerse my readers into my thoughts, experiences, and reflections as a Latinx student and educator. As a Puerto Rican born in Belgium, I am uniquely positioned to be American yet not American enough because my native language is Spanish, and I was born outside the United States. This intention positions me alongside education researchers who use autoethnography to ask, How might my experiences of culture, learning, and education inform my approaches to curriculum and pedagogy? (Hughes et al., 2012). I am using critical autoethnography (Boylorn & Orbe, 2014) as a way to examine and interrogate my oppressive lived experiences to use theory to challenge dominant narratives in the U.S. education system. I offer my individual autoethnography as a conversation with others' stories, in the hope of creating a dialogue on the intersection of language bias, racism, and elitism.

Narratives

I situate my narratives (all people, places, and schools are pseudonyms) within the literature. In sharing my experiences, I might shed light on the collective experiences of Latinx educators. My stories are not extraordinary; many minorities face similar challenges in their educational experience and teaching. What's different is the pattern noticed: the forms of oppression I received as a student, including white privilege, the myth of meritocracy, and erasure—topics I could interrogate with my students as a teacher.

Navigating My Ethnic Identity Growing Up

In this narrative, I share my understanding of my lived experiences as a Puerto Rican growing up in the U.S. education system. The context described by Phinney (1990) as a theory on ethnic identity development, looks at the psychological relationship of ethnic and racial minority group members, examining personal and within-group views. Through my ethnic identity, I explore my sense of self as an educator in the United States, exploring my ethnic identity through my culture and language (Syed et al., 2013). I understand that my ethnic identity is a social construct and others impact how I affirm and reaffirm the boundaries of who I am (Kibria, 2000; Lyman & Douglas, 1973). In placing myself at the margins of my ethnic identity, I am able to integrate how culture and language influenced my role as an educator.

> *From Kindergarten until I graduated with my master's in education, I never had a Latinx teacher. Even worse, my education did not include my culture in my learning. This created a divide early on, between who I was at home and who I was at school. As early as elementary school, I unintentionally, but by design, navigated a hierarchy of which culture schools preferred. My proud Puerto Rican parents raised me in a Spanish-speaking working-class household. My father was in the military and we attended schools primarily with other military children all over the United States and the world. Often, I was the only student in my class who was Latinx. Throughout my K–12 education, I went to five elementary schools, two middle schools, and two high schools. Each time I went to a new school—because my parents marked Spanish as a language spoken at home—I would be pulled out of class and asked to pass an English proficiency test. Each time triggered questions in my head, "How many times do I have to pass this so I never have to prove myself again? Am I going to pass? Will they find out I don't know English well enough? Am I enough?"*

My experiences in education positioned English as the only language needed to be successful academically, consistent with monoglossic ideologies of subtraction bilingualism. García (2009) describes subtractive bilingualism: "When monoglossic ideologies persist, and monolingualism and monolingual schools are the norm, it is generally believed that children who speak a language other than that of the state should be encouraged to abandon that language and instead take up only the dominant language" (p. 51). My bilingualism was devalued, considered an obstacle that must be quickly removed. Flores and Schissel (2014) discuss the standards in the United States in which it mandates teachers to perpetuate the monoglossic language ideologies and urged educators to move toward more heteroglossic language ideologies. The historically encouraged viewpoint is to abandon the native language and instead take up the dominant language. Due to these monoglossic ideologies, as early as kindergarten, I was being positioned as a bilingual student navigating between my cultural and linguistic identities.

Spelling Test Blues and White Privilege

To examine my lived experiences and oppression as a student, I share a story from second grade. I attended a U.S. school in a classroom with a white monolingual teacher. I had feelings of being inferior and not working hard enough due to a deficit framework, very common with bilingual students (Chavez, 2012; Flores & Schissel, 2014; Lamar, 2019).

> *In second grade, I was the worst at spelling. I would study so hard, having my parents quiz me throughout the week. Yet on the day of the test, I would fail. The sounds in my head just didn't quite match the letters on the page. One day, after failing another spelling test, I got so frustrated, I ripped up my paper and threw it in the trash can outside the classroom. To make it worse, I would see my teacher congratulating my monolingual peers on how great they did. "Way to go, Mattie and Josh, you must have studied so hard." My white teacher found the ripped-up test and called me up to her desk. "Jennifer, you simply need to study harder and do better. Maybe your Spanish is hindering your learning."*
>
> *Because of this constant reminder that English was not my native language, as a student, I was hesitant to participate in class. When my teacher would call on me to read, my cheeks would get red from the anxiety of having to read aloud. I was so nervous that I would not read the words correctly and students would make fun of me. So, when I went into education, it stunned my family. No one in my family was an educator, but they supported me in my decision to become a teacher. My first experience of becoming an educator would happen after graduating with my bachelor's degree.*

In my experience of being told I was not working hard enough, my teacher was participating in the myth of meritocracy, a component of CRT. Bernal (2002) explains meritocracy: Individuals are assured that if they just work hard enough, no matter their race, ethnicity, or class, they can achieve anything. This advice does not consider the advantages of whites over historically marginalized groups.

My second-grade teacher's beliefs led her to think in these "American" ideals, devaluing my cultural and linguistic background. Her status as a white female meant she had white privilege. White privilege is "an invisible package of unearned assets" (McIntosh, 1997, p. 120). Tatum (1999) asserts that white privilege, although invisible, is real, infusing all areas of our lives. My linguistic knowledge was undervalued and even viewed as a deficit by my monolingual teacher. The design of standards in an education curriculum includes the invisibility of white privilege, devaluing "other" norms (Flores & Schissel, 2014). Additionally, Bernal (2002) summarizes, "The insidious nature of a Eurocentric epistemological perspective allows it to subtly (and not so subtly) shape the belief system and practices of researchers, educators, and the school curriculum while continuing to adversely influence the educational experiences of Chicanas/Chicanos and other students of color" (p. 202). As a teacher, I empathized with students because of these experiences, critically reflecting as I created lesson plans and considered the academic progress of my Latinx and all students (see narrative below).

The Decision to Become a Teacher

My desire to become a teacher was influenced by optimistic ideals common to other marginalized populations—"transformative pedagogical concepts and revolutionary curriculum" that disrupt the status quo (Lamar, 2019, p. 148). The following narrative charts the serendipitous path that led me to become a teacher.

After graduating with my bachelor's degree in psychology, a professor told me about an opportunity to teach in Spain. After speaking with him, I applied and got the job. Surprised to see they accepted me; I began the process of my visa so I could live in Spain for the next school year. Rather quickly, I moved to Spain for a year to teach English to middle and high school students. This would be my first job as an educator. In Puerto Rico, we often call Spain "la Madre España" [the Mother Spain] as it was a huge part of colonization. Having ancestral ties to Spain, I thought it would be a way to connect with my heritage. Once in Spain, I took that time to dig deeper not only into the Spanish language but also to learn about Spanish literature. I even joined a book club. In the book club with other teachers at the school, we would read books by Spanish authors in Spanish and then have discussions. These book club meetings reoriented me to the beauty of my native language and how it, too, is academic. Until that point, I had only thought of Spanish as a social language, not academic. Years of a U.S. education had made me devalue my bilingualism. I had absorbed the message that speaking English was the singular route toward academic success. Through this experience, I could find value in my heritage and felt inspired to become a teacher in the United States. It was the first time I saw people who looked like me teaching and it was powerful. That example showed me I, too, could be a teacher. This experience got me excited to come back to the United States to complete a master's in education and become a teacher. I had hopes I could bring some unique ideas into the classroom that encouraged multiculturalism and multilingualism. I was not yet aware of the strict guidelines in the curriculum I would have to follow, the scripted curriculum, or the pressures of standardized tests.

When you connect or see yourself in a profession, you are more likely to go into that field (Irizarry & Donaldson, 2012). For me to decide to become an educator in the United States, I first had to see people like me teaching. I navigated my ethnicity through exposure to Spanish literature in the book club. That is how I understood the world and later connected this important concept to my teaching. Lizárraga and Gutiérrez (2018) declare that the borders, *napantlas*, that multilingual and multicultural students negotiate should hold value in literacy. Stories and words transform learners' unique experiences, allowing them to "…navigate cultural, emotional, and cognitive borderlands" (p. 39). I rooted my beliefs in teaching to include stories and storytelling, a communal context, relating to the realities of students' lives (Ladson-Billings, 1995).

Silencing Ethnicity to Conform to Dominant Culture

Next, I discuss my experience at a Florida school where demographics were shifting. The oppression my Latinx students received translated into a form of silencing. Latinx students silence their ethnic identity as a mode of self-preservation to conform to the dominant culture and to be successful in school (Espin, 1993; García, 2009; Yosso, 2005).

When I got the fifth-grade teaching job at La Fresa Elementary, I was told that I was exactly "the type" of teacher "these kids" needed and offered the job. I accepted. Later I found out the school's demographics were changing, from being a primarily white monolingual school to one that included a higher Latinx population labeled as English Learners (ELs), meaning their primary language was not English.

During my first week working, teachers had that week before the students arrived to get their classrooms ready and attend faculty meetings. As an icebreaker activity with the staff, we divided into groups of five and did a faculty scavenger hunt. We went around the school completing different tasks. The last task was to take a picture as a group. When I looked at our picture, I noticed that I was the only Latinx person in the picture, with brown hair, tan skin, and brown eyes. The rest of the teachers were white with blond hair.

A few months into the start of the school year, three new students joined my class around the same time. None of them spoke English. As I got to know them, I learned that two had primary languages of Spanish and one Haitian Creole. This would be the first time I had students who knew little English. Curious about how best to help them, I spoke with my English language resource teacher. She was one of the few other Latinx teachers designated to assist in our school with students who were labeled "EL." The school received extra funding to provide extra assistance to learn English. I asked, "What can I do to better help my students during class?" She responded, "I'll create a time where I will pull them out of class or give you a website to put them on." Not feeling satisfied with her answer because it did not help when I was in class, I asked other teachers in the school what they did. The responses I got were horrifying, "The demographics in this place are changing, and not for the better," "The glory days are behind us," "They will either sink or swim," and "What do they want us to do, go to Haiti and learn the language?" I felt confused and frustrated because I did not have support for such injustice.

One morning I was working with one of my labeled ELs, Xavier. One of my newest students who had recently immigrated, his native language was Spanish, and he was attempting to do his work with his dictionary. This is a common practice among ELs; the school would provide an English/Spanish dictionary to all Spanish-speaking students. I asked him, "How are you doing?" Xavier told me, "Sé que tendré que olvidar mi español para aprender inglés" ["I know I will need to forget my Spanish to learn English"]. In shock, I said, "¿Por qué dices eso?" [Why do you say that?] He replied, "Pues, Mateo me dijo que para que él aprendiera inglés, tenía que olvidar su español. ["Well, Mateo (another student in the class) told me that for him to learn English, he had to forget his Spanish"]. His response affected me in such a way that I immediately reflected on my own experiences and what I could do as a teacher to help support his native heritage. How did a school with so many Latinx students not have a better system in place? I wanted social justice to challenge the inequities that schools perpetuate.

According to Freire (2000), education can be an instrument to enforce conformity or to transform oppression. Xavier's comment about forgetting Spanish to learn English reproduced conformity. The goal is not to merely tolerate non-dominant cultures and languages but to celebrate and value all cultural and linguistic knowledge (García, 2009; Ladson-Billings, 1995). The teachers I spoke to reminded me of my second-grade teacher. They exhibited the CRT tenets of white privilege, the devaluing of other languages, and the myth of meritocracy. They were all white, monolingual English speakers who saw Spanish as a challenge to overcome instead of as a valuable resource to bridge knowledge. Additionally, they believed that if students worked hard enough, they could succeed and would either "sink or swim."

Using Latinx Knowledge as a Tool of Resistance in Pedagogy

An element of CRT is the call for social justice in education (Delgado & Stefancic, 2001). In this next narrative, my Latinx background helped me seek social justice in my curriculum and to value culture and language, constantly asking questions of representation and whose story gets prioritized. My experience with Xavier inspired me to challenge the curriculum and think more critically about my teaching pedagogy. By sharing this narrative, I aim to help address the complexities of multicultural multilingual students by accepting and affirming their ethnic identities while developing critical perspectives that challenge inequities that schools (and other institutions) perpetuate (Ladson-Billings, 1995).

Social studies was the last subject of the day and often cut short or eliminated altogether due to dismissal. Interestingly, it was the only subject that included multicultural values in its standards. Because of the subject, it was a perfect way to infuse my multicultural ideas into the classroom and prioritize this time. The school had given us a workbook as a resource to help us teach social studies, almost like an afterthought that was formulaic. The lessons or curriculum never included how students could bridge multicultural and multilingual values to learn new content. During a social studies lesson, the topic was immigration and coming to an unknown land. The lesson was straightforward, discussing conquistadors and historical dates but not asking students to reflect on their own lived experiences, especially those who had immigrated to the United States. I yearned to figure out a way that would combine my students' culture and linguistic expertise.

Read alouds would be something my elementary students love. Introducing a social studies lesson included strategically selecting books to read aloud to situate the topic, but also to access prior knowledge. This was a common practice among teachers, but I was going to include community knowledge of my students from their multicultural and multilingual lives. I searched for all the multicultural resources I could find while still adhering to the standards. I had to look beyond what the school provided. To celebrate diverse backgrounds, I looked for bilingual books. My local library had a range of bilingual books in all the languages represented in my classroom (Spanish and French). Besides the book I would read aloud in class, I would also set out different bilingual books in our classroom library for students to explore independently.

The first experience reading a bilingual book to my students, I read the English part, and then I read the Spanish part. Dan, a student who was white and monolingual, said, "I didn't understand a word you said. Why did you even read that?" Connecting to our immigration topic as a class, we discussed how it might feel to come to the United States and not know English. Xavier said, "Es muy difícil dejar todo que tu sabes pero nosotros queremos una vida mejor." [It is difficult to leave all you know, but we wanted a better life.] The class got quiet for a second as students reflected on that. After that conversation, Dan said, "Wow, that must be really hard."

Freire (2000) maintains that the motivation behind teaching is never neutral—you either challenge the inequities or allow them. I challenged iniquities by developing positive school expectations, fostering a sense of belonging, and improving subsequent educational outcomes (Antrop-González & De Jesús, 2006). By purposefully selecting bilingual books to bring multicultural and multilingual stories into our classroom, the motivation behind my teaching was not neutral. My Latinx background uniquely positioned me to tap into my knowledge of culture and language to bring a more multicultural education for my students. Since I came from a community similar to that of my students, I took ownership and pride in my multicultural students' education but was also deeply knowledgeable of their histories, language, and traditions (Flores & García, 2017).

Discussion, Conclusions and Implications

This chapter is an examination of the experiences of one Latinx student and educator and how my experiences shaped the way I taught students in the classroom. This story illustrates the need for more salient research concerning Latinx teachers, and how their unique cultural and linguistic backgrounds set the stage for both representation and understanding (Bristol & Martin-Fernandez, 2019; Goldhaber et al., 2019).

The intention of this chapter is not to be generalizable. Instead, this story has transferability. My experiences are relatively common throughout limited research (Lamar, 2019). But my story lends depth and personalization to a better understanding of Latinx teacher experiences. Although this chapter focuses on one teacher, I feel it should be a stepping stone to further research in this important area of the broader subject of multiculturalism education. Centralizing the voices and stories of historically marginalized scholars facilitates understanding of how the normalization of oppression and inequality persist in education (Duncan, 2005) and functions to produce particular teacher identities. Hence, recognizing inequality, specifically race and language bias in American schools cannot be examined without capturing the narratives of those who have lived through these experiences (Chavez, 2012). Implications include highlighting the need for more diverse teacher stories and experiences. Future research should explore connections with marginalized teachers and experiences in the classroom, with broader implications of fostering multicultural values in teacher education programs and professional development. Vellanki and Prince (2018) noted silences in education in their exploration of multicultural teacher education programs. There is great potential for the application of this method to future interviews, discussion panels, and teacher preparation programs, employing a wider sample than this one autoethnographic work.

A particular strength of sharing my narratives concerning navigating my ethnic identity growing up, spelling test blues and white privilege, the decision to become a teacher, silencing ethnicity to conform to the dominant culture, and using Latinx knowledge as a tool of resistance in pedagogy is that they serve as a powerful reference to help researchers examine Latinx teachers. My story provides a data source for examining the potential impact of Latinx teachers on Latinx students, as well as the broader role of Latinx teachers in education.

My story offers many anecdotes to show how school policies regarding multicultural and multilingual pedagogy limit the educator and students alike. There is a considerable lack of research on Latinx teachers and students. Historically, the Latinx community in the United States is part of negative popular discourse, described by Carter (2014) as The Latino Threat Narrative (LTN). Politically this threat attacks language and culture. With some strides made in states like California and Arizona that just reversed English-only laws, it may be possible to find ways for deeper social integration of historically marginalized populations into school environments. The increasingly high growth rate of the proportion of Latinx students in the United States presents a unique backdrop of cultural context for research. Representation matters—we hear it so often that we may become desensitized to its significance. Representation of minoritized groups in education is incredibly powerful, changing the way we think and breaking dominant power structures.

Thus, additional research is required to generate possible multicultural and multilingual responses to the Latinx population and to answer the call for more research that includes marginalized voices (Bristol & Martin-Fernandez, 2019; Goldhaber et al., 2019; Gomez & Rodriguez, 2011). Missing from teacher education programs is a more welcoming and supportive context for Latinx students to become educators, and for Latinx and other pre-service teachers of color to explore how their identities connect to teaching (Gomez & Rodriguez, 2011). This research calls for teacher educators to make spaces in their classrooms for students to listen to and share stories of their experiences, particularly stories that can highlight ethnic backgrounds describing disadvantages or privilege. These experiences promise to create a much-needed dialogue among all future teachers by creating school cultures that are inclusive of all cultures, ethnicities, and languages starting as early as elementary school. Building support networks within the community that value the families and students who attend the school will create inclusive spaces, address the opportunity gap, and provide positive associations with multiculturalism in the school environment (Ladson-Billings, 1994, 1995). CRT and autoethnography are the manners in which I think about the world and the ways I have described my experiences. A person's multicultural and multilingual identity should be celebrated as a superpower, not denigrated as an obstacle.

The impact of these findings on future research helps share counter-stories of minority teachers in the classroom. In the United States, a push for diverse teachers in the classroom has been discussed yet our teacher prep programs do not reflect that. In this chapter, I discuss my Latinx knowledge as a tool of resistance in pedagogy that serves as a powerful reference to help researchers examine Latinx teachers. My story provides a data source for examining the potential impact of Latinx teachers on Latinx students, as well as the broader role of Latinx teachers in education.

References

Antrop-González, R., & De Jesús, A. (2006). Toward a theory of critical care in urban small school reform: Examining structures and pedagogies of caring in two Latino community-based schools. *International Journal of Qualitative Studies in Education, 19*, 409–433.

Aveling, N. (2006). "Hacking at our very roots": Rearticulating White racial identity within the context of teacher education. *Race Ethnicity and Education, 9*(3), 261–274. https://doi.org/10.1080/13613320600807576

Bartolomé, L. I. (2004). Critical pedagogy and teacher education: Radicalizing prospective teachers. *Teacher Education Quarterly, 31*, 97–122.

Bartolomé, L. I. (2008). Authentic cariño and respect in minority education: The political and ideological dimensions of love. *The International Journal of Critical Pedagogy, 1*(1), 1–16.

Bell, D. (1995). Who's afraid of critical race theory? *University of Illinois Law Review, 1995*(4), 893–910. https://doi.org/10.1177/0011392109342205

Bernal, D. (2002). Critical race theory, Latino critical theory, and critical raced-gendered epistemologies: Recognizing students of color as holders and creators of knowledge. *Qualitative Inquiry, 8*(1), 105–126. https://doi.org/10.1177/107780040200800107

Bochner, A. P. (2012). On first-person narrative scholarship: Autoethnography as acts of meaning. *Narrative Inquiry, 22*(1), 155–164.

Bochner, A. P., & Ellis, C. (1996). Talking over autoethnography. In C. Ellis & A. Bochner (Eds.), *Composing ethnography: Alternative forms of qualitative writing* (pp. 13–45). AltaMira Press.

Boylorn, R. M., & Orbe, M. P. (Eds.). (2014). *Critical autoethnography: Intersecting cultural identities in everyday life*. Left Coast Press.

Bristol, T., & Martin-Fernandez, J. (2019). The added value of Latinx and Black teachers for Latinx and Black students: Implications for policy. *Policy Insights From the Behavioral and Brain Sciences, 6*(2), 147–153. https://doi.org/10.1177/2372732219862573

Carter, P. M. (2014). National narratives, institutional ideologies, and local talk: The discursive production of Spanish in a new U.S. Latino community. *Language in Society, 43*(2), 209–240. https://doi.org/10.1017/S0047404514000049

Chavez, M. (2012). Autoethnography, a Chicana's methodological research tool: The role of storytelling for those who have no choice but to do critical race theory. *Equity and Excellence in Education, 45*(2), 334–348.

Clanindin, D. J., & Connelly, F. M. (2000). *Narrative inquiry: Experience and story in qualitative research*. Jossey-Bass.

Coker, J., & Cain, L. (2018). Southern disclosure: One southern-and-queer middle school teacher's narrative. *Middle Grades Review, 4*(3), 1–9.

Covarrubias, A., & Lara, A. (2014). The undocumented (im)migrant educational pipeline: The influence of citizenship status on educational attainment for people of Mexican origin. *Urban Education, 49*(1), 75–110. https://doi.org/10.1177/0042085912470468

Delgado, R., & Stefancic, J. (2001). *Critical race theory: An introduction*. University Press.

Denzin, N. K. (1997). *Interpretive ethnography: Ethnographic practices for the 21st century*. Sage.

Duncan, G. A. (2005). Critical race ethnography in education: Narrative, inequality, and the problem of epistemology. *Race, Ethnicity & Education, 8*(1), 93–114.

Ellis, C., & Bochner, A. (2000). Autoethnography, personal narrative, reflexivity: Researcher as subject. In N. Denzin & Y. Lincoln (Eds.), *Handbook of qualitative research* (pp. 733–768). Sage.

Flores, N., & García, O. (2017). A critical review of bilingual education in the United States: From basements and pride to boutiques and profit. *Annual Review of Applied Linguistics, 37*(2017), 14–29. https://doi.org/10.1017/S0267190517000162

Flores, N., & Schissel, J. (2014). Dynamic bilingualism as the norm: Envisioning a heteroglossic approach to standards-based reform. *TESOL Quarterly, 48*(3), 454–479. https://doi.org/10.1002/tesq.182

Freire, P. (2000). *Pedagogy of the oppressed* (30th anniversary ed.). Continuum (Original work published 1970).

García, O. (2009). *Bilingual education in the 21st century: A global perspective*. Basil/Blackwell.

Goldhaber, D., Theobald, R., & Tien, C. (2019). Why we need a diverse teacher workforce. *Phi Delta Kappan, 100*(5), 25–30. https://doi.org/10.1177/0031721719827540

Gomez, L., & Rodriguez, T. L. (2011). Imagining the knowledge, strengths, and skills of a Latina prospective teacher. *Teacher Education Quarterly, 38*(1), 127–146.

Heath. S. B., & Street, B. V. (2008). *Ethnography: Approaches to language and literacy research*. Teachers College Press.

Hughes, S. A., Pennington, J. L., & Makris, S. (2012). Translating autoethnography across the AERA Standards: Toward understanding autoethnographic scholarship as empirical research. *Educational Researcher, 41*, 209–219.

Iglesias, E. (1997). Forward: International law, human rights, and LatCrit theory. *University of Miami Inter-American Law Review, 28*, 177–213.

Irizarry, J., & Donaldson, M. L. (2012). Teach for America: The Latinization of U.S. schools and the critical shortage of Latina/o teachers. *American Educational Research Journal, 49*(1), 155–194. https://doi.org/10.3102/0002831211434764

Kehly, M. J. (1995). Self-narration, autobiography and identity construction. *Gender & Education, 7*(1), 23–31.

Kibria, N. (2000). Race, ethnic options, and ethnic binds: Identity negotiations of second-generation Chinese and Korean Americans. *Sociological Perspectives, 43*, 77–95. https://doi.org/10.2307/1389783

Ladson-Billings, G. (1994). *The dreamkeepers: Successful teachers of African American children*. Jossey-Bass Publishers.

Ladson-Billings, G. (1995). Toward a theory of culturally relevant pedagogy 2.0: Aka the remix. *Harvard Educational Review, 84*(1), 465–491.

Lamar, A. (2019). An irregular verb that cannot be conjugated: One Latina's autoethnographic journey out of teaching. In C. R. Rinke & L. Mawhinney (Eds.), *Opportunities and challenges in teaching recruitment and retention* (pp. 147–171). Information Age Publishing.

Lizárraga, J. R., & Gutiérrez, K. D. (2018). Centering nepantla literacies from the borderlands: Leveraging "in-betweenness" toward learning in the everyday. *Theory Into Practice, 57*(1), 38–47. https://doi.org/10.1080/00405841.2017.1392164

Lyman, S. M., & Douglas, W. A. (1973). Ethnicity: Strategies of collective and individual impression management. *Social Research, 40*, 344–365.

McIntosh, P. (1997). White privilege: Unpacking the invisible knapsack. In B. Schneider (Ed.), *An anthology: Race in the first person* (pp. 119–126). Crown Trade Paperbacks.

National Center for Educational Statistics. (2018). *Digest of educational statistics, 2018*. Department of Education. https://nces.ed.gov/fastfacts/display.asp?id=28

Phinney, J. S. (1990). Ethnic identity in adolescents and adults: Review of research. *Psychological Bulletin, 108*, 499–514. https://doi.org/10.1037/0033-2909.108.3.499

Solórzano, D., & Yosso, T. J. (2001). Critical race and LatCrit theory and method: Counter-storytelling. *International Journal of Qualitative Studies in Education, 14*(4), 471–495. https://doi.org/10.1080/09518390110063365

Solórzano, D., & Yosso, T. J. (2002). Critical race methodology: Counter-storytelling as an analytical framework for education research. *Qualitative Inquiry, 8*(1), 23–44. https://doi.org/10.1177/107780040200800103

Syed, M., Walker, L. H., Lee, R. M., Umaña-Taylor, A. J., Zamboanga, B. L., Schwartz, S. J., et al. (2013). A two-factor model of ethnic identity exploration: Implications for identity coherence and well-being. *Cultural Diversity & Ethnic Minority Psychology, 19*, 143–154. https://doi.org/10.1037/a0030564

Tatum, B. (1999). *Why are all the Black kids sitting together in the cafeteria? And other conversations about race*. Basic Books.

Vellanki, V., & Prince, S. P. (2018). Where are the "People Like me"?: A collaborative autoethnography of transnational lives and teacher education in the U.S. *The Teacher Educator, 53*(3), 313–327. https://doi.org/10.1080/08878730.2018.1462873

Yazan, B. (2019). Toward identity-oriented teacher education: Critical autoethnographic narrative. *TESOL Journal, 10*(1), 1–15.

Yosso, T. (2005). Whose culture has capital? A critical race theory discussion of community cultural wealth. *Race Ethnicity and Education, 8*(1), 69–91. https://doi.org/10.1080/1361332052000341006

Jennifer M. Barreto is an Assistant Professor at Eastern Michigan University in the department of Teacher Education. Her research interest includes equity and diversity and how it pertains to identity development with multicultural and multilingual students.

Open Access This chapter is licensed under the terms of the Creative Commons Attribution 4.0 International License (http://creativecommons.org/licenses/by/4.0/), which permits use, sharing, adaptation, distribution and reproduction in any medium or format, as long as you give appropriate credit to the original author(s) and the source, provide a link to the Creative Commons license and indicate if changes were made.

The images or other third party material in this chapter are included in the chapter's Creative Commons license, unless indicated otherwise in a credit line to the material. If material is not included in the chapter's Creative Commons license and your intended use is not permitted by statutory regulation or exceeds the permitted use, you will need to obtain permission directly from the copyright holder.

Chapter 29
New Zealand: The Experiences of Māori Teachers as an Ethnic Minority in English-Medium Schools

Hana Turner-Adams and Christine Rubie-Davies

Abstract This chapter discusses the experiences of Māori teachers who are currently or were previously employed in English-medium schools and early childhood centers in New Zealand. The New Zealand education system has a long history of failing to meet the educational needs of Māori students, and the demand for teachers to improve students' academic outcomes has increased. Māori teachers connect and engage more readily with Māori students due to their shared culture and background. In contrast, many Pākehā/New Zealand European teachers have a limited understanding of Māori language, knowledge systems, values, and customs, and often hold low expectations for Māori student achievement. Findings from our study revealed that Māori teachers carried a substantial cultural and pastoral workload. On average, teachers reported spending at least 5½ hours per week working with Māori students and their whānau (family) in addition to their full-time teaching responsibilities. Although most teachers were acknowledged for their contributions through additional remuneration or time-release, others received no recognition. Participants were committed to their students but often worked in unwelcoming and unsupportive Eurocentric environments. Teachers were also disheartened by the general lack of commitment of their non-Māori colleagues to Māori language, culture, and values, yet were expected to guide, support, and educate these colleagues on how to meet their obligations to Māori students. The chapter concludes with suggestions for how school principals, center managers, and other teachers, could better support Māori teachers so that they continue making valuable contributions to their students' education and remain employed in the teaching profession.

H. Turner-Adams (✉) · C. Rubie-Davies
University of Auckland, Auckland, New Zealand
e-mail: h.turner@auckland.ac.nz

Introduction

Māori teachers occupy a unique place in New Zealand English-medium schools and centers. Although Māori comprise 16.5% of the New Zealand population, only 10% of teachers are Māori compared with 73% of Pākehā (NZ European) and 10% of teachers of other ethnicities (Education Counts, 2020). The English-medium system, where most Māori teachers work, has failed generations of Māori students and their families (Controller Auditor-General, 2016; Ministry of Education, 2012b, 2013b). Any enactment of Māori language and culture in English-medium settings occurs within the structural and cultural constraints of Pākehā-dominated, Eurocentric organizations.

The low number of Māori teachers employed in English-medium schools and centers means that many are culturally isolated, with no other Māori colleagues for support. Individual Māori teachers are commonly assigned responsibility for all Māori-related matters. These include cultural and pastoral leadership, kapa haka (Māori performing arts), rituals such as pōwhiri (traditional welcoming ceremony), and supporting non-Māori colleagues with Māori students and curriculum queries (Whitehead et al., 2000). Māori teachers' extra responsibilities are often in addition to a full teaching load, and may lack any time allowance or further remuneration (Torepe et al., 2018; Torepe & Manning, 2018). For many Māori teachers, the heavy workload has led to job dissatisfaction and attrition (Mitchell & Mitchell, 1993). Therefore, it is crucial that more teachers are recruited to boost the Māori teaching population, and that those currently employed are appropriately supported to remain in the profession.

Research Objective

This qualitative research study aimed to provide insights into the experiences of Māori teachers who were currently (or previously) employed in English-medium early childhood education centers, primary (elementary) schools, or secondary (high) schools in New Zealand. The study also sought to identify the personal benefits and challenges of being a Māori teacher and the extra contributions they made to their students and school community. Teachers with previous English-medium experience were included to uncover the reasons why Māori teachers might leave the profession or change to a different sector (e.g., Māori-medium education). It is also important to investigate how school leaders could better support and acknowledge Māori teachers' contributions, retain current teachers, and attract more Māori teachers to the profession.

The research questions guiding this study were:

1. What are the benefits and challenges for Māori teachers working in an English-medium school or center?
2. What changes need to be made within schools/centers and in education more broadly, to attract and retain Māori teachers within the profession?

The New Zealand Context

New Zealand is an island nation of five million people, situated in the South Pacific. Australia and the Pacific Islands of Fiji, Tonga, and New Caledonia are its closest neighbours. Māori people are Indigenous to New Zealand, but following British settlement in the early 1800s, their culture has been systematically marginalized through colonization and assimilatory educational policies.

Since European-style schooling began in 1816, the New Zealand education system has primarily reflected the language, beliefs, and values of the dominant Pākehā ethnic group while actively discouraging Māori language, ideas, and knowledge. Historically, the purpose of schooling for Māori until the mid-twentieth century was to educate students for manual labour and the low-skilled workforce. Māori were not perceived by Pākehā to be capable of further education or professional occupations.

Māori Teachers

The numbers of Māori teachers employed in New Zealand has historically been low. In Native Schools (rural schools in Māori communities that operated between 1867 and 1969), teachers were initially Pākehā (and not always qualified). Local Māori who had 1–2 years of high school education were employed as junior teaching assistants. In the mid-1900s, it became challenging to recruit Pākehā beginning teachers as they were reluctant to be posted to Native schools. Consequently, principals recommended that suitably qualified Māori assistants be trained as teachers. The government introduced a Māori quota system, and in 1940, the first four Māori students entered teacher training (Calman, 2012; Fletcher, 1948; Walker, 2016). Following World War II, teacher shortages led the government to increase the Māori quota from the initial four teachers to approximately 60 teachers per year (Walker, 2016). According to Walker (2016):

> These teachers constituted the second wave of graduates and intellectuals who engaged in the praxis of liberating Māori from educational subjection. Their objective was to carefully incorporate elements of Māori culture (including art and songs) into their classrooms while avoiding a Pākehā backlash (p. 28).

Māori boarding schools, one of the few options for Māori students to obtain a high school education, also supported the entry of Māori teachers into the profession. Some students stayed on at school until they had qualified as teachers and later were employed at the boarding schools they had attended as students. Old Girls' Association scholarships also supported the training of further Māori teachers (Jenkins & Morris Matthews, 1998).

Māori-driven educational initiatives such as Te Kōhanga Reo (Māori-medium language nests/preschools), Kura Kaupapa Māori (Māori-medium elementary schools), and wharekura (Māori-medium high schools) were instituted in the 1980s to support the revitalization of te reo Māori (Māori language) and increase the numbers of Māori language speakers (Tocker, 2015). These kura (schools) needed trained teachers who were fluent in te reo Māori. Today, Māori students who attend Māori medium education achieve at higher levels in national qualifications than Māori students in English-medium schools (Education Counts, 2021). However, fewer Māori students are enrolled in Māori-medium education (more than 95% of Māori students attend English-medium education). In English-medium schools where kaupapa Māori (Māori philosophies) and relational pedagogy have been introduced, there have also been improved levels of academic success for Māori (Bishop et al., 2003).

Since the early 2000s, demand has increased for teachers to respond to and meet the educational needs and aspirations of Māori students (Ministry of Education, 2008, 2013a). Some researchers have argued that Māori teachers are a vital element in improving and advancing the educational outcomes of Māori students (Lee, 2005, June 24; McNaughton, 2020). Māori teachers can connect and engage more readily with Māori students due to their shared culture and background. In contrast, many Pākehā teachers have limited awareness of Māori language, knowledge systems, values, and customs (Bishop et al., 2003; Bishop & Glynn, 2011; McKinley, 2002), and struggle to relate to Māori students.

Despite the recent focus on improved educational outcomes for Māori, achievement disparities between Māori and non-Māori persist (New Zealand Qualifications Authority, 2017). In many schools, deficit theorizing and low expectations for Māori students endure (Turner et al., 2015), along with resistance by some teachers and academic scholars to incorporate Māori history, knowledge, and relational pedagogy into the curriculum (Rata, 2012). Like their students, Māori teachers navigate an English-medium, mainstream system, where their culture, knowledge, and language are sidelined in favor of the dominant Pākehā culture. At the same time, Māori teachers are expected to guide non-Māori colleagues to integrate Māori language and knowledge into their programmes and to understand their obligations under the Treaty of Waitangi (Gilgen, 2016; Mitchell & Mitchell, 1993; Torepe & Manning, 2018).

The Treaty of Waitangi was an agreement signed in 1840 between 540 Māori chiefs and representatives of the British Crown that promised to provide equal rights for Māori and Pākehā in New Zealand. When Māori signed the Treaty, they agreed to allow the Crown to govern but retained authority over their lands, villages, and all their treasures. Differences in the Māori and English texts of the Treaty have led to ongoing disputes about the level of authority Māori retained and what they ceded to the Crown (Barrett & Connolly-Stone, 1998). Although the Treaty has always been a critical point of reference for Māori, it was not honored by the Crown or considered within New Zealand law or government policies (including education) until near the end of the twentieth century (Tomlins-Jahnke & Warren, 2011).

Within education currently, teachers are expected to meet their Treaty of Waitangi obligations through the principles of partnership, participation, and protection. Partnership means that Māori are equal decision-makers in all educational issues that involve Māori students and their families. Participation ensures that Māori students have equality of access and opportunity to participate fully in all levels of education and schooling. Finally, protection ensures Māori knowledge, interests, values, and treasures are protected. The survival and safeguarding of Māori language for future generations is an important aspect of the protection principle (Ministry of Education, 2012a; Tomlins-Jahnke & Warren, 2011).

To maintain their teacher registration and practicing certificate, New Zealand teachers are required to use te reo me ona tikanga Māori (Māori language and culture/customs) in their practice (Education Council of Aotearoa New Zealand, 2017, p. 17). However, evidence suggests that this is not always happening (Tito, 2008). The limited implementation of Māori language and knowledge in New Zealand schools and centers is exacerbated by the low numbers of non-Māori teachers who speak te reo Māori and understand Māori culture (Bishop & Glynn, 2011).

Initial teacher education programmes have begun to introduce more Māori language into their courses. However, these courses are often at an elementary level (e.g., basic pronunciation, greetings, colors, and numbers). Consequently, they do little to increase the level of te reo Māori spoken in English-medium schools/centers unless teachers commit time to Māori language learning. Some training institutions offer a Bachelor of Education in Māori-medium education for students already proficient in te reo Māori. However, most graduates of Māori-medium programmes go on to work in Te Kōhanga Reo and Kura Kaupapa Māori, not English-medium education (Education Counts, 2020). Therefore, all teachers in English-medium schools/centers must meet the requirements for implementing te reo me ona tikanga Māori, and the Treaty of Waitangi into their practice to help reduce the workload on Māori teachers who are over-burdened supporting their colleagues in these areas.

Māori Teachers' Experiences in English-Medium Schools and Centers

There is limited research that focuses on the experiences of Māori teachers in English-medium education. Mitchell and Mitchell's (1993) study explored why Māori teachers left the profession, and Lee's (2008) doctorate researched high school te reo Māori teachers' experiences. Other studies in this field are primarily Master's theses (Coffin, 2013; Gilgen, 2016). An exception is the research of Torepe and colleagues (Torepe et al., 2018; Torepe & Manning, 2018). They investigated the experiences of Māori teachers who returned to teaching in mainstream schools after completing a Māori immersion/bilingual teaching qualification. Further research is needed to confirm whether Māori teachers' current workload and conditions are consistent with those found in earlier studies.

Methodology

This study utilized a generic qualitative inquiry approach—a research methodology that investigates participants' experiences and seeks their views, attitudes, beliefs, thoughts, or reflections about those experiences. It works well with data collected via surveys (Percy et al., 2015) as in the current study. Our survey transcripts were analyzed thematically following the steps outlined in Braun and Clarke's (2006) inductive approach for analyzing qualitative data.

Participants

The participants were 16 teachers of Māori descent who completed an anonymous online survey about their experiences in English-medium education. All teachers were currently teaching or had previously taught in English-medium schools or centers. Fourteen participants were female, and two were male. Participants were from the elementary (10/16), high school (2/16), or the early childhood sector (3/16). One teacher had taught across both the elementary and high school sectors. Teaching experience ranged from less than 6 years to more than 20 years, with 50% of teachers in the 1–5 years range. The most common qualification was a Bachelor's degree (12/16), three teachers had a Master's degree, and nine had diplomas or postgraduate diplomas.

Procedure

Through advertisements posted on social media and teaching networks, Māori teachers were invited to complete a survey about their current or previous experiences teaching in English-medium education. An online, anonymous, open-ended survey was selected as it enabled the efficient collection of data from teacher participants throughout New Zealand. Another benefit of online surveys is that they provoke more honest answers from participants who may answer in more socially acceptable ways if interviewed face-to-face (Fricker & Schonlau, 2002). An open-ended survey has the added advantage of eliciting a wide range of spontaneous and varied responses from participants. In contrast, closed questions limit participants to answers that are provided by the researcher (Reja et al., 2003). A list of the survey questions is provided in Fig. 29.1.

Findings and Discussion

This section reports the thematically analyzed data from the teachers' online surveys and discusses how each theme aligns with existing research literature. The eight themes are displayed in Fig. 29.2. The first five themes describe Māori teacher-identified benefits and challenges of teaching in English medium education. The final three themes discuss why Māori teachers leave teaching and suggest changes to improve retention and conditions for Māori teachers.

> **Open-ended online survey questions**
> - How does your school/center acknowledge the work you do with/for Māori students/children? (e.g., management units, bonus payments, non-contact time, no acknowledgement, etc.
> - What have been the greatest challenges for you as a Māori teacher in an English-medium school/center?
> - Have you seriously considered leaving teaching (or have you gone on extended leave)? If so, what were the reasons?
> - What do you think English-medium schools/centers or the Ministry of Education could do to attract more Māori teachers or to retain more Māori teachers in the profession?

Fig. 29.1 Survey questions

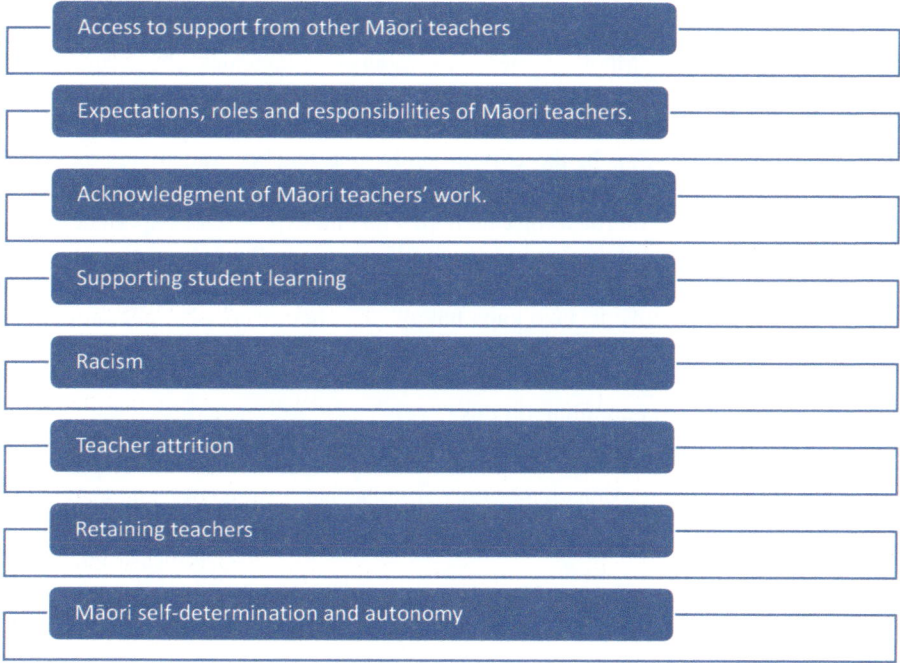

Fig. 29.2 Themes from the data analysis

Access to Support from Other Māori Teachers Participants reported that the number of Māori teachers employed in their schools or centers ranged from 1–10 teachers; the average was 3.8. For teachers who were the sole Māori teacher in a school or center (5/16), "Not having other Māori teachers to feed off" was a challenge. All three early childhood education participants identified that they were the only Māori teacher in their centers. However, nine teachers were in schools with four or more Māori colleagues, and they relished the support and the opportunities for collaboration. For example, "I had a great team (Māori teachers) to work with. We would always get together to have a chat about anything". This finding differed from prior research (Mitchell & Mitchell, 1993; Torepe, 2011), where teachers frequently reported that they experienced cultural isolation and loneliness as the only Māori teacher in a school. It is pleasing that schools are employing more than one Māori teacher. However, collegial support also needs to be a focus for English-medium early childhood centers.

Expectations, Roles, and Responsibilities of Māori Teachers Along with teaching their students and planning lessons, Māori teachers were responsible for a wide range of cultural activities in their school or center. Table 29.1 presents a list of the teachers' roles and responsibilities and the number of teachers who reported each type. The time teachers spent weekly on these tasks, over and above their general teaching responsibilities, ranged from 1 hour to 30 hours, with an average time of 5½ hours per week.

A common issue for Māori teachers was leaders or colleagues who assumed that being Māori made them an expert or authority on all aspects of Māori culture and knowledge. Participants in Torepe's (2011) research referred to this as being "a one-stop-Māori-shop" (p. 77). In the current study, one teacher said it was expected "[That] I know absolutely everything to do with 'things' Māori". Other teachers were pressured to take on roles for which they had no expertise or experience. One said, "Some schools send the hard-to-teach Māori kids to the Māori teacher to 'fix up'… or, you are Māori, you take kapa haka. …If they looked at my CV, you will see no mention of 'I love to take kapa haka'". Teachers were also uncomfortable when they were expected to speak on behalf of all Māori. For example, one teacher wondered, "How one person like me can speak on all the issues of Māori and tikanga… Am I Māori enough to do this?"

Table 29.1 Māori teachers additional roles and responsibilities

Role or responsibility	Number of participants
Interacting with and advocating for whānau Māori/organizing whānau hui[a]	6
Kapa haka[b]	8
Pōwhiri[c]	3
Te reo me ona tikanga Māori[d] consultant/specialist	6
Karakia[e]	1
Management role (e.g., HOD; senior leader)	4
Bilingual/whānau unit	2
Responsible for all things Māori in their school	4

[a]A meeting that involves families; [b]Māori performing arts; [c]Traditional welcoming ceremony; [d]Māori language and culture; [e]Chanted incantation or prayer (not necessarily religious)

Finally, some participants' relational skills with Māori students and whānau led others to assume that they could support students and families from all non-dominant ethnic groups in their schools or centers. One teacher said she was the "Overall advocate for Māori whānau and Pasifika families [those originating from the Pacific Islands], and minority groups".

The wide range of demands on Māori teachers because of their ethnicity are described by Padilla (1994) as 'cultural taxation'. Other studies (Torepe, 2011; Torepe et al., 2018; Torepe & Manning, 2018) have also acknowledged that multiple additional roles, for which Māori teachers often felt a cultural obligation, came at a personal and professional cost. Many teachers reported feeling 'burned out' or unable to maintain high standards in other aspects of their work (Torepe, 2011). It was evident that there needed to be greater support and acknowledgement of Māori teachers' work.

Acknowledgment of Māori Teachers' Work To acknowledge the time spent on additional tasks for Māori students and whānau, nine of the participants in this study received management units (MU; $5000 per unit per annum), a middle management allowance (MMA; $2000 per allowance per annum), or a Māori Immersion Teacher Allowance (MITA; $4000 per annum). Management units provide teachers with an extra hour of non-contact time, but there is no time allowance attached to MMAs or MITAs (PPTA, 2020).

One teacher who reported spending an additional 30 hours per week on her further responsibilities referred to her school's unwillingness to allocate management units to Māori. She said:

> You could grow tomatoes, call yourself Head of Environment and receive a Management unit. [But] for me to argue that the bilingual unit should receive a management unit? I had to walk away from my job and give that role to someone else because the top didn't want me to have more [management units] than the DP [Deputy Principal].

Some participants received extra non-contact time in addition to management units, whereas other teachers only received time off or were thanked in staff meetings. Two participants did not receive any acknowledgement or payment for their additional roles and responsibilities.

Previous research has reported that the cultural labor of Māori teachers is consistently unrecognized, inadequately supported, or unpaid (Mitchell & Mitchell, 1993; Torepe & Manning, 2018). Although more than half the teachers in the current study received some form of extra payment, none came close to compensating the actual time that teachers expended. Nonetheless, participants were strongly committed to supporting their students' learning.

Supporting Student Learning Teachers valued the opportunity to share Māori language and culture in their schools or centers and reported that most of their students enjoyed it. Other teachers reflected positively that Māori language and culture now had its rightful space in mainstream education, after being excluded for so many decades. For example:

We have a culturally diverse kindergarten,[1] and I love that I am able to share what I know with our tamariki [children] from all over the world. I love that our language is celebrated as this was certainly not the case when I was growing up.

As Māori teachers, participants were particularly committed to teaching Māori students and ensuring their success. One teacher explained, "I love the children, all children, but I am drawn to upholding the mana [status] of Māori children …. playing my part in setting them up with high expectations for their future education".

Teachers were especially proud of Māori students who they observed navigating successfully between the Māori and Pākehā worlds. For example, "Working with tauira Māori [Māori students] who naturally converse in te reo or English, depending upon who they are conversing with—seeing our tauira Māori me kaiako [Māori students and teachers] carrying their culture with them throughout the day". Durie (2001) argued that education must prepare Māori students to be successful in both te ao Māori (the Māori world) and te ao Pākehā (the Pākehā world). Māori teachers have an essential role in ensuring that students have access to Māori language, knowledge, and culture to increase their opportunities for dual success by the time they finish their education. Unfortunately, racism continues to impede Māori teachers working in English-medium education.

Racism Most participants had been subjected to or had witnessed racism in their schools or centers. Sometimes, the discrimination was blatant. For example, one teacher said, "On my first day in a new school, my team leader referred to Māori and Pasifika students as 'bloody coconuts'. I should have called him out, but I was just too shocked…" Other teachers reported that school/center leaders and those in governance positions were racist. For example, "A BOT [Board of Trustees][2] member took his kids out of our school because I was opening another bilingual class. His statement: 'it's getting too *Māori* here'. At the time, we had 86% Māori students". Another teacher said, "The BOT and Senior Management hold ideas that frankly are racist…Schools make the 'culture' uninviting to anyone who isn't white; it's toxic. But the Pākehā teachers don't understand this because it is a white-cultured school".

Teachers reported that there was a sense that Māori language and culture had a low priority in their schools and centers. For example, "We always come beneath English" and "You always had to push for Māori rights using school policies". In some cases, teachers felt alone in supporting Māori students and families. One teacher said, "[There was a] lack of commitment from the other teachers to ensuring whānau Māori [Māori families] and Pasifika and minority groups were valued, respected, and honored. Although there were some teachers who tried, the majority did not and were racist." Unsurprisingly, racism and a lack of support led to teacher attrition.

---

[1] In NZ, Kindergartens are early childhood education/preschools.

[2] In NZ, schools are self-managing and governed by a Board of Trustees which is made up of elected representatives from the school community (primarily parents of students) and the principal. The Ministry of Education funds, resources, and monitors schools, but has no direct authority as long as schools operate within the law (Wylie, 2012).

Teacher Attrition For the participants who had left English-medium education, or seriously considered leaving, their reasons included insufficient support, a lack of commitment to the Treaty of Waitangi, and being worn down through mental or physical exhaustion. One teacher said, "Māori teachers get hōhā (annoyed) or burnt out having to deal with so much". Attrition is common across the research on Māori teachers. Mitchell and Mitchell's (1993) study found that Māori teachers who had left the profession, did so for various reasons including stress due to excessive workloads. Subsequent studies have highlighted similar findings (Whitehead et al., 2000), and recent research by Torepe and colleagues (Torepe, 2011; Torepe et al., 2018; Torepe & Manning, 2018) reported that 50% of their original participants had left teaching.

One teacher in the current study who had left English-medium education to work in Māori-medium education was not interested in returning. She said,

> I won't work in mainstream early childhood education again. I left because there is a noticeable lack of authentic commitment to Te Tiriti o Waitangi (the Treaty of Waitangi). Whānau Māori were not respected—including myself—yet [we] were expected to be performing seals on certain occasions…

The expectation for Māori teachers to perform pōwhiri or other Māori rituals in English-medium schools or centers aligns with existing research (Stewart, 2020; Stewart et al., 2015). It can be difficult for Māori teachers to reconcile their leaders' or colleagues' desire to include these rituals in the school culture while simultaneously holding racist, disrespectful, and deficit beliefs about Māori students and their whānau (Stewart, 2020). Engagement with Māori culture should not be tokenistic or only on display for celebratory or public-facing events (Torepe & Manning, 2018). A genuine commitment to Māori teachers, students, and their whānau comes from respecting and normalizing Māori culture in schools/centers.

Retaining Teachers The Māori teachers who remained working in English-medium education stayed because of a "passion for their students". They had not considered leaving because, as one teacher said, "There's still too much to do!" However, teachers understood the challenges of teaching in the mainstream. One teacher said, "Kaiako Māori (Māori teachers) who leave the profession do so because they work in schools where colonization remains the status quo, and they become powerless". She encouraged Māori teachers to "…work alongside more kaiako Māori, [where they] have the collective strength to make changes – and be happier in their work. Maybe then, they'll stick around as long as I have (39 years)."

Participants recognized that for Māori teachers to be attracted to teaching or retained in English-medium schools and centers, major culture shifts were required. For some organizations, acknowledging that Pākehā culture was entrenched and that current practices were not inclusive or supportive of Māori was an essential first step. Furthermore, self-determination and autonomy were seen as a solution for improving English-medium education settings for Māori.

Māori Self-Determination and Autonomy Participants strongly asserted that educational success for Māori students depended on Māori involvement and decision-making. One teacher said, "I firmly believe in the catch cry: 'By Māori, for Māori, with Māori' 'cos Pākehā don't know, nor will they ever know, what it means to be Māori… they won't break down the barriers that constrain us…" Some participants also noted that Māori teachers needed to be in leadership to ensure success for their students. For example,

> My one reason for moving into 'management' in 2013 was to safeguard the establishment of the reo rua (bilingual) unit which was initiated and co-founded by myself and my teina (younger sibling) …In true consultation with our Māori community, we built a kaupapa (philosophy) which focused on tauira Māori learning as Māori to enable high Māori student achievement.

Finally, several teachers emphasized the importance of working in schools where Māori people, histories, and world views were valued and where they could *be Māori*. One teacher explained, "Māori teachers need to be in safe spaces where being Māori is respected and honored".

The assertion that Māori-led initiatives will lead to the best outcomes for Māori is supported in the literature relating to kaupapa Māori education (Tocker, 2007, 2015). However, in English-medium education, where most Māori are located, the Pākehā-centric structures and culture obstruct self-determination and autonomy for Māori. Notwithstanding, Lee (2008) argued that Māori teachers in English-medium education can achieve relative autonomy through enacting kaupapa Māori philosophies. Māori-centric educational interventions in English-medium schools (Bishop et al., 2003) have also supported self-determination for Māori.

Conclusions and Implications

This qualitative study utilized an open-ended online survey to explore Māori teachers' experiences in English-medium schools and centers. The inclusion of teachers from early childhood education, elementary, and high school sectors aimed to gain insights into the benefits and challenges that current and previous teachers faced. The study investigated the benefits and challenges for Māori teachers (research question 1) and what changes were needed in schools, centers, and education more broadly to attract and retain teachers in the profession (research question 2).

A key finding from this study was that Māori teachers spent many hours supporting the pastoral, cultural, and academic needs of Māori students and whānau. Although some teachers' work was acknowledged through management units and non-contact time, it did not adequately compensate for the time expended.

Participants were positive about including Māori language and culture in their school or center programs, but many reported that Māori initiatives had a low priority. Cultural shifts needed to occur at school or center level, as the decisions made by management and Boards of Trustees had the greatest impact on a teacher's everyday working environment.

To attract and retain Māori teachers in English-medium schools and centers, leaders first need to acknowledge the extent of teachers' cultural labor, and then provide appropriate and extensive support that reflects their work's value. Support for teachers should allow them to be effective practitioners and give them the time, space, and resources needed to contribute to Māori students, whānau, and their school community. Furthermore, roles and responsibilities should be shared equitably between staff in the school. As cited earlier, all teachers in New Zealand schools and centers, not just Māori teachers, have a duty to use te reo Māori me ngā tikanga-a-iwi in their practice and to meet the cultural, pastoral, and academic needs of Māori students. In 2019, the New Zealand government (Te Puni Kōkiri, 2019) set the goals:

- By 2040, one million New Zealanders will be able to speak basic te reo Māori; and
- 150,000 Māori aged 15 and over will use te reo Māori as much as English.

These goals are in addition to the demands on teachers to improve the educational outcomes of Māori students. Meeting these aspirational goals relies heavily on having sufficient numbers of Māori teachers, and currently, there are not enough. The findings in this study have shown that there are dedicated and committed Māori teachers working in English-medium schools and centers, but they are overworked and under-appreciated. To achieve improved outcomes for Māori students, and to protect and revitalize the Māori language, Māori teachers must be supported to continue their valuable work.

Our findings demonstrated the dedication and commitment of overworked Māori teachers in English-medium settings. Increased Māori teacher recruitment may help ease future cultural and pastoral workload. Nevertheless, reducing attrition by supporting currently employed teachers is essential. Future research could explore ideal conditions for Māori teachers and the resourcing and support needed. However, non-Māori teachers and principals need to assume and share responsibility for Māori students/children. Improved Māori outcomes cannot be achieved by Māori teachers alone. Future research, therefore, could investigate the school cultures where Māori teacher retention is high and where teachers experience high levels of support from non-Māori colleagues. This research could benefit schools that need guidance to attract, support, and retain Māori teachers.

Glossary

Aotearoa	The Māori name for New Zealand
English-medium/mainstream schools	English-medium or mainstream schools are schools where the language of instruction is English
Hōhā	Annoyed
Iwi Māori	Māori people
Kaiako	Teacher
Kapa haka	Māori performing arts
Karakia	A ritual chant or prayer
Kaupapa	Philosophy
Kura	School
Kura Kaupapa Māori	Schools where the language of instruction and philosophies are Māori
Mana	Authority/power
Māori	Indigenous people of Aotearoa, New Zealand
Pākehā	A non-Māori New Zealander of European or British descent
Pasifika	Refers to the people, cultures, and language of Pacific groups including Sāmoa, Tonga, the Cook Islands, Niue, Tokelau, Tuvalu, and other smaller Pacific nations – Who are now living in New Zealand
Pōwhiri	A traditional welcoming ceremony
Reo Rua	Bilingual unit in a school where the instruction is in te reo Māori and English
Tamariki	Children
Tauira Māori	Māori students
Teina	A younger sibling of the same sex
Te ao Māori	The Māori world
Te ao Pākehā	The Pākehā world
Te Kōhanga Reo	Māori-medium language nests/preschools
Te reo Māori	The Māori language
Tikanga Māori	Māori culture/customs/values
Waiata	Song
Whānau	Family/extended family
Whānau hui	Family meeting
Whānau unit	A multi-level grouping of Māori students in a school, designed to be a like a family who care and support each other
Wharekura	Māori medium high school

References

Barrett, M., & Connolly-Stone, K. (1998). The treaty of Waitangi and social policy. *Social Policy Journal of New Zealand, 11*, 29–48.

Bishop, R., & Glynn, T. (2011). *Culture counts: Changing power relations in education*. Cengage Learning.

Bishop, R., Berryman, M., Tiakiwai, S., & Richardson, C. (2003). *Te Kōtahitanga: The experiences of year 9 and 10 Māori students in mainstream classrooms*. Ministry of Education.

Braun, V., & Clarke, V. (2006). Using thematic analysis in psychology. *Qualitative Research in Psychology, 3*(2), 77–101.

Calman, R. (2012). Māori education – mātauranga – The native schools system, 1867 to 1969. In *Te Ara – The Encyclopedia of New Zealand*.

Coffin, R. M. (2013). *Kia mau ki tō Māoritanga – The role of Māori teachers in English medium primary schools*. Unpublished Master's thesis, University of Waikato.

Controller Auditor-General. (2016). *Summary of our education reports for Māori*. Office of the Auditor General.

Durie, M. (2001, February). *A framework for considering Maori educational advancement*. Opening address Hui Taumata Matauranga, Turangi and Taupō.

Education Counts. (2020). *Teaching staff*. Ministry of Education. https://www.educationcounts.govt.nz/statistics/schooling/teaching_staff

Education Counts. (2021). *School leaver's attainment*. Ministry of Education. https://www.educationcounts.govt.nz/statistics/school-leavers

Fletcher, T. (1948). *Report of the senior inspector of Māori schools* (1 AJHR E-3). New Zealand.

Fricker, R. D., & Schonlau, M. (2002). Advantages and disadvantages of Internet research surveys: Evidence from the literature. *Field Methods, 14*(4), 347–367.

Gilgen, R. (2016). *Tīhei Mauri Ora: Negotiating primary school teachers' personal and professional identities as Māori*. Unpublished Master's thesis, University of Waikato.

Jenkins, K., & Morris Matthews, K. (1998). Knowing their place: The political socialisation of Maori women in New Zealand through schooling policy and practice, 1867–1969. *Women's History Review, 7*(1), 85–105.

Lee, J. B. J. (2005, June 24). Cultural sustainability: Māori teachers in 'mainstream' schools. In The international diversity conference, Beijing, China.

Lee, J. B. J. (2008). *Ako: Pūrākau of Māori teachers' work in secondary schools*. Unpublished PhD thesis, University of Auckland.

McKinley, S. (2002). *Māori parents and education: Ko ngā ātua Māori me te mātauranga*. NZCER Press.

McNaughton, S. (2020). *The literacy landscape in Aotearoa New Zealand: What we know, what needs fixing and what we should prioritise*. Office of the Prime Minister's Chief Science Advisor. Retrieved from https://cpb-ap-se2.wpmucdn.com/blogs.auckland.ac.nz/dist/f/688/files/2020/01/The-Literacy-Landscape-in-Aotearoa-New-Zealand-Full-report-final.pdf

Ministry of Education. (2008). *Ka Hikitia: Managing for success: The Māori education strategy 2008–2012*. https://www.education.govt.nz/assets/Documents/Ministry/Strategies-and-policies/Ka-Hikitia/KaHikitia2009PartOne.pdf

Ministry of Education. (2012a). *NZ curriculum update: The New Zealand curriculum treaty of Waitangi principle*. Retrieved from https://nzcurriculum.tki.org.nz/Curriculum-resources/NZC-Updates/Issue-16-January-2012

Ministry of Education. (2012b). *Statement of Intent 2012–2017*. Retrieved from https://assets.education.govt.nz/public/Documents/Ministry/Publications/Statements-of-intent/2012StatementOfIntent.pdf

Ministry of Education. (2013a). *Ka Hikitia – The Māori Education Strategy: Accelerating success 2013–2017*. http://www.minedu.govt.nz/theMinistry/PolicyAndStrategy/KaHikitia.aspx

Ministry of Education. (2013b). *Tau mai te reo: The Māori language in education strategy 2013–2017*. https://www.education.govt.nz/our-work/overall-strategies-and-policies/tau-mai-te-reo/.

Mitchell, H. A., & Mitchell, M. J. (1993). *Māori teachers who leave the classroom*. New Zealand Council for Educational Research.

New Zealand Qualifications Authority. (2017). *New Zealand qualifications authority annual report on NCEA and New Zealand scholarship data and statistics*. New Zealand Government. Retrieved from http://www.nzqa.govt.nz/assets/About-us/Publications/stats-reports/ncea-annualreport-2016.pdf

Padilla, A. M. (1994). Research news and comment: Ethnic minority scholars; research, and mentoring: Current and future issues. *Educational Researcher, 23*(4), 24–27.

Percy, W. H., Kostere, K., & Kostere, S. (2015). Generic qualitative research in psychology. *The Qualitative Report, 20*(2), 76–85.

PPTA. (2020, February 12). *Units, MMAs and SMAs*. https://www.ppta.org.nz/advice-and-issues/your-pay/units-mmas-and-smas/

Rata, E. (2012). The politics of knowledge in education. *British Educational Research Journal, 38*(1), 103–124.

Reja, U., Manfreda, K. L., Hlebec, V., & Vehovar, V. (2003). Open-ended vs. close-ended questions in web questionnaires. *Developments in Applied Statistics, 19*(1), 159–177.

Stewart, G. T. (2020). A typology of Pākehā "whiteness" in education. *Review of Education, Pedagogy, and Cultural Studies, 42*, 1–15.

Stewart, G. T., Tamatea, K., & Mika, C. (2015). Infinitely welcome: Education pōwhiri and ethnic performativity. *MAI Journal, 4*(2), 91–103.

Te Puni Kōkiri. (2019). *Maihi Karauna, the crown's strategy for Māori language revitalisation, 2019–2023*. Retrieved from http://www.tpk.govt.nz/docs/tpk-maihi-karauna-en-2018.pdf

Tito, J. (2008). *Māori language use in New Zealand secondary schools: What are the issues for teachers and students?* Unpublished Master's thesis, Victoria University of Wellington, NZ.

Tocker, K. (2007). Kura kaupapa Maori experiences. *New Zealand Journal of Educational Studies, 42*(1/2), 65–75.

Tocker, K. (2015). The origins of kura kaupapa Māori. *New Zealand Journal of Educational Studies, 50*(1), 23–38. https://doi.org/10.1007/s40841-015-0006-z

Tomlins-Jahnke, H., & Warren, K. T. R. (2011). Full, exclusive and undisturbed possession: Māori education and the treaty. In V. Tawhai & K. Gray-Sharp (Eds.), *Always speaking: The Treaty of Waitangi and public policy* (pp. 21–34). Huia Publishers.

Torepe, T. (2011). *The cultural taxation of Māori teachers: Māori teachers reflect upon their teaching experiences in the Waitaha (Canterbury) region, New Zealand*. Unpublished PhD thesis, University of Canterbury.

Torepe, T., & Manning, R. (2018). Cultural taxation: The experiences of Māori teachers in the Waitaha (Canterbury) province of New Zealand and their relevance for similar Australian research [Article]. *Australian Journal of Indigenous Education, 47*(2), 109–119. https://doi.org/10.1017/jie.2017.20

Torepe, T., Macfarlane, A. H., Macfarlane, S., Fletcher, J., & Manning, R. (2018). Leading schooling in Aotearoa New Zealand: Understanding and supporting the weight of culture for Māori teachers. *Journal of Educational Leadership, Policy & Practice, 33*(2), 48–59. https://ezproxy.aut.ac.nz/login?url=https://search.ebscohost.com/login.aspx?direct=true&db=edb&AN=136455294&site=eds-live

Turner, H., Rubie-Davies, C. M., & Webber, M. (2015). Teacher expectations, ethnicity and the achievement gap. *New Zealand Journal of Educational Studies, 50*(1), 55–69. https://doi.org/10.1007/s40841-015-0004-1

Walker, R. (2016). Reclaiming Māori education. In J. Hutchings & J. Lee-Morgan (Eds.), *Decolonisation in Aotearoa: Education, research and practice* (pp. 19–38). New Zealand Council for Educational Research.

Whitehead, A., Ryba, K., & O'Driscoll, M. (2000). Burnout among New Zealand primary school teachers. *New Zealand Journal of Psychology, 29*(2), 52–60.

Wylie, C. (2012). *Challenges around capability improvements in a system of self-managed schools in New Zealand*. WestEd. Retrieved from https://files.eric.ed.gov/fulltext/ED541649.pdf

Hana Turner-Adams is a lecturer in the Faculty of Education and Social Work at the University of Auckland, New Zealand. Her research interests are Māori student success, teacher expectations, teacher-student relationships, and the disparities in educational achievement between Māori and non-Māori students. She has experience researching with Māori and non-Maori in educational settings, using both quantitative and qualitative research methodologies. Her PhD research focused on the schooling experiences of high achieving Māori and non-Māori senior secondary school students, and the factors that contributed to their academic success. Hana has 18 years' experience teaching across the primary, secondary and tertiary sectors, and she has taught at schools in both New Zealand and Australia.

Christine Rubie-Davies is a Professor of Education in the Faculty of Education and Social Work at the University of Auckland, New Zealand. Her main research interests are teacher expectations and beliefs that moderate expectancy effects. Christine focuses on class-level teacher expectations and the associations with student outcomes. She also has a strong interest in teacher expectation effects for disadvantaged groups. Christine has published six books and over 100 articles and chapters in prestigious presses, has won national and international awards for research, teaching, and service, and is a Fellow of both the American Psychological Association and the Association for Psychological Science.

Open Access This chapter is licensed under the terms of the Creative Commons Attribution 4.0 International License (http://creativecommons.org/licenses/by/4.0/), which permits use, sharing, adaptation, distribution and reproduction in any medium or format, as long as you give appropriate credit to the original author(s) and the source, provide a link to the Creative Commons license and indicate if changes were made.

The images or other third party material in this chapter are included in the chapter's Creative Commons license, unless indicated otherwise in a credit line to the material. If material is not included in the chapter's Creative Commons license and your intended use is not permitted by statutory regulation or exceeds the permitted use, you will need to obtain permission directly from the copyright holder.

Chapter 30
Transformation or 'Training the Dog'? Approaches to Access Within an Historically White University in South Africa

Dina Zoe Belluigi and Gladman Thondhlana

Abstract This chapter provides insights into the intractable ethico-political nature of 'access' in post-colonial, post-conflict higher education (HE), through the reflections of Black academics and women academics who have lived experience of the minority-majority transitions of academic communities in post-apartheid South Africa. To address the lack of 'diversity' of under-represented demographics within historically white institutions, those institutions who provided access to these hand-picked academics did so requiring that they undergo rigorous professional development and socialisation programmes for the purposes of assuring their quality. Critical discourse analyses were undertaken of the qualitative responses of these academics made in response to a questionnaire on this subject, which were then confirmed and deepened within small group discussions. In this chapter we discuss how their responses revealed: (1) the mis-educational reception of *structural access* for troubling homogeneous institutional cultures; (2) the risks encountered in the politics of belonging of an individual's *access for success*; and (3) the problematic weight of transformative expectations when conditions mitigate against empowering agents *access to challenge*. Situated within an historical narrative of academic development and the national drives in that country for an HE sector 'transformed' from its historical legacies of injustice and inequality, the chapter highlights the implications of these three constructions of access for disrupting the machinations of the hidden macro- and meso-curricula of power and whiteness.

D. Z. Belluigi (✉)
Queen's University Belfast, Belfast, Northern Ireland, UK
e-mail: d.belluigi@qub.ac.uk

G. Thondhlana
Rhodes University, Makhanda, South Africa

Questions of Equity in Faculty Development

Questions of access, authorship and uncertainty are appropriate for problematizing the interpretative frames of the university, as the intractable conditions of inequality and crises of representation continue to feature. Simmering below the surface of distinctions between access and equality are hidden curricula which socialize and construct participants in HE, their communities and knowledge(s) as de/legitimate or mis/recognised. This in turn impact on how such participants may be positioned as dominant or marginalised within the institutions. This study provides global readership insights from South African academics almost three decades into that country's democratization, when students and staff are continuing to actively voice disquiet about the problematics, politics and costs of having gained access to institutions with explicit legacies of exclusion – particularly, historically white universities (HWI).

In this chapter, we posit academic development as a site where national and institutional priorities, interests, and pressures for access are negotiated against what is valued for equity and justice. Characterized by rates of low participation and high attrition (Fisher & Scott, 2011), academic development in South Africa has become an active terrain of academic and professional practice (Skead, 2017). With barriers to access framed primarily in terms of *student learning*, this educational emphasis has manifested in foci on the micro-curriculum of teaching enhancement and curriculum review. As we discuss in this chapter, one of the problematics is that approaches that were utilized to address barriers to access for students marginalised within apartheid education policies and practices, have been applied to staff. Only recently has the gaze of those within this applied area of Higher Education Studies, extended to the meso- and macro-level cultures and structures which continue to privilege, legitimate and reinforce established apartheid, colonialist and cold war cultural hegemonies.

Presenting a series of narratives wherein literature and the responses of participants are interwoven to probe the reception and perception of access, in this chapter we differentiate approaches to access in this context, to expose the ways in which they have enabled the persistence of a problematic hidden curriculum. The nuanced insights of the lived experiences of academics deemed 'other' unveil the macro-aggressions enacted through the might of institutional quality assurance at an HWI, and call into question: in whose image the excellence of academic staff is constructed, and how do such aesthetics of identification operate in the quest for a transformed, equitable university?

Methodological Approach

The study involved the participation of a very particular group of heterogeneous individuals situated at various positions along the academic ladder. What binds them is their positioning as academic staff whose access to an historically white

English-medium, settler colonial institution[1] in South Africa, was made possible as recipients of various academic development programmes. These programmes aimed to address the legacies of exclusion of those academics categorised within demographic groups identified by the State and equity policies as under-represented within HWIs. As we discuss within the next section of this chapter, the apartheid regime had created an inversion of the national demographics of the majority Black populations to privileged white, male South Africans, and as such the inclusion of Black academics and of women academics in such programmes was in a bid to address the minoritisation of such 'previously disadvantaged' and 'previously marginalised' groups within HWIs particularly. Such elitist patterns of stratification are not uncommon to many postcolonial contexts.

The explicit 'development' purpose of the programmes was to both support career advancement and assure the quality of the academic practices of the selected Black and woman academics. In their 18 years of their piloting and implementation, programme titles have varied due to political rhetoric or aims ('accelerated development', 'next generation', 'equity agenda', funders et cetera). Common to all was that augmented mentorship, professional development and evaluation occurred *prior* to their selection for tenured employment, which differing to the standard employment practices. Drawing from the positive outcomes of the various iterations of these Programmes, funding shifted from external to national sources in 2015, with three centralised versions of the Staffing South Africa's Universities Framework (SSAUF) for Black nationals and, where underrepresented, women: the 'New Generation of Academics Programmeme' (nGAP) for early career staff, 'Existing Academics Capacity Enhancement Programmeme' for mid-career staff, and 'Higher Education Leadership & Management Programmeme' for managerial positions. Recipients of such Programmes encouraged us to explore their differing receptions of group membership and staff evaluation, at an event when the authors presented findings of a study about societal asymmetries in student assessment dynamics (Thondhlana & Belluigi, 2016).

Both of the chapter authors have had direct experience with the national context: one author had been a programme recipient, and the other had worked within academic development. Acknowledging the inadequacy of our authoritativeness in this area, we invited our participants to embark on this study as central authorities to ensure that "those who are socially-marginalized… determine what is critical" (Berry, 2017, p. 63). Our interactions were thus characterized by critical dialogue between peers, rather than conventional researcher-respondent dynamics. Critical Discourse Analysis was utilised to differentiate between the 'acts of narration' of our contributors to the larger institutional and sectoral discourses which they negotiated in their everyday academic lives, and which pervade the HE sector nationally and globally. This approach allowed us to recognise the agency of these academics to resist, collude, shape, counter and call out such discourses; but also to read such

---

[1] The study was awarded ethical approval, and policy briefs have been presented to relevant committees and authority. However, we have made concerted effort to reduce risk to the participants by removing identifiers of the particular institution and the specificity of the Programs.

larger discourses as artefacts of culture, to be explored for both their meanings and for how they operate in creating conditions within contexts. Within this, is a recognition of inherent power dynamics and the limits of critical consciousness of actors in times of rapid change.

The data generation process followed a report-and-respond approach (Stronach & Piper, 2004) to constructions of dominant institutional and national policy discourses of transformation, access, peer evaluation, and group membership. These were presented firstly in a questionnaire, followed by two small group discussions of our interpretations for member-checking and further exploration. Of the 53 recipients from 2000–2017, 27 responding positively to our invitation; 13 were not contactable; and 10 indicated their entry to the institution was too recent to be valid. Twenty-one chose to provide qualitative responses to this chapter's discussion on access and equity for academic staff (see Belluigi & Thondhlana, 2021 for a shorter meditation on this subject against concerns of racialised 'diversity' within UK HE).

The participants' reader-responses of those dominant discourses probed the misfit between the policy discourses, and their experiences of the meso-curriculum. Iterative analysis alongside these participants led to findings about the gaps between the espoused and the experienced discourses of transformation (Belluigi & Thondhlana, 2019) and intersectional insights into the politics of belonging as minoritised academics (Belluigi & Thondhlana, 2020). In this chapter, we discuss how over-arching approaches to access were categorized as (1) 'structural access', (2) 'access for success' and (3) 'access to challenge', which have shaped this chapter's structure. This grounded analysis of the participants' responses is interwoven with concepts and studies from academic literature which resonate with their problematizing of diversity and belonging. These were most often informed by Critical Race Theory (CRT), post-colonial and conflict theory, as these underpinning theoretical orientations challenge systems of racism, sexism, inequality and hegemony.

Findings and Discussion

'Window-Dressing': Participants' Reception of Structural Access

While many contexts have long grappled with massification and structural access, South African HE only began the project in the wake of its negotiated political settlement in the mid 1990s. As the vast majority of the population had been excluded from tertiary education, the issue of whom counted as 'under-represented' was not as fluid a concept as argued elsewhere (Reisberg & Watson, 2010). The concerted effort to dismantle the legacy of racial segregation and subjugation of apartheid ideologies and structures, inevitably led to a focus of affirmative action in the demographics of race and gender in national discourses, policies, and funding formula (Higher Education of South Africa, 2011; Ramrathan, 2016).

Initial emphasis was placed on structural access for student entrants at HWI, with less concerted scrutiny and pressure on the academic staff composition. As a gesture for the short-term, many HWI institutions hired non-national Black academics whose qualifications were assured elsewhere, rather than South African historical Black institutions, and who were perceived as more manageable than those who may be politically active (Sebola, 2015). A few HWIs piloted a range of development programmes, models of which were imported and funded by philanthropic organizations in the minority world of the Global North, tracing colonialist and cold war ties with democratic, capitalist leanings. Although tenured positions were the norm, these intensive development programmes offered employment on a contractual basis with significantly more scrutiny than the norms required for mainstream academic staff. They thereby assured that the altering of institutional demographics would be done in stable ways, while not relinquishing the long-held constructions of quality associated with their branding as leading national institutions.

Despite being small scale, these were billed as sustainable affirmative action pathways to eventual 'transformation' (Badat, 2008). One participant articulated how this rhetoric created the "disproportionate… phenomenon [where the] 'first black' or 'only black' is often treated as a major achievement" (#4). Two decades after democracy, the slow rate of change to the composition of the professoriate was described at national level as "the most glaring collective failure of the sector" (Transformation Strategy Group and Transformation Management Group, 2015, p. 11), because whites made up more than half (53.2%) of the academic staff against a national demographic of majority (79.2%) Black South Africans (Department of Higher Education and Training, 2015). Due to the persistent "poor picture" (Govinder et al., 2013, p. 5) produced from "institutional resistance to transformation" of HWIs (Booi, 2016: 78), one participant asserted that while "transformation is not just a numbers game, numbers are necessary" (#3).

In the questionnaire responses, a large majority of participants wrote about how the HWI intentionally mis-represented its stasis by parading these few selected Black staff as "window dressing" (#14) and "tokens" (#25) to "make the department look good" (#25) and "get the numbers looking good rather than changing the way in which power operates at the university" (#14). All participants indicated discomfort at being positioned as *representatives* of diversity and/or of transformation at the institution.

I merely had to be hired into a previously untransformed space, for the space to be considered transformative, and that was all the transformation they were willing to undergo (#19).

Within the small group discussions, participants spoke at length about their internal conflict from having benefited materially from such positioning while not having "signed-up" to the interests and ends it served, and being without sufficient power and networks to solidarity to resist such collusion.

Discourses of structural access were seen as mis-educational about equality. They reaffirmed perceived tensions between equity and quality, particularly because the criteria for access "implicitly assumes and implies that those staff members (mostly white) who don't go through the programme are ready to teach in a rapidly transforming high education landscape" (#12). Participants described how this created conditions where negative associations of affirmative action were projected on participants, particularly those located on the basis of their race. Membership of the Programmes became "tantamount to 'labeling' which unintentionally creates a situation of having 'others' in the system" (#12). Emphasizing gains in numeric access retained the historic legacy of the thinking and practices of the majority, whom then continued to reproduce the whiteness hegemony characteristic of their own schooling (Belluigi, 2012; Paasche, 2006).

Globally, 'superficial inclusion' and 'visual diversity' is recognized as problematic for social justice (McDowell & Hernández, 2010). Yet few studies have recognised how affirmative action policies position and conflate heterogeneous individuals through their skills level and social locations (Fryer & Loury, 2010). Participants of this study were particularly concerned that the State's focus on staff composition (Republic of South Africa, 1998; HESA, 2011) was insufficient to address the relationships between race and class, echoing calls for racial and social quotas in other contexts in the Global South (Osorio, 2009) with fraught relationships between inequality and HE economics. The data for this study was generated against the backdrop of ongoing campus unrest due to the unresolved issue of tuition fees and educational 'access for all', with tension between the African National Congress government and the younger generation (Maserumule, 2016). Many of the participants of this study argued that intersectional lenses are required to not limit structural access, and in turn identity, to the parameters established by the apartheid and colonial gaze. As is discussed in the section titled 'chipping away', some explicitly saw decoloniality as a "confrontation with the racial, gender, and sexual hierarchies that were put in place or strengthened by European modernity as it colonized and enslaved populations through the planet" (Maldonado-Torres, 2007, p. 261).

'Training the Dog': Participants' Reception of 'Access for Success'

Recognizing that superficial notions of access would maintain disadvantage, South Africa's Council for Higher Education early on positioned 'equal opportunity' against the historical legacy of inequality (Sikhosana, 1993). Following students' structural access, high attrition rates confirmed the legacy of Bantu education in poor secondary schooling. Emphasis on equity was initially placed on additional support structures, leading to a proliferation of writing centres for those students identified as 'at risk'. Working directly with students within initiatives which soon became critiqued as functioning ghettos, 'educational developers' were positioned as marginal to the academic structures they were tasked to decode for their charges, with vulnerable employment arrangements reinforcing their reduced agency (Boughey, 2007). In countries where such individuals are in the minority, non-social marginal models may be possible. They proved largely impractical and unsustainable in South Africa, as the majority of entrants fell within the umbrella category of 'underprepared', diagnosed into subcategories of perceived deficiency ('first generation' status, 'previously disadvantaged'), and positioned within zero-sum dichotomies (related to secondary schooling, language, literacy, rural/urban et cetera). More systemic approaches sought to infuse epistemological access (Morrow, 2009) within the curricula, theorizing equity as membership of academic discourses rather than generic academic literacy. And so 'academic development' evolved as its reach enlarged to workshops, formalised courses and centers for the development of teachers and the curricula. At the HWI of this study, educational developers utilized 'diversity' discourses to wrestle 'access for success' away from the autonomous deficit positioning of Black students, with 'inclusion' discourses valorizing the ways in which the more subtler aspects of learning cultures and inclusive dynamics might increase belonging (Hurtado et al., 2015). It took considerably longer to broaden such positively-framed 'belonging' discourses to the meso-currriculum of institutional culture and staff relations, perhaps because success-driven approaches rarely acknowledge the politics of belonging. However, beyond this national context, such discourses have been critiqued when it comes to student participation, from entry (Maunder et al., 2013) through to postgraduate study (Holley, 2013). Problematics emerge, such as conflating talent with advantage, myths of the autonomous self, and constructing the ideal knower in the image of curriculum authors. These should have acted as a warning for how academics might be similarly mis-constructed.

Approaches of 'access for success' for student educational development, were translated to the curricula of the Programmes to which the participants of this study were recipients. As staff similarly located within 'previously disadvantaged' communities, the Programmes pre-emptively satisfied the oft held critiques of affirmative action (Kravitz et al., 1997) as equality at the cost of quality. Quality assurance and professional advancement dovetailed with the national drive. Through various stop-starts, the approaches utilized for minority academics 'of color' within US HEIs were implemented, despite the contextual inversion of racial representation nor the scholarly critique that such professional socialization models emphasize "worker adaptation to the work environment [where] reproduction of organizational norms engenders the most rewards" (Sulé, 2014, pp. 432–433). As we unpack in this section, this critique was echoed within the responses of the participants of this study, who felt that in-group membership characteristics had not been disrupted from the predominant norms of the past. Those who exhibited a stronger sense of belonging had similar familial and school socialization to their white colleagues, while recipients' rejection or resistance to belonging was primarily influenced by experiences of alienation, exclusion and self-identification. White domination at the HWI was re-enforced from random acts to more enduring patterns, with micro-aggressions ranging from exclusion from departmental social media and events through to persistent administrative blunders. These created unwanted oscillations in participants' emotions between righteous anger through to self-doubt about rejection-sensitivity. Substantive access as "active inclusion" was "safeguarded" for white staff (#11). Similar persistent patterns of tacit intentionality in the UK (Gillborn, 2005) and the US (Leonardo, 2004) were discussed at length at the small group discussion.

To be expected of individuals coming from a range of disciplines, backgrounds and positions along the academic hierarchy, participants varied in their opinions about *how* institutional culture(s) might be addressed. A minority felt it was not the institution's remit to "create the necessary space for transformation" because "the institution cannot change if the individuals within it are unable to do so" (#17). A similar situationist position was taken by the leading practitioner Badat (2009, p. 456) when he argued that "different social agents and actors acting in cooperation and/or conflict within HE and its institutions" impact on "the pace, nature and outcomes of institutional change". Such arguments fail to recognize that a central element of the Programmes' curriculum was its assessment literacy, which coerced these academics into conforming to the requirements for success. None of the mainstream academics were subjected to such evaluation nor mentorship regimes, with their academic autonomy protected by the 'collegial rationality' evaluation approach practiced in many of the country's HWIs (Luckett, 2006).

Assessment began with a strongly scrutinizing and competitive selective process, which marketed itself as ensuring only the "brightest" and most "talented" of the applicants were permitted access. Similar to what has been described as the myth of 'the supernegro' in a US study (Baldridge, 2016), hero narratives of individualist exceptionalism emerged in metaphors of being the 'poster child' (#12), where "being exceptional works to justify and historicize the ongoing racialized societal structure of land theft, human subjugation, and wealth accumulation" (Patel, 2016: 398). The deficit positioning of the communities to which the recipients were located, locked them into subservience where "I ought to be grateful for even getting my foot in the door" (#19). This liberalist ethos constructs equity as extending opportunities available to the privileged 'us' to pathologized 'others' (Burman, 2003), which one participant explained "required me to consider myself as otherwise underqualified and undeserving of the space I now occupied" (#19).

Such characterization is insulting, demeaning and in some cases dehumanizing... How do you challenge those in power and certain ways of thinking about the meaning of transformation if you are coming from a position of inferiority? (#12).

The assessment regime continued once recipients gained access. Senior academics were empowered with formative and policing functions: to *support* access by "decoding the unsaid requirements of assimilation" (#19) within the ontological dimensions of the institutional habitus; and to *enforce* submission to such performance management parameters through their evaluations. Modelled on hierarchical master-apprentice, dominant-subordinate power dynamics (Booi, 2016), one participant described how the problematic nature of the relationship "crudely reproduced institutional hierarchies, i.e. young Black female scholars on the programme mentored by senior white males" (#16). Peer assessment was characterized on a continuum, from having "a slight undertone" (#19) of bias, to "actively silencing" the recipients through "threats of disciplinary action and/or discrimination" (#14).

While the criteria for assessment by their mentors were transparent, participants questioned the authority of

> *whose standards? In my opinion the access for success perspective suggests that those 'previously disadvantaged' entering the system, whether staff or students, are urged to "become" (and not be) more competent (#8).*

Familiarity with, and performance of, institutional habitus was a requirement for both in-group membership, and for being seen to have the capacity to attain the levels of quality required. Ensuring the continuation of an "otherwise perfect system", the top-down focus on fixing the deficit 'mentees' from their initial status as an "unknowledgeable 'developmental candidate'" (#16) was not experienced as empowering: "It implies that a person is deficient and needs to be trained (as in training a dog)" (#12). Excessive evaluation led some to "regret signing up for the programme, believing that if I had applied for the job simply on the basis of my academic results I would have felt a stronger sense of self belief, and ownership over the process of my growth within the academy" (#16).

Underpinning the access for success approach is assimilation at the level of group membership. Emphasizing 'sameness' to reduce tension and promote harmony (Gaertner & Dovido, 2012) is a reconciliatory position that has been adopted for stability in other post-conflict contexts (Ferguson & McKeown, 2016). Inclusion discourses of benevolent "helping relationships" (Burman, 2003: 294) often leave unacknowledged their inherent power dynamics and social account where identity pathologies difference. Participants of this study were at pains to state that these dynamics should be acknowledged.

> *[Such] conditions left me feeling as a newcomer that my voice could not penetrate a culture so 'sutured' and unchallenged by those acting as my mentors. With or without the [Programme], I know that many young black staff feel that, when transformation is pursued, the integration of black staff is problematized as opposed to the environments that they are entering into (#16).*

Similar approaches to inclusion in other contexts have been found to reinforce the status quo of the dominant group, reducing recognition of unfair group-based disparities (Banfield & Dovidio, 2013). A participant within this study who recognized this dynamic, wrote about how their mentor did not feel powerful enough to raise consciousness about the politics of belonging at that HWI (#25). Identity politics perform in the interests of the group to which the individual deemed 'diverse' must assimilate to replicate group norms (Ryan et al., 2007; Verkuyten, 2006). 'Diversity' and 'inclusion' in assimilationist models of access have been found in the US to reap more benefits to those within the establishment than the intended recipients (Peralta, 2015). Participants highlighted the inappropriateness of assimilationist models in an HWI shaped by settler colonialism and apartheid, particularly as "assimilation allows existing oppressive ideologies to continue. X [HWI] opts for assimilation strategies rather than allowing students and staff to become active participants in transforming this space" (#14). The Transformation Strategy and Management Group (2015, p. 17) which oversees change in HE in the country, have argued it is imperative to unearth the hidden curriculum of "who controls the material, academic, organizational and social instruments to reproduce the faculty and the university?" Participants felt that the institution's embrace of 'access for success' allowed for untroubling the dynamics of meritocracy, which both reduced recipients' power to act as agents of transformation and relinquished the institution of its responsibilities for change.

> *In as much as I have not internalized my role as a black academic, the institution has perhaps not internalized its role as an institution/system in a specific context. (#8).*

In this section, we discussed how our participants exposed the validity of this construction of access as impoverished, because 'success' is predicated on privileging the very racist, gendered and classist systems which have subjugated the majority of the population of the country.

'Chipping Away at the Rock Face': Participants' Reception of the Conditions for 'Access to Challenge'

Following on from almost three decades of the access and success approach for a minority of the majority of the country, a growing intellectual mass in the country has been asking: what is the point of access to HE, if not for substantive transformation? Many argue access should be emancipatory: to dismantle the cultures and structures of apartheid, legacies of colonialism and cold war conflict, challenge the continued epistemic violence of the Eurocentric university, and to resist neoliberal interests of 'third world' labor and human capital for the global market place.

Frustrated with the limitations of 'opportunities' provided from structural access, and the pathological orientation of access for success, academic and student activists in South Africa have taken on the mantel of calling for 'decolonizing the curriculum' since 2015, a discourse which has rippled globally. Because of the country's educational development's focus on teaching-and-learning, as discussed in the previous sections, this call has often been translated as about pedagogical or disciplinary review. Discussions on access often focus at the micro-level: on the politics of representation (Okundaye, 2017), epistemologies of inclusion (Sulé, 2014), and of participation (Hall & Smyth, 2016). As indicated by critiques of the individualist approaches for success, discussed in the section above, participants recognized micro-level concepts of equity as distributive justice were limited and limiting.

With rare exception, HEIs seem to avoid direct confrontation or acknowledgment of their own complicity at the macro- or meso-level. In this study, a participant expressed this as "the elephant in our room is X [the color of the HWI's brand identity]" (#25). Participants characterized the institutional culture as strongly replicating the macro-aggressions of its inherited, exclusionary, homogeneous past. The concept of the macro-curriculum enables unearthing the ideologies of white race-privilege in academia (Solomona et al., 2005) and its relation to machinations of domination and macro-aggressions, from which micro-aggressions emerge (Huber & Solorzano, 2015). Macro-level considerations discern access in relation to sociological theories of power, conflict and collective action, to foreground justice in the analysis of social change. As a principle, distributive justice has informed leadership and development of HE in the Global South (McDowell & Hernández, 2010). Albeit that academic developers are often positioned as marginal, mediating and vulnerable; key players within that applied field in South Africa are informed by more critical leanings than their mainstream academic colleagues (Belluigi, 2012), encouraging pedagogies which question their complicity in reproducing privilege and marginality (Bozalek, 2011). Moreover, many within the higher education landscape share the belief, along with critical conflict theorists and critical race theorists, that the very firmament of formal education is problematic.

A number of participants raised concerns about "superficial, and dangerous assumptions" (#17) that their structural access would contribute to the national drive of "intellectual and academic decolonization, de-racialization and de-gendering of the inherited intellectual spaces of South Africa's universities" (Higher Education of South Africa, 2011, p. 11). Visual diversity often does not equate to rupture, particularly if mental colonialisation is reinforced by assimilationist conditions which militate against recipients' agency, where

those who have been 'oppressed' maintain the status quo, as their immersion in the ways of the other, propels the continuation of an oppressive history and way of thinking (#17).

Spivak (2008) positions the university's 'making' of an academic as constraining the extent to which the agent is able to reject the way they are produced. Structurally reproductive agency entails choices that either reinforce the status quo or replicate prevailing social patterns, thereby diminishing transformative agency to purposefully alter social patterns (Sulé, 2014, p. 437). Participants cited aversion to the "professional risk" (#25) which the assessment literacy of the 'access for success' approach engendered, forcing them to act in their own self-interests to

ensure that our careers and reputations are not compromised… When challenges were made [it opened] a can of worms. I was not safe to talk to, I was shunned… I am told to be careful of career suicide and boundaries (#25).

The conditions for risk-aversion and enculturation of the institution's meso-curriculum of access for success led many participants to choose not to align themselves with the more radical notions of 'access to challenge'. Common-group identity, prevalent to belonging discourses, has been found to dull motivation for challenging injustices and for exposing what underlies intergroup conflict (Banfield & Dovidio, 2013). Such vulnerability tangibly constrained the recipients' ability to challenge injustices when they or their colleagues experienced them. It also impacted on their acting in solidarity with Black students, because "How do you help when you know the very structures are set up, [so that even] you do not get heard?" (#25). This was articulated as the "awkward position" (#8) of being "illegitimate representatives" (#1) of social justice.

Those recipients who self-identified with the approach of 'access to challenge' were those who experienced the greatest role conflict. Conditions at the HWI exacerbated such conflict as "the reality is uncomfortable even for those in power espousing it" (#27). Identity politics wreaked havoc with these participants' sense of self, as they walked a "tight rope" (#8) between expectations, that they embody diversity and were responsible for transforming the institution, and crushing pressures to assimilate into the current culture and satisfy rigorous performance management targets. Rather than "disturbing the paradigm of exclusion" (Sulé, 2014, p. 437), a participant's choice of the idiom "chipping away at that rock face" (#25) better represented the frustrations of these academics' "futile" (#25) impact on transformation at that HWI. The myths of evolutionary progress, which underpinned theories of change within the institution, were seen to result "in a LACK of substantive change since it relies on gradual evolution, and there is no clear evolutionary path between "untransformed" and "transformed" states" (#4). Liberalist understandings of incremental change run counter to arguments that racism, in particular, requires sweeping and radical change (Ladson-Billings, 1998) through disruption (Nwadeyi, 2016). Many of these participants exhibited the psychological stress symptoms of battle fatigue (Smith et al., 2016) common to those marginalized in HE in other national contexts (Alemán & Gaytán, 2017), and those with intergenerational collective memories of discrimination and violence (Maldonado-Torres, 2007).

It is argued that such "subaltern passions [should be viewed] as political resources that challenge hegemonic conditions and formulate strategic counter-hegemonic responses" (Zembylas, 2013). This potential may be realized within larger collective projects of decolonisation across the country in time, if they are not domesticated. These participants' narratives pointed to the insufficient conditions of their 'access to challenge' the cultures, social formations and knowledge formations at that HWIs. Rather, such agency was relinquished by self-preservation within the system of exchange inherent to the assessment regimes of the Programmes.

I chose to silence myself a lot of the time to avoid conflict and to integrate into the department and find some sort of sense of belonging. While I became an easier colleague to work with (as mentioned by many of my colleagues), I felt that I had compromised my own values, ethics, and beliefs. My sense of belonging increased, but my sense of self diminished (#14).

Conclusions and Implications

Whilst trans-ontological hopes of "generous interaction among subjects" may be aspired to in the decolonial project (Maldonado-Torres, 2007, p. 260), this chapter reveals how such conditions were painfully elusive for these academics in this supposedly 'post'-colonial, 'post'-apartheid, 'post'-racial context. These participants' insights into the lived realities of institutionalized machinations of domination, reaffirmed the "threadbare" nature of "settler narratives of linearity, progress, and mobility" (Patel, 2016: 399) which underpinned the approaches to access in this HE context. Finding themselves problematically positioned by the conservative mainstream as embodying transformation through their superficial diversity in the 'structural access' approach, and as agents of transformation by those committed to emancipatory visions of 'access to challenge', the reality of the constraining 'access for success' model effectively reduced the agency of these individuals to *be* or to *effect* change within the historically white institutions' cultural expectations and norms.

Although social justice as a term abounds in the espoused, every day and scholarly discourses of South African Higher Education Studies, this study points to the significance of academic development's blinkered focus on educational outcomes (Patel, 2016; Wuetherick & Ewert-Bauer, 2012) over moral, ethical and political obligations. Participants of this study revealed the problematic nature of the measured and conservative projects of success within the academy when the figure of focus remains individualist. Academic development requires a shift towards 'critical academic development' if unjust conditions are to be challenged within. Participants' insights call for authorial accountability at the meso-level for the continuity of the macro-curriculum of the country's exclusionary past in the present. Avoidance of accusation mimics the ways in which individualistic hero narratives (Baldridge, 2016) and white privilege discourses (Leonardo, 2004) detract readers from the important task of examining the machinations of domination and systemic oppression of global racism. The insights emerging from these reflections on the lived experiences and concerns of these potentially powerful insiders in South African HE, serve as a warning for those espousing discourses of diversity, inclusion and belonging in contexts with legacies of conflict, oppression and inequality.

This study by confirms the importance of exploring the gaps between what is espoused, by those in power, and what is experienced, by the intended beneficiaries, of what is implemented in practice. When it comes to academic development in post-conflict contexts, questions should be asked when approaches for the academic success of underrepresented students are mis-translated into staff programmes in the name of historic redress. Critical analysis of approaches to the access and participation of minoritised and marginalised academics should consider whether such inclusion has had transformative impact on mainstream hegemonic norms. This is of importance for justice, diversity, equity and inclusion policy and practice, and for the democratisation of higher education.

References

Alemán, S. M., & Gaytán, S. (2017). 'It doesn't speak to me': Understanding student of color resistance to critical race pedagogy. *International Journal of Qualitative Studies in Education, 30*(2), 128–146.

Badat, S. (2008). *Redressing the colonial/apartheid legacy: Social equity, redress and higher education admissions in democratic South Africa*. In Conference on affirmative action in higher education in India, the United States and South Africa, New Delhi. https://core.ac.uk/download/pdf/49241217.pdf

Badat, S. (2009). Theorising institutional change: Post-1994 south African higher education. *Studies in Higher Education, 34*(4), 455–467.

Baldridge, B. J. (2016). "It's like this myth of the Supernegro": Resisting narratives of damage and struggle in the neoliberal educational policy context. *Race Ethnicity and Education, 20*(6), 1–15.

Banfield, J. C., & Dovidio, J. F. (2013). Whites' perceptions of discrimination against blacks: The influence of common identity. *Journal of Experimental Social Psychology, 49*(5), 833–841.

Belluigi, D. Z. (2012). Provoking ethical relationship. In L. Quinn (Ed.), *Re-imagining academic staff development: Spaces for disruption*. SunMedia.

Belluigi, D. Z., & Thondhlana, G. (2019). 'Why mouth all the pieties?' Black and women academics' revelations about discourses of 'transformation' at an historically white south African university. *Higher Education, 78*(6), 947–963.

Belluigi, D. Z., & Thondhlana, G. (2020). "Your skin has to be elastic": The politics of belonging as a selected black academic at a 'transforming' south African university. *International Journal of Qualitative Studies in Education, 35*, 141–162.

Belluigi, D. Z., & Thondhlana, G. (2021). In whose interest is 'training the dog'? Black academics' reflection on academic development for 'access and success' in an historically white university in South Africa. In D. S. P. Thomas & J. Arday (Eds.), *Doing equity and diversity for success in higher education: Redressing structural inequalities in the academy. Palgrave studies in race, inequality and social justice in education* (pp. 265–275). Palgrave Macmillan.

Berry, T. R. (2017). The intersections of Africana studies and curriculum theory: A counter-Western narrative for social justice. *Journal of Curriculum Theorizing, 32*(1) http://journal.jctonline.org/index.php/jct/article/view/462

Booi, M. (2016). *Accelerated development programmemes for black academics: Interrupting or reproducing social and cultural dominance?* (Master of art in political and international studies). Rhodes University.

Boughey, C. (2007). Educational development in South Africa: From social reproduction to capitalist expansion? *Higher Education Policy, 20*(1), 5–18.

Bozalek, V. (2011). Acknowledging privilege through encounters with difference: Participatory learning and action techniques for decolonising methodologies in southern contexts. *International Journal of Social Research Methodology, 14*(6), 469–484.

Burman, E. (2003). From difference to intersectionality: Challenges and resources. *European Journal of Psychotherapy & Counselling, 6*(4), 293–308.

Department of Higher Education and Training. (2015). *Staffing South Africa's universities framework* (pp. 1–30). Department of Higher Education and Training. http://www.justice.gov.za/commissions/FeesHET/docs/2015-Staffing-SAUniversitiesFramework.pdf

Ferguson, N., & McKeown, S. (2016). Social identity theory and intergroup conflict in Northern Ireland. In *Understanding peace and conflict through social identity theory* (pp. 215–227). Springer.

Fisher, G., & Scott, I. (2011). *Closing the skills and technology gap in South Africa background paper 3: The role of higher education in closing the skills gap in South Africa*. The World Bank. https://glenfisherdotorg.files.wordpress.com/2016/03/world-bank-2011_highered-fisher-and-scott_final.pdf

Fryer, R. G., & Loury, G. (2010). *Valuing identity* (Working Paper No. 16568). National Bureau of Economic Research. https://doi.org/10.3386/w16568

Gaertner, S. L., & Dovido, J. F. (2012). Reducing intergroup bias: The common ingroup identity model. In P. A. M. Van Lange, A. W. Kruglanski, & E. T. Higgins (Eds.), *Handbook of theories of social psychology* (pp. 439–457). Sage.

Gillborn, D. (2005). Education policy as an act of white supremacy: Whiteness, critical race theory and education reform. *Journal of Education Policy, 20*(4), 485–505.

Govinder, K. S., Zondo, N. P., & Makgoba, M. W. (2013). A new look at demographic transformation for universities in South Africa. *South African Journal of Science, 109*(11/12), 1–12.

Hall, R., & Smyth, K. (2016). Dismantling the curriculum in higher education. *Open Library of Humanities, 2*(1).

Higher Education of South Africa. (2011). *A generation of growth*. Proposal for a national programme to develop the next generation of academics for South African Higher Education. Higher Education of South Africa. http://www.usaf.ac.za/wp-content/uploads/2017/03/12430-HESA-Next-Generation-V4.pdf

Holley, K. A. (2013). How diversity influences knowledge, identity, and doctoral education. *New Directions for Higher Education, 2013*(163), 99–105.

Huber, L. P., & Solorzano, D. G. (2015). Racial microaggressions as a tool for critical race research. *Race Ethnicity and Education, 18*(3), 297–320.

Hurtado, S., Ruiz Alvarado, A., & Guillermo-Wann, C. (2015). Creating inclusive environments: The mediating effect of faculty and staff validation on the relationship of discrimination/bias to students' sense of belonging. *Journal Committed to Social Change on Race and Ethnicity, 1*(1), 60–80.

Kravitz, D. A., Harrison, D. A., Turner, M. E., Levine, E. L., Chaves, W., Brannick, M. T., Denning, D. L., Russell, C. J., & Conard, M. A. (1997). *Affirmative action: A review of psychological and behavioral research*. https://works.bepress.com/maureen_conard/8/

Ladson-Billings, G. (1998). Just what is critical race theory and what's it doing in a nice field like education? *International Journal of Qualitative Studies in Education, 11*(1), 7–24.

Leonardo, Z. (2004). The Color of Supremacy: Beyond the discourse of 'white privilege'. *Educational Philosophy and Theory, 36*(2), 137–152.

Luckett, K. M. (2006). *The quality assurance of teaching and learning in higher education in South Africa: An analysis of national policy development and stakeholder response*. Thesis, University of Stellenbosch, Stellenbosch. http://scholar.sun.ac.za/handle/10019.1/1127

Maldonado-Torres, N. (2007). On the coloniality of being. *Cultural Studies, 21*(2–3), 240–270.

Maserumule, M. H. (2016, November 1). Why the notion of free higher education in South Africa is misplaced. *The Conversation*. http://theconversation.com/why-the-notion-of-free-higher-education-in-south-africa-is-misplaced-67408

Maunder, R. E., Cunliffe, M., Galvin, J., Mjali, S., & Rogers, J. (2013). Listening to student voices: Student researchers exploring undergraduate experiences of university transition. *Higher Education, 66*(2), 139–152.

McDowell, T., & Hernández, P. (2010). Decolonizing academia: Intersectionality, participation, and accountability in family therapy and counseling. *Journal of Feminist Family Therapy, 22*(2), 93–111. https://doi.org/10.1080/08952831003787834

Morrow, W. E. (2009). *Bounds of democracy epistemological access in higher education*. HSRC Press.

Nwadeyi, L. C. (2016, June 29). Lovelyn Nwadeyi's empowering message: The onus is on us to disrupt the status quo | Opinion. *Mail and Guardian Online*. https://mg.co.za/article/2016-06-29-we-all-have-agency-and-we-must-use-it-to-disrupt-the-status-quo

Okundaye, J. O. (2017, October 25). The 'decolonise' Cambridge row is yet another attack on students of colour. *The Guardian*. https://www.theguardian.com/commentisfree/2017/oct/25/decolonise-cambridge-university-row-attack-students-colour-lola-olufemi-curriculums?CMP=Share_iOSApp_Other

Osorio, R. G. (2009). Class, race and access to higher education in Brazil (Classe, raça e acesso ao ensino superior no Brasil) (R. Dinham, Trans.). *Cadernos de Pesquisa, 39*(138), 867–880. https://doi.org/10.1590/s0100-15742009000300009

Paasche, K. I. M. (2006). *An analysis of South Africa's education policy documents: Self-definition and definition of the "Other"*. E. Mellen Press.

Patel, L. (2016). Pedagogies of resistance and Survivance: Learning as Marronage. *Equity & Excellence in Education, 49*(4), 397–401.

Peralta, A. (2015). *A market analysis of race-conscious university admissions for students of color* (SSRN Scholarly Paper ID 2584481). Social Science Research Network. https://papers.ssrn.com/abstract=2584481

Ramrathan, L. (2016). Beyond counting the numbers: Shifting higher education transformation into curriculum spaces. *Transformation in Higher Education, 1*(1), 8.

Reisberg, L., & Watson, D. (2010). Access and equity. In P. Altbach (Ed.), *Leadership for world—Class universities: Challenges for developing countries* (pp. 1–36). Boston College. http://www.gr.unicamp.br/ceav/revista/content/pdf/Watson_Reisberg-Access_and_Equity_en.pdf

Republic of South Africa. (1998). Employment Equity Act No 55. Government Gazette 400 No. 19370. Cape Town. https://www.labour.gov.za/DocumentCenter/Acts/Employment%20Equity/Act%20-%20Employment%20Equity%201998.pdf

Ryan, C. S., Hunt, J. S., Weible, J. A., Peterson, C. R., & Casas, J. F. (2007). Multicultural and colorblind ideology, stereotypes, and ethnocentrism among Black and White Americans. *Group Processes & Intergroup Relations, 10*(4), 617–637.

Sebola, M. P. (2015). Scarce skills expatriates in South African universities: Rhetoric and realities of the of the "Messianic" academics. *The Journal for Transdisciplinary Research in Southern Africa, 11*(4), 180–192.

Sikhosana, M. (1993). *Affirmative action: Its possibilities and limitations* (Education Policy Unit EPU Working Paper 1). University of Natal.

Skead, M. (2017). What's next? Experiences of a formal course for academic developers. *Higher Education Research & Development, 37*(2), 390–403.

Smith, W. A., Mustaffa, J. B., Jones, C. M., Curry, T. J., & Allen, W. R. (2016). 'You make me wanna holler and throw up both my hands!': Campus culture, Black misandric microaggressions, and racial battle fatigue. *International Journal of Qualitative Studies in Education, 29*(9), 1189–1209.

Solomona, R. P., Portelli, J. P., Daniel, B.-J., & Campbell, A. (2005). The discourse of denial: How white teacher candidates construct race, racism and 'white privilege'. *Race Ethnicity and Education, 8*(2), 147–169.

Spivak, G. C. (2008). *Outside in the teaching machine*. Routledge.

Stronach, I., & Piper, H. (Eds.). (2004). *Educational research: Difference and diversity*. Ashgate.

Sulé, V. T. (2014). Enact, discard, and transform: A critical race feminist perspective on professional socialization among tenured Black female faculty. *International Journal of Qualitative Studies in Education, 27*(4), 432–453.

Thondhlana, G., & Belluigi, D. Z. (2016). Students' reception of peer assessment of group-work contributions: Problematics in terms of race and gender emerging from a South African case study. *Assessment in Higher Education, 42*(7), 1118–1131.

Transformation Strategy Group and Transformation Management Group. (2015). *A transformation barometer for South African higher education*. Universities South Africa.

Verkuyten, M. (2006). Multicultural recognition and ethnic minority rights: A social identity perspective. *European Review of Social Psychology, 17*(1), 148–184.

Wuetherick, B., & Ewert-Bauer, T. (2012). Perceptions of neutrality through a post-colonial lens: Institutional positioning in Canadian academic development. *International Journal for Academic Development, 17*(3), 217–229.

Zembylas, M. (2013). Revisiting the Gramscian legacy on counter-hegemony, the subaltern and affectivity: Toward an emotional pedagogy of activism in higher education. *Critical Studies in Teaching and Learning, 1*(1), 1–21.

Dina Zoe Belluigi is a Reader at Queen's University Belfast (Northern Ireland) and a Visiting Professor at the Chair for the Critical Study of Higher Education Transformation at Nelson Mandela University (South Africa). Her work relates to the agency and ethico-historical responsibility of artists and academics in contexts undergoing transitions in authority and in the shadow of oppression. Shaped in part by her experiences as a practitioner in creative arts higher education and later in academic development in her country of South Africa, she is concerned with the complexity of the conditions for the development of critical consciousness and critical hope in those who bare the responsibility for representation. She is committed to the growth of pan-African and international networks for advancing Critical University Studies, where committed scholars, practitioners and policy makers across the globe actively pursue an emancipatory imagination for the future university.

Gladman Thondhlana is an Associate Professor in Environmental Science at Rhodes University, South Africa. His research focus on improving human well-being, which he has undertaken with extensive field research experience with indigenous and local communities in rural parts of South Africa and Zimbabwe. Beyond his disciplinary research, he has a commitment to transformation and civic engagement in higher education, with a particular interest in the interactional dynamics between academic colleagues and within student group work. Thondhlana's lived experiences provided invaluable solidarity with the participants' whose reflection shaped the study included in this book, as a fellow of such programmes.

Open Access This chapter is licensed under the terms of the Creative Commons Attribution 4.0 International License (http://creativecommons.org/licenses/by/4.0/), which permits use, sharing, adaptation, distribution and reproduction in any medium or format, as long as you give appropriate credit to the original author(s) and the source, provide a link to the Creative Commons license and indicate if changes were made.

The images or other third party material in this chapter are included in the chapter's Creative Commons license, unless indicated otherwise in a credit line to the material. If material is not included in the chapter's Creative Commons license and your intended use is not permitted by statutory regulation or exceeds the permitted use, you will need to obtain permission directly from the copyright holder.

Chapter 31
Minority Status, Majority Benefits: Stories of Minority Teachers in U.S and What They Bring to the Classroom

Atifa Manzoor

Abstract With more emphasis placed on culturally responsive teaching, the field has become aware of recognizing the cultural capital students bring into the classroom but what about the teacher? This study closely examined the "lived stories" of three minority women seeking to answer the question: How does their cultural identity influence their teaching in regards to classroom curriculum, environment and relationships with students? With three participants, the researcher included, the main method of research was narrative inquiry, using interviews to gain insight on their background, teaching, and experiences with culture in the classroom. In addition to interviews, journals were employed to evidence researcher experiences. After a clean transcription, all data was then coded to reveal major themes. After researching the cultural identity of minority teachers, there was an awareness of their culture influencing their classroom. Major themes to emerge from the data were: minority teachers as role models and culturally responsive teaching. Although not obvious to participants but only through reflection, minority teachers had something more to offer students. They provided a unique perspective to which some students might relate. With an ever-changing demographic, it is advantageous to have diversity among educators that mirrors that of the student population.

Introduction

It is the summer of 2020 and the vision of the United States, our direction and our education is more blurry than ever. In the past 6 months COVID has run rampant through the states as has riots and the fight for social justice and equality. May 25, 2020, an African-American man, George Floyd, dies at the hands of police officers after allegedly using a counterfeit bill to pay for cigarettes. Not the first to die in police custody, but a death that would trigger a movement for social justice. For me, it once again brought into question: What is it to be minority in the United States? Living in a place you call home only to feel like an outsider? With Floyd's death

A. Manzoor (✉)
University of Houston, Houston, TX, USA

came an insurgence of rage, an awareness of blatant inequality, and for many, the realization that "we" can do better.

When I accepted the invitation to write for this book, I didn't think I had much to offer. It was prior to the recent events described above and I wrote a dissertation 3 years ago, which I had thought, only benefited myself. It was based on the questions I had about my life experiences and I was simply curious to know if others felt the same way. Now, with the state of the union in question, it has become more apparent that minority teachers, their experience, stories and the knowledge they have to share will be vital in moving society towards the direction of progress.

My research into minority teachers began close to home. It was a personal topic: how I straddle the line of two cultures as well as its effects on me personally and professionally. Growing up, I thought culture was only about religion and ethnicity, not knowing that culture extends to nations, social groups and institutions (Culture, n.d.). Students enter the classroom with cultural baggage that affects their learning styles and behaviors. Why wouldn't it be the same for educators? Teachers do not enter the classroom as blank slates with no past or background; they enter with their own cultural baggage. Teachers are individuals with a background, affiliations, and identities outside of the classroom. Although much research has been conducted on minority students' culture and its influence on learning and the classroom, less research has been done on minority teachers' culture having an influence on teaching and the classroom. In this study, I explored the role a minority teacher's culture plays in the classroom. More specifically: How their cultural identity shaped by their background and experiences, influences their teaching in regards to classroom curriculum, environment and relationships with students?

As I delved into the reflection of my own teaching practices and the influence my culture has on my teaching, I sought to gain more insight into this phenomenon by speaking with two other minority teachers: one Hispanic teacher coming from a border town in Texas and the other, an African American woman teaching in Houston. Both had families that had lived in the U.S. for generations in contrast to mine, both held varying teaching styles, goals, and focus as their culture shaped their ideology, classroom, and relationships with students.

Minority Teachers in the United States

Although the population of public school teachers has become more diverse over the years, it is not as racially diverse as the larger population or that of students. According to the National Center for Education Statistics, in the 2017–2018 school year, 48% of students were White, 15% Black, 27% Hispanic and 5% were Asian with the number of minority students projected to increase by 2029 (2020). Unfortunately this does not mirror the demographics of teachers in the United States which showed 7% of teachers being Black, 9% Hispanic and 2% classified as Asian in comparison to 80% of the teachers being White (NCES, 2019). The benefits of having minority teachers in the classroom is becoming more apparent through research yet we still encounter a diversity gap. Such a significant gap between students and teachers can be attributed to "education requirements, low pay, unhappy workplaces, and lack of respect" (Meckler & Rabinowitz, 2019). The path from high school to teaching in the classroom weens minority students out of the process of becoming educators. Students of color are less likely to enroll in college, teacher preparation programs, take the certification exam and graduate (US Department of Education, 2016).

So what of the minority teachers currently working in schools? Since my initial investigation, there has been more research compiled regarding minority teachers and their experiences. Leah Schafer writes for the Graduate School of Education at Harvard and looks into the experiences of minority teachers, focusing her attention on Black and Latino teachers (2018). Adam Wright (2017) and Constance Lindsay (2017) conducted two separate studies correlating the positive outcome of minority students when they have teachers of the same race. These studies also focused on the African American population. One study conducted by Danielle Magaldi, Timothy Conway and Leora Trub (2018) included participants from Puerto Rican, Jamaican, African, Dominican and Black American. Within the study, they found teachers to feel overlooked and unprepared with minimal multicultural training/courses during their teacher preparation programs. When it came to looking for a South Asian perspective, particularly teachers of Pakistani origin within the United States, the research falls short.

Methodology

I was a qualitative researcher before I even knew what a doctorate was. My father worked for the airlines since I was five. This allowed us many opportunities to fly across the world. What I loved the most amongst the chaos of the airport crowds was observing people, wondering who they were and where they were going. It's on these trips that I would learn people's stories just by sharing an armrest. On a flight from Los Angeles to Salt Lake City, seat 32B would become more than a number but a face with a story to tell. To me, there was no other choice than to conduct a qualitative study. As explicated by Polkinghorne (2005), "qualitative research is inquiry aimed at describing and clarifying human experience as it appears in people's lives" (p. 137). Its methods are often used to answer "the *whys* and *hows* of human behavior, opinion, and experience" (Guest et al., 2012, p. 1). Within qualitative research, the best way to conduct my study was through narrative inquiry and by telling the stories of these two teachers alongside my own.

Narrative inquiry is much more than a simple method in which researchers are "just telling stories." "Narrative is a way of characterizing the phenomena of human experience and its study" (1990, p. 2). Clandinin and Connelly made it clear that narrative inquiry is a way of understanding experience (Clandinin, 2013). It is an approach to the study of human lives that honors and gives credence to lived experience as an important source of knowledge. Clandinin and Connelly explained,

"People by nature lead storied lives and tell stories of those lives, whereas narrative researchers describe such lives, collect and tell stories of them, and write narratives of experience." (1994, p. 2). How else would I know more about a teacher, their life and the way they teach unless I got to know them, ask questions and gain more insight into who they are personally and professionally?

With my methodology decided, I began data collection consisting of me journaling my past as well as keeping a researcher reflective journal to capture my thoughts and interactions with the students. With the basis of narrative inquiry in the telling and retelling of stories, interviews were conducted with the two participants to hear and use their stories as the main source of my data. As Seidman (2006) stated, the purpose of in-depth interviewing is not to obtain answers or evaluate but to gain an understanding of the "lived experience of other people and the meaning they make of that experience" (p. 9). Following the three-interview model adapted from Dolbeare and Schuman (Schuman, 1982), enabled the establishment of the context of the participants' experience. Teacher backgrounds were obtained as well as their sense of ethnic culture and self-described identities (Seidman, 2006). Participants reconstructed their current experiences in the classroom making possible connections to previous stories and experiences. This process allowed participants to reflect on the meaning of their shared experiences.

With much of the data consisting of interviews with participants, a thematic and structural analysis approach was used. Prior to determining themes, interviews were coded using a clean transcript. Coding, as described by Richards and Morse (2012), is the first step to opening up meaning. "It leads you from the data to the idea, and from the idea to all the data pertaining to that idea" (p. 137). Analytical coding, coding that comes from interpretation and reflection on meaning, is a prime way of gathering categories and themes as well as the data needed to explore them (Richards, 2009, p. 103). Codes were categorized, then analyzed, and overarching themes identified.

Three teachers participated in this study: a Hispanic elementary school teacher, an African American middle school teacher, and me, an American Muslim middle school teacher. The inquiry began with a self-study to reflect on my teaching and cultural influences in the classroom. It was soon apparent that collecting narratives from other teachers of cultures differing from my own, would be beneficial to exploring the research question. Two participants were chosen based on convenience. Both participants were teachers that had been teaching for over 5 years, were minorities, and willing to share stories about themselves and to reflect on their teaching. They were also two teachers with whom I had a rapport, which facilitated establishing a comfortable interview environment.

Elena Elena (pseudonym) was a 32-year-old Hispanic teacher who taught second grade in a suburban elementary school. Originally from a Texas border town, Elena had the opportunity to attend a college in the southeast and returned to Houston upon her college graduation. For 8 years, Elena taught at a Title I school in the same district. This was her first year "across the river" at a new elementary school located in an economically advantaged area.

Dominique Dominique (pseudonym) was a 30-year-old African American teacher who taught U.S. history in a Houston middle school with grades seven and eight. Growing up in the Deep South (Georgia) and then moving to Texas, Dominique was southern through and through. Her school, O'Hare Middle (pseudonym) was a suburban school with approximate 1200 students. As reported in the *Texas Tribune*, students performed below the state average in passing TAKS scores in 2010 and teachers had less experience than the state average.

Atifa At the time of this inquiry, I taught at the school located in Northeast Houston in the district in which I lived. Out of the 65 teachers on our campus, 54 were White making up 94.6% of the teacher population, one was African American, one Hispanic, and one was Asian (TEA website). The one Asian making up 2% of the population was me.

Findings and Discussion

As a researcher, you try not to let your own research agenda get in the way. I set out to explore how other minority teacher's culture influenced their classroom. With my previous experience, I was curious to see if they had negative experiences as well. I was secretly hoping I was not alone in my experiences. Where I was seeking to find commonalities in our negative experiences, I actually found the beauty of being a minority teacher. Personally this study changed the lenses through which I viewed being a minority teacher. Socially, the implications of this study further justified the need for minority teachers and what districts needed to do in a time of racial inequality and social unrest. Through coding and categorizing, themes began to emerge. The two most significant themes were: (1) minority teachers as role models and (2) culturally responsive teaching.

Theme One: Minority Teachers as Role Models

Growing up as a minority, it can be difficult to figure out where you "fit in". It's as Dominique described as being "too Black for the White folks and too White for the Black folks." It was hard enough trying to relate to the peers around you who were different than you, let alone trying to relate to the teachers. I can count on one hand how many minority teachers I had in public school. Through interviews with participants, I became aware that I was not the only one that felt the way I did growing up. Those emotions and insecurities growing up, led us to become the teachers we are today. Teachers that wanted to impress upon their students to accept who they are, complete with all their quirks, and go forward in life confidently.

Elena grew up with her grandmother who would "dress to the nines" and dye her hair blonde to "keep up with the Joneses" in a time and place where it wasn't accepted to speak Spanish outside your home or share your ethnic heritage. It was a time where she felt she had to fit into White American society. Growing up bicultural and having a grandmother with this mindset, Elena often questioned her own appearance when she was younger. She recalls, "My hair was different. All of theirs was straight and thin; mine is thick and curly. They were so skinny. I felt like I was hairier too because you would see it so much easier than theirs." With age came self-esteem and self-assurance but Elena wondered if she would have been more opinionated and confident at an earlier age if she learned to embrace her difference instead of comparing herself to others as she tried to fit in.

Now coming into a new school, Elena felt she still stood out among the staff in her appearance and the way she dressed; she felt she was "much more unique looking". She usually comes to school in crocs, not a lot of jewelry, a silly or thought provoking shirt and her hair as she would describe it, curly and "all over the place". When asked what she hopes students gain from her appearance and how she dressed, she hoped "that they can feel comfortable being themselves too. We like seeing who you are and enjoy being part of that."

Surprisingly, the concept of beauty and natural hair came up with Dominique as well. She shared her thoughts on beauty. "We are so tied to these Eurocentric values and that straight hair is professional, straight hair is valued as a sign of beauty," she offered. Dominique's mother had been putting a perm in her hair to achieve the straight sleekness since she was 12 and Dominique has continued doing it ever since. It's not until recently that Dominique began wearing her hair "natural", although not without resistance and questions from others. This resistance not only came from the outside community but within her own family. Wearing her hair natural is met with mixed emotions. Her mother's side of the family is quite supportive while her father's side sees it as unprofessional.

Dominique recognized the power of appearance as well, especially with wearing her hair natural. She described it best by saying, "Even though you're not intentionally trying to send a message or make a statement, [you do and you should]." She explained:

> I had a student come up to me, it was not my kid and she was just like "Thank you so much for wearing your hair like that. It's really pretty and it makes me feel like its ok for me to wear my hair like that too."

For Dominique, it was important for Black girls to see people they interact with, particularly professional educated Black women, with natural curls especially when they are "given images that they're not pretty or that society is not going to accept them unless they look like this." She found it comforting to be surrounded by Black women who have natural hair and she knew the students felt the same. When asked if being a "proud Black woman" was something instilled at an early age, she responded with it being "something I grew into."

For me, the concept of beauty tied in with being and feeling different. I knew early on that I was different than most of the kids I went to school with. I was not as skinny, as blonde and not as light skinned as they were. Much like Elena, I too felt that I had more hair on my body than my friends, when their hair was actually much lighter and less noticeable. As a young kid, particularly a young girl, you do not want to be different. You grow up with Barbies and society ingraining in you its notion of beauty. Nobody in the media looked like I did and I, much like other ethnic girls, strived to be a type of beautiful that I was not, nor ever would be.

Natural hair was something that had been an issue with me and journaled about as well. With my hair being naturally wavy, I straightened it regularly to "fit in". As the other two teachers mentioned, embracing natural hair confidently as something beautiful became easier as I got older. I wanted to show students that even though it may appear to some as messy and "unkempt" to have my hair in frizzy curls, as Dominique mentioned in her interview, "it does not make me any less professional, beautiful or educated. It is simply how my hair grows out of my head."

Being a role model was never more apparent to me than with my Southwest Asian students. I had Southwest Asian parents, mothers particularly, excited about me being their daughter's teacher. They wanted their daughters to see a highly-educated woman that was similar to themselves. One parent in particular kept in contact with me regularly and would often say, "Can you tell my daughter that? She does not believe me but she'll listen to you." For my young Southwest Asian girls who were most often so quiet in class, I unknowingly became a role model; an example of confidence and what they could achieve.

As a nation, we must increase the minority representation within the demographics of our educators. "Many believe that minority teachers are best situated to counter negative stereotypes and to serve as role models, mentors, or cultural-translators" (Egalite & Kisida, 2015, p. 1). The teachers within this study demonstrated their ability to be the role models, mentors and cultural translators our students need. The benefits of having minority teachers are far more than we can imagine. In an article written for *Educational Leadership*, Mary Futrell said, "It is essential for *all* teachers to have the knowledge, skills, and training to successfully teach diverse student populations. But it is equally important for *all* students to have the opportunity to be taught by teachers who reflect their diversity (1999, p. 30)". As I listened to the stories and responses from participants and journaled about my own experiences, Mary's sentiment became more apparent to me. Minority teachers have something different to offer, as evidenced in participants' natural ability to relate to and advocate for minority students.

Theme Two: Culturally Responsive Teaching

Out of the few minority teachers I had growing up, I never encountered a teacher of Southwest Asian ancestry. Of course, I had caring teachers along the way but not one who brought my culture into the classroom, let alone someone who truly understood the struggles of an immigrant child from Pakistan. The same was true for participants Dominique and Elena. Being a minority as a child was difficult, and as an adult it continued to bring hardships. On the other hand, as a teacher, being minority provided an advantage in the classroom. Along this line of thought was the most prominent theme that emerged among the three participants: culturally responsive teaching.

Geneva Gay defines culturally responsive teaching as "the cultural knowledge, prior experiences, frames of reference, and performance styles of ethnically diverse students to make learning encounters more relevant to and effective for them" (2018). In addition, culturally responsive teaching is "designed to help empower children and youth by using meaningful cultural connections..." (Vavrus, 2008). Under the umbrella of culturally responsive teaching, two sub themes arose: awareness and understanding of being minority as well as validating and empowering students.

Awareness and Understanding of What It Is to Be a Minority

Being bicultural can be a mix of any two cultures with which one identifies. Ethnically speaking, it is likely to mean having a culture at home that is most likely different than the mainstream culture in which one lives. When you grow up with a subculture, you frequently question why you are required to do certain things and others do not. Then as a young adult, there is often a tendency to "play both sides" or to create a third culture by merging the two cultures together. Although a bicultural identity was more pronounced with Dominique and myself, cultural differences between Elena's home and that of her friends were still apparent.

Being a fourth-generation Hispanic living in El Paso, the mainstream culture of the town was blended into Elena's family culture. However, many aspects still differed. Attending church, remained an expectation, as was participating in CCD or Confraternity of Christian Doctrine classes, something her friends didn't have to do and she questioned often. Religiously, her parents had everything blessed, they had a crucifix up in the house and would put up a palm on Palm Sunday. Again, things her friends did not do. Her family was also more affectionate than those of her friends, offering hugs and a kiss goodnight.

Dominique referred to herself as an "Oreo," somebody who was black on the outside but had mannerisms and "acted" white on the inside. Playing both sides, so to speak, was something with which Dominque was familiar. She was conscious of how she acted differently around her White friends versus Black friends to ensure she would be accepted by both groups. This was something she noticed in her Asian students. Dominique explained that her school had a small Asian population with the rest of the school's population split between half Hispanic and half African American. Most of the Asian students had grown up in the surrounding neighborhood and "[were] able to float back and forth between what it means to be Asian and how you have to carry yourself, then what it means to be able to function in the school." Finding it "weird" to watch the students' transition among groups made Dominique recognize these students as a younger version of herself. She had to know how to function in different settings based on the culture of the students she was around. Asked if she believed "playing sides" was more specific to minority groups, she replied, "Definitely." Dominique elaborated:

> Seeing my Asian students, you know, when they're all together, they're "Asian" and they listen to k-pop and share stories about things their parents do to them as far as discipline or that they have to go to cultural school this weekend. But then when they get out and they go to their normal classes where they're mixed in, just having to, I guess, assimilate…

With my campus being majority White, there were not many large pockets of other races. The students that stood out to me the most were the Southwest Asian students. Some of my students attended the same mosque as I did and it was very interesting to see them assimilate in different contexts. They abided by mainstream norms in hopes of blending in while at school and then outside of school they attended mosque and followed the Islamic culture. Watching my students brought me back to when I was in school and the struggle of making sure I fit in with mainstream culture while keeping my ethnic culture at home.

I once had twin students in my class who I suspected to be from Pakistan but through all our conversations in class about my heritage, they never brought it up. I finally had a conversation with them and mentioned they never shared they were from Pakistan. One student responded, "Eh, yeah, we don't share that information much." I did not react the way I should have by telling them they should not be afraid to share their heritage. I knew I was afraid too at their age; afraid of being different, scrutinized and ostracized. Truth is, there were moments even as an adult when I was scared to share my heritage because of some of the same reasons.

Validating and Empowering Students

The idea of validating and empowering students came across as one of the most important and powerful sub-themes of culturally relevant teaching among the three participants. Teacher participants mentioned celebrating and appreciating differences among students by taking an interest in who they were as individuals and ensuring differences were appreciated and embraced to empower students.

What came through most in interviews was Elena taking an interest in and learning who her students were as a whole. Teaching the second grade, Elena wanted to learn about students from the first day. In her reflection on culture she wrote, "I am very aware in particular of how unique and individual my students are and what value that brings into my classroom in terms of learning-academically, linguistically, emotionally, socially, etc." She shared that they take time to get to know each other, their families, interests and special characteristics. One way she accomplished this was through "Student of the Week." Giving each student a week to have the spotlight and share about themselves. Elena focused on making sure what makes a child different was seen positively, appreciated, and embraced, not just by their peers but the students themselves.

I look to find what they find special or what they think is unique and special about them and draw that out. I try to do that in the way we talk about things with myself. So, I tell them, "Oh look, I have big crazy curly hair and I should not feel weird about that." I think that's what I would like them to feel comfortable doing too.

Being in a school district representing so many different cultures, Dominique wanted her students to understand that she respected them and was always ready to celebrate with them. Dominique took an interest in who her students were and, much like Elena, learned about them beginning on day one. She asked them questions about their heritage, cultural traditions and life events taking place outside of school. "I want to know my kids and their cultures" she said. She had students who attended Vietnamese school on the weekends and talked to her about how much they disliked it. She also had students that participated in dragon performances for the Chinese New Year. Dominique attended Quinceañera celebrations for some of her Hispanic students and attended different churches with some of her African American students. When she had a Muslim student come in with henna on her hands, she made it a point to ask questions to learn more about her culture. Dominique loved that her students had different cultures because to her, that was what made them individuals. She let them crack jokes about their culture and have fun with it, letting them embrace it, and see that culture was part of who they were.

Being a Muslim in American schools left me feeling like I didn't quite belong. In my classroom, I made it a point to learn about my students, where their families came from and to empower them to be themselves. Teaching World Cultures, it was easy to bring their different heritages into the classroom. We started out by creating a "selfie" that displayed students' cultures, their interests and what made them unique. When we studied the part of the world from which their family came or students had visited, we took time to share what knowledge, pictures, and artifacts students brought to class. The biggest thing for me was recognizing where they were from and taking an interest. One time it was as simple as letting a student (Ibrahim) know on the first day of school that I was going to pronounce his name in Arabic, not knowing he was from Egypt. Never having a teacher address his culture or share similar traits, he had a big grin on his face. Sometimes that's all it takes to build a relationship and have them invested in my class.

In addition to bringing their students' culture into the classroom, participants recognized the need for multicultural education. As students, participants did not grow up with multicultural education in school. Even though Elena grew up in a city where minorities make up the majority of the population, the curriculum was Eurocentric with a focus on rote learning. Dominique grew up learning more about Black history at home and from books she read versus what she learned in school. Although I was Muslim, I was expected to participate in the Christmas play, make Christmas presents, and hunt for Easter eggs. Now as teachers, the three participants make conscious efforts to provide a multicultural education.

Elena understood the importance of history and multicultural education and was a proponent of history through literacy; using books to teach what she might not have time to during the regular day. When asked if this was automatically built into the curriculum, she said it was not. She included books such as *Something Beautiful*, where the main character found what was beautiful where she lived or *One Green Apple* where the main character wore a hijab. Elena also used activist books written for kids. With each book, students discussed the story, discovered and appreciated the differences of the characters and related it to themselves.

Dominique's biggest task with the curriculum was to provide the students an opportunity to form their own opinions and realize that there was no right or wrong. She wanted to make sure her "students have an opinion and it's not just the opinion of a textbook." When asked how much she taught out of the textbook, her answer was simple, she did not. Dominique utilized a lot of primary sources in her teaching, providing students a chance to read different accounts of events and topics that were covered in the curriculum. When it came to teaching history, Dominique was very straightforward with her students. She shares the good, the bad, and the ugly parts of history for all ethnic groups involved. Where the curriculum and textbook left off was where Dominique filled in the gaps with resources and class discussion.

Tied to culturally responsive teaching is the idea of cultural sensitivity. Whether it be unknowingly or not, participants reported there being a lack of cultural sensitivity among staff members. With the increase in globalization, trainings and workshops on cultural sensitivity and cultural awareness have become the new 'must' for major corporations and businesses (Sifter, 2013). It should be no different in education. How can we expect the future generation to invest in their country if they are being met with degradation and exclusion beginning in grade school?

The lack of cultural sensitivity was more obvious with some than others at Elena's school. Elena was the type of teacher who wanted as much diversity in her classroom as possible. She loved looking at the roster in the beginning of the year and seeing which kids would walk in the door the first day. Reflecting on students that other teachers would consider troublesome or different, Elena said, "I want those kids. I like those kids." There was a student in first grade from India who wore a turban on his head, since he was of the Sikh faith. Having traveled to India years prior and loving the culture, Elena excitedly wondered if she would have him in class. As she shared her roster with other teachers, she shared her excitement aloud. When another teacher didn't know what the Sikh faith was, Andrea shared her knowledge and let her know it was the boy who wore a turban on his head. Andrea shared,

> The other teacher said, "Oh that one kid that wears a towel on his head?" [Elena laughs and shakes her head at me] The other teacher goes, "I think I have the kid with the towel." I said "He's Sikh, yes but you should call it a wrap or if it's a turban, that's appropriate. They [Google] said turban so ok you can call him the boy with the turban. Do not say towel."

As Elena proceeded to tell her how certain ways the turban was wrapped meant different things, the other teacher simply passed it off, appearing to not care to learn more about the culture of her future student.

Dominique shared a story about a White coworker who once said, "I do not see race. I had a Black nanny growing up," as though that fact counteracted the things she said and did in her classroom. Dominique described how, with good intentions, the coworker showed her students documentaries such as the one on Emmett Till

(14-year-old African American boy lynched in 1955 after being falsely accused of flirting with a White woman) because, as she explained it, "They need to know this." Reflecting on her coworkers' wanting to show the video in class, Dominique says she did not consider the fact that the Black Lives Matter movement was at its height with police brutality on the news daily. Although Till's story was important, explained Dominique, her coworker did not take into account the school's demographics or that it might hit home for her students, possibly causing a stir of emotions.

My school was located in a predominantly White, Christian area and the staff reflected the same demographics. Last summer I was asked to lead a professional development session. Based on my interest, a slightly changing demographic, and noticing a need, I suggested that I lead a session on culturally responsive teaching and multicultural education. The table of teachers, all White, looked at me in silence. As much as I would have liked to think that we progressed to be able to discuss matters of race and ethnicity in the classroom, it still seemed to be taboo; something teachers still feared to discuss. By the looks on everyone's faces, it was clear that I needed a new topic. When I changed the subject of my session, there was much more praise and acceptance of the new idea.

As we ended the 2019–2020 school year remotely, those sentiments still held true. At our last staff meeting of the year, we discussed the uncertainty of the upcoming school year and how the school district would be planning to tackle going to school in the midst of COVID. Nothing was mentioned about race riots and how our country was in shambles and hurting. When I asked if there was going to be any direction on multicultural education, professional development or addressing the race inequality, there was a quick "no" and change of topic.

Conclusion and Implication

Often, discussions on race, diversity and multiculturalism are sprinkled throughout a preservice teacher's coursework but "teachers continue to exit their teacher preparation programs not prepared to effectively teach all students" (Hayes & Juarez, 2012, p. 3). Although unclear whether minority teachers are naturally inclined to be culturally responsive teachers, the participants within this study appeared to be aware of culturally responsive pedagogy and its implementation in the classroom. As shared by Geneva Gay (2000), for teachers to successfully teach *all* students, not just those in the mainstream, it is important for teachers to have the knowledge, skills and dispositions to effectively implement culturally responsive pedagogy.

I began this chapter by asking what it was to be minority in the United States. More specifically I wanted to go back to my research and look at the experiences of being a minority teacher and its effects on the classroom. Being a Pakistani Muslim teacher allowed me to share my culture and experiences with my students but also opened me up to scrutiny. It was the scrutiny that caused me to shy away from being the teacher I naturally was and should continue to be.

Through the research process, the benefits of having minority teachers in the classroom became obvious as did the need for minority teachers in the classroom, and this is a point that should be debated in future studies. Although, the most significant finding from the research was personal: the realization that being a minority teacher would allow for negative experiences but if the minority teacher is open to it, it could lead to something more positive and monumental for the students.

References

Clandinin, J. (2013). *Engaging in narrative inquiry*. Left Coast Press, Inc.
Clandinin, D. J., & Connelly, F. M. (1994). Personal experience methods. In N. Denzin & Y. Lincoln (Eds.), *Handbook of qualitative research* (pp. 413–427). Sage.
Connelly, F. M., & Clandinin, D. J. (1990). Stories of experience and narrative inquiry. *Educational Researcher, 19*(5), 2–14.
Culture in the classroom. (n.d.). Retrieved October 24, 2015, from http://www.tolerance.org/culture-classroom
Egalite, A., & Kisida, B. (2015, March 6). *The benefits of minority teachers in the classroom*. Retrieved October 26, 2015, from https://www.amren.com/news/2015/03/the-benefits-of-minority-teachers-in-the-classroom/
Futrell, M. H. (1999). Recruiting minority teachers. *Educational Leadership, 56*(8), 30–33.
Gay, G. (2018). *Culturally responsive teaching: Theory, research, and practice*. Teachers college Press.
Gay, G., & Howard, T. C. (2000). Multicultural teacher education for the 21st century. *The Teacher Educator, 36*(1), 1–16.
Guest, G., Namey, E. E., & Mitchell, M. L. (2012). *Collecting qualitative data: A field manual for applied research*. Sage.
Hayes, C., & Juarez, B. (2012). There is no culturally responsive teaching spoken here: A critical race perspective. *Democracy and Education, 20*(1), 1.
Lindsay, C. A., & Hart, C. M. D. (2017). Exposure to same-race teachers and student disciplinary outcomes for black students in North Carolina. *Educational Evaluation and Policy Analysis, 39*(3), 485–510. https://doi.org/10.3102/0162373717693109
Magaldi, D., Conway, T., & Trub, L. (2018). "I am here for a reason": Minority teachers bridging many divides in urban education. *Race Ethnicity and Education, 21*(3), 306–318.
Meckler, L., & Rabinowitz, K. (2019, December 27). America's schools are more diverse than ever: But the teachers are still mostly white. *The Washington Post*. https://www.washingtonpost.com/graphics/2019/local/education/teacher-diversity/
National Center for Education Statistics. (2019). *Spotlight A: Characteristics of public school teachers by race/ethnicity*. Retrieved February 12, 2021, from https://nces.ed.gov/programs/raceindicators/spotlight_a.asp#f1
National Center for Education Statistics. (2020). *Racial/ethnic enrollment in public schools*. Retrieved February 12, 2021, from https://nces.ed.gov/programs/coe/indicator_cge.asp
Polkinghorne, D. E. (2005). Language and meaning: Data collection in qualitative research. *Journal of Counseling Psychology, 52*(2), 137–145.
Richards, L. (2009). *Handling qualitative data: A practical guide*. Sage.
Richards, L., & Morse, J. M. (2012). *Readme first for a user's guide to qualitative methods*. Sage.
Schuman, D. (1982). *Policy analysis, education, and everyday life*. Heath.
Seidman, I. (2006). *Interviewing as qualitative research: A guide for researchers in education and the social sciences*. Teachers College Press.

Sifter, M. (2013, April 1). Cultural awareness training: A new 'must' for businesses. *Philadelphia Business Journal*. Retrieved from http://www.bizjournals.com/philadelphia/blog/guest-comment/2013/04/cultural-awareness-training-a-new.html

US Department of Education. (2016). *The state of racial diversity in the educator workforce*. https://www2.ed.gov/rschstat/eval/highered/racial-diversity/state-racial-diversity-workforce.pdf

Vavrus, M. (2008). Culturally responsive teaching. In *21st century education: A reference handbook* (Vol. 2, pp. 49–57).

Wright, A., Gottfried, M. A., & Le, V.-N. (2017). A kindergarten teacher like me: The role of student-teacher race in social-emotional development. *American Educational Research Journal, 54*(1_suppl), 78S–101S. https://doi.org/10.3102/0002831216635733

Atifa Manzoor graduated with her Ed.D. from the University of Houston in Curriculum and Instruction with specialization in Social Education. She is currently a middle school social studies teacher in Texas and adjunct Professor with the University of Houston-Downtown (USA).

Open Access This chapter is licensed under the terms of the Creative Commons Attribution 4.0 International License (http://creativecommons.org/licenses/by/4.0/), which permits use, sharing, adaptation, distribution and reproduction in any medium or format, as long as you give appropriate credit to the original author(s) and the source, provide a link to the Creative Commons license and indicate if changes were made.

The images or other third party material in this chapter are included in the chapter's Creative Commons license, unless indicated otherwise in a credit line to the material. If material is not included in the chapter's Creative Commons license and your intended use is not permitted by statutory regulation or exceeds the permitted use, you will need to obtain permission directly from the copyright holder.

Conclusions and Implications

Mary Gutman, Wurud Jayusi, Michael Beck, and Zvi Bekerman

Reading the literature, it becomes apparent that since the late 1960s and early 1970s educational research has attended to the need for more teachers from minority ethnic, religious, and national groups in public education settings. Attention to this issue arose in response to growing ethnic, religious, and national diversity in public education systems. A review of the existing literature was published over two decades ago (Quiocho & Rios, 2000), and apparently things have not changed much since then. Calls for the inclusion of minority teachers in mainstream schools are still being heard and there is a sense that the need is growing. Although there has been a steady increase in research on this subject since the 1980s, a web search using Google Scholar algorithms for composites of concepts such as "minority teachers," limited to the years 1900–2020 offers over 16,000 results; limiting the same search request to the years 2010–2020 yields only 6000. Indeed, this is a rather new area of research, but one which is already well-populated. This volume is a modest attempt to support what is already known and add some complexity to an already ambivalent education issue.

Alongside the conspicuous scarcity of research on minority teachers, there is a growing number of research institutes and academic publications focusing on immigration and mobility as a global phenomenon. This should come as no surprise: for thousands of years and multiple reasons, people have moved around the globe in search of food, fleeing from war, or in pursuit of riches, disseminating their languages, cultures, skills, and genes along the way. In recent times and after the decline of international migration during the interwar years, the improved economic conditions of the postwar era brought about a renewed impetus in world migration. Paradoxically, while today's globalization seems to facilitate the movement of goods, services, and capital, international migration of people, which is also about movement, provokes intense political debate in western democracies (Breunig et al., 2012). As Brettell and Hollifield (2014) have argued, migration is the political mirror of trade and finance: while the wealthier states push hard for protection to keep foreign labor flows out, many poorer states push for openness (although rarely explicitly). Nevertheless, a recent United Nations report estimates that the total number of international migrants keeps increasing. In the year 2000, total world migration was estimated at 150 million people; by 2010, the number had risen to 214 million, and by 2019 to almost 272 million globally, comprising mostly of labor migrants. However, this figure only represents 3.5% of the world population, meaning that still today over 95% of the global population is living in the country of birth (United Nations, International Organization for Migration, 2020).

Naturally, this situation emphasizes the complexity of so-called majority-minority relationships, which are felt in all spheres of life and public services. The education system is the first to experience such relationships because it absorbs immigrant descendants and integrates them into classrooms. This process involves the absorption of suitable staff that is fluent in the verbal and mental languages of the groups coming into school. Although the education and teaching profession is easily perceived as mobile, since there is always a global demand for teachers and educators, evidence in the field points to the myriad challenges immigrant teachers face in accepting jobs in world education systems—even if such evidence is not made official or published in academic formats.

A critical examination of the 31 chapters in this book enables us to identify similar struggles experienced by minority teachers, regardless of their geographical location and the educational policies that prevail where they practice. Thus, for example, studies discussed in the **first part** support the claim that the education system is a significant social factor. Its role is to impart to students the patterns of behavior, norms, and values that will enable them to live in a diverse society in line with the claims made by Rubenko (2018). However, although there is widespread agreement about the contribution of teachers from immigrant backgrounds in this regard, as shown in Chaps. 8 and 10, this issue is hardly addressed by policy-makers. Sometimes it creates distress, a sense of not belonging, and loneliness, in line with the findings of the studies presented in Chaps. 2, 3, 5, and 9. Looking at the existing literature, Howard's (2010) study is noteworthy in that it shows that American students in a predominantly white milieu believe that teachers of Asian origin can provide them with a broader cultural understanding, which is required in a society where nearly half of the citizens are "of color." Another study (Ferlazzo, 2018) argued that encounters between teachers and students in the education arena have a positive effect on the majority group's perception of the minority (to which the teacher belongs), and on the minority group's perception of the majority. A study produced in South Africa by Davids (2018) supports a similar claim, arguing that students who are not exposed to such diversity in education will have difficulty in the future with global citizenship tasks and attaining the verbal skills required today in most corporations; they may be left unprepared for self-realization in a variety of social and professional contexts.

Looking at the studies in the first section shows that a similar conclusion emerges in Chaps. 4, 6 and 7, which examine the current reality in the US. These chapters illustrate some personal and professional challenges faced by minority teachers who are recent arrivals to the US, emphasizing the importance of a preparatory program to help teachers integrate into schools.

A broader look at the concept of "minority teachers" reveals some surprises. In many contexts, teachers feel – and are identified as – minorities because they differ from their peers and students not just in terms of their mastery of the official language of the state, but also because of religion, nationality, and social trends. Similarly, it is not uncommon to see bilingual, independent, and complementary education institutions in which native teachers feel like minorities who serve as mediators of local curricula, language, and heritage, as discussed in the **second part** of this book.

Whereas initially, the focus of this area of research might have been on what the colonial powers and settlers called "indigenous teachers," the main focus of the book is on what national institutions call "immigrant teachers." The term "minority" can serve as a synonym for both immigrants and indigenous people. However, the first two sections of this book treat native and immigrant teachers separately, examining each as a minority, while the interrelationships between them and students, peers, and principals are interpreted through the lens of minority-majority relations. Chapter 11, which compares the status of Palestinian-Israeli teachers in bilingual and Hebrew-speaking schools, shows that these interrelationships affect their levels of satisfaction and the willingness of the system to accept minority teachers. This conclusion is directed at policy-makers, arguing for the need to increase support and guidance for minority teachers, both in multicultural and in majority education settings.

The importance given to greater inclusion of these teachers in complementary and independent school settings, as argued in Chaps. 12 and 13, stems from the assumption that native teachers integrated into these schools would address diversity issues more adequately and professionally than teachers belonging to the same group as the students. This thinking is consistent with recent studies (King & Butler, 2015; Kumar et al., 2015) that claim that a diversity of teaching power provides minority students with the role models needed to strengthen a democratic society. It was also believed that their presence would benefit the "regular" faculty, the schools, and school communities as a whole (Cherng & Halpin, 2016; Ginsberg et al., 2017). The presence of a diverse professional teaching corps provides minority students with identification points that help them grow into professional and responsible roles in their communities (Liu & Ball, 2019). The two studies presented in Chaps. 14 and 15, which were conducted in Argentina, also show that minority-oriented teaching based on strategies morgere compatible with the original culture of minority students facilitates learning processes and has a positive impact on student achievement.

The third part of the book examines the journeys of international teacher educators. Here, the belief is confirmed that when these minority faculty members are integrated into teacher education institutions as representatives of a minority group, they develop the ability to educate for values of tolerance and inclusion, and serve as role models for the majority and minority pre-service teachers (Gutman, 2019). Thus, when teacher training institutions ensure the cultural diversity of academic staff, there is a greater chance that pre-service trainees and teachers will internalize the message, choose to integrate into leadership roles, and promote a tolerant and pluralistic view, thereby contributing to the creation of shared spaces in schools. Since the school serves as a microcosm of society, the creation of these spaces is important.

When considering possible solutions, it has been suggested that efforts should be made to identify teacher educators who are suitable for this task, including training teachers overseas and enabling them to serve as mentors and international teacher educators. This conclusion corresponds with the ethnographic chapters presented in this section, all but one of which takes place in different US contexts.

The fourth part of the book relies on the assumption that adequate representation of ethnic minority teachers and the provision of language assistance directly and indirectly affect student achievement and social learning. For example, Anderson (2015) examined students' perceptions of their teachers and the parameters that were important to them, and found that there is a great preference for teachers from a minority group, even though they only constitute 17% of all teachers in the school and are neither in management nor in positions of authority. This is because these teachers are more caring; they understand what troubles the students and make them feel motivated. The study found that this is especially critical at the middle school age, which is a time of identity formation, when teachers can provide greater confidence among those students who are self-conscious about identity issues. Thus, in an atmosphere of trust and inclusion of difference—whether it is based on origin, spoken language and accents, financial ability, marital status, various learning disabilities, emotional, or social abilities—the classroom becomes a safe place for every student. This conclusion emerges in the last ten chapters of this book, with the emphasis in most on positive discrimination of minority staff in diverse educational settings, including Turkey, Czech Republic, South Africa, Finland, Sweden and the USA. (The exception is Chap. 26 in which the US-born teacher is presented in a privileged position as a minority teacher in the People's Republic of China.)

The above should help us contextualize our understanding of the phenomenon studied in this volume. When considering immigrant, minority, or indigenous teachers and education, we are discussing teachers who are from or who serve peripheral populations: refugees, displaced people, "traditional" groups, and/or non-westernized communities. In short, we are focusing on the non-privileged, the racialized, and the subalterns—those lacking economic and political power in their present contexts. It is true that not all immigrant teachers are representatives of these groups; some (e.g., "foreign" teachers in international schools) are themselves representatives of privileged classes and serve their students, but the great majority does not fall into this category.

The studies in the present volume cover related issues in different ways in 15 countries: Israel, Switzerland, Germany, Austria, USA, South Africa, Argentina, Netherlands, Canada, Turkey, Czech Republic, China, Finland, Sweden, and New Zealand. Within these countries, 18 ethnic, religious, or cultural groups are mentioned as having been included in the studies. In Israel, they are Ethiopian and

Russian Jews, and Arab Palestinians; in the USA, Koreans, Mexicans, Chinese, Puerto Ricans, and Africans. In German-speaking countries, they are Turks and Serbians; in New Zealand, Maoris; in Finland and Sweden, Muslims; in Argentina the Toba/Qom, Germans, and Italians; and in Turkey, Kurds. In China, they are North Americans; in South Africa, Zimbabweans; in the Netherlands, Polish and Chinese; and in the Czech Republic they are Roma.

The fact that this book refers to 15 countries out of the 195 represented in the United Nations is not a reflection of laziness on the editors' part. Of the 58 countries in the African continent, only one is represented, namely South Africa; of the 14 countries in Oceania, only New Zealand is represented; of the 33 countries in Latin America and the Caribbean, only Argentina is represented; of the 44 countries in Europe, seven are represented, excluding Switzerland and all members of the European Union; and of the five countries in North America, only Canada and the USA are represented. We tried hard to get more, and although we are certain other countries could have been represented, the ones included reflect the power relations discussed above.

Over the years, research has validated these assumptions and encouraged policy-makers to increase their efforts to engage and include more minority teachers to serve the growing number of minority students studying in national education settings. However, the studies included in this book reveal failures among these efforts and therefore, in the long run, the presence of minority teachers may be reduced despite the continuing increase in the participation of minority students.

We believe that these studies will contribute to the understanding of these difficulties, and that they will highlight the circumstances that prevent minority teachers from joining the teaching force, thus enabling readers to reflect on the measures required to change this situation. The studies reveal that among the barriers minority teachers mentioned are: the low status of the profession and its declining popularity; limited chances of promotion; low salary; the need to prove oneself to the authorities by investing greater efforts than their "regular" colleagues, and more. In addition, poor training of minority students in schools and their consequent inability to enter university was also mentioned as a barrier to preparing greater numbers of minority teachers. Moreover, conflicts between the teachers' ideologies and those inherent in the curriculum have been shown to hinder their smooth integration into the host schools (Parker & Stovall, 2004; Carver-Thomas, 2018). This claim seems to be supported by the studies in this book and constitutes one of its conclusions.

For the most part, the research reported in this volume replicates previous findings. We are clear about the importance of replication as a central tool of verification in the empirical sciences, which adds to the credibility and value of scientific research (Fabrigar & Wegener, 2016). However, the fact that little new knowledge is gained—other than the undeniable importance of the particular cases reported—leads us to ask what else we can do as researchers to advance the cause of the minority, immigrant, indigenous teachers and students we care so much about. In this volume, we offer a few critical insights we believe are worthy of consideration for future research.

This anthology was created on the understanding that there is a dearth of studies dealing with these and other issues concerning the existence of minority teachers in the classroom and in the teachers' room, and with knowledge of the impact these teachers have on the students of the social majority group. The main issues underlying the deep social awareness that develops among these teachers inhere in the process of integration, acculturation, and assimilation into a foreign culture, the optimal educational climate, which the teachers generate. We recommend an in-depth reading of these studies that present different shades of majority-minority relations. Finally, we ask whether a more critical approach to our subjects of research, and a reconsideration of the main categories that our contexts offer, might help us suggest better policies to overcome the many obstacles confronted by the population.

References

Anderson, M. (2015). Why schools need more teachers of color—For white students. *The Atlantic*.

Brettell, C. B., & Hollifield, J. F. (Eds.). (2014). *Migration theory: Talking across disciplines*. Routledge.

Breunig, C., Cao, X., & Luedtke, A. (2012). Global migration and political regime type: A democratic disadvantage. *British Journal of Political Science, 42*(4), 825–854.

Carver-Thomas, D. (2018). *Diversifying the teaching profession: How to recruit and retain teachers of color*. Learning Policy Institute.

Cherng, H. Y. S., & Halpin, P. F. (2016). The importance of minority teachers: Student perceptions of minority versus White teachers. *Educational Researcher, 45*(7), 407–420.

Davids, N. (2018). Researchers feel excluded from South Africa's schools by race and culture. *The Conversation – Academic rigour, journalistic flair*, April, 2018.

Fabrigar, L. R., & Wegener, D. T. (2016). Conceptualizing and evaluating the replication of research results. *Journal of Experimental Social Psychology, 66*, 68–80.

Ferlazzo, L. (2018). The importance of 'White students having Black teachers': Gloria Ladson-Billings on education. *Education Week, 20*.

Ginsberg, A., Gasman, M., & Samayoa, A. (2017). The role of minority serving institutions in transforming teacher education and diversifying the teaching profession: A literature review and research agenda. *Teachers College Record, 119*(10), 1–31.

Gutman, M. (2019). International mobility and cultural perceptions among senior teacher educators in Israel: 'I have learned to suspend judgment'. *Journal of Education for Teaching, 45*(4), 461–475.

Howard, J. (2010). The value of ethnic diversity in the teaching profession: A New Zealand case study. *International Journal of Education, 2*(1), 1.

King, E., & Butler, B. R. (2015). Who cares about diversity? A preliminary investigation of diversity exposure in teacher preparation programs. *Multicultural Perspectives, 17*(1), 46–52.

Kumar, R., Karabenick, S. A., & Burgoon, J. N. (2015). Teachers' implicit attitudes, explicit beliefs, and the mediating role of respect and cultural responsibility on mastery and performance-focused instructional practices. *Journal of Educational Psychology, 107*(2), 533.

Liu, K., & Ball, A. F. (2019). Critical reflection and generativity: Toward a framework of transformative teacher education for diverse learners. *Review of Research in Education, 43*(1), 68–105.

Parker, L., & Stovall, D. O. (2004). Actions following words: Critical race theory connects to critical pedagogy. *Educational Philosophy and Theory, 36*(2), 167–182.

Quiocho, A., & Rios, F. (2000). The power of their presence: Minority group teachers and schooling. *Review of Educational Research, 70*(4), 485–528.

Rubenko, R. (2018). The influence of teachers from a social minority group on students from the social majority group. *Merhavim Institute* (in Hebrew).

United Nations, International Organization for Migration. (2020). *World migration report 2020*.

Printed by Printforce, the Netherlands